A BOOK ABOUT
AMERICAN POLITICS

Books by George Stimpson

A BOOK ABOUT THE BIBLE

A BOOK ABOUT A THOUSAND THINGS

INFORMATION ROUNDUP

A BOOK ABOUT AMERICAN HISTORY

A BOOK ABOUT
AMERICAN POLITICS

BY

GEORGE STIMPSON

HARPER & BROTHERS PUBLISHERS

New York

Library of Congress catalog card number: 52-5472

Dedicated
to
MARVIN JONES

PREFACE

Under a democratic form of government politics touches every phase of human life and is everybody's business.

When Americans meet they usually start the conversation by talking about the weather and wind up talking politics. Nobody expects to do much about the weather, but nearly everybody thinks something ought to be done about politics.

It would be hard to find two persons who agree on what politics is. The term seems to cover a multitude of sins and virtues. *Politics* in the sense of the art and science of government is derived from Greek *polis,* "city." *Policy, polity, police* and *politic* are from the same root. Originally a politician was a person who helped manage the affairs of a city, just as a statesman was one who helped manage the affairs of a state.

Although at first *politician* and *statesman* meant about the same thing, the former term gradually came to mean a lower order of leader than did the latter. Like many other terms of general application, *politics* has a broad and a narrow meaning, a good and a bad one.

Basically we can never get away from politics. Those who talk about eliminating politics from government overlook the fact that politics is government in action, and that politics of the right kind is the only means of perpetuating freedom.

Already in the time of Shakespeare *politician* had acquired unfavorable connotations. Shakespeare himself used *politician* only five times in his works and always in the unfavorable sense. In *I Henry IV* Hotspur was "stung with pismires" when he heard of "this vile politician—Bolingbroke." Hamlet, referring to a skull thrown up by the First Gravedigger, says to Horatio: "It might be the pate of a politician which this ass now o'er-reaches; one that would circumvent God." Mad Lear told blind Gloucester: "Get thee glass eyes; and, like a scurvy politician, seem to see the things thou dost not."

Neither *politics* nor *politician* occurs in the King James version of the Bible, but the Hebrew chroniclers understood very well the persons and the practices that these terms represent. According to *I Samuel 22:2,* when David was making head against King Saul in the cave Adullam, "every one that was in distress, and every one that was in debt, and every one that was discontented, gathered themselves unto him; and he became a captain over them: and there were with him about four hundred men."

Apparently David's son Absalom was also a consummate politician, for in *II Samuel 15:1-6* we are told how he stole the hearts of the men of Israel from his royal father:

"And it came to pass after this, that Absalom prepared him chariots and horses, and fifty men to run before him. And Absalom rose up early, and stood beside the way of the gate: and it was so, that when any man that had a controversy came to the king for judgment, then Absalom called unto him, and said, Of what city art thou? And he said, Thy servant is of one of the tribes of Israel. And Absalom said unto him, See, thy matters are good and right; but there is no man deputed of the king to hear thee. Absalom said moreover, Oh that I were made judge in the land, that every man which hath any suit or cause might come unto me, and I would do him justice! And it was so, that when any man came nigh to him to do him obeisance, he put forth his hand, and took him, and kissed him. And on this manner did Absalom to all Israel that came to the king for judgment: so Absalom stole the hearts of the men of Israel."

Many business, military and professional men who seek to enter public life are fond of insisting that they are "not politicians," a phrase that may indicate envy rather than contempt of the professional and practical politicians. And even many great politicians have continually protested that they knew nothing about politics. In 1807, for instance, former President John Adams, who certainly was a politician if there ever was one, said: "I do not say when I became a politician—for that I never was." The real politician knows that he must be a good politician before he can be elected to high office and become a statesman—if he has it in him. Lincoln became a great statesman only because he first had been a great politician.

A hundred years ago a rising young politician named Rutherford B. Hayes made the following curious comment in his diary:

"Politics is no longer *the topic* of this country. Its important questions are settled—both on the construction of the Constitution and the fundamental principles which underlie all constitutions. Consequently, the best minds hereafter are to be employed on other matters; or if upon political or semipolitical questions it will not be upon those which are to determine who are to govern, to hold office, etc. Government no longer has its ancient importance. Its duties and its powers no longer reach to the happiness of the people. The people's progress, progress of every sort, no longer depends on government."

What the future President failed to see then was that the Federal Government would grow as the country grew, and would gain more and more control over the people and their affairs, with the result that all problems would become political. Instead of less politics, as Hayes predicted, we got more politics.

I first saw politics in action on a large scale at the Republican National Convention at Chicago in 1920. I was then only a cub reporter on a small-town newspaper and understood very little of what happened behind the scenes. I saw the Punch-and-Judy show but did not see the hands that pulled the wires and made the political puppets dance. But I did learn that what actually happens in politics is often quite different from what the cold record shows.

I arrived in Washington on January 29, 1922. It was the morning after Washington's greatest disaster, the collapse of the Knickerbocker Theater roof, which crushed 98 persons to death. As I looked out from Union Station I saw the snow-covered dome of the Nation's Capitol. Then and there I made up my mind I was going to get acquainted with and learn the ways of the men who work in that building. In Washington I found the nominees of that Chicago convention, Harding and Coolidge, and the men who manipulated it, managing the affairs of the nation. My thirty years of experience as reporter, editor and Washington correspondent has reinforced the lesson I learned in 1920, that there is too often a discrepancy between the printed record and what actually happens.

This book is, in a general way, a nonpartisan history of American politics. My purpose in writing it is to put between two covers the greatest number of answers to questions that are most often asked in this field. You will find here the history of American political life in terms of the odd, the unusual and the interesting. No book on politics like this has ever been written before, and none like it probably will ever be written again. How useful it is may be debated, but few, I think, will say it is not interesting to know these things. It may even teach an occasional lesson.

The plan of this book was conceived a quarter of a century ago. My technique, such as it is, is to answer thousands of oft-asked questions under a few hundred headings. I feel constrained to caution my readers against taking the leading questions too seriously. A critic of my former books accused me of asking a simple question and then, after answering it, rambling all around Robin Hood's barn. Nothing could be further from the truth. Of course there is no rambling in this book. Each article is well organized and based on careful and prolonged research. My purpose has been to compress the greatest amount of interesting and authentic information within the smallest possible space.

I have dealt with caucuses and conventions, committees and campaigns, songs and slogans, parties and platforms, politicians and propaganda, Presidents and would-be Presidents. At the same time I have woven into it most of the basic facts of our political history.

Incidentally I have had much to say about the origin of many political words, phrases and sayings. Many slang words and phrases come and go in the course of the ever-changing political situation in America. Most such words and phrases are completely forgotten in a short time. Others are embalmed in the history of the events and retain only a historical significance, while now and then some gain a permanent place in the language.

Many of our American political terms are borrowed from England, but in most cases they have changed in meaning. On the other hand, many American political terms have been introduced into England and often with the meaning changed.

The whole history of a period can be told in terms of a few catch-words that serve as handles for the memory. For instance, the Wilson era can easily be brought to mind and into focus by ten such terms: The New Freedom, Watchful Waiting, Little Group of Willful Men, Freedom of the Seas, Too Proud to Fight, Lusitania, He Kept Us Out of War, Make the World Safe for Democracy, War to End Wars, and The Fourteen Points.

This is not a political dictionary, nor encyclopedia, nor handbook, but it comprises some of the features of all. Politics, government and history are closely related and not easily separated. In this volume I have dealt with matters purely political. I have dealt with history in *A Book About American History,* and I hope to deal with government in a future volume.

It would be impracticable to mention by name all those persons who lent a helping hand through the years the book was in preparation. A list of such names—would make a sizable volume in itself. Two, however, I shall mention—Charles A. Grefe, who helped in research and editing during the last seventeen years, and Russell McFarland, who helped see the book through the press.

I have dedicated this book to Marvin Jones, whose friendship has been one of my most precious possessions for thirty years.

The Index at the end will give a good idea of the great variety of matters considered.

I only wish that you may have as much fun reading this book as I have had writing it.

GEORGE STIMPSON

January 29, 1952
National Press Building
Washington, D.C.

A BOOK ABOUT

AMERICAN POLITICS

A BOOK ABOUT
AMERICAN POLITICS

Is the United States a republic or a democracy?

Whether the United States is a democracy or a republic is good for an argument in almost any American gathering. Many people still insist that the United States is a republic and not a democracy.

The question is academic because the two terms as now used are not susceptible of definitions sufficiently exact to form the basis of a satisfactory argument. They are not altogether mutually exclusive, are often used interchangeably and may be applied to the same form or system of government. Neither term is used as part of the official title or name of the United States. It is an interesting fact that many modern sovereign states call themselves *republics* officially, while not one uses *democracy* in its official name.

Republic is derived from Latin *res*, "thing" or "affair," and *publicus*, "public," and literally means the "commonweal." *Democracy* is derived from Greek *demos*, "people," and *kratein*, "to rule," and literally means rule of the people. The independent city-states of ancient Greece were called democracies, while the city-state of Rome, which became master of a vast empire, was called a republic. In the Greek democracies the freemen or qualified voters met together and exercised their authority in person, while in the Roman republic the freemen or qualified voters chose agents to exercise their authority. Suffrage in both was greatly restricted and only a small per cent of the population took part in government. But historically *democracy* connoted more direct participation by the people in government than *republic* did.

Democracy and republic were little used by English-speaking people in the English Colonies in reference to their own governments, because they lived, except for a brief period, under a monarchy. Even during the time of Cromwell the Colonists did not refer to their governments as republics or democracies. As early as 1647, however, it was declared that, "The form of government established in Providence Plantations is democratical." *Democracy* acquired an unfavorable connotation and became almost synonymous with mobocracy or rabble rule. In 1636 John Cotton wrote: "Democracy I do not conceive that ever God did ordain as a fit government either for church or commonwealth." In the *Somers Tract* (1686) we find: "The democratical man . . . is never quiet under any government." *Democratic* was only occasionally applied to American institutions in Colonial times. On August 16, 1744, Dr. Alexander Hamilton of Maryland wrote in his diary at Boston in reference to Massachusetts: "The government is so far democratic as that the election of the Gouvernour's Council and the great officers is made by the members of the Lower House or representatives of the people." In the same year Dr. Hamilton wrote at Newport in reference to Rhode Island: "Their government is somewhat democratick, the people choosing their governour from among their own number every year by pole vote."

The American people who regarded themselves as Whigs before the Revolution generally regarded themselves as Republicans after the adoption of the Declaration of Independence. In fact after the Declaration of Independence was adopted the United States became a loose confederation of thirteen republics with the Continental Congress as their central agency. Virtually all those who had supported the Revolution favored a republic and only a small minority favored a monarchy. In 1777, when only twenty years old, Alexander Hamilton wrote to Gouverneur Morris from Washington's headquarters at Morristown: "A representative democracy, where the right of election is well secured and regulated, and the exercise of the legislative, executive, and judiciary authorities is vested in select persons, chosen really and not nominally by the people, will, in my opinion be most likely to be happy, regular and durable." Even in the Philadelphia Convention of 1787 Hamilton did not advocate adopting a monarchy in America. After stating why he thought republican governments were weak, he said: "Whatever may be my opinion, I would hold it, however, unwise to change that form of government." Elbridge Gerry, with the Shays' Rebellion fresh in his mind, admitted that perhaps he had previously been "too republican," but insisted that he was still republican. Yet he said that "It would seem to be the maxim of democracy to starve the public servants," and "The evils we experience flow from the excess of democracy." But George Mason said: "Notwithstanding the oppressions and injustices experienced among us from democracy, the genius of the people is in favor of it, and the genius of the people must be consulted."

For more than three hot summer months the delegates in the

Constitutional Convention worked behind closed doors at their task of framing a new constitution for the United States. During that same year a rumor was circulated that the Continental Congress had secretly approached Prince Henry of Prussia, brother of Frederick the Great, with a view of offering him the crown of an American monarchy. The delegates of the convention kept their secrets so well that very few outsiders knew anything about the document they were drafting. After signing the document on September 17, 1787, and completing their work, the delegates decided to dine together at the City Tavern before dispersing to their homes throughout the various States. They left the convention hall more or less in a body. In the sketchy minutes of the proceedings kept by James McHenry of Maryland is this footnote: "A lady (Mrs. Powell of Philadelphia) asked Dr. Franklin well Doctor what have we got a republic or a monarchy. A republic replied the Doctor if you can keep it." At that time it would have been unthinkable to call the American government a democracy.

Neither *republic* nor *democracy* occurs in the Declaration of Independence, the Articles of Confederation or the Constitution. In *The Federalist Papers* (1788) James Madison set forth the generally accepted meaning of *democracy* and *republic* at that time:

The true distinction between the two forms . . . is, that in a democracy, the people meet and exercise the government in person; in a republic, they assemble and administer it by their representatives and agents. A democracy, consequently, will be confined to a small spot. A republic may be extended over a large region.

And again:

From this view of the subject it may be concluded that a pure democracy, by which I mean a society consisting of a small number of citizens, who assemble and administer the government in person, can admit of no cure for the mischiefs of faction. . . . Hence it is that such democracies have ever been found incompatible with personal security or the rights of property; and have in general been as short in their lives as they have been violent in their deaths. Theoretic politicians, who have patronized this species of government, have erroneously supposed that by reducing mankind to a perfect equality in their political rights, they would, at the same time, be perfectly equalized and assimilated in their possessions, their opinions, and their passions.

At that time Madison thought of the new system of government as a "confederate republic." In fact the Philadelphia Convention had voted down a national government in favor of a federal government, notwithstanding Madison himself was at that time a Nationalist and wanted a national government. In the years following "federal republic" was regarded as the most satisfactory description of the American system of government.

Although *republic* does not occur in the Constitution, Article IV, Section 4 of that document says, "The United States shall guarantee to every state in this Union a republican form of Government." Thomas Jefferson, often referred to as the Father of American Democracy, used *democratic republic* and *democracy* in his notebooks before the Revolution, but he never used those terms in public statements and rarely used them in private correspondence. *Democracy* after the Revolution continued to mean "pure democracy" in America and was generally used in a disparaging sense even by men who regarded themselves as "democratic republicans." Some writers still refer to democracy in the original sense as "pure democracy," as Madison did, and democracy in the later sense as "representative democracy," as Hamilton did. Bishop James Madison of William and Mary College, a cousin of the Father of the Constitution, so disliked monarchy that he refused to think of Heaven as a Kingdom and in his discourses referred to "that great Republic where there is no distinction of rank, and where all men are free and equal."

Before the adoption of the Constitution a party division of sorts existed in the Continental Congress. There were nationalists and state-righters, conservatives and radicals, etc., but these groups were not labeled as parties and were little more than factions. Similar divisions existed in most of the thirteen States. For instance, from about 1780 those in Pennsylvania who advocated changing the State constitution were known as republicans. In a general way, however, it may be said there were no political parties in the United States from 1776 to 1787. There were factions but no national parties in the modern sense. The first great division of political opinion arose during the struggle over the adoption of the Constitution in 1788. The Constitution itself does not so much as allude to political parties.

In the convention itself those who supported a national government were called Nationalists, while those who supported a federal system were called Federalists. But after the Constitution was submitted to the States those who favored it were called Federalists and those who opposed it were called Antifederalists for want of a better name. Thus the original Federalists became the Antifederalists. Madison himself later explained that the new system of government under the Constitution, "being a novelty and a compound, had no technical terms or phrases appropriate to it, and that old terms were to be used in new senses, explained by the context or the facts of the case." As early as January 9, 1788, the Pennsylvania *Gazette* declared, "It is the duty of the anti-federalists in Pennsylvania to learn wisdom from the conduct of the republican party." Governor George Clinton and his followers in New York who opposed adoption of the Constitution called themselves Federal Republicans. After the Constitution went into effect in 1789 *federalist* and *antifederalist* became meaningless in their original senses because virtually everybody took the new system of government for granted and supported it. A new division then arose regarding the interpretation of the Constitution and on social and economic questions. In a sense the chief question was whether the new government should be an aristocratic republic or a democratic republic. The original Federalists—who had favored adoption of the Constitution—and others who supported the administrations of George Washington and John Adams continued to call themselves Federalists. The original Antifederalists—those who opposed adoption of the Constitution—and others who were dissatisfied with the administration called themselves at first Antifederalists and then Republicans. The Federalists believed in a strong central government, loose construction of the Constitution and a reasonable degree of aristocratic formality, while the Antifederalist or Republicans believed in States' rights, strict construction of the Constitution and republican ways of conducting public business. On January 12, 1790, before Jefferson returned from France, William Maclay of Pennsylvania wrote in his diary that he told the Senate: "That I, as a republican, was, however, opposed to the whole business of echoing speeches."

But two distinct major parties did not begin to develop until after Jefferson became Secretary of State on March 22, 1790. Secretary of the Treasury Hamilton was the leader of the Federalists and Jefferson became the natural leader of the Republicans. President Washington, though often referred to as a Federalist, never regarded himself as the member of a political party and tried to be neutral between the two party leaders in his Cabinet. The framers of the Constitution had not considered the possibility of powerful political parties and that document as originally drafted was not adapted to party government. In his Farewell Address President Washington, fearful the Federal Government would be destroyed by factions, warned the American people against the dangers of dividing into political parties.

At first Jefferson and most of his political adherents referred to themselves simply as Republicans, although occasionally they were called Democratic-Republicans. They favored republican principles and practices and accused the Federalists of favoring aristocratic principles and practices. But the causes of the division into two parties lay deeper than that. Later Jefferson himself explained the basis of the first two parties in the United States. In a letter to Henry Lee in 1824 he wrote:

Men in their constitutions are naturally divided into two parties: 1. Those who fear and distrust the people, and wish to draw all powers from them into the hands of the higher classes. 2. Those who identify themselves with the people, have confidence in them, cherish and consider them as the most honest and most safe, although not the most wise depository of the public interests. In every country these two parties exist and in every one where they are free to think, speak, and write, they will declare themselves.

The French Revolution that started in 1789 divided the French people sharply into two classes, and the French coined two new words to describe these classes—*aristocrates* and *démocrates*. *Democracy* and *democratic* and *aristocracy* and *aristocratic* were old words in the English language, but *democrat* and *aristocrat* were formed from the new French *démocrate* and *aristocrate* and were introduced in the United States after 1790. On March 13, 1792, Lafayette wrote to President Washington from France: "I do not speak only of those which the democrats might desire and bring about." Many Americans, particularly the Jeffersonian Republicans, sympathized with the French *démocrates* and rejoiced at the turn of affairs in France. When war started between England and Revolutionary France the Federalists were generally pro-British or neutral and the Republicans were generally pro-French. In many cities pro-French organizations sprang up, calling themselves variously Republican, Democratic or Democratic-Republican clubs or societies. During this period newspapers began to take the names *Democrat, Republican* and *Republic*.

The excesses of the French Revolutionists, particularly during the Reign of Terror in 1793-1794, embarrassed the pro-French Democratic clubs in the United States and dampened their ardor. *Democrat* and *democratic* took on an unpleasant connotation and the Federalists passed by no opportunity to associate the Jeffersonian Republicans with the unpleasantness in Europe. Federalist editors pinned *democrat* on the Republicans wherever and whenever they could. On October 16, 1793, President Washington wrote to Governor Henry Lee of Virginia in reference to the Democratic societies:

I have not, as you will perceive, touched the subject of politics in this letter. The reasons are, your letter of the 17th has expressed precisely my ideas of the conduct, and view of those, who are aiming at nothing short of the subversion of the Government of these States, even at the expense of plunging this

Country in the horrors of a disastrous War; and because I wish to wait a little longer to see what may be the sense of the legally constituted bodies at the meetings which are about to take place.

On April 11, 1795, after Jefferson had resigned from the Cabinet, President Washington wrote to Secretary of State Edmund Randolph: "The first fruit of the Democratic Societies begins, more and more, to unfold itself." The British joined the Federalists in trying to discredit the Jeffersonian Republicans by sneeringly and contemptuously calling them Democrats. On November 27, 1795, John Quincy Adams, son of the Vice President, wrote in his diary in London that George Hammond, British Undersecretary of State, "said he heard *the democrats* were quite cock-a-whoop—talked very high of impeaching the President." Four days later Adams wrote of Hammond: "What sort of soul does this man suppose I have? He talked about the Virginians, the Southern people, the democrats; but I let him know that I consider them all in no other light than as Americans." Out of the Cabinet, Jefferson continued his political activities quietly. He, Madison and the other leaders of the party continued to refer to themselves as Republicans.

In the Presidential elections of 1788, 1792 and 1796 only one ticket of electors was nominated in each State. Under this system the Republicans were at a great disadvantage. Although no formal nominations were made, it was understood in the election of 1796 that Adams was the Federalist and Jefferson the Republican candidate for President. The slogans used in that campaign were "Peace and Prosperity" for Adams, and "The Rights of Man" for Jefferson. The electoral vote was 71 for Adams, 68 for Jefferson and 137 scattered for 11 other men. Under the Constitution as it then stood this made Adams President and Jefferson Vice President. In those days each elector voted for two men for President and the electors were not pledged in advance to vote for any particular candidate to the extent they were later. Despite the fact that Virginia and North Carolina were overwhelmingly for Jefferson, one elector from each of these States exercised his personal independence and voted for Adams instead of Jefferson. In addition, according to Jefferson himself, the vote of one elector in Pennsylvania was diverted from him to Adams by questionable practice. Two of these three electoral votes would have made Jefferson instead of Adams President and the Republicans felt they had been cheated out of the Presidency. For this reason the Republicans decided to put up separate lists of electors in 1800. This was really the beginning of the two-party system in the United States in the modern sense of the term.

Although the Federalists continued to call the Republicans *Demo-*

crats in ridicule, the Jeffersonians continued to call themselves Republicans. *Democratic-Republican* was seldom used. There were no national conventions or committees or other party authority empowered to adopt a name. Consequently the Federalists and Republicans of those days never had an official designation that all units agreed upon. The followers of Jefferson went by different names in different States. In spite of the sneers of their political enemies, here and there a Republican took pride in being called a Democrat.

In 1800 the Republicans put up their own slate of candidates for electors and it was understood that Vice President Jefferson was their candidate for President and Aaron Burr of New York their candidate for Vice President. The Federalists supported Adams to succeed himself and agreed upon Charles C. Pinckney of South Carolina as their candidate for Vice President. The Republicans won but again ran into technical difficulties. Under the system then in effect each elector voted for two men for President and none for Vice President. When the electoral votes were counted Jefferson and Burr were ahead of Adams and Pinckney but were tied with seventy-three votes each. This meant that the House of Representatives, voting by States and not as individuals, had to decide whether Jefferson or Burr would be President. The Federalist members of the House, forced to choose between two Republicans, voted for Burr, with the result that there was a deadlock. After a long struggle the deadlock was finally broken, largely because Hamilton, who hated Burr more than he feared Jefferson, influenced a number of Federalists to change their votes, and Jefferson was chosen on the thirty-sixth ballot. This has been the only time in American history that a Vice President defeated a President for the Presidency. John Adams was the only President elected by the Federalist Party and he was elected over Jefferson in 1796 by a majority of only three electoral votes, at least one of which, according to Jefferson, was irregular.

At last a Republican was President and what amounted to a political and social revolution followed. The election of 1800 decided that the government of the United States would be a democratic republic instead of an aristocratic republic. On March 4, 1801, the day Jefferson was inaugurated, Chief Justice John Marshall wrote: "I wish however more than I hope that the public prosperity and happiness may sustain no diminution under democratic guidance. The democrats are divided into speculative theorists and absolute terrorists." On the same day Jefferson declared in a conciliatory inaugural address that "We are all republicans; we are all federalists." *Democrat* and *Democratic-Republican* were more often applied to the Jeffersonians after Jefferson took office. Members of the party in Pennsylvania boldly called themselves Democrats and rejoiced in the name. But Jefferson himself and Madison and Monroe still called themselves Republicans in public statements.

Thomas Moore, the Irish poet, who visited Washington in 1804 and who acquired a dislike for Jefferson from the Federalists and Britishers with whom he associated, referred to him as "the present Democrat President." On February 1, 1805, Senator John Quincy Adams used *republican cause* and *republican principles* in his diary. Later he abandoned the Federalists and joined the Republicans because he preferred Jefferson's foreign policy to that of the New England Federalists. On January 20, 1808, he wrote: "Mr. Bradley delivered me a printed invitation to attend the meeting of the *republican* members of both Houses . . . to consult respecting the next presidential election." On April 23 of the same year he thought the Constitution "would become more democratic." To punish him for his apostasy the Massachusetts legislature chose his successor long before the required time, whereupon Adams resigned from the Senate in June, 1808, more than eight months before the expiration of his term.

"We are democratic altogether, and I hold democracy in its natural operation to be a government of the worst," wrote George Cabot, the arch-Federalist, in 1804. Jefferson was slow to use *democrat* and *democratic-republican*. After he retired from the Presidency he did use them in private correspondence, but very sparingly. After Associate Justice William Cushing died in 1810, Jefferson wrote President Madison suggesting that he appoint to fill the vacancy on the Supreme Court "a democratic-Republican with nothing equivocating about him." In 1816 he wrote to Dupont de Nemours: "We in the United States are constitutionally and conscientiously democrats." "Democrats," he wrote William Short in 1825, "consider the people as the safest depository of power in the last resort; they cherish them, therefore, and wish to leave in them all the powers to the exercise of which they are competent." But apparently he never referred to the *Democratic Party*. He died in 1826 still a *Republican*. But *democracy* in a general sense was creeping into American usage. The term still meant something bad to former President John Adams. In his retirement at Quincy he wrote: "Democracy has never been and never can be as desirable as aristocracy or monarchy, but while it lasts, is more bloody than either. Remember, democracy never lasts long. It soon wastes, exhausts and murders itself. There never was a democracy that did not commit suicide." But his Republican son was more in tune with the times. On May 12, 1820, Secretary of State

[9]

John Quincy Adams wrote: "Senator Jonathan Roberts 'was bred to a mechanical profession, and is one of those men who, by their talents, and by the prevalence of democracy in Pennsylvania, have risen to the high distinction of his present station. . . .' But no popularity lives long in a democracy." On August 26, 1822, Adams, referring to William H. Crawford's candidacy for the Presidency, wrote: "Democracy, Economy, and Reform are the watch-words for his recruiting service—Democracy to be used against me, Economy against Calhoun, and Reform against both." The Secretary of State wrote on September 11 of the same year that the Washington *Republican* printed an article that said President Monroe "had a private account to settle with the Democratic party." On January 23, 1823, Adams, himself a candidate for President as a Jeffersonian Republican, complained that "all parties disown me—the Federalists as a deserter, the Democrats as an apostate." He had a talk with James Reed of Massachusetts on May 1, 1824, and noted in his diary: "I asked him if he thought there was a doubt of my election by a large majority of the electoral votes but for an opposition from the Republican party on the very ground of my being suspected of too much federalism. He said there was not. I told him I had originally been a federalist, just such as President Washington had been."

The Federalist candidates for President were overwhelmingly defeated by the Democratic-Republicans in 1804, 1808, 1812 and 1816. Even as early as 1807 the Federalists realized that the name of their party was a handicap. In that year the New York Federalists called their State ticket "the American Ticket." A prominent member of the party suggested publicly that it might be wise to drop the obnoxious name Federalist altogether. Most of the Northeastern Federalists opposed the War of 1812 and made the name more unpopular than ever. Members of the party who supported the war revived an extinct name and called themselves Federal Republicans. *Federalist* became more and more odious until it became almost synonymous with *Tory*. The Federalists as a national party threw in the sponge after the election of 1816 and lingered only as a local party in a few spots until the 1830's. *Federalist,* however, continued to be a term of reproach in politics. During the famous log cabin and hard cider campaign of 1840 one of the charges made by the Democrats against General Harrison was that he had once been a Federalist, a charge that he emphatically denied. On July 18, 1840, Philip Hone, the New York Whig leader, wrote in his diary:

Federalism. . . It is strange that this term, by which was designated in former times, the purest, the wisest, and the most patriotic political party which ever existed, should continue to be a term of reproach and the means of exciting the bad feelings and prejudices of the people even now, when it has ceased to be a bond of union or badge of party, and when all but those who use it for sinister purposes are more ignorant of its meaning than they are of the Talmud. The fact is that the Federal party, as it was originally constituted, embraced nearly all the great and glorious spirits of the Revolution, and all the real friends of the people .... But the great party is extinct.

In the election of 1824 there were four candidates—Adams, Andrew Jackson, Crawford and Henry Clay. They were all members of the same party, variously called Republican, Democratic-Republican and Democratic. None of the four received a majority of the electoral votes and Adams, who ran second to Jackson in both electoral and popular votes, was chosen President by the House of Representatives. In theory President Adams was head of the party variously called Republican, Democratic-Republican and Democratic. He tried to strengthen his weak position as leader of the party by appointing Clay Secretary of State, a position that had been the steppingstone to the Presidency. Crawford was in poor health and soon passed out of the political picture. But Jackson, who had received the most electoral and popular votes in 1824, soon decided to run against Adams in 1828. The next four years was a bitter struggle between the Adams-Clay and the Jackson factions of the Republican Party. The issue of the campaign was largely whether President Adams had been party to a "corrupt bargain" when he appointed Clay Secretary of State in return for Clay's support in the House when it chose Adams President. In 1828 the Republican Party did not nominate a candidate. It had two candidates who nominated themselves and the campaign that followed split the Republican Party into two irreconcilable factions. Jackson defeated Adams overwhelmingly in the election of 1828. Within a year or two the Adams-Clay faction joined with the remaining Federalists and other anti-Jackson elements and formed a separate party known as the National Republican Party. In 1832 the National Republicans nominated Clay for President and John Sergeant of Pennsylvania for Vice President, and they were defeated by Jackson and Martin Van Buren.

The Jackson faction, which gained control of the government in 1829, regarded itself as the true heir of the Jeffersonian party and continued to call itself variously Republican, Democratic-Republican and Democratic, but there was already a growing tendency to call it Democratic-Republican or Democratic more often than Republican. As early as September 22, 1830, former President Adams referred to the two parties in Massachusetts as "Federal and Democratic," but on October 13 of the same year he says the "Republicans" and "National Republicans" both called conventions in the Quincy district. Both parties were reluctant to give up the name *Republican,* the name preferred by Jefferson, Madison and Monroe. On March 13, 1832, Adams, alluding to the Jacksonians, referred to "the political frauds and hypocrisy of the party calling itself *the* Republican Party." Up to this time *Democrat* had been little used since the days of Jefferson's administration. During the campaign of 1832 Duff Green, editor of the *Telegraph* and a Clay man, began to hurl *Democrat* at the Jacksonians on the theory that the word still had a sting in it. But the word had lost its sting and many Jacksonians began to call themselves Democrats. On September 26, 1833, William Dunlap wrote in his diary: "I told him (Washington Irving) that I had always been a Democrat." More and more the Jacksonians were called Democratic-Republicans to distinguish them from the National Republicans. On December 24, 1832, Adams wrote: "Mr. Hoffman is a New Yorker, of Dutch descent, a lawyer, of the Democratic Republican party of the Albany Regency, and now a Van Buren man." Adams wrote on October 9, 1834: "New Hampshire is governed by a knave of the name of Isaac Hill, editor of a newspaper, mail contractor, and now a Senator of the United States—just cunning enough to grow rich by railing against the rich, and to fatten upon the public spoils, bawling Democracy." Still Adams reported on January 7, 1835, that the "Jackson Republicans of both Houses of Congress had a dinner at Brown's Hotel." The former President, now a member of Congress, had as hard a time to decide what to call the Jacksonians as they had themselves. On June 15, 1835, he referred to "the issue of the Democratic convention at Baltimore," and on August 18 of the same year he wrote:

I received from Washington a Richmond *Enquirer* containing the address of the Baltimore Van Buren Convention to the Democratic Republicans of the United States. There is something extraordinary in the present condition of parties throughout the Union. Slavery and democracy, especially the democracy, founded, as ours is, upon the rights of man, would seem to be incompatible with each other. And yet at this time the democracy of the country is supported chiefly, if not entirely, by slavery.

Democracy was beginning to be identified with the philosophy and principles of Jefferson and *Democrat* was becoming more common as a designation of a Jacksonian. On July 10, 1835, a few days after the famous Chief Justice died, Adams wrote that "Marshall has cemented the Union which the crafty and quixotic democracy of Jefferson had a perpetual tendency to dissolve." In that year the French writer Alexis de Tocqueville published a book entitled *Democracy in America*. On June 8, 1838, Adams referred to "George H. Keim, a Pennsylvania German Democrat." In the same year Representative Robert Barnwell Rhett of South Carolina said:

In this connection I must say I object to the name democrats as applied to us or our party. It has been more particularly appropriated to those who have adhered to the administration while we have assumed the name of State rights and Republican party. In truth the name democrat better applies to the North than the South, and as usually understood means those who are in favor of the government of the absolute, numerical, majority to which I am utterly opposed and the pursuance of which would destroy our system and destroy the South.

In his *Disquisition on Government* John C. Calhoun also objected to *Democratic* as the name of his party because the term connoted "an enforcement of the rule by the mere preponderance of heads."

The national convention of 1840 that renominated Van Buren referred in its platform to "the cardian principles in the Democratic faith," but did not go so far as to proclaim itself the Democratic Party. On April 16 of that year the Washington *Globe* reported, "The Republican party is sound to the core in this section of the state." It was not until the convention of 1844, which nominated James K. Polk for President, that the party boldly asserted that it was "The American Democracy" and "the Democratic party of the Union." The stone that had been rejected nearly fifty years before at last became the head of the corner. The *Democratic* Party has been the official name ever since.

In 1848 the antislavery faction of the Democratic Party of New York met at Syracuse and adopted the name *Free Democracy*. Their delegation was offered half of New York's vote in the Democratic convention that nominated Lewis Cass for President, but they were dissatisfied with this concession and held another convention and nominated Van Buren for President. Later this nomination was confirmed by the Free Soil Party, which absorbed most of the Free Democracy. In 1860 the Democratic Party was split into two factions—popularly called the Northern Democrats and the Southern Democrats. The Northern Democrats nominated Stephen A. Douglas for President and Benjamin Fitzpatrick of Alabama for Vice President. Fitzpatrick declined the nomination and the Northern Democratic Committee named Governor Herschel V. Johnson of Georgia to take his place on the ticket. The Southern Democrats held a convention at Baltimore under the name National Democratic Convention and nominated Vice President John C. Breckinridge of Kentucky for President and General Joseph Lane of Oregon for

Vice President. Both factions called themselves the Democratic Party. Little confusion was caused by this because they did not put up competing nominees for electors in individual States. The Democratic Party put up Douglas electors in the Northern States and the Democratic Party put up Breckinridge electors in the Southern States. During the Civil War those Democrats in the North who supported the war and favored the Union were known as Union Democrats or War Democrats, while those Democrats in the North who opposed the war and thought it was still possible to save the Union by compromise were called Peace Democrats. The original slogan of the latter was: "The Constitution as it is and the Union as it was." After the war the Democrats of the South came back into the Democratic Party.

Democracy as generally used from 1844 to 1912 meant the Democratic Party and what it stood for. In a letter to William S. Bissell on February 15, 1894, when the Democratic Party was split into two factions—the Gold Democrats and the Silver Democrats—President Grover Cleveland wrote: "The Ship of Democracy, which has weathered all storms, may sink through the mutiny of those on board." It was Woodrow Wilson more than any other one person who popularized *democracy* in the sense of the republican form of government in the United States. Since his administration *democracy* in the sense of the Democratic Party has fallen into disuse.

During the early days of the Republic it was considered a breach of propriety to refer or even allude to political party divisions on the floor of the House and Senate, but this squeamishness disappeared before the Civil War.

How did *hustings* originate?

Hustings is derived from Anglo-Saxon *hus*, "house," and *thing*, "assembly," and originally a husting was a royal household council as distinguished from a people's assembly. Later the term was applied to a court held in English cities before the magistrates. Local courts held in various cities in Virginia are still called Hustings Courts. The Hustings Court of London was at one time the supreme court of the city and was held in the Guildhall before the Lord Mayor, Recorder, Sheriffs and Aldermen. In the eighteenth century the platform at the upper end of the hall where the magistrates sat came to be called the husting. *Husting* became associated with political campaigning and electioneering because, before the Ballot Act of 1872, Parliamentary candidates were nominated and addressed the voters from the husting in the Guildhall. In the United States *hustings,* plural in form but construed as singular, was applied first to any place where political speeches were made and then to campaigning and electioneering in general. The term is now synonymous with *stump,* and *on the hustings* is equivalent to *on the stump.*

Why did the Patriots call themselves Sons of Liberty?

Sons of Liberty was first applied to the Colonial Patriots by an Englishman, not by an American. During the debate in the House of Commons on the Stamp Act in 1765 Colonel Isaac Barre, one of the handful who opposed the measure, had a passage at arms with Charles Townsend in which he apostrophized the Colonial radicals as "Sons of Liberty." Later in the same year the Patriots, first at Boston and then throughout the Colonies, organized themselves into clubs called The Sons of Liberty. In some Colonies the Sons of Liberty were popularly known as Liberty Boys.

Colonel Barre, who entered Parliament in 1761, was a one-eyed veteran of the French and Indian War and was present when Wolfe died at Quebec in 1759. His name is commemorated in the name of Barre, Vermont; in that of Wilkes-Barre, Pennsylvania, and in other place names in the United States.

Americans borrowed many of their ideas and symbols of liberty from the ancient Greeks and Romans. In Roman mythology Libertas was the goddess and personification of freedom. The root of the name is *liber,* "free" or "independent." In early Roman art Libertas was represented as a beautiful and richly adorned matron, and hence the female figures in "liberty heads" and statues of liberty.

The national headdress of the ancient Phrygians was a limp, close-fitting conical red felt cap with the apex turned forward. When a Roman slave was emancipated a Phrygian cap (*pileus*) was placed on his head to indicate that he was a *libertinus,* "freedman," and that his name was registered with members of the city tribes. When Saturninus, about 100 B.C., took refuge in the Capitol he hoisted a Phrygian cap on his spear to indicate that slaves who joined his party would be freed. In time the Phrygian cap became a republican symbol. After Julius Caesar was killed, the conspirators marched forth in a body with a freedmen's cap raised on the point of a spear as an emblem of liberty. The American Sons of Liberty adopted the liberty cap as their emblem, and the French Revolutionists used the cap of liberty (*bonnet rouge*) to symbolize their freedom from royal authority.

[15]

Poles and trees crowned with liberty caps were widely used by the Sons of Liberty. There were liberty trees and liberty poles in Boston, New York, Philadelphia, Charleston and other Colonial cities. Large numbers of poplar and other species of trees were planted by the Patriots during the Revolution as symbols of growing freedom, and the French Revolutionists also planted liberty trees. During the troublesome times before the Revolution the Sons of Liberty informed one another of meetings by posting handbills on the Liberty Tree in Boston, and sometimes they met around the Liberty Tree. On November 13, 1787, Thomas Jefferson wrote to W. S. Smith: "The tree of liberty must be refreshed from time to time with the blood of tyrants. It is the natural manure."

Why is an office seeker called a candidate?

Candidate comes from Latin *candidus,* "shining" or "white." *Candid, candle* and *incandescent* are from the same root. In ancient Rome it was customary for a person seeking a consulship or other high elective office to appear among the citizens in the Forum, Campus Martius and other public places dressed solely in a white toga. The simple toga, with the natural wool further brightened with chalk, symbolized purity of purpose, while the absence of a tunic or undergarment symbolized humility and made it easy to show battle scars to voters. A person clothed in white and publicly soliciting votes was called by the Romans *candidatus,* which became *candidate* in English. Shakespeare describes the Roman custom in *Coriolanus* and uses *candidatus* in *Titus Andronicus.* Standing or running for office came to be called first *candidateship* and then *candidature* in British usage. Americans at first used *candidature* but gradually substituted *candidacy.*

How did *Tory* originate?

Tory is believed to be derived from Gaelic *toraidhe* or *toraighe,* meaning "pursuer" or "hunter," from *toir,* "to pursue." About 1648 the term was applied to the Irish who were dispossessed by the British and who were forced to hide in the bogs and live by robbing and plundering the English settlers and soldiers. In English *Tory* became synonymous with robber, bandit, spoiler and outlaw. Since the Irish Tories were Catholics the term was extended to designate all Irish Papists.

During the reign of Charles II, the Protestants introduced in Parliament a bill to exclude the Duke of York, the King's brother and a Catholic, from the succession to the throne. The bill passed the House of Commons in 1679, whereupon the King first prorogued and then dissolved Parliament. It passed the Commons again in 1680 but was rejected by the House of Lords. When Charles II died in 1685 the Duke of York succeeded to the throne as James II. During the struggle over the Exclusion Bill those who supported the hereditary rights of James regardless of his faith were called Tories. After "The Glorious Revolution of 1688," which deposed James II and put William and Mary on the throne, *Tory* became the name of the more conservative of the two great Parliamentary parties.

In *A Select Glossary of English Words* (1859) Richard Chenevix Trench, Archbishop of Dublin, wrote:

> It is curious how often political parties have ended by assuming to themselves names first fastened on them by their adversaries in reproach and scorn . . . . *tories* was a name properly belonging to the Irish bogtrotters, and during our Civil Wars robbed and plundered, professing to be in arms for the maintenance of the royal cause; and from them transferred, about the year 1680, to those who sought to maintain the extreme prerogative of the Crown.

The English Tories were the spiritual heirs and successors of the Royalists and Cavaliers. Under date of October 24, 1681, Oliver Heywood noted in his diary: "A gentleman had a red Ribband in his hat . . . he said it signified that he was a Tory. What's that? said she. He answered, An Irish rebel . . . I hear that . . . instead of Cavalier and Roundhead, they are now called Torys and Whigs."

In the English Colonies in America, *Tory,* like *Whig,* had little political significance until after Parliament passed the Stamp Act of 1765. All members of both the Tory and Whig parties professed loyalty to the King and opposed taxation by Parliament. The chief difference between them was that the Whigs advocated resistance to the tax while the Tories advocated patience and nonviolence until Parliament had heard their petitions and had a fair opportunity to repeal the Stamp Act. Up until that time the Whigs were not much more liberal than the Tories nor the Tories much more conservative than the Whigs on most questions. But the radical patriots, realizing the term had a somewhat derogatory implication, denounced as Tories all conservatives who advocated that the courts and ports be opened without the use of stamps and that business go on as usual. It was good political strategy to encourage the belief that the office holders and American Tories were themselves responsible for the detested tax. But during the next nine years there was no great difference in the views of the Tories and Whigs. They agreed substantially on the rights and liberties of the Colonies and both professed to oppose taxation by Parliament and to favor reconciliation with the mother country. They differed only in the methods by which these objectives were to be attained.

After 1774 there could be no neutrals but only Patriots and Loyalists in the eyes of the Patriots. As early as 1774, John Adams, while attending the First Continental Congress at Philadelphia, wrote: "A Tory here is the most despicable animal in the creation. Spiders, toads, snakes are their only emblems." In November, 1775, Philip Vickers Fithian wrote in his diary at Stephensburgh in western Virginia that "no Tories are permitted to vent their Sentiments, the Name of *Whig* has the Port of Majesty." After the Revolutionary War started in 1775, and especially after the Declaration of Independence was adopted in 1776, most of the Whigs and a part of the Tories joined the rebels. All those who refused to accept independence after it was declared and continued to favor British rule were called Tories regardless of previous political affiliations. *Royalists* and *Loyalists* were slightly less offensive synonyms for the term.

It is a mistake to suppose that all those called Tories were office-holders, aristocrats and people of wealth. The Tories represented all classes. In the Northern Colonies many of the merchants, landowners and professional men were Tories, while the lower classes were more likely to be Patriots; but in the Southern Colonies most of the landed aristocrats, who had been Whigs, were Patriots, while the lower classes in many cases were Tories. On December 25, 1845, Representative John Quincy Adams recorded in his diary:

I had a visit from Mr. James Buchanan, Secretary of State. He told me that he had formerly visited my father at Quincy, and said that in speaking to him of some of the Tories during our Revolutionary War, he said they were men of great respectability, fine talents, and excellent private character, but that they were all deplorably loyal—an epithet which Mr. Buchanan said had greatly diverted him.

It is estimated that nearly a third of the 2,000,000 white inhabitants—600,000—remained Loyalists at heart during the Revolution. John Adams thought at least a third of the people did not want independence and another third was neutral at the outset of the Revolution. To Thomas McKean he wrote on August 31, 1813:

Upon the whole, if we allow two thirds of the people to have been with us in the revolution, is not the allowance ample? Are not two thirds of the nation now with the administration? Divided we have ever been, and ever must be. Two thirds always had and will have more difficulty to struggle with the one third than with all our foreign enemies.

On June 2, 1816, his son, John Quincy Adams, then American minister to England, wrote:

Sir James Mackintosh asked me if I thought Dr. Franklin had been sincere in the profession which he made here, that he lamented the Revolution which was to separate the colonies from Great Britain which he said he did the day before he had left London, even in tears. I told him I did not believe Dr. Franklin wished for the Revolution—nor Washington. He asked me if any of the leading men had. I said perhaps my father, Samuel Adams, and James Otis.

About 70,000 Tories, it is estimated, left the United States during the Revolution and settled in England, Canada, Florida, the West Indies or elsewhere in the British Empire. When General Sir William Howe evacuated Boston on March 17, 1776, and sailed for Halifax he took with him 1,100 Tories, including eighteen clergymen of the Church of England; and when the British surrendered Charleston, South Carolina, to General Anthony Wayne in 1782 they took away with them 3,700 Loyalist men, women and children and 500 slaves belonging to them. About 10,000 Tories fled to Florida, which remained loyal to the British, but when the territory was ceded to Spain in 1783 most of these Tories left with the British flag and settled in the Bahamas. Maintenance of the thousands of American refugees in England became a serious problem. "There will scarcely be a village in England without some American dust in it by the time we are all at rest," lamented one Loyalist. The number of Tories who settled in Canada is estimated at between 35,000 and 40,000. For years the Tory refugees in Canada were known as "The United Empire of Loyalists."

It has been contended with all seriousness that as many Americans served in the British as in the American forces during the Revolution. Although that is undoubtedly an exaggeration, it is probable that some 50,000 Loyalists served in the British army and navy from 1775 to 1783. New York City, occupied by the British for seven years during the Revolution, was a Tory stronghold. Few of the local Tories left and many Tories from other parts of the country sought refuge there. Anticipating this use of New York City when he evacuated the city in 1776, General Washington wanted to burn it, but could not get the consent of the Continental Congress. It has been estimated that New York contributed 23,500 men to the British military and naval forces during the war. Most of the 1,000 British troops killed, wounded or captured at King's Mountain were Loyalists recruited in the Carolinas. At that time there were 6,000 Loyalists serving under Cornwallis in the South. About 500 American Loyalists surrendered with Cornwallis at Yorktown. These figures show to what extent the American Revolution was a civil war. Benjamin Franklin's only son, William Franklin, was a Loyalist. Royal Governor of New Jersey when the Revolution started, William Franklin was arrested and held in prison in Connecticut until exchanged in 1778, after which he went to England and never returned to America. In his will Benjamin Franklin left his Nova Scotia land to his Loyalist son in England. A brother of Gouverneur Morris was a major general in the British army and married to the Duchess of Gordon. Eliza Kortwright Monroe, wife of the fifth President of the United States, was the daughter of a Loyalist officer in the British army.

Of course, most of the Tories did not leave the country and all of them did not lose all their property. Some of those who did leave eventually returned and prospered. John Wickham, who served in the British army during the Revolution, became head of the Richmond (Virginia) bar and was one of Aaron Burr's counsel in his treason trial. The Provisional Treaty between the United States and Great Britain, signed November 30, 1782, provided that Congress would "earnestly recommend" to the States that they revise their laws confiscating the property of Tories and that it would try to bring about a restoration of property to the Loyalists who had not borne arms. The inability of Congress to persuade the States to do this produced friction between the United States and Great Britain for decades. In New York Governor George Clinton was an effective Tory baiter and confiscated £260,000 of their personal goods and lands worth more. Alexander Hamilton as a lawyer helped the Tories get their legal rights and won a notable court decision on the question of the property rights of Tories.

Naturally *Tory* was not perpetuated in America as the name of a political group. No party has been willing to accept the obnoxious name. But the term survives as a synonym for a dyed-in-the-wool conservative and is often hurled by politicians at their enemies as a term of general opprobrium. *Tory* was applied contemptuously to the New England Federalists who opposed the War of 1812. South Carolinians who opposed Nullification in 1832-1834 were called Tories by the Nullifiers.

On December 24, 1832, John Quincy Adams wrote in his diary in reference to Duff Green, Washington editor: "His *Telegram* has lately had some violent publications against the Union men in South Carolina, of whom Blair is one. To make them odious, it designates them as *Tories*—a name of special abhorrence there from remembrance of the Revolution." Three days later Philip Hone in New York commented in his diary: "Gen. Blair, member of Congress from South Carolina, attacked Duff Green in the street at Washington on Monday last, beat him unmercifully with a cudgel, and fractured his arm. Blair was a member of the Union Party, and from his own statement he had no private griefs to complain of, but resorted to this brutal and unwarrantable act in revenge for Green having in his paper stigmatized the Union Party as 'Tories.' " On April 30, 1834, after Representative James Blair of South Carolina had shot himself, Adams wrote: "He had paid three hundred dollars fine for beating and breaking the bones of Duff Green because he had charged the Union party of South Carolina with being Tories."

Tory was applied in 1861 to Unionists in the South, in 1896 to advocates of the gold standard, and in 1933 to opponents of the New Deal. In his acceptance speech on June 27, 1936, President Franklin D. Roosevelt indirectly designated his wealthy and powerful political opponents "economic royalists." Among other things the President said in that speech:

In 1776 we sought freedom from the tyranny of a political autocracy—from the eighteenth century royalists who held special privileges from the crown . . . . Since that struggle, however, men's inventive genius released new forces in our land which reordered the lives of our people. . . . Out of this modern civilization economic royalists carved new dynasties. New kingdoms were built upon concentration of control over material things. . . . The whole structure of modern life was impressed into this royal service.

In Great Britain *Tory* as a party name was superseded by *Conservative* in 1830. After 1886 a part of the Conservative Party became known as Unionists. Although both terms are widely used in their political sense in America, *Conservative* and *Liberal* have never been adopted as the official names of major political parties in the United States. The Democrats who opposed the subtreasury system in the special session of Congress called by President Van Buren in the fall of 1837 were known as Conservatives. On October 11, 1837, Representative John Quincy Adams wrote in his diary that James M. Mason of Virginia "spoke for the party called the Conservative, or, in other words, the State Bank party," On October 14 of the same year Adams referred to Representative John C. Clark as "one of the New York Conservatives, as they are now called." The former President also used *liberal*, but in a humorous sense. On January 17, 1838, he wrote: "Mr. Rariden's resolution, to furnish new members of the House with the books which have been furnished to the veterans, to be paid for from the contingent expenses of the House, was the unfinished business of the morning hour. The usual debate between the economists and the liberals, commenced yesterday, was now continued, till the expiration of the hour." The Republicans who opposed the reconstruction program of the Radical Republicans after the Civil War were called Conservative Republicans, and a fragment of the Republican Party in 1872 called itself the Liberal Republican Party. In that year the Liberal Republicans nominated Horace Greeley for President and B. Gratz Brown for Vice President, nominations that were confirmed by the Democratic Party. During the reconstruction period some Southern Democrats were called Conservatives, but the term fell into disuse after 1872.

After the close of the Second World War it was reported that many British Conservatives felt the name of their party had outlived its usefulness and a new one should be adopted. Some unidentified wit defined a liberal as a person who has both feet firmly planted in the air. Ralph Waldo Emerson defined a conservative as "a Democrat grown old and gone to seed," while Elbert Hubbard's definition of a conservative was "a man who is too cowardly to fight and too fat to run." In *Iolanthe* (1882) Sir William Schwenck Gilbert wrote:

> I often think it's comical,
>> How nature always does contrive
> That every boy and every gal,
>> That's born into the world alive,
> Is either a little liberal,
>> Or else a little Conservative.

When Winston Churchill was charged in 1946 with being a "reactionary," he replied in a debate on the Greek situation in the House of Commons: "An armed Communist advances upon you and you react against him. Therefore you are a reactionary."

A proverb says that a rolling stone gathers no moss and a "hidebound" conservative is called a *mossback,* a term believed to have been first applied in 1885 to an Ohio conservative Democrat. It may have been suggested by a motionless turtle lying in the water with its back covered with mosslike vegetation.

When did *stump speech* acquire its political meaning?

Stump in connection with political oratory is of American origin and goes back to the early part of the nineteenth century. It was suggested by the fact that in pioneer days on the western frontier candidates for office sometimes resorted to the stump of a tree as a rostrum or platform from which to harangue the backwoods voters. At first the term was associated with rough-and-tumble political speeches made to open-air gatherings by a candidate himself. The earliest use of *stump* in this connection recorded by *The Dictionary of American English* is dated 1816. In that year the *Annals of Congress* reported that one Congressman said of another: "His arguments are better calculated for what is called on this side of the river STUMP, than for this committee." The idea supplied the American political vocabulary with a whole series of convenient terms still in use—*stump speech, stump speaker, stump orator, stump oratory, stumper, take the stump, on the stump, to stump it* and *to stump the State* or *nation.*

How were John and Samuel Adams related?

John Adams and Samuel Adams, Revolutionary statesmen, were second cousins. They were descended from Joseph Adams, who came to America in 1626 and who had two sons, Joseph and John. President John Adams was the grandson of Joseph and Samuel Adams was the grandson of John. On one occasion Samuel Adams said to his distinguished relative: "Cousin John, you were born to build up; I was born to tear down."

Who were the Know Ye Men?

The paper-money faction in Rhode Island from 1783 to 1789 was known as the Know Ye Men because one of their pamphlets addressed to the people began with those words.

Did Washington receive all the electoral votes for President?

It is customary and substantially correct to say that George Washington was elected President of the United States twice unanimously, although he did not receive all the electoral votes cast for President. The Presidential electoral system did not operate when Washington was elected President as it did later. In its original form the Constitution provided that the electors should "vote by ballot for two persons, of whom one at least shall not be an inhabitant of the same State with themselves," that "the person having the greatest number of votes shall be President, if such number be a majority of the whole number of electors appointed," and "after the choice of the President, the person having the greatest number of votes of the electors shall be the Vice President." From this it will be seen that the electors did not vote separately for President and Vice President, but each elector cast two votes for President. The number of votes cast for President was twice the number of the electors and under this system it was impossible for one person to receive all the electoral votes for President, although he might receive one of the two votes of every elector.

On September 13, 1788, the Congress under the Articles of Confederation set January 7, 1789, for choosing electors and February 4 of the same year for their voting for President. Since the Constitution fixed the number of Representatives that each State was entitled to in the First Congress under the new system, the number of electors in the first electoral college was also fixed. If all the thirteen original States had participated in the election of 1789 there would have been 91 Presidential electors and 182 electoral votes. But North Carolina, entitled to seven electors, and Rhode Island, entitled to three, had not ratified the Constitution, and, though named in the Constitution, could not participate in the first Presidential election. Therefore only eleven States with 81 electors and 162 electoral votes were eligible to take part. But New York, entitled to eight electors and sixteen electoral votes, failed to choose electors owing to a political dispute between the State senate and house of representatives. Accordingly only ten States with 73 electors and 146 electoral votes participated. On February 4, 1789, the day the electoral colleges met in their respective States, four electors, two in Maryland and two in Virginia, failed to vote because they were delayed by ice in the rivers they had to cross. This reduced the number of electors who voted to 69 and the number of electoral votes cast for President to 138. The result of the election was: Washington, 69; John Adams, 34; Samuel Huntington, 2; John Jay, 9; John Hancock, 4; Robert H. Harrison, 6; George Clinton, 3; John Rutledge, 6; John Milton, 2 and James Armstrong, Howard Telfair and Benjamin Lincoln, 1 each. Every elector voted for Washington once and in that sense only he was elected unanimously. It is only a natural presumption that Washington was the first choice of every elector. At any rate, Washington's election was taken for granted and the electors probably exercised their independent judgment only in casting their second-choice votes, which would determine who would run second for President and therefore become Vice President. Adams received only 34 electoral votes for President, one less than a majority of the remaining votes, but since he had a greater number than any of the other ten he was declared Vice President. Since it was understood that every elector would vote once for Washington, the 34 electors who voted also for Adams for President realized in effect they were voting to give him second place.

By the time of the election of 1792 North Carolina and Rhode Island had ratified the Constitution and Vermont and Kentucky had been admitted to Statehood. The fifteen States in the Union were entitled to 132 electors and 264 electoral votes and every elector voted. At that time the country was slowly dividing into two major political parties— the Federalists headed by Hamilton and the Antifederalists or Republicans headed by Jefferson. The Antifederalists, who opposed Hamilton's financial policies, centralization of Federal power and domination of Washington's administration, knew they could not defeat Washington for a second term if they wanted to, so they concentrated their efforts on displacing Adams for second place by voting for George Clinton. The result was: Washington, 132; Adams, 77; Clinton, 50; Thomas Jefferson, 4 and Aaron Burr, 1. Again every elector voted for Washington once and in that sense he was re-elected unanimously. Adams received a plurality of 27 over Clinton and a majority of 22 over Clinton, Jefferson and Burr and was again declared Vice President. In both 1789 and 1793 Washington received all the electoral votes that the electors could cast for him, although each elector also cast another vote for President besides the one he cast for Washington.

When was a political canvass first called a campaign?

For some years after the adoption of the Constitution in 1789 Americans continued to use the British *canvass* as the name for a pre-election contest. During the early 1800's American politicians began to compare a political canvass to a military operation and called it an *electioneering campaign*. The earliest use of the term recorded by *The Dictionary of American English* is dated 1809. *Campaign* is derived from Latin *campus,* "field," and German *Kampf* and English *camp, campus, champion* and *champagne* all stem from the same root. *Electioneering campaign* soon became simply *campaign,* which gradually supplanted canvass in American political usage. Later *strategy, battle, camp, high command, war chest* and other military terms were borrowed for political use. In 1896 William Jennings Bryan referred to the East and especially New York as "the enemy's country." He decided to "invade" New York and "carry the war" into "the enemy's country" by accepting the Democratic nomination for President at Madison Square Garden. Bryan called his book about this campaign *The First Battle.* Campaign *oratory, speech, manager, club, fund, textbook* and *button* came into use after the Civil War.

Did Hamilton favor government by the rich and well born?

According to Robert Yates, who made notes of the proceedings of the Constitutional Convention, Alexander Hamilton said in a speech on June 18, 1787:

All communities divide themselves into the few and the many. The first are *the rich and well born,* the other the mass of the people. The voice of the people has been said to be the voice of God; and however generally this maxim has been quoted and believed, it is not true in fact. The people are turbulent, and changing; they seldom judge or determine right. Give therefore to the first class a distinct, permanent share in the government. They will check the unsteadiness of the second, and as they cannot receive any advantage by a change, they therefore will ever maintain good government.

Later John Adams wrote that "the rich, the well born and the able will acquire an influence among the people that will soon be too much for simple honesty and plain sense in a House of Representatives." After Hamilton and Adams became the leading Federalists, the Jeffersonian Republicans never let them forget these references to the rich and well born. In fact, the phrase contributed materially to the elimination of the Federalist Party from national control.

In the Constitutional Convention Hamilton favored a strong central government with checks and balances—a moderate one between the extremes of despotism and democracy. He wanted the President and Senators to serve during good behavior and to be chosen by electors selected by popular vote. He also wanted the President to have an absolute veto and the Governors of the States to be appointed by the Federal Government. According to Madison's notes, Hamilton said in the speech just quoted, "In his private opinion he had no scruple in declaring, supported as he was by the opinions of so many of the wise & good, that the British Govt was the best in the world; and that he doubted much whether any thing short of it would do in America," and, "Their house of lords is a most noble institution." On April 8, 1837, John Quincy Adams wrote in his diary: "If Hamilton were now living, he would not dare, in an assembly of Americans, even with closed doors, to avow the opinions of this speech, or to present such a plan even as a speculation."

Why is a ballot called a ticket?

Ticket is a corrupted form of French *etiquette*. The root of *etiquette* signified "to stick" and hence the term came to mean a label, bill, card, sign or notice stuck on a post or wall. In the time of Louis XIII visitors at Fontainebleau were warned to observe carefully the *etiquettes* or signs indicating the paths and flower beds. Persons received at court were given cards of directions and regulations and those who wanted to do the proper thing were careful to follow the directions on the *etiquettes.* Hence *etiquette* came to mean prescribed court ceremonial, protocol, the usage of diplomatic and military intercourse and the correct thing to do in polite society. Louis XIII was such a stickler for court etiquette that when he visited Cardinal Richelieu, who was sick, he lay down on the bed beside him—it was unthinkable for a subject to lie while his king stood or sat, and since the subject was sick and could not rise, the king lay down. The Duchess of Noailles, mistress of ceremony at the court in Marie Antoinette's time, was known as Mme. Etiquette because of her rigid enforcement of court procedure.

"That's the ticket," meaning "that's the right thing," is a survival of the original meaning of *ticket.* "That's the card" is similar in meaning and origin. *A la carte* means "according to the card." *Ticket* in its political sense is of American origin. A list or slate of candidates nominated for office by a party or faction was called a ticket as early as 1711, but the term was uncommon until the nineteenth century. On November 12, 1807, Senator John Quincy Adams wrote in his diary: "This was committed at the motion of Mr. Bradley, who circulated among the friends to his opinions on the affair a *ticket* to be voted for as members of the committee." *Straight ticket, scratched ticket, split ticket, mixed ticket* and *general ticket* all date from the early part of the nineteenth century.

What were the Yazoo Land Frauds?

Georgia originally claimed the Mississippi River as her western boundary. What now constitutes most of Alabama and Mississippi was known as the Yazoo territory, from the Yazoo River, a two-hundred-mile-long tributary of the Mississippi. *Yazoo,* an Indian term of unknown meaning, was the name of an extinct tribe and town on the lower part of the river that came to bear that name.

In 1795 Georgia granted thirty-five million acres of Yazoo lands to four companies for $500,000 on condition that settlements be formed after the Indian titles were extinguished. It was learned that every member of the Georgia legislature except one had a financial interest in the grants when he voted for the bill. A howl of protest followed and all Georgia was in an uproar over the scandal. James Jackson resigned his seat in the U.S. Senate and was elected to the State legislature to fight the fraud and to reclaim the Yazoo lands for the State. His death in 1806 is attributed to the many wounds he received in duels that his attacks upon the Yazoo grants brought upon him.

The new legislature in 1796, headed by Jackson, declared the grants null and void, and two years later this nullification was written into the State constitution. Meanwhile, however, the Yazoo companies sold the lands in large tracts to speculators throughout the country at an average price of fourteen cents an acre. Georgia denied the legality of these sales, while the Yazoo companies insisted that under the Federal Constitution the State legislature could not impair the obligation of a contract. Georgia would not entertain suits and the buyers of the Yazoo lands suffered heavily. In 1798 the Federal Government, after having acquired · undisputed jurisdiction over the Alabama-Mississippi region, created the Territory of Mississippi. A commission composed of Albert Gallatin, James Madison and other prominent officials appointed by President Jefferson recommended that $1,250,000 be paid to Georgia from the proceeds of the sale of lands in the Territory and that five million acres be set aside to satisfy private claims against that State. A bill to carry out this compromise was blocked in Congress in 1803 and 1805 by John Randolph of Roanoke, who hinted that Jefferson had improper motives in favoring the compromise. In 1810 Chief Justice Marshall, in *Fletcher vs. Peck,* upheld the original Yazoo grants and declared that Georgia's nullification act violated the "impairment of contracts" provision in the Federal Constitution. But President Madison had no means of enforcing the decision against Georgia. Finally, in 1814, after Randolph had been defeated for re-election, Congress passed a bill authorizing up to $8,000,000 to settle the various Yazoo claims.

What was the Essex Junto?

Spanish *junta,* ultimately from Latin *jungere,* "to join," means an administrative or legislative council or committee. In the seventeenth century the English borrowed the term in the altered form of *junto* and used it in the sense of a cabal, coterie, clique, faction or group of persons combined for political purposes. It was applied to the cabinet council of Charles I, the Rump Parliament, and a group of Whig leaders during the reigns of William III and Anne. In 1727 Benjamin Franklin formed a self-improvement club in Philadelphia called the Junto. Before the Revolution a group of men in Essex County, Massachusetts, who were opposed to the royal governor, were called the Essex Junto, and the same term was applied to some of the political opponents of Governor John Hancock in the early 1780's.

After 1797 George Cabot, Timothy Pickering, Fisher Ames, Theophilus Parsons and other New England Federalists followed the leadership of Alexander Hamilton instead of President John Adams. It happened that most of the anti-Adams faction lived in Essex County, Massachusetts, and the President, reviving an old term in his State, called it the Essex Junto. He also referred to the group as the "pro-British party" because they opposed his French policy and sympathized with England. In the end the President broke completely with the Essex Junto and dismissed Pickering from his Cabinet. After Adams's defeat in 1800 *Essex Junto* became synonymous with the New England ultra-Federalists in general. It was the Essex Junto in this sense that led the Federalist Party to its final ruin. The group of men who promoted the original candidacy of Andrew Jackson for President were known as the "Nashville Junto."

How was national election day chosen?

Selection of the first Tuesday after the first Monday in November as national election day appears to have been governed by several considerations.

The Constitution provides that "Congress may determine the *time of choosing the electors,* and the day on which they shall give their votes; which day shall be the same throughout the United States." A law approved March 1, 1792, fixed the first Wednesday in December as the day for the electors to meet and cast their votes for President and Vice President. That law also provided that the electors should be "appointed" in each State "within thirty-four days preceding the first Wednesday in December in every fourth year succeeding the last election."

In the early days the legislatures of most of the States chose the Presidential electors and the exact date on which the electors of the States were chosen was not important. After the election of 1824 nearly all the States that had not already done so gave up the old method of choosing Presidential electors by the legislature. With a few exceptions the Presidential electors have since been chosen by popular vote in all States. Before 1845 there was no national election day and each State fixed its own date for "appointment" of Presidential electors within thirty-four days of the meeting of the electors. All the States chose their electors in November, but the dates varied. New York held her election for electors on the first Tuesday after the first Monday; New Jersey, on the first Tuesday and the day following. In two States the second Monday was election day; in fourteen, the first Monday; in two, the second Tuesday, and in two, the Friday nearest the first of November.

This lack of uniformity led to abuses. The results in one State were used to influence those in other States. In contiguous States "repeating" was easy and common. By traveling from State to State one person could vote for Presidential electors several times. This practice led to what were known as the "pipe-laying scandles" of 1840 and 1844, when both the Democrats and Whigs were accused of sending gangs of voters across State lines. The frequency of such election frauds created a popular demand for a uniform national election day.

On January 23, 1845, President John Tyler approved an act of Congress providing that "the electors of President and Vice President shall be appointed in each State on the Tuesday next after the first Monday in the month of November of the year in which they are to be appointed." The act of 1792 still required the electors to meet on the first Wednesday in December, and in fixing a uniform day Congress wished to make the time as close as possible to thirty days before that date. Public sentiment was opposed to holding elections on Sunday or traveling to the polls on that day. Therefore it was desirable to have one day intervene between Sunday and election day because many voters lived far from the polls and in those days it was often necessary to start out the preceding day. Since many voters would object to traveling on Sunday to go to the polls, Monday was excluded. The first Tuesday was excluded because it might fall on the first of the month and inconvenience businessmen. The second Tuesday might fall on the 14th, which would leave only twenty-two days between election day and the meeting of the Presidential electors. It was discovered that the first Tuesday after the first Monday in November, the date already chosen by New York, would always place election day not later than November 8 and always about thirty days before the meeting of the electors on the first Wednesday in December. Representative Alexander Duncan, an Ohio Whig and author of the election bill of 1845, said in the debate on the subject that "Public sentiment has appointed this time" because harvesting is over by November and winter weather has not yet made the roads impassable. He objected to the first Tuesday in November because it "might in some cases be more than 30 days from the first Wednesday in December." The first Tuesday after the first Monday in November was accordingly accepted.

In 1848, when Zachary Taylor and Millard Fillmore were the successful candidates for President and Vice President, all the States chose their electors on this uniform date, although South Carolina chose its electors by the Legislature instead of popular vote. On Tuesday, November 7, 1848, President James K. Polk wrote in his diary:

This is the day appointed by law for the election of President and Vice-President of the United States. Heretofore the people of the several States have by State laws fixed the period of holding the election in each State. Since the last Presidential election Congress for the first time exercised the power vested in them by the Constitution, and fixed the same day for holding the election in all the States. There will probably be not less than three million of votes polled in this election.

Actually the total popular vote in that election was 2,875,408. The act of 1792 provided that, "when any State shall have held an election for the purpose of choosing electors, and shall fail to make a choice on the day aforesaid, then the electors may be appointed on a subsequent day in such manner as the State shall by law provide," and that provision continued effective.

The first Tuesday after the first Monday in November remains national election day, notwithstanding the fact that the original reasons for that particular date no longer exist, the time of the meeting of the electors having been changed three times since then. Election day is either a full or a half holiday in most of the States.

How did *vote* originate?

Vote is derived from Latin *votum,* "vow," "prayer," "wish" or "desire." *Votive, votary* and *vow* are from the same source. *Vote* in the sense of casting a ballot was used in English in the sixteenth century, but does not occur in Shakespeare. When Coriolanus stood for consul he asked the people for their voices, not their votes.

Who said: "Millions for defense, but not one cent for tribute"?

"Millions for defense but not one cent for tribute" is inscribed on the cenotaph to the memory of Charles Cotesworth Pinckney (1746-1825) in St. Michael's Church in Charleston, South Carolina, and the saying is popularly, but wrongly, attributed to him.

The saying originated during the "quasi war with France" between 1797 and 1800. By the French Alliance of 1778 the United States bound itself in return for French aid against England to help France in future wars against England if England was the aggressor. It was understood under the agreements of 1778 that the United States would aid France in holding her West Indian possessions against British aggression. This was one of the prices the United States had offered to pay for French aid in winning her independence.

After the French Revolution of 1789 this alliance with France became embarrassing to the United States. France declared war against England on February 1, 1793, and insisted that the United States was under treaty obligations to come to her aid. Opinion in the United States as to what to do was divided. Some people favored England, others favored France, and still others were neutral. President Washington was in a quandary. He did not want to embroil the United States in a fruitless European war, but how could the United States renounce the treaties of 1778 without showing bad faith? Secretary of the Treasury Alexander Hamilton, who was pro-British, wanted Washington to advise Genet, the French Minister in America, that the treaties of 1778 were made with the King of France and were no longer binding because the King was dead. Secretary of State Thomas Jefferson, who was pro-French, insisted that the treaties were made with the French government and were still binding. On April 22, 1793, the President issued a proclamation, which was drafted by Attorney General Edmund Randolph. In spirit it was a proclamation of neutrality, although the word itself was carefully avoided, because Washington's desire was, as he wrote Patrick Henry, "to comply strictly with all our engagements, foreign and domestic."

When John Adams became President in 1797 Franco-American relations were nearing the breaking point. France particularly resented the Jay Treaty of 1794, which patched up Anglo-American relations temporarily. In December, 1798, President Washington had appointed Charles Cotesworth Pinckney minister to France in the hope of settling differences between the two nations. When Pinckney reached Paris the French government refused to receive him and later he was compelled to leave the country. Shortly thereafter France gave her permission to attack American shipping. President Adams called a special session of Congress to deal with the problem and sent Elbridge Gerry, John Marshall and Pinckney to Paris to try to stop French attacks on American commerce.

The French Directory refused to recognize the American commissioners, but on October 6, 1797, one of Foreign Minister Talleyrand's secret agents named Hottenguer whispered to Pinckney that the Directory would talk business with the American commissioners if they would advance a *douceur* (bribe) of fifty thousand pounds sterling to the Directory and make a large loan to the French government. It was at this juncture that Pinckney is supposed to have uttered the historic saying, "Millions for defense, but not one cent for tribute." According to his own story, his reply was, "Not a sixpence, sir." In later meetings with the American commissioners French agents repeated the suggestion that a bribe and a loan would bring the Directory around to an agreement. In their official report to President Adams, Pinckney, Gerry and Marshall said: "M. X. again returned to the subject of money. Said he, gentlemen, you do not speak to the point; it is money; it is expected you will offer money. We said that we had spoken to that point very explicitly. No, said he, you have not; what is your answer? We replied, it is no; no, not a sixpence."

In January, 1798, Marshall related the incident in a strong note to Talleyrand. When President Adams sent the correspondence to Congress he did not name the three French officials involved but designated them simply as M. X., M. Y. and M. Z., and when the documents became public the incident became known as "The XYZ Affair." Naturally the incident created a national sensation. Marshall returned to the United States to find himself very popular with the Federalists. On June 18, 1798, the Federalist members of Congress gave a banquet in Marshall's honor at O'Eller's Tavern in Philadelphia, then the seat of government. At this banquet sixteen toasts were offered, many of them breathing defiance to France. The eleventh toast was: "The American eagle; may it regard with disdain the crowing of the Gallic cock." Robert Goodloe Harper (1765-1825), a native of Virginia but a Federalist member of Congress from South Carolina, offered the thirteenth toast, which was: "Millions for defense, but not one cent for tribute." The *American Daily Advertiser*, a Philadelphia newspaper, printed all sixteen of the toasts in its issue of June 20, 1798, and credited to Harper the one that became famous. Pinckney did not hear of it until he returned from Europe later. He died in 1825 at the age of seventy-nine. Before his death he told Thomas Grimke that his reply to Talleyrand's secret agent was simply "Not a sixpence, sir," and not another word. He said he had never used the expression, "Millions for defense, but not one cent for tribute," but that Harper had done so at a public meeting. The old Revoluntionary statesman and general explained that he had never corrected the report because "The nation adopted the expression, and I always thought there would have been more ostentation in denying than in submitting to the report." Harper, apparently the true author of the famous saying, afterward explained that he did not even have Pinckney's reply in mind when he offered the toast at the Marshall banquet. He said he had in mind only the general thought that the United States should use for national defense the millions it was losing to French privateers. The saying is more characteristic of the eloquent and flamboyant Harper than it is of the modest and self-effacing Pinckney. Harper later removed to Maryland, married a daughter of Charles Carroll of Carrollton and represented Maryland in the U.S. Senate. He, like Pinckney, died in 1825.

On July 9, 1798, Congress abrogated the treaty of 1778 and other treaties with France and authorized American war vessels and privateers to attack French armed ships. Taxes were increased, the Alien and Sedition Acts were passed, naval affairs were removed from the War Department and placed under a new Navy Department, an increase in the army was authorized and Washington was made nominal commander-in-chief. During the two and a half years of the undeclared war with France, Americans captured eighty-five French ships and lost only one. In 1799 Napoleon Bonaparte, who had become dictator of France, adopted a more conciliatory attitude toward the United States. Talleyrand intimated to Williams Vans Murray, American minister to the Netherlands, that France was willing to receive another American Minister. In February, 1799, President Adams appointed Murray, William R. Davis and Chief Justice Oliver Ellsworth to negotiate with Napoleon. The treaty they negotiated became effective December 21, 1801. Although the American Colonies aided the mother country in wars against France before the Revolution, the United States, since it became an independent nation, has never declared war against France.

Which Vice President was chosen by the House of Representatives?

Aaron Burr has been the only Vice President chosen by the House of Representatives.

In the election of 1800, before the Twelfth Amendment to the Constitution was adopted and when each elector voted for two persons for President and none for Vice President, Thomas Jefferson and Burr each received seventy-three electoral votes, which was eight more than the number received by John Adams and nine more than the number received by Charles Cotesworth Pinckney. Article II of the Constitution provided: "The person having the greatest number of votes shall be President, if such number be a majority of the whole number of electors appointed; and if there be more than one who have such majority, and have an equal number of votes, then the House of Representatives shall immediately chuse by ballot one of them for President; . . . after the choice of the President, the person having the greatest number of votes of the electors shall be Vice President." It also provided that "in chusing the President, the votes shall be taken by States, the representation from each State having one vote, a quorum for this purpose shall consist of a member or members from two-thirds of the States, and a majority of all the States shall be necessary to a choice."

On the thirty-sixth ballot the House chose Jefferson President and under the Constitution Burr then automatically became Vice President. Since the House had to choose a President from the two, it in effect chose a Vice President as well as a President.

How did *doughface* originate?

Doughface was popularized if not coined by John Randolph of Roanoke, who applied the term to Northern politicians who truckled to the Southern slavery men. He branded the Missouri Compromise of 1820 as "a dirty bargain," helped on by "eighteen Northern doughfaces." The New Brunswick *Times* on April 12, 1820, quoted Randolph as saying: "I knew these would give way. They were scared at their dough-faces. We had them." The term quickly became current. On December 3, 1824, Secretary of State John Quincy Adams wrote in his diary: "He spoke of the efforts yet making to bring over the dough-faces to the caucus."

Adams used the term several times in his diary after he became a Representative in Congress. On November 12, 1838, he wrote: "I had thought it apparent that they [Southern Congressmen] generally held in contempt the Northern members who truckled to them, such as John Randolph had nicknamed 'dough-faces.'" Old Man Eloquent had no patience with Northerners who were subservient to the South. On November 20, 1841, when the exclusion of antislavery petitions and the annexation of Texas were burning questions, Adams wrote: "I look forward to both these designs with alarm and anguish—not for the power of the South, which can effect nothing by itself, but from experience of the treachery of the Northern representatives, both to Northern interests and principles." He noted in his diary on February 28, 1843: "The vote was partisan sectional, except Cushing's, which was Northern, servile, or dough-face." James Russell Lowell defined *doughface* as a "contented lickspittle, a common variety of Northern politician." During the Civil War the term was applied to a Northerner who favored the South.

One authority suggests that possibly Randolph was improperly quoted and that what he really meant was *doeface,* referring to the proverbial meekness and timidity of the doe. But the first element in the term was invariably spelled *dough* and not *doe* in early usage. It is more probable that in its first application the term compared certain pliable and yielding politicians with the kneadable character of dough. In pioneer days, especially in the South, it was common for country people to make masks or false faces for Hallowe'en and other sportive occasions by putting dough or flour over their faces. Such masks were called *doughfaces.* This practice is mentioned in Edward Eggleston's *The Hoosier Schoolboy* (1883). Possibly Randolph had the practice in mind when he coined *doughface* in its political sense. He may have intended to compare the hypocrisy of certain Northern Congressmen with the expressionlessness of a dough mask.

Later politicians of the type described by Randolph as doughfaces were known as "Northern men with Southern principles," a phrase of unknown authorship. Apparently President Martin Van Buren was the first politician to be called "a Northern man with Southern principles." On March 14, 1838, Adams wrote in his diary: "He [W. Cost Johnson] touched on nullification, and was called to order by the Speaker, who, since Calhoun's chop round to the Northern man with Southern principles, has become tenderly observant of the feelings of the Nullifiers." During the Presidential campaign of 1840 a committee of seventy-six Democratic-Republicans addressed "to the citizens of the Southern States" a forty-page pamphlet entitled *A Northern Man with Southern Principles and a Southern Man with American Principles.* Three of the Democratic Presidential nominees after Van Buren—Lewis Cass in 1848, Franklin Pierce in 1852, and James Buchanan in 1856—were "Northern men with Southern principles." During the campaign of 1852 John Y. Mason of Virginia urged the South "to cherish and defend Northern men like Pierce who had risked so much for the maintenance of Southern rights and honor."

Who were the Coodies?

The majority of the members of the Federalist Party were opposed to the War of 1812 against Great Britain. Federalist opposition to the war reached its acme with the Hartford Convention late in 1814. The minority of Federalists who favored and supported the war were known derisively as Coodies. This odd name was suggested by a series of articles published in a New York newspaper in 1814 by Gulian Crommelin Verplanck (1786-1870) under the nom de plume *Abimeleck Coody*. The writer pointed out the impropriety of opposing the war and urged the Federalists to help defend their country. Verplanck was an editor, author, Shakespearean scholar and was prominent in the New York literary life of his time. Like his father before him, he was a member of Congress. Roger Brooke Taney, of Maryland, afterward Chief Justice of the United States, was called "King Coody" or "the King of the Coodies."

How did *gerrymander* originate?

A gerrymander is an unnatural and unfair division of a State, county or other governmental unit into distorted representative districts to give undue advantage to the political party in power. Hostile voters are placed in districts certain to go against the dominant party and friendly voters in districts where the parties are more equally divided.

Gerrymander is a blend of *Gerry,* a proper name, and *salamander,* the name of a spotted lizard-like animal. It originated in Massachusetts in 1812 when Elbridge Gerry was Governor of the State. On February 11, 1812, the Democratic-Republican legislature of Massachusetts passed a bill redistricting the State in irregular senatorial districts to give the Democratic-Republican candidates a decided advantage in the coming spring election. Notwithstanding frequent statements to the contrary, Governor Gerry did not sponsor this measure and he signed it reluctantly, but nonetheless his name became associated with it.

Essex County in the northeastern corner of the State was divided into two senatorial districts. A two-member district was rather compact and included "sure" Federalist "towns," but a three-member district was abnormally shaped and ran around the western and northern edge of the entire county from seacoast to seacoast. This distorted arrangement was intended to make it possible for the heavy Democratic-Republican vote in Marblehead to overcome the Federalist majorities in the other eleven towns. When the Democratic-Republican legislature got through with its work this Essex County district somewhat resembled a dragon in outline. Naturally the infuriated Federalists accused Governor Gerry of having been behind the redistricting measure, and they called the distorted district a "Gerrymander."

According to legend, Benjamin Russell, Federalist editor of the Boston *Centinel,* hung up in his office a map showing the proposed new senatorial districts. One day the famous artist Gilbert Stuart went into the *Centinel* office and noticed the queer shape of the upper Essex County district on the map on the wall above Russell's desk. Taking a pencil he added a head, wings and claws, at the same time observing, "That will do for a salamander!" "Better say *Gerrymander*," replied Russell. Another version of the legend is that it was a miniature painter and engraver named Elkanah Tisdale who drew the head, wings and claws on the map and that it was either Richard Alsop, one of the "Hartford Wits," or James Ogilvie, a well-known lecturer, who suggested *Gerrymander*. At any rate, a new term entered the American political vocabulary that year. It was popularized by the Federalists during the following campaign by the circulation of a caricature representing the Essex County senatorial district as a winged monster with Governor Gerry's profile in the background.

The Gerrymander of 1812 in Massachusetts worked. In the April election the Federalist candidates for State senator received 51,766 votes in the State as against 50,164 for the Democratic-Republican candidates; but, thanks to the Gerrymander Bill, twenty-nine State senators were elected by the Democratic-Republicans and only eleven by the Federalists. Governor Gerry himself, however, was defeated for re-election. Two months later he was nominated for Vice President on the Madison ticket and was elected. He died in office and was buried in the Congressional Cemetery, being the only Vice President to be buried in Washington. The Gerrymander act of 1812 was repealed a year after it was passed. As early as April 2, 1813, the Boston *Gazette* reported that *gerrymander* was being used "throughout the United States as synonymous with *deception*." In its issue of June 2, 1813, the *Massachusetts Spy* declared: "The manner in which they have obtained a majority is by a species of gerrymandering." A British writer once suggested that perhaps *gerrymander* was derived from an American politician named Jerry Mander.

Gerry's name is pronounced with a hard *g* as in *Gerrit*. Although *gerr-ee-*MANN-*der* was long the preferred pronunciation of *gerrymander*, it is now widely pronounced JERR-*ee-*MANN-*der*.

Elbridge Gerry signed the Declaration of Independence, was a member of the Constitutional Convention of 1787, although he refused to sign the final document, and was one of the American commissioners to France during the XYZ Affair. His disposition was to oppose almost everything. He was not a member of the Massachusetts convention that ratified the Federal Constitution, but as one of its framers he was invited to "sit on the floor" to answer "such questions as may be propounded to him." Gerry was so active in the debates that this privilege was rescinded and he was requested to leave the convention. He was small in stature, dressed dapperly, and was known as the "Columbian Patriot." In 1786, when he was forty-two, he was married to Ann Thompson, "the handsome and exceedingly amiable" seventeen-year-old daughter of a New York merchant. She lived until 1849 and was the last surviving widow of a signer of the Declaration of Independence. After Gerry's death in 1814, Senator Christopher Gore of Massachusetts introduced a bill providing for the payment of the Vice President's salary to his widow for the remainder of his term. The bill was passed by the Senate but rejected by the House. Peter Goelet Gerry, who served in the House and Senate from Rhode Island several terms between 1913 and 1947, was a great-great-grandson of Elbridge Gerry.

Although *gerrymander* was a new term in 1812, the practice it described was old. When the Federalists got back into power in Massachusetts they did some gerrymandering on their own account. On September 22, 1830, when he was a candidate for Congress, John Quincy Adams wrote in his diary: "I asked how it happened that Quincy had been cast into the Plymouth district for elections to Congress. He said he attributed it to Mr. Thomas Greenleaf, who was in the Council when the thing was done, and the object of it was to make Plymouth a certainly federal district; but now, what with Anti-Masonics and Jackson men, parties were all broken up, and no one could tell what any man was." In 1890 William McKinley was "gerrymandered out of Congress." Six years later he was elected President of the United States. One of the most notorious gerrymanders in American history was the famous Mississippi "Shoe String District," which was five hundred miles long and only forty wide. A glance at the Congressional district maps in the current *Congressional Directory* indicates that gerrymandering is not a lost art among American politicians, although Congressional districts often are irregularly shaped for geographic and population as well as for political reasons.

Why is a preliminary meeting called a caucus?

Caucus, meaning a secret preliminary meeting of the leaders of a political party or group, is supposed to be derived from the name of a pre-Revolutionary club in Boston. How the original club got its name has never been determined and several theories have been advanced to explain it. Perhaps the term, variously spelled, antedated the club and a word already current was taken for the name of the political society.

The Boston *Evening Post* of August 19, 1745, announced that a "general meeting" of "lay brethren" would be held "at West-Corcus in Boston." This quotation has led some to suppose that *Caucus* may have been the name of a now forgotten locality in that city. During the year 1760 the *Boston Gazette* used *Corcas* several times. For instance, "Nothing of the least significance was transacted at a late meeting of the New and Grand Corcas," and, "Votes are to be given away by the delicate hands of the New and Grand Corcas." In February, 1763, John Adams wrote in his diary:

This day learned that the Caucus Club meets, at certain times, in the garret of Tom Dawes, the Adjutant of the Boston Regiment. He has a large house, and he has a movable partition in his garret which he takes down, and the whole club meets in one room. There they smoke tobacco till you cannot see from one end of the garret to the other. There they drink *flip,* I suppose, and there they choose a moderator, who puts questions to the vote regularly; and selectmen, assessors, collectors, wardens, pre-wards, and representatives, are regularly chosen before they are chosen by the town. Uncle Fairfield, Story, Buddock, (Samuel) Adams, Cooper, and *rudis indigestaque moles* of others are members. They send committees to wait on the merchant's club, and to propose and join in the choice of men and measures. Captain Cunningham says they have often solicited him to go to these caucuses; they have assured him benefits in his business, etc.

On March 14, 1763, the *Evening Post* referred to the secret gathering in Tom Dawes's attic to make up a slate of candidates and measures for the town meeting as the *Corkass.* By 1775 Boston had "The North End Caucus," "The South End Caucus" and "The Middle District Caucus."

In *The History of the Rise, Progress, and Establishment of the Independence of the United States of America,* published in four volumes in London in 1788, William Gordon, an English clergyman who lived in America during the Revolution, wrote in a note:

The word *caucus* and its derivative *caucusing,* are often used in Boston. The last answers much to what we style *parliamenteering* or *electioneering.* All my repeated applications to different gentlemen have not furnished me with a satisfactory account of *caucus.* It seems to mean a number of persons, whether more or less, met together to consult upon adopting and prosecuting some scheme of policy for carrying a favorite point. The word is not of novel invention. More than fifty years ago Mr. Samuel Adams's father and twenty others, one or two from the north end of the town, where all the ship-business is carried on, used to meet, make a *caucus,* and lay their plan for introducing certain persons into places of trust and power. When they had settled it they separated, and used each their particular influence within his own circle. He and his friends would furnish themselves with ballots, including the names of the parties fixed upon, which they distributed on the days of election. By acting in concert, together with a careful and extensive distribution of ballots, they generally carried the elections to their own mind. In like manner it was that Mr. Samuel Adams first became a representative for Boston.

The earliest theory derived the word from *caulker*, meaning one who drives oakum or old rope into the seams of vessels. According to this theory, which was favored by John Pickering in 1814, *Caucus Club* was merely a corruption of *Caulkers' Club* and the members were contemptuously called caulkers by their enemies because most of them were identified in one way or another with the shipping interests of Boston. Later Pickering made a note that Benjamin Russell told him that Samuel Adams and Paul Revere had said that *caucus* was made up from the initial letters of five of the original members—Cooper, Adams, Urann, Coulson, Urann and Symmes.

Because it has long been a common practice to adopt classical names for organizations, some derive *caucus* from Latin *caucus* (Greek *kaukos*), "cup" or "drinking vessel." Adams's reference to drinking flip at the Caucus Club is pointed out as evidence of the appropriateness of the Latin and Greek term that might suggest classical conviviality. *Flip* in those days was the name of a concoction made by mixing beer or ale with hard cider or rum, adding eggs beaten to a froth and sugar or syrup for sweetening and then boiling the whole with a red-hot poker to give it a bitter or burnt taste. With drink like that a caucus could easily put over its slate of candidates.

Since it was also a common practice to give clubs Indian names, others follow a similar line of reasoning and derive the name from the Algonquin Indian *caucauasu*, which, according to J. Hammond Trumbull, in the Virginia dialect of the Algonquin tongue signified "elder," "counselor" or "one who advises, urges, encourages, pushes on." Still others try to connect the term with Indian *kaw-kaw-was*, "talk."

But there is insufficient evidence to support any of these theories. One man's guess is about as good as another's, and the origin of this curious and interesting Americanism remains one of the unsolved puzzles of etymology.

Caucus was introduced into general circulation in England in 1878 when Disraeli misapplied it to "The Liberal Association of Birmingham." Now the British apply the term to the managing or steering committee of a political party or faction. While in America a caucus is a secret preliminary meeting, in England it is a "political machine."

The Democratic Party organization in the House of Representatives is officially called "The Democratic Caucus." The corresponding Republican Party organization in the House, as well as both the Democratic and Republican organizations of the Senate, is officially called a "Conference." These caucuses meet to nominate persons for House and Senate offices at the beginning of a new Congress and occasionally at other times to get the sense of the party on a pending measure. The chairmanship of the caucus or conference usually goes to a party wheelhorse.

When were candidates first nominated by conventions?

In the years immediately following the adoption of the Federal Constitution there were no national political parties in the United States and candidates were not formally nominated for President and Vice President. Until the Twelfth Amendment to the Constitution became effective in 1804 each elector voted for two persons for President. The one who received the most votes became President and the one who received the second largest number became Vice President, provided the number was a majority of the total. Under this system George Washington and John Adams were elected President and Vice President respectively in 1788 and 1792, and Adams and Thomas Jefferson were elected President and Vice President respectively in 1796. Adams and Thomas Pinckney were the recognized Federalist candidates for President and Vice President in 1796 without formal nominations, but Jefferson, the choice of the Republicans without a formal nomination and without a running mate, received the second largest number of electoral votes and became Vice President.

The earliest party division on a national scale was between the Federalists, who favored the new Constitution, and the Antifederalists, who opposed it. The next party division was between the followers of Alexander Hamilton, who retained the name Federalists, and the followers of Jefferson, who adopted the name Republicans. In 1800 the Federalists and Republicans put up separate lists of candidates for electors and undertook to tell their list of electors, in the event they were chosen, whom to vote for for President and Vice President, even though the electors could not vote for these officers separately. The obvious candidates for President were President Adams for the Federalists, and Vice President Jefferson for the Republicans. There was a general understanding among the Federalist leaders in and out of Congress that their electors should vote for Adams as first choice and Charles Cotesworth Pinckney as second choice. In the spring of 1800 the Republican members of the Senate and the House of Representatives met in

Philadelphia, then the national capital, and recommended that their electors vote for Jefferson as first choice and Aaron Burr as second choice. This Republican meeting was called a "congressional convention," but it was the beginning of the caucus system of making nominations. The successful electors could not vote for President and Vice President separately and the election of 1800 demonstrated the impracticability of the original electoral scheme under a party system. Adams received 65 electoral votes, Pinckney received 64, and Jefferson and Burr each received 71, with the result that the House of Representatives had to decide between the latter two. One Federalist elector had taken the precaution to vote for John Jay instead of Pinckney to prevent Adams and Pinckney from being tied in the event of success, but no Democratic-Republican elector had taken that precaution in respect to Burr. The Twelfth Amendment, which became effective in 1804, provided that each elector should vote for President and Vice President separately and made separate nominations for President and Vice President practicable.

In 1804 Vice President Burr was no longer acceptable to the Republicans as their choice for second place. Accordingly the Republican members of Congress held a caucus and nominated President Jefferson to succeed himself—a mere formality—and nominated George Clinton for Vice President. The Federalist members of both houses of Congress also held a caucus and nominated Thomas Pinckney for President and Rufus King for Vice President. This established the Congressional caucus system as the method of nominating candidates for the two highest offices.

John Quincy Adams gives us an intimate glimpse of the Republican caucus of 1808, which he calls a "convention." On February 23, 1808, Senator Adams, who had just switched from the Federalists to the Republicans, wrote in his diary:

I dined with Mr. Bradley [Senator Stephen Row Bradley of Vermont] at his lodgings, and in the evening attended the convention of the members to nominate suitable persons as candidates for the offices of President and Vice President. There has been much question as to Mr. Bradley's authority to call this convention, which it seems he contends was given him at a convention on the last presidential election, four years ago. The New York members especially are extremely averse to it. There were, however, about ninety members who assembled under Mr. Bradley's summons; upon which he stated the authority formerly given him, and his reasons for calling the meeting. But he said that, as exception had been taken to his exercise of that authority, it was now at an end, and the meeting must proceed at their own pleasure. He said that he had issued his circulars to every republican member of both Houses; indeed, to every member, excepting five of the Senate and twenty-two of the House of Representatives. Nor should I have omitted them, said he, but that they have never been in the habit of acting with us.

Mr. Giles moved that Mr. Bradley should take the chair; which he accordingly did. It was agreed that the members present should be counted, and Mr. Milledge and Mr. Varnum were appointed tellers. The members present were found to be eighty-nine. Mr. Bradley proposed the appointment of a clerk. Mr. Burwell and Mr. G. W. Campbell were successively chosen, and excused themselves from serving. Mr. Johnson, of Kentucky, was then chosen, and accepted. After some question whether there should be a viva voce nomination and a subsequent ballot, it was at last agreed to vote by ballot without nomination. On taking the ballots for the office of President there were eighty-three votes for James Madison, three for James Monroe, and three for George Clinton. Before the ballot for Vice-President, Mr. Pope made a speech recommending unanimity for the choice of this office. The votes were seventy-nine for George Clinton, five for Henry Dearborn, three for John Langdon, and one for J. Q. Adams. The chairman then declared James Madison duly nominated by a great majority of votes, as candidate for the office of President, and George Clinton for that of Vice-President.

A committee of correspondence was then chosen, consisting of a member from each State, but Connecticut and Delaware, not being present, had no members chosen. A resolution was then offered by Mr. Giles, and adopted, for publication, stating this nomination, and the reasons which induced the meeting to make it, after which the meeting adjourned without day, and I came home. Many of the persons who attended the meeting thought it precipitately called. Many refused to attend. The number present was a bare majority of the whole number of members. Twenty-seven federalists where not invited; about sixty others were absent, among whom were all the Virginians, or Randolph minority. Dr. Mitchill told me that Mr. Bradley's ardor in favor of Madison was stimulated by his personal views, and that he was now soliciting offices for his son, and for his brother-in-law, by the name of Atwater. From the appearances at the meeting I judged it to be called in concert, and probably at the instigation of Virginian Madisonians, and particularly Messrs. Giles and Nicholas. I suppose their particular object to be to aid the canvass of Mr. Madison's friends for electors of President and Vice-President, which is now going on in the Virginia Legislature.

In the same year the Federalist Congressional caucus renominated their candidates of 1804—Pinckney and King. At that period State legislatures, legislative caucuses or conventions often lent a helping hand by endorsing the candidates nominated by the Congressional caucuses. In May, 1812, the Republican Congressional caucus renominated Madison for President and nominated John Langdon for Vice

President. Langdon, then seventy-one years old and Governor of New Hampshire, declined the nomination, whereupon the Republicans substituted Elbridge Gerry.

In 1812 the Federalists, who had been defeated in three successive elections, decided to take a different tack. War against England had been declared in June and there was considerable opposition outside the Federalist Party to the war and the re-election of President Madison. Instead of relying on a Congressional caucus, the Federalist leaders met in New York City in September for consultation about a Presidential candidate. This Federalist convention was attended by about seventy self-appointed "delegates" from eleven of the eighteen States then in the Union. As a challenge to the Congressional caucus that renominated Madison, the Republicans of the New York legislature had nominated De Witt Clinton for President, and the Federalists of the Pennsylvania legislature had nominated Jared Ingersoll for Vice President. The Federalist convention in New York made no formal nominations, owing to the opposition of Rufus King, but, under the leadership of Harrison Gray Otis, passed a resolution declaring, "That we highly approve of the nomination by the State of New York, of De Witt Clinton (a citizen of the State, possessing distinguished talents and long tried Patriotism) for the next Presidency, and Jared Ingersoll, of Pennsylvania, for the office of Vice President." The Federalist meeting in 1812 is sometimes called the first national nominating convention, but it was hardly that. It was a secret meeting and more in the nature of a regional caucus than a national convention. This was the first Presidential election in wartime and the incumbent was re-elected. The electoral vote was 128 for Madison and 89 for Clinton, who was an anti-Madison Republican rather than a Federalist.

The first serious contest in the Republican Congressional caucus occurred in 1816. James Monroe was nominated but received only eleven votes more than William H. Crawford. Daniel D. Tompkins was nominated for Vice President. The Federalists did not try the convention method again. Their Congressional caucus nominated King for President and John Eager Howard for Vice President. King, who had been the Federalist Vice-Presidential candidate in 1804 and 1808, received only 32 electoral votes and Howard only 22. After that the Federalists ceased to be a national party and never made another nomination for President or Vice President either by caucus or convention. In 1820 there was only one national political party left and the Republican caucus was meaningless, because President Monroe's re-election was taken for granted. The caucus that year was called by a small group who wanted to replace Vice President Tompkins by Henry Clay. Only forty members of Congress attended and the caucus merely voted unanimously not to make any nominations.

During the next four years the caucus system of making nominations became unpopular. People were getting tired of having their Presidents and Vice Presidents named by an inner circle of Congressmen. As early as 1819 Secretary of State John Quincy Adams had written in his diary that the Congressional caucus was objectionable because it invited ambitious men to curry favor with Senators and Representatives, placed the President in a position of subserviency to Congress and caused cabals and corrupt coalitions. By 1823 opposition to the caucus system had become serious and in 1824 it was an important political issue. At the outset there were five strong candidates to succeed President Monroe—Adams, Clay, Jackson, John C. Calhoun and Crawford. The first four opposed the caucus system and decided to run for President without formal nominations by any national group, but Crawford, who appeared to be the strongest of the five, favored it. The chief objection to the system was that it was undemocratic. Jackson's supporters referred to it sneeringly as "King Caucus," a monarch to be dethroned in democratic America. The Tennessee, Alabama and Maryland legislatures passed resolutions condemning the caucus system, but many States refused to commit themselves, while the Maine legislature went on record as approving the system.

To head off the rising anti-caucus movement, the Crawford supporters, knowing they outnumbered any one of the others, called a Congressional caucus early in 1824 to nominate their man. The caucus met in the hall of the House of Representatives on February 14. Most of the supporters of the other candidates boycotted the caucus and only 68 out of 261 members of Congress attended. Sixty-four voted to nominate Crawford for President and Albert Gallatin for Vice President. After that Crawford was scoffingly called the "caucus candidate." Gallatin, Swiss born, had no prospect of election and was persuaded to withdraw from the ticket. Calhoun, seeing how the political wind blew, dropped from the Presidential race and became informally the candidate for Vice President on the tickets of the other four factions. In the election Crawford, the caucus candidate, ran third. None of the four candidates received a majority of the electoral votes, and, notwithstanding the Twelfth Amendment, an election again was thrown into the House of Representatives, which chose Adams, who had run second to Jackson. The election of 1824 killed King Caucus and demonstrated that this method of nomination was effective when it followed but not when it tried to lead public opinion.

Jackson, who had received more electoral votes than any other candidate, was the natural opponent of President Adams in 1828. Vice President Calhoun was accepted without formal nomination as the Jackson candidate to succeed himself. There was no need to nominate Adams formally to succeed himself, although both he and Jackson were endorsed by several State legislatures, legislative caucuses and conventions. A State convention at Harrisburg, Pennsylvania, endorsed Adams for President and Richard Rush for Vice President and after that Rush was accepted by the Adams people as their candidate for Vice President. With the exception of the Federalist-Republican fusion ticket in 1812, which nominated De Witt Clinton of New York and Ingersoll of Pennsylvania, it had been an unbroken practice to nominate a Northerner and a Southerner on each party ticket. Rush was Secretary of the Treasury and President Adams liked him personally but regretted that a Northern instead of a Southern man was his running mate. Calhoun was already Vice President and there was little the Jackson men could do about his candidacy for re-election. The result was that for the first time both tickets were sectional—Jackson and Calhoun from the South, and Adams and Rush from the North.

The Republican Party was split into two parties by the election of 1828—the supporters of Adams, who later called themselves National Republicans, and the supporters of Jackson, who later called themselves Democrats. In 1830 the supporters of Daniel Webster, who wanted him to be the National Republican candidate against President Jackson in 1832, considered a revival of the Congressional caucus to give their favorite a head start in the race. Adams told Webster that a caucus nomination would harm him more than it would help him, and his supporters abandoned the plan. King Caucus was dead, but as yet no satisfactory substitute had been suggested. Finally the Anti-Mason Party showed the way. In 1830 this new party held a national convention in Philadelphia to discuss its program. On September 26, 1831, it held another national convention in Baltimore and nominated William Wirt for President and Amos Ellmaker for Vice President. This was the first national convention composed of delegates representing the people and called to nominate candidates for the highest Federal offices. It is surprising that national nominating conventions had not been held before. Conventions were not new and the Federalists in 1812 had indicated their possibilities. The Stamp Act Congress of 1765 and the First Continental Congress in 1774 were really inter-Colonial conventions. The Revolutionary legislatures of 1776 were in effect State conventions at first, and in many States political conventions were recognized institutions. Perhaps the ill-starred Hartford Convention of 1814-1815 had made national conventions unpopular.

At any rate, the National Republicans decided to follow the example set by the Anti-Masons. In December, 1831, they held a national convention at Baltimore and nominated Clay for President and John Sergeant for Vice President. Although Jackson's candidacy to succeed himself for President was taken for granted, the Democrats needed a formally nominated candidate for Vice President. A caucus of the Democratic members of the New Hampshire Legislature called a Democratic national convention to meet in Baltimore in May, 1832. This convention, endorsed Jackson for President as a matter of course and nominated Martin Van Buren as his running mate. In May, 1835, the Democratic National Convention met in Baltimore and nominated Van Buren for President and Richard M. Johnson for Vice President. The new Whig Party held no national convention in 1836 and made no national nominations, although William Henry Harrison was the favored Whig candidate for President by virtue of being endorsed by Whig caucuses and conventions in many States. The Congressional caucus, which dictated Presidential and Vice-Presidential nominations from 1800 to 1824, was never revived. Since 1832 all nominations for President and Vice President have been made by conventions. It is an interesting fact that the first three national nominating conventions were held in Baltimore, which continued to be the favorite place for such meetings for many years, and which became known as "The Convention City." Baltimore was probably chosen because the delegates to the early conventions were largely Federal officeholders who wanted to meet as near to Washington as possible without actually meeting in the Federal capital. Baltimore also had the advantage, more important in 1832 than now, of being located about halfway between the Northern and the Southern States.

Since the modern Republican Party held its first national convention in 1856, it has been an unbroken custom for that party to hold its convention at an earlier date than the Democratic convention.

What Vice President was indicted for murder?

Aaron Burr (1756-1836) was indicted for murder while he was Vice President. After he mortally wounded Hamilton in a duel July 11, 1804, he was indicted in New York County, New York, for violating a statute against sending challenges, and he was indicted for willful murder in Bergen County, New Jersey, where the duel was fought. He was never tried on either charge.

Although a good lawyer himself, Burr several times employed lawyers to defend him in brushes with the law. After he killed Hamilton the Vice President was virtually an exile from his own State. He fled first to Philadelphia and then southward. When Congress convened December 3, 1804, Burr was in the chair as President of the Senate. Senator William B. Giles of Virginia circulated a petition among Senators asking the Governor of New Jersey to have the indictment for murder quashed. During the 1804-1805 Senate session Burr, himself under indictment for murder, presided over the impeachment trial of Associate Justice Samuel Chase of the Supreme Court of the United States. On March 2, 1805, two days before his term as Vice President expired, Burr, "feeling an indisposition coming over him," took leave of the Senate in a remarkable farewell address. Of this speech Senator John Quincy Adams noted in his diary: "Immediately after finishing this speech, he left the chair and the room. It was delivered with great dignity and firmness of manner, but without any apparent emotion or sensibility. Many of the members appeared deeply affected, and two of them, Mr. Wright and Mr. Smith, of New York, were moved even to tears." On March 4, 1805, when George Clinton was sworn in as his successor as Vice President, Burr was present as a visitor in the Senate gallery.

In 1806, while Burr was on his first trip down the Mississippi, he was arrested twice in Kentucky and once in Mississippi, but in all three cases was released. Henry Clay defended Burr twice after being assured that the latter had no treasonable intentions. The next year Burr was arrested in Mississippi Territory and tried on charges of treason in the U.S. Circuit Court at Richmond, Virginia, with Chief Justice John Marshall presiding as circuit judge. After being acquitted of treason, Burr was tried on charges of misdemeanor and again acquitted. He was also indicted for treason in Ohio and gave bail, but after the Richmond trials he jumped bail in Ohio and went to Europe. From 1808 to 1812, when he returned to New York and resumed his law practice, Burr was in England, Denmark, Sweden, Germany and France. While in England he was arrested for debt and spent three days in prison.

Burr was a son of Aaron Burr, a president of the College of New Jersey (afterward Princeton University), and a grandson of Jonathan Edwards, one of the foremost theologians and metaphysicians in American history. In 1782, while a colonel in the Continental army,

Burr was married to Mrs. Theodosia Barstow Prevost, widow of a former British army officer and ten years older than himself. Mrs. Prevost then had five children and two of her young sons were in the British service. She had three children by Burr but only one, Theodosia, born June 21, 1783, survived childhood. In 1801 Burr's daughter Theodosia was married at Albany to Joseph Alston, a prominent South Carolinian. Their only child, Aaron Burr Alston, was born May 29, 1802, and died of fever on June 30, 1812. On December 30, 1812, Theodosia Burr Alston sailed from Georgetown, South Carolina, in the *Patriot* to visit her father in New York, but neither the ship nor anybody on board was ever heard from again. Consequently there are no living direct descendants of Aaron Burr.

In 1833, when Burr was seventy-seven, he was married to fifty-eight-year-old "Betsey Bowen Jumel," who was the widow of a French wine merchant named Stephen Jumel and whose maiden name was Eliza Brown. They were married by the Reverend David Schuyler Bogart of the Dutch Reformed Church who had performed the ceremony fifty-one years before when Burr was married to Mrs. Prevost. On Wednesday, July 8, 1833, Philip Hone noted in his diary: "The celebrated Col. Burr was married on Monday evening to the equally celebrated Mrs. Jumel, widow of Stephen Jumel. It is benevolent in her to keep the old man in his latter days. One good turn deserves another." Mme. Jumel, as she is generally known in history, obtained a divorce from Burr three years later and the decree bore the date of his death.

Who were the Bluelight Federalists?

Some leaders of the Federalist Party in New England went so far in their opposition to the War of 1812 that they advocated secession of their section from the Union and discouraged enlistments in the army, the buying of Government bonds and all other forms of co-operation in the war effort. Early in the war Commodore Stephen Decatur's squadron was bottled up at New London, Connecticut, by a British blockading fleet. In December, 1812, newspapers printed the following from one of Decatur's dispatches to the Secretary of the Navy:

Some few nights since the weather promised an opportunity for this squadron to get to sea, and it was said on shore that we intended to make the attempt. In the course of the evening two blue lights were burned on both the points at the harbor's mouth as signals to the enemy; and there is not a doubt but that they have, by signals and otherwise, instantaneous information of our movements.

Decatur did not say specifically that the blue lights were burned by traitorous Americans and there is no evidence that antiwar Federalists had anything to do with them, but some of the Federalist leaders were so pronounced in their pro-British sentiments and went so far in their opposition to all war measures that the Democratic-Republicans easily created the impression that New England Federalists were making signals to the British fleet. Antiwar Federalists were called "Bluelight Federalists" and the opprobrious nickname was kept alive by the Democrats as long as there was a Federalist Party. Later *bluelight* became synonymous with *rock-ribbed, dyed-in-the-wool* and *ultraconservative.* John Quincy Adams referred in his diary to "a bluelight federalist" as late as 1833.

Who were the Quids?

The Quids or Quiddists were a faction of the Democratic-Republican party who followed John Randolph of Roanoke in opposing Jefferson's administration.

This name is from Latin *tertium quid,* "a third something." In ancient philosophy the Greek equivalent of *tertium quid* was applied to some indefinite or unknown thing that was related in some way to two definite or known things, but distinct from both. Pythagoras is reputed to have said: "A man is a biped, so is a bird, and a third thing, which shall be nameless." Iamblichus, fourth-century Syrian Neoplatonic philosopher in Alexandria, suggested that the *tertium quid* or third thing was Pythagoras himself. In chemistry a substance formed by the chemical union of two substances, as a neutral salt produced by mixing an acid and an alkali, is called a *tertium quid.* The term came to be used colloquially and humorously to signify a third thing or person of anomalous nature or ambiguous status.

John Randolph, who about 1810, when he settled permanently on his Virginia estate called "Roanoke," added "of Roanoke" to his name to distinguish himself from a detested kinsman of the same name as his, was the administration leader in the House of Representatives from 1801 to 1805; but in the latter year he broke with Jefferson and after that he and a handful of followers were very critical of administration policies. In a speech in Congress in 1806, wrote Henry Adams, Randolph "avowed himself to be no longer a republican; he belonged to the third party, the quiddists or quids, being that *tertium quid,* that third something, which had no name, but was really an anti-Madison movement." The eccentric Virginian was quite a classical scholar and was fond of quoting Latin and Greek in his speeches. After he used *tertium quid* in this speech he and his followers were known as Quids, that is, neither Federalists nor Republicans, but members of a third, nameless party.

The Quids advocated extreme states' rights, opposed attempts to acquire West Florida, favored Monroe against Madison for President in 1808, resisted the embargo on imports, and made bitter verbal attacks on Jefferson. In New York the Quids were led by Governor Morgan Lewis, veteran Revolutionary soldier and son-in-law of Robert R. Livingston, head of the "Livingston interests." Nathaniel Macon of North Carolina, Speaker of the House from 1801 to 1807, was one of the ablest but least spectacular of the Quids. Under date of February 23, 1808, Senator John Quincy Adams refers in his diary to the Quids as "the Virginia, or Randolph minority," who refused to attend the Democratic-Republican Congressional caucus. Randolph had little ability as a political organizer and he was temperamentally unsuited for national leadership. His Quid movement, the first "third party" in American politics, petered out about 1812 and the sometime Quid leader remained in public life only as a free-lance thorn in the side of whatever group happened to be in power. On May 25, 1812, President Madison wrote to Thomas Jefferson: "To go to war with England and not with France arms the Federalists with new matter, and divided the Republicans, some of whom, with the Quids, make a display of impartiality."

Randolph was frail in body and unstable in mind. At times, according to the testimony of those who knew him best, he was virtually insane. But his talents bordered on genius and he was noted for his invective and sarcasm. In 1833 John Quincy Adams wrote that the eccentric Virginian turned disease into commodity and "for forty years was always dying." On March 11, 1828, President Adams wrote in his diary of Randolph: "The rancour of this man's soul against me is that which sustains his life, and so it is of W. E. Giles, now governor of Virginia. The agony of their envy and hatred of me, and the hope of effecting my downfall are their chief remaining sources of vitality. The issue of the presidential election will kill them to the gratification of their revenge." Randolph believed that Daniel Webster had accused him of impotence. Of Webster he said: "I would not attempt to vie with the honorable gentleman from Massachusetts in a field where every nigger is his peer and every billygoat his master." He is reputed to have said of Edward Livingston, one of Jackson's Secretaries of State: "He is a man of splendid abilities but utterly corrupt. He shines and stinks like rotten mackerel by moonlight."

Third party was used soon after two major parties took form. In 1801 Fisher Ames wrote: "There are but two divisions of party in the United States; and he is a very weak or very presumptuously vain man who can think of organizing a third party that shall rule them both." The political balance between two major parties has been maintained through the years so completely that all other parties are sometimes referred to as "third parties." But it is customary to apply *third party* only to new political movements that challenge the two major parties. Third-party movements have generally failed because their following fell off after the first test of strength. In only five elections since 1836 have more than two Presidential candidates received electoral votes—1856, 1892, 1912, 1924, and 1948. More attention is attached to third parties in the United States than in most countries because a sizable third party could throw the election into the House of Representatives, but that has not happened since 1824 when the two-party system broke down temporarily.

A political party that remains in the field of election after election but remains small is called a "minor party." The Prohibition Party and the Socialist Party have long been in this class. A temporary small party is known as a "splinter party." Most third and minor parties start out with the hope of becoming major parties. In 1936 Representative William Lemke of North Dakota received 882,479 popular votes as the Presidential candidate of the Union Party. In 1900 there were a total of eleven Presidential and Vice-Presidential candidates in the field, and in 1948 there were also eleven. Some political parties have been restricted to a single State or region. The Farmer-Labor Party formed in 1920 never attained national strength and had little strength except in Minnesota and bordering States. The United Labor (Single Tax) Party was limited largely to New York, where Henry George received a sizable vote as its candidate for mayor of New York City in 1886 and as secretary of state in 1887. The American Labor Party is largely a New York State party.

What was the O Grab Me Act?

O Grab Me in this connection is merely *embargo* spelled backwards. *Embargo* is of Spanish origin and literally means "to restrain." The original Spanish embargoes were official orders forbidding ships from leaving port for a specified period.

The United States passed a general embargo act in 1807, when the British and French were seizing American ships under the British orders in council and the French Berlin and Milan decrees. President Jefferson believed that both the warring nations depended on American foodstuffs to such an extent that they would have to relax their regulations if all ships were prohibited from leaving American ports. It was commercial warfare and the Democratic-Republican administration's substitute for actual war. Congress acceded to the President's request and after considering the proposal only four days passed the Embargo Act of December 21, 1807, which prohibited all international trade with American ports, whether in domestic or foreign ships.

Some of the Federalist opponents of the measure ridiculed it as the "O Grab Me Act" and contemptuously called those who favored it Embargoroons. At first the farmers favored the measure and the commercial interests opposed it. In 1808 the Embargo Act was extended to cover inland waters and land commerce to prevent the increased trade with Canada resulting from stoppage of European commerce. This was the first time in history that such a complete embargo had been attempted, and it failed. The United States was unable to enforce the act effectively, and when an enforcement act was passed in 1809 there was much talk in New England of seceding from the Union. American ships avoided home ports and traded between ports of other countries. Exports from the United States shrank to one-fifth of what they had been. Enforced idleness in commercial centers resulted in much suffering and discontent.

After two years the Embargo Act was terminated as of March 4, 1809, which was the end of Jefferson's term in office, and the Non-Intercourse Act was substituted. This act, which prohibited commerce only with England and France and forbade ships and goods of these nations and their colonies to enter American ports, was supplanted in 1810 by the Mason Bill No. 1, which authorized the President to restrict the commerce of one belligerent if and when the other revoked its decrees against neutrals. All of these acts failed in their objective, which was to prevent war, but in the long run they had the effect of stimulating American manufactures.

The Federalists called the events preceding the War of 1812 "The Terrapin War," because they said the United States with its Embargo and Non-Intercourse acts, abandoned its foreign commerce and drew within its shell like a turtle or terrapin.

Who were the War Hawks?

War Hawk in the sense of one clamorous for war was the American forerunner of the English *jingo*. The term appears to have been coined by Thomas Jefferson and was first applied in 1798 to certain Federalist leaders who favored war with France. On April 26, 1798, Jefferson wrote to James Madison: "At present, the war hawks talk of septemberizing, deportation, and the examples for quelling sedition set by the French executive." Jefferson wrote to Madison on the following June 21: "Doctor Logan . . . sailed for Hamburg—he very unwisely made a mystery of it. . . . This was seized by the war hawks and given out as a secret mission."

The term was applied specifically to a group of members of the twelfth Congress (1811-1813) who advocated war with Great Britain. The War Hawks were all Democratic-Republicans and chiefly from the South and the West. They belonged to the post-Revolutionary generation and most of them were under thirty-five years of age. Among them were Henry Clay and Richard Mentor Johnson of Kentucky; John C. Calhoun, Langdon Cheves, William Lowndes and David Rogerson Williams of South Carolina; William Rufus DeVane King of Alabama; Felix Grundy of Tennessee; Peter Buell Porter of New York, and John A. Harper of New Hampshire. The War Hawks said sneeringly that President Madison "could not be kicked into a war." "The militia of Kentucky alone are competent to place Montreal and Upper Canada at your feet," shouted Clay, the leader of the War Hawks, who had been chosen Speaker of the House on the war issue the first day he took his seat. "I believe," seconded Calhoun, "that in four weeks from the time a declaration of war is heard on our frontier, the whole of Upper Canada and a part of Lower Canada will be in our power." By 1812 this "war party within the Democratic-Republican party" was strong enough to force the reluctant hand of the peaceful President and they got their "second war of independence," although the results were quite different from what they hoped for and expected. The Federalist press called it "Mr. Madison's War," but the President didn't want war and was pushed into it by the War Hawks. "I was not in public life at the time it was declared," wrote Thomas H. Benton, "but have understood from those who were, that, except for the exertions of two men (Mr. Monroe in the Cabinet and Mr. Clay in Congress), the declaration of war could not have been obtained."

When Clay resigned his seat in the House in 1815 to serve as one of the peace commissioners, he was succeeded in the Speakership by another War Hawk, Langdon Cheves, who had fourteen children and who pronounced his last name CHIVV-as. None of the War Hawks later became President but three of them became Vice President— Calhoun, Johnson and King. Johnson was one of the few War Hawks who took the field and fought in the war he had advocated. He was wounded five times in the Battle of Thames.

How were Thomas Jefferson and John Marshall related?

Thomas Jefferson and John Marshall are often referred to as cousins. Their closest kinship was through their mothers and they were only second cousins once removed. Jefferson was the great grandson and Marshall the great-great-grandson of William Randolph.

Jefferson as Governor of Virginia signed Marshall's license to practice law, but the two men became personal and political enemies. According to an apocryphal story, Vice President and President-elect Jefferson called upon Secretary of State Marshall to congratulate him upon his appointment as Chief Justice. Marshall was out and Jefferson hurriedly scribbled on a card that he had been so *lucky* as not to find Marshall in. Noticing the error in the note, Jefferson changed it to *unlucky*. "That is the first time," observed Marshall upon receiving the note, "that Jefferson came near to telling the truth." Jefferson wrote of Marshall to James Madison in 1810: "His twistifications in the case of Marbury, in that of Burr, and the Yazoo case show dexterously he can reconcile law to his personal biases." On July 10, 1835, after the great Chief Justice's death, John Quincy Adams wrote in his diary:

Marshall has cemented the Union which the crafty and quixotic democracy of Jefferson had a perpetual tendency to dissolve. Jefferson hated and dreaded him. Marshall kept Jefferson much under the curb—sometimes, as perhaps in the case of Aaron Burr's conspiracy, too much so; but Marshall's mind was far better regulated than that of Jefferson.

Who coined the phrase *entangling alliances?*

This phrase is popularly attributed to George Washington. But Thomas Jefferson, not Washington, was the author of it.

In his first inaugural address, March 4, 1801, President Jefferson said: "Peace, commerce, and honest friendship with all nations—*entangling alliances* with none." In a letter dated December 21, 1787, Jefferson, then American minister in Paris, wrote: "I know, too, that it is a maxim with us, and I think it is a wise one, not to entangle ourselves with the affairs of Europe."

So far as known Washington never used the words *entangling alliances,* although he approved of the idea expressed by it. In his Farewell Address, published September 17, 1796, President Washington said: "Why forego the advantages of so peculiar a situation? Why quit our own to stand upon foreign ground? Why, by interweaving our destiny with that of any part of Europe, entangle our peace and prosperity in the toils of European ambition, rivalship, interest, humor, or caprice?"

When Washington made that statement the United States was bordered on the North, the West and the South by territory controlled directly by European nations, and war with France or England or both appeared to be imminent. The treaty of alliance made with France during the Revolution was still in effect, but the first President wanted to terminate it and remain neutral in the wars between France and England. On October 9, 1795, Washington asked Patrick Henry to become Secretary of State. In his letter to Henry, who declined the appointment, Washington wrote:

My ardent desire is, and my aim has been (as far as depended upon the executive department), to comply strictly with all our engagements, foreign and domestic; but to keep the U. States free from political connexion, with every other country, to see them independent of all and under the influence of none. In a word, I want an American character, that the powers of Europe may be convinced that we act for ourselves, and not for others. This, in my judgment, is the only way to be respected abroad, and happy at home; and not, by becoming partisans of Great Britain or France, create dissensions, disturb the public tranquillity, and destroy, perhaps forever, the cement which binds the Union.

The following quotation is often attributed to Washington: "When, our institutions being firmly consolidated and working with complete success, we might safely and perhaps beneficially take part in the consultations held by foreign states for the advantages of the nations." The statement has none of the earmarks of Washington's style and there is no evidence that he ever made such a statement.

Who was Albert Gallatin?

Albert Gallatin (1761-1849) was born in Geneva, Switzerland, and came from a family prominent in public affairs at that place for centuries. He was christened Abraham Alphonse Albert Gallatin, but used only the shorter form of his name. Although orphaned at nine, he received a good education and graduated from the Academy of Geneva in 1779. In the latter year he refused a lieutenant-colonelcy in a Hessian regiment being raised to fight in America for George III because he did not wish "to serve a tyrant."

On May 24, 1780, Benjamin Franklin in Paris wrote to his son-in-law, Richard Bache in Philadelphia: "Messieurs Gallatin and de Serre, two young gentlemen of Geneva of good families and very good characters, having an inclination to see America, if they should arrive in your City I recommend them to your Civilities, Counsel and Countenance." Gallatin and his chum, Henri Serre, landed at Boston later the same year. The Swiss youths brought with them, of all things, a consignment of tea to pay their expenses and to start in business. Americans had no taste for tea at that time and Gallatin and his chum were unsuccessful in their first business venture in America. Gallatin served in the militia briefly but did not "fight in the Revolution," as often said. For a time Gallatin tutored Harvard students in French for a living.

In 1785, upon receiving his patrimony at the age of twenty-five, he engaged in a speculation in western lands with Robert Morris. Out of this venture he came out with only a seven-hundred-acre tract of land in what is now Fayette County in western Pennsylvania. There he established "Friendship Hill," his home for forty years. While in Richmond on land business, he eloped with his landlady's daughter, Sophie Allegre, whom he took to his rustic house on the Monongahela. His bride died within a few months and Gallatin plunged into politics to forget the life of bliss he had hoped for. He founded near-by New Geneva and in 1797 with two partners established there the first glass factory west of the Alleghenies. In 1793 Gallatin married Hannah, daughter of Commodore James Nicholson of the U.S. Navy. She bore him a daughter and two sons.

As a member of the Pennsylvania Legislature in 1790-1792 Gallatin served on thirty-five committees at the same time and wrote every bill and report handled by each. It was then that he laid the foundation of his reputation as a genius of public finance. In 1792 the legislature chose him a U.S. Senator and he took his seat on December 2, 1793. As a member of the Pennsylvania ratification convention in 1787 he opposed adoption of the Federal Constitution, and in the Senate he incurred the further ire of the Federalist majority by demanding financial reports from Secretary of the Treasury Alexander Hamilton and in other ways needling the Washington administration. By a vote of fourteen to twelve on February 28, 1794, his election as a Senator was voided on the technical ground that he had not been a citizen the nine years required by the Constitution. The Jeffersonians regarded this as an unfair interpretation of the Constitution and Gallatin became a political martyr.

Gallatin opposed Hamilton's excise tax on whisky and was implicated in the Whisky Rebellion. He himself confessed later that his acting as clerk to a meeting of protesting farmers was his "only political sin." The Federalists tried to make it appear that Gallatin was one of the leaders of the disturbers when actually he had counseled against violence and used his influence to bring about a satisfactory settlement. He served in the U.S. House of Representatives from 1795 to 1801, and in 1797 succeeded James Madison as Democratic-Republican leader in that body. In the Congress he specialized in finance and had the standing committee on ways and means established to handle appropriations and revenue measures. He played an important part in 1801 in breaking the deadlock in the House between Thomas Jefferson and Aaron Burr. President Jefferson appointed him Secretary of the Treasury and he served in that position until 1814, when he became a peace commissioner. Henry Adams wrote that the Treaty of Ghent was "the special and peculiar triumph of Albert Gallatin." He was American minister to France (1815-1823) and to Great Britain (1826-1827).

Gallatin spoke and wrote excellent English, but had a decided French accent, which handicapped him politically in the United States but helped him diplomatically abroad. He was very serious and his son says he rarely laughed. He was greatly hurt when Louis XVIII told him in broken English: "Your French is more perfect than mine, but my English is far better than yours." Gallatin's son James wrote in his diary:

The poor old King is far more gregarious; he really seems to enjoy father's society, and certainly shows him great favour. He laughingly said to him the other day, 'I wish you would give us French lessons and we will give you English ones.' Poor father's French accent is so strong in English. I sincerely believe it is one of the reasons he is so disliked in America.

His foreign birth and accent closed the doors of the White House to him. On June 16, 1820, when the State Department was regarded as a steppingstone to the Presidency, Secretary of State John Quincy Adams wrote of Gallatin in his diary: "His foreign nativity was at the opening of Mr. Madison's Administration, the insuperable bar to his obtaining the Department of State, and thereby cut off forever his prospects of coming to the Presidency." In 1824 an effort was made to put Gallatin in the White House through the back door. Although the Twelfth Amendment to the Constitution, which became effective twenty years earlier, specifically declared that "no person constitutionally ineligible to the office of President shall be eligible to that of Vice President," the Democratic-Republican Congressional Caucus nominated Gallatin for Vice President on the ticket with William H. Crawford, who was in poor health and not expected to live out his term if elected President. During the campaign the Swiss-born Vice Presidential candidate was greatly abused by his political opponents as "a foreigner." President Monroe and other party leaders thought that no person of foreign birth could be elected Vice President. Martin Van Buren, a Crawford campaign leader, advised Gallatin that he was weakening the ticket and induced him to withdraw from the race shortly before election day. At the time

Gallatin's son wrote: "Father, although he never admits it, I am certain feels very deeply the gross injustice and prejudice that shuts the door of the Presidency to him simply because he was not born in America."

In 1815 John Jacob Astor, the richest man in America offered to make Gallatin his partner in business. Gallatin refused the offer, but in 1832, upon Astor's recommendation, became president of the National Bank of New York, later named the Gallatin Bank. His last years were devoted to writing on finance and American Indians. He died at eighty-eight in his daughter's home at Astoria on Long Island, and was buried in Trinity Churchyard, where the rival of his earlier years, Hamilton, had been buried forty-five years earlier. Ninety years later, in 1939, Congress authorized a statue of Gallatin to be erected on the north plaza of the Treasury building in Washington as a counterpart to that of Hamilton on the south plaza. On October 2, 1884, ex-President Rutherford B. Hayes wrote in his diary:

Mr. Fish as a boy met often Albert Gallatin; heard him say that when he became Secretary of the Treasury he determined to undo about all that Alexander Hamilton had done—was greatly prejudiced against Hamilton. Soon found he had better go slow, and at the end of thirteen years, left Hamilton's work almost entirely undisturbed; convinced of the great ability and wisdom of Hamilton.

When was the Era of Good Feeling?

The administration of President James Monroe (1817-1825), particularly his first term (1817-1821), is known as "The Era of Good Feeling." From Washington's to Madison's administrations inclusive there had been two major parties—Federalists and Republicans. The Federalists, after being defeated twice by Jefferson and twice by Madison, began to lose ground rapidly because they had opposed the War of 1812 and because Madison had adopted many of their domestic policies. Rufus King, the Federalist candidate for President in 1816, received only 34 electoral votes, while Monroe, the Republican candidate, received 183.

Shortly after his inauguration in 1817 President Monroe, dressed in a uniform such as he wore as a Revolutionary soldier, toured New England, the last stronghold of the Federalists. One of those who took a leading part in honoring the President when he visited Boston was Benjamin Russell (1761-1845), editor of a semiweekly newspaper called the *Columbian Centinel*. Russell had served in the Continental army and was a member of the military guard at the execution of Major John Andre. Although an ardent Federalist, he wrote an editorial favorable to the Republican President and printed it in his paper dated July 12, 1817, under the heading "The Era of Good Feelings." The President liked the phrase coined by Russell. With the final *s* dropped the phrase was picked up and used as a sort of slogan for the Monroe administration.

The fusion of the two parties continued and in 1820 the Federalists did not nominate a candidate for President, with the result that Monroe received all the electoral votes except one. Monroe himself took the "Era of Good Feeling" seriously and thought that political parties in the United States were dead and of no further use. But Thomas Jefferson did not agree. "You are told," wrote the Sage of Monticello to Albert Gallatin, "that there are no longer parties among us; that they are all now amalgamated; the lion and the lamb lie together in peace. Do not believe a word of it." Secretary of State John Quincy Adams, who had his eye on the Presidency, also saw the political storm ahead. On January 8, 1820, he wrote in his diary: "In short, as the first Presidential term of Mr. Monroe's Administration has hitherto been the period of the greatest national tranquility enjoyed by this nation at any portion of its history, so it appears to me scarcely avoidable that the second term will be among the most stormy and violent." Party spirit was merely in abeyance and it was really a period of suppressed bad feeling. One of the fiercest Presidential contests in history was brewing beneath the surface. The panic of 1819 and the controversy over the Missouri Question in 1820 were indications that the Era of Good Feeling was only a calm before a storm. A political party cannot live without opposition and the disappearance of the Federalists caused the Republican Party to split into factions. Five strong men—Andrew Jackson, John Quincy Adams, Henry Clay, William H. Crawford and John C. Calhoun, began to build up personal parties with a view of being chosen President in 1824. All these men called themselves Republicans, although Adams had once been a Federalist and was suspected of still being one at heart.

Why wasn't President Monroe re-elected unanimously?

When James Monroe was re-elected President in 1820 he received all the electoral votes except one—231 out of 232. It was generally expected that he would be re-elected unanimously because no candidate opposed him. Many writers say that one elector withheld his vote from Monroe to prevent him from sharing an honor previously granted only to George Washington. That is a myth.

William Plumer, Sr., of New Hampshire, was the elector who refused to vote for Monroe. On November 24, 1820, after the Presidential electors had been chosen, Secretary of State John Quincy Adams wrote in his diary that Representative William Plumer of New Hampshire had spoken to him about the approaching election of President and Vice President.

His father [wrote Adams] is chosen one of the electors for the State of New Hampshire, and has intimated to him that there and in Massachusetts there are persons unwilling to vote for the re-election of D.D. Tompkins as Vice-President, and disposed to vote for me; not with the expectation or intention of success, *but with a prospective view of holding up my name to view at a future period;* and inquired whether it was with my approbation. I answered, certainly not; that my wish was that both Mr. Monroe as President and Mr. Tompkins as Vice-President should be re-elected unanamiously; but, however that might be, that there should not be a single vote given for me, and I requested him to write so immediately. As to Massachusetts, I told him it would be peculiarly disagreeable to me that any such votes should be given, because my own father had been chosen one of the electors.

William Plumer, Sr. then proceeded to vote for Adams for President and former Attorney General Richard Rush for Vice President and in a letter to his son dated January 8, 1821, he explained his reasons for doing so. "I was," he wrote, "obliged from a sense of duty and a regard to my own reputation to withhold my vote from Monroe and Tompkins; from the first because he had discovered a want of foresight and from the second because he had grossly neglected his duty." He added that he regarded Monroe as a weak President and condemned him because during his administration we had reached "the same spirit of profusion and waste in granting money here, as in England."

On February 14, 1821, Adams made this interesting observation in his diary:

This was the ninth Presidential election since the existence of the present Constitution of the United States, and is already the second instance of a crisis in the election. On the former occasion it happened at the very tug of conflict between the national parties for the mastery. Now it happened at an era far more extraordinary—when that party conflict had performed its entire revolution, and that unanimity of choice which began with George Washington had come round again in the person of James Monroe. In the survey of our national history the latter unanimity is much more remarkable than the first. In this last unanimity there is the exception of a single vote, given by William Plumer, of New Hampshire, and that vote, to my surprise and mortification, was for me. If there was an electoral vote in the Union which I thought sure for Mr. Monroe, it was that of Mr. Plumer. I deeply regretted the loss of Mr. Plumer's vote, because it implied his disapprobation of the principles of the Adminis-tration, and although by giving the vote for me he obviously exempted my share in the Administration from any essential portion of the censure, I could take no pleasure in that approbation which, though bestowed on me, was denied to the whole Administration.

The younger Plumer told Adams on January 2, 1822, that he favored a Northern man to succeed Monroe in 1824 and personally favored Adams himself, which indicates that the Plumers were pro-Adams from the beginning. In his *Life of William Plumer* William Plumer, Jr., wrote:

In the exercise of this duty, he voted for John Quincy Adams instead of James Monroe, who received every other electoral vote in the Union. This single vote against Monroe (for it was regarded chiefly in that light) excited much wonder, and some censure at the time . . . . He thought Mr. Monroe's capacity by no means equal to the place. "We mistake," he said, "if we suppose that any but the ablest men are fit for the highest place. The government of weak men must always be disastrous. Wo to thee, O land, when thy king is a child!"

From these statements it will be seen that Plumer cast his electoral vote in 1820 against Monroe because he regarded him as a weak man and for Adams because he wanted to hold up his name for a future election. It is an interesting fact that Adams, whom the elder Plumer cast a sole electoral vote for in 1820, was chosen President in 1825, and when Adams ran for re-election in 1828 Rush, for whom Plumer cast a sole electoral vote for Vice President in 1820, was his running mate. The theory that Plumer withheld his vote from Monroe to prevent him from sharing an honor before granted only to Washington was not mentioned until long afterward.

What President wrote his own epitaph?

Thomas Jefferson wrote his epitaph, specified the size and material of his tombstone and chose the exact spot for his grave. The epitaph and specifications for his monument, including a sketch, were on an undated sheet of paper written about a year before his death on July 4, 1826. He suggested that "the following inscription & not one word more" be placed on his tombstone: "Here was buried Thomas Jefferson, Author of the Declaration of American Independence, of the Statute of Virginia for Religious Freedom & Father of the University of Virginia." Jefferson had been a member of the Continental Congress, Governor of Virginia, Minister to France, Secretary of State, Vice President and President, but his epitaph mentioned only his authorship of two documents and the founding of a university, "because by these, as testimonials that I have lived, I wish most to be remembered."

For a monument Jefferson specified "a plain die or cube of 3 feet without any moulding, surmounted by an Obelisk of 6 feet height, each of a single stone" and "of the coarse stone of which my columns are made that no one might be tempted hereafter to destroy it for the value of the material." Despite Jefferson's precaution, the original stone over his grave at Monticello was destroyed by relic hunters, but the epitaph was placed on the present shaft, which is protected by a high iron fence. Jefferson's wife died in 1782, ten years after their marriage, and he wrote the epitaph for her tombstone. Four lines of the epitaph were in Greek.

In their youth Jefferson and his friend Dabney Carr built a rustic seat under a great oak on Monticello (Little Mountain) and spent many happy days there studying, talking and looking at the scenery. They made a boyish compact that the one that died first should be buried by the other under that oak. The tie of friendship was strengthened by Dabney's marriage to Jefferson's favorite sister. Both were elected to the legislature and both cast their lot with Patrick Henry and the anti-King party. On one occasion Dabney made an eloquent speech favoring a union of all the Colonies and was hailed throughout Virginia as the Patriot leader. But Dabney died before the Revolution had fairly begun. Jefferson was absent and Dabney was buried at Shadwell, but when he returned he had the body removed to Monticello. More than fifty years later Jefferson was buried beside his boyhood friend.

What Vice Presidents held office under two Presidents?

Only two men have held the office of Vice President under two different Presidents. George Clinton, of New York, who died in office, was Vice President during Jefferson's second term and part of Madison's first term. John C. Calhoun of South Carolina who resigned the Vice Presidency to represent his State in the Senate, served in the office during John Quincy Adams's one term and most of Jackson's first. Franklin D. Roosevelt was the only President to have three Vice Presidents—Garner, Henry A. Wallace and Truman. Seven Presidents—Jefferson, Madison, Jackson, Lincoln, Grant, Cleveland and McKinley—had two Vice Presidents each.

Who was the Old Man Eloquent?

John Quincy Adams is known as the Old Man Eloquent. John Milton coined the phrase and applied it to Isocrates, an Athenian orator, in a sonnet written about 1645 and addressed to Lady Margaret Ley.

> Till the sad breaking of that Parliament
> Broke him, as that dishonest victory
> At Chæronea, fatal to liberty,
> Kill'd with report that old man eloquent. . . .

The legend was that Isocrates died at ninety-nine of mental shock and grief upon hearing that Philip of Macedon had defeated the allied Greek army at Chæronea in 338 B.C. The fact seems to be, however, that Isocrates, after getting the tidings of the defeat, went on a "hunger strike" and died of voluntary starvation four days after the battle.

John Quincy Adams was not an eloquent orator in the sense that Webster, Clay and several other public men of his day were, and it is not known when or by whom *Old Man Eloquent* was first applied to him. A Harvard graduate and a classical scholar, Adams became a lawyer by profession, but spent most of his life in public service as diplomat, Senator, Secretary of State, President and Representative. In 1806 he became the first Boylston Professor of Rhetoric and Oratory at Harvard. He has been the only person to serve in the House of Representatives after retiring from the White House. During his nearly seventeen years in that body Adams became the champion of free speech and the right to petition, and it was during that period that his effectiveness as a speaker developed.

On October 24, 1843, a Harvard student named Rutherford B. Hayes heard John Quincy Adams address a Whig audience at Dedham and the next day wrote in his diary:

> His speech contained little politics but much abolitionism. Some of it was very good, much of it unreasonable and very unfair. My opinion of the venerable but deluded old man was not (at) all changed. His speech was rather dry; contained some good hits and exhibited some sparks of the internal fires which, when aroused into flames, render him the impersonation of "the old man eloquent." I do not wonder that he is regarded a dangerous adversary in a more personal encounter. He is quick, sharp, fearless, and full of the wit and learning of all ages. He is not at all times an interesting or eloquent speaker, but when aroused by the repeated attacks, the sneers and taunts of his bitter foes, he is truly a most formidable man.

On November 10 of the same year Philip Hone in his diary wrote of Adams that "every city and town at which he arrives sends out its multitudes to welcome 'the old man eloquent.'"

Old Man Eloquent was a harsh critic of himself. On June 4, 1819, when he was Secretary of State, he wrote in his diary: "I am a man of reserved, cold, austere, and forbidding manners; my political adversaries say, a gloomy misanthropist, and my personal enemies, an unsocial savage." Adams said he was industrious but slow in comprehension, and all his life he lamented his inability to speak extemporaneously. From time to time he refers to his speeches in and out of Congress as unskillful, tedious and unsystematic, and his delivery as slow, hesitating, incoherent, confused and drowsy. On one occasion he wrote that "I spoke with shame and mortification for about ten minutes." and on another, "I made a very incoherent speech, without order and without self-collection." When called upon unexpectedly in London for an after-dinner speech, Adams said he "got through without discredit only by re-volving during dinner-time what to say; a process not remarkably favorable to the enjoyment of the conviviality of the table." Vice President Aaron Burr was bored by long speeches in the Senate. After Senator Adams had made a long speech, the President of the Senate asked that when Senators were going to make such speeches they give him notice so "that he might take the opportunity to warm himself at the fire."

Theodore Parker thought Old Man Eloquent was "seldom eloquent." Ralph Waldo Emerson marveled that a speaker with such a poor voice could be so effective. He was simple in habits and unostentatious in manners, but spoke without dignity or grace, and often resorted to invective. "He has peculiar powers as an assailant," said Rufus Choate, "and almost always, even when attacked, gets himself into that attitude by making war upon his accuser; and he has, withal, an instinct for the jugular and the carotid artery, as unerring as that of any carnivorous animal." In small gatherings Hone found that Old Man Eloquent could be talkative, gay, witty, instructive and entertaining. His natural modesty and reserve did not prevent the President from writing in his diary on August 31, 1826: "There is at this time in this Commonwealth a practical school of popular oratory, of which I believe myself to be the principal founder by my own orations and lectures, and which, with the blessing of Him who reigns, will redound to the honor and advantage of this nation and to the benefit of mankind." Perhaps Hone put his finger on Adams's weakest spot when he wrote in his diary on June 13, 1833, that, "He wanted tact."

Long after Adams's death *Old Man Eloquent* was applied in England to William E. Gladstone.

Which President was a poet?

Several of the Presidents wrote verse in their youth, and some of the poetical efforts of Abraham Lincoln are extant, but John Quincy Adams had been the only President who continued to dabble in verse throughout life. He was a skillful but not distinguished poet. Two of his best-known poems are "The Wants of Man" and "The Pen." His translation of Christoph Martin Wieland's *Oberon* from German in English verse is regarded by critics as excellent. On March 8, 1831, the poet President wrote in his diary:

In a few instances I have suffered the publication of my effusions, and I am accredited as one of the smallest poets of my country. Very short and fugitive pieces and translations are the only rhymes I have ever committed to the press; one short poem, the lines to Mrs. Hellen on the death of her two children, and one translation, the thirteenth satire of Juvenal, have been favourably noticed. One satirical song, overlooked when first published, was dragged into light twenty years afterwards, for political effect against me, because it laughed at the party Lama—Jefferson. All the rest of my published poetry has passed from the press into the waters of Lethe.

Who was the Millboy of the Slashes?

Henry Clay (1777-1850) was known as "The Millboy of the Slashes." He was born and brought up in Hanover County, Virginia, in a neighborhood called "the Slashes." *Slashes* in the South was applied to clearings in the woods covered with underbrush and to damp swales, sloughs, marshes and swampy bottom lands overgrown with thickets. Robert Beverly used *slash* in this sense in his history of Virginia in 1705. *Slash* is of echoic origin and in this case may have originally referred to the slashing sound made in cutting down trees or to that made by underbrush striking against one walking through it. There were many slashes in the vicinity of Clay's boyhood home. As a boy he used to carry sacks of grain on mule- or horseback to a near-by grist mill for use in making bread, cornpone and hoecake. From this he received his earliest sobriquet, which did much to increase his popularity among the common people in his political campaigns. Legend says Clay overcame a stammer and developed his speaking powers by haranguing cattle he herded in the Slashes.

Clay was given many nicknames by friend and foe and he probably had more of them than any other American politician. He picked up some of them from the then common practice of toasting distinguished men at banquets. Nearly every stage of his long and colorful career is represented by a nickname and the story of his life can be brought to mind by merely listing them. The Millboy of the Slashes became successively "The Cock of Kentucky," "The War Hawk," "The Great Kentuckian," "Harry of the West," "Prince Hal," "The Judas of the West," "The Compromiser," "The Farmer of Ashland," "The Great

Compromiser," "The Old Prince," "The Great Commoner" and "The Great Pacificator." In 1841 Henry A. Wise of Virginia attacked Clay in a speech in the House of Representatives in which he called him "Rumor."

Clay was the son of a Baptist preacher, but was not a member of any church until three years before his death, when he joined the Episcopal Church. His mother gave birth to nineteen children—eight by his father and eleven by her second husband. Clay married Lucretia Hart, a cousin of Thomas Hart Benton, in 1790 when he was twenty-three and she bore him eleven children—five sons and six daughters. All of his daughters and one son died before he did. His son Henry was killed in the battle of Buena Vista. Another son went insane due to an accident. Clay played brag and whist, liked dancing, was fond of the ladies, loved horse-racing, drank whisky, dipped snuff, owned fifty slaves and fought duels. He challenged Humphrey Marshall and both were slightly wounded in a duel on the Indiana side of the Ohio. When he was Secretary of State he fought a farcical duel with Senator John Randolph of Roanoke. On January 20, 1819, the Senate adjourned so its members could go to the House chamber and hear Clay speak on the Seminole War.

Several times Clay lost large sums at cards, and often was in financial straits. At one time he owed $50,000 on a note in the Northern Bank of Kentucky at Lexington. Clay could not make it good and repeatedly had it renewed. Unknown to Clay, wealthy friends in the East raised the money and sent a young man with it to Lexington. Without calling on Clay or letting him know he was in Kentucky, the young man paid the note in full on condition that Clay never know who did it. When Clay told the bank that he could not raise the money and offered them his home Ashland, in satisfaction, he was informed that he owed nothing, but that the names of his benefactors could not be disclosed because they did not wish him to be under obligations to them. "My God!" exlaimed Clay. "Did any man ever have such friends!" The mysterious bearer of the money was William Pennington, afterward Governor of New Jersey and Speaker of the U.S. House of Representatives.

On March 9, 1821, Secretary of State John Quincy Adams wrote in his diary the following severe but just estimate:

Clay is an eloquent man, with very popular manners and great political management. He is, like almost all the eminent men of this country, only half educated. His school has been the world, and in that he is a proficient. His morals, public and private, are loose, but he has all the virtues indispensable to a popular man. As he is the first very distinguished man that the Western country has presented as a statesman to the Union, they are proportionately proud of him, and being a native of Virginia, he has all the benefit of that clannish preference which Virginia has always given to her sons. Clay's temper is impetuous, and his ambition impatient. . . . Clay has large and liberal views of public affairs, and that sort of generosity which attaches individuals to his person. As President of the Union, his administration would be a perpetual succession of intrigue and management with the legislature. It would also be sectional in its spirit, and sacrifice all other interests to those of the Western country and the slave-holders. But, his principles relative to internal improvements would produce results honorable and useful to the nation.

Four years after writing this Adams, as President, appointed Clay to succeed him as Secretary of State.

A tedious and long-winded Congressman from Virginia named Alexander Smyth said to Clay: "You, sir, speak for the present generation; but I speak for posterity." "Yes," retorted Clay, "and you seem resolved to speak until the arrival of your audience."

In 1859 Abraham Lincoln referred to "Henry Clay, my beau-ideal of a statesman." But perhaps John C. Calhoun sized Clay up as well as any. He is reputed to have observed: "I don't like Henry Clay. He's a bad man, an imposter, a creature of wicked schemes. I wouldn't speak to him, but, by God, I love him."

What was the American System?

After the War of 1812 Henry Clay, with an eye on the Presidency, tried to unite politically Eastern commercial interests and the Western people by advocating a protective tariff, extensive internal improvements, a strong national bank, and distribution among the States according to their population of the proceeds from the sale of public lands. This program, which later formed the basis of the platform of the National Republican and Whig parties, was called the American System because it was calculated to make the United States more self-sufficient and less dependent on foreign countries. Apparently Clay himself first used *American System* during the debates in the House of Representatives on the Tariff Bill of 1824. His theory was that the Federal Government's first duty was to help its people.

A few years later, after the tariff became a burning political issue, *American System* was applied specifically to the protective tariff. On October 14, 1830, Philip Hone recorded in his diary that "Tristam Burgess, the great champion of the American (protective tariff) system delivered an address." Eight years later Hone referred to Hezekiah

Niles, editor of *Niles' Register,* as "the father of the American System." In his annual message of 1848 President James K. Polk, who had opposed Clay's program as a young member of Congress in 1830, said the American System was a departure from earliest American policy, depended on an enlargement of the Federal powers, and was not warranted by a just interpretation of the Constitution.

Who said: "I had rather be right than be President?"

It is popularly supposed that Henry Clay uttered these historic words in the U.S. Senate in the debates on the Compromise of 1850. According to the legend, another Senator interrupted the Millboy of the Slashes and alluded sneeringly to his Presidential ambitions. Clay, then seventy-three years old, is said to have replied haughtily: "Sir, I had rather be right than be President."

That story is fictitious, although it has found its way into many reference works. The famous quotation did not originate on the floor of the Senate.

In February, 1839, Clay delivered a notable speech in the Senate against the abolitionists. Before making the speech he consulted his friend, Senator William Preston of South Carolina, and in that interview between the South Carolinian and the Kentuckian the famous saying was born. The first knowledge the public had of Clay's epigrammatic utterance came through a speech that Senator Preston made when he addressed a Whig meeting in Philadelphia sometime later in the same year. In the course of an eloquent eulogy of the Whig leader Senator Preston said:

On one occasion Mr. Clay did me the honor to consult me in reference to a step he was about to take, and which will, perhaps, occur to your minds without more direct allusion. After stating what he proposed, it was remarked that such a step might be offensive to the ultras of both parties, in the excitement which then existed. To this Mr. Clay replied: "I trust the sentiments and opinions are correct; I had rather be right than be President."

On April 20, 1839, Colonel James Thomas had a chat with John Quincy Adams, who under that date wrote in his diary:

He said . . . that his (Clay's) only prominent supporter at the South now was Mr. Preston, but yesterday the most furious champion of nullification. It is indeed curious that Preston has avowed in a speech at a Whig meeting and in a published letter, that he was one of a small party of friends to whom Clay read his anti-abolition speech before he delivered it in the Senate.

Grover Cleveland is reputed to have said, "I care more for principle than the Presidency." On April 19, 1884, former President Rutherford B. Hayes wrote in his diary: "Clay would rather be right than be President. Blaine would gladly be wrong to be President."

Once, during a heated debate in the U.S. House of Representatives, Representative William M. "Bounding Bill" Springer, Illinois Democrat, shouted: "I am right. I know I'm right, and I say with Henry Clay, 'I'd rather be right than be President.'" Speaker Thomas B. Reed, who disliked Springer, observed *sotto voce:* "The gentleman needn't worry, he'll never be either."

Who was Old Bullion?

Thomas Hart Benton (1782-1858) was nicknamed "Old Bullion" because he advocated "hard money" and opposed bank notes, "shin-plasters" and other paper currency. Bullion is uncoined precious metal in lumps, bars or ingots. Thomas Jefferson fixed the ratio between gold and silver at fifteen to one, but, since the market price of gold was greater than that in respect to silver, very little gold circulated as money. Benton sponsored a bill that made the ratio between gold and silver sixteen to one to encourage the coining of gold bullion and increase the circulation of gold coins. Either as the result of a slip of the tongue or an attempt to make a pun, Old Bullion once referred to gold coins as "mint-drops," and when the Treasury issued new gold coins in 1834 the public called them "Benton's Mint-Drops." Missouri used to be called the Bullion State from the favorite nickname of "The Great Missourian," who was also called "Old Ironclad" and "The Old Mastiff." His enemies called him "Gold Humbug" and "The Prince of Humbugs."

Benton was born in North Carolina, attended Chapel Hill College (now the University of North Carolina), studied law at William and Mary, practiced in Tennessee and served in the State Senate. In a tavern brawl at Nashville in 1813 he or his brother Jesse fired a pistol ball into the left upper arm of Andrew Jackson, who did not have the bullet removed until after he became President. Five of Benton's brothers and sisters died of tuberculosis and he had the same disease in its incipient stage, but camp life during the War of 1812 restored his physical vigor and he died of cancer at seventy-six. In 1815 he removed to St. Louis, Missouri, where he edited a newspaper and practiced law. Two years later he was challenged by Charles Lucas, a youthful U.S. district attorney, whom he wounded in the duel. Against the advice of the seconds and in violation of the code, Benton forced Lucas to fight a second duel, in which the district attorney was killed.

When Missouri was admitted to statehood in 1821, Benton was chosen one of the first two U.S. Senators. His name was placed before the legislature by a son of Daniel Boone. He was the first Senator to serve five full six-year terms, a total of thirty years. Old Bullion was aggressive, egotistical, vain, dogmatic and humorless, but independent and usually forthright. Although a slaveholder, he was "against the institution of slavery" and opposed to its extension to new territories. He was a Westerner rather than a Southerner in his views and put the Union above all sectional interests. Much of his energy was used in promoting the exploration and development of the West, but he never traveled farther west than Missouri. He made up with Jackson when they were both Senators and later became Old Hickory's stanchest supporter and Senate floor leader. In January, 1832, a surgeon removed from President Jackson's arm the bullet put there by one of the Benton brothers. An apocryphal story says that Francis P. Blair sent the bullet to Benton, who declined to accept the souvenir on the ground that under the common law the President had acquired clear title to it by twenty years' of peaceful possession.

During the War of 1812 Benton was Jackson's aide for a short time, colonel of a regiment of Tennessee volunteers for about four months, and lieutenant colonel of the Thirteenth U.S. Infantry for a year, but saw no combat service. During the Mexican War President Polk and Senator Benton concocted a scheme to make the latter commander-in-chief of the army for political purposes. Generals Scott and Taylor were both being talked of for the Whig nomination for President in 1848. The plan was to create the rank of lieutenant general, appoint Benton to the office, make him a synthetic military hero and nominate him for President to succeed Polk. The President recommended the bill and it passed the House, but it was too much for some of the Democrats to swallow and it was defeated in the Senate by three votes. When Benton was reminded that Scott and Taylor might object to being outranked by a newly created officer, he seriously pointed out that his rank of lieutenant colonel in the War of 1812 predated those of both the generals! After the bill was rejected, he said to Polk on January 23, 1847, according to the President's diary: "Sir! seeing what I have today, I will go as a Major-General or a Lieutenant-Colonel, or in any other rank, provided I can have the command of the army, and if I can have such command I will close the war before July." Then Polk nominated and the Senate confirmed Benton as a major general, but Old Bullion refused to accept it because it did not give him rank over the four other major generals, make him commander of the army in Mexico and give him full powers to make a peace treaty.

For some unknown reason Benton insisted that the correct pronunciation of his surname was *bayne-tun* and he always pronounced it that way. In 1856 Benton remained faithful to the Democratic Party and supported James Buchanan for President against John C. Frémont, the Republican candidate, who was the husband of his famous daughter, Jessie. Benton hated John C. Calhoun personally and politically for more than twenty years. When the Great Nullifier died in 1850 Benton was asked by a reporter if he cared to comment. "No, sir," he is reputed to have replied, "when God Almighty lays his hand upon a man, I take mine off."

Who was "the boy Governor of Michigan"?

Stevens Thomson Mason (1811-1843), a great-grandnephew of George Mason of Gunston Hall, is known as "the boy Governor of Michigan" because he was the first Governor of that State when he was only twenty-five years old. He was born near Leesburg, Virginia, on October 27, 1811, and spent his youth in Kentucky. His father, John Thomson Mason, was appointed secretary of Michigan Territory in 1830 by President Jackson. About a year later the secretary resigned to go to Texas to manage a large tract of land he had acquired there. It was widely believed, though never proved, that he went to the Southwest as Jackson's secret agent to lay the groundwork for the annexation of Texas.

President Jackson promptly appointed the son to the vacant secretaryship and was severely criticized for doing so. Stevens Thomson Mason, generally known as "Tom Mason," took the oath as secretary of Michigan Territory July 25, 1831, when he was nineteen years and nine months of age. Shortly thereafter Lewis Cass, who had been Governor of Michigan Territory for eighteen years, resigned to become Secretary of War in Jackson's Cabinet, and Mason was acting Governor or Governor ex officio of the Territory during the next five years with the exception of two months while George B. Porter was Governor. He distinguished himself particularly in his fight for statehood and his leadership of the faction that asserted Michigan's claim to the Toledo strip. When Michigan was admitted into the Union January 26, 1837, Mason became the first elected Governor of the State at the age of twenty-five. His political fortunes having sunk to a low ebb at the end of his second term, he did not run again, but practiced law in New York City, where he died at the age of thirty-one. In time the first Governor of the State became a legendary figure in Michigan, and in 1905 his body was removed from New York City and reinterred in Capitol Square at Detroit, which had been the capital of Michigan until 1847.

In 1778 James Jackson (1757-1806), a native of England, was elected Governor of Georgia by the legislature when he was only twenty-one and had been in America only six years, but he declined to serve on the ground that he was too young and inexperienced. Twenty years later, after he had served both as a Representative and a Senator in the U.S. Congress, he was again elected Governor and served in that office until he returned to the U.S. Senate in 1801.

The second youngest person to serve as Governor of a State was William Sprague (1830-1915), who became Governor of Rhode Island in 1860 at the age of twenty-nine. He later became a Senator and married Secretary of the Treasury Salmon P. Chase's daughter Kate. Harold E. Stassen was thirty-one when sworn in as Governor of Minnesota January 1, 1939. William Eustis Russell was elected Governor of Massachusetts in 1890 at the age of thirty-three. On March 22, 1891, former President Rutherford B. Hayes called on Governor Russell in Boston and wrote in his diary: "A young, cheery, hopeful, gentlemanly man—said to be of sound and level head—with a future. How strange. The ancient commonwealth, the home of conservative opinion and conduct, with its boy governor!" Huey P. Long became Governor of Louisiana in 1928 at the age of thirty-four.

Some State constitutions are silent on the subject, but the majority of them, like the Federal Constitution, prescribe a minimum age as one of the qualifications of the chief executive. These minimum age requirements range from twenty-five to thirty-five years.

The oldest person to serve as Governor of a State was Walter S. Goodland, who was born December 22, 1862, and who was Governor of Wisconsin when he died March 11, 1947, at the age of eighty-four. Benjamin Franklin became President of the Executive Council of Pennsylvania—then equivalent to Governor—when he was seventy-nine and served until he was eighty-two. Luren D. Dickinson succeeded to the Governorship of Michigan on March 17, 1939, and served until January 1, 1941, when he was eighty-one years, eight months and fifteen days old.

What was the Anti-Mason Party?

The Anti-Mason Party, though short-lived, was one of the most curious political movements in the United States. In a sense it was the first "third party."

It grew out of agitation over the mysterious disappearance of William Morgan in 1826. Very little is known for certain about Morgan. He is supposed to have been born in 1774 in Virginia, where he served an apprenticeship as a stonemason. After living in Kentucky and again in Virginia he went north about 1823. In the latter year he appears to have been working as a brick-and-stone mason in Rochester and Batavia in New York. He took an active interest in Freemasonry and on May 31, 1825, became a Royal Arch Mason at Le Roy in the same State.

The next year it was rumored that Morgan was writing a book to expose the secret ritual of Freemasonry and that David C. Miller of Batavia would publish it. On August 14, 1826, Morgan applied for a copyright on a book entitled *Illustrations of Masonry*. Just what Morgan's reputation in the community was is hard to determine. Afterward some people testified that he was a respected citizen, while others said he was a heavy drinker and a ne'er-do-well. He was sued for debt several times during that summer. On September 11, 1826, he was arrested and taken to Canandaigua, seat of Ontario County, to answer charges of petty theft. Morgan never returned from Canandaigua and what became of him has never been ascertained definitely.

Almost at once a story was circulated that Freemasons, to prevent publication of the exposé of their order, had seized Morgan after his release by the court, taken him in a closed carriage to Fort Niagara, murdered him and thrown his body into the Niagara River. The disappearance of Morgan caused great excitement in western New York. At that time there was considerable public sentiment against secret orders of all kinds. Since 1738 Catholics had been strictly forbidden, under penalty of excommunication, to join societies of Freemasons or in any way to promote such organizations. But Catholics were not numerous in the United States in those days and they played virtually no part in the anti-Masonic agitation in the early part of the nineteenth century. The Lutherans, Dutch Reformed, Mennonites, Dunkards, Quakers and many other Protestant denominations and sects discouraged membership in secret orders. In 1823 the General Methodist Conference in Pennsylvania prohibited its clergy from joining the Masons. About the same time the Baptists were divided into two factions on the issue. Prejudice against the Masons was particularly strong because so many members of that order held high political offices. Many people, charging that Masons were bound by oath to support one another politically, would not vote for Masons on the theory they put the tenets of their order above the laws of their country and therefore were unfit to hold public office. Several political leaders were quick to sense this feeling and to make political capital of it. Prominent Masons denied that members of their order had any part in the disappearance of Morgan. Governor DeWitt Clinton, a high officer of the Masonic order in New York, offered a reward of $1,000 for the discovery of the whereabouts of Morgan if he was alive and twice that sum for the discovery and conviction of his murderers if he was murdered. Public feeling increased and both factions formed committees to procure evidence.

The flames were still further fanned when in the fall of 1826 Miller published *Illustrations of Masonry,* which was widely circulated in English as well as in foreign languages. Some Masons said Morgan's book was substantially true but was unimportant because it was little more than a plagiarism of *Jackim and Boaz,* published in London in 1762. Others charged that it was really the work of Miller himself who had rewritten and corrected the manuscript of the illiterate Morgan. Feeling against the Masons became so strong that many members withdrew from the order while many others demanded revision of the rules of the order. The National Republican Party of New York nominated a State ticket without a single Mason on it. Notwithstanding this gesture, the Anti-Masons held a convention at Le Roy in 1827 and nominated their own ticket. Millard Fillmore, later Vice President and President of the United States, was elected to the New York Legislature as an Anti-Mason. At first the Anti-Masons received a comparatively small vote, but the movement spread and by 1830 the Anti-Mason Party was the chief competitor of the Albany Regency and Martin Van Buren's Democratic-Republican party for political power in the State.

Anti-Masonry spread from New York into Pennsylvania and New England. Early in 1828 the White House began to hear about the new political party, which troubled President John Quincy Adams, who was not a Mason and who was running as the National Republican candidate to succeed himself. On October 25, 1827, the President wrote in his diary:

Dr. Watkins called with a letter from A. H. Tracy, the former member of Congress from the western part of the State of New York, inquiring, with great solicitude, whether I am, and also whether General Jackson is, a Freemason. He says that it is circulated there with an indefatigable assiduity that I am, and that he is not, a Mason; that the object of these reports is to influence the elections; and that they do more powerfully operate upon it there than all other electioneering topics put together. About fifteen months since, a man by the name of William Morgan published, or attempted to publish, at Batavia, a book professing to divulge the secrets of Freemasonry. He was shortly afterward kidnapped, carried away, murdered and thrown into Lake Ontario, where his body has within a few days been found. No positive proof of his death had been till now produced; but as there has been ample evidence of a conspiracy among the Freemasons, which succeeded in carrying him away, and had the purpose of destroying him, the consequence has been a universal excitement and popular fermentation in that vicinity, which has extended throughout New York, and has at length brought a mass of obloquy upon the institution of Masonry itself. I told Watkins he might answer Tracy that I am not, and never was, a Freemason, but whether General Jackson is or not I do not know.

Andrew Jackson was a Mason and took a militant pride in his record in the order. The body that had been found near Oak Orchard in the Niagara River below the Falls was never proved to be that of Morgan. His wife swore that it was his body and one of his extracted teeth was fitted into the jaw. Some other witnesses testified that the body was that of Morgan beyond all doubt, but others were equally certain that it was the body of another man who had disappeared from the community. After doubt was thrown on the identity of the body found, Thurlow Weed, the Anti-Mason leader in New York, who was determined to destroy Van Buren and the Albany Regency, was reported as observing, "A good enough Morgan for me till after the election," and "a good enough Morgan" passed into the political vocabulary in the sense of a real or supposed barefaced imposition.

Masonry was becoming a national issue. On January 22, 1828, Adams wrote:

Mr. Tracy, . . . and Dr. Watkins called together. Mr. Tracy's object was to ask of me a renewed declaration that I was not a Freemason. I had already told him that I was not; and he made many apologies for repeating the question, but said that in the western part of New York this was now the only test of elections; and he read me a part of a letter from one of his friends, who wrote him that although a positive denial had been published that I was a Mason, the assertion that I was had been republished, with promises to produce extracts from the books of the lodge to which I belonged. This is a sample of electioneering falsehoods. I had received this morning two letters full of anxiety for the effect which the belief of my Masonry would have against me, and one of them entreating me to give a denial of it under my own hand. I told Tracy that if I should deny it I should not be surprised if they were to produce a forged extract from some imaginary lodge to counteract my denial. Such are the morals of electioneering.

On January 30, 1828, Adams wrote:

Mr. Garnsey, member of the House from the western part of the State of New York, came to ask me the question whether I was a Mason. This question absorbs all others upon the electioneering canvass in that part of the country; and the slander-mongers there, disregarding all other lies, only pledge their words and their oaths that they know me to be a Mason. Garnsey told me that he was himself one; and he gave me to understand that in the event of the formation of a new Territory, carved out of Michigan, he would like the appointment of Governor of it.

On April 18, 1828, President Adams wrote:

Governor Barbour [Secretary of War] called with the Ontario *Messenger,* a newspaper published in the western part of the State of New York. It contained a statement made by persons sent by the authority of the Government of New York into the Territory of Arkansas in pursuit of three persons suspected as accomplices in the murder of Morgan. The statement charges Colonel Cummins, commandant of the post at Cantonment Towson, with having collusively facilitated the escape of a man named King, acting as sutler to the troops, and the most deeply implicated of them all in the suspicion of the murder. It is even asserted that Colonel Cummins denied the authority of the Secretary of War to give the instructions with which the pursuers had been furnished, ordering him to give all the aid in his power to detect and arrest the suspected culprits. This order had been given the last autumn, at the request of the late Governor Clinton. The Governor had received this newspaper yesterday, and another copy of it had been forwarded to me. He said he had immediately written to the publisher of the paper, and to the person by whom the statement was made, asking further particulars relating to the allegations against Colonel Cummins. This I approved, and advised that a copy of the statement should be sent to Colonel Cummins himself, and that he should be called upon to defend himself against the allegations it contains.

On May 14, 1828, the President wrote:

I gave Governor Barbour the memorial to Congress of the Anti-Masonic Convention at Le Roy, addressed to Congress, and which the House of Representatives, by resolution, the day before yesterday, referred to me. B.O. Tyler came, it seems, to talk of the Anti-Masonic Le Roy Convention memorial, which gives him great concern. He is himself a Mason, and sympathizes with their troubles. Colonel King, the sutler who contrived to make his escape, was a friend, and had been a boarder of Tyler's, who thinks him entirely innocent. Tyler read me a piece which he had prepared for publication in defense of King. There were some imprudent remarks in it, which I advised him not to publish; and he said Mr. Bateman, the Senator from New Jersey, had given him the same advice.

[78]

Jackson defeated Adams in the election of 1828, but the activities of the Anti-Masons did not cease. By 1831 the Anti-Masons thought they were strong enough to make a bid for the Presidency and called a national convention to meet in September at Baltimore. Former President Adams, Former Secretary of the Treasury Richard Rush, Associate Justice John McLean of the Supreme Court, and former Attorney General William Wirt were most prominently mentioned as presidential possibilities on the Anti-Mason ticket. In June, 1831, Adams declined an invitation to make the Fourth of July address at an Anti-Mason meeting in Boston, but in his letter to the committee he "expressed the opinion that the institution ought to be dissolved, or to discard their secrets, oaths, penalties, and pageantries," although he refused to make this opinion public "for the present." Rush, like McLean, declined the Anti-Mason nomination for the Presidency. "The most stirring passage in Rush's letter," wrote Adams on July 11, 1831, "is the statement that not one of the men convicted in the State of New York of agency in the kidnapping of Morgan had been expelled from the lodge to which he belonged." On June 10, 1831, Adams wrote: "The dissolution of the Masonic institution in the United States I believe to be really more important to us and our posterity than the question whether Mr. Clay or General Jackson shall be the President chosen at the next election." On May 20 of that year Adams had attended an Anti-Masonic meeting in Faneuil Hall and for several weeks thought and talked continually on the subject. By August 27 he, like John C. Calhoun, had indicated clearly that he, while not desirous of the Anti-Mason nomination for President, would accept it if it were offered to him by the Baltimore convention. In *Autobiography of Seventy Years* (1903) George F. Hoar wrote: "The ex-President, I think, about the year 1832, published a pamphlet in which he savagely attacked the Masonic Order. He met Mr. Samuel Hoar in Boston and asked him what he thought of it. Mr. Hoar answered: 'It seems to me, Mr. Adams, there is but one thing in the world sillier than Masonry. That is Anti-Masonry.' "

The Baltimore convention nominated Wirt for President and Amos Ellmaker of Pennsylvania for Vice President on a platform that declared against secret societies and imprisonment for debt and for a protective tariff, canal improvements and exemption of banks from regulatory taxes. The Anti-Masons made no particular appeal to the Catholics, who were opposed to secret societies by the tenets of their Church. Instead the Anti-Masons appealed to Protestant orthodoxy and opposed Universalism and other forms of religious liberalism. Jackson, the Democratic-

Republican nominee to succeed himself, and Henry Clay, the National Republican candidate, were both Masons, although Clay, in the cant of the day, was what was called an "adhering Mason," that is, he had joined a Masonic lodge but had not been active in it and had never withdrawn from it or renounced Masonry. Some of the Anti-Masons were or had been Masons, and even Wirt, their presidential candidate, had been a Mason in his younger days, although he had little contact with the order in later years. It appears that Wirt, who had removed from Virginia to Maryland, was not much interested in Anti-Masonry as such and accepted the nomination on the theory that he could be nominated by the National Republicans also and be the candidate of both parties against Jackson. When the National Republicans persisted in nominating Clay in December at their Baltimore convention, Wirt wanted to withdraw as the Anti-Mason candidate, but could hardly do so honorably, and from that time he was an unwilling candidate. In the election of 1832 Wirt and Ellmaker received a total of 100,000 popular votes and only the seven electoral votes of Vermont, where the popular vote was 13,106 for Wirt, 11,152 for Jackson and 7,870 for Clay. The Anti-Mason ticket also ran ahead of Jackson in Massachusetts.

In 1833 Adams was nominated for Governor of Massachusetts by the Anti-Masons but finally withdrew his name. He was also supported by the Anti-Masons in his early races for Congress, and on March 27, 1834, he was chosen chairman of a bloc of Anti-Mason members of Congress. In the Phi Beta Kappa Society Representative Adams led the fight to amend the constitution and bylaws to abolish injunctions of secrecy. In 1836 the National Republicans made no national nominations and cast their votes for William Henry Harrison and three other candidates. Harrison, by far the leading Whig candidate, was reputed to be an Anti-Mason sympathizer. On December 16, 1835, the Pennsylvania Whigs and Anti-Masons held separate conventions at Harrisburg. Both conventions nominated Harrison for President. The Anti-Mason convention, however, united on Francis Granger for Vice President and he received enough votes to throw the Vice Presidency into the Senate, which chose Richard M. Johnson, the leading Democratic-Republican candidate for Vice President. In 1835 a combination of Anti-Masons, led by Thaddeus Stevens, and National Republicans elected Joseph Ritner Governor of Pennsylvania. After the election of 1836 the remnant of the Anti-Mason Party was gradually absorbed by the other parties, particularly the Jacksonians, who had begun to call themselves Whigs instead of National Republicans and who were knitting their forces for the battle of 1840. As late as 1837 Adams conferred with a group of

Anti-Masons from Pennsylvania in Brown's Hotel in Washington. Two prominent Anti-Mason leaders—William H. Seward and Thaddeus Stevens—remained in public life until after the Civil War.

Just what happened to William Morgan has never been determined to the satisfaction of everybody. Several trials of persons who were charged with implication in the case failed to reveal the facts. Some people believe that he was never murdered at all but that he merely absconded when things got too hot for him. From time to time for many years stories were circulated that he had been seen in various places, as an Indian chief in the Rocky Mountains, as a hermit in Canada, as a Mohammedan mufti in the Levant, as a merchant in Smyrna and as a pirate hanged at Havana. It is said that his wife became one of the "spiritual wives" of Joseph Smith, founder of Mormonism, who had once lived at Canandaigua, where Morgan mysteriously disappeared. For generations "Morgan Tower," a square tower near Youngstown, New York, near where the Niagara River empties into Lake Erie, was pointed out as the last place where William Morgan was seen alive.

Why was Andrew Jackson called Old Hickory?

Just how Andrew Jackson got his famous nickname is not known. It is generally supposed that he was first called Old Hickory in 1813 by his soldiers because of his physical toughness and sturdiness. The earliest known reference in print to *Old Hickory* as a nickname of Jackson occurs in Samuel Putnam Waldo's *Memoirs of Andrew Jackson,* printed by Silas Andrus at Hartford, Connecticut, in 1818, three years after the Battle of New Orleans.

That work contains the following passage:

The troops before New Orleans embraced many of the first young gentlemen, in point of talents, education, family, and fortune, in the states of Kentucky, Tennessee, Louisiana and Mississippi; and among them were, of course, many of a rougher character. The pleasant raillery, which is the very zest of life, when played off by one gentleman upon another, was unfortunately practised upon a captain of a company, who took it in high dudgeon. In imitation of the names of Indian chiefs, his men called him Capt. Flat-foot. He remonstrated against it to General Jackson, who pleasantly remarked—: "Really, Captain, it is difficult getting along with these gay young fellows; but so long as they toil at the lines with such vigour, and fight the enemy with such courage, we officers must overlook a little innocent levity. Why, Captain, they call me Old Hickory; and if you prefer my title to your's I will readily make an exchange." The Captain retired, proud of the title of Capt. Flat-foot.

In his life of Andrew Jackson (1859) James Parton wrote:

The name was not an instantaneous inspiration, but a growth. First of all the remark was made by some soldier who was struck with his commander's pedestrian power, that he was tough. Next, it was observed that he was as tough as hickory. Then he was called *hickory*. Lastly, the affectionate adjective *old* was prefixed and the general thereafter rejoiced in the completed nickname.

And in *Andrew Jackson, the Border Captain* (1933) Marquis James, citing Parton as his authority, said the nickname originated in the early part of 1813, about two years before the battle of New Orleans, when Jackson was returning from Natchez to Tennessee with his militia after the War Department had advised him that his services would not be needed at New Orleans.

The column moved at the pace of veterans—in a wilderness where streams had to be bridged and the road hacked through swamps [wrote James]. Jackson was everywhere—up and down the toiling line, with the sick, where the rations were distributed—and always on foot, until the men began to offer their horses. "He's tough," an admiring voice observed in the ranks after the General had passed by. "Tough as hickory," said another naming the toughest thing he knew. The word somehow seemed to suit the tall, striding man in a mussed uniform and muddy boots. "Hickory" he became to that company. The sobriquet took and before the first settlements were reached was the property of the army with the affectionate prefix "Old" for completeness.

But James, like Parton before him, was only guessing. Soldiers have their own way of appraising generals and it is possible that the nickname was not at first entirely complimentary or affectionate but was applied to Jackson because of his stubborn and unyielding disposition and harsh discipline rather than because of his strong and wiry physique and sturdy character. The quotation from Waldo, the earliest known reference to the subject in print, intimates that the nickname was originally uncomplimentary and bestowed in "innocent levity." William Allen, an old neighbor who messed with Jackson during the Creek War of 1813-1814, told a different story of the origin of the nickname. According to Allen, a captain of a militia company at the time, the army was moving rapidly through a cold rain and sleet to surprise the Indians. The army had no tents and General Jackson, still suffering from a pistol bullet fired by one of the Benton brothers and afflicted with a severe cold, tried to sleep on the muddy ground with his men. Captain Allen and his brother John cut down a hickory tree, peeled off the bark and with it made a covering for the General. The next morning a drunken man stumbled over the bark hut and knocked it over. As Jackson crawled out the drunk said: "Hello, Old Hickory! Come out of your bark and jine us in a drink." Another yarn is that Jackson was called Old Hickory because he set his men the example of subsisting on hickory nuts when provisions ran low. Still another attributes the nickname to the alleged fact that on one occasion Jackson failed to beat an assailant because his rattan cane was too light and brittle, whereupon his friends gave him a hickory cane in the hope he would have better luck the next time.

Old Hickory did not become nationally known as Jackson's nickname until he became an active candidate for President, when "General Hickory Clubs" were formed and Jackson men paraded with hickory poles. In its issue of June 20, 1827, the Hallowell (Maine) *Gazette* said: "He was in favor of amending the constitution, so as to let the people vote for 'Old Hickory.'" Washington Irving, in 1829, wrote: "As to the old general, with all his hickory characteristics, I suspect he has good stuff in him." The Presidential campaign of 1828 was known as the "Hickory Pole Canvass" because the Democratic-Republicans used a hickory pole as an emblem. In some sections of the country supporters of the Hero of New Orleans were called hickories. Dr. Robert Mayo told John Quincy Adams in 1837 that he proposed to publish a book entitled *Eight Years' Residence in Washington*—"a secret history of the Kitchen Cabinet, the Hickory Club, and the Administration of Andrew Jackson." Adams, who had been defeated by Jackson in 1828, wrote in his diary on November 17, 1837: "Dr. Mayo is one of those office-hunters and busybodies, who, during Jackson's Administration, under the mask of reform, were in a continual struggle to turn out of the Executive office all the incumbents except his devoted tools, and to put themselves, and such as themselves, in their places. Mayo was the principal agent of the Hickory Club, acting under the impulse of Amos Kendall." At the height of his power Jackson was called "Saint Andrew" and "King Andrew the First" by his political enemies, but he was "The Man of the People" to his followers.

An attempt was made by the Democrats to attach the nickname "Young Hickory" to James K. Polk, a Tennessean nominated for President in 1844 as a protégé of Old Hickory. On June 3 of that year Representative Stephen A. Douglas said of Polk: "He is emphatically a Young Hickory—the unwavering friend of Old Hickory in all his trials." But Polk was small in stature, had never been a soldier, had never fought a duel, did not drink liquor, nor use tobacco, and the nickname was not appropriate and did not stick to him long. Franklin Pierce of New Hampshire was hailed by the Democrats in 1852 as "The Young Hickory of the Granite Hills," which hardly outlasted the campaign.

Hickory is of Algonquin Indian origin. Captain John Smith spelled the word *pawcohiccore*. The Virginia Indians applied it to a preparation of pounded nut kernels, but the English applied it, in a shortened and altered form, to the shaggy-barked walnut tree that produced the nuts. This tree is common in North America and because of its hard, flexible wood its name is applied to many things characterized by hardness and toughness. *Hickory* is a common place-name in America. It is the name or part of the name of nearly a score of post offices, and *Old Hickory* is the name of a county in Mississippi and of towns in that State and North Carolina. American hickory surpasses all other woods for axes, hammers and other tool handles. It has all the qualities a striking tool handle should have—stiffness, hardness, resiliency, shock-resistance and toughness—and it has played an important part in building America.

What President's wife smoked a pipe?

Mrs. Andrew Jackson, wife of the seventh President, was a habitual pipe-smoker, but she never presided over the White House as First Lady of the Land. She died late on December 22, 1828, on the evening of the day before her husband had planned to set out for Washington to assume the duties of the Presidency on March 4, 1829. A Nashville seamstress had just made Mrs. Jackson new clothes for her life in the White House and according to tradition she was buried in a white satin dress that she expected to wear at her husband's inauguration in Washington.

In Colonial days and until the middle of the nineteenth century many American women of all classes used tobacco privately. Mrs. Mary Ball Washington, mother of the Father of His Country, and Mrs. Nellie Conway Madison, mother of the Father of the Constitution, both smoked pipes habitually. Mrs. Dolly Payne Todd Madison, wife of the President was a habitual snuff-user. Early in Jefferson's first administration, when Madison was Secretary of State, Vice President Aaron Burr wrote to his daughter Theodosia: "Mrs. Madison is still pretty, but oh that unfortunate propensity to snuff-taking." In his *Autobiography* (1929) Calvin Coolidge says of his grandfather, Calvin Galusha Coolidge: "He took me one time to see her sister, his very aged aunt, whom we found sitting in the chimney corner smoking a clay pipe. This was so uncommon that I always remembered it. I thought tobacco was only for men, though I had seen old ladies outside our neighborhood buy snuff at the store." Somebody once asked Speaker Joseph G. Cannon, who was born in North Carolina, what he thought of women smoking cigarettes. "Uncle Joe" replied that he saw no objection to it since his mother smoked a pipe.

There is ample evidence that Mrs. Jackson was a habitual pipe-smoker. Her maiden name was Rachel Donelson and her first husband was named Lewis Robards. In *The Life of Andrew Jackson* Marquis James indicates that Rachel Donelson began to smoke when she was quite young. Referring to about 1789, James writes: "Perhaps Mrs. Robards dipped snuff instead of smoking a pipe as her border-bred daughter-in-law did, but she liked Rachel." James Parton, Jackson's first important biographer, said it was not uncommon for Jackson and his wife to sit for hours smoking their pipes before their fire in the Hermitage near Nashville. "After supper," says Marquis James, "she must join the gentlemen over their brandy by the fire. Jackson would fill a fresh clay pipe and light it for her with a coal, the same as when they were alone." In 1823 Rachel Jackson's favorite sister, Jane Hays, wrote to her: "How does my dear sister Jackson do? I cannot take up my bonnet and meet you at sister Betsys or sister Marys . . . smoke our pipes, laugh and talk." In 1825, when Jackson was in Washington waiting for the House of Representatives to decide whether he was to be President, he wrote to General John Coffee: "Mrs. J. and myself at home smoking our pipe." Four years later, after Jackson was certain of the Presidency, Washington society was gossiping about Mrs. Jackson. In January, 1829, Margaret Bayard Smith wrote to her sister: "We spent the evening at Dr. Simm's last night. All present were Jacksonians—Dr. Simm the most ardent and devoted. He had lately received a letter from Gen. J. which he promised to show me. I wanted to see it immediately, suspecting, as I told him, if he deferred showing it, it would be with the intention of correcting the orthography. He laughed and joked on the subject very good naturedly and about Mrs. J. and her pipe in the bargain." Mrs. Smith did not know that Mrs. Jackson was in her coffin and that during her last illness she had her maid Hannah help her to her chair by the fire and fill a pipe with tobacco. Marquis James suggests that Mrs. Jackson also smoked cigars. While General Jackson was military governor of Florida he and his wife lived at Pensacola. "And to prove that no human experience is wholly barren," says James, "Rachel had brought away from Florida a preference for Spanish cigars."

It is often said that Mrs. Zachary Taylor, wife of the twelfth President, was a habitual pipe-smoker and that she was known to smoke a pipe occasionally in private while mistress of the White House, but there is no evidence that this is true and it is contrary to family tradition. Mrs. Taylor's maiden name was Margaret Smith and she was a daughter of

Walter Smith, a planter of Calvert County, Maryland. Sarah Knox Taylor, one of the daughters of President and Mrs. Taylor, was the first wife of Jefferson Davis. The second Mrs. Jefferson Davis wrote that Mrs. Taylor not only did not smoke but would not permit even the members of her family to smoke in her presence. According to tradition, General Taylor himself did not smoke because of his wife's objection to the habit. Herbert C. Wood, Jr., a grandson of President and Mrs. Taylor who at one time lived with the family said that Old Rough and Ready did not smoke, and Holman Hamilton, in his *Zachary Taylor, Soldier of the Republic* (1841), says this was "probably out of deference to Mrs. Taylor, whom smoke made actively ill."

What President was married to the same woman twice?

Andrew Jackson was married to Rachel Donelson Robards twice. In 1785 Rachel Donelson was married to Captain Lewis Robards, a resident of the Kentucky District of Virginia. On December 20, 1790, the Virginia legislature passed a bill granting Robards permission to sue for divorce in the proper court provided he could prove sufficient grounds. Under the mistaken notion that this ex parte divorce proceeding had been completed, Jackson and Rachel were married in August, 1791, at Natchez, Mississippi. After Jackson and Rachel had lived together for some time they learned that the divorce proceeding had not been completed and that technically she was a bigamist. On January 17, 1794, after Robards had received a divorce decree from a Virginia court, Jackson and Rachel were remarried in a ceremony at Nashville.

The charge that the Jacksons had lived together in adultery for more than two years disturbed their peace of mind for the rest of their lives. In 1817 Nashville friends appointed a committee to investigate the charge, and this committee absolved the Jacksons from all blame in respect to their original marriage, but much was made of the matter by political enemies during his campaigns for the Presidency. Mrs. Jackson was sensitive about such publicity and her husband believed that it hastened her death. "I assure you," she told a friend, "I would rather be a doorkeeper in the house of my God than to live in that place in Washington." She died in 1828 after her husband was elected President but before he was sworn in. Part of the epitaph Jackson had inscribed on her tombstone was the following: "A being so gentle, and yet so virtuous, slander might wound, but could not dishonor."

The mistress of the White House during most of Jackson's administration was Emily Donelson, wife and cousin of Andrew Jackson

Donelson, son of one of Rachel's six brothers and adopted son and secretary of the President. Mary, the daughter of Andrew Jackson Donelson and his wife, was known as "Sunshine of the White House." When Jackson was asked for a token to place in the cornerstone of the Treasury building in Washington, he sent a lock of Mary's hair.

On April 18, 1831, former President John Quincy Adams wrote in his diary that "Jackson lived some time in adultery with his wife," and about two months later referred to the President of the United States as "an adjudicated adulterer."

Jackson was the first President who married a divorcee. The second and only other one who did so was Warren G. Harding. In 1878, when she was eighteen, Florence Kling, daughter of a Marion businessman named Amos O. Kling, was married to Henry DeWolfe, by whom she had a son, Marshall DeWolfe. Mrs. Henry DeWolfe was divorced from her husband by a decree that restored her maiden name, and in 1891, after her former husband had died, Florence Kling, then thirty-one, was married to Harding, who was five years younger than she.

What President deliberately shot a man to death?

Andrew Jackson has been the only President to fight a duel and the only one known to kill anybody in personal encounter. On May 30, 1806, Jackson and a twenty-seven-year-old Nashville attorney fought a duel in Kentucky just across the Tennessee line. The original quarrel grew out of a misunderstanding over a horse race. During the controversy Dickinson made a slighting remark about Mrs. Jackson's matrimonial history. When confronted by Jackson, Dickinson apologized and said he had been drinking when he made the remark. But Jackson heard repetitions. Finally Dickinson published a statement in a newspaper in which he called Jackson "a worthless scoundrel, a poltroon, and a coward."

Jackson challenged Dickinson, who chose pistols at twenty-four feet. Dickinson, a quick and good shot, fired instantly after the word was given. Jackson was a thin man and Dickinson was deceived as to the location of his heart by his loose frock coat. Even so the bullet lodged so near Jackson's heart that it could never be removed. Jackson, a slow and not particularly good shot, deliberately withheld his fire. Despite his serious wound, he raised his pistol calmly, aimed carefully and fired a shot that mortally wounded Dickinson.

Although Jackson was in several brawls and personal fights and issued and declined several challenges, he fought only one other formal duel. In 1795 he fought a duel with Waitsell Avery, an opposing lawyer in a lawsuit, over an argument that started in the courtroom. Neither was touched and it was suspected that both fired wild intentionally. In 1812 Jackson exchanged shots with Thomas and Jesse Benton in a Nashville tavern and received two wounds in the same arm and shoulder. One of the Benton bullets stayed in his shoulder, and the General started the Creek campaign that year with one arm in a sling and two bullets in his body.

During his Presidential campaigns Jackson was represented by his enemies as a hot-tempered barbarian, who drank liquor, owned and bet on fighting cocks and race horses, chewed and smoked tobacco, and shot people down at the drop of a hat. The voters were reminded in print and pictures that Jackson had approved the execution of six militiamen and seven regulars under his command, had ordered the execution of two British subjects in Florida, and had permitted the killing of men, women and children during a battle with the Creek Indians. The authors of the campaign documents omitted to include among Jackson's victims the two thousand British soldiers killed or wounded at New Orleans, the only ones that interested the majority of voters. Jackson's opposition resented his popularity with the people. On June 13, 1833, Philip Hone, a New York National Republican and Whig leader, wrote: "Talk of him as the second Washington! It won't do now. Washington was only the first Jackson." A sample of the stories circulated about the Hero of New Orleans was recorded by Hone in his diary on May 20, 1834:

On the arrival of the stage in one of the towns of the interior of Pennsylvania, during the President's far-famed journey to the East, the crowd assembled in the bar-room of the tavern collected around the driver with the usual inquiry, "What news?"—"Why, haven't you heard?" said the waggish driver. "The General made his grand entry yesterday into Philadelphia in a barouche drawn by four gray horses; and the crowd pressing around him so as to obstruct his progress, he just stepped out of the carriage, drew his sword, and run one fellow clean through the body."—"The damned fool," exclaimed one of the auditors, "why didn't he stand out of the General's way."

Men differed violently in regard to Jackson. Apparently Jefferson and Jackson misliked and mistrusted each other. Jackson's temporary friendship for Aaron Burr did not increase Jefferson's confidence in him. As early as 1806, while on the way to the Dickinson duel, Jackson observed that Jefferson "was the best republican in theory and the worst in practice" he had ever known. President Monroe considered General Jackson for Minister to Russia. On April 8, 1818, Secretary of State John Quincy Adams, after talking with the President, wrote in his diary: "He said also when in Virginia last autumn, he had enquired of Mr. Jefferson how it would suit to appoint General Jackson to the Russian mission. His answer was, 'Why, good God! he would breed you quarrel before he had been there a month.' " Daniel Webster visited Jefferson in 1824 and quoted the Sage of Monticello as having said to him:

I feel much alarmed at the prospect of seeing General Jackson President. He is one of the most unfit men I know of for such a place. He has had very little respect for laws or constitutions, and is, in fact, merely an able military chief. His passions are terrible. When I was President of the Senate, he was a Senator, and he could never speak, from the rashness of his feelings. I have seen him attempt it repeatedly, and choke with rage. His passions are, no doubt, cooler now; he has been much tried since I knew him, but he is a dangrous man.

In 1840 Hone referred to Jackson as a "vindictive old man, whose administration of the government will be marked in the annals of the country as the period of her disgrace and humiliation," and the "hoary disturber of his country's peace." On June 17, 1845, after learning of Jackson's death, Hone wrote in his diary: "Now, to my thinking, the country had greater cause to mourn on the day of his birth than on that of his decease." But on January 12, 1837, Thomas H. Benton had said on the floor of the Senate: "Where is there a chief magistrate of whom so much evil has been predicted and from whom so much good has come?" In his *Life of Andrew Jackson* (1859) James Parton wrote: "He was the most American of Americans—an embodied Declaration of Independence—the Fourth of July incarnate."

What was the Kitchen Cabinet?

Kitchen Cabinet in its political sense is supposed to have been coined by John Randolph of Roanoke and is the popular name applied to a small group of intimate advisers of President Andrew Jackson during his early years in the White House. The original Kitchen Cabinet was composed of several able journalists and pamphleteers who had promoted Jackson for the Presidency and who continued to support him in Washington. Although these men held no important offices at that time, they advised the President in making appointments and in forming administration policies.

The first six Presidents leaned heavily on their Cabinets for advice. Often they accepted the judgment of the majority of the Cabinet instead of their own in making important decisions. Presidents Madison, Monroe and John Quincy Adams seldom acted on any matter without consulting and receiving the support of their Cabinets. But President Jackson paid much less attention to the advice of his official advisers. His Kitchen Cabinet had more influence on his actions than did his Cabinet.

Jackson's "appointing council" was called the Kitchen Cabinet because it was said that when they visited the President they went through the back or kitchen door of the White House to avoid public notice. Randolph, a caustic critic and coiner of stinging phrases, declared that this little coterie of newspapermen, politicians and minor officials decided the great affairs of state while the members of the official Cabinet were asleep. The idea was not new with Randolph. In 1806, after he had turned against President Jefferson, he said: "I speak of backstairs influence. . . . There is no longer any Cabinet."

The moving spirit and the ablest and most influential member of the Kitchen Cabinet was Amos Kendall of Kentucky, Fourth Auditor of the Treasury, who later became Postmaster General and who was the only one of the group to attain actual Cabinet rank. Other members were General Duff Green of Missouri, editor of the *United States Telegraph*, the administration organ in Washington; Major William B. Lewis of Tennessee, one of the original promoters of Jackson for the Presidency, Second Auditor of the Treasury; Andrew Jackson Donelson, Rachel Jackson's nephew and the President's adopted son and secretary, and, later, Francis P. Blair, Sr., of Kentucky, who was editor of *The Globe*, which was established in 1830 to supersede the *United States Telegraph* as the "court journal" in the Capital.

Historians do not agree upon the exact personnel of the Kitchen Cabinet because the term was applied to a continually changing group of Jackson's intimate and informal advisers. One of Jackson's most active advisers and secretaries during the campaign of 1828 was Henry Lee, son of "Light-Horse Harry" Lee and a half brother of Robert E. Lee, but he was early eliminated from the Kitchen Cabinet by his appointment as consul to Algeria, a position for which the Senate refused to confirm him. Likewise Duff Green soon lost his influence with Jackson and was supplanted in the "appointing council" by Blair. James Alexander Hamilton, third son of Alexander Hamilton, is sometimes included in the Kitchen Cabinet. As a Tammany politician and intimate of Jackson he had much to do with Martin Van Buren's appointment as Secretary of State. Tradition assigns a place in the Kitchen Cabinet to Isaac Hill, former Senator and editor of the *New Hampshire Patriot*, but contemporary evidence hardly supports the tradition.

In 1832 a writer alluded to Van Buren as "the most despicable of all the Protogees of the Kitchen Cabinet." Nicholas Biddle, president of the

Bank of the United States, wrote to Robert Lenox on July 3, 1833; "When we begin we shall crush the Kitchen Cabinet at once." On December 6, 1833, John Quincy Adams wrote in his diary: "What an illustration of a Government by a Kitchen Cabinet. To turn out Cranston from the post-office, Pearce addressed himself, not to Barry, the Postmaster General, but to Amos Kendall, an auditor of the Treasury. Amos turns out the Postmaster, and then betrays Pearce, his informant." Thirteen days later Representative Richard H. Wilde of Georgia moved to deny the Treasurer, Register, Comptroller and Auditor the privileges of the floor of the House, and Adams noted, "His real object was a cut at Lewis, the Second Auditor of the Kitchen Cabinet, who, Wilde thought, was spending too much of his time in the House." Philip Hone wrote in his diary on May 4, 1835, that President Jackson "has rewarded the favorite member of his kitchen cabinet, Amos Kendall, by appointing him to the important and responsible office of Postmaster General, by which he secures the enormous patronage of that department in all its ramifications in his favor." One of the early members of the Kitchen Cabinet was Dr. Robert Mayo. On November 17, 1837, Adams wrote: "Dr. Mayo paid me a morning visit, with a prospectus of a book which he proposes to publish under the title of *Eight Years' in Washington*—that is, a secret history of the Kitchen Cabinet, the Hickory Club, and the Administration of Andrew Jackson." In the July 18, 1839, number of the *Democratic Review* William Cullen Bryant, poet and editor wrote:

The driving energy of Jacksonian democracy, like that of any aggressive reform movement, came from a small group of men, joined together by essential sympathies in a concerted attempt to transform the existing order. Communion among these men was frank and free, and the men themselves were utterly loyal to the cause. Few nationally known politicians, available for cabinet posts, could meet the necessary standards of selflessness and candor. As a result, Jackson had to turn away from his cabinet for his most confidential counsel to men more basically dissatisfied with the existing order. There thus sprang into existence the celebrated Kitchen Cabinet, "an influence at Washington," as one member of the official cabinet ominously described it, "unknown to the constitution and to the country."

Did Jackson threaten to hang Calhoun?

A popular story says that when Andrew Jackson was on his deathbed he told a clergyman that the two regrets of his life were that he had not had Henry Clay shot and John C. Calhoun hanged.

The story is apocryphal but characteristic of Jackson, for he hated both men intensely. During the Nullification crisis in 1832 President Jackson did talk about hanging the Nullifiers. To a South Carolina Congressman who called at the White House before leaving for home at the end of the session in July, 1832, the President is reputed to have asked him to tell the Nullifiers that "if one drop of blood shall be shed there in defiance of the laws of the United States, I will hang the first man of them I can get my hands on to the first tree I can find." On August 30 of the same year the President wrote Van Buren that Calhoun's "best former friends say . . . he ought to be hanged."

Congressman Robert P. Letcher of Kentucky called on President Jackson to sound him out on a compromise. In *Thirty Years View* Thomas H. Benton wrote that the President answered that he "would admit of no further delay, and was determined to take at once a decided course with Mr. Calhoun (an arrest and trial for high treason being understood)." Jackson's statement to Letcher was circulated as, "If one more step is taken, I will try Calhoun for treason, and if convicted, hang him as high as Haman." In June, 1833, President Jackson told the Mayor of Boston that "he thought he would have to hang some of them and he would have done it." On another occasion Jackson said: "This was only the pretext and disunion and a Southern Confederacy the real object. The gallows ought to be the fate of all who involve the country in civil war."

Jackson disliked Clay almost as intensely as he did Calhoun. He never forgave the Kentuckian for leaving the Speaker's chair in the House, descending to the floor and denouncing Jackson's invasion of Florida. Clay was author of the Senate resolution censuring Jackson for his handling of the United States bank question. Besides Jackson believed that Clay had a hand in the circulation of slanders on Mrs. Jackson during the campaign of 1828. There is nothing improbable in the story that Jackson said in conversation later in life that he regretted that he had not had Clay shot and Calhoun hanged.

It is often said that during the Nullification crisis medals were struck off in South Carolina with Calhoun's portrait and the inscription, "John C. Calhoun, First President of the Southern Confederacy." No such medals were struck off. The fictitious story was published by Amos Kendall, Francis P. Blair and other Jacksonian editors to discredit Calhoun. Actually Calhoun never advocated secession, although after listening to Webster's Fourth of March Speech with approval, he observed that he could not see how two peoples so different and hostile could live together in the same Union.

Calhoun was in public service almost continually for forty-two years—

as State representative, U.S. Representative, Secretary of War, Vice President, Secretary of State and U.S. Senator. He and Aaron Burr are rivals for the distinction of having been the ablest and most famous Vice President who did not become President.

The Great Nullifier, as Calhoun was called after 1832, was extremely serious and had little sense of humor. "Mr. Calhoun," wrote Harriet Martineau in 1838, "looks as if he had never been born and could not be extinguished." A story was circulated in Charleston that when he was courting the woman who became his wife he wrote a poem, each stanza of which began with "Whereas." Calhoun married his cousin Floride Calhoun and they had nine children.

In January, 1849, Calhoun had one of several fainting spells in the Senate and was carried to the Vice President's room and placed on a sofa. There he told Representative James Barnwell Rhett that he was almost played out and that younger men such as he would have to take over. The Congressman assured him that the South still needed him, whereupon Calhoun said, "The South, the poor South! God knows what will become of her." These words are often incorrectly said to have been uttered just before his death in a Washington boarding house on March 31, 1850, at the age of sixty-eight. Rhett was chosen to succeed him in the Senate. Calhoun's last formal address had been read to the Senate on March 4 by Senator James Murray Mason of Virginia as its author sat silent in his seat.

What is meant by the removal of the deposits?

In 1816 Congress chartered the second Bank of the United States for twenty years. The Government owned part of the stock, appointed some of the directors and received $1,500,000 from the bank for granting it the privilege of being the Government depository and fiscal agency. By the terms of the charter the Secretary of the Treasury could at his discretion discontinue the use of the bank as the depository of Federal funds if he gave Congress satisfactory reasons for doing so.

President Andrew Jackson hated the bank chiefly because Nicholas Biddle (1786-1844) used his position as its president for political purposes. "I long for retirement & repose on the Hermitage," wrote Old Hickory. "But until I can strangle the hydra of corruption, the Bank, I will not shrink from my duty on my part." In July, 1832, he vetoed a bill to recharter the bank nearly four years before its old charter was to expire, and in the Presidential election that year defeated Henry Clay, the Whig candidate and sponsor of the bank bill.

Jackson then upon his own responsibility undertook to deal "the monster" a solar plexus blow by repudiating it as the Federal fiscal agency. Since under the law only the Secretary of the Treasury could issue such an order, the President in May, 1833, appointed William J. Duane as head of the Treasury department. Duane had expressed opinions unfavorable to the bank, but when the time came refused to sign the order, whereupon the President dismissed him on Setember 23, 1833, and on the same day appointed in his place Roger Brooke Taney, who a few hours after taking office signed the order.

This is called the order for "the removal of the deposits," which is a misnomer. At that time the Federal funds in the bank amounted to nearly $10,000,000. The order directed the revenue collectors to cease making deposits in the Bank of the United States and to make future deposits in designated State banks, known as "pet banks." Federal funds in the bank were not suddenly *removed* but were left to be drawn out by the Government in the usual way as needed in the normal course of business. The Whig-controlled Senate regarded Taney's reasons for discontinuing Federal deposits in the bank as unsatisfactory, and in retaliation formally censured the President and refused to confirm Taney's appointment as an associate justice of the Supreme Court. President Jackson waited nine months after the order was issued before he discontinued his personal account with the bank, although he started a new account on January 8, 1833, with a "pet bank" in Washington. In July of the same year he wrote a personal check for $1,137.21 and closed his account with the Washington branch of the "hydra of corruption."

"Old Nick," as Jackson called Biddle, got the bank rechartered in 1836 by the Pennsylvania legislature under the name "Bank of the United States, of Pennsylvania." In 1841, three years after Biddle retired, the bank failed, and the former director and president was indicted in connection with it, but was never tried. He spent his last like his earlier years in writing, for which he had considerable talent.

What was the Expunging Resolution?

In July, 1832, President Andrew Jackson vetoed Henry Clay's bill to recharter the Bank of the United States nearly four years before the expiration of its old charter. The veto was sustained by Congress and Jackson defeated Clay in the Presidential election later the same year on the recharter issue. In September, 1833, Jackson caused to be issued an order discontinuing government deposits in the bank. Under date of December 12, 1833, Representative John Quincy Adams wrote in his diary:

The Senate yesterday, at the motion of Mr. Clay, sent a message to the President asking a copy of his written communication to his Cabinet, made on the

18th of September last, about the removal of the deposits from the United States Bank; and he has sent them this morning a flat refusal. There is a tone of insolence and insult in his intercourse with both Houses of Congress, especially since his re-election, which was never witnessed between the Executive and the Legislature before. The domineering tone has heretofore been usually on the side of the legislative bodies to the Executive, and Clay has not been sparing in the use of it. He is now paid in his own coin.

On March 28, 1834, the Senate adopted by a vote of 26 to 20 Clay's resolution of censure, which read: "That the President, in the late executive proceedings relating to the revenue, has assumed upon himself authority and power not conferred by the Constitution and laws, but in derogation of both."

Jackson bitterly resented this "imputation of my private as well as upon my public character," and sent to the Senate a solemn protest, which the Senate by formal vote refused to receive. Senator Thomas H. Benton, more Jacksonian than Jackson himself, immediately announced his intention of introducing someday an "expunging resolution against the sentence of the Senate," which, he said, in effect adjudged and pronounced the President guilty of an impeachable offense.

On January 14, 1837, nearly three years later, Benton introduced a resolution providing "That the said resolve be expunged from the journal; and, for that purpose, that the Secretary of the Senate, at such time as the Senate may appoint, shall bring the manuscript journal of the session 1833 '34 into the Senate, and, in the presence of the Senate, draw black lines around the said resolve, and write across the face thereof, in strong letters, the following words: 'Expunged by the order of the Senate, this 16th day of January, 1837.' " Old Bullion was begged to accept in lieu a resolution rescinding the obnoxious resolution of 1834, but he had the votes and would not budge. Nothing short of physical obliteration of the official record would satisfy him. The unprecedented and unique Expunging Resolution was adopted and its provision carried out at midnight the same day in the presence of visitors in the crowded galleries and lobbies. John Tyler had resigned his seat in the Senate rather than obey the Virginia legislature's instructions to vote for the rescinding resolution. Old Hickory, whose term was to expire in less than sixty days, was delighted and satisfied when Benton gave him the pen used to destroy the obnoxious record. "The Senate," moaned Clay, "is no longer a place for a decent man."

Expunge, meaning to strike out, blot out or erase, comes from *expungere,* signifying to point or prick out, as marking a word or name with dots for deletion or omission.

When were the most Presidents together under one roof?

Lafayette died on May 20, 1834, and on December 30 of that year John Quincy Adams delivered an oration on his life and character to both houses of Congress in the old House chamber in the Capitol. Eight men whose names occur in the list of Presidents were together in the same room on that occasion. They were: John Quincy Adams, ex-President and Representative; President Andrew Jackson; Vice President Martin Van Buren; Senators John Tyler and James Buchanan, and Representatives James K. Polk, Millard Fillmore and Franklin Pierce. These eight men constituted one-fourth of the first thirty-two Presidents from Washington to Truman inclusive. With the exception of the one year and five months of the William Henry Harrison and Zachary Taylor administrations, these eight Presidents occupied the White House continuously during the thirty-six years between the James Monroe and Abraham Lincoln administrations. John Quincy Adams served in the House of Representatives with a total of five future Presidents—Polk, Fillmore, Pierce, Lincoln and Andrew Johnson. Former Presidents William Howard Taft and Woodrow Wilson, President Calvin Coolidge, and future President Herbert Hoover attended the funeral of Warren G. Harding in 1923.

What does Jackson Day commemorate?

Jackson Day—January 8—does not commemorate Andrew Jackson's birthday, as many people suppose, but his final victory over the British at New Orleans in 1815. Even Governor Alfred E. Smith of New York, while an aspirant for the Democratic nomination for President, alluded to the event as Jackson's birthday when he was chief speaker at a Jackson Day gathering in Washington. Jackson was born March 15, 1767.

The anniversary of the final battle of New Orleans was celebrated locally to some extent soon after Jackson's victory, and January 8 is a legal State holiday in Louisiana, but it was not until after General Jackson's rise as a political figure that it became customary for his followers to hold their political rallies and banquets on that date and to make it a "party festival."

On Christmas Eve, 1814, John Quincy Adams and three other American commissioners signed a treaty of peace with Great Britain at Ghent in Belgium. Napoleon had been defeated, the British were sending more forces to America, the public buildings in Washington had been burned, the Government was bankrupt, the war was going badly, and the Americans were willing to sign almost any treaty that left the United States independent. Great Britain, in her hour of victory, granted generous terms, but the Americans left Ghent hurt and humiliated. Adams had hardly heard the name of Andrew Jackson, but, upon reaching Paris, he learned of the victory at New Orleans and his heart swelled with pride and happiness. He was able to go over to England with his head up. Naturally he conceived a great admiration for the victor of New Orleans. As Secretary of State he championed General Jackson in the Cabinet and easily found ways of justifying him when he was under fire for high-handed and rash acts.

In 1824 Secretary of State Adams sponsored a dinner in Washington on New Orleans Day in honor of Jackson. On January 6 of that year Adams wrote in his diary: "We have invited all the members of both Houses of Congress excepting Alexander Smyth and John Floyd. Their personal deportment to me has been such that I could not include them in the invitations." President Monroe declined to accept because General Jackson was being promoted for the Presidency and the President didn't take Jackson's candidacy seriously. On January 8, 1824, Adams wrote in his diary:

This being the anniversary of the victory at New Orleans we gave an evening party or ball to General Jackson, at which about one thousand persons attended. General Jackson came about eight o'clock and retired after supper. The dancing continued till near one in the morning. The crowd was great, and the house could scarcely contain the company. But it all went off in good order, and without accident.

A year later—January 8, 1825—Adams wrote that he "attended an evening ball at General Brown's, given to General Jackson in honor of the day—the anniversary of the battle of New Orleans. The house was crowded, and the apartments oppressively hot."

In the election of 1824 Jackson received a plurality of the popular and electoral vote, but none received a majority, and on February 9, 1825, the House of Representatives chose Adams. That evening at President Monroe's reception at the White House General Jackson shook hands with Adams and congratulated him very cordially on his election. William H. Crawford, another defeated candidate, when he heard of this, observed: "That was a useless piece of hypocrisy. It deceived no one. Shaking hands was very well—was right—but the congratulatory speech might have been omitted." Adams and Jackson never met again. Jackson felt that Adams, with the aid of Henry Clay, had cheated him out of the Presidency and the two men became bitter personal and political enemies.

Adams took no more part in Jackson Day festivities and never said another good word about Old Hickory. In 1828 Jackson defeated Adams and after that January 8 was observed only by his political followers. On January 8, 1829, Philip Hone in New York wrote in his diary: "A great dinner was given this day in honor of the victory of New Orleans and the successful result of Jackson's election. It was held at Tammany Hall. Mr. Benjamin Butler presided. A ball was also given at the Bowery Theater on the same occasion."

Nicholas Biddle, president of the Bank of the United States, proposed a plan whereby the national debt would be extinguished January 8, 1833. Since Jackson was keen to have the national debt paid off and was sentimental about New Orleans Day, Biddle thought his subtle suggestion might cause the President to withdraw his opposition to rechartering the bank. Jackson did not take the bait, but proceeded to fight the bank until he had killed it, although the Democrats, then still called Republicans, did celebrate the extinguishment of the national debt on January 8, 1835, the twentieth anniversary of the Battle of New Orleans. This "Republican Celebration" consisted of a public dinner at Brown's Hotel in Washington. According to James Parton, this was the day that Jackson "esteemed the most glorious of his Presidency." The affair was attended by Vice President Martin Van Buren; James K. Polk, afterward President; the entire Cabinet; prominent Democratic Senators and Representatives, and more than two hundred other notable party leaders. There was band music, delicious food at one dollar a plate, plenty of stimulating drink, interminable speeches and one hundred toasts. President Jackson was not present, but he sent a brief message, to which was appended a toast, which read: "The payment of the national debt: Let us commemorate it as an event which gives us increased power as a nation, and reflects lustre on our Federal Union, of whose justice, fidelity and wisdom, it is a glorious illustration." That night John Quincy Adams wrote in his dairy: "The Jackson Republicans of both Houses of Congress had a dinner at Brown's Hotel to celebrate conjointly the victory of New Orleans and the extinction of the national debt. Both of which they hold as belonging to the glorification of Andrew Jackson."

It became customary, when the Democrats were in the majority, for Congress to adjourn on "Old Hickory Day." On January 8, 1841, Representative Adams wrote, "Turney moved to adjourn, because it was the 8th of January." And a year later he wrote, "Campbell, of South Carolina, then observed that it was the 8th of January, and moved an adjournment—which was carried." Observance of Jackson Day was discontinued during the Civil War but was later revived. It became customary for the Democrats to hold a Jackson Day dinner and rally in Washington. On Presidential election years prospective candidates were asked to speak and "sound the keynote" for the coming convention and campaign.

Beginning in 1935 and every year thereafter until the events were suspended because of the Second World War, the Democratic Party held Jackson Day Dinners to raise funds for the party. The "parent dinner" in Washington cost $100 a plate, and other dinners, at lower prices, were held throughout the country. President Franklin D. Roosevelt addressed the parent dinner in person and his message was carried by radio to the other dinners and to the people at large. This arrangement, suggested by a country editor in Florida named D. C. Hodgkin, brought large sums into the party treasury. In 1942 the party dinners were held on February 23 and called George Washington dinners. After that the dinners were held later in the year and known as Jackson-Jefferson dinners. Abraham Lincoln's birthday—February 12—is used to some extent by the Republicans as a party rally day.

Who said: "To the victor belong the spoils"?

This saying, at least in its political application, originated in a speech delivered in the U.S. Senate on January 21, 1832, by William Learned Marcy. It is often misquoted, "To the victor *belongs* the spoils," but good grammar requires the plural verb, *belong*.

Most of the early Presidents had not removed Government clerks and other minor officers for purely party purposes, and President Andrew Jackson, supposedly under the influence of Secretary of State Martin Van Buren of New York, had been the first frankly to make party loyalty a qualification for continuing to hold as well as for receiving positions in the Federal service. When Van Buren's name was before the Senate on January 21, 1832, for confirmation as Minister to Great Britain, Henry Clay spoke in opposition, and among other things said:

I believe, upon circumstances which satisfy my mind, that to this gentleman is principally to be ascribed the introduction of the odious system of proscription for the exercise of the elective franchise in the Government of the United States. I understand that it is the system on which the party in his own State, of which he is the reputed head, constantly acts. He was among the first of the Secretaries to apply that system to the dismission of clerks in his Department, known to me as to be highly meritorious, and among them one who is now a Representative in the other House. It is a detestable system, drawn from the worst periods of the Roman republic; and if it were to be perpetuated, if the offices, honors, and dignities of the people were to be put up to the scramble, to be decided by the result of every Presidential election, our Government and institutions, becoming intolerable, would finally end in a despotism as inexorable as that at Constantinople.

Marcy, the junior Senator from New York, could not let pass unnoticed this reflection on his State and on a political ally and friend. In his reply to Clay the same day he said:

It may be, Sir, that the politicians of the United States are not so fastidious as some gentlemen are, as to disclosing the principles on which they act. They boldly preach what they practice. When they are contending for victory, they avow their intention of enjoying the fruits of it. If they are defeated, they expect to retire from office. If they are successful, they claim, as a matter of right, the advantages of success. They see nothing wrong in the rule, that to the *victor belong the spoils of the enemy.*

Marcy's speech was delivered in executive session and was not at first printed. When it was finally printed, the saying, "to the victor belong the spoils," immediately caught the public fancy. Never before had the practice been so openly and boldy justified nor the principle on which it operated so aptly stated. Stripped of all superfluous verbiage, as most popular sayings are, the "rule," as Marcy called it, was discussed by everybody and the practice that it described thereafter became known as the "spoils system."

Van Buren, who had actually assumed his duties as Minister in London, failed of confirmation. But the vote against him, intended to give him a political setback, turned out to be a kick upstairs. He returned to be elected Vice President and then President to succeed Jackson in 1837.

Marcy later had a distinguished public career as Governor of New York, Secretary of War in Polk's Cabinet and Secretary of State in that of Pierce. When he entered Pierce's Cabinet the "spoils system" had been recognized by all parties.

Spoils system, suggested by Marcy's famous saying, is the systematic and wholesale filling of public offices on the basis of party loyalty and service rather than on merit. The term also connotes improper use of public position and the appointing power for personal and political purposes. A politician who practices the spoils system is called a spoilsman.

The spoils system was not an invention of Jackson but evolved gradually. In a sense it dated from the organization of the Federal Government. At first all Federal offices were new and President Washington filled them with friends and persons whom he considered favorable to the Constitution. The First Congress decided that officers appointed by the President were removable by him at his pleasure. Since all the first appointments were made by President Washington, during his administration Government officers were removed only for cause, with the result that there were practically no removals at all. President John Adams followed the same policy in respect to Government clerks and minor officers, but during his administration party spirit was increasing and he appointed only Federalists to fill vacancies and new places.

The first change of political parties in the Presidency occurred in 1801 when Adams was succeeded by Jefferson, who resented the fact that Federalists held all the offices, and who was the first President to remove Federal officeholders to provide places for his partisans. A committee of merchants headed by Elias Shipman wrote to President Jefferson protesting against the removal of the Federalist collector at New Haven, Connecticut. On July 12, 1801, the President wrote to this committee: "If a due participation of office is a matter of right, how are vacancies to be obtained? Those by death are few; those by resignation, none. Can any other mode than that of removal be proposed? This is a painful office, but it is my duty and I meet it as such." "Few die and none resign" became the popular and simplified version of Jefferson's statement. On November 11, 1869, Governor Rutherford B. Hayes of Ohio wrote, in reply to a request that he support a certain person's application for a consulship, that "I was told that consulates are all gobbled up long ago— that his only chance is the death or resignation of the present incumbents; and you know 'few die and none resign.' "

Jefferson explained in his letter to the New Haven committee that he intended to remove only enough Federalists to give the Republicans a fair proportion in the Government service. He virtually abandoned his removal policy after his first two years in office. Actually he removed only about half of the minor Federal officeholders and about one-fourth of the postmasters when their number was comparatively small, but he continued to appoint only Republicans to fill vacancies and new places.

President Jefferson advocated "rotation in office"; that is, a periodic turnover in executive offices. His theory was that fresh men in such offices would be more responsive to the wishes of the people and would be free from the corruption and indifference that comes from long-continued officeholding. His rotation-in-office principle ignored the importance of expert and trained administrators and was used later by spoilsmen to justify their system. On February 21, 1821, Secretary of State John Quincy Adams wrote in his diary: "Eustis has republican principle enough to admire rotation in office, and patriotism enough to serve his country as collector of customs at Boston. Dearborn is equally patriotic but not just now so much an admirer of rotation. This principle is, indeed, more congenial to republicans out of than to those in office."

James Madison and James Monroe regarded themselves as political heirs of Jefferson and followed his policy of filling vacancies and new offices chiefly with Democratic-Republicans. Monroe was opposed in principle to removals from office and was too kindly disposed to remove any officer except for serious cause. During the Era of Good Feeling party spirit subsided and there were few vacancies to fill. There were no retirement or pensions for civil servants and men continued in office as long as they lived. On May 15, 1820, President Monroe approved an act of Congress limiting the terms of many classes of Federal employees to four years. Monroe's Secretary of the Treasury, William H. Crawford of Georgia, was accused by his enemies of using the patronage of his department to promote his campaign for the Presidency in 1824.

At first President Adams regarded himself as a Democratic-Republican and followed the policy of Madison and Monroe. On January 21, 1825, President Adams wrote in his diary: "I assured Bradley that I should turn out no person for his conduct or opinions in relation to the election." He refused even to dismiss Postmaster General John McLean, who had been appointed by Monroe and who supported Jackson against Adams in 1828. But Adams filled vacancies and new offices with his friends and partisans, and, like his father twenty-eight years before, sent nominations to the Senate till his last day in office.

The bitter Adams-Jackson contest of 1828 split the Democratic-Republicans into two parties, and Jacksonians looked upon Adams supporters as little better than the old Federalists. Van Buren, moving spirit in the Albany Regency, was an old hand at using executive patronage to control elections, and he had advocated appointing postmasters for political reasons, but Jackson's nature was such that his Secretary of State needed no witchcraft to convince him that friends should be rewarded and enemies punished. Both Jackson and Van Buren believed in the spoils system, but neither favored a "clean sweep," because many office-holders had supported them and many others were susceptible to conversion with little pressure. Jackson may have been a spoilsman, but his spoils system had the virtue of frankness. He did what Jefferson had done but did it more openly. "We give no reasons for our removals," Van Buren said. On November 17, 1837, Adams wrote in his diary:

Dr. Mayo is one of those office-hunters and busybodies who, during Jackson's Administration, under the mask of reform, were in a continual struggle to turn out of the Executive offices all the incumbents except his devoted tools. Mayo was the principal agent of the Hickory Club, acting under the impulse of Amos Kendall. But in his purposes of reform he assumed a principle which did by no means suit them, and that was, removals should be made only for moral or official misconduct or open abuse of the Administration; and that it should be applied equally to individuals of their own party as well as to others. He offered to the club a resolution to that effect, which, he says, was almost unanimously rejected.

Actually Jackson removed fewer than a thousand officeholders out of more than ten times that many. Some of those removed held the higher offices, which everybody expected him to replace with his partisans, and some of the lower officeholders, including many postmasters, were removed for good cause. Since the number of Federal employees had greatly increased, Jackson's percentage of removals was probably lower than Jefferson's. Jackson's enemies naturally exaggerated the ruthlessness of his policy and the number of his removals.

On May 11, 1832, the National Republican Young Men's Convention, which endorsed Henry Clay against Jackson, declared that the "indiscriminate removal of public officers for a mere difference of political opinion is a gross abuse of power, and that the doctrine boldly preached in the United States Senate that 'to the victor belong the spoils of the vanquished,' is detrimental to the interests, corrupting to the morals, and dangerous to the liberties of the country." Senator John C. Calhoun, on February 9, 1835, submitted a report condemning Jackson's arbitrary removals and recommending a bill requiring the President, when he nominated anybody to fill a vacancy caused by a removal, to tell the Senate why he had made the removal. But the spoils system was so well established under Jackson that it continued to prevail for generations. Although in 1857 James Buchanan succeeded another Democrat, he announced he would observe the principle of rotation in office and reman the civil service.

Civil service was borrowed from British usage. About 1785 the term began to be applied to that part of the service of the East India Company that did not belong to the army or the navy. Later it was applied, in the language of the Oxford dictionary, to "all the unwarlike departments of the public administrative service of the state." In America *civil service* came to mean all the civilian employees in the executive departments.

Thomas J. Jenckes, a Republican Representative from Rhode Island, is sometimes called the father of civil service reform. On December 20, 1865, he made a speech in Congress on the subject and introduced a bill "to regulate the civil service of the United States." The next year Senator B. Gratz Brown of Missouri introduced a resolution providing for "such changes in the civil service as shall secure appointments to the same after previous examination by proper Boards, and as shall provide for promotion on the score of merit, or seniority." After this civil service

[103]

reform was demanded by "liberals" in both the Republican and Democratic parties.

A rider on an appropriation act approved March 3, 1871, authorized the President to

... prescribe such regulations for the admission of persons into the civil service of the United States as may best promote efficiency therein and ascertain the fitness of each candidate in respect to age, health, character, knowledge, and ability for the branch of the service in which he seeks to enter; and for this purpose he may employ suitable persons to conduct such inquiries, prescribe their duties, and establish regulations for the conduct of persons who may receive appointments in the civil service.

Under this authority President Grant appointed George William Curtis and six others to compose the National Civil Service Commission. The Republican platform of 1872 declared that

... any system of the civil service under which the subordinate positions of the Government are considered rewards for mere party zeal is fatally demoralizing, and we therefore demand a reform of the system by laws which shall abolish the evils of patronage and make honesty, efficiency and fidelity essential qualifications for public positions, without practically creating a life tenure of office.

Rutherford B. Hayes, elected in 1876 as a civil service reformer, was one of the most nonpartisan Presidents since Washington. In his inaugural address on March 5, 1877, he said: "He serves his party best who serves his country best." Under him Government employees were reasonably secure in their jobs if their official and private conduct was good. On August 5, 1877, the President wrote in his diary:

I grow more conservative every day on the question of removals. On ex parte statements, I have made mistakes in removing men who, perhaps, ought to have been retained, and in appointing wrong men. Not many removals have been made. Less than any new Administration since John Q. Adams. But I shall be more cautious in future; make removals only in clear cases, and appoint only on the best and fullest evidence of fitness.

But Hayes's nonpartisan policy displeased many Republicans and got little support from Democrats, who had slight interest in the success of an administration they had not elected. Senator Roscoe Conkling, a spoilsman of the first water, sneeringly referred to President Hayes as "Granny" and to civil service as "snivel service," and observed: "When Dr. Johnson called patriotism the last refuge of a scoundrel he forgot the possibilities contained in the word Reform." Hayes appointed to the National Civil Service Commission Theodore Roosevelt, Sr., father of the President of the same name, but his nomination was blocked in the Senate by the Conklingites.

Dorman B. Eaton, an early advocate of civil service reform, who had succeeded Curtis as chairman of the National Civil Service Commission in 1873, drafted a new civil service bill, which was introduced by George H. Pendleton, Democratic Senator from Ohio. President Chester A. Arthur, who had been part of Conkling's New York political machine, approved the Civil Service Reform Act on December 18, 1883. Under this act the old National Civil Service Commission was succeeded by the new United States Civil Service Commission. The Pendleton Act, amended from time to time, became the foundation of the present civil service system.

But the Pendleton Act did not establish civil service reform overnight. The movement still had hard sledding. The majority of politicians regarded public offices as so much political plunder. Many Government job-holders depended upon "political pull," and "It isn't what you know but who you know," remained the motto of applicants. During his first two years in office, President Grover Cleveland appointed Democrats to all but 8,000 of the 57,000 civilian jobs in the Government. Theodore Roosevelt, later President, was appointed a member of the U.S. Civil Service Commission by President Benjamin Harrison in 1889 and he has been the most famous person to serve on that commission.

In the early days political parties were run largely by Federal officeholders. As early as February 22, 1841, the Senate engaged in a spirited debate on a proposal of Senator John R. Crittenden of Kentucky "to prevent the interference of officeholders in elections." President Hayes, to the dismay of many of his fellow Republicans, issued an executive order forbidding Federal officeholders to take part in party politics and also forbidding political parties and leaders to levy assessments on officeholders. On July 14, 1886, President Cleveland sent to all department heads a circular letter in which he said:

I deem this a proper time to especially warn all subordinates in the several departments and all officeholders under the general Government against the use of their official positions in attempts to control political movements in their localities. Officeholders are the agents of the people, not their masters. Officeholders are neither disfranchised nor forbidden the exercise of political privileges; but their privileges are not enlarged, nor is their duty to party increased to *pernicious activity* by officeholding. They have no right as officeholders to dictate the political action of their party associates or to throttle freedom of action within party lines by methods and practices which pervert every useful and justifiable purpose of party organization.

But there were those who doubted that "pernicious activity" could be eliminated from politics. In an interview in the New York *World* in 1890, John J. Ingalls, Republican President Pro Tempore of the Senate, was quoted as making this cynical statement:

The purification of politics is an irridescent dream. Government is force. Politics is a battle for supremacy. Parties are the armies. The Decalogue and the Golden Rule have no place in a political campaign. The object is success. To defeat the antagonist and expel the party in power is the purpose. The Republicans and Democrats are as irrevocably opposed to each other as were Grant and Lee in the Wilderness. They use ballots instead of guns, but the struggle is as unrelenting and desperate and the result sought for the same. In war it is lawful to deceive the adversary, to hire Hessians, to purchase mercenaries, to mutilate, to destroy. The commander who lost the battle through the activity of his moral nature would be the derision and jest of history. This modern cant about the corruption of politics is fatiguing in the extreme. It proceeds from tea-custard and syllabub diletanteism and frivolous sentimentalism.

The following rule was incorporated in the Civil Service Regulations:

No person in the executive civil service shall use his official authority or influence for the purpose of interfering with an election or affecting the results thereof. Persons who by the provision of these rules are in the competitive classified service, while retaining the right to vote as they please and to express privately their opinions on all political subjects, shall take no active part in political management or in political campaigns.

An act of Congress, approved in 1907, provided:

It shall be unlawful for any national bank, or any corporation organized by authority of any laws of Congress, to make a money contribution in connection with any election to any political office. It shall also be unlawful for any corporation whatever to make a money contribution in connection with any election in which Presidential and Vice-Presidential electors or a representative in Congress is to be voted for or any election of a United States Senator.

In 1939 Congress passed the Political Activities Act, sponsored by Senator Carl D. Hatch, New Mexico Democrat. This act extended the provisions of the Civil Service Regulations respecting political activities to all Federal employees below the "policy-making" level. The penalty for violating this provision is the loss of position and the right to hold a Government position in the future. The act grew out of a proposal to protect relief workers from political pressure. Senator Hatch himself said its purpose was to free Federal workers from "the domination by fear of losing their jobs and of political reprisal." President Franklin D.

Roosevelt approved the Hatch "Clean Politics" Act reluctantly. Ordinarily a President sends a message to Congress with a bill only when he vetoes it, but when he approved this bill on August 2, 1939, President Roosevelt sent it to Congress with an interpretive message, in which he said: "It is because for so many years I have striven in public life and in private life for decency in political campaigns, both on the part of government servants, of candidates, of newspapers, of corporations, and of individuals, that I regard this new legislation as at least a step in the right direction." He was confident, the President said, that Congress intended that the act should be so administered so that "the rights of free speech shall remain, even to those who serve their government, and that the government itself shall have full right to place all facts in its possession before the public."

The Second Hatch Act, approved in 1940, extended the "pernicious political activity" provision to all State and local employees who get part of their income from Federal funds. The Hatch Act also limited campaign contributions of individuals to $5,000 and expenditures of each political party or organization to $3,000,000, within any calendar year, and imposed severe penalties for violations. But there are more ways than one of skinning a cat. It was still legal for several members of a family to make individual contributions up to $5,000 and for independent organizations to spend up to $3,000,000. Notwithstanding passage of the Hatch acts in 1939 and 1940, it was estimated that about $23,000,000 was spent in connection with the political campaigns in 1944.

Who said: "Politics makes strange bedfellows"?

This common saying is of unknown authorship. It was suggested by a passage in Shakespeare. In *The Tempest* the jester Trinculo, as he crawls under Caliban's gaberdine for shelter during a sudden storm, says: "Misery acquaints a man with strange bedfellows." As early as July 9, 1839, Philip Hone wrote in his diary in reference to Martin Van Buren: "During the President's stay in New York he has visited most of the public places in the constant custody of a set of men who are not (unless he has greatly changed) the sort of folks he would have chosen for his associates; but party politics, like poverty, bring men 'acquainted with strange bedfellows.' " The saying in its later and more compact form, "politics makes strange bedfellows," occurs in Charles Dudley Warner's *My Summer in a Garden* (1870).

[107]

What was the Buckshot War?

The Buckshot War was a violent election dispute in Pennsylvania that almost resulted in civil war. In 1835, when the Democrats were split, Joseph Ritner was elected Governor by the Anti-Masons and Whigs. Three years later, in the first election under a new State constitution, Ritner was defeated by the Democratic nominee, David Rittenhouse Porter. Thaddeus Stevens, Ritner's campaign manager and Whig and Anti-Mason leader, insisted that Porter was elected by fraud. Charles J. Ingersoll, the Democratic leader, charged that Stevens was trying to keep Ritner in office despite his defeat at the polls.

After the election in the fall of 1838 a Democratic candidate for Congress in a Philadelphia County district attributed his defeat to the fraud and corruption of the Whigs, whereupon the Democratic election judges declared the Democrat elected. At the same time they certified the election of eight Democrats as members of the State house of representatives. The Whig election judges then met on their own account and certified the election of the Whig candidate for Congress and eight Whig members of the State house of representatives.

When the Legislature assembled at Harrisburg on December 4, 1838, two sets of representatives from Philadelphia County, eight Democrats and eight Whigs, presented credentials and claimed membership. The membership from the rest of the State was so evenly divided that the contested eight seats from Philadelphia County would give either party a majority. At that time both U.S. Senators from Pennsylvania—Samuel McKean and James Buchanan—were Democrats; but McKean's term would expire March 3, 1839, and the Whigs were determined to choose a Whig as his successor. The State senate was overwhelmingly Whig but control of the house of representatives was essential to the Whig program. The Democrats, including the eight Democratic claimants from Philadelphia County, met in the house chamber in the State capitol, took charge of the records and organized as the lawful house. Under the leadership of Stevens, the Whigs, including the eight Whig claimants from Philadelphia, met in the same chamber and also chose a speaker and organized as the lawful house. Utter confusion and bedlam followed. A mob crowded into the senate chamber and prevented the senate from doing business. A demagogue named John McCahan even took the presiding officer's chair and harangued the mob. Meanwhile Pennsylvania had two houses of representatives with quorums to transact business.

Feeling was intense throughout the State and even the whole nation.

Large numbers of persons of both parties from Philadelphia and elsewhere went to Harrisburg and increased the size of the disorderly mob in and around the capitol. Rioters crowded into the legislative chambers and threatened the members with physical violence. Many of the partisans on both sides were armed and the city was in an uproar. On one occasion Stevens escaped from the mob by jumping out of a capitol window. Governor Ritner proclaimed a "lawless, infuriated, armed mob" had seized Harrisburg to intimidate the State government, called upon the militia to be ready to march and asked President Van Buren to send Federal troops to suppress the insurrection. The President refused to intervene, but the militia responded and restored order.

The deadlock was broken when three Whigs deserted their body and joined the Democrats, leaving the Whig house without a quorum and making one for the Democratic house without counting the contested representatives from Philadelphia County. Most of the other Whigs and Anti-Masons, except the contested members, then took their seats and the senate recognized the Democratic house as the duly constituted one, but the seat of Stevens was declared vacant and he was not reseated until he had been re-elected by his constituents. Porter, the successful Democrat, was inaugurated Governor on January 15, 1839, without further disorder, but the Legislature was not able to elect a U.S. Senator until January 14, 1840, when Daniel Sturgeon, a Democrat was chosen.

This comic-opera episode, in which not a shot was fired and nobody suffered more than bruises, was called the Buckshot War because the militiamen called to disperse the mob and to restore order loaded their guns with buckshot and a member of the Whig house expressed the hope that it would be used freely on the Democrats. In the December 27, 1838, issue of *The Volunteer,* published at Carlisle, Pennsylvania, the following was printed under the caption, *Last Days of Governor Ritner:*

> Come up and come down,
> Come from country and town,
> And obey the fat Deatchlaender's writ, sir,
> Come one and come all
> With buckshot and ball
> And take care of Governor Ritner.

Can one vote for President and Vice President separately?

The same electors choose the President and the Vice President and there is no way a voter can vote for the Presidential candidate of one party and the Vice-Presidential candidate of another party. The electors themselves vote for President and Vice President separately, but since they are under a moral obligation to vote for the candidates nominated by their own party, a voter in marking his ballot cannot "split the ticket" in respect to Presidential and Vice-Presidential candidates.

When did *favorite son* originate?

Favorite son is almost as old as the Federal Government. On May 1, 1789, the New York *Daily Gazette* hailed the first President as, "Washington, the favorite son of liberty," and in the same year the Massachusetts *Centinel* called him "Columbia's favorite son." In *The Life of John Randolph of Roanoke* (1850) H. A. Garland quoted another as saying in 1825: "John Randolph thought himself unkindly treated by his native State. He will now, I trust, see in himself her favorite son," In his diary Philip Hone referred to Vice-President-elect Martin Van Buren as "New York's favorite son" in quotation as early as January 6, 1835, and on July 4, 1835, when Vice President Van Buren was being talked of as President Jackson's successor, Hone attended a dinner given by the Corporation of New York City, and on that day wrote in his diary: "The President's health was received with all the fire and vivacity which brandy or champagne can inspire, but the great burst of feeling was reserved for New York's favorite son, 'the Vice President.' " Van Buren proved to be not only New York's favorite son but also the nations's favorite and was chosen President in the next election.

After the convention method of nomination was adopted *favorite son* was applied to an aspirant for the Presidential nomination who is supported at the party's national convention by only the delegates of his own State and who has little or no prospect of success. A delegation may vote for a favorite son on the first few ballots either to compliment him or to withhold its vote from one of the leading aspirants until it sees how the wind is blowing. In *The American Commonwealth* (1888) James Bryce wrote that *a favorite* "is a politician well known over the Union, and drawing support from all or most sections,"while *a favorite son* is one "respected or admired in his own State, but little regarded beyond it."

Who were the Loco-focos?

In 1834 a New Yorker named John Marck patented a self-lighting cigar, which was ignited by means of a chemical composition inserted in the end. The inventor, desiring a catchy trade name for his product, hit upon *Loco-foco*. Just how he arrived at the term is not known for certain, but it is supposed that he took *loco* from *locomotive* on the supposition that it meant "self-moving" instead of "moving from place to place," and *foco* from Latin *focus*, which means "hearth" or "fireplace," but which he apparently thought meant "fire." Marck's patented self-lighting cigar was not successful, but the public took up his trade name and applied it to the friction match, which had been invented in England by John Walker in 1827 and had recently been introduced in America. Thus the friction match called a lucifer in Europe became known as a Loco-foco in the United States.

In 1835 the Democratic Party in New York split into two factions, the Regulars and the Radicals. On the evening of October 29 of that year the Democrats met in Tammany Hall to nominate a slate of candidates. The Regulars favored Gideon Lee and the Radicals Charles G. Ferris for Congress. During the tumultuous meeting the Regulars declared their candidates nominated and the meeting adjourned. It is said that the Regular chairman deliberately brought about a state of confusion during which the gas lights in the hall were put out to thwart the designs of the Radicals, who had arrived in large numbers. The Radicals, forewarned of the trick, had come prepared with candles and Loco-foco matches concealed in their pockets. Lighting their candles, they proceeded with the meeting and nominated their candidates.

Some of the newspapers, after this incident, sneeringly dubbed the Radicals *Loco-focos*, a name the Radicals eventually accepted. In the election Lee, the Regular candidate for Congress, won, but Ferris, the Loco-foco candidate, received a substantial vote and encouraged the faction to continue its fight for control of the party. From 1835 to 1837 the Loco-focos were practically a third party in New York. They favored labor in its struggle with capital and were against monopolies and the banking interests. On October 10, 1837, Representative John Quincy Adams wrote in his diary in reference to a speech made in the House by Francis W. Pickens of South Carolina: "He said he supposed he should pass for a Loco-foco; but he had recently heard it said that John Milton was a Loco-foco. Then he passed a panegyric upon John Milton as the intrepid supporter of the *rights of man,* and concluded that if John Milton was a Loco-foco he was content to be called so too." Adams reported that Caleb Cushing, who replied to Pickens, "said if there was to be an alliance between the slaveholders of the South and the Loco-focos of the North, it would not be an alliance between equals, but of masters and slaves."

Ultimately the Regular and Radical Democrats got together again under the leadership of President Van Buren, but the Whigs continued to call all Northern Democrats Loco-focos, or Locos for short. In 1839 Philip Hone referred in his diary to "the Loco-foco rabble who have gotten possession of his (Van Buren's) person." During the Harrison-Van Buren campaign of 1840 Abraham Lincoln in his speeches invariably referred to the Democrats as Locos. In 1841 John Quincy Adams in his diary referred to John B. Weller of Ohio as "a prince of the mock Democracy, now called Loco-foco," and the next year he wrote of "the Loco-foco Democracy of the North and West voting with the slave-breeding South." On June 2, 1844, Rutherford B. Hayes wrote his sister that "some faint attempts are being made to excite enthusiasm for the nominees of the Loco-foco convention, Polk and Dallas." In 1847 Hayes called the Democrats "Lokies" and Hone described two men as "disciples in the sect of the Loco-focos." The Whigs were still referring to the "Loco-foco ticket" in 1855, and echoes of this name for the Democrats were occasionally heard as late as the campaign of 1860.

How did *up Salt River* originate?

A defeated candidate is said to be sent or rowed "up Salt River." Although *Salt* is a common name for rivers and creeks, early examples of the phrase indicate that the Salt River up which defeated candidates are sent to oblivion was originally an imaginary rather than real stream.

The earliest use of the phrase found so far is in the following sentence in Frances M. Trollope's *Domestic Manners of the Americans,* published in London in 1832: "This was one of those threats which in Georgia dialect would subject a man to 'a rowing up salt river.' " Mrs. Trollope, who was the mother of Anthony and Thomas Adolphus Trollope, had lived in Cincinnati three years a decade earlier and must have picked up the phrase in the early 1820's. The English writer did not capitalize the name of the river and took the phrase to be "Georgia dialect."

The second earliest known use of the phrase occurs in *Banks of the Ohio* (London, 1833) by James K. Paulding, who wrote: "See if I don't row you up Salt River before you are many days older." He capitalized the name as if a real river was meant. In *A Tour Down East* (1834) David Crockett wrote: "Judge Clayton made a speech that fairly made the tumblers hop. He rowed the Tories up and over Salt river." The next year (1835) a man named Flint wrote in the *Athenaeum* that there is "a well-known rivalry between the collectors of the Downing dialect of New England, and the Crockett or Salt River dialect of the South &

West." By 1843 *crick* (creek) was being substituted for *river*. In that year R. Carlton wrote in *The New Purchase*: "If I don't row you up Salt Crick in less or no time, my name's not Sam Townsend." In the seventeenth century *salt river* (or creek) was applied to any coastal stream up which the tide comes to or almost to its source. *Up Salt Creek* may have originated in vulgar slang and *Salt* in the phrase may be merely a euphemism for some unprintable word.

To row up used to signify to get the better of, to beat, to treat severely, to attack vigorously, to rebuke, to punish with words, or to make uncomfortable. In 1838 James Russell Lowell wrote that when he recited Lock, Mr. Frost "generally spends three quarters of the time endeavoring to row up that delectable writer," and in 1845 the New York *Tribune* declared that it would like "to row up the majority of Congress as it deserves in regard to the practice." Whether *to row up* in this sense is a clipped form of *to row up Salt River,* or *to row up Salt River* is an elaborated form of *to row up*, is not known. John Russell Bartlett in 1859 and Schele De Vere in 1872 derived *to row up* from the practice of punishing refractory slaves by making them row heavy keelboats up the powerful currents of the Southern and Western rivers.

At an early date *up Salt River* was identified with Salt River in Kentucky, a stream that flows into the Ohio at West Point below Louisville. "The several streams and branches of Salt River (Rolling Fork, East Fork and the Beech River)," wrote John Filson in 1784, "afford excellent mill sites." In his *Notes on Virginia,* published the same year, Thomas Jefferson wrote: "Salt River is at all times navigable for loaded batteaux 70 or 80 miles. It is 80 yards wide at its mouth, and keeps that width to its fork, 25 miles above."

Many improbable stories have been told to account for the origin of *up Salt River*. One traces it to an alleged incident in the life of Henry Clay, when he was running for President against Andrew Jackson in 1832. It is said that the Whig candidate hired a boatman to row him up the Ohio to Louisville, where he was scheduled to make an important campaign speech. The boatman was a Jackson man and "accidentally on purpose" rowed Clay up the Salt River and caused him to miss his engagement. Another version is that the phrase was suggested by the fact that Clay, after his defeat, took a trip up the Salt River to forget and be forgotten for a while. Another story traces the phrase to the fact that pirates on the Ohio River were in the habit of rowing their booty up Salt River to avoid capture. Still another story identifies the phrase with Salt River in Missouri. This three-hundred-mile stream rises in Schuyler County and flows into the Mississippi in Pike County about three miles above the town of Louisiana. It is said that in the 1840's a Pike County man named Jackson was defeated several times in succession for the Missouri legislature and after each defeat moved farther up Salt River. These stories, like many others of the kind, are probably fanciful attempts to account for the origin of the phrase and most of them are discredited by the date of the quotation from Mrs. Trollope.

What President was the first not born a British subject?

Martin Van Buren, the eighth President, was the first President born after the adoption of the Declaration of Independence in 1776 and consequently was the first President of the United States not born a British subject. He was born in 1783 and served one term—1837 to 1841. In his inaugural on March 4, 1837, President Van Buren said: "Unlike all who have preceded me, the Revolution that gave us existence as one people was achieved at the period of my birth; and while I contemplate with gratified reverence that memorable event, I feel that I belong to a later age and that I may not expect my countrymen to weigh my actions with the same kind and partial hand."

Van Buren's immediate successor, William Henry Harrison, was born a British subject in 1773, but all the Presidents who followed him were born after the adoption of the Declaration of Independence. John Tyler, who was born in 1790 and who was President from 1841 to 1845, was the first President born after the establishment of the Federal Government under the Constitution in 1789. Only two later Presidents, Zachary Taylor and James Buchanan, were born before the Constitution went into effect.

George III died on January 29, 1820, after a reign of sixty years. On March 14, 1820, Secretary of State John Quincy Adams wrote in his diary: "George the Third had reigned sixteen years the sovereign of this country. I suppose there are about half a million souls in this Union who were once his subjects; four-fifths of that number born his subjects—of whom I was one."

John C. Calhoun, who was born in 1782 and who was Vice President from 1825 to 1832, was the first Vice President not born a British subject. All his predecessors in the Vice Presidency were born British subjects and all his successors were born after the adoption of the Declaration of Independence.

All of the Presidents and Vice Presidents have been born on soil that was or eventually became part of continental United States.

Who was the Little Magician?

Martin Van Buren (1782-1862), like Henry Clay, picked up a large variety of nicknames in the course of his long political career. Most of them were suggested by his small stature, his place of residence, or his reputation as a smooth and shrewd politician. "The Little Magician" is his most famous nickname. A poem printed on April 29, 1831, when Van Buren was Jackson's Secretary of State, referred to him as "the magician," and on January 25, 1833, John Quincy Adams called him "the little magician."

Van Buren was born at Kinderhook, New York, in his father's tavern, which was the village polling place. In his autobiography Van Buren wrote: "My family was from Holland, without a single marriage with one of different extraction from the time of the first emigrant to that of the marriage of my eldest son, embracing a period of over two centuries and including six generations." The immigrant, Marten Cornelissen van Burrmalsen, came over in 1631 as a servant indentured to Van Rensselaer, the first patroon, and later changed his surname to Van Buren. Van Buren belonged to the Dutch Reformed Church and married a kinswoman of his mother. He was often called "The Flying Dutchman."

In his younger days Van Buren earned the dubious nickname "Blue Whisky Van" because he could drink large quantities of whisky without the customary effects. He was in debt when he started to practice law but retired from law practice at forty with a fortune of $200,000. Although a good conversationist and a fair public speaker, Van Buren seldom committed himself on controversial questions. In December, 1821, when Van Buren was about to go to Washington as a Senator, Rufus King wrote of him: "He will not be there two weeks until he will know every man's opinion, but none will know his." When a Senator asked him whether he believed the rumor that the sun rises in the east, Van Buren was reputed to have replied: "I understand that is the common notion, but since I never get up until after dawn I can't say." In 1835 David Crockett wrote of the Vice President: "It is said that at a year old he could laugh on one side of his face and cry on the other at one and the same time. . . . It would be difficult to say from his personal appearance whether he was man or woman, but for his large red and gray whiskers." John Randolph of Roanoke said Van Buren "rowed to his objective with muffled oars." *Vanburenism* was used as a synonym of "noncommitalism." Van Buren was so sly that they called him "The

Fox" and "The Red Fox of Kinderhook." Of course, he didn't escape being called Van and Little Van; Mat and Little Mat, Matty and Little Matty, and Marty and Little Marty. Other nicknames were "The Wizard of Kinderhook," "The Sage of Kinderhook," and after he acquired his new place at Kinderhook, "The Sage of Lindenwald." He was also called simply "Old Kinderhook," and some suppose that O.K. in the sense of "all right" originated as the initals of *Old Kinderhook*. After he became President he was called "King Martin the First" by his political enemies.

Van Buren was twice challenged to duels but never fought one. "America's first real politician," Holmes Alexander calls him in *The American Talleyrand; The Career and Contemporaries of Martin Van Buren, Eighth President* (1935). At least he was the first professional politician to become President. Although a great political tactician and strategist, he himself was never a popular candidate. His policy was to try to back winners and not let personal friendship stand in the way of political success. Adams thought Van Buren was "a demagogue with a tincture of aristocracy." He started out as a Federalist. In 1824 he supported William H. Crawford's forlorn hope, but between elections he stepped on Andrew Jackson's coattail and rode on it for the next twenty years. Stroking the leonine mane of Old Hickory the right way brought him the Secretaryship of State, the Governorship of New York, the Ministership to England, the Vice Presidency and the Presidency. His wife died in 1819 and he was able to weather the storm over Peggy O'Neal Eaton and keep Jackson's friendship largely because he had no wife to interfere with his social life. He never succeeded in politics again after Jackson repudiated him because of his straddling on the Texas Question. Occasionally The Fox outsmarted himself. In 1836 he sponsored the two-thirds rule, which kept him from getting the nomination in 1844.

A persistent legend says Van Buren was a natural son of Aaron Burr. Some writers suppose that John Quincy Adams had this in mind when he wrote of Van Buren in his diary on May 12, 1827: "He is now acting over the part in the affairs of the Union which Aaron Burr performed in 1799 and 1800, and there is much resemblance of character, manners, and even person, between the two men." Neither this nor any other statement in the diary can be fairly said to indicate that Adams thought there was blood relationship between Van Buren and Burr. After the Adams diary was published by his son in 1874-1877, several facts were pointed out to show that the legend might have some basis. Burr was a frequent visitor at the Van Buren tavern in Kinderhook during the year before Martin's birth. Martin bore little physical and mental resemblance to any members of his family but many to Burr. Both were small, slender men and looked enough alike to be father and son. When Van Buren went to New York City to study law he visited "Richmond Hill" and, according to his own autobiography, Burr "treated me with much attention." Later Van Buren learned practical politics from Burr and finally took Burr's place as political boss of the State. After Burr returned from his exile in Europe he often stayed with Van Buren. But these facts do not prove that Van Buren was a natural son of Burr or that Van Buren was even aware that he was supposed to be so. Abraham Van Buren, the tavern-keeper, was a thirty-nine-year-old bachelor when he married a twenty-nine-year-old widow named Mary Van Alen, who had three daughters by a former marriage. She had borne Abraham Van Buren two daughters and was thirty-five when Martin was born. To say the least, the legend that Burr and Van Buren were father and son is hard to believe.

President Van Buren's oldest son, Abraham, was a West Pointer and spent much of his life as an army officer. He married Angelica Singleton, a cousin of Dolly Madison. He was his father's secretary in the White House and during the latter part of the Van Buren administration his wife acted as First Lady.

The President's second son, John, "The Young Fox," was a brilliant lawyer, orator and politician. When Van Buren went to England in 1831 as Minister John went with him as his secretary, and remained in London two years with the American legation. The handsome, debonair youth made a great hit in London society. In 1838, while his father was President, John Van Buren went abroad again, this time with a letter of introduction to the Duke of Wellington from Andrew Jackson. A court circular giving the guests at a state dinner listed John Van Buren's name among princes, dukes and other bigwigs. He danced with Queen Victoria, and the Whigs, to hurt his father politically, circulated a story that he was engaged to her and referred to him as "Prince John." "John Van Buren," wrote John W. Forney in *Anecdotes of Public Men*, "was the despot of the dinner-table. He had a way of assuming the command that made him resistless, and he had the bearing, the voice, and the domination that seemed to give equity to the title of Prince, bestowed by his enemies and adopted by his friends." Owing to a confusion of names it is often said that Prince John served a term in Congress. John Van Buren (1799-1855) of Kingston, New York, who served in the House of Representatives from 1841 to 1843, was not related to the President. The only important public office ever held by Prince John was that of Attorney General of New York.

What was the Albany Regency?

The Albany Regency was the nickname of a political machine that controlled the Democratic Party in New York from about 1825 to 1855 and influenced the national party for many years. The leaders in the Albany Regency were Martin Van Buren, William L. Marcy, Azariah C. Flagg, Benjamin F. Butler, Edwin Croswell, Michael Hoffman, Silas Wright and John A. Dix. Four of these—Van Buren, Marcy, Wright and Dix had served as Governor, although Dix did not hold that office until 1873, after he had become a Republican. In 1820 Van Buren acquired indirect control of the Albany *Argus* and under Croswell's editorship it became the organ of the Albany Regency, which was so called by political enemies because most of its members started as State officials and operated from the State capital. Every Governor of New York was Democratic from 1801 till the Whigs made William H. Seward Governor in 1839.

Who was the Expounder of the Constitution?

Daniel Webster (1782-1852) was known as "The Expounder of the Constitution" and "The Great Expounder." As a constitutional lawyer and orator he greatly influenced the Supreme Court in interpreting the Federal Constitution, and he did as much as any one man to inspire Americans to regard that document with reverence. On March 16, 1837, Webster's friends and admirers referred to him as "the man whom all (without regard to party) acknowledge as the eloquent and patriotic expounder and supporter of the Constitution."

Webster was five feet nine inches tall and weighed about 155 pounds in his prime, but his large head and shoulders made him appear taller and larger than he was. He was dark-complexioned and swarthy, and when at college, where he was often taken for an Indian, he acquired the nickname "Black Dan." Later he was called "Daniel the Godlike" and "The Godlike Daniel" by his political enemies. On November 14, 1843, Rutherford B. Hayes, then a Harvard law student, wrote in his diary: "Daniel Webster has been styled 'the godlike' in derision. But if any man born of woman deserves the epithet, it is Daniel Webster. The majesty of pure intellect shines forth in him." He was also called "The Giant of Massachusetts" and "The Great New Englander."

Born on a New Hampshire farm, Webster graduated from Dartmouth, read law and taught in an academy. He served in the U.S. House of

Representatives from districts in both New Hampshire and Massachusetts, served two stretches in the U.S. Senate and was twice Secretary of State. Webster, who had his weather eye on the Presidency for forty years, never received a national party nomination for that office. In 1836 the Massachusetts legislature nominated him as a Whig candidate for President, but he received only the fourteen electoral votes of Massachusetts.

Thomas Carlyle met Webster at breakfast in England in 1839 and found him "a magnificent specimen," "a dignified, perfectly bred man," whom "As a logic-fencer, advocate, or Parliamentary Hercules, one would incline to back . . . at first sight against all the extant world." Carlyle thought, "God Almighty never created a man half so wise as he looks." Sidney Smith observed, "Good heavens. He is a cathedral all by himself." But he also said, "Daniel Webster struck me much like a steam-engine in trousers." Ralph Waldo Emerson, who heard Webster make his Second Bunker Hill oration on June 17, 1843, wrote of him on that occasion: "His countenance, his figure, and his manners were all in so grand a style that he was, without effort, as superior to his most eminent rivals as they were to the humblest. He alone of all men did not disappoint the eye and the ear, but was a fit figure in the landscape. There was the Monument, and there was Webster."

William Henry Harrison had a penchant for quoting the classics. He submitted his inaugural address, interlarded with references to the Romans, to Webster for criticism. That night the Secretary of State-designate came home and lay down on a sofa, telling his family and friends that he was dog-tired from the labor of killing seventeen consuls and twelve proconsuls as dead as smelts.

Some of Webster's speeches in the Senate lasted serveral hours a day for several days. Although Webster had a cigar named after him, he did not smoke. He entertained lavishly, liked good food, and sometimes drank too much. On the night of August 8, 1846, President James K. Polk, a teetotaler, who went to the Capitol to sign bills at the close of the session of Congress, wrote in his diary: "Great confusion, I learned, prevailed in both houses during the night's session and what is deeply to be regretted several members as I was informed were much excited by drink. Among others I was informed that Senators Webster and Barrow were quite drunk, so much so that the latter gentleman, it was said, was noisy and troublesome." Webster was lax in private money matters. Emerson wrote: "Thirty years ago when Mr. Webster at the bar and in the Senate filled the eyes and minds of young men, you might often hear cited as Mr. Webster's three rules: first, never to do today what he could defer till tomorrow; secondly, never to do himself what he could make another do for him; and, thirdly, never to pay any debt today." Although Webster did not care for the details of public office, he did a prodigious amount of work. His writings were published in eighteen large volumes. He spent freely, lost money in speculations, and was often financially embarrassed. He supported the Bank of the United States both in principle and as a lucrative client. In 1841, when he became Secretary of State, he still owed that bank more than $110,000. Because Webster was slow in accounting for $10,000 of State Department funds, Charles J. Ingersoll, Pennsylvania Democrat, moved his impeachment, but the House of Representatives rejected the motion by an overwhelming vote. Webster accepted considerable sums of money from friends and admirers without compunction and felt that his public services and the expenses he was put to entitled him to such help. On September 17, 1841, ex-President John Quincy Adams wrote in his diary of the Secretary of State: "Such is human nature, in the gigantic intellect, the envious temper, the ravenous ambition, and the rotten heart of Daniel Webster."

Webster opposed slavery but put the Union above everything else. In his Reply to Hayne in 1830 he said: "Liberty and Union, now and forever, one and inseparable." He supported Henry Clay's Compromise of 1850, and, speaking "not as a Massachusetts man, not as a Northern man, but as an American," delivered his Seventh of March Speech, the only speech remembered by the date on which it was delivered. It infuriated his Northern antislavery followers, and John Greenleaf Whittier wrote *"Ichabod,"* one of the most scathing poems ever written by a great poet about a great statesman during his life.

When Millard Fillmore became President in 1850 he made Webster Secretary of State again, and in that office the Great Expounder died on October 24, 1852, at Marshfield, his estate in Massachusetts. To the very last he had hoped to get the Whig nomination for President in 1852. "How will this look in history?" he asked when a telegram informed him that on the fifty-seventh ballot Winfield Scott had received 159, Fillmore 112 and he only 21 votes. As he lay on his deathbed, he asked his wife, doctor, son and friends: "Have I, on this occasion, said anything unworthy of Daniel Webster?" He overhead the doctor tell an attendant to give him some brandy if he was alive in an hour. When the attendant returned he said, "I still live," his last distinguishable words. His life went out with the tide in the early morning. In the following national election Daniel Webster, nearly two weeks dead, received more than seven thousand votes for President. Webster was of Puritan stock but not active in any church. The day before he died he dictated the following, which was put on his tombstone at Marshfield:

Philosophical argument, especially that drawn from the vastness of the universe, in comparison with the apparent insignificance of the globe, has sometimes shaken my reason for the faith that is in me; but my heart has always assured and reassured me that the gospel of Jesus Christ must be Divine Reality. The Sermon on the Mount cannot be a mere human production. This belief enters into the very depth of my conscience. The whole history of man proves it.

Webster had five children—two daughters and three sons by his first wife, Grace Fletcher. Both daughters died of tuberculosis, one, Grace, in childhood, and the other, Julia (Mrs. Samuel A. Appleton), in New Orleans in 1848. His youngest son, Charles, died at two in 1824. Although never a soldier himself, two of his sons died in war. Major Edward Webster commanded a regiment of Massachusetts Volunteers during the Mexican War and died of disease near Mexico City in 1848. At the outbreak of the Civil War Colonel (Daniel) Fletcher Webster, Webster's only son to survive him, was killed at the head of his regiment in the First Battle of Bull Run.

Who were the Bucktails?

From 1817 to 1828 the Democratic-Republican Party in New York State was divided into two factions. The supporters of Governor De Witt Clinton (1769-1828) were known as the Clintonians and his opponents as the Bucktails. During the Revolution the tail of a deer was often worn in the headgear of men as a symbol of Americanism. On June 6, 1775, Philip Fithian wrote in his *Journal* at Winchester, Virginia: "Mars, the great God of Battle, is now honoured in every Part of this spacious Colony, but here every Prescence is warlike, every Sound is martial! Drums beating, Fifes & Bag-Pipes playing, & only sonorous & heroic Tunes—Every Man has a hunting-Shirt, which is the Uniform of each Company—Almost all have a Cockade, & Bucks-Tale in their Hats, to represent that they are hardy, resolute, & invincible Natives of the Woods of America." At the same place Fithian wrote on June 17 of the same year: "This Town in Arms. All in a Hunting-Shirt Uniform & Bucks Tale in their Hats.—Indeed they make a grand Figure."

St. Tammany, a legendary Delaware Indian chief, was regarded as the patron saint of America, and the Tammany Society adopted an Indian motif for its ritual, costumes and paraphernalia. Members of the Tammany Society wore part of the tail of a buck in their hats as an insigne on certain occasions. Since the Tammany Society was opposed to Governor De Witt Clinton politically, his followers called all members of that organization Bucktails. In his *Travels in the United States* (1818) J. M. Duncan wrote: "Tammany Hall is one of the public hotels, and noted for the public meetings of the Democratic party, or Bucktails, as they are called." Eventually *Bucktails* was applied to all the anti-Clintonians throughout the State. The Bucktails opposed building the Erie Canal, Clinton's favorite project, which they called "Clinton's Big Ditch." On January 5, 1822, John Quincy Adams, Secretary of State and candidate for the Presidency, wrote in his diary that Postmaster General Return J. Meigs, Jr., had appointed General Solomon Van Rensselaer postmaster at Albany because "twenty-two members of the New York delegation, eleven of whom were Bucktails, seven Clintonians, and four federalists, had signed a written recommendation of him." In that year the Bucktails became the dominant Democratic-Republican organization and passed under the leadership of Martin Van Buren and the Albany Regency. On December 9, 1826, Adams, then President, wrote that General Jacob J. Brown "urges that Clinton and his friends will support the Administration of the General Government, and that Van Buren and his Bucktails will be inveterate in their opposition."

What was the first Federal foreign-aid act?

An act approved March 3, 1812, appropriating $50,000 for the relief of Venezuelans in distress because of an earthquake, was the first Federal foreign-aid act passed by Congress. Some Congressmen opposed the act on the ground the Constitution did not authorize such legislation. On March 3, 1820, Secretary of State John Quincy Adams wrote in his diary that President Monroe had said to him: "Some years ago Congress had appropriated a sum of money to the relief of the inhabitants of Caracas, who had suffered by an earthquake. There was no express grant of authority to apply the public money to such a purpose. It was by an implied power." Congress was equally reluctant to pass legislation for domestic relief. On February 4, 1794, it voted $5,000 for the relief of San Domingo refugees in the United States. The first social welfare legislation passed by Congress was an act in 1798 authorizing the deduction of twenty cents a month from the wages of American seamen for building marine hospitals. During the exceptionally cold winter of 1829 the Federal authorities in the District of Columbia directed that fifty cords of firewood be distributed to the poor.

What was the Toledo War?

The "Toledo War" was a spirited boundary dispute between the State of Ohio and Michigan Territory in 1835. The Ordinance of 1787 for the government of the Northwest Territory provided that a line running due west from the southern bend of Lake Michigan was to be the southern boundary of Michigan and the northern boundary of Ohio, Indiana and Illinois. When Ohio was admitted into the Union this provision was disregarded and the northern boundary was located far enough north to include the site of Toledo within Ohio. This area between the two lines comprised about six hundred square miles and was known as the Toledo strip.

Both Michigan and Ohio claimed the Toledo strip, but the controversy lay dormant until 1835, when Michigan Territory, without waiting for an enabling act, formed a constitution and demanded statehood. Stevens Thomson Mason, the twenty-four-year-old acting Territorial Governor, gained wide popularity as the leader of the faction that asserted Michigan's claim to the Toledo strip, and his energetic part in the controversy was the source of embarrassment to President Jackson and the Democratic Party, because Indiana and Illinois took the part of Ohio and thirty-five electoral votes in the coming Presidential election were at stake.

The Ohio legislature directed Governor Robert Lucas to take possession of the disputed territory by force, and the legislative council of Michigan Territory resolved to resist by force. Both sides called out the militia and conflict and bloodshed appeared inevitable. Richard Rush and Benjamin C. Howard were sent by President Jackson as conciliators to try to persuade Michigan and Ohio to keep the peace. Attorney General Benjamin F. Butler wrote an opinion in which he declared that Ohio had no right to seize jurisdiction over the disputed territory by force, that Congress, by assenting to the Ohio constitution, had reserved to itself the right to assent later to the proposed boundary, and that the President should prevent Michigan from resisting the force offered by Ohio. Ohio commissioners proceeded to establish the line and the State extended its jurisdiction over the disputed area. Congress refused to admit Michigan to statehood until the dispute was settled in favor of Ohio. In 1836 Congress passed an act providing for the admission of Michigan into the Union on condition that a convention called by the people of the Territory for that express purpose should assent to the change in the southern boundary. A convention called by the Michigan legislature met in September, 1836, and rejected the condition imposed by Congress. Two months later another convention, chosen by a spontaneous movement among the people, voted to assent to the condition. Ohio won her point, and the Toledo War was over, but Congress detached the Upper Peninsula from Wisconsin Territory and granted it to Michigan as compensation for her loss of the Toledo strip.

Who was author of "Old Tippecanoe and Tyler Too"?

"Tippecanoe and Tyler Too," one of the most famous and effective campaign slogans in American politics, is believed to have been originated by Alexander Coffman Ross (1812-1883), a jeweler and amateur songwriter of Zanesville, Ohio.

In December, 1839, the Whig convention at Harrisburg nominated William Henry Harrison of Ohio for President and John Tyler of Virginia for Vice President, and in May, 1840, the Democratic convention at Baltimore renominated Martin Van Buren for President but left Vice President Richard Mentor Johnson to seek re-election without a convention nomination. Harrison's large vote against Van Buren in 1836 foreshadowed a hot contest but neither Whigs nor Democrats could have foreseen that it would set the pattern for Presidential campaigns for the next century.

Harrison defeated Henry Clay for the nomination and for several months after the convention many Clay Whigs nursed the hope that the sixty-seven-year-old General would step aside for the popular favorite. On March 23, 1840, the Baltimore *American,* a Van Buren paper, printed a squib to the effect that no doubt Harrison would be willing to withdraw and spend the rest of his days in a log cabin if given a $2,000-a-year pension and a barrel of hard cider. This was the first appearance of *log cabin* in political campaigns.

Harrison was not born in a log cabin but in a Tidewater Virginia mansion, and he never lived in a real log cabin, although as a soldier on the Northwestern frontier he lived in stockades and other log structures. After his marriage to the daughter of a wealthy landowner he and his wife moved into his father-in-law's five-room log house at North Bend on the Ohio. Soon after the close of the War of 1812 Harrison built a large house around this old log house where he and his wife had spent their honeymoon. The General, for sentimental reasons, called the new house, a mansion in the eyes of the neighbors for miles around, "The Log Cabin," and he was fond of opening a closet door and showing guests some of the logs from the original house. He was a moderate drinker and distilled whisky on his farm for sale, but hard cider was a plebeian drink and it is not probable that it was served to guests at North Bend before the 1840 campaign.

After serving as army officer, secretary of the Northwest Territory, Delegate in Congress, Governor of Indiana Territory, Major General in command of American troops in the Northwest, U.S. Representative, State senator, U.S. Senator and Minister to Colombia, he settled down on his 2,800-acre farm at the age of fifty-six. He had a large family, entertained freely and was often short of ready cash. To supplement the income from his farm he sought and obtained the Hamilton County court clerkship, which paid no salary but which brought him from $6,000 to $10,000 a year in fees. In dress, bearing and manners he was a mixture of the Virginia gentleman and aristocrat and the frontier soldier and farmer, but he liked to think of himself as a plain man of the people. In 1836 he wrote to Solomon Van Rensselaer: "The Clerk of the Court of Common Pleas of Hamilton County at your service. But, I have news still more strange to tell you, if you have not already heard. Some folks are so silly as to have formed a plan to make a President of the United States out of this Clerk and Clodhopper."

In 1811 General Harrison marched with nine hundred men against the hostile Indians, who had their headquarters near the juncture of Tippecanoe Creek and the Wabash. "The Kickappos are encamped near the Tippecanoe," wrote Harrison in a letter that was sent to Congress by President Madison. Just before daybreak on November 7, 1811, the Indians under the Prophet attacked Harrison's camp with great fury. The Indians got inside Harrison's lines and his camp was in great confusion while the fighting continued. It is believed that about one thousand warriors took part in the battle and that about sixty of them were killed, although the number of Indians engaged and the number of their losses is not known definitely, because they withdrew at dawn. Harrison lost about sixty in killed and twice that many in wounded. As commander of the American forces at the Battle of the Thames in Canada on October 5, 1813, Harrison won a decisive victory over the British and Indians and became a national hero. It was in fact the only important land battle won by the Americans during the War of 1812 before the peace treaty was signed. But Colonel Johnson, the Democratic candidate for Vice President in 1836 and 1840, was played up as the killer of Tecumseh and the hero of the Battle of the Thames, and Harrison's admirers preferred to identify him with the less decisive victory over the Indians at a place with the musical and fascinating name of Tippecanoe. To them, twenty-five years after the battle, the old warrior became "Old Tippecanoe" or "Old Tip."

The Whigs were the political heirs of the Federalists and their leaders represented business and wealth. They had adopted no platform and their loosely knit followers were united only in their desire to oust the Democrats from the White House, where, under various names, they had lodged for forty years. The deliberate policy of the Whigs was to play up their candidate as a homespun frontiersman and war hero and to ridicule Van Buren as an aristocrat and dandy. Van Buren was born in a tavern in a humble family with little means, but as a lawyer and politician he had acquired considerable wealth and lived more like an aristocrat than a democrat. He was sleek in person, oily in conversation, polished in manners, and he liked fine food, good liquor, fashionable clothes, and elegant surroundings. "Mr. Van Buren is growing inordinately fat," reported John Quincy Adams after a visit to the White House on December 26, 1839. A story circulated that the President was wearing corsets to retain his figure.

On April 14, 1840, Representative Charles Ogle of Pennsylvania began a three-day speech in Congress in which he struck the keynote of the Whig campaign. He charged that the President was keeping "a royal establishment at the expense of the nation." He said: "Let us enter this palace and survey its spacious courts, its glittering and dazzling saloons with all their magnificence and sumptuous array of gold spoons and silver plate, of crimson and orange, of blue and violet." The Whig orator itemized the amounts Van Buren had spent for flowers, window curtains, French china and other White House luxuries.

Whig leaders woke up to the fact that they had a powerful psychological weapon in the log cabin and hard cider sneer. All over the country "Tippecanoe clubs" sponsored stump-speakings, barbecues, mass meetings, processions and torchlight parades. An invariable feature of the parades was a log cabin on wheels with the latchstring out. Beside the log cabin was a barrel of hard cider and a large ball in motion. Often on top of the log cabin was a tree with a live raccoon in it. The coon was the Whig emblem and Whigs wore coonskin caps and called themselves coons. Canoes (suggested by *Tippecanoe*) were also used as emblems. Everywhere "The Old Farmer of North Bend" was toasted with mugs of hard cider. "Hard cider has become the fountain of Whig inspiration," wrote Philip Hone on April 10. The Whig meetings became so immense that newspapers reported the size of the crowds "by the acre." The campaign was so violent that it hurt business. "There is a revolution in the habits and manners of the people," wrote John Quincy Adams. "Where will it end?"

The Democrats tried in vain to stem the Whig tide. In response to arguments the Whigs yelled "Hurrah for Harrison." Horace Greeley changed the name of his *Jeffersonian* to *The Log Cabin,* and other papers adopted the same name. In many cities meeting places were constructed in the form of enormous log cabins. Old Tip, said the Whigs, could live comfortably on what Van Buren spent for his wardrobe. They represented the President as standing for hours before a mirror primping himself and making his dainty toilet. The Whigs proclaimed that they would "teach the palace slave to respect the log cabin." They charged that Van Buren's policy was fifty cents a day and French soup, while that of Harrison was two dollars a day and roast beef.

For the first time badges, ribbons and banners were used on a large scale in political demonstrations, but the most remarkable innovation was the wholesale use of band music and songs. Hundreds of songs, most of them on the Whig side, were composed for the campaign. A hundred were printed in a single volume. Whigs sang, "Farewell, dear Van, you're not our man," "With Tip and Tyler we'll burst Van's biler," and

> Old Tip, he wears a homespun coat,—
> He has no ruffled shirt—shirt, shirt;
> But Mat he has the golden plate,
> And he's a little squirt—squirt, squirt.

George Pope Morris, author of "Woodman, Spare that Tree," wrote, to the tune of Samuel Woodworth's "Old Oaken Bucket":

> The iron-armed soldier, the true-hearted soldier,
> The gallant old soldier of Tippecanoe.

But Ross wrote the most popular song of the campaign and gave the Whigs their most effective slogan. Tyler, former Democrat turned Whig because he disliked Van Buren and Andrew Jackson, meant little to Northern Whigs. Ross, however, felt that he must be dragged into the song somehow. It is said that the snapper line of his song came to him while in church and thinking more of politics than the sermon. His song, which made an immediate hit at a Zanesville Tippecanoe meeting, ran in part as follows:

> What has caused this great commotion, motion, motion
>   Our country through?
> It is the ball a-rolling on, on
> For Tippecanoe and Tyler too, Tippecanoe and Tyler too.
> And with them we'll beat Little Van, Van Van.
>   Van is a used up man.
> And with them we'll beat Little Van.

Like the rushing of mighty waters, waters, waters,
On it will go
And its course will clear the way
For Tippecanoe and Tyler too.

Later during the campaign the chairman of a Whig meeting in Lafayette Hall in New York City called for some one to sing a song before the speaking started. The Buckeye jeweler happened to be present and responded with his new song, which made a prodigious hit, and soon was being sung by Whigs everywhere. Whigs paid their candidates the highest compliment in their power by naming spans of horses and yokes of oxen Tip and Ty. The log cabin did for Harrison what the hickory pole had done for Jackson, and Harrison won by a landslide. Van Buren, who was beaten in a game for which he had helped write the rules, never entirely lived down his reputation as a Sybarite. Ten years later Thomas H. Benton visited the ex-President at Lindenwald. "I am a little chary of new customs," Old Bullion said afterward, "but when I saw Mr. Van Buren dip the tips of his fingers in the bowl and wipe them daintily on a napkin, I just raked back my sleeves and took a good plain Republican wash."

In the log cabin and hard cider campaign the Vice Presidential candidates were both slaveholders and the Presidential candidates were both the sons of slaveholders.

What First Lady never saw her husband as President?

Mrs. William Henry Harrison was absent from the national capital all the time her husband was President and never saw him while he held that office.

In 1795 Harrison was married at North Bend, Ohio, to Anna, daughter of Colonel John Cleves Symmes, Revolutionary soldier and statesman, chief justice of New Jersey and founder of the Miami Settlement in Ohio. The Harrisons had ten children—six sons and four daughters. When Harrison was elected President in 1840 he was sixty-eight and his wife was sixty-five.

Mrs. Harrison was indisposed when her husband went to Washington to be inaugurated on March 4, 1841, but she expected to join him in the White House in the following May. Worn out by a hard campaign and by the solicitations of office seekers, President Harrison, after eight days of illness, died of pneumonia on April 4, one month to a day after taking the oath of office. The President's widowed daughter-in-law, Mrs.

William Henry Harrison, Jr., and his niece, Mrs. Thomas Taylor, acted as White House hostesses. On April 4, 1841, the day of the President's death, John Quincy Adams wrote: "The bereavement and distress of his family are felt intensely, albeit they are strangers here and scarcely known to any one. His wife had not even left his residence at North Bend, Ohio, to join him here. An express was sent for her two or three days since; but the tidings of death must meet her before she can reach this city."

It is suspected that illness and advanced age alone did not prevent Mrs. Harrison from going to Washington with her husband. She probably had seen enough of politics during the spectacular log cabin and hard cider campaign of 1840 and desired to avoid the hubbub that accompanies a new administration in the national capital. Whatever the reason, neither she nor any of their many children ever saw Harrison as President. Mrs. Harrison lived to a greater age than any other woman who was the First Lady of the Land. She was eighty-nine when she died in 1864.

When were there three different Presidents in the same year?

Twice the United States has had three different Presidents within the same calendar year—1841 and 1881. William Henry Harrison succeeded Martin Van Buren on March 4, 1841, and was succeeded by John Tyler on April 30 of the same year. In 1841 there were three different Presidents within a period of thirty-one days. A child born on March 3, 1841, would have lived under four Presidents when he was four years and one day old—Van Buren, Harrison, Tyler and Polk. James A. Garfield succeeded Rutherford B. Hayes on March 4, 1881, and was succeeded by Chester A. Arthur on September 10 of the same year. A child born on March 3, 1877, would have lived under five Presidents when he was eight years and one day old—Ulysses S. Grant, Hayes, Garfield, Arthur and Grover Cleveland.

What Vice President was chosen by the Senate?

Richard Mentor Johnson (1781-1850) of Kentucky, who was Vice President under Martin Van Buren, has been the only Vice President chosen by the Senate.

The Twelfth Amendment to the Constitution, which became effective in 1804, provides that a candidate must receive a majority of the whole number of electoral votes to be elected Vice President. If no candidate for Vice President receives such majority the Senate must then choose a Vice President from the two candidates who have received the highest number of the electoral votes, a majority of the whole number of Senators being necessary to a choice.

In the election of 1836, when Van Buren was elected President, the candidates for Vice President and the number of electoral votes received by each were: Johnson, 147; Francis Granger, 77; John Tyler, 47, and William Smith, 23. The total number of electoral votes received by Granger, Tyler and Smith was 147, the same number received by Johnson, and no candidate had a majority of the whole number. Therefore the choice devolved upon the Senate, which cast thirty-three votes for Johnson and sixteen for Granger.

The Twentieth Amendment to the Constitution, which became effective in 1934, provides that "The Congress may by law provide . . . for the case of the death of any persons from which the Senate may choose a Vice President whenever the right of choice shall have devolved upon them," but up to the present Congress has passed no law under this authority.

Richard M. Johnson, the only Vice President chosen by the Senate, played an active and important part in State and national politics for more than forty years. After attending Transylvania College at Lexington, he studied law and was admitted to practice. He became a member of the State house of representatives at twenty-three and a member of the U.S. House of Representatives at twenty-six. During the War of 1812, while a Congressman, he was commissioned a colonel of volunteers and commanded a regiment of Kentucky mounted riflemen under General William Henry Harrison in Lower Canada. In the Battle of the Thames on October 5, 1813, five bullets struck and wounded him severely and five others struck his clothing and his horse. On April 4, 1818, Congress voted Johnson a sword in recognition of "the daring and distinguished valor displayed by himself and the regiment of volunteers under his command in charging and essentially contributing to vanquish the combined British and Indian forces." President Monroe formally presented the sword to Johnson in a White House ceremony on April 19, 1820. His admirers called him "Tecumseh Johnson" because they credited him with killing the famous Indian chief Tecumseh in the Battle of the Thames, but to his familiars he was known as "Dicky Johnson."

The red-haired, much-wounded Colonel became a member of the Senate in 1819 and was an aspirant for the Presidency or the Vice Presidency for the next thirty years. He advocated abolition of imprisonment for debt and other measures that appealed to the working classes.

He never wore a cravat and was careless in dress and informal in manners, but he was affable and likable. Politically he was an opportunist, perhaps somewhat of a demagogue, and he and his two brothers, who also served in Congress, were suspected of putting their private interests above those of the public. On February 18, 1820, Secretary of State John Quincy Adams wrote in his diary, after the Kentucky Senator had recommended William Duane for an appointment in the foreign service for which Adams thought he was clearly unsuited: "Johnson is a man who can refuse no favor to any man. He would recommend ten persons for one and the same place rather than say no to any one of them." Adams, a severe critic but a good reporter, wrote on March 10, 1821:

Johnson's politics are too deeply involved with his private interests, and too dependent upon them. His popularity and influence in Kentucky have neutralized Clay's hostility, and perhaps prevented the opposition which Clay at one time intended to have raised against the re-election of Mr. Monroe. I am afraid that this advantage has been purchased by compliance with private interests and speculation of Johnson and his relatives in which the public interests have not been so rigidly guarded as they ought to have been. Colonel R. M. is a man of great intrigue and management, and, I believe, warm and honest-hearted, but plunged irrevocably into private bank, land and money speculations, till he has lost the thread of his morals.

In 1824, when Andrew Jackson, William H. Crawford, Henry Clay and Adams were the Presidential candidates, Johnson shocked the New Englander by telling him frankly that he wanted to be on the side of the winner. Johnson professed friendship for both Adams and Jackson after the election but sometimes had difficulty in covering up his political tracks. On December 8, 1825, President Adams wrote: "Colonel R. M. Johnson, the Senator from Kentucky, has just arrived. He declared that the stories of his having been electioneering against the Administration were all slanders. The Colonel is disposed to keep on good terms with all parties." By the early 1830's Johnson was so popular with the Democrats that he was regarded as the political heir of President Jackson and was being groomed as the Democratic candidate to succeed Old Hickory in 1836. On December 24, 1831, Adams, then a Representative in Congress, wrote that William Babcock told him that Johnson "may be plastered up into a hero, and that will be enough to fashion him into a candidate for the office of President." The Democratic National Convention of 1836 nominated Vice President Van Buren for President and Johnson for Vice President. Since Van Buren had no military record, the Democrats played up the martial achievements of their Vice Presidential candidate to offset those of General Harrison, the leading Whig candidate for President, who had commanded the American forces at the Battle of the Thames, in which Johnson had covered himself with glory. During the campaign the Democrats sang:

> Rumpsey, Dumpsey,
> Colonel Johnson killed Tecumseh.

Johnson would have received a clear majority of the electoral votes over Granger and Tyler, and the choice would not have devolved upon the Senate, had not the Virginia electors bolted the ticket and voted for William Smith of Alabama.

Serious opposition to the Vice President began to develop soon after he took office. On October 27, 1837, Edward Wyer, the Senate doorkeeper, told Adams "that of all vulgar men in the world, the most vulgar man, in his judgment, was the Vice President of the United States," and on December 26, 1839, Adams referred to "Colonel R. M. Johnson, whose Vice Presidential chair, it is said, is gently to be drawn from under him at the next Presidential election." Van Buren's renomination for President in 1840 was taken for granted, but even former President Jackson suggested that Governor James K. Polk of Tennessee be substituted for Johnson to strengthen the ticket. The Democratic convention of 1840 renominated Van Buren but was unable to renominate Johnson. In lieu of a nomination for Vice President, the convention adopted the following unprecedented resolution:

Whereas, Several of the States which have nominated Martin Van Buren as a candidate for the Presidency, have put in nomination different individuals as candidates for Vice-President, indicating diversity of opinion as to the person best entitled to the nomination; and whereas some of the said States are not represented in this Convention, Resolved, that the Convention deem it expedient at the present time not to choose between the individuals in nomination, but to leave the decision to their Republican fellow-citizens in the several States, trusting that before the election shall take place, their opinions will become so concentrated as to secure the choice of a Vice-President by the Electoral College.

The purpose of this curious resolution was to permit Johnson to run in the East and West, where he was still popular, and Polk in the South, but Polk refused to be a party to this arrangement, with the result that Van Buren had no formally nominated running mate. In the log cabin and hard cider campaign of 1840 the Democrats again played up Johnson's military prowess to offset that of General Harrison, this time the regularly nominated Whig candidate for President. In the election

Van Buren received sixty electoral votes and Johnson forty-eight. The eleven South Carolina electors voted for Littleton W. Tazewell of Virginia for Vice President and one Virginia elector voted for Polk. But Van Buren and Johnson were decisively defeated by Harrison and Tyler and the difference between Van Buren's and Johnson's electoral votes did not affect the result.

The refusal of the convention of 1840 had more behind it than the fact that the Vice President of the United States did not wear a cravat. He was eliminated from the national political scene because of his private rather than his public life. Personal scandal was at the bottom of most of the opposition to him in his own party.

Johnson never married and is regarded as the only bachelor Vice President. When he was a young man he fell in love with a Yankee schoolteacher. For some reason his mother objected to the match and succeeded in breaking it up. At the time Johnson told his mother that she would regret this interference in his personal plans. In the distribution of his father's estate he came into possession of a mulatto slave girl named Julia Chinn, whom his mother had reared. Later he took this slave girl as his mistress, placed her at the head of his household and treated her and publicly referred to her as his wife. By Julia Chinn he had two daughters, Imogene and Adeline, who were so light that they could pass for whites and whom Johnson had educated by a white tutor. Both in Kentucky and in Washington Johnson attempted to introduce his mulatto mistress and his quadroon daughters into white society. When he failed in this he virtually ceased to go out socially himself, Julia Chinn died of cholera during an epidemic in Kentucky in 1833. Both of Johnson's acknowledged colored daughters married white men and he deeded each one of them a plantation as a dowery. Adeline died in 1836, but Imogene survived her father. Johnson's relatives never recognized Julia Chinn as his legal wife or Imogene and Adeline as his legal daughters, and after his death they had a Kentucky court declare that he was without descendants. After Julia Chinn's death Johnson had other colored mistresses. On August 22, 1839, Amos Kendall sent President Van Buren a letter written by a Kentuckian in which it was stated that the Vice President was then living with a third colored mistress, the young sister of a colored mistress whom he had sold for infidelity.

Johnson's private life was discussed in the newspapers, on the hustings and even in Congress. On March 22, 1838, Adams reported from the House of Representatives: "Halstead had alluded yesterday to R. M. Johnson the Vice-President's swarthy wife and dingy children in a manner which he thought witty, but which provoked Bynum and Boon beyond all measure, and they, savage-like, took their revenge." Many Democrats shuddered at the political consequences if President Van Buren should die in office and Johnson should move his colored family into the White House. But the Colonel's Kentucky neighbors never went back on him. They sent him to the legislature again after he retired from the Vice Presidency and were still talking about him for President when he died in 1850 at the age of sixty-nine.

What President studied medicine?

William Henry Harrison, the ninth President, studied medicine in his youth with the intention of becoming a doctor. In 1797, when only fourteen, he entered Hampden-Sidney College in Virginia but left after a year. After studying medicine in the office of Dr. Andrew Leiper in Richmond, he was sent to Philadelphia in April, 1791, to pursue his medical studies under Dr. Benjamin Rush, professor of medicine in the newly organized University of Pennsylvania. Benjamin Harrison requested Robert Morris, the financier of the Revolution, to be his son's guardian while at school in Philadelphia, then the seat of the Federal Government. Rush, Morris and the elder Harrison all three had signed the Declaration of Independence.

When William Henry Harrison arrived in Philadelphia he learned that his father had died. His brother Benjamin wrote the student that notwithstanding the father had left him three thousand acres of land there would be no further funds with which to continue his schooling. After attending Dr. Rush's classes for only a short time the medical student decided, without consulting either his guardian or family, to enter the army. With the influence of Governor Henry Lee, Harrison, still only eighteen years old, obtained a commission as ensign in the regular army. His commission was dated August 16, 1791, and was signed by President Washington. On July 20, 1839, he wrote: "In 24 hours from the first conception of the idea of changing my profession, I was an ensign in the 1st U.S. Regt of Infantry."

In 1794 Harrison was promoted from lieutenant to captain for heroic action in the Battle of Fallen Timbers. John Cleves Symmes, judge and soldier, objected to Harrison's marriage to his daughter Anna on the ground that the young man had no source of income except that of the pay of an army captain. A year after Harrison married Anna, Judge Symmes wrote to Robert Morris of his son-in-law; "He can neither bleed, plead, nor reach, and if he could plow I should be satisfied. His best prospect is in the army; he has talents, and if he can dodge well a few years, it is probable he may become conspicuous."

What are the "fatal twenties" in Presidential elections?

By a strange coincidence, beginning with 1840 every man elected to the Presidency of the United States in a year represented by a date ending in zero died in office. In other words, the President elected in 1840 and the one elected every twentieth year thereafter failed to complete his term or terms in office—six of them in all. Their names, with the dates of their election, are as follows:

1840, William H. Harrison
1860, Abraham Lincoln
1880, James A. Garfield
1900, William McKinley
1920, Warren G. Harding
1940, Franklin D. Roosevelt

Zachary Taylor, the only other President to die in office, was elected in 1848, took office March 4, 1849, and died July 9, 1850.

What was the Liberty Party?

The Liberty Party was the first organized effort to make the abolition of slavery a partisan political issue and was the first third party in the United States to decide a Presidential contest.

At an antislavery meeting in 1839 at Cleveland, Ohio, Myron Holley, who, despite the difference in the spelling of his name, claimed descent from the man after whom Halley's Comet was named, moved that candidates for President and Vice President be named. This motion was rejected because a majority of the delegates agreed with William L. Garrison and other antislavery leaders that slavery was a moral and not a political issue. At that time only a minority of the abolitionists advocated political action. Later in the same year at an antislavery meeting at Warsaw, New York, Holley renewed his motion and the delegates nominated James Gillespie Birney (1792-1857) for President and Francis Julius LeMoyne (1798-1879) for Vice President. Birney and LeMoyne declined to accept the nominations on the ground that the Warsaw meeting was insufficiently representative of the country as a whole to constitute a national convention. On April 1, 1840, a larger antislavery convention, composed of delegates from six States, met at Albany, New York and formed a party that came to be known as the Liberty Party. Salmon P. Chase, of Ohio, who had defended so many fugitive slaves that he was called the "attorney general for runaway Negroes," was one of the chief organizers. This convention adopted no platform and took no position on political issues in general. It merely declared itself in favor of abolishing slavery and nominated Birney and LeMoyne for President and Vice President.

Birney was born in Kentucky, educated at Princeton and admitted to the bar in Philadelphia; practiced law in his native State; served in the Kentucky and Alabama legislatures, where he sponsored emancipation measures; freed his own slaves; was agent of the American Colonization Society; organized the Kentucky Anti-Slavery Society; published *The Philanthropist* at New Richmond, Ohio; in 1837 became the executive secretary of the American Anti-Slavery Society and moved to New York City. LeMoyne was a physician of French descent whose house at Washington, Pennsylvania, was an Underground Railroad station. This first serious attempt of the abolitionists to adopt political action and to write abolition into law attracted little attention in 1840, the year of the famous log cabin and hard cider contest between William Henry Harrison and President Martin Van Buren. Birney and LeMoyne received only about 7,000 popular votes.

In August, 1843, the Liberty Party met in convention at Buffalo, New York, with delegates from twelve States. This time it adopted a militant platform in the spirit of Garrison. The platform, largely the work of Chase, not only denounced slavery but declared the purpose of the abolitionists to be, "whether as private citizens or as public functionaries sworn to support the Constitution of the United States to regard and to treat the third clause of the fourth article of that instrument, whenever applied to the case of a fugitive slave, as utterly null and void, and consequently as forming no part of the Constitution of the United States, whenever we are called upon or sworn to support it." For President the Liberty Party again nominated Birney, for Vice President, Thomas Morris (1776-1844), who had served many years in the Ohio legislature and one term in the U.S. Senate and who had been read out of the Democratic Party for his antislavery views and his fight for the right of petition. In the election of 1844 Birney and Morris received a total of 62,263 popular votes. The Democratic and Whig nominees for President were James K. Polk and Henry Clay respectively. If Clay had carried New York he would have been elected, but Polk carried that State by a plurality of 5,106. Birney, who had received only 2,798 votes in New York in 1840, received 15,812 in 1844. It is presumed that most of the Birney votes would have gone to Clay had Birney not been a candidate and Clay would have been elected. The electoral vote in Michigan was also probably switched from Clay to Polk by Birney's vote in that State. Both Polk and Clay were slave owners and their views on the extension of slavery were not sufficiently different to matter much to the abolitionists, but the effect of their efforts was to elect to the Presidency the less desirable of the two major candidates from the abolition point of view. In the country as a whole Polk defeated Clay by only 38,901 votes and thus became a minority President.

Birney's public career ended in 1845 when he fell from a horse and was partially paralyzed. His son, William Birney (1819-1907) recruited and commanded Negro troops in the Federal army during the Civil War and became a general.

In 1847 the Liberty Party's nominee for President was John Parker Hale, of New Hampshire, who had served one term in the U.S. House of Representatives as a Democrat and who had just been elected as the first outright antislavery member of the U.S. Senate. Senator Hale declined the nomination and in 1848 the majority of the members of the Liberty Party decided to unite with the Conscience Whigs and antislavery Democrats to form the Free Soil Party. A minority, confined almost entirely to New York, and known as "the true Liberty Party men" and as "the Liberty League," nominated Gerrit Smith for President and Charles Foote for Vice President, but Smith, whose sister-in-law was Birney's second wife, declined the nomination and the last remnant of the Liberty Party ceased to exist as a separate organization.

When the antislavery men of the North who favored organized political action saw that the Liberty Party would not succeed they organized the Free Soil Party. The beginning of this movement was a meeting of Barnburners—New York antislavery Democrats—at Herkimer, New York, in October, 1847. Apparently at this meeting was born the slogan, "Free Trade, Free Labor, Free Soil, Free Speech and Free Men." The Free Soil Party was formed in a convention at Buffalo, New York, in August, 1848. The keynoter of this convention was Chase, who had been active in the Liberty Party during its eight years of existence. It was a gathering of men who had been affiliated with all the existing parties and factions. It differed from the Liberty Party in taking a position on issues other than slavery and in confining its slavery demands to restriction of the extension of slavery. The platform, written largely by Chase, declared for "no more slave States and no more slave territory." Resolution 16 of Chase's Free Soil platform declared "That we inscribe on our banner, 'Free Soil, Free Speech, Free Labor, and Free Men,' and under it we will fight on, and fight ever, until a triumphant victory shall reward our exertions." Former President Martin Van Buren, who had been defeated by Harrison in 1840 and who had lost the Democratic nomination to Polk on the slavery issue in 1844, was nominated for President. His running mate was Charles Francis Adams, son and grandson of a President, who was permanent chairman of the convention. On August 11, 1848, President Polk wrote in his diary: "I learned tonight that the Buffalo Convention of Whigs, Abolitionists, and Barnburners have nominated Charles F. Adams, the son of the late John Quincy Adams, who is an avowed Abolitionist, for the Vice-Presidency on Mr. Van Buren's ticket, the latter having been nominated for the Presidency. Mr. Van Buren is the most fallen man I have ever known."

In the election of 1848 Van Buren and Adams received 291,263 popular votes. Again a third party, without receiving an electoral vote, decided a Presidential contest. The Free Soil Party took enough votes from Lewis Cass, the Democratic nominee, in New York and Pennsylvania to give the electoral votes of those States to Zachary Taylor, the Whig nominee, and to elect him. Van Buren's large popular vote made Taylor another minority President.

In 1852 the Free Soil Party's nominee for President was Senator Hale, who in 1847 had declined the Liberty Party's nomination. The nominee for Vice President this time was George Washington Julian, of Indiana, who had been one of the Free Soilers elected to the U.S. House of Representatives in 1848. In the election of 1852, when Franklin Pierce and Winfield Scott were the Democratic and Whig candidates respectively, Hale and Julian received 156,149 popular votes—not enough to make Pierce a minority President. Charles Sumner, of Massachusetts, one of the founders of the Free Soil Party, who had been defeated for the U.S Senate in 1848, was elected to the Senate in 1852 by a combination of Free-Soilers and antislavery Democrats. In 1854 the Free Soil Party became the nucleus of the new Republican Party. After the first Republican National Convention met in Philadelphia in June, 1856, and nominated John C. Frémont for President, the new party, which the Free-Soilers joined, adopted a modification of the old Free Soil Party slogan as its own—"Free Speech, Free Press, Free Soil, Free Men, Frémont, and Victory."

Why does Maine elect Congressmen in September?

Maine elects its Representatives and Senators in Congress as well as its State officials on the second Monday in September instead of on the first Tuesday after the first Monday in November as the other States do, but it is required by law to choose Presidential electors on the same date that the other States do, with the result that the State holds two elections in Presidential election years—one in September for the election of Representatives and Senators in Congress and State officials, and one in November for the election of Presidential electors. The original constitution of Maine, adopted in 1819, fixed the second Monday in September as election day for both State and Federal officials and that provision has never been changed.

When Congress in 1845 fixed the first Tuesday after the first Monday in November as the date for choosing Presidential electors in the States it did not fix a date for choosing Representatives in Congress. Several States continued to hold their elections for State officials and members of Congress at a date earlier than the Presidential election every fourth year. Pennsylvania, Ohio and Indiana elected members of Congress and State officials on the second Tuesday in October and in political parlance they were known as the "October States." The October elections for members of Congress and State officers in these "key States" were supposed to foreshadow public sentiment and served as a "test" or a "straw" vote for the November election. It was customary for political parties to make especially intensive campaigns in the October States with a view of making a good showing and influencing the "bandwagon vote" throughout the country in the national election. On October 30, 1856, Rutherford B. Hayes wrote in his diary: "I feel seriously the probable defeat of the cause of freedom in the approaching Presidential election. Before the October election in Pennsylvania and Indiana, I was confident Colonel Frémont would be elected. But the disastrous results in those States indicate and will probably do much to produce his defeat. The majorities are small, very small, but they discourage our side."

Electing members of Congress at different times in different States proved unsatisfactory and in 1872 Congress enacted that the States and Territories should elect their Representatives and Delegates in Congress on the first Tuesday after the first Monday in November of 1876 and on the same day every second year thereafter; but it was provided that this should not apply to States whose constitutions would have to be amended to effect the change. Senators were not included in that provision, because they were elected by the State legislatures until the Seventeenth Amendment to the Constitution became effective in 1913. But the act of 1872 did contain a provision applicable to the failure of election of a Senator by a State legislature when one house voted for one person and the other for another and were unable to reach an agreement. The act directed that in such cases the two houses of the State legislature should meet in joint sessions on a fixed day and continue to meet every day until a Senator was chosen.

In 1872 only three States—Maine, Arkansas and Oregon—had provisions in their constitutions requiring the election of Representatives to Congress on dates other than national election day. Arkansas and Oregon, considering it more convenient and practical to hold Congressional elections every fourth year on the same day as the Presidential election, changed their constitutions to conform to the act of 1872. Several other States continued to hold their elections for State officials at a date earlier than the Presidential election every fourth year. This practice was abandoned by Indiana in 1880 and by Ohio in 1884. Maine, however, did not amend her constitution or change the date of her State election but clung to the old election day for both Congressional and State offices and is the only State to continue to hold these elections on a different day.

Election day in Maine was placed in September during the early days when traveling facilities were poor and when bad roads and cold weather frequently prevented the rural inhabitants from going to the polls late in the fall. Even at the present time climatic conditions may contribute toward the retention of the September date for the State and Congressional elections in Maine. Some advocates of the earlier date maintain that the present system in Maine serves the purpose of separating State from National issues in Presidential years.

Because of its earlier election date Maine supplanted the October States as a sort of political index or barometer for the whole nation. The notoriety provided by this "political oddity" may have something to do with the retention of the September election date by Maine. After the Roosevelt landslide of 1936 discredited the saying "As Maine goes, so goes the country," an unsuccessful attempt was made in the Maine legislature to discard the early election date for State and Congressional offices. It was then estimated that the traditional election day cost the taxpayers of the State $60,000 extra on Presidential years, because another election is necessary to elect Presidential electors on the first Tuesday after the first Monday in November, as in all the other States.

For more than a century the Maine election in September has been watched with keen interest for a hint as to how the political wind may be blowing. This started in 1840, when Maine had been a State only twenty years. The State had gone Democratic several times before the famous log cabin and hard cider campaign. Former Governor Edward Kent was the Whig candidate for Governor in Maine and the Whigs in other States rejoiced when Kent received a plurality in the September election. They thought it forecast a victory for Harrison in November and "Maine went hell-bent for Governor Kent" became a common saying.

As a matter of fact none of the candidates for Governor in Maine that year received a clear majority at the polls and Kent was finally chosen Governor by the legislature, but in the November election Harrison defeated Van Buren.

Statistics show that the early Maine election is not a dependable political barometer for the whole country, or even for New England, and its results are of little value for practical forecasting. Maine first went Republican in the September and November elections in 1856, but it did not forecast a Republican national victory. During the next seventy-six years the State usually went Republican and so did the nation. Not one of the five Democratic Presidential victories from Buchanan in 1856 to Wilson in 1916 was preceded by a Democratic victory in Maine's September election. In 1880 Maine in September chose a Democratic Governor by a majority of 164, but in November it gave Garfield a popular majority of 6,000 over Hancock. The earliest known record of "As Maine goes, so goes the country," occurs in 1888, during the first Cleveland-Harrison campaign, and apparently it dates from that time.

Many political observers continue to watch Maine on the theory that, although the State is almost sure to go Republican, the majority by which it goes Republican in the September election is fairly indicative of how the major parties will fare in the nation as a whole in the No-vember election. In other words, the early Maine election does not hinge on a Republican victory or defeat but on the size of the Republican majority. Statistics, however, indicate that the relationship between the shifts in the early Maine vote and the later national vote has generally been too slight to form the basis of a dependable forecast.

What was the Wilmot Proviso?

David Wilmot (1814-1868) is remembered almost solely because he introduced an amendment that never became law. On August 8, 1846, the House of Representatives considered a bill to appropriate $2,000,000 for the President's use in making peace with Mexico. Wilmot, a Free-Soil Democrat from Pennsylvania, tossed a bombshell into the forum by offering the following amendment:

Provided, That, as an express and fundamental condition to the acquisition of any territory from the Republic of Mexico by the United States by virtue of any treaty which may be negotiated between them and to the use by the Executive of the moneys herein appropriated, neither slavery nor involuntary servitude shall ever exist in any part of said territory, except for crime whereof the party shall first be duly convicted.

This short amendment, known as the Wilmot Proviso, split the Democratic Party wide open. It infuriated John C. Calhoun and other Southern proslavery leaders and supplied a rallying point for the increasing antislavery feeling in the North. President James K. Polk in his diary referred to "the slavery proviso" as "a mischievous and foolish amendment," and regarded it as a trick to embarrass him in dealing with Mexico.

After an exciting debate the House adopted the Wilmot Proviso by a vote of 83 to 64 and passed the appropriation bill by a vote of 87 to 64. Polk said the amendment was passed by "the Whigs and Northern Democrats, who had been opposed to making the appropriation." On August 10, 1846, the date that had been agreed upon for the adjournment of Congress, the Senate took up the appropriation bill. A motion was made to strike out the Wilmot Proviso and Senator John Davis of Massachusetts was still speaking against the motion when adjournment time came. "Had there been time," wrote Polk, "there is but little doubt the Senate would have struck out the slavery proviso and that the House would have concurred." At the next session a bill to appropriate $3,000,000 for the same purpose was introduced in the House, and Wilmot, after broadening his amendment to include all territory that the United States might acquire, reintroduced it. On February 15, 1847, the House adopted the amendment by a vote of 115 to 105, but later the amendment was struck out by a narrow margin in the Senate, which passed the bill. Philip Hone, the New York Whig leader, proved himself a good prophet when he wrote in his diary on February 16, 1847: "It is an important measure, which may alter the whole organization of political parties in the country." When Wilmot introduced his Proviso in 1848 as a separate resolution it was laid on the table.

Wilmot, who in 1848 supported the Free Soil ticket headed by former President Martin Van Buren, helped form the Republican Party. In the Philadelphia Convention of 1856, which nominated John C. Frémont for President, he drafted the Republican platform. On the first and only ballot for Vice President, Wilmot received 42 votes, Abraham Lincoln, 110 and William L. Dayton, 259. Wilmot went to the Republican Convention of 1860 in Chicago as a Lincoln delegate from Pennsylvania and was chosen temporary chairman and keynoter. He declined a Cabinet post in Lincoln's administration, but when Simon Cameron became Secretary of War in 1861, Wilmot filled out his Senate term. In 1863 Lincoln appointed him to the U.S. Court of Claims.

Whether Wilmot himself wrote his famous Proviso is a controversial subject. Twenty years later Jacob Brinkerhoff of Ohio, who had been a Free-Soil Democratic member of the House in 1846, claimed that he drafted the "Wilmot Proviso" and for political reasons asked Wilmot to introduce it. When the resolution to annex Texas was considered in 1845 Brinkerhoff proposed an amendment providing that "as a fundamental condition . . . the existence of slavery shall be forever prohibited in one-half of all the annexed territory." At the same time Julius Rockwell of Massachusetts proposed an amendment providing "That within the State, by this resolution admitted into the Union, slavery or involuntary servitude, except for crime, shall be prohibited, and all the provisions of the said Constitution inconsistent with this proviso shall be null and void." One story is that a small group of antislavery Democrats, including Brinkerhoff, "cooked up" the amendment and chose Wilmot to introduce it because he was on good terms with President Polk and friendly with the proslavery Democrats in the House. Authorship of the amendment is not important, because both thought and language were borrowed from the Ordinance of 1787. Wilmot won a place in history because the amendment bearing his name crystallized an issue that ultimately caused civil war. The language of his Proviso, broadened to cover the whole nation, became substantially that of the Thirteenth Amendment to the Constitution.

How did *Whig* originate?

The origin of *Whig* as a political term is obscure and several theories have been advanced to explain it. *Whig* was a North English and Scottish provincialism meaning "sour whey" or "buttermilk." In *Curiosities of Literature* (1791-1823) Isaac Disraeli wrote:

The friends of the court and the advocates of lineal succession, were, by the republican party, branded with the title of *tories,* which was the name of certain Irish robbers: while the court party in return would find no other revenge than by appropriating to covenanters and the republicans of that class, the name of the Scotch beverage of sour milk, whose virtue they considered so expressive of their disposition and which is called *whigg.*

But most authorities suppose *Whig* to be derived from *whiggamore,* the original form of which appears to have been *whiggamaire,* which signified "driver" or "drover." The first element of this obsolete term was *whig,* meaning "to drive," "to urge on" or "to jog along." When a Scot in the fifteenth century wanted to urge a horse forward he said *whiggam,* just as modern Englishmen and Americans say *gee-up* or *gid-*

up. According to some authorities, *more,* the last element in *whiggamore,* signifies "horse."

Whatever the exact meaning of the term, the Scots in the southwestern shires who drove north to trade at Leith were called *Whiggamores* by the northern Scots. In 1648 the Presbyterian ministers incited a rebellion in the southwestern counties against the King, the Duke of Hamilton and the court party. About 6,000 men, with the Marquis of Argyle at their head, marched to Edinburgh. In *My Own Times* (1723) Gilbert Burnet, Bishop of Salisbury, wrote that they came up "with an unheard of fury, praying and preaching all the way as they came." This threat to the authorities at Edinburgh was called the "Whiggamores' Inroad," and after that members of the anticourt party in Scotland were called *Whiggamores,* which was soon shortened to *Whigs.* About 1657 *Whig* was applied contemptuously to all Presbyterians and Covenanters in Scotland. In this sense the term became common in England and after the Restoration of Charles II in 1660 the Roundheads were called Whigs to distinguish them from the Cavaliers.

During the contest over the Exclusion Bill in 1679-1680 those who opposed the succession of the Duke of York on the ground he was a Catholic were called Whigs, and after the "Glorious Revolution of 1688" *Whig* became the name of one of the two great political parties in England and remained so until it was supplanted by *Liberal* in 1831, when there was a realignment of the two great parties. The Whigs in England advocated popular rights, the privileges of Parliament over those of the Crown and toleration to dissenters, and the term became synonymous with moderate liberalism. In 1824 Thomas Jefferson wrote: "The difference between the Whig and Tory of England is, that the Whig deduces his rights from the Anglo-Saxon source, and the Tory from the Norman."

Whig, like *Tory,* was introduced into the English Colonies as a party name early in the eighteenth century, although at first it had little political significance other than to indicate that a person who called himself a Whig sympathized with the Whig Party in the mother country. Most of the Colonists who resisted the Stamp Act of 1765 and later Parliamentary encroachments upon Colonial rights called themselves Whigs. In 1768 William Livingston of New Jersey began to write under the pen name "American Whig." The next year "The American Whig Society" was founded at Princeton. When the American Revolution started the Whigs in America produced the majority of "Patriots" and the Whigs of Great Britain produced the majority of the "friends of America." After the Revolution, during which the Tories, Loyalists and

Royalists were eliminated, *Whig* fell into disuse because there were no distinct political parties in the United States. But *whig* was occasionally used as a synonym for *republican* or *liberal*. On May 15, 1791, Jefferson wrote to Madison that "we have been trying to get another weekly or half weekly paper set up excluding advertising, so that it might go through the states, & furnish a whig vehicle of intelligence," and in 1796, when the sedition bill was pending, he wrote Madison that its purpose was "the suppression of the Whig press."

During the administration of James Monroe (1817-1825) the Federalist Party disappeared from the national stage and only the Democratic Republican Party founded by Jefferson remained. In the election of 1824 all four Presidential candidates—Andrew Jackson, John Quincy Adams, William H. Crawford and Henry Clay—professed to be members of the Democratic-Republican Party. In the election of 1828 President Adams and Jackson were the only candidates for President and their supporters did not have distinctive party names. After Adams's defeat in 1828 the opponents of Jackson adopted the name National Republican Party, while the Jacksonians gradually abandoned the name Democratic-Republican Party in favor of the Democratic Party. On December 13, 1831, the National Republican Convention at Baltimore nominated Clay for President and John Sergeant of Pennsylvania for Vice President.

After the defeat of Clay and Sergeant by Jackson and Martin Van Buren in 1832 the National Republicans began to give thought to the organization of a party that could effectively oppose the Jacksonians. There was a widespread feeling among the National Republicans that the name of their party was unsatisfactory. Duff Green's Washington *Telegraph,* which supported Clay, shortened *National Republicans* to *Nationals,* but the name did not catch the popular fancy. Then *Democratic Whig* was suggested and used to some extent in 1832 and 1833, but it also failed of general adoption. Finally the National Republicans gradually began to call themselves Whigs, a term that had just been abandoned as a party name in Great Britain and that recalled memories of the Patriots of Revolutionary days. Just who suggested the revival of *Whig* is not known for certain. The suggestion is variously attributed to Duff Green, James Watson Webb, editor of the *Morning Courier* and New York *Enquirer* and Philip Hone, New York businessman and one of the Whig leaders. Hone himself claimed the distinction of having named the party. The first time he used it in his diary was under date of April 8, 1834, when he wrote that "the Whig Party, whose candidate for mayor is Mr. Verplanck, are active, zealous and confident of success." After that he used *Whig* to the exclusion of *National Republican*. On June 18,

1840, Hone wrote: "Even Gen. Harrison, in whose support all the good men of the country who are banded together under the name of Whigs (a name, by the by, to which I stood godfather, having been the first to use it at a political meeting of which I was president at Washington Hall)..." One of the earliest known uses of the new name in print occurs in Niles' *Register* for April 12, 1834: "In New York and Connecticut the term *Whigs* is now used by the opponents of the administration when speaking of themselves." About the same time the Jacksonians began to refer to their opposition as Whigs. John Quincy Adams was slow to accept the new name of the party that had fallen to pieces under his leadership. *Whig* does not occur in his diary until 1835. On March 27 of that year he wrote, "The Whigs are to have a convention at Baltimore next December to nominate a candidate," and on November 18, 1836, he referred to "The Whigs, as they now call themselves." Even as late as September 10, 1837, Old Man Eloquent wrote that Stephen C. Phillips "told me that there has been a meeting of a small number of the members of the party now calling themselves Whigs . . ." But the majority of the members of the party quickly adopted the name Whig in 1834 soon after it had been proposed. Webb, whom some credit with reviving the old term as a party name thought it appropriate because the party was opposed to Jackson's "executive usurpation" and historically the term was associated in both England and America with opposition to royal authority.

The formation of the new Whig Party was due largely to Henry Clay and Daniel Webster. In a sense the Whigs in the United States were the spiritual heirs and successors of the defunct Federalists. Adams, referring to a Jacksonian victory in Connecticut, wrote on April 11, 1835: "It is another downfall of federalism under the name of Whigs." *Federalist,* however, was an odious term at that time and the supporters of William Henry Harrison emphatically denied that their candidate had ever been a Federalist. Clay was the patron saint of the new Whig Party and his "American System" was presumed to be its cornerstone. But in another sense it was a loose confederation rather than a fusion of former Federalists, former National Republicans, former Anti-Masons, Jackson's personal enemies and others opposed to his regime. It was a party of expediency without real objects and united only in a common desire to oust Jackson from power. It advocated rechartering the Bank of the United States, internal improvements, a protective tariff and keeping the slavery issue out of partisan politics.

Clay, who had done more than any other man to promote the new Whig Party, did not think Vice President Van Buren, Jackson's candi-

date for President to succeed him in 1836, could be beaten and did not seek the Whig nomination, with the result that no national Whig convention was held and the strength of the new party was divided among four Whig candidates who had been nominated only by State legislatures and conventions. The fact is that if the Whigs had united on one candidate he probably could have won. Even as it was, William Henry Harrison, without a national nomination, received 736,656 popular votes as against Van Buren's 761,549. Van Buren received 170 electoral votes; Harrison, 73; Hugh L. White, 26; Daniel Webster, 14, and Willie P. Mangum, 11. What is more significant is that the Whigs elected 115 members of the House of Representatives as against 117 Jacksonians. Since 10 independents were elected to the House this meant that the Jacksonians lost control of Congress.

With victory in sight for the Whigs, Clay wanted the nomination in 1840, but Harrison's good showing in 1836 made him the natural candidate and he was nominated by the Whig National Convention that met in Harrisburg, Pennsylvania, in December 1839. This convention met in the Zion Lutheran Church and Harrison has been the only successful Presidential candidate of a major political party nominated in a church. When messengers from Harrisburg told Clay that Harrison had been nominated, he said: "I am the most unfortunate man in the history of parties; always run by my friends when sure to be defeated, and now betrayed for a nomination when I, or anybody, would be sure of an election." Clay, as a National Republican and a Whig, had a large following in the South and many of the "landed aristocrats" of the South adhered to the Whig Party. It has been estimated that two-thirds of the slaves in the United States were owned by the Whigs in 1840. To attract the votes of conservative Whigs and anti-Jacksonians in the South the Whig convention of 1839 nominated John Tyler, a Virginia slaveowner, for Vice President. Tyler had served as a U.S. Representative, Governor, and U.S. Senator as a Democratic-Republican and was not really a Whig at all, but he was opposed to Jackson and often referred to as a Whig.

In the election of 1840 the popular vote was 1,275,017 for Harrison, 1,128,702 for Van Buren and 7,000 for Birney. But Harrison received 234 electoral votes as against only 60 for Van Buren, and the Whigs elected a majority in both houses of Congress. Harrison "died of the Presidency" 30 days after he took office, before the Whigs could put through their program, and Tyler, at heart a States' Rights Democrat rather than a Whig, became President "by act of Providence." All the Whigs except Secretary of State Webster got out of the Cabinet and the President vetoed the bank bill and opposed most of the other Whig measures. The

Whigs deserted Tyler and the Democrats refused to support him. With only "a corporal's guard" of supporters, he became "a President without a party."

As early as November 5, 1841, John Quincy Adams wrote at Boston: "The Whig party, as they call themselves, is splitting into a thousand fragments." But Clay thought the Whigs had a chance to win again in 1844 and accordingly sought and obtained the Whig nomination for President. His running mate was Theodore Frelinghuysen of New Jersey. They were nominated in a church in Baltimore. The Democrats, after discarding former President Van Buren by use of the two-thirds rule, nominated James K. Polk for President and George Mifflin Dallas of Pennsylvania for Vice President. President Tyler, though elected as a Whig, was a States' Rights Democrat at heart and wanted the Democratic nomination himself, but the Democrats would not consider him. A Tyler convention composed of several hundred delegates met at Baltimore at the same time as the Democratic convention and nominated Tyler for President, but made no nomination for Vice President. Shortly thereafter, however, Tyler withdrew and he and most of his handful of supporters joined the Democrats. In the election of 1844 the popular vote was 1,377,243 for Polk, 1,299,068 for Clay and 62,300 for Birney. Polk received 170 electoral votes and Clay 105. The Democrats elected a majority in both houses of Congress.

In 1848 the Whigs passed by Clay and nominated Zachary Taylor for President and Millard Fillmore of New York for Vice President. Before the Whig convention met the Baltimore *Clipper* quoted a Kentucky backwoodsman as saying: "The national convention be damned—I tell you General Taylor is going to be elected by spontaneous combustion!" The Democrats nominated Lewis Cass of Michigan for President and William O. Butler of Kentucky for Vice President. Taylor received 1,360,601 popular votes and Cass 1,220,444. The electoral vote was 163 for Taylor and 127 for Cass, but the Whigs failed to elect a majority in either house of Congress. Taylor died fifteen months after taking office and Fillmore became President. It was Fillmore, the third and last Whig President, who signed the bills known as the Compromise of 1850, sponsored by Clay as a final solution of the slavery question. But the slavery question would not stay solved and it was this issue that finally wrecked the Whig Party.

In 1846 a Boston merchant named Thomas G. Carey opposed a set of antislavery resolutions under consideration in the Massachusetts legislature on the ground they would offend the South and hurt business. Ebenezer Rockwood Hoar of Middlesex replied that he thought the legislature should represent the conscience as well as the cotton of the commonwealth. After that members of the party in the North who opposed slavery were known as "Conscience Whigs" and those who put the preservation of the Union above all other issues were known as "Cotton Whigs." The Cotton Whigs were also called "Snuff-Takers," from the fact that snuff-pinching was more common in the South than in the North. Another name for the Conscience Whigs was "Woolly-Heads," an allusion to their sympathy for the Negro slaves. Whigs in general were nicknamed "Coons," which was suggested by the fact that during the Harrison log cabin and hard cider campaign in 1840 the Whigs adopted the raccoon as their emblem. DOWN WITH THE COONS was an inscription on a banner carried in a Democratic parade in New York City in 1844. Conservative Whigs, who adhered to the original principles of the party, were known as "Old-Line Whigs."

In 1852 the Whigs nominated General Winfield Scott for President and William A. Graham of North Carolina for Vice President, while the Democrats nominated Franklin Pierce of New Hampshire for President and William Rufus King of Alabama for Vice President. The popular vote in the election was 1,601,474 for Pierce, 1,386,578 for Scott, and 156,159 for John P. Hale, the Free Soil candidate. Pierce received 254 electoral votes and Scott 42. After this defeat, despite the large popular vote received by Scott, the Whig Party was so demoralized that it never nominated another candidate for President. Most of the Southern Whigs joined the Democratic Party, while the majority of the Old-Line Whigs of the North joined the new Republican Party, although some of them took temporary refuge in the American Party. The American Party convention met at Philadelphia on February 20, 1856, and nominated Millard Fillmore for President. What was left of the Whig Party held a convention at Baltimore on September 17 of the same year and endorsed the American Party's nominations.

During the less than twenty years the party was in existence under that name the Whigs elected only two Presidents. Both of them were military heroes and both died in office.

Who were the Barnburners and Hunkers?

In the early 1840's the Democrats in New York split into two factions over the use to be made of canal revenues. The conservatives, later called Hunkers, wanted to use these funds to complete the canal system, while the radicals, later called Barnburners, wanted to use such funds to pay the State debt. When the Hunkers came out for annexation of Texas and the extension of slavery and the Barnburners for the Wilmot Proviso and restriction of slavery the split became irrevocable.

The Barnburners received their nickname because their opponents compared them to the Dutch farmer who burned down his barn to get rid of the rats. The implication was that they were willing to scuttle the canal and public improvement program to get rid of the abuses connected with it. At that time *Hunker* was synonymous with "conservative." In some children's games the goal, home, den or base was called the *hunk,* from Dutch *honk,* "post." When a player reached the home base he cried "honk" or "hunk," meaning he was "safe." *Hunker* came to signify "in a safe place" or "in a good condition or position." By extension it acquired the meaning of a conservative, one satisfied with conditions or one opposed to innovations, new issues, change or progress. A person who was "all right" or O.K. was said to be *hunky.* Some authorities suppose that *hunky* in *hunky-dory* is from the same source. In 1859 John Russell Bartlett defined *Hunkers* as "Those who cling to the homestead or to old principles." The theory that Hunkers were so called because they "hankered" after public office and patronage appears to be without foundation.

Former President Martin Van Buren and Silas Wright were leaders of the Barnburners, while William L. Marcy and William C. Bouck were the leaders of the Hunkers. In 1847 the two factions held separate conventions and in 1848 they both sent delegations to the Democratic National Convention, from which the Barnburners withdrew and supported the Free Soil Party, which nominated Van Buren for President and Charles Francis Adams for Vice President. In the end most of the Barnburners joined the Republican Party. The Hunkers, who had gotten control of the State party machinery, themselves split into two factions during the campaign of 1852. The "Hardshells" or "Hards" supported Pierce, while the "Softshells" or "Softs" opposed him. Francis P. Blair, Jr., who voted for Van Buren in 1848, established a free-soil newspaper in Missouri known as *The Barnburner.*

What is a whipping boy?

A whipping boy is a scapegoat, one punished for the shortcomings of another. The original whipping boy was a boy educated with a young prince. When the student prince, whose royal person was inviolable, committed an offense worthy of punishment his companion was flogged in his stead. *Whipping boy* in this sense is traced by the Oxford dictionary to 1647. Barnaby Fitzpatrick was whipping boy for Edward VI and

Mango Murray for Charles I of England when they were crown princes. In *Gil Blas* Le Sage says that Raphael, the Italian Renaissance painter, was whipped for the son of the Marquis de Leganez, but the budding artist, seeing no justice in the whipping-boy arrangement, ran away. Whipping one person symbolically for the sins of others was an ancient practice. Figuratively, a cabinet officer, a military commander or other public official is often made the scapegoat or whipping boy for conditions for which he is not personally responsible. On February 20, 1943, Thomas L. Stokes, Washington columnist, wrote: "The bureaucrat is an ideal whipping boy, impersonal and aloof." Secretary of Labor Lewis B. Schwellenbach said that "an attempt is being made to make labor the whipping boy for the high cost of living."

What was the Know-Nothing Party?

There never was a political party in the United States officially known as the Know-Nothing Party. That was merely the nickname of a native American movement that first attracted public attention in the early 1840's.

Most of the original settlers in the thirteen English Colonies in America were Protestants. The majority of them were anti-Catholic, but Catholics were not numerous enough in the Colonies, except in Maryland, to play a large part in politics and Catholicism was seldom a serious issue. In the pre-Revolutionary period Catholicism first became a national issue in 1774, when the British Parliament passed the Quebec Act, which virtually established the Catholic Church in the Northwest Territory. But during and immediately after the Revolution the question subsided and attracted little attention until after large numbers of Catholic immigrants began to settle in America.

In 1834 a mob attacked and burned the Ursuline Convent at Charlestown near Boston, and in 1838 a serious clash took place between "natives" and Irish in New York City. "The Society of Native American Citizens" in New York City, composed chiefly of Whigs, took an active part in supporting William Henry Harrison for President in 1840. The next year Governor William H. Seward of New York recommended and the legislature passed an act authorizing the use of State money to establish separate schools for the children of foreigners and to pay the salaries of teachers of their own faith and language. There was a storm of disapproval. Bishop John Hughes, a native of Ireland, who in 1850 became the first Catholic archbishop of New York, was charged by the natives with having inspired the act, which was repealed by the next legislature.

On October 29, 1841, Bishop Hughes delivered an address in Carroll Hall in which he advocated State support of religious schools and urged Catholic voters in New York to act together to obtain their ends. Soon thereafter a secret political party known first as the American Republican Party and finally as the Native American Party sprang up in New York and spread to New England, Pennsylvania and other States. Lewis Charles Levin (1808-1860), who had been born and educated in South Carolina, helped form the Native American Party in Pennsylvania and published at Philadelphia a "penny daily" called the *Sun* to promote the movement. In 1842 a mob in New York City attacked the house of Bishop Hughes. On November 7, 1843, Philip Hone wrote in his diary at New York:

The election was held today. Besides the two great party tickets, there is a new party which has polled most unexpectedly five or six thousand votes. They call themselves the American party, and are opposed to the extension of suffrage to foreigners; . . . with this powerful demonstration of popular opinion in their favor, I should not be surprised if ere long they should swallow up the Whig party. This new movement has occasioned a great defection from both parties.

Hone on April 13, 1844, reported:

Charter Election. The Native Americans have carried everything. An overwhelming torrent, which a twelfthmonth since was an insignificant rivulet, has swept away Whig and Loco-focos. Mr. James Harper is elected mayor by a majority of 4,000 over Mr. Caddington; the strongholds of the old belligerents are broken up by this new irruption, and nobody knows where he stands or who are his associates.

During the summer of 1844 friction between the Native Americans and Catholics resulted in a series of riots in Philadelphia in which twenty-four persons were killed and two churches were burned and other Catholic property destroyed. These disorders almost reached the proportions of civil war and were suppressed only by State troops. Daniel J. Desmond, consul general of the Papal States in the United States, whose house was in Philadelphia, appealed to Secretary of State John C. Calhoun for protection as a recognized diplomatic representative. Calhoun did not share Desmond's apprehensions of personal danger and told him that there never had been "a single instance known, where diplomatic or consul representatives, or any public functionary residing here had been molested, during public outbreaks." While the riots were in progress Levin counseled his followers to be moderate and to respect Catholic property to maintain the honor of the movement. There were, during the same period, anti-Catholic riots in Baltimore and New Orleans. On June 29, 1844, Representative John Quincy Adams wrote in his diary:

I requested of the clerk . . . a copy of the memorial of A. De Kalb Tarr and 179 citizens of Philadelphia, praying for an alteration of the naturalization laws so as to require twenty-one years of residence for foreigners before admitting them to all the privileges of native Americans. This was the first memorial presented to the House on the subject. . . . I declared in the House that I should not hold myself bound to support the demand in the House; but at the next session the Native American party will be heard in both Houses . . .

On the following July 4 Adams wrote:

I wrote this day a letter to W. D. Barnes and A. De Kalb Tarr, in answer to that which they addressed to me with the memorial calling for alteration of the naturalization laws . . . . The Native Americans are falling into the blunders of the abolition societies. They have an excellent cause, which they will ruin by mismanagement. The Native Americans, like the Anti-Masons, will have a momentary and limited success, but the staff will break in their hands and lay them in the dust.

Hone noted in his diary on November 5, 1844: "State election. The Whigs abandoned all their local candidates and went en masse for the Native Americans." In Philadelphia Levin was elected to Congress on the Native American ticket. The Whigs suffered politically from their apparent alliance with the Native Americans in the election of 1844. Some authorities believe that it was this issue that turned the tide in favor of James K. Polk, the Democratic nominee, and against Henry Clay, the Whig nominee. Immigrants were entering the country by the thousands and the activities of the Native Americans caused nearly all foreign-born citizens to support the Democrats.

Under the leadership of Congressman Levin, the Native Americans held a Pennsylvania State convention at Harrisburg on February 22, 1845, and a national convention at Philadelphia later in the same year. During his three terms in Congress, Levin was untiring in his efforts to extend the party throughout the Union. In December, 1845, a coalition of Native Americans and Whigs chose Josiah Quincy, Jr., mayor of Boston, "the Natives having observed," in Hone's words, "that they and the Whigs were of the same family."

During the next few years very little was heard of the Native Americans, but members of the movement in different States organized units variously known as "The Sons of '76," "The Order of the Star-Spangled Banner" and "Order of the United Americans," which were secret, oath-bound societies with grips and passwords. After the adoption of the Compromise of 1850, which was supposed to be a permanent settlement of the slavery question, and especially after 1852, when the Whigs were defeated in the Presidential election and began to break up as a party, there was a resurgence of Native Americanism.

In 1859 John Russell Bartlett quoted the New York *Times* as saying that the Native Americans received their nickname in 1853, after their leader in New York, who called himself Ned Buntline, instructed members of the organization to guard its secrets carefully and when asked by outsiders what they stood for to reply, "I don't know" or "I know nothing about it." From this circumstance people began to call them, first, "Don't Knows" and finally "Know-Nothings." *Know-nothing* in the sense of an ignorant person, one "green as a pumpkin vine," had been used as early as 1828. *Harper's Magazine* for August, 1854, said: "A secret combination designated as 'Know-Nothings' have operated with much success in local elections in many of the larger places." In the same year the *Southern Literary Messenger* predicated that "This-Know-Nothing movement will prove to be a giant evil."

Passage of the Kansas-Nebraska Bill in 1854 brought the slavery issue to the fore more acutely than ever. Northern Whigs opposed to the extension of slavery were called Anti-Nebraska Men. In the election of 1854 the Know-Nothings showed considerable strength and created consternation among the old parties. Until then the Know-Nothings had not been taken seriously as a political force and they slipped up on the Whigs and Democrats unawares. Although they had met in secret, chosen their candidates behind closed doors, published no platform and campaigned only by word of mouth, they carried Massachusetts, Pennsylvania and Delaware in the State elections and came close to defeating Horatio Seymour for Governor in New York. About this time the Native Americans began to be called "Hindoos," from the fact that their candidate in New York, Daniel Ullman, was charged by his enemies with having been born in Calcutta, India, and not being a native of America. For some unknown reason, perhaps because of the Know-Nothing's professed attachment to Uncle Sam, a member of the secret party was called "Sam." At Cincinnati, Ohio, Rutherford B. Hayes wrote to his Uncle Sardis Birchard on October 13, 1854: "Anti-Nebraska, Know-Nothings, and general disgust with the powers that be, have carried this county by between seven and eight thousand majority! How people do hate Catholics, and what happiness it was to thousands to have a chance to show it in what seemed a lawful and patriotic manner."

George Frisbie Hoar, in *Autobiography of Seventy Years* (1903) wrote in reference to 1854:

This (Kansas-Nebraska Bill) created strong excitement among the people of Massachusetts, and the Know-Nothing movement came that fall, inspired more by the desire of the people to get rid of the old parties and form a new anti-slavery party, than by any real opposition to foreigners, which was its avowed principle. The party swept Massachusetts, electing all the State officers and every member of the State Legislature except two. . . . They had rather a sorry Legislature. It was the duty of the outgoing Governor to administer the oath to the Representatives and Senators-elect. Governor Washburn performed that duty, and added: "Now, gentlemen, so far as the oath of office is concerned, you are qualified to enter upon your duties."

Among the Know-Nothings elected to the legislature was Henry Wilson, afterward Vice President of the United States. Hoar also wrote:

It is a remarkable fact that of the men known to join the Know-Nothing Party, no man, unless he were exceedingly young and obscure when he did it, ever maintained or regained the public confidence afterward, with the exception of Henry Wilson, Anson Burlingame and Nathaniel P. Banks. These men all left it after the first year. Wilson and Burlingame denounced it with all the vigor at their command, and Banks led the forces of the Republican Party to its overthrow.

Until after the State and Congressional elections of 1854 the Know-Nothings had tried to continue as a secret political organization that favored restrictions on "undesirable immigration," extension of the waiting time for citizenship to twenty-one years and the exclusion of naturalized citizens from public office. Irish Catholic immigrants were coming into the country by the thousands and the Know-Nothings were primarily opposed to them. The slogan of the Know-Nothings was "Americans must rule America." Naturally the foreign-born, Protestants as well as Catholics, distrusted the Whigs, because many of the Know-Nothings were Whigs in disguise. The effect of the activities of the Know-Nothings was to drive most of the foreign-born citizens into the Democratic fold and to discredit the Whig Party.

By 1855 the Know-Nothings began to discard much of their secrecy and to come out in the open as a political party under the name of "The American Party." In that year the party split over the slavery question. At a meeting of the national council in Philadelphia the Southern delegates, called "South Americans," obtained adoption of a resolution declaring it the policy of the organization "to maintain the existing laws upon the subject of slavery." Many of the Northern Know-Nothings, known as "North Americans," were opposed to the extension of slavery in the territories and seceded from the party and formed their own organization.

On August 24, 1855, Abraham Lincoln, an "Old-Line Whig," wrote to Joshua F. Speed: "Our progress in degeneracy appears to me to be pretty rapid. As a nation, we began by declaring that 'all men are created equal.' . . . When the Know-Nothings get control, it will read, 'All men are created equal except Negroes and foreigners and Catholics.' "

"South Americanism" spread rapidly in Delaware, Kentucky, Alabama, Georgia, Tennessee and other slave States. The Know-Nothings were so strong in Virginia in 1855 that the regular Democrats despaired of success and didn't nominate a candidate for Governor, but Henry A. Wise, who had served in Congress as a Whig, a Democrat and a Tylerite, was nominated by a combination of Tidewater and trans-Allegheny delegates and beat the Know-Nothings after a spectacular campaign. On one occasion, at a political mass meeting in an open field, Wise, while orating how the poor and downtrodden of Europe had sought liberty in this land of the free and home of the brave, saw a foreign-born peddler in the crowd. Intending to hold up this immigrant as an illustration of his theme, Wise pointed at the peddler and asked: "Is it not true, my friend, that you left your native country and came across the sea to America to enjoy the blessings of liberty and our free institutions?" To Wise's chagrin, the peddler replied: "No, sir, Governor, I came to America to sell ready-made clothing cheap."

On February 2, 1856, Nathaniel P. Banks of Massachusetts, elected to Congress as a member of the American Party, was chosen Speaker of the U.S. House of Representatives. Rutherford B. Hayes wrote to his friend Guy M. Bryan in Texas on April 16, 1856: "Not being a K. N. (Know-Nothing) I am left as a sort of waif on the political sea with symptoms of a mild sort towards Black Republicanism." In February, 1856, the American Party held it first national convention and nominated for President former President Millard Fillmore, who was then traveling in Europe. His running mate was Andrew Jackson Donelson of Tennessee, a nephew of Rachel Jackson, who had been brought up virtually as a son of Andrew Jackson at the Hermitage and who had served as his secretary in the White House. Fillmore, who had been elected to the New York legislature in 1828 as an Anti-Mason, attributed his defeat for Governor in 1844 to "the Abolitionists and foreign Catholics." "Peace at Any Price; Peace and Union" was the campaign slogan of the American Party. This party provided a convenient halfway house for those Whigs who had not made up their minds on the slavery question and in September, 1856, a remnant of the Whig Party, a mere ghost of the party that had elected two Presidents, held a convention in Baltimore and confirmed the nominations of Fillmore and Donelson, the American Party nominees. The conservative Whigs who supported Fillmore were known as "Silver Grays," from a remark that an unusually large number of the delegates who walked out of the New York State Whig convention were gray-haired men. But many antislavery Whigs refused to support Fillmore and joined the new Republican Party. The American Party platform condemned truckling to European powers and advocated immediate removal from office of all "foreigners and ultraists," while the Democratic platform rebuked the American Party for its "political crusade against Catholic and foreign-born." The North Americans held a separate convention and endorsed Frémont, the Republican candidate, for President, but nominated a candidate of their own for Vice President. In the election of 1856 the popular vote was 1,838,169 for James Buchanan, Democrat; 1,341,264 for John C. Frémont, Republican, and 874,534 for Fillmore, American. Buchanan received 174 electoral votes and Frémont 114, while Fillmore received only the eight electoral votes of Maryland.

After its defeat in 1856 the American Party had little strength except in a few Eastern cities and in the Border States. In 1857 the Know-Nothings became active in Texas, and the next year they gained control of Kentucky. By this time most of the Northern Know-Nothings had joined the Republicans, but the Border-State Unionist unwilling to join the Democrats, still remained in the American Party. The Congress that met on December 5, 1859, contained twenty-seven American Representatives, all but four of whom were from the South, and two "South American" Senators.

When the Northern and Southern Democrats split in 1860 and nominated Stephen A. Douglas and John C. Breckinridge for President and Vice President respectively, the remnant of the American Party joined the new Constitutional Union Party, which held a convention at Nashville and nominated John Bell of Tennessee for President and Edward Everett of Massachusetts for Vice President. Bell, who had been both Democrat and Whig, was a former Speaker of the U.S. House of Representatives, Secretary of War and U.S. Senator. This "fourth party" advocated "the Union, the Constitution and the enforcement of the laws" and was a more moderate proslavery party than the regular Southern Democrats. In the election of 1860 Bell received 591,900 popular votes and the 39 electoral votes of Virginia, Kentucky and Tennessee, all border proslavery States. Lincoln, Republican, received 106 electoral votes and 1,865,913 popular votes; Breckinridge, Southern Democrat, received 72 electoral votes and 848,404 popular votes, and Douglas, Northern Democrat, received 12 electoral votes and 1,374,664 popular votes. The Know-Nothings who joined the Republican Party between 1856 and 1860 probably made the nomination of Lincoln possible. William H. Seward, once an Anti-Mason, had opposed the anti-foreign program of the Native Americans and they did much in the convention to stop Seward and to pave the way for Lincoln's nomination.

Know-Nothingism was swallowed up by slavery, secession and other issues and as an organization rapidly disappeared after the war started in 1861. But there were echoes of the movement many years after the war. During the Hayes-Tilden campaign the Republican nominee was charged by the Democrats with having been a Know-Nothing in his younger days. On September 15, 1876, Governor Hayes wrote Carl Schurz: "I was not a Know-nothing when my political associates generally ran off after that ephemeral party." And on October 12 Hayes wrote Schurz: "Your reply to the Know-nothing charge is ample, and fully authorized by me and the facts. We should set off against it the Gray Nuns Act of Tilden." What Hayes referred to as the Gray Nuns Act was a bill passed early in 1875 by the New York legislature authorizing a Catholic order of Gray Nuns to grant teaching certificates acceptable in the public schools of the State. Governor Tilden had not sponsored the bill but signed it. There was so much protest that the legislature repealed the act in 1876 and Tilden signed the repeal.

Why is a phony candidate called a stalking-horse?

The original stalking-horse was a horse used as a blind by hunters in stalking game. Wild animals and birds generally take horses for granted and hunters concealed themselves behind a trained horse to get within shooting range without alarming their quarry. *Stalking-horse* was applied to a horse used in this manner by fowlers as early as 1519. Sometimes a dummy horse or a portable screen resembling a horse was used instead of a real horse. Figuratively the term came to mean decoy, sham, pretext or any person or thing put forward to conceal or mask real intentions, designs or plans. Shakespeare uses the term only once. In *As You Like It* the banished Duke says of Touchstone: "He uses his folly like a stalking-horse and under the presentation of that he shoots his wit." Politically, a stalking-horse is a candidate who runs to split the opposition and without expecting to win himself. In *Garner of Texas* (1948) Bascom N. Timmons, referring to Vice President John N. Garner's candidacy for President in 1940, wrote: "He said that he would not be a stalking-horse and if he did allow the use of his name he would mean what he said about his candidacy."

Are election bets legal?

Courts have held that a wager by a participant on the outcome of an election is against public policy and void on the ground it tends to corrupt the election. Several States have laws that disqualify a person who has bet on the result from voting if he is challenged at the polls.

During the campaign of 1864 August Belmont, New York banker and sportsman, who was chairman of the Democratic National Committee at the time, made two wagers on the outcome of the Lincoln-McClellan contest. He bet $10,000 that if Lincoln was elected the war would last through his second term and the Union would be broken up, and the same amount that if McClellan was elected peace would be made and the Union restored before the end of his term. On election day Belmont's right to vote in New York City was challenged on the ground he had bet on the result of the election. The chairman of the Democratic National Committee left the polling place without voting.

Martin Van Buren was a born gambler and was fond of betting on the outcome of elections. On November 3, 1836, former President John Quincy Adams wrote in his diary: "This bolstering up of mediocrity would seem not suited to sustain much enthusiasm; but a practice has crept in of betting largely upon the issue of elections, and that adds a spur of private, personal, and pecuniary interest to the impulse of patriotism. This is the exciting cause of all the ardor which we have met with throughout the journey."

Freak election bets are an old American custom. In 1856 Ben Perley Poore, Washington correspondent and columnist, declared publicly that if former President Millard Fillmore, the Know-Nothing candidate for President, did not carry Massachusetts in the election he would wheel a barrel of apples from Newburyport, his home town, to Boston. Although this was not a bet, Poore kept his promise. In a two-day trip he trundled a barrel of apples from Newburyport to the State House in Boston, where a cheering crowd waited for him.

Betting on national elections, individually and through brokers, is now "big business" in the United States and totals many millions of dollars. The "betting odds" are often taken as an indication of the outcome of an election.

Why is an ultraconservative called a die-hard?

Die-hard in its political sense was borrowed from British usage. To *die hard* is an old English phrase meaning to die with a struggle or fighting for life and resisting death to the last gasp.

During the Peninsular War a British, Portuguese and Spanish army under General Beresford defeated a French army under Marshal Soult at Albuera in Spain on May 16, 1811. Just before the battle Colonel William Inglis of the 57th Foot, a West Middlesex regiment, said in an address to his men: "Die hard, my lads of the 57th, die hard!" The Colonel himself was wounded, his banner pierced by 30 bullets, and 23 officers out of 24 and 414 men out of 584 were killed or wounded. After that the 57th Foot Regiment was known as the Die-Hards.

In the nineteenth century *die-hard* was applied in England to the Tories who stoutly resisted all reform of the House of Lords and the Unionists who fought Irish Home Rule to the last ditch. From this *die-hard* came to signify any extreme and uncompromising partisan in politics, particularly an ultraconservative who never says die. In American politics the term is synonymous with *standpatter, bourbon, old guard, stalwart* and *irreconcilable.*

How did the rooster become a Democratic emblem?

In 1840 a man named Joseph Chapman was the Democratic candidate for the Indiana legislature from Hancock County. It was soon after the panic in Van Buren's administration and prospects looked gloomy for the Democrats. William Henry Harrison, who had been defeated by Van Buren in 1836, was again the Whig candidate against "the Little Magician."

George Pattison, editor of *The Constitution,* an Indianapolis newspaper, wrote the following letter to William Sebastian of Greenfield on June 12, 1840:

I have been informed by a Democrat that in one part of your County thirty Van Buren men have turned for Harrison. Please let me know if such be the fact. Hand this letter to General Milroy. I think such a deplorable state of facts cannot exist. If so, I will visit Hancock and address the people relative to the policy of the Democratic Party. I have no time to spare, but I will refuse to eat or sleep or rest so long as anything can be done. Do, for heaven's sake, stir up the Democracy. See Chapman, tell him not to do as he did heretofore. He used to create unnecessary alarms; *he must crow;* we have much to crow over. I will insure this County to give a Democratic majority of two hundred votes. Spare no pains. Write instanter.

This letter was secretly copied at the post office by a Whig and on June 16 of the same year it was printed in the Indianapolis *Semi-Weekly Journal,* the leading Whig newspaper in the State, with a view of ridiculing the Democrats.

But it had just the opposite effect. "Crow, Chapman, crow" became the slogan of the Indiana Democrats. The phrase caught the popular ear and became known all over the nation. When the *Indiana State Sentinel*, a Democratic paper, was launched at Indianapolis on July 21, 1841, the masthead included a large picture of a rooster with the legend CROW, CHAPMAN, CROW. Although the Democrats were soundly trounced by the Whigs in the election of 1840, the rooster became the popular emblem of the Democratic Party and still is used as the party emblem on the tickets in several States.

Although the Chapman incident undoubtedly popularized the rooster as the Democratic emblem, some authorities believe that the bird was associated with the Democrats before publication of Pattison's letter to Sebastian and that it was adopted because the cock has been regarded since ancient times as the herald of dawn, a new day and victory. In his life of Lincoln, Albert Beveridge wrote: "June 4, 1840, a monster Whig demonstration took place in Springfield. Processions paraded the streets. Hardin marched holding high a banner with the device of a dead rooster on its back." That date is twelve days earlier than the publication of Pattison's letter in which he referred to Chapman. But there is no evidence that the rooster was used as the Democratic emblem earlier than the campaign of 1840. "The Democratic papers," reported the Quincy *Herald* on June 2, 1843, "announce every victory with the heading of a crowing rooster." Some Democrats insist that the Democratic emblem is the gamecock rather than the ordinary barnyard variety of rooster.

What former Speaker of the House became President?

James Knox Polk (1795-1849), a native of North Carolina but a resident of Tennessee when elected, has been the only Speaker of the House of Representatives who later became President.

He was first elected to Congress in 1824 and served as Speaker of the House from 1835 to 1839, when he retired from Congress to become Governor of Tennessee. In 1844 he was elected President on the Democratic ticket with George M. Dallas, of Pennsylvania, as Vice President. He served one term and refused to run for a second. Polk was President during the Mexican War, which the Whigs called "Polk's War." He was a teetotaler and Sam Houston said of him that he was "a victim of the exclusive use of water as a beverage."

Although most Speakers of the House are regarded as potential candidates for the Presidency, no person has been nominated for the Presidency while Speaker. Three former Speakers—Henry Clay of Kentucky,

John Bell of Tennessee and James G. Blaine of Maine—were nominated for the Presidency by major parties but were defeated, while four Speakers—Thomas B. Reed of Maine, Joseph G. Cannon of Illinois, Champ Clark of Missouri and John N. Garner of Texas—were active aspirants for the Presidency but failed to be nominated. In 1844, when the Democrats nominated Polk and the Whigs nominated Clay, both candidates were former Speakers and that has been the only campaign in which that occurred.

When did political parties first adopt platforms?

Party platforms originated at the same time that national nominating conventions did. It is often said that the Jeffersonian Republicans adopted the first national party platform in 1800, but no platforms in the modern sense of the terms were adopted by American political parties until after 1830.

The Anti-Masonic Party in 1831, at the first national nominating convention in the United States, adopted an address to the people, and in a sense this was the first written platform of a national political party. The National Republican convention that met later in the same year and nominated Henry Clay for President did not adopt a platform, but it issued an address to the people and a call for another convention to meet in Washington, D.C., the next spring. The address to the people favored internal improvements, a protective tariff, renewal of the charter of the United States Bank and removal of the Cherokee Indians from their lands in the South to the territory west of the Mississippi. The ratifying convention at Washington on May 11, 1832, known as the Young Men's National Republican Convention, endorsed Clay for President and adopted a formal platform, which consisted of ten resolutions embodying the principles and policies of the party.

The first Democratic National Convention, which met in 1832, followed suit and adopted a platform of sorts. In 1836 the Democratic National Convention adopted a platform, but the new Whig Party, which held no national convention, did not do so. The Democratic National Convention of 1840 again adopted a platform, but the Whig National Convention at Harrisburg in 1839, which nominated William Henry Harrison for President, deliberately refrained from adopting a platform or issuing an address to the people. At that time the Whigs were agreed upon only one thing—a common dislike of Andrew Jackson and Martin Van Buren—and they realized that a "declaration of principles" would split up the loosely knit party. So the convention merely emphasized the merits of their candidates—Harrison and John Tyler—and promised nothing. Senator Thomas H. Benton of Missouri observed that "Availability was the only ability sought by the Whigs." Both the Democrats and Whigs adopted platforms in 1844. In 1848 the Democrats adopted a platform, but the Whig convention, which nominated Zachary Taylor for President and Millard Fillmore for Vice President, was composed of many discordant elements and stood for so little that it could not agree upon a platform. After that it became a regular practice for all political parties to adopt a series of resolutions containing a declaration of party principles and policies.

The platform of the Northern Democratic Convention of 1860, which nominated Stephen A. Douglas for President and Hershel V. Johnson for Vice President, was only 360-words long and probably has been the shortest platform adopted by a political party since platforms became an established custom. National parties did not begin to adopt long and elaborate platforms until after the Civil War. Although platforms or substantial parts of them are often taken seriously and carried out when possible, they are designed primarily to "catch votes" and to win the election. The typical platform "points with pride" to the party's record; "views with alarm" what the opposition proposes to do; takes a positive stand on dead issues; straddles important issues on which public opinion is doubtful, and endorses strongly a few proposals that a majority of the voters are believed to favor. In a speech at Des Moines in 1901 President McKinley said: "Our differences are policies, our agreements principles." A train conductor once told a passenger that the platform is to get in on, not to stand on, and many politicians work on that theory.

The earliest known use of *platform* in this peculiar political sense occurs in one of the resolutions which the Democratic National Convention of 1844 adopted and which read: "The Whigs, whether on the Lexington platform or some other non-committal platform, will be and must be at once known as the party that opposed their country in her just and generous war." One might naturally suppose that *platform* in this sense was suggested directly by the wooden platform on which a candidate stood at political meetings and appealed for votes, but such was probably not the case.

Platform is derived from Old French *plateforme*, which literally meant a plane or a flat form. Figuratively the term came to signify first a ground plan, chart, map, blueprint or a draft to build by and then a written outline, sketch, scheme, design or a plan of action. A scheme of philosophy, a system of moral conduct, an ecclesiastical constitution or a plan of church government was called a platform. In *Advancement of*

Learning (1623) Francis Bacon wrote: "The wisdom of a lawmaker consisteth not only in a platform of justice, but in the application thereof." Richard Hooker, in *On the Laws of Ecclesiastical Polity,* mentioned opinions "conformable to the platform of Geneva." A book entitled *A Platform of Church Discipline* was published in London in 1653. Two years later Oliver Cromwell wrote "the things did not work forth your platform." In *Parable of the Pilgrim* (1687) an English controversialist named John Patrick wrote: "He can soon quit the way wherein he was, and become religious, after the manner of this novel platform." *Platform* in the sense of a raised surface formed of planks or boards was common already in the sixteenth century.

When American political parties began to hold national nominating conventions and to adopt platforms the term was familiar in both senses. In the second edition of his *Dictionary of Americanisms* (1859) John Russell Bartlett, quoting Noah Webster's dictionary, says under *platform:* "In some parts of the New England States, an ecclesiastical constitution, or a plan for the government of churches; as, the Saybrook platform.—Webster. The same use of this word is made by English divines." But Bartlett added: "Of late years the word has got into very common u. ᵊ throughout the country to denote the collection of principles avowed by a pᴏᶫᵗical party." Many Americans, with a tendency to interpret figures of speech literally, thought of a political platform as the wooden platform for speakers in a convention hall. As early as 1848 a single declaration in a political platform was already called a plank. A few years later an editor referred to "every plank and splinter of the platform." It was several generations before *platform* in its peculiar political sense was naturalized in England.

Which President was born farthest south?

Andrew Jackson, who was born in the Waxhaw settlement on the North Carolina-South Carolina border, was born farther south than any other President. Zachary Taylor, a native of Virginia, was a resident of Baton Rouge, Louisiana, in 1848 and was living farther south than any other President when elected. Chester A. Arthur, who was born at Fairfield in northern Vermont, was born farther north than any other President and Vice President. Franklin Pierce, who was born at Hillsboro, New Hampshire, was a resident of Concord in the same State when elected and his residence was farther north than any other President. The most southernly born Vice President was John N. Garner of Texas.

What is a dark horse?

Politically speaking, a dark horse is a little-known person who gets a nomination unexpectedly. The term is applied particularly to a person who is not generally mentioned as a possible candidate before a convention but who is unexpectedly nominated as a compromise after the delegates fail to agree upon one of the leading candidates.

The dark horse is generally, although not always, a more or less colorless politician who has not reached national prominence, but who is favorably known in his own State or section as a faithful party wheel horse and is therefore regarded as a "safe" compromise candidate to nominate with a view of harmonizing opposing factions. At national conventions occasionally a mere "favorite son," who at the outset has the support of only his State delegation, turns out to be a dark horse in the race.

Although *dark horse* was not used so early in the sense of a surprise candidate, James Knox Polk, nominated by the Democrats in 1844, is regarded as the first dark horse elected President. His nomination was engineered largely by George Bancroft, the historian, after the Democratic convention became deadlocked on former President Martin Van Buren and Lewis Cass. Van Buren received a majority of the votes but could never get the required two thirds. In *Anecdotes of Public Men* (1872) John W. Forney wrote: "That convention was James Buchanan's first appearance as an aspirant for President, and had he remained in the field he would assuredly have been the candidate against Mr. Clay." During the campaign the Whigs, who nominated Henry Clay, asked sarcastically, "Who is James K. Polk?" in order to create the impression that Polk was "a mediocre nobody."

Actually Polk was already a minor national figure and his nomination was not so accidental as is sometimes supposed. He had served twelve years in the U.S. House of Representatives, had been chairman of the Ways and Means Committee and had been Speaker two terms. He had also served one term as Governor of Tennessee, and was so effective as a campaign speaker that he was known in his own State as "The Napoleon of the Stump." In 1840 Polk was an aspirant for the Vice-Presidential nomination on the Van Buren ticket and had the support of Andrew Jackson, but on that occasion no nomination for Vice President was made. Several years later President Tyler felt out Polk for Secretary of State but the Tennessean was not interested. Polk was again an aspirant for the nomination for Vice President in 1844 and again had the support of Andrew Jackson. When Old Hickory withdrew his support of Van

Buren for President shortly before the convention, largely because the attitude of the Little Magician toward the Texas Question was unsatisfactory, Polk became the candidate of Old Hickory, Silas Wright and other Democratic leaders, who were energetic behind the scenes in grooming Polk for the Presidential nomination, and the fact that he was, before the convention, the choice of Van Buren men for Vice President, made his choice for President easier than it would have been otherwise. In other words, Polk in 1844 was known to nearly every politician in the country and was not so dark at that time as he has been painted. But even so Polk's nomination was a surprise to the country. On July 21, 1846, President Polk wrote in his diary: "Mr. Andrew Jackson, I was informed, said at Baltimore when my nomination was suggested that it was a 'humbug.' "

In general Polk was quite successful as President. He was largely successful in carrying out the four major planks of his platform—a reduction in the tariff, the acquisition of California, the settlement of the Oregon boundary question, and the establishment of an independent treasury. More territory was added to the United States during his administration than during any other administration except that of Jefferson. On November 19, 1845, President Polk, according to his diary, told James Buchanan that it was his "belief that no man would ever be elected President who was prominently before the public for that office for two or three years or a longer time before the nomination." In other words, he thought all future Presidents would be nominated as dark horses like himself. But Buchanan persisted in seeking the nomination and was nominated and elected in 1856.

The second successful dark horse Presidential candidate was Franklin Pierce of New Hampshire, whose surprise nomination in the Democratic convention at Baltimore in 1852 was largely the work of Caleb Cushing. Lewis Cass, James Buchanan, Stephen A. Douglas and William L. Marcy were the leading candidates when the balloting began. Pierce received no votes until the thirty-fifth ballot, and he was nominated on the forty-ninth. When a friend congratulated Pierce upon his nomination, he replied, "Sir, you could not congratulate a more astonished man." The Democrats told the Whigs, "We Polked you in 1844 and we shall Pierce you in 1852," and they did. The successful nominee had served two terms in the U.S. House of Representatives and nearly one term in the U.S. Senate, and was a brigadier general during the Mexican War. On November 8, 1852, Rutherford B. Hayes, wrote to his sister Fanny: "As to the result, Who cares? is a question as hard to answer as was a few months ago, 'Who is General Pierce?' "

Hayes, Republican nominee in 1876, and James A. Garfield, Republican nominee in 1880, were both successful Presidential dark horses in the sense that they did not conduct preconvention campaigns and were not seriously considered for the nominations by the majority of the delegates when the conventions opened. Warren G. Harding, Republican nominee in 1920 is sometimes included among the successful dark horses, but he entered the convention with a bloc of votes and was backed by an organized group of men who were determined to win if possible.

It was natural for political writers and politicians to compare a Presidential contest to a horse race and to borrow terms from the race track. On May 14, 1844, before Polk was nominated, Philip Hone wrote in his diary:

These opinions [of Clay and Van Buren] have left a door open for other would-be candidates, who would struggle upward by means of the most unscrupulous conduct. In this number is General Cass, who after having made himself ridiculous by interfering in affairs with which he had no concern, comes out now in favor of the measure [annexation of Texas] in all its length and breadth, declaring war against Mexico, threatening Great Britain, and scoffing at all the old-fashioned notions in favor of union and harmony. This is the horse on which this demagogue would ride into power.

Dark Horse was originally English racing slang. In the phrase, *dark* means "secret," "hidden" or "unknown." A dark horse is a winning animal about which little is known before the race. It has been suggested that the term may have originated from an old trick practiced by jockeys who dyed the hair of well-known fast horses in order to enter them in races under other names. Such horses were generally dyed black. The jockeys and their friends would then bet large money on the "dark horse" and make a cleanup, much to the surprise of other betters. There appears to be no evidence to support the oft-repeated story that *dark horse* was first applied to a coal-black horse named "Dusky Pete" whose Tennessee owner, Sam Flynn, used to clean up at local races by entering this speedy racer as a mere nondescript nag.

The earliest recorded use of the term that has been found is in Benjamin Disraeli's *The Young Duke* (1831). Disraeli wrote "The first favorite was never heard of, the second favorite was never seen after the distance post, all the ten-to-oners were in the rear, and a dark horse, which had never been thought of, and which the careless St. James had never even observed in the list, rushed past the grand stand in sweeping triumph." In *The Adventures of Philip,* published thirty years later, William Makepeace Thackeray wrote: "Who is the dark horse he has in his stable?" *Dark horse* in its political sense is believed to have been first applied to Hayes in 1876. A writer in *The Century Magazine* for November, 1884, said: "Perhaps he is that mysterious personage known as the 'dark Horse.' " *Race, favorite, runner-up* and *grooming a candidate* are other political terms borrowed from racing.

Why is a conservative referred to as dyed in the wool?

Dyed in the wool originated in the days of vegetable dyes and homespun clothes. When the raw wool was dyed before weaving the coloring lasted better than when the cloth was dyed after weaving. Apparently, however, the dye was not too firm in either case. In 1797 Daniel Webster rode from his father's New Hampshire farm to Dartmouth College at Hanover. "I had the *blues* many days after my arrival," said Webster long afterward, "because a drenching rain had washed the indigo from my new suit dyed in the wool at home, into my skin, coloring it deeply, darkly, beautifully blue." At any rate, *dyed in the wool* came to signify ingrained, thorough or complete.

In its political sense the phrase dates from the Jackson era. On May 22, 1830, Representative John Quincy Adams, referring to a Jefferson birthday dinner in Washington, wrote in his diary: "Eight members of the Pennsylvania delegation, Jefferson Republicans dyed in the wool, agre d to go." In its issue of May 24, 1847, the New York *Commercial Advertiser* reported: "The democrats . . . are beginning to claim General Taylor as a democrat dyed in the wool, as a democrat of the Jeffersonian order of 1798." Now *dyed in the wool* is applied to any uncompromising partisan, particularly a conservative "of the deepest dye."

What was the two-thirds rule?

For more than a century Democratic national conventions operated under the "two-thirds rule"; that is, they required a majority of two-thirds of the votes for nominating candidates for President and Vice President.

The requirement of a two-thirds majority had no precedent in ancient Greek and Roman or in British parliamentary history and was an American invention. It was incorporated into the Federal Constitution of 1787 as one of the devices known as "checks and balances" to protect minorities against majorities. A majority of two thirds was required in Congress for conviction on impeachment, for expelling members, for proposing Amendments to the Constitution, for confirming treaties, and for overriding vetoes.

The first Democratic national convention, held in Baltimore in 1832, adopted the two-thirds rule for making nominations as evidence of party unanimity. This convention renominated Andrew Jackson for President and nominated Martin Van Buren for Vice President, both foregone conclusions. The two-thirds rule was adopted again in 1835, when the Democratic national convention nominated Van Buren for President and Richard M. Johnson for Vice President. Apparently the two-thirds rule was not formally adopted by the convention of 1840, when Van Buren's renomination was a foregone conclusion, and when no Vice-Presidential nomination was made.

Van Buren was defeated for re-election in 1840. By 1844 he had offended many proslavery delegates by his attitude on the Texas Question and they and their allies were determined to block his nomination. Accordingly, before the convention was completely organized, adoption of the two-thirds rule was rushed through on the theory that it had already become a precedent. Adoption of the two-thirds rule sealed Van Buren's political doom. On the first ballot he received a majority of twenty-six but was unable to get closer than thirty-two votes to a two-thirds majority, with the result that James K. Polk, the first "dark horse," was nominated. The proslavery block recognized the two-thirds rule as the surest means of preventing nominations objectionable to their interests and insisted on its retention in later conventions. Under this rule any group controlling one more than a third of the votes could prevent the nomination of a candidate even though a majority favored him. A combination of Southerners and supporters of minor candidates and 'favorite sons" had little difficulty in controlling more than a third of the votes in a convention until an objectionable favorite was eliminated from the balloting. The two-thirds rule gave a minority an effective veto in party councils.

The two-thirds rule discouraged all candidates not acceptable to the Southern States from entering the contest. It survived the Civil War and the fact that a candidate who received simple majority almost invariably received a two-thirds majority was used as an argument for retaining the rule. In only two instances after 1844 did a candidate who received a majority of the votes fail to get the nomination for lack of two-thirds—Stephen A. Douglas in 1860 and Champ Clark in 1912.

At the outset there were 303 votes in the Charleston Democratic Convention of 1860 and 202 were required to nominate under the two-thirds rule. Because of objection to the slavery plank in the platform, which had been adopted by a simple majority, fifty delegates from

Southern States withdrew from the convention before the balloting began. The remaining delegates adopted a motion requiring two-thirds (202) of a full convention (303) to make nominations. On all of the fifty-seven ballots Douglas received a clear majority of the 153 votes cast, and on five ballots he received $152\frac{1}{2}$, which was a majority of the full convention as originally constituted. Benjamin F. Butler of Massachusetts went to the convention instructed to vote for Douglas but voted 56 times for Jefferson Davis and not once for Douglas. Davis never received any other votes in the convention except the half vote of another delegate on several ballots. This convention was unable to make a nomination for President and adjourned to meet later at Baltimore, where many of the Border State delegates withdrew before the balloting began. Douglas was finally nominated by two-thirds of the remaining delegates and became the nominee of only a fragment of the Democratic Party.

The two-thirds vote required for nominations in Democratic conventions after the Civil War was not two-thirds of the total number of votes accredited to a convention, but two-thirds of the number of votes actually cast, a quorum being present. In the Democratic convention at Baltimore in 1912 Champ Clark received a majority of all the votes on eight different ballots but lost the nomination to Woodrow Wilson. That was the only instance after 1860 that a candidate for President in a Democratic convention received a majority without ultimately receiving a two-thirds majority while that rule was in effect. It is often said that Alfred E. Smith and William G. McAdoo were defeated by the two-thirds rule in the hectic Democratic National Convention in New York City in 1924, but neither one of these aspirants ever received a simple majority on any of the 103 ballots taken between June 30 and July 9. McAdoo's highest vote was 530 on the sixty-ninth ballot and was eighteen votes short of a simple majority of the total of $1,095\frac{1}{2}$ cast. Smith's highest was 368 on the seventy-sixth ballot and was 181 short of a simple majority of the 1,097 cast in that ballot.

In 1920, when the two-thirds rule was not specifically mentioned in the resolution adopting the rules, the convention held that it was a requirement "authorized through immemorial usage." In 1884 and 1924 motions to suspend the rules and abrogate the two-thirds rule failed to carry. On January 9, 1936, the Democratic National Committee recommended that the next national convention abolish the two-thirds rule. The convention that met in Philadelphia later in the same year acted favorably on this recommendation and the 104-year-old two-thirds rule was abandoned in favor of nominations by simple majorities, which had been the practice in Republican national conventions since 1856.

What is a rock-ribbed Republican?

Rock-ribbed means having ribs of or like rock and has long been used figuratively in the sense of strong, sturdy, stoutly built or solidly established. Shakespeare uses "ribs of iron" and "ribs of steel" and refers to "strong-ribbed barks" and a "flinty ribbed" castle. In *Thanatopsis* (1817) William Cullen Bryant has, "the hills, rock-ribbed, and ancient as the sun," and in *Landing of the Pilgrim Fathers* (1826) Felicia Dorothea Hemans has, "On a stern and rock-bound coast." "The rock-ribbed coast of Maine" is an old expression. An unyielding partisan in politics, especially a conservative, is said to be rock-ribbed.

Who coined *manifest destiny*?

The earliest known use of *manifest destiny* occurs in an editorial in the July-August, 1845, issue of the New York *United States Magazine and Democratic Review*. This editorial denounced the opponents of the annexation of Texas and declared that "our manifest destiny is to overspread the continent alloted by Providence for the free development of our yearly multiplying millions." There is no doubt that this editorial was written by the editor of the paper, John L. O'Sullivan (1813-1895), lawyer, journalist and diplomat, who was born on a British warship at Gibraltar. O'Sullivan also edited the New York *Morning News* and in the December 27, 1845, issue of that paper he wrote an editorial in which he asserted that the strongest claim that the United States had to the Oregon country was "by right of our manifest destiny to overspread and to possess the whole of the continent which Providence has given us for the . . . great experiment of liberty." *Manifest destiny* was picked up by the territorial expansionists and used as an effective slogan by those who believed that it was inevitable and proper that the United States would ultimately control not only North America but Cuba and other neighboring islands as well.

In a speech in the House of Representatives on January 3, 1846, favoring acquisition of Oregon, Robert C. Winthrop referred to "That new revelation of right which has been designated as the right of our manifest destiny to spread over the whole continent." James G. Blaine, in *Twenty Years of Congress,* said that Stephen A. Douglas was injured politically in the Democratic convention of 1852 "by his partial committal to what was known as the doctrine of 'manifest destiny,'—that indefinite acquisition of territory southward, especially in the direction of the West Indies." Former President Millard Fillmore is reputed to have said in a speech in 1853 that the United States would welcome Canada and Mexico into the Union "for it is the manifest destiny of this government to embrace the whole North American continent." In *Following the Drum* (1858) E. L. Vielé observed: "Buildings of every description bore the marks of inevitable progress, or go-aheadativeness, otherwise called 'manifest destiny.' " "That word, 'manifest destiny,' which is profanely used," wrote Ralph Waldo Emerson in 1865, "signifies the sense all men have of the prodigious energy and opportunity lying idle here."

M. Schele de Vere, in *Americanisms; the Language of the New World* (1872) wrote of the phrase:

Designed originally for the expression of a perfectly justifiable doctrine, that America was intended by Providence to be a republic, and a refuge for all who wished to be free, it was seen to be a convenient cloak for every measure of aggrandizement or violence. It was *Manifest Destiny* that conquered part of Mexico and purchased Alaska; it is *Manifest Destiny* that Cuba should be annexed and Canada ceded to the United States. J. R. Lowell terms it justly a phrase characteristic of "that national recklessness as to right and wrong," of which Mr. Birdofredum Sawin, in the *Bigelow Papers,* is the very incarnation.

On May 25, 1879, President Rutherford B. Hayes notes in his diary:

The annexation to the United States of the adjacent parts of the continent both north and south, seems to be, according to the phrase of 1844, our "manifest destiny." I am not in favor of artificial stimulants to the tendency. But I think I see plainly that it is now for the interest of both Canada and the United States that properly and in order with due regard to the feelings of Great Britain, the two countries should come under one government.

Manifest destiny was revived during William McKinley's administration and for that reason McKinley is often erroneously credited with coining the term. When the United States annexed Hawaii in 1898 McKinley is reputed to have told his assistant secretary, George Cortelyou, that it was "manifest destiny." After the conquest of Cuba, Puerto Rico, Guam, the Philippines and other Spanish possessions, *Imperialism* was substituted for *manifest destiny.* The Democrats and many "antiexpansionist" Republicans insisted that the McKinley administration was making the United States a "colonial power" and entangling it in world politics. Although William Jennings Bryan had supported the treaty with Spain after the Spanish-American War, as the Democratic nominee for President against McKinley in 1900 he made "Imperialism" the issue, but the Republicans easily won with "the Full Dinner Pail."

In a speech at Buffalo on September 5, 1901, the day before he was shot, President McKinley said: "*Isolation* is no longer possible or desirable. God and man have linked the nations together. No nation can longer be indifferent to any other." After the First World War those who favored the historic American foreign policy of aloofness and isolation from World affairs and nonparticipation in international action became known as *isolationists,* a term of reproach coined at that time to designate those who opposed entrance into the League of Nations.

On January 27, 1936, in his second speech of acceptance, President Franklin D. Roosevelt said, "This generation of Americans has a rendezvous with destiny," which was probably suggested by Alan Seager's poem entitled "I Have a Rendezvous with Death."

What is the origin of *ballot?*

Ballot is derived through French from Italian *ballotta,* the diminutive of *balla,* "ball" and literally means "little ball." *Bullet* comes from the same source. In many of their elections the ancient Greeks voted by tossing pieces of shell *(ostrakons),* potsherds or pebbles into an urn. The Italian *ballotta* was applied to round objects or little balls used in elections and hence we have *ballot* in the sense of a ticket or a vote. The Federal Constitution provides that the Presidential electors, and the House of Representatives when the choice falls on it, shall vote "by ballot."

Suffrage in the sense of the right to vote has a similar origin. The root of Latin *suffragium* from which the term is derived is supposed to signify something broken off, such as a piece of shell or potsherd used in voting, and hence it came to mean a voting tablet and the right to vote. The right to vote or the suffrage was called the *franchise,* from Old French *franc,* "free," because only freemen enjoyed the right to vote.

What is a roorback?

A roorback is a fictitious story or forged report circulated to injure a candidate on the eve of an election when refutation is difficult if not impossible before the votes are cast.

The roorback lie received its name from a story published in 1844 to injure the reputation of James K. Polk, the Democratic candidate for President who was a slaveholder. Just before the election the Ithaca (New York) *Chronicle* printed what purported to be an extract from *A*

Tour Through the Western and Southern States, by Baron Roorback. The extract contained a description of a camp of slavedrivers on Duck River, and stated that forty-three of the unfortunate slaves "had been purchased by the Honorable J. K. Polk, the present Speaker of the House of Representatives, the mark of the branding iron, and the initials of his name, on their shoulders, distinguishing them from the rest." The pretended extract was reprinted by the Albany (New York) *Journal* and the other Whig papers. Later part of the extract was proved to be a forgery, the work of an Ithaca abolitionist named Linn. He took the description of the camp of slave drivers from George William Featherstonbaugh's *Excursions Through the Slave States,* which had just been published. Featherstonbaugh was an English geologist and author who spent many years traveling in North America. *Duck River,* was substituted for *New River,* the name of a tributary of the Kanawha, and the statement about the forty-three slaves branded with the initials of Polk was forged. There never was any such writer as Baron Roorback, but ever since *roorback* has been applied to a last-minute lie or canard published on the eve of an election.

The "Morey Letter" of 1880 was a typical roorback. Two weeks before the election there was published a letter purporting to have been written by James A. Garfield, the Republican nominee for President to "H. L. Morey" of the Employers' Union of Lynn, Massachusetts. The fictitious letter favored continued immigration of Chinese and was calculated to alienate labor from Garfield.

Another typical roorback was the "Murchison Letter." During the Presidential campaign of 1888, when President Cleveland and Benjamin Harrison were the Democratic and Republican nominees respectively, a man named Murchison, inspired by Republican politicians, wrote a letter to Sir Lionel Sackville-West, British minister at Washington. The writer pretended to be a naturalized Englishman who sought advice as to how he could best serve Great Britain in casting his vote. He pointed out instances in which Cleveland had been friendly to the British but expressed doubts about his position on the fisheries question. The minister took the bait and in his reply hinted that a vote for Cleveland would be useful to Great Britain. This correspondence was released to the press at Los Angeles on October 21, 1888, and produced a sensation. It is supposed to have contributed to Cleveland's defeat by alienating Irish and other voters by seeming to confirm the Republican contention that the British were behind the reduction in tariff. The President gave the British minister his passports after his government refused to comply with a request to recall him.

How did *bolt* get into politics?

Bolt was borrowed from horse-racing in the days when most politicians were racing fans. *Race* for a political campaign, *dark horse* for an unexpected nominee, and *"running* for office" all came directly from the race course. *Bolt* is an old English term meaning a metal pin, an arrow or a shaft. A horse that ran away suddenly or got out of the control of its rider was said to bolt, presumably it acted in its speed like an arrow or perhaps a bolt of lightning. In the diary of John Quincy Adams we see the term in the process of moving from the race course to the political arena. On April 9, 1808, when the U.S. Senate disposed of a resolution to expel Senator John Smith of Ohio for implication in the Burr conspiracy, Senator Adams wrote: "As the concurrence of two-thirds of the members is necessary to carry a resolution for expulsion, this was lost by a single vote. Dr. Mitchill and Mr. Bradley were both absent, doubtless intentionally; unwilling to vote on either side. This is sometimes called *bolting,* and sometimes flying the course."

A political leader bolts when he repudiates his party's platform or candidate and joins the oppositon. On December 4, 1833, Representative John Quincy Adams wrote in his diary that "At last, Archer, of Virginia, bolted from the party." The term now is generally applied to the temporary desertion of a politician who has been disappointed in getting a nomination or the recognition he thinks he is entitled to. Rarely is it applied to a common voter who leaves his party and votes for the oppositon ticket. "Several of our contemporaries," reported the St. Louis *Democrat* on April 3, 1871, "have announced it as a well-established fact, that Carl Schurz has *bolted* from the Republican party." Under date of January 26, 1888, former President Rutherford B. Hayes wrote: "Revolutions and *bolts* are alike. They are sacred when the facts justify them. When not so justified they are blunders of the sort that is worse than crime."

Who was "the general who never surrenders"?

On February 22, 1847, on the eve of the Battle of Buena Vista, **General Santa Anna**, whose Mexicans outnumbered the Americans nearly four to one, summoned General Zachary Taylor to surrender. Thomas Leonidas Crittenden, Taylor's kinsman and aide, carried to Santa Anna the American commander's reply: "General Taylor never surrenders." The next day Taylor won a decisive but costly victory. Largely on the strength of this victory Taylor was nominated for President by the Whigs in 1848 and "General Taylor never surrenders" was used as their campaign slogan.

One of the objectives of James K. Polk's administration was to acquire the Oregon country, California and New Mexico and to extend the Union to the Pacific. War resulted and General Taylor's part in that war made him President. On March 5, 1849, the retiring President rode to the Capitol in an open carriage with his successor. That night Polk wrote in his diary:

On going up to the Capitol California was alluded to . . . .Something was said which drew from General Taylor the expression of views and opinions which greatly surprised me. They were to the effect that California and Oregon were too distant to become members of the Union, and that it would be better for them to be an independent government. . . . These are alarming opinions to be entertained by the President . . . General Taylor's opinions as expressed, I hope, have not been well considered. General Taylor is, I have no doubt, a well-meaning old man. He is, however, uneducated, exceedingly ignorant of public affairs, and, I should judge, of very ordinary capacity.

What Presidential candidate did not learn of his nomination till a month after the convention had adjourned?

Zachary Taylor, President of the United States from March 4, 1849, till his death July 9, 1850, did not learn officially of his nomination for President for about a month after the convention that nominated him had adjourned.

General Taylor, a hero of the Mexican War, was living on his plantation near Baton Rouge, Louisiana, when the Whig convention nominated him for President on the fourth ballot in June, 1848. The chairman of the convention immediately sent a letter to the candidate in Louisiana notifying him of the nomination. At that time telegraph communications with the Southwest had not been established. Postage stamps were comparatively new and in those days postage was still often collected in money directly from the sender or from the recipient when the mail was delivered. In 1845 the postage rate had been fixed at five cents for a half-ounce letter for three hundred miles or less and ten cents for any greater distance.

A large number of people had been writing to Taylor at his expense, and one day he got tired of paying ten cents apiece for fan and crank letters and refused to accept a large bundle of letters in the Baton Rouge post office. A few days later, after thinking the matter over, he decided that the bundle might contain important letters and that it would be advisable to investigate. Meanwhile, however, the postmaster had sent the letters to the Post Office Department in Washington as unclaimed mail. It so happened that the bundle contained the notification letter from the chairman of the Whig convention, and consequently it was about a month before the candidate learned officially of his nomination.

What President never voted?

It is supposed that Zachary Taylor (1784-1850), the twelfth President, never voted in his life, although he was Constitutionally eligible to vote in ten Presidential elections from 1808 to 1848 inclusive.

Born in Virginia and reared in Kentucky, Taylor entered the Army in his early twenties and remained in the service until a short time before his election to the Presidency, when he retired to Baton Rouge, Louisiana, where he owned a plantation. As a professional soldier he never stayed in one place long enough to qualify for voting. General Taylor did not attach himself very firmly to any political party or faction. After he had become a national hero because of his exploits in the Mexican War the Whig party managers had considerable difficulty in getting the famous soldier to say definitely that he was a Whig. In 1847 he admitted that he had never voted for President, but went so far as to say that had he voted in 1844 he would have voted for the Whig candidate, Henry Clay. Throughout the campaign he insisted that if elected he "would not be the President of a party, but the President of the whole people." There is no evidence that he voted even in the election of 1848, when he was the candidate for President.

Why was Zachary Taylor nicknamed "Old Rough and Ready"?

Zachary Taylor (1784-1850) was called "Old Rough and Ready" because he was a plain, unpretentious, forthright, fearless and efficient army officer. In 1837, when he had been in the regular army nearly thirty years and was still a colonel, Taylor took command of the field forces against the Seminoles in Florida. On Christmas Day of that year he fought a fierce battle with the Indians in the Everglades north of Lake Okeechobee. In recognition of his services he was made a brigadier general by brevet, and in 1838 succeeded General Thomas S. Jesup in command of the department, a position he held until 1840.

Sometime during the Seminole War Taylor was first called Old Rough and Ready. Just when and by whom he was given the nickname is not known. *Rough and ready* is an old phrase found in print in its general sense as early as 1810. A sergeant named Harris said General Taylor was called Old Rough and Ready because he "treated the redskins in the roughest way and in the readiest manner." Apparently the nickname did not get into print and become nationally known until after Taylor took command in Texas. He fought the Battle of Resaca de la Palma, about four miles from Brownsville, on May 9, 1846. In *Captain Sam Grant* (1950) Lloyd Lewis wrote: "In a private letter written by a soldier after Resaca, and widely published, there had been a sentence that had taken the nation by storm—'we call him Old Rough and Ready.'"

Taylor was contemptuous of pomp, uniforms, regalia, insignia and other trappings of war. General U. S. Grant, who served under Taylor in the Mexican War, wrote in his *Memoirs:* "General Taylor never made any great show of parade, either of uniform or retinue. In dress he was probably too plain, rarely wearing anything in the field to indicate his rank, or even that he was an officer . . . I can call to mind only one instance when I saw him in uniform, and one other when I heard of his wearing it. On both occasions he was unfortunate." One of these was at a grand review of the army, which had to be called off because General William J. Worth refused to participate until a point of precedence was officially determined. The other occasion recalled by Grant was when Taylor met Commodore David Conner of the Gulf squadron for a routine conference in May, 1846, after the battles of Palo Alto and Resaca de la Palma.

While the Army was on the River [wrote Grant], the Flag Officer sent word that he would call on the General to pay his respects on a certain day. General Taylor, knowing that naval officers habitually wear all the uniform the "law allows" on all occasions of ceremony, thought it would be only civil to receive his guest in the same style. His uniform was therefore got out, brushed up, and put on, in advance of the visit. The Flag Officer, knowing General Taylor's aversion to the wearing of the uniform, and feeling that it would be regarded as a compliment should he meet him in civilian's dress, left off his uniform for this occasion. The meeting was said to have been embarrassing to both, and the conversation was principally apologetic.

According to Grant, General Taylor "dressed himself entirely for comfort" and "was very much given to sit his horse side-ways—with both feet on one side—particularly on the battlefield." He often appeared among his troops wearing a straw hat, checked gingham coat and blue trousers. His men, who loved him, more often called him "Old Zach" than "Old Rough and Ready." A town in Nevada County, California, was named Old Rough and Ready by miners in 1849 when Taylor was

President, and a railway station in Georgia near Atlanta was given the same name.

Did any President "affirm" instead of "swear"?

The Constitution gives the President the choice of taking a prescribed "oath or affirmation." Madison's notes indicate that "or affirmation" was inserted after "oath" in the Constitution without debate on August 30, 1787, only eighteen days before the Philadelphia convention adjourned.

An affirmation is a solemn declaration made by a person who for conscientious reasons refuses "to swear." In law it is equivalent to an oath and is administered in the same manner. Apparently it was inserted in the Constitution as an alternate to the oath in deference to Quakers and members of other religious sects who object to taking oaths in the customary form.

Oddly enough, the only President who has affirmed was nominally an Episcopalian, while the only Quaker to become President swore. Franklin Pierce, who joined the Episcopal Church after he was President, has been thus far the only President to choose the alternative "affirm" instead of the usual "swear" when he assumed office. Herbert Hoover, a Quaker, "swore" when inaugurated on March 4, 1929.

Pierce was born on Friday, November 27, 1804, was inaugurated on Friday, March 4, 1853, and died on Friday, October 8, 1869. He served in the New Hampshire legislature while his father was Governor of the State. His wife, Jane Appleton Pierce, was the daughter of Jesse Appleton, president of Bowdoin College, from which Pierce graduated in the class of 1824, a year ahead of Henry Wadsworth Longfellow and Nathaniel Hawthorne. Pierce was a heavy drinker, and Hawthorne, who wrote his campaign biography in 1852, got him to promise to be moderate in his drinking during his Presidency, a promise he did not keep too well. Pierce did not stop drinking entirely until he formally joined the Episcopal Church about two years before his death. The Pierces had three sons. One died in infancy and another at the age of four. On January 6, 1853, President-elect Pierce, his wife and their eleven-year-old son Benjamin, traveled on the Boston and Maine Railroad from Andover to Lawrence in Massachusetts. When the car in which they were riding was thrown off the track the boy was dashed against some rocks on the roadbed and instantly killed within sight of his parents. Two months later President Pierce alluded to this personal tragedy in his inaugural address, which began with the sentence: "It is a relief to feel that no heart but my own can know the personal regret and bitter sorrow over which I have been borne to a position so suitable for others rather than desirable for myself."

What was John C. Frémont's religion?

John C. Frémont was an Episcopalian. He was born near Savannah, Georgia, January 21, 1813, while his parents were camping on a journey among the Southern Indians. His mother, whose maiden name was Ann Beverly Whiting, was a member of an old Virginia family. She was a member of the Episcopal Church and brought her children up in that faith. Frémont's father, Charles Frémon, was a political refugee from France. He was not a Roman Catholic, as popularly supposed. In 1929 Allan Nevins, author of *Frémont, the West's Greatest Adventurer,* wrote the author as follows: "Frémont's father was unquestionably a French Huguenot. All the family records and traditions agree upon this point, and Frémont himself so stated." It was John C. Frémont who anglicized the French family name by adding the *t*. Because of his four exploring expeditions in the West, Frémont was known as "The Pathfinder," which was one of the nicknames of Natty Bumppo, a central figure in James Fenimore Cooper's *The Pathfinder* (1840) and other Leatherstocking Tales.

The erroneous belief that John C. Frémont was a Catholic dates from 1856, when he was the Republican nominee for President. His political enemies circulated, with considerable effect in certain parts of the country, a report that Frémont was a practicing Catholic in secret in order to injure him with the Know-Nothing Party, which was strongly anti-Catholic. Frémont's French name and several other circumstances lent color to the false report. He refused to make a public statement on the subject and took the position that, regardless of what his own religion was, no religious faith disqualified anybody from office under the Constitution. On October 19, 1841, he had been married in Washington to Jessie Benton by Father Van Horseigh, a Dutch Catholic priest. It was a runaway marriage and the couple applied to the priest only after several Protestant clergymen had refused to perform the ceremony on the ground that it was a secret marriage to which Senator Thomas Benton was bitterly opposed. Further "evidence" that Frémont was a Catholic was found in the fact that he had carved a cross on Rock Independence during his first expedition in the West. Frémont described the incident in his journal under date of August 23, 1842:

Yesterday evening we reached our encampment at Rock Independence, where I took some astronomical observations. Here, I engraved on that rock of the Far West a symbol of the Christian faith. Among the thickly inscribed names, I made on the hard granite the impression of a large cross, which I covered with a black preparation of India rubber, well calculated to resist the influence of wind and rain.

Incidentally, Senator Benton, a dyed-in-the-wool Democrat, who had supported his son-in-law in all his exploration work, refused to vote for him as the Republican Presidential nominee.

Who was Old Fuss and Feathers?

Winfield Scott (1787-1866) was called "Old Fuss and Feathers" in his later years. He was six feet five inches tall and weighed over three hundred pounds. Once he wrote a hotel to "please give me a bed at least six feet six inches in length or one without a foot-board."

Born and reared in Virginia, Scott studied law briefly in the College of William and Mary, pursued his legal studies in a law office, and, after some militia service, joined the regulars as a captain in 1809. During the War of 1812, while still in his twenties, he became a regular brigadier general and a brevet major general. He was injured at Queenstown and captured. After being exchanged, he distinguished himself at Chippewa, and at Lundy's Lane within sound of Niagara Falls he had two horses shot under him and was carried from the field with two severe wounds. In a war with few land victories he became a national hero. Congress voted him a gold medal, and New York and Virginia a medal and a sword.

After the war he studied and observed military operations in Europe. He became known as the Pacificator because he stood by in South Carolina during the Nullification crisis (1832), commanded against the Seminoles in Florida (1836), supervised transfer of the Cherokees to Indian Territory (1838), quieted the disturbances in connection with the *Caroline* affair on the Canadian border (1838), pacified both sides in the Aroostook War between Maine and New Brunswick (1839), and settled the controversy over San Juan Island in Puget Sound (1859). The soldier diplomat is credited with preventing three wars between the United States and Great Britain.

On February 9, 1825, the day the House of Representatives chose John Quincy Adams President, Scott attended President Monroe's regular Wednesday levee. President-elect Adams, two of his late rivals, General Jackson and Speaker Clay, and other big shots were there. The White

House "was crowded to overflowing" reported Adams. Scott had drawn $800 from the bank in anticipation of a trip, and in the dense throng his wallet with the $800 disappeared from his pocket. There was "much mirth," wrote Margaret Bayard Smith, "occasioned by the idea of pick-pockets at the President's Drawing room."

General Scott favored the substitution of light wines and beer for ardent spirits in the army and is credited by some with having started the temperance movement. In 1832 he was sent West with about 950 men to command in the Black Hawk War. On the way his men were struck by Asiatic cholera. The general was convinced of a direct connection between the disease and the personal habits of the men. After the first deaths at Fort Armstrong near Rock Island, Scott issued his famous Order No. 16, which read in part:

It is believed that all these men were of intemperate habits. The Ranger who is dead, it is known, generated this disease within him by a fit of intoxication. . . Sobriety, cleanliness of person, cleanliness of camp and quarters, together with care in the preparation of the men's messes, are the great preventives. . . The Commanding General . . . therefore peremptorily commands that every soldier or Ranger who shall be found drunk or sensibly intoxicated, after the publication of this order, be compelled, as soon as his strength will permit, to dig a grave at a suitable burying place, large enough for his own reception, as such grave cannot fail soon to be wanted for the drunken man himself or some drunken companion. This order is given as well to serve for the punishment of drunkenness as to spare good and temperate men the labor of digging graves for their worthless companions.

Against the advice of his army doctors, Scott exposed himself by ministering personally to his stricken men.

Scott wanted to run for Congress in 1822 and after that continually hankered for political honors. He was a serious aspirant for the Whig nomination for President every time that party was in the field—1840, 1844, 1848 and 1852. In 1852 he was nominated but received the electoral votes of only four States. As late as 1860 he still hoped to become President.

For both personal and political reasons President Polk, a dyed-in-the-wool Democrat, did not want Scott to command in Mexico. The President was infuriated in May, 1846, when the senior major general in the army wrote Secretary of War William L. Marcy that, "I do not desire to place myself in the most perilous position—a fire upon my rear from Washington, and the fire in front from the Mexicans." In the abuse of his enemies "a fire upon my rear" was distorted into "a shot in the rear." About the same time Marcy sent Scott a peremptory note by messenger while the general was eating in a Washington restaurant near the war office. Scott wrote in his reply that he had just stepped out to take "a hasty plate of soup." Democratic newspapers picked up the phrase in ridicule and Scott did not hear the last of the "hasty plate of soup" for years.

Polk finally gave him the command in Mexico. After he had captured Vera Cruz and started to fight his way to Mexico City, the eighty-three-year-old Duke of Wellington said: "Scott is lost! he has been carried away by successes. He can't take the city, and he can't fall back upon his base." Santa Anna was banished in 1845 and lived in Havana. On the strength of vague promises made by Santa Anna through an emissary that he would make a satisfactory peace with the United States if restored to power, President Polk ordered the squadron blockading the Gulf ports of Mexico to permit the dictator to land at Vera Cruz. The result was that Santa Anna commanded the armies against both Generals Taylor and Scott. At Springfield on October 8, 1847, Daniel Webster said that "the President must be gratified to know that in the subsequent battles, which have cost so much blood and treasure, the commanding general on both sides was of his own choosing."

Scott returned again a national hero. His rival for fame in the Mexican War, Zachary Taylor, as President treated Scott coolly, but when Millard Fillmore succeeded to the Presidency in 1850, he took General Scott's hand and told him his persecutions were over. Two years later Congress gave him the rank and pay of lieutenant general, a rank held by none since Washington. That year Scott was the successful rival of President Fillmore for the Whig nomination for President.

When and by whom Scott was first called Old Fuss and Feathers is uncertain. It is generally assumed that his men so called him affectionately because he wore plumes in his hat and was fussy in enforcing the regulations regarding dress and decorum. But it is probable that he was called Old Fuss and Feathers derisively by his political enemies when a candidate for President. He was proud, irritable and outspoken, spent years bickering over his rank and precedence, and made enemies by his tendency to talk and write about his personal grievances. A giant in stature and handsome and imposing in person, General Scott was fond of all the pomp and circumstance of the military profession. In full dress uniform, with elaborate embroidery and epaulets, ribbons and gold braid, shining buttons, medals and spurs, glittering sword, cocked hat decked with five white plumes to indicate his rank, he was a sight to behold when mounted on a spirited charger. It was in such regalia that he rode into the conquered Mexican capital.

As early as 1846 he was referred to as "old granny." When running for President "the military dabbler in politics" was called "the peacock of politics, all fuss and feathers, and fireworks." Some authorities say his most famous sobriquet was pinned on him during this period by Mrs. June Casneau, editor of a Washington Democratic newspaper called the *Daily States.* The old beplumed and fussy soldier was compared to an old hen dusting herself in a sand lot. "Fuss and Feathers has more style than any man who ever lived," said the October, 1860, number of *Knickerbocker's Magazine* in the earliest recorded use of the exact phrase that has been found. It was perpetuated by its alliteration.

Although a Virginian, he remained loyal to the Union and incurred the hatred of his native State and the South. In 1861 he was old and too infirm to ride a horse, but he gave some direction to military preparations and tried in vain to induce Robert E. Lee to accept command of the Union field forces. On November 1, 1861, he was retired with the rank and pay of a lieutenant general and was succeeded by George B. McClellan as commander-in-chief.

In 1864 Scott, who was a voluminous writer, published his *Memoirs* in two volumes. To Ulysses S. Grant, who had served under him in Mexico, he inscribed a set: "From the Oldest to the Greatest General." Though he never attended any military school, Scott died at West Point, fifteen days under eighty, and was buried there. He was married to Maria D. Mayo of Richmond, who bore him two sons and five daughters. One daughter and the two sons died in childhood. His daughter Virginia became a Catholic and in 1844 entered a convent in Georgetown, D.C. where she died two years later at twenty-four. The other daughters married and survived him.

Who was the youngest Vice President?

John Cabell Breckinridge of Kentucky, who was born January 21, 1821, and who qualified as Vice President March 4, 1857, at the age of thirty-six—only a year above the Constitutional minimum—was the youngest person to be Vice President between 1789 and 1949.

Theodore Roosevelt of New York, who was born October 27, 1859, was forty-two years, four months and six days old when he took the oath of office March 4, 1901, and he ranks second among the Vice Presidents in point of youth. John C. Calhoun of South Carolina, who qualified in 1825 at the age of forty-three years and fourteen days, ranks third in this respect. Daniel D. Tompkins of New York was forty-three when he qualified in 1817, but he was older than Calhoun.

Vice President Breckinridge was nominated for the Presidency in 1860 by the proslavery seceders from the Democratic convention and received seventy-two electoral votes. As Vice President he presided over the joint meeting of Congress that counted the votes and it fell to his lot to announce the election of one of his successful rivals, Abraham Lincoln. When the youngest Vice President's term expired on March 4, 1861, he became a member of the Senate, where he paid lip service to the United States flag, but opposed Lincoln's war policies and took such a dubious part in debate that he was accused of being disloyal. At that time Kentucky was trying to be neutral between the North and South, but on September 21, 1861, she voted to remain in the Union and ordered Confederate sympathizers to leave the State. Eleven days later the Kentucky legislature adopted a resolution asking Breckinridge and his colleague, Lazarus W. Powell, to resign their seats, and, in the event they refused, asking the Senate to investigate their conduct and to expel them if found to be disloyal. Powell did not resign, but was found loyal and permitted to serve out his term ending in 1865. Meanwhile Breckinridge had left the State and joined the Confederate army. In the July special session the Senate had declared vacant the seats of all Senators from Confederate States but had applied no opprobrious terms to them. Of all the Senators who joined the Confederacy, Breckinridge alone was formally "expelled" and declared a traitor. On December 4, 1861, the Senate resolved that "John C. Breckinridge, the traitor, be and is hereby expelled from the Senate."

Breckinridge rose to the rank of major general and distinguished himself in many campaigns and engagements, and finally became Secretary of War in Jefferson Davis's cabinet in 1865. When Robert E. Lee surrendered at Appomattox, Breckinridge refused to surrender; when Joseph E. Johnston surrendered in North Carolina, Breckinridge again refused to surrender. He went to Georgia with Davis and other members of the cabinet. With several young officers and their servants he set out for Europe by way of Cuba, which he reached after weeks of wandering and adventure. In 1866 he returned to Kentucky, where he practiced law and was very popular. The only other former Vice President of the United States who joined the Confederacy was John Tyler of Virginia.

How large was the Little Giant?

Stephen Arnold Douglas (1813-1861), whose name is linked with that of Abraham Lincoln, was called the Little Giant because he was a giant in the political arena and small in stature. He had short legs and was only five feet tall but had disproportionately large head, neck, shoulders and chest. Although his personal appearance was against him, he was eloquent and forceful as a public speaker. Some authorities regard the short and stocky Douglas the best debater America ever produced. His chief fault was that he often lost his temper in rough and tumble debate. When Thomas H. Benton was asked whether the Little Giant could be elected President, Old Bullion replied, "No, sir, his coattails reach too close to the curbstone." The *Illinois Register* at Springfield quoted a Whig politician as referring to Douglas as "the little giant" as early as 1839, and in the postscript of a letter to Representative John T. Stuart on December 23 of the same year Lincoln wrote, "The Democratic giant is here, but he is not now worth talking about."

Douglas's father, a Vermont doctor, died when Stephen was an infant, and in his youth he was apprenticed to a cabinetmaker. After attending Canandaigua Academy in New York, Douglas settled in Illinois, taught school, studied law and began to practice. At twenty-seven he was elected a member of the State supreme court and won the title "Judge." At one time Douglas and Lincoln were both suitors for the hand of Mary Todd. In 1836-1837 Douglas and Lincoln served together in the State legislature. Douglas served in the U.S. House of Representatives from 1843 to 1847 and in the U.S. Senate from 1847 until his death in 1861. On February 14, 1844, John Quincy Adams wrote in his diary this prejudiced picture of the Little Giant in action in Congress:

At the House, Stephen A. Douglas, of Illinois, the author of the majority report from the Committee of Elections, had taken the floor last evening, and now raved out his hour in abusive invective upon the members who had pointed out its slanders, and upon the Whig party. His face was convulsed, his gesticulation frantic, and he lashed himself into such a heat that if his body had been made of combustible matter it would have burnt out. In the midst of his roaring, to save himself from choking, he stripped off and cast away his cravat, unbuttoned his waistcoat, and had the air and aspect of a half-naked pugilist. And this man comes from a judicial bench, and passes for an eloquent orator!

But the Little Giant appealed to millions of Americans, particularly young people, and was known as "Young America." At thirty-five he was already taken seriously as a Presidential candidate. He received votes in the Democratic convention of 1848, was a runner-up in 1852 and 1856, and was nominated by the Northern wing of the party in 1860. Though disappointed, he was a good loser, pledged his wholehearted support to Lincoln, and died in Chicago of typhoid fever at the age of forty-seven while on a western trip, made at Lincoln's request, to arouse Union sentiment.

What is meant by the band-wagon vote?

The collective votes of those who vote for a candidate merely because they think he will win is called "the band-wagon vote."

Band wagon was originally applied to a high and usually bizarrely ornamented wagon on which a band of musicians rode at the head of a circus parade. The term appears to be an Americanism and the earliest known use of it occurs in a book written in 1855 by P. T. Barnum, the famous showman, who wrote: "At Vicksburg we sold all our land conveyances except four horses and the band wagon." During the log cabin and hard cider campaign of 1840 the Whig supporters of General Harrison took a hint from the circus and used a band wagon to lead their parades. Local candidates rode on the band wagon with the musicians. Office seekers and other self-servers who wanted to identify themselves conspicuously with a candidate who they expected to win in the election "climbed on the band wagon," while ordinary voters merely "joined the procession." Hence persons who, after waiting to see which way the cat will jump, join the forces of an obvious winner are said to get on the band wagon. When large numbers of delegates in a convention switch to a winning candidate and get on the imaginary band wagon they are said to "stampede." *Band wagon* in its political sense did not become common until around the turn of the century. On September 4, 1906, the New York *Post* referred to "Many of those Democrats who rushed into the Bryan bandwagon."

Politicians recognize the fact that many people like to be on the winning side and therefore they insist to the last minute that their side is going to win, but climbing on the band wagon is more characteristic of office seekers and political leaders, who hope for political plums, than it is of ordinary voters.

Who was Robert Barnwell Rhett?

Robert Barnwell Rhett (1800-1876) was a noted Southern "fire-eater" and is sometimes referred to as "the father of secession." He was a son of James Smith, a descendant of Landgrave Smith, Colonial governor of

Carolina. Robert Barnwell Rhett was elected to the U.S. House of Representatives in 1836 and served in that body until 1849. In 1837, when he was a member of Congress, the family, with the later approval of the South Carolina legislature, changed its name from Smith to the less common one of a distinguished ancestor, Colonel William Rhett.

Rhett had 190 slaves on his plantations, lived as a Southern aristocrat and was a fiery and eloquent disunionist long before the Civil War. On September 30, 1837, Representative John Quincy Adams, an unfriendly witness, wrote in his diary: "Robert Barnwell Rhett (Smith heretofore) moved a long amendment and literally howled a nullification speech. I say howled, for his enunciation was so rapid, inarticulate, and vociferous that his head hung back as he spoke, with his face upward, like a howling dog." Rhett was elected to the U.S. Senate in 1850 to succeed John C. Calhoun but resigned two years later. He was such a storm center in South Carolina politics that the State was facetiously called "Rhettsylvania." After playing a prominent part in the Confederacy, which he did as much as any one man to create, he removed to Louisiana in 1867 and died there.

How did the modern Republican Party get its name?

When and where the Republican Party was born and who first suggested the name are disputed questions. The movement that led to the organization of the Republican Party was spontaneous and the party was not formed and named in a particular meeting. The immediate cause of the Republican movement was passage of the Kansas-Nebraska Bill.

In 1852 the Whig candidate for President, Winfield Scott, received 1,386,576 popular votes and 42 electoral votes, while the Democratic candidate, Franklin Pierce, received 1,601,474 popular votes and 254 electoral votes. Although the Democrats elected large majorities in both houses of Congress, the showing of the Whigs, who had elected Presidents in 1840 and 1848, was not particularly discouraging. But the Whig Party had always been neutral on the slavery question and antislavery sentiment in the North was growing rapidly. After the election of 1852 many antislavery people began to feel that the Whig Party could not again provide effective opposition to the Democratic Party.

There was an outburst of indignation in the North when a combination of Democrats and Whigs passed Stephen A. Douglas's Kansas-Nebraska Bill, which upset the Missouri Compromise of 1820 and the Compromise of 1850 and permitted slavery in territory that had been free for thirty-four years. Bitter debate on the bill in Congress aroused antislavery people to a high pitch and both Conscience Whigs and Anti-Slavery Democrats began to talk about forming a national party designed specifically to oppose the further extension of slavery. Opponents of the Kansas-Nebraska Bill were known as "Anti-Nebraska Men" or simply "Anti-Nebraskas."

It is said that Alvan E. Bovay, a young lawyer at Ripon, Wisconsin, suggested as early as February, 1854, that a new national party be formed and that it be called the Republican Party. Many years later Bovay himself wrote:

I set to work in the most systematic way that I could contrive, to dissolve the Whig Party and all other parties opposed to the slave power, and to organize the Republican Party right here in Ripon, because I was fully convinced that sooner or later others would take similar steps elsewhere, and that in a few months we should have a great irresistible Northern party organized on the simple issue of the non-extension of slavery.

A group of Conscience Whigs, Anti-Nebraska Democrats, Free-Soilers and Abolitionists held a meeting in a schoolhouse at Ripon on March 20 of that year and resolved, if the Kansas-Nebraska Bill became law, "to throw old party organizations to the winds and organize a new party on the sole basis of the non-extension of slavery." Bovay was a friend of Horace Greeley and he is reputed to have written to the editor of the New York *Tribune* after the March 20 meeting at Ripon suggesting that *Republican Party* be adopted as the name for the new party in process of formation. A small frame building on the campus of Ripon College at Ripon is referred to as the place where the Republican Party was born and named. While that is true in a sense, the Republican Party was not actually formed at that meeting.

On May 9, 1854, the day after the Kansas-Nebraska Bill passed the House, Representative Israel Washburn of Maine called together some thirty antislavery Congressmen at the rooms of two Massachusetts members. This group, composed chiefly of Conscience Whigs, took steps toward organizing a new party and agreed informally upon the name Republican Party, a name that Washburn used soon afterward in a public speech at Bangor.

On July 6, 1854, five thousand delegates, "irrespective of political organization," held a meeting in Jackson, Michigan. The number of delegates was so great that they could not get a hall large enough to hold them and they met for two days "under the oaks." They condemned the Kansas-Nebraska Bill, formed a new party and named it the Republican Party. This was the first formal adoption of this name. On July 6, 1904,

Secretary of State John Hay delivered an address in Jackson, Michigan, at what was regarded as the fiftieth anniversary of the "birth of the Republican Party" at that place. On July 13, 1854, similar mass conventions were held in Madison, Indianapolis, Columbus and Montpelier, and during the weeks following Maine, Iowa, Illinois, New York and other States followed suit. The Anti-Nebraska idea spread like wild fire and the movement completely disrupted the Whig Party and threatened to break up the Democratic Party in the North. So many mass meetings were held to condemn Douglas that he himself said, "I could travel from Boston to Chicago at night by light of my own burning effigies. When the Little Giant returned to Illinois to defend himself the people were in no mood to listen to him. At Chicago, while he was trying to address a crowd of 10,000 angry people, church bells tolled and ships on Lake Michigan lowered their flags to half-mast. Great orator and able debater that he was, Douglas was so hooted and jeered that he finally abandoned his attempts to be heard. It was late Saturday night and he is reported to have taken out his watch and said in disgust: "It is now Sunday morning; I am going to church and you can go to hell."

The Republican Party started as a spontaneous movement, a mere coalescence of dissenters on the warpath. As Horace Greeley wrote in the New York *Tribune* on July 9, 1859; "The Republican Party . . . was called into being solely to resist the encroachments of slavery upon the free territory of the Union and upon the free States. It was a combination of men of varying political antecedents; some had been Whigs, some Democrats, some Americans, some Abolitionists, some had always kept aloof from politics." In 1854 the Republican Party had no national organization or name, lacked cohesion and was in fact only a series of State parties. It had been launched by the people without the help of professional politicians and did not have a single leader with a national reputation. In some States the Republicans were little more than the Whigs under a new name.

George Frisbie Hoar, in *Autobiography of Seventy Years* (1903) wrote:

In 1854, the passage of the measure known as the Kansas-Nebraska Bill offered a new opportunity. A meeting of citizens of Concord appointed a committee of which Mr. Hoar was Chairman, and A. G. Fay, Secretary, who called a meeting of prominent persons from different parts of the State to meet at the American House in Boston, to make measures for forming a new party and called a State Convention. The Convention was held at Worcester on the 7th of September, and formed a party under the name of Republican, and nominated candidates for State offices. The meeting has been claimed to be the foundation of the Republican Party of Massachusetts, and its 25th anniversary was celebrated accordingly in 1879. But it effected little more than to change the name of the Free Soil party. Few Whigs or Democrats united in the movement.

The New York unit of the party did not adopt the name Republican until 1855. But all members agreed in their opposition to the extension of slavery and the Democratic Party that sponsored it. In the Congressional and State elections of 1854 the Republicans polled popular majorities in fifteen of the thirty-one States and elected eleven U.S. Senators and ninety-two Representatives. From this time it was obvious that the new party would have national leaders and would supplant the Whig Party as the major opposition to the Democrats.

In December, 1855, the State Republican committees of Ohio, Massachusetts, Pennsylvania, Vermont, Wisconsin and Michigan issued a call for a national meeting in Pittsburgh on February 22, 1856. Of course those who called the meeting did not realize that the date was the birthday of a new member of the party and would become a red-letter day in the American calendar. By this time nearly all groups in the new party had decided to accept the name Republican. *Whig* was thought undesirable because it was associated with neutrality on the slavery question and would discourage Democrats and others by giving members of the old Whig Party seniority. Since the National Republicans had adopted *Whig* in the 1830's and the Jacksonians had finally discarded *Democratic-Republican* in favor of *Democratic* in 1844, *Republican* was no longer the name or part of the name of a national party and was available for any party that wanted to use it. The term had been preferred by Jefferson, Madison and Monroe and had connotations that appealed to the divergent groups composing the new party. Besides most of the State organizations of the new movement had already adopted *Republican* as the party name.

The Pittsburgh meeting formally adopted *Republican Party* as the official name of the new organization, formed a national committee, perfected a national organization and made arrangements for a national nominating convention later in the year. The first Republican National Convention met in Philadelphia on June 17, with only a handful of delegates from the Southern States present. The convention was in agreement on one issue only—that slavery should not be extended—and that was the basic plank in the platform. But the leaders realized that this issue alone was not enough on which to build a new party in opposition to the Democrats. The convention, besides declaring it "the right and the duty of Congress to prohibit in the territories those two twin relics of barbarism—Polygamy and Slavery," went on record in favor of the principles of Washington and Jefferson, Federal aid to a Pacific railroad, and Congressional appropriations for "the improvement of rivers and harbors of a national character."

The convention nominated John C. Frémont, "the Pathfinder of the West," for President on the first ballot, and William L. Dayton of New Jersey for Vice President. Abraham Lincoln, who had waited nearly two years before abandoning the Whig Party to join the new party, received 110 votes for Vice President on the first and only ballot. "Free Speech, Free Press, Free Soil, Free Men, Frémont, and Victory!"—a modification of the old Free Soil Party slogan, was adopted by the Republicans. The Democrats nominated James Buchanan for President and John C. Breckinridge of Kentucky for Vice President. The American Party (Know-Nothings) nominated former President Millard Fillmore for President and Andrew Jackson Donelson of Tennessee for Vice President, while a remnant of the Whig Party held a national convention at Baltimore and indorsed the American Party candidates. Many men who had been elected to office as Whigs continued to use that name, but the Whig Party as a national organization ceased to exist. On most issues except slavery the Republican Party had become both the political and spiritual heir of the Whig Party in the North. Most of the Southern Whigs joined the Democratic Party.

Because of their supposed fondness for Negroes and because they were supported by the Abolitionists, members of the new party were called Black Republicans by the Southern Democrats. As early as January 3, 1856, Representative George Abel Simmons of New York, who had been elected in 1852 as a Whig, said in a speech in Congress: "Now, these gentlemen denounce us as 'Black Republicans.'" But most of the Republicans did not resent the term and adopted it. On April 16, 1856, Rutherford B. Hayes wrote to his friend Guy M. Bryan in Texas: "Not being a K.N. (Know-Nothing) I am left as a sort of waif on the political sea with symptoms of a mild sort toward Black Republicanism." In a speech in Washington, D.C. Anson Jones, last President of the Republic of Texas, said, "I consider Black Republicans as synonymous with abolitionism." Years before the Conscience Whigs had been called Woolly Heads by Southerners for similar reasons.

The campaign of 1856 was a bitter one. Know-Nothing sentiment was at its peak, and Frémont, of French Huguenot descent, was accused of being secretly a Catholic. Even the Republican candidate's paternity was an issue. Sex appeal was used in a national political campaign for the first time. Jessie Benton Frémont, daughter of Senator Thomas H. Benton of Missouri, was with her husband continually during the campaign and pictures of Frémont and his wife appeared side by side on so many posters and banners that many people were under the impression that she was running for Vice President. Frémont's supporters sang

> Oh! we'll give 'em Jessie
> When we rally around the polls . . .

and "Give 'em Jessie" became a slogan. Much was made of the fact that Senator Benton, who was opposed to the extension of slavery, refused to support his son-in-law and remained loyal to the Democrats. In the election of 1856 the electoral and popular vote was: Buchanan, 174—1,838,169; Frémont, 144—1,341,264 and Fillmore, 8—874,534. The Republicans elected twenty Senators and ninety-two Representatives to Congress. Although the Democrats won, the Republicans received enough electoral and popular votes to justify the hope of victory in 1860.

Several events helped the Republicans during the next four years—the assault upon Senator Charles Sumner of Massachusetts in the Senate Chamber by Representative Preston S. Brooks of South Carolina, the Dred Scott decision, John Brown's raid on Harper's Ferry, attempts of the Democratic administration to enforce the Fugitive Slave Act rigidly, and the breach between Douglas and the Southern Democrats. At the age of thirty-five Douglas was widely talked of as the Democratic candidate for President in 1848. In the Democratic National Convention of 1852 he received more votes than any other man except Lewis Cass until Franklin Pierce, a dark horse, was nominated on the forty-ninth ballot, and in the convention of 1856 he had received more votes than any other man except Buchanan. At that time it was taken for granted that the Little Giant would be the Democratic nominee for President in 1860. Douglas sponsored "Popular Sovereignty" in the hope that it would unite behind him both the Northern and Southern Democrats. Until then he was very popular with the Southern Democrats, who called him "Young America." But his "Popular Sovereignty" and Kansas-Nebraska Bill displeased many Northern and nearly all Southern Democrats. In 1847 Douglas married Martha Denny Martin, daughter of Colonel Robert Martin, who owned large plantations in North Carolina and Mississippi. When Colonel Martin died in 1848 Mrs. Douglas inherited his plantations, including 150 slaves. This connection with the Southern aristocracy made Douglas popular in the South but was a political liability in the North. Mrs. Douglas died in 1852 and for several years Douglas became careless in dress, bitter in speech and generally dejected. After making an extended tour of Europe he returned much refreshed and more ambitious politically than ever before. On November 20, 1856, shortly after the election, the forty-three-year-old widower with two sons married Adele Cutts, the charming and attractive daughter of James Madison Cutts of Washington, D.C., and a grandniece of Dolly Madison. The second Mrs. Douglas was a devout Catholic and that fact probably influenced American political history more than can ever be demonstrated. Know-Nothingism had spread to the South and the Know-Nothings saw to it that the fact that Douglas's wife was a Catholic was widely advertised.

The Republicans made substantial gains in the Congressional and State elections of 1858 and *Whig* virtually disappeared as a political label. In 1860 the Republican National Convention met in Chicago on May 16 with all the Northern and Border States represented. The convention adopted the platform of 1856 in substance and, after denouncing the threats of secession by Southern States, added planks favoring a protective tariff and a homestead law. Abraham Lincoln was nominated for President and Hannibal Hamlin of Maine for Vice President. The Democrats held their national convention at Charleston. Douglas led on all fifty-seven ballots but could not get the necessary two thirds. Seven State delegations withdrew from the convention and the Democratic Party was split wide apart. At a later convention in Baltimore the Northern Democrats nominated Douglas for President and Herschel V. Johnson of Georgia for Vice President. The Southern Democrats, meeting in the same city, nominated John C. Breckinridge for President and Joseph Lane of Oregon for Vice President. The Constitutional Union Party (essentially the Know-Nothings and Americans under a new name) nominated John Bell of Tennessee for President and Edward Everett of Massachusetts for Vice President. With four major parties in the field for the first time, the campaign was confused and extremely bitter. Hamlin, the Republican Vice-Presidential candidate was swarthy in complexion and the story was successfully circulated in the Southern and Border states that he was of part Negro blood. Lincoln was lampooned and cartooned as an ape. Anti-Catholics whispered around that Douglas while on his European tour had stopped in Rome and "kissed the foot of the Pope." Republicans sang:

> Old Abe Lincoln came out of the wilderness,
> Down in Illinois.

The electoral and popular vote in 1860 was: Lincoln, 180—1,865,913; Douglas, 12—1,374,664; Breckinridge, 72—848,404, and Bell, 39—591,900. Although Lincoln received a decided minority of the total popular vote, he received a clear majority of the electoral vote. The Republican Party started as a third party, quickly became a second party, gained control of the Government six years after its beginning, and remained in control of the Government without interruption for twenty years.

Who said: "There is a higher law than the Constitution"?

This statement was made by William Henry Seward (1801-1878), antislavery Senator from New York, in a speech in the U.S. Senate during the debate on the Compromise of 1850. Daniel Webster, who hoped that adoption of the compromise measures introduced by Henry Clay would prevent a sectional war and save the Union, delivered a notable speech on March 4. Since indorsement of the compromise put Webster in the position of favoring a more drastic fugitive slave law, the abolitionists and other antislavery people of the North were very bitter toward him and accused him of selling out to the slaveholding South. Seward, then a new member and, like Webster and Clay, a Whig, spoke on March 11. Among other things he said:

I know there are laws of various kinds, which regulate the conduct of men. There are constitutions and statutes, codes mercantile and civil; but when we are legislating for States, especially when we are founding States, all these laws must be brought to the standard of the laws of God. The Constitution regulates our stewardship; the Constitution devotes the domain to union, to justice, to defence, to welfare, to liberty. But *there is a higher law than the Constitution,* which regulates our authority over the domain.

The context of Seward's speech shows clearly that he meant that the Senate, in dealing with the fugitive slave act and the slavery question in general, should consider moral as well as constitutional law; but he was accused of advocating measures outside and beyond the Constitution. Not only the Democrats, but also many of the Whigs, including former Representative Abraham Lincoln, thought that Seward had gone too far when he made his "higher law" statement. It is believed that this "catch phrase" cost Seward the Republican nomination for the Presidency in 1856, when John C. Frémont was nominated but not elected.

The "higher law" theory was not original with Seward. In 1835, when the Southern States were applying to the Federal Government to protect them against the circulation of abolitionist literature through the mails, Postmaster General Amos Kendall said in a letter to the postmaster at Charleston, South Carolina: "We owe an obligation to the laws, but a higher one to the community in which we live, and if the former be perverted to destroy the latter, it is patriotism to disregard them."

On October 25, 1858, in a speech at Rochester, New York, Seward said of the slavery struggle: "It is an *irrepressible conflict* between opposing and enduring forces, and it means that the United States must and will, sooner or later, become either entirely a slave-holding nation, or entirely a free-labor nation." This catch phrase, *irrepressible conflict,* widely interpreted as meaning that the slavery question could not be settled without a dissolution of the Union, further alienated moderate anti-slavery people among Seward's followers in the North and probably cost him the Republican nomination in 1860, when Lincoln was nominated and elected. Yet Seward's statement was substantially the same as Lincoln's "house-divided-against-itself" statement. On June 16, 1858, more than four months before Seward spoke at Rochester, Lincoln had said at Springfield: "I believe this government cannot endure permanently half slave and half free. I do not expect the Union to be dissolved. I do not expect the house to fall, but I do expect that it will cease to be divided. It will become all one thing, or all the other." When Lincoln heard that Seward had adopted his opinion he nodded approval. But Seward had gone further than Lincoln had in condemning the institution of slavery itself. James G. Blaine said of Seward long afterward that "everything he had said was remembered to his injury."

What was the mudsill theory of society?

A mudsill is the lowest sill or foundation timber of a structure, such as a house, bridge or dam, and is generally embedded in the soil or mud. Railroad crossties, the timbers laid on the roadbed to form the foundation for the rails, used to be called mudsills. Just before the Civil War *mudsill* was used to denote the lowest class of society, particularly those who did the hard work.

Early in 1858 Senator William H. Seward of New York boasted that in the future the North would rule the South as a conquered province. On March 4, 1858, Senator James H. Hammond of South Carolina replied to the New Yorker. Hammond, the son of a native of Massachusetts, had declared that slavery was "the cornerstone of our republical edifice" and had advocated the death penalty for abolitionists. Among other things the South Carolinian said in his reply to Seward:

In all social systems there must be a class to perform the drudgery of life,— that is, a class requiring but a low order of intellect, and but little skill. Such a class you must have, or you would not have that other class which leads progress, civilization, and refinement. It constitutes the very mud-sill of society and of political government; and you might as well attempt to build a house in the air, as to build either the one or the other except on this mud-sill. Fortunately for the South, she found a race adapted to that purpose. . . . We use them for that purpose and call them slaves. . . . But I will not characterize that class at the North with that term; but you have it. It is there; it is everywhere; it is eternal.

Mudsill came to Hammond's mind in this connection because he had been supervising the construction of buildings on his South Carolina plantation.

The Republicans promptly charged the Southern leaders with branding the farmers and workingmen of the North as *mudsills,* which became a sort of political battlecry. A banner carried by supporters of Abraham Lincoln for the Senate in Illinois bore the legend: SMALL-FISTED FARMERS, MUD-SILLS OF SOCIETY, GREASY MECHANICS, FOR A. LINCOLN. The New York *Evening Post* reported that the miners and workingmen of California who supported Senator David C. Broderick were organizing themselves into associations styled "Mud-sill Clubs." The catchy term worried politicians even in the Border States. In May, 1858, the Richmond *Enquirer* quoted Governor Henry A. Wise as saying in a a speech:

It is time that Virginia was turning her attention to manufacturers, mechanics, mining, and foreign commerce. No country, no State can live upon one only of the five cardinal powers of production. She must resort to all the five combined, and she is doing it. I say that labor is not the 'mud-sill' of society; and I thank God that the old colonial aristocracy of Virginia, which despised mechanical and manual labor, is nearly run out.

In 1859 Lincoln made a speech entitled *Mud-sill Theory of Labor* in which he said:

By some it is assumed that labor is available only in connection with capital— that nobody labors unless somebody else owning capital, somehow, by the use of it, induces him to do it. . . . But another class of reasoners . . . hold that labor is prior to, and independent of, capital; that, in fact, capital is the fruit of labor, and could never have existed if labor had not first existed without capital.

Who said: "If any one attempts to haul down the American flag, shoot him on the spot"?

When the Southern States began to secede and to seize Federal property William Hemphill Jones was sent to New Orleans as U.S. Treasury Department agent. Captain Breshwood of the revenue cutter *Robert*

McClelland had refused to obey instructions to take the vessel north and was suspected of having designs of turning her over to the Confederates. Jones asked for further instructions from Washington, but his position was hopeless after Louisiana seceded on January 26, 1861. On January 29, John Adams Dix (1798-1879), who had become President Buchanan's Secretary of the Treasury only fourteen days before and who was then living in the White House as the President's guest, sent Jones the following telegram:

Tell Lieut. Caldwell to arrest Captain Breshwood, assume command of the cutter, and obey the order I gave through you. If Capt. Breshwood, after arrest, undertakes to interfere with the command of the cutter, tell Lieut. Caldwell to consider him a mutineer, and treat him accordingly. If any one attempts to haul down the American flag, shoot him on the spot.

The unarmed Treasury clerk in the midst of a secessionist hotbed would have been powerless to carry out the peremptory order. Actually the telegram fell into Confederate hands and never reached him. All Federal property in New Orleans was seized, the American flag hauled down, and the amiable agent left without shooting anybody on the spot or elsewhere. But Dix's message was published and the last sentence became the rallying cry of Unionists all over the country.

Dix fought in the War of 1812 and was a captain when he left the Army in 1828. He became a lawyer and writer, and in 1845 was chosen U.S. Senator as an antislavery Democrat. After he retired as Secretary of the Treasury on March 3, 1861, when he was sixty-three years old, he was appointed a major general by Lincoln. He was Minister to France three years, and in 1872, though a Democrat and seventy-five years of age, he was nominated and elected Governor of New York by the Republicans.

When were the most ex-Presidents living?

Between March 4, 1861, when Abraham Lincoln became President, and January 18, 1862, when John Tyler died, there were five living ex-Presidents, a greater number than at any other time. They were Martin Van Buren, Tyler, Millard Fillmore, Franklin Pierce and James Buchanan.

In 1861 ex-President Pierce suggested that the five ex-Presidents appeal to the Federal Government to grant an armistice with a view of devising steps to save the Union without civil war. Fillmore and Tyler favored the proposal, but Van Buren, the senior ex-President, refused to join in such action without assurances that it would be agreeable to the Lincoln administration. Buchanan, whose inaction was partly responsible for the crisis, was hardly in a position to be giving counsel to his successor. Upon the suggestion of Tyler the Virginia legislature proposed a convention of the Border States to attempt conciliation between the North and the South. The convention met in Washington in February, 1861, and Tyler acted as its chairman. Neither of these proposals came to anything.

The unusually large number of ex-Presidents living at that time was due chiefly to the fact that no President chosen between 1836 and 1856 inclusively served longer than four years. All five of the ex-Presidents in 1861 were one-termers.

Between March 4, 1825, when John Quincy Adams became President, and July 4, 1826, when Thomas Jefferson and John Adams died, there were four living ex-Presidents—James Monroe, James Madison, Jefferson and John Adams. President Monroe always sent copies of his messages to Congress and other important state papers to the three ex-Presidents, and he consulted Jefferson and Madison as "elder statesmen" and as a sort of super-Cabinet.

There have been only four short periods since Washington retired from the Presidency when there has not been at least one former President living. Washington was the first ex-President as well as the first President. When he died December 14, 1799, he had been ex-President for two years, nine months and ten days, and for the rest of John Adam's term there was no living ex-President. This situation did not occur again for more than seventy-four years. When Ulysses S. Grant became President on March 4, 1869, three ex-Presidents were living—Fillmore, Pierce and Andrew Johnson. Fillmore died in 1868, Pierce in 1874, and Johnson on July 31, 1875. Thus during the latter part of Grant's second term—from July 31, 1875, to March 4, 1877, when Rutherford B. Hayes became President, there was no ex-President living.

Ex-President Grover Cleveland died June 24, 1908, and there was no ex-President living from that date until March 4, 1909, when William Howard Taft succeeded Theodore Roosevelt. This happened again in 1933. Calvin Coolidge died January 5, 1933, and from that date until March 4, 1933, when Franklin D. Roosevelt succeeded Herbert Hoover, there was no living ex-President. Hoover has been the only ex-President living since March 4, 1933, until the present time (1952).

John Adams was ex-President longer than any other man. He was ex-President from March 4, 1801, to July 4, 1826, a period of twenty-five years and four months. He lived to see three successors, all Virginians, to serve a total of twenty-four years, and died during the administration of his own son. Van Buren was ex-President twenty-one years, four months and twenty days. He was the eighth President and lived to see eight Presidents succeed him, all of them being from different States—Harrison of Ohio, Tyler of Virginia, Polk of Tennessee, Taylor of Louisiana, Fillmore of New York, Pierce of New Hampshire, Buchanan of Pennsylvania and Lincoln of Illinois. This is remarkable in view of the fact that from Washington to Harry S. Truman only thirteen States sent men to the Presidency. Millard Fillmore was ex-President for twenty-one years and four days.

James K. Polk was ex-President a shorter time than any other man. He died on June 15, 1849, three months and twelve days after his term expired. He was fifty-three years, seven months and thirteen days old and died at an earlier age that any other ex-President. Robert C. Winthrop, Speaker of the House and Senator from Massachusetts, wrote in 1894 when he was eighty-five: "I have known, and many of them intimately, every one of the twenty-three Presidents, except Washington, who died nine years before I was born."

What ex-President's death passed without official notice?

John Tyler, President from 1841 to 1845, has been the only President whose death was not the subject of a special announcement or proclamation by the President of the United States in office.

In 1861 former President Tyler was sent by Virginia as a commissioner to President James Buchanan to try to neutralize Fort Sumter. Later in the same year he was a delegate to and president of the Peace Congress in Washington called by Virginia to devise means of preventing war between the North and the South. After its failure he joined the Confederacy and served in the Provisional Confederate Congress. On November 8, 1861, the Richmond *Enquirer* reported that John Tyler, the tenth President of the United States, had been elected to the House of Representatives of the Confederacy and had "received a majority of 215 over all his opponents and outnumbered his nearest competitor more than two to one." He died on January 18, 1862, a month before the first session of the regular Confederate Congress opened, and was buried on January 20 with Episcopal services. President Jefferson Davis, Vice President Alexander Stephens and all members of the Confederate cabinet attended his funeral, but President Lincoln took no official notice of his death. It was not until October 12, 1915, that a monument to Tyler in Hollywood Cemetery in Richmond was authorized by act of the U.S. Congress.

Tyler was the only former President who joined the Confederacy. His family claimed descent from the fourteenth-century English rebel Wat Tyler. Two of his sons by his second wife, J. Alexander Tyler and

David Gardiner Tyler, enlisted in the Confederate army as privates when they were fifteen and sixteen respectively. Later these two sons of of President Tyler studied in Germany, and J. Alexander Tyler served with the German Uhlans during the Franco-Prussian War. The latter died in New Mexico in 1883.

What does "twisting the lion's tail" mean?

Abusing the British to curry favor with anti-British voters is known in American political slang as twisting the lion's tail. The shield of England contains a lion *passant gardant,* as it is called in heraldry. Consequently the king of beasts is regarded as the national emblem of Great Britain and the symbol of the British people. "Twisting the British lion's tail" was originally applied in America to anything said or done to annoy the British and to please their enemies, especially the Irish. At first the phrase had a much more serious meaning than it has at present. Between the War of 1812 and the Civil War anti-British sentiment was widespread in the United States. Fire-eaters in and out of Congress were continually demanding war with England. Demagogues quickly learned how to whip up anti-British feeling for political purposes. They found that giving the lion's tail another twist or two didn't disturb the British much but was very effective in getting votes in the Third Ward.

When Thomas R. Marshall was Governor of Indiana the legislature passed and the Governor signed a bill requiring that "The Star Spangled Banner" be sung in its entirety in all of the State schools, but the act appropriated no funds to supply words and music of the song to the school children. In *Recollections* (1925) Marshall wrote:

Some months after the General Assembly had adjourned I was called on by a friend of Irish descent who asked me to inform him when the act was to be put into effect. I explained the financial situation. I said to him that for patriotic reasons I was extremely sorry that it could not be done. Whereupon, with the frankness that always marks the conduct of a man of Irish descent, he notified me that the act had been prepared and presented by the Clan na Gael; that they had no patriotic purpose in it whatever, but that they desired it sung in its entirety because there was one verse in it that gave the British Lion's tail a particularly vicious and nerve-racking twist.

What is a fire-eater?

Fire-eater in the sense of a juggler who pretends to swallow fire was used as early as 1670. It is believed that fire-eaters accomplish their apparent magic by means of tricks and sleight-of-hand substitution of materials, although it is said that some of them can hold burning coals in the mouth several minutes at a time without injury by previously treating the mouth and lips with compounds that make them impervious to heat. Early in the nineteenth century *fire-eater* came to be used in the sense of a duelist, a hotspur, a firebrand, and a hotheaded person who will fight at the drop of a hat. After the admission of Texas into the Union in 1845 Northerners applied *fire-eater* to the extreme and violent Southern partisans, such as Robert Barnwell Rhett of South Carolina, Robert Lowndes Yancey of Alabama and others who openly advocated disruption of the Union. In the second edition of *Dictionary of Americanisms* (1859) John Russell Bartlett said the term in this sense was "of recent introduction." "The fire-eaters in the territory and the fire-eaters outside," reported the Lecompton (Kansas) *Democrat* in November, 1857, "do not at all agree in their views of what is proper to be done in reference to voting on the constitution."

Who was "Extra Billy" Smith?

"Extra Billy" was the nickname of William Smith (1797-1887), Virginia lawyer, businessman, Congressman, Governor and soldier. In 1827 he organized a coach service between Fairfax and Culpeper and within a few years was operating mail and passenger coaches between Washington, D.C., and Milledgeville, Georgia. During a Congressional investigation in 1834, Senator Benjamin W. Leigh of Virginia noticed the frequent extra payments made by the Post Office Department on mail contracts with Smith and referred to him as "Extra Billy," a sobriquet that stuck. Extra Billy Smith was severely wounded in the Battle of Antietam and commanded the Confederate "Light Brigade" at Gettysburg while he was Governor-elect of Virginia.

What was the National Union Party?

The National Union Party was a temporary coalition of the Republicans and War Democrats from 1863 to 1866. Abraham Lincoln was elected President the first time as a Republican, but the second time as a National Unionist.

When the Republican Party gained control of the Federal Government in 1861 it was a minority party not only in the country as a whole but even in the loyal States. It was also a comparatively new party that had not had time to consolidate as an effective political organization. That the Republican Party was only a sectional party that did not represent the entire country was a common charge made by the Democrats. President Lincoln recognized the justice of this charge and from the beginning appointed some Union Democrats to high Federal office. After the outbreak of hostilities the Republican leaders realized they would need the help of the War Democrats and Independents to carry on the war successfully.

In 1862 secret Union political societies began to spring up in the Northern and Border States to counteract the activities of the Copperheads, Knights of the Golden Circle and other secret organizations disloyal to the Union. Their declared purpose was to organize and consolidate loyalty to the Union and to make it effective. They urged support of the Lincoln administration regardless of party, minimized the idea that the war was being fought to free the slaves and appealed to the War Democrats by emphasizing the importance of saving the Union. William Osborn Stoddard took an active part in organizing the various local Union Leagues and Loyal Leagues into the Union League of America. All members of the organization took oaths to vote only for Union men for office. The next year Union League clubs were organized in various cities. In Philadelphia and Chicago these organizations survived as Republican social clubs.

There was precedent for using *Union* as a party label. Those in South Carolina in 1832 who opposed Nullification and favored the Union were known as Unionists. References to "the Union Party" of South Carolina occur frequently in the reports of the time. Mass meetings of persons friendly to the Union and in sympathy with the Union Party in South Carolina were held in Northern cities. Philip Hone and others formed the "Union Club" in New York City. Many Northern Whigs continued to call themselves "Unionists" for several years. Those who nominated John Bell of Tennessee for President in 1860 called their temporary and makeshift party "the Constitutional Union Party."

Although the Republicans in 1863 retained their national and State political organizations, they began to refer to themselves in many parts of the country as Unionists instead of Republicans. By nominating War Democrats as well as Republicans the "Union Party" won in most of the elections in Ohio and the Border States in 1862 and 1863. On April 10, 1863, Rutherford B. Hayes wrote to his wife, "I am glad as anybody that the Union ticket (in Cincinnati) was carried," and on October 21 of the same year he wrote to his mother from Camp White in West Virginia, "The men of my regiment and my brigade were both unanimous for the Union ticket."

At one time it appeared doubtful whether President Lincoln could even be renominated as the Republican candidate. Horace Greeley wrote an editorial suggesting that Lincoln withdraw in favor of some other man such as John C. Frémont or Benjamin Butler. "Mr. Lincoln is already beaten. He can never be elected," wrote the famous editor of the New York *Tribune*. On February 25, 1864, the Union members of the Ohio legislature held a caucus and declared for Lincoln's renomination and that started the ball rolling in favor of the President. Shortly thereafter the Republicans decided to suspend the name *Republican Party*. The National Union Party was never quite a political party or a coalition of two political parties in the usual sense of those terms. Actually it was little more than a label to induce War Democrats and Independents to join the Republicans on the single question of saving the Union. Although the Republican National Committee retained its identity as such, nearly everywhere the Republicans gave up their name temporarily and campaigned under the name of the National Union Party. It is doubtful whether Lincoln could have been re-elected as a straight Republican.

A group of anti-Lincoln Republicans invited "the radical men of the nation" to meet in convention at Cleveland on May 31, 1864. This convention was composed of several hundred delegates representing fifteen States. The delegates represented anti-Lincoln Republicans, radical Democrats, abolitionists and western Germans. They favored the Union and vigorous prosecution of the war and agreed in their opposition to the Lincoln administration. Others were personal admirers of John C. Frémont, who had been the Republican candidate in 1856, who had been relieved of his military command chiefly because he had undertaken to free slaves on his own responsibility, and who disliked Lincoln personally. The convention, after denouncing the Lincoln administration, adopted a platform calling for the suppression of the rebellion, preservation of habeas corpus, the right of asylum and the Monroe Doctrine, a Constitutional Amendment prohibiting slavery, the confiscation of the land of rebels and its distribution of such land among actual settlers, election of the President by direct popular vote, and a single term for the President. Although this "third party" was called "The Radical Democracy" and "the Radical Men," it adopted the name Independent Republican Party. It nominated Frémont for President and General John Cockrane of New York for Vice President.

When Lincoln was told that only four hundred delegates had met in Cleveland instead of the thousands expected, the President opened a Bible and read I Samuel 22:2, which reads: "And every one that was in distress, and every one that was in debt, and every one that was discontented, gathered themselves unto him; and he became a captain over them: and there were with him about four hundred men." But Frémont had many followers among the radicals and Lincoln and the Republican leaders were worried about his independent candidacy, which looked as if it might split the Union Party.

The Republican National Convention met at Baltimore on June 11 and nominated Lincoln for President and Andrew Johnson of Tennessee for Vice President on the ticket of the National Union Party. Johnson was a slaveowner and a Democrat who had received the twelve votes of Tennessee in the Southern Democratic convention of 1860 and who had voted for John C. Breckinridge in the election that year. The Republican convention of 1864, composed of both Republican and Democratic Unionists, wanted to refute the charge that it represented only a section, to give significance to the name National Union Party and to appeal to War Democrats. To what extent Lincoln had a hand in discarding Vice President Hannibal Hamlin of Maine and in choosing Johnson is a disputed question. Some authorities say Lincoln wanted Johnson as his running mate and engineered his nomination, while others insist that the President meant exactly what he said when he advised his henchmen that he had no choice in the matter and the question as to who should be the candidate for Vice President was entirely up to the convention. Johnson was the only Southerner who remained loyal to the Union and kept his seat in the Senate after his State seceded and the war had begun in earnest. The Tennessean remained in the Senate at the risk of his life, and Lincoln so admired his courage that he appointed him military governor of his State. In the convention Henry Jervis Raymond, a friend of Lincoln's and later chairman of the Republican National Committee, took an active part in the nomination of Johnson for Vice President.

The military situation was temporarily unfavorable to the North and Lincoln was gloomy about the prospects of his re-election. On July 12, 1864, a month after his renomination, President Lincoln stood on a mound in the suburbs of Washington and watched a battle in which about 980 Federal and Confederate soldiers were killed or wounded. On August 23, 1864, before the Democratic National Convention met, the President had each member of his Cabinet sign a piece of paper so folded that they could not read the contents. He then put this paper in a safe place. Later it was learned that this paper read: "This morning, as for some days past, it seems exceedingly probable that this administration will not be reelected. Then it will be my duty to so cooperate with the President-elect as to save the Union between the election and the inauguration; as he will have secured his election on such ground that he cannot possibly save it afterwards. A. Lincoln."

The Democratic National Convention, controlled by the Peace Democrats, met at Chicago on August 29 and nominated General George B. McClellan for President and Representative George H. Pendleton of Ohio for Vice President on a platform declaring the war a failure and demanding a cessation of hostilities and a negotiated peace. Frémont, though anti-Lincoln, was strongly pro-Union, and saw that his candidacy would operate merely to divide the Unionists and help McClellan and the Peace Democrats. After indirect negotiations with Lincoln, Frémont and Cockrane withdrew on September 21 and the Independent Republican Party dissolved. Lincoln then requested and received the resignation of Postmaster General Montgomery Blair, who was objectionable to the Independents, and appointed William Dennison of Ohio in his place. From that time the campaign of 1864 was a contest between the National Union Party and the Democratic Party with no minor parties in the field. A series of Federal military victories rapidly improved Lincoln's prospects for re-election during the last weeks of the Presidential campaign. Lincoln and Johnson, the National Unionist candidates, received 2,216,007 popular votes and 212 electoral votes, while McClellan and Pendleton, the Democratic candidates, received 1,808,725 popular votes and only the electoral votes of New Jersey, Delaware and Kentucky.

After Lincoln was assassinated Vice President Johnson became President. Although he was a war Democrat, he then became the titular head of the nebulous National Union Party, composed of Republicans, War Democrats and Independents. On December 1, 1865, Representative Rutherford B. Hayes noted in his diary: "A caucus of the Ohio Union delegation held at Mr. Delano's rooms tonight." The Union League of America declined in the North after the war, but in the South it was a powerful influence until its activities were curtailed by the Ku Klux Klan. In the South the Union League of America developed into a powerful organization of Federal officials, carpetbaggers, scalawags and Negroes. It was estimated that two years after the close of the war the organization had a membership of 200,000 in the former Confederate States.

President Johnson soon lost the support of the Radical Republicans, who comprised a large majority in the Republican Party. The Conservative or Johnson Republicans and the War Democrats, with the support of many former Peace Democrats and Copperheads, tried to keep alive the fictitious National Union Party, of which President Johnson was the nominal head. Beaten in Congress by the Radical Republicans, Johnson's supporters sponsored an "off-year" convention of the National Union Party at Philadelphia in August, 1866. This was called "The Arm-in-Arm Convention" because the delegates from Massachusetts and

South Carolina entered the convention hall together arm in arm. Even Henry J. Raymond, chairman of the Republican National Committee, upon the suggestion of William H. Seward and other Conservative Republican leaders supporting Johnson, attended the Arm-in-Arm Convention and helped write its declaration of principles. The chief issue between the National Union Party and the Radical Republicans was Johnson's reconstruction policies. The Radical Republicans, who controlled both Congress and the Republican Party, refused to participate in the Philadelphia convention, and the National Union Party, which had served its purpose of uniting Union men during the war, soon petered out.

In 1868 President Johnson sought the Democratic nomination, but the Democratic National Convention, again attended by Southern as well as Northern delegates, nominated Horatio Seymour of New York for President and Francis Preston Blair, Jr., of Missouri for Vice President. The Republican Party, which had abandoned the National Union Party label, nominated Ulysses S. Grant for President and Schuyler Colfax of Indiana for Vice President. There were no minor parties in the field in 1868 and the contest was solely between the Republican Party and the Democratic Party. Grant and Colfax received 3,015,071 popular votes and 214 electoral votes, while Seymour and Blair received 2,709,613 popular votes and 80 electoral votes.

Who was Thaddeus Stevens?

Thaddeus Stevens (1792-1868) was the son of a thriftless Vermont shoemaker and was raised and educated by his mother. The family name was spelled *Stephens* and he was named for Thaddeus Kosciusko, the Polish Revolutionary hero. Thaddeus was sickly as a child and had a clubfoot and limped throughout life. He was a good swimmer and once he said he could swim the Hellespont as easily as did the club-footed Byron. After graduating from an academy and Dartmouth College and attending the University of Vermont, Stevens taught in an academy in York, Pennsylvania, studied law, and practiced first at Gettysburg and then at Lancaster.

In politics he was successively an Anti-Mason, a Whig, a Free-Soiler and a Republican. A remarkably effective speech in the Pennsylvania legislature in 1835 is credited with having saved the free public school system of the State. During the "Buckshot War" he escaped from a mob by leaping out of the window of the capitol at Harrisburg. He was denied his seat for his part in that controversy but was readmitted after being re-elected by his constituents. From youth he nursed a fierce hatred of slavery and as a lawyer aided fugitive slaves to escape. At Lancaster in 1853 he founded a newspaper called the *Independent Whig*.

Stevens was in Congress from 1849 to 1853 and from 1859 till his death in Washington. He helped organize the Republican Party and was one of the bitterest partisans who ever served in Congress. Coming into an election committee meeting late on one occasion, he asked what the point of the case under consideration was. When a colleague told him, "There isn't much point to it—they are both damned scoundrels," Stevens replied, "Which is the Republican damned scoundrel?—I want to go for him."

When the clouds of civil war were lowering over the country early in 1861, while Stevens's fellow-townsman, James Buchanan, was still President, he exclaimed, "Oh, for six months of stern old Jackson." The public edited this into, "Oh, for one hour of Andrew Jackson." Fitz-Greene Halleck, the poet, said: "Would to God we could have my old friend Jackson back again, to put down this accursed rebellion and restore the blessings of peace to our bleeding country."

In 1861 Stevens became chairman of the ways and means committee and Republican leader of the House. Up till then all money bills, including appropriations, were handled by that standing committee. Later, when he was failing in health and the burden becoming too much for him, Stevens had part of the work transferred to a new standing committee on appropriations, of which he became chairman.

As Radical Republican leader in the House, Stevens advocated racial equality, confiscation of rebel property, arming the slaves, and issuance of an emancipation proclamation by the President immediately. His hatred of the South was intensified after June, 1863, when General Lee invaded Pennsylvania and General Jubal A. Early destroyed Stevens' Caledonia ironworks near Chambersburg. Early had his Confederate soldiers work for several days to destroy completely the property of "the enemy of the South." The damage was estimated at $50,000, and Stevens had to provide for the hundred people who were made homeless and jobless. Stevens thought Lincoln was a dead duck politically, and when the President and his party went to the Gettysburg battlefield later in 1863 he refused to go along, saying, "Let the dead bury their own dead." He favored Salmon P. Chase in place of Lincoln as the Republican candidate for President in 1864.

After the war Stevens talked of reducing the Southern States to a "territorial condition" and treating them like "conquered provinces." He sponsored the Fourteenth Amendment to the Constitution, the

Freedman's Bureau Act, the Reconstruction Act and the Tenure of Office Act. It is probable that he did more than any other person to create "the Solid South."

He introduced the resolution to impeach President Johnson and was chairman of the House managers appointed to prosecute the President before the Senate. His eyes flashing with vengeance, the seventy-eight-year-old enemy of the South was wheeled to the President's trial in a chair, but he was a dying man and unable to take much part in the proceedings. He never married and his private morals were often questioned, but he was a man of ability and had loyal supporters and a national following. Some called him "the Great Commoner." More feared than loved, he had few intimate friends and companions, and when he died only a nephew and his colored housekeeper were at his bedside.

In his will the political nemesis of the South requested that he be buried in a private cemetery rather than a public one that denied Negroes burial. The following epitaph, written by himself, was engraved on his tombstone in Schreiner's Cemetery at Lancaster: "I repose in this quiet and secluded spot, not from any natural preference for solitude, but finding other cemeteries limited by charter rule as to race, I have chosen this that I might illustrate in my death the principles which I advocated through a long life—Equality of Man before his Creator."

Who was "Little Napoleon"?

General George Brinton McClellan (1826-1885), twice commander of the Army of the Potomac, was called "Little Napoleon" and "Young Napoleon" by his admirers. He resembled Napoleon Bonaparte in being slightly under medium height and squarely and powerfully built. Because he took the comparison of himself with Napoleon seriously he was ridiculed by his critics by the nickname "Macpoleon." He was an able organizer, maintained excellent discipline and morale among his troops and was popular. Although he could train an army, he was accused of being slow and overcautious in using it in battle and in following up an advantage. One of his weaknesses was his tendency to underrate his own resources and to overrate those of the enemy. General Robert E. Lee understood McClellan's strength as an organizer and his weakness as a fighter. After McClellan was replaced with Burnside in November, 1862, Lee remarked that he regretted to part with him, "for we always understood each other so well. I fear they may continue to make these changes until they find someone I don't understand." But later when asked who was the best Federal commander he had ever faced, he replied, "McClellan, by all odds." After the failure of his Peninsular campaign in 1862, McClellan's initials were sarcastically interpreted as standing for "Gun Boat" in allusion to his inclination to depend too much upon naval support for his army. His most friendly nickname was "Little Mac."

McClellan graduated No. 2 in the West Point class of 1846, served during the Mexican War and remained for several years in the regular army. He went abroad as a member of a board of officers to study European military systems and was an observer during the siege of Sevastopol in the Crimea in 1855. In his report he proposed a new type of saddle, modeled after that used in the Hungarian army. The basic features of the saddletree had been designed by Major Samuel Ringgold of the U.S. Army. The "McClellan saddle," with slight alterations, continued to be used in the Army until recent times.

When McClellan was removed from command the second time he was ordered to report at Princeton and wait for further orders, but he was never given another assignment. In 1864 the Democratic National Convention at Chicago nominated General McClellan for President. His running mate was Representative George Hunt Pendleton, of Ohio, who married Alice Key, daughter of Francis Scott Key and niece of Chief Justice Roger B. Taney, and who was known as "Gentlemen George" because he was descended from the Virginia Pendletons and inherited some of their natural dignity.

One plank of the Democratic platform was:

That this Convention does explicitly declare, as the sense of the American people, that after four years of failure to restore the Union by the experiment of war, during which under the pretense of a military necessity, a war power higher than the Constitution, the Constitution itself has been disregarded in every part, and public liberty and private rights alike trodden down, and the material prosperity of the country essentially impaired, justice, humanity, liberty, and the public welfare demand that immediate efforts be made for a cessation of hostilities, with a view to an ultimate convention of all the States, or other peaceable means, to the end that at the earliest practicable moment peace may be restored on the basis of the Federal Union of the States.

In his letter of acceptance McClellan ignored the demand for a cessation of hostilities, and the declaration that the war was a failure. He virtually disavowed the principal plank in the platform and declared: "The re-establishment of the Union in all its integrity is and must continue to be the indispensable condition in any settlement." McClellan did not resign his commission as a major general in the Federal army until election day. McClellan and Pendleton received 1,808,725 votes, but carried only three States—New Jersey, Delaware and Kentucky—with only 21 electoral votes. Lincoln and Johnson received 2,216,067 votes, and carried 19 States with 212 electoral votes. From 1878 to 1881 McClellan was Governor of New Jersey, the only nonslave State he had carried in 1864. His son of the same name was a member of Congress and Mayor of New York City.

The Battle of Antietam (Sharpsburg) on September 17, 1862, is regarded as the bloodiest one-day fighting during the Civil War. Total casualties were more than 20,000. The Federals under McClellan lost 11,832 out of 46,000 engaged, and the Confederates under Lee lost over 8,000. When the Antietam battlefield was dedicated after the war, General McClellan was not even invited to attend the ceremonies, and later when the battlefield was dedicated as a National Park, President Theodore Roosevelt spoke for an hour without mentioning or alluding to the man who commanded the Army of the Potomac on that bloody day.

Who was Ben Butler?

Two unrelated Benjamin Franklin Butlers were noted American lawyers and politicians. The lesser-known Benjamin F. Butler (1795-1858) was a New Yorker and was a law partner of Martin Van Buren at Albany. He turned down several high public offices because he preferred to practice and to teach law, but he was Attorney General of the United States under Andrew Jackson and Van Buren from 1833 to 1838. He founded the law department of the University of the City of New York.

The other Benjamin F. Butler (1818-1893) was a stormy petrel of American politics for thirty years. He was born in New Hampshire and taken to Massachusetts by his mother when he was ten years old. After graduating from Waterbury College (now Colby University) in Maine, he became a lawyer at Lowell, which continued to be his home. He spoke in a clear, racy and simple style, had a quick but coarse wit, could use original or borrowed epigrams effectively, was resourceful in all the defensive devices of the law, and made a fortune as a criminal lawyer. A good orator with a flair for publicity, he had a genius for personal controversy. One of his favorite tricks was to do or say something to draw attacks upon him and then use his talents to confound his assailants. "Mr. Butler, are you trying to show your contempt for this court?" asked a judge. "No, your honor," retorted Butler, "I'm trying to conceal it."

Butler served in the State house of representatives in 1853 and in the senate in 1859 and incurred the ire of the Brahmins of both parties by currying favor with Roman Catholics and advocating reduction of the working day to ten hours. He went to the Democratic National Convention at Charleston in 1860 instructed for Stephen A. Douglas, but violated his instructions and voted for Jefferson Davis on thirty-seven consecutive ballots. In the election that year he supported John C. Breckinridge, the Southern Democratic candidate.

When Fort Sumter was fired upon Butler was a brigadier general in the Massachusetts militia. At a time when it appeared doubtful whether it was to be a sectional or a party war, the eloquent and energetic Butler did much to swing Democrats behind the Lincoln administration. Washington was almost defenseless and isolated from the North after the Sixth Massachusetts Regiment had to fight its way through a pro-Southern mob in Baltimore and suffered many casualties on its way to the capital. General Butler with the Eighth Massachusetts landed at Annapolis, bypassed Baltimore and reached Washington without firing a shot, much to the relief of Lincoln. From that time Butler was almost continually in the news.

On May 13, 1861, General Butler with nine hundred men occupied Baltimore, and three days later was made a major general of volunteers. As commander at Fort Monroe, he was repulsed at Big Bethel in Virginia but took the Hatteras forts on the North Carolina coast. He commanded the land forces against New Orleans and was military governor for eight months after the capture of the city in May, 1862. His regime in New Orleans was efficient but severe and unpopular. He seized $800,000 in bullion that had been deposited by Southerners in a foreign consulate. On June 1, 1862, the military governor hanged H. B. Mumford for pulling down an American flag that Commodore Farragut had placed over the United States mint.

The women of New Orleans treated the Union soldiers with scant respect. It is said that one of their methods of insult was to throw slop on them from upper-story windows. General Butler countered with his famous Order No. 28, which read: "When any female shall by word or gesture, or movement, insult or show contempt for any officer or soldier of the United States, she shall be regarded and held liable to be treated as a woman of the town plying her avocation." Prime Minister Palmerston, secretly pro-Confederate, said in Parliament that "any Englishman must blush to think that such an act has been committed by one belonging to the Anglo-Saxon race." Butler's activities at New Orleans were cited as examples of tyranny the South might expect if conquered by the North. In December, 1862, Jefferson Davis denounced Butler as a "felon deserving capital punishment." To Southerners the able but erratic soldier-administrator became "Beast Butler." Several foreign nations protested against Butler's activities in New Orleans. Wherever Butler was there were rumors and charges of financial irregularities, corruption, frauds, illicit trading with the enemy and nepotism. A tradition says that he even stole the spoons from a home where he was staying. In December, 1864, Butler commanded the first expedition against Fort Fisher near Wilmington, North Carolina, and was charged with bad judgment and mismanagement. Later in the same year he was put in command of the Army of the James, but on January 7, 1865, after having bottled his army up in Bermuda Hundred, he was relieved by General Grant for the good of the service.

The cantankerous and turbulent general knew how to capitalize on his military record for political purposes. He served in the U.S. House of Representatives from 1867 to 1875 as a Radical Republican and from 1877 to 1879 as an Independent Greenbacker. He sponsored the Civil Rights Bill and was one of the most active House managers in charge of the impeachment of President Johnson. In Congress Butler often acted as spokesman for President Grant, who as commander-in-chief had removed him from command of an army. On one occasion Samuel Sullivan ("Sunset") Cox attacked Butler savagely. When Butler spoke he took no notice of the attack until he closed his speech, when he said: "There is no need for me to answer the gentleman from New York. Every Negro minstrel just now is singing the answer, and the hand-organs are playing the tune, *Shoo, Fly, Don't Bodder Me*." The song referred to was composed by Thomas Brigham Bishop, set to music by Frank Campbell and popularized in the late 1860's by Billy Reaves. After making many efforts to win that office, Butler was elected Governor of Massachusetts in 1882 for one term with Democratic and Greenback support, and in 1884 he ran for President on the Anti-Monopoly and Greenback tickets.

How did Carl Schurz pronounce his name?

Carl Schurz (1829-1906) pronounced his surname as if it were spelled *shoorts,* an approximation of the German. Americans had difficulty in pronouncing the name and called him variously *Shurz, Shirts, Skirz* and *Skirts.* When Lincoln was reviewing Hooker's army in April, 1863, General Darius M. Couch, on horseback beside the President, observed as Schurz came up with his division: "Mr. President, this is General *Schurz.*" Lincoln replied: "Not *Shurz,* General Couch, but *Shoorts.*"
Schurz was born near Cologne, Germany, and attended the Jesuit

Gymnasium at Cologne and the University of Bonn. Through his friend and patron Professor Gottsfried Kinkel, he became involved in the Revolution of 1848 and took the field. When Rastatt fortress surrendered to the Prussians, Schurz escaped to Zurich. The next year he helped Professor Kinkel escape from Spandau prison near Berlin and aided him to get to Scotland. Then he became a newspaper correspondent in Paris, but was expelled from France in 1851 as a dangerous foreigner. After teaching German in England, he and his wife migrated in 1852 to Philadelphia.

Within five years after his arrival in America Schurz spoke and wrote English fluently and soon gained a reputation as a writer, orator and politician. In 1856 he went to Wisconsin, identified himself with the Republican Party, and a year later was nominated for Lieutenant Governor before he was an American citizen. He spoke for Lincoln against Douglas in the Illinois Senatorial campaign of 1858, and later in the same year was admitted to the bar and began to practice law in Milwaukee. In the Chicago convention of 1860 he was chairman of the Wisconsin delegation, which supported Seward to the end, and was chairman of the committee that notified Lincoln of his nomination.

Schurz was the recognized German-American leader and is credited with having kept Missouri in the Union at the outset of the Civil War. Lincoln appointed him Minister to Spain in 1861, but he resigned the next year to enter the army. He commanded troops at Second Bull Run as a brigadier of volunteers and at Chancellorsville, Gettysburg and Chattanooga as a major general. During the 1864 Presidential campaign he was one of the most eloquent and effective speakers for Lincoln. He returned to the army and served till the end of the war. Many officers were jealous of the German-born general who was in continual communication with the President.

In 1865 President Johnson chose him to make a survey of conditions in the South. After the war he was Washington correspondent of the New York *Tribune,* editor of the Detroit *Post,* and editor and part owner of the St. Louis *Westliche,* a German language daily. In 1869 Schurz became the first German-born U.S. Senator. George F. Hoar, who was in the House while Schurz was in the Senate, wrote of him: "He was admirably equipped for public service. Although a native of Germany, he had a most excellent, copious and clear English style. No man in either House of Congress excelled him in that respect. He was a clear reasoner, and not lacking on fit occasions to a stirring eloquence."

The tall, lanky Schurz, who had a fine sense of humor, was temporary chairman and keynoter of the Republican National Convention that nominated Grant in 1868. Later he broke with Grant, helped organize the Liberal Republican Party, and presided over the convention that nominated Horace Greeley for President in 1872. His chief interests were readjustment in the South, civil service reform, conservation of natural resources, and "sound money." He supported Hayes and was his Secretary of the Interior. In 1884 he headed the Mugwumps who bolted Blaine in favor of Cleveland. He supported McKinley in 1896, but supported Bryan in 1900. His latter years were devoted chiefly to literary pursuits. In an address in Faneuil Hall on April 18, 1859, he said: "Ideals are like stars. You will not succeed by touching them with your hands. But like the seafaring man on the desert of waters, you choose them as your guides, and following them will reach your destiny."

What was the Force Bill?

This term was originally applied to a "revenue collection measure" empowering the President to deal with Nullification. The bill was called "the Force Bill" and "the Bloody Bill" by the Nullifiers because it authorized the President to use military and naval force in case of need to collect the revenues and execute the Federal laws in South Carolina. Henry Clay's "Compromise Tariff Bill" became effective the same day that the Force Bill did—March 2, 1833, and President Jackson never exercised any of his powers under it. In 1870 "Force Bill" was applied by its opponents to a bill to enforce the Fourteenth and Fifteenth Amendments to the Constitution in the South. It was also applied to the "Ku Klux Klan Bill" of 1871, which authorized the President to use military force and suspend the writ of habeas corpus to suppress disorders intended to deny citizens their Constitutional rights. "Force Bill" was applied again to a bill introduced in 1890 by Representative Henry Cabot Lodge "to amend and supplement the election laws of the United States and to provide for their more efficient enforcement." Since then the term has been used to designate several bills interpreted as being designed to coerce the Southern States to give Negroes civil rights.

Who said: "The way to resume is to resume"?

"The way to resume is to resume" is a popular version of, "The way to resumption is to resume," which occurs in a letter dated March 17, 1866, written by Chief Justice Salmon P. Chase to Horace Greeley, editor of the New York *Tribune*. During the Civil War, when Chase was Secretary of the Treasury, the Government issued more than $400,000,000 in legal-tender notes known as greenbacks, and after the war the best method of resuming specie payments was a burning question. The Resumption Act, approved January 14, 1875, directed the resumption of specie payments on January 1, 1879. Since John Sherman took a leading part in the debates on the question as Chairman of the Senate Finance Committee and was Secretary of the Treasury when the act went into effect, the famous epigram, "The way to resume is to resume," is often erroneously attributed to him. In his *History of the United States* (Volume 6, Page 230) James Ford Rhodes, probably through a slip, ascribed the saying to Greeley.

Who were the carpetbaggers?

A carpetbag is a traveling bag, carryall or holdall, such bags having been originally made of carpeting or similar material. Burton Stevenson quotes Sir Walter Raleigh as having written shortly before his execution in 1618:

Eat slowly; only men in rags
And gluttons old in sin
Mistake themselves for carpet-bags
And tumble victuals in.

Carpet bag in the sense of a traveling bag became common in the United States in the 1830's. In 1851 Benjamin Penhallow Shillaber, creator of *Mrs. Partington,* began to edit a humorous weekly called the *Carpetbag.* On September 17, 1854, Rutherford B. Hayes, then practicing law at Cincinnati, wrote to his uncle Sardis Birchard: "When you get to the Hamilton depot take your carpetbag in hand, the walk is is short, save your quarter, and keep along the south side of Sixth Street till you get to No. 383, next house east of Glenn's." *Carpetbagger* in the sense of a visitor or stranger "traveling light" was used in 1848, and in 1857 the following appeared in the Lawrence (Kansas) *Herald of Freedom:* "Early in the spring several thousand excellent young men came to Kansas. This was jokingly called the carpet bag emigration."

After the Civil War and during the Reconstruction period Southerners applied *carpetbagger* to Northerners who went into the Southern States to obtain political influence, offices and spoils by pandering to the colored voters. It is supposed that Colonel Joseph Hodgson, editor of the Montgomery (Alabama) *Mail* was the first to apply the term to this particular class. The carpetbaggers were so called because they were often adventurers without property and their only possessions were carried in their carpetbags. In *Twenty Years of Congress* (1886) James G. Blaine wrote "out of these circumstances there came into political power the class of men known as 'Carpet-Baggers'—so described from the insulting presumption that the entire worldly estate of each one of the class was carried in a carpet-bag, enabling him to fly at any moment of danger from the State whose domestic policy he sought to control."

In English politics *carpetbagger* is applied to a candidate for Parliament who is a stranger in the district in which he seeks election.

Who were the Copperheads?

During the early days of the Civil War persons in the North who sympathized with the South or were opposed to its conquest by arms were sneeringly called copperheads by the Republicans and Unionists. Before the close of the war the term was extended to all Democrats who did not openly and actively support the Lincoln administration and its war measures.

The allusion was to a species of very venomous snake, common in the Eastern part of the United States and known as the copperhead because of the copper-colored markings on its head. It is a member of the same family as the rattlesnakes and vibrates its tail when annoyed, but, unlike the typical rattlesnakes, it has no rattles on its tail and strikes from ambush without previous movement or warning. The copperhead is popularly supposed to lie in wait to strike at passers-by and therefore has become symbolic of traitors or secret foes. It is also sometimes called the "highland moccasin."

There seems to be no foundation for the oft-repeated story that *copperhead*, as used during the Civil War, was derived from the custom among members of secret antiwar societies of wearing on their coats buttons made of copper one-cent pieces and bearing the likeness of the Goddess of Liberty. The name copperhead no doubt suggested these buttons instead of the buttons suggesting the name.

The term seems to have been applied to Northern sympathizers with the Confederates as early as the first year of the war. In 1871 Schele de Vere wrote: "In the year 1861, a Mr. Burtt, then Quartermaster in the United States Army, is said to have first applied the term to a class of so-called Anti-War Democrats, Northern sympathizers with the Southern rebellion, though it is not unlikely that in his patriotic zeal he may have rather compared them to the venomous and noisome serpent, which is also known under the name of Copperhead."

On May 5, 1862, Rutherford B. Hayes, then a Union officer on duty in western Virginia, wrote to Colonel E. P. Scammon: "Captains Hunter and Lovejoy have arrived. They report Captain Foley died of his wounds. This will be a deathblow to the 'Copperheads.' All the people tell us we need apprehend no bushwhacking this side of that gang, either here or in front of us." Under date of July 30, 1862, the Cincinnati *Gazette,* referring to the Indiana State Democratic convention, announced that "The Copperhead Bright Convention meets in Indianapolis today." The next day the same newspaper referred to "a glorious sequel to the Copperhead convention." On October 1, 1862, the Cincinnati *Commercial* printed an article entitled "Comfort to Copperheads." On March 24, 1863, Hayes wrote: "The peace men, sympathizing with the Rebels, called Copperheads or Butternuts, are mostly of the Democratic party."

Newspapers quickly took up the new term. Before the close of the war *copperhead,* as employed by the Republicans and Unionists, was virtually synonymous with *Democrat,* and many Democrats assumed the name with pride and defiance. It carried the same stigma in the North that *Unionist* did in the South.

At one time the Yankees applied *copperhead,* for entirely different reasons, not only to the Indians but also the the descendants of the Dutch settlers in New York. In *Knickerbocker's History of New York* (1809) Washington Irving wrote: "The Yankees sneeringly spoke of the round-crowned burghers of the Manhattoes as the Copperheads."

On June 24, 1938, President Franklin D. Roosevelt said in a "fireside chat" to the nation:

Never in our lifetime has such a concerted campaign of defeatism been thrown at the heads of the President and Senators and Congressmen as in the case of this Seventy-Fifth Congress. Never before have we had so many Copperheads—and you will remember that it was the Copperheads who, in the days of the War Between the States, tried their best to make Lincoln and his Congress give up the fight, let the Nation remain split in two and return to peace—peace at any price.

Who were the scalawags?

Scalawag is sometimes applied as an opprobrious epithet to a low-down or dishonest politician, a sense it acquired immediately after the Civil War when Southern Democrats applied the term contemptuously to native white Southerners who joined the Republican Party and co-operated with the carpetbaggers and Negroes in carrying out the reconstruction program and in controlling the politics of the former Confederate States. Naturally the Democrats of the South resented being governed by a combination of carpetbaggers, scalawags and former slaves supported by Federal bayonets. But all the so-called scalawags were not dishonest turncoats who changed sides after the war to feather their own nests. Many of them honestly thought that their course was the right thing for the best interests of the South.

The term is of obscure origin. The earliest known uses of *scalawag* or variants of it occur in the 1840's. Two early spellings, *scallawag* and *scallywag,* still occur in British usage. It is generally supposed that *scalawag* is of American origin and that it was coined as an "artificial word." In the 1850's its most usual sense was a rascal, a scapegrace, or a mean, worthless, good-for-nothing fellow. In his *Dictionary of Americanisms* (1859) John Russell Bartlett wrote: "A scallawag has been defined to be, 'like many other wags, a compound of a loafer, blackguard, and scamp.' " Some authorities think it may be akin to Scandinavian *scallag,* "a menial." But one of its earliest senses was "a runt" or "stunted animal." A domestic animal that was worthless or of little value because undersized from lack of proper feeding was called a scalawag. This had led some authorities to suggest the theory that *scalawag* is merely a corruption of *Scalloway,* the name of a town and district on one of the Shetland Islands, where breeds of small ponies, cattle and sheep are bred. This theory seems to receive some support from the fact that *scalawag* was formerly sometimes spelled *scallaway.*

What is "a swing around the circle"?

When the President of the United States makes a tour of the country for political purposes he is said to take " a swing around the circle."

This expression was popularized during the administration of Andrew Johnson. In the summer of 1866 President Johnson was invited to go to Chicago and be present at the laying of the cornerstone of a monument to Stephen A. Douglas, and he decided to take advantage of the trip to address the people of the North face to face and to attempt to gain popular support in his fight with Congress. Petroleum V. Nasby, the humorist, observed that the tour was undertaken "to arouse the people to the danger of concentrating power in the hands of Congress instead of diffusing it through one man." James Russell Lowell called it "an advertising tour of a policy in want of a party."

President Johnson left Washington August 28, 1866, and was accompanied by several members of his Cabinet, Admiral Farragut, General

Grant and many other distinguished men. The tour extended as far north as Detroit and as far west as St. Louis. At Cleveland, September 5, the President said in part: "I tell you, my countrymen, I have been fighting the South and they have been whipped and crushed and they acknowledge their defeat and accept the terms of the Constitution; and now, as I *go around the circle,* having fought traitors at the South, I am prepared to fight traitors at the North."

The President was heckled unmercifully on this occasion and when he was impeached this speech was named in the indictment as one of the three public addresses made by him that "had brought his office into contempt, ridicule and disgrace." He used "swinging round the circle" and "swinging around the circle" in several other speeches on this tour, and six months earlier he had declared: "Now as we *swing around the circle* of the Union . . . the Government must stand unshaken and unmoved on its basis."

Newspapers and his political enemies repeated "swing around the circle" in ridicule and applied it to the Western tour. It seems that it was an old Tennessee political phrase that meant "thinking a thing through" and which President Johnson was fond of using. There is reason for believing that Johnson employed it during a campaign for the Governorship in 1855. Oliver P. Temple, who ran against Johnson for Congress in 1847, long afterward wrote as follows in *Notable Men of Tennessee,* in this case referring to Johnson in 1860. "To use Mr. Johnson's favorite figure, when these scared Democratic veterans looked across the *circle* and saw their old Whig enemies standing on the Democratic camping ground, directly facing them, it must have been a curious as well as a puzzling reflection to Johnson's followers to know how the Whigs got there."

Johnson, who started out as a humble tailor with no formal education, was proud of the fact that he had held consecutively the offices of alderman, mayor, State representative, State senator, Representative in Congress, United States Senator, Governor, Military Governor, Vice President and President. On one occasion, it is said, he declared that he had "swung around the entire circle from alderman to President." He held more public offices—Federal, State and local—than any other President.

Presidential tours began soon after the adoption of the Constitution. In the fall of 1789 President Washington, to use his own words, made a "tour through the Eastern States during the recess of Congress to acquire knowledge of the face of the Country, the growth of agriculture thereof and the temper and disposition of the inhabitants towards new government." Washington confined his tour to the three New England States then in the Union—Connecticut, Massachusetts and New Hampshire. Rhode Island ratified the Constitution on May 29, 1790, and later in that year the President visited that State. In the spring of 1791 he made a similar tour through the Southern States, when he traveled 1,900 miles in seventy-eight days—an average speed of four miles an hour. These dignified and nonpartisan tours by President Washington were criticized by some of the Jeffersonians as imitations of "the royal progresses" made by European sovereigns. But Democratic Presidents made similar tours. Early in his first administration President Monroe made what his critics styled a royal progress throughout the country. In 1832 President Jackson made a trip to Massachusetts to receive an honorary degree from Harvard University. These early Presidential tours, however, were dignified and stately, and no references to politics were ever made in connection with them. President Johnson was the first President to use such a tour for purely political purposes.

Who was Blue Jeans Williams?

James Douglas Williams (1808-1880), Indiana Congressman and Senator, was known as "Blue Jeans Williams" because he was a farmer and habitually wore bibless blue overalls.

The homely, old-fashioned-sounding word *jeans* smacks of a native American origin, but etymologists derive it from Genoa (Old French *Janne* and Modern French *Gênes*), the Italian city, where a twilled fabric so called was manufactured and exported at an early date. In England this fabric was called "jean" or "jean cloth." In America jean cloth was so widely used in overalls for farmers and working men that *jeans* became synonymous with *overalls*. The term survives chiefly in the expression "to dig down into one's jeans." Jeans were generally colored blue because that dye was cheap.

Although Blue Jeans Williams had little schooling, he was far from being a "hayseed" or "hick." He owned 4,000 acres of land and ran a sawmill, gristmill and pork-packing plant in connection with his farms. Between 1843 and 1873 he served five terms in the State house of representatives and three in the State senate, where his chief interests were education, agriculture and government economy. In 1874 he was elected to the U.S. House of Representatives. Even in Congress he continued to wear blue jeans made of cloth woven from the wool of his own sheep.

In 1876 the Democrats nominated him for Governor. The campaign was a notable one in Hoosier politics. It was the year of the memorable Hayes-Tilden contest and Indiana was a "pivotal State" in the Presidential race. Blue Jeans Williams was a picturesque candidate. He was six feet four inches tall, had large hands and feet, was awkward and ungainly in gait, was dressed in pioneer style, had a pleasing voice and kindly manner, and spoke plainly and bluntly. Lew Wallace wrote that Blue Jeans wore a "tall stovepipe hat, that was threadbare and dyed the color of subdued tobacco juice" by wind, rain and mud. The Democratic candidate had been critical of the Lincoln administration and the Republicans branded him a "Copperhead." His opponent was Benjamin Harrison, Indianapolis lawyer, whom the Democrats called "the man in the kid gloves." Blue Jeans won, resigned from Congress and was Governor until his death. Harrison achieved enough prominence in the colorful campaign to start him on the road to the Presidency of the United States.

What States comprise the Solid South?

Political experts differ as to just what States comprise the Solid South. In the strictest sense of the term the Solid South comprises the eleven former Confederate States—Virginia, North Carolina, South Carolina, Georgia, Florida, Alabama, Mississippi, Tennessee, Louisiana, Arkansas and Texas. The name was suggested by the fact that from 1876 to 1920 every one of these States gave its electoral vote to the Democratic nominee for President.

Although Solid South did not come into general use until more than a decade after the end of the Civil War, the political fact that it expresses was recognized by politicians as early as 1854, when it had become apparent that all the Southern States would vote as a unit on slavery, states' rights and certain other sectional issues. Some of the former Confederate States went Republican in 1868, 1872, and 1876, owing to the influence of carpetbaggers and the limitations on the franchise imposed by the Federal Government during the Reconstruction Period. After 1876 the Solid South was not broken as a political unit in Presidential elections until 1920, when Tennessee gave its electoral vote to Warren G. Harding, the Republican nominee. In 1924 the Solid South was solid again in its support of the Democratic nominee; but in the "Republican landslide of 1928" it was smashed, politically speaking, when Florida, North Carolina, Virginia, Tennessee and Texas all went Republican.

In a broader sense, Maryland, Kentucky and Missouri, which were slave States before the Civil War, are included in the Solid South. But these three States, none of which was at any time an undisputed member of the Confederacy, are classed as Border States and they are often regarded as doubtful in a Presidential race. Kentucky, for instance, went Republican in 1896, 1924 and 1928, while Missouri went Republican in 1904, 1908, 1920, 1924 and 1928. Maryland also broke away from the Solid South in several elections during that period. Delaware and West Virginia were slave territory before the Civil War but have never been regarded as part of the Solid South. Oklahoma, which did not become a State until 1907, has been influenced politically more by the South than the North.

After the Civil War the famous Virginia ranger commander Colonel John S. Mosby invariably supported the Republican candidates for President. During the Tilden-Hayes contest of 1876 a former Confederate comrade in arms wrote to Mosby urging him to support Tilden. In a letter written August 6 of that year and published in the New York *Herald* six days later Mosby said: "But suppose Hayes is elected with a *solid South* against him; what are you going to do then?" That appears to be the earliest recorded use of *solid South* as applied to the political unity of the former Confederate States.

The Republican nominee had foreshadowed Mosby's phrase. On July 8, 1876, Rutherford B. Hayes wrote in his diary: "Our adversaries reckon on *a united South.*" Several times during the campaign Hayes referred to the former Confederate States as *a united South.* But on August 5, 1878, President Hayes wrote to William Henry Smith: "Colonel Kellar is winning victories in Memphis, you notice. I am sorry it is mixed up with soft money, but as it divides the solid South, I think we may welcome it." In a speech at Madison, Wisconsin, in July, 1879, James A. Garfield said: "Why does the South make this issue? I answer: They have a solid South, and only used to carry Ohio and New York to elect a President, and they trust to carry these States by the means they best know how to use."

Deep South, which came into use after the First World War, is a songwriter's rather than a politician's phrase. It generally refers to South Carolina, Georgia, Florida, Alabama, Mississippi, Louisiana, Arkansas and Texas.

Why is a political leader called a boss?

Boss in the sense of a politician who controls his party in a city, district or State is from Dutch *baas,* which originally meant "uncle" but which now means "head of a household," "chief," "overseer" and "master." The term was borrowed from the Dutch in New York and spelled *boss*. As early as 1679 an Englishman named Philipse wrote in *Early Voyage to New Netherland:* "Here they had their first interview with the female *boss* or supercargo of the vessel."

During the Jeffersonian era *boss* began to supplant *master* in common speech in New York. *Master* connoted the master-slave relationship and was regarded as inappropriate for application of one freeman to another in a democracy. At first *boss* was applied particularly to the employer of laborers, the superintendent of mechanics or the head of a gang of workers. *Master-carpenter* became *boss-carpenter, master-bricklayer, boss-bricklayer,* etc. The earliest use of the term in this sense recorded by *The Dictionary of American English* is dated 1806. In 1819 an English traveler named John Palmer listed *boss* in this sense as peculiar to the United States. With the construction of canals and railroads the term was carried from New York into adjoining States and finally all over the country. In *The American Democrat* (1838) James Fenimore Cooper protested against the widespread use of *boss* in lieu of *master*. The New York boot and shoemakers adopted a resolution in 1850 referring to "capitalists or bosses."

John Russell Bartlett in the second edition of his *Dictionary of Americanisms* (1859) quoted a writer as using the phrase "boss politicianer." But *boss* in its political sense did not become common until after the Civil War. M. Schele De Vere did not notice this use of the term in his comprehensive *Americanisms* (1872). The first politician to be widely known as a boss was William Marcy Tweed (1823-1878), who gained control of Tammany Hall in the 1860's and who defrauded New York City out of sums variously estimated at $30,000,000 to $200,000,000. A Committee of Seventy was formed at a mass meeting to fight the corrupt Tweed Ring, but it was defeated in the city election of 1871. Tweed is reported to have said: "As long as I count the votes, what are you going to do about it? Say." In *"The Boss"* James Russell Lowell wrote:

> Skilled to pull wires he baffles nature's hopes,
> Who sure intended him to stretch a rope.

Boss Tweed was finally indicted for complicity in robbery and fraud. The jury in the first trial disagreed, but in a second trial in November, 1873, he was convicted and sentenced to twelve years in prison on Blackwell's Island and to pay a fine of $12,759. After he had served a year the State court of appeals reduced the sentence to one year's imprisonment and the fine to $250. Tweed was released from prison in

January, 1875, but was immediately rearrested on civil charges brought by the State to recover $6,000,000 the Tweed Ring had stolen from the City. Bail was fixed at $3,000,000, which Tweed could not raise, whereupon he was lodged in the Ludlow Street Jail. The famous political boss was treated leniently while in jail. He was permitted to take daily rides in his carriage and even to visit his home in the company of turnkeys. On December 4, 1875, while on one of these visits to his home, he disappeared out of the back door as the turnkeys sat in the parlor. With the help of friends Boss Tweed got to Cuba and finally to Spain disguised as a sailor. Spanish officials identified him from one of Thomas Nast's pictures in *Harper's Weekly* and he was arrested and sent back in a warship. Since judgment had been entered against him during his absence in November, 1876, and he could not meet it, he was confined in Ludlow Street Jail, where he died in his cell on April 12, 1878.

From Boss Tweed *boss* acquired unsavory political connotations it has never completely lost.

What was the Whisky Ring?

Ring in the sense of a combination of persons for political and business purposes is an Americanism which dates back at least to 1862. The unmasking and breaking of the Whisky Ring was one of the sensational scandals during Grant's administration. In 1874 a secret investigation made by Secretary of the Treasury Benjamin H. Bristow showed that a combination of distillers, Federal agents and politicians had defrauded the Government of several million dollars during the preceding five years by avoiding the payment of taxes. On May 10, 1875, the records of sixteen suspected distilleries and rectifying places in St. Louis, Chicago and Milwaukee were seized. Criminal and civil charges were filed against two hundred and fifty-three persons and one hundred and ten were convicted. Three went to the penitentiary.

Orville E. Babcock, Grant's private secretary, had communicated with and had received costly gifts from Whisky Ring leaders. When an implicating letter to Babcock was shown to Grant, he wrote on its back: "Let no guilty man escape. If Babcock is guilty, there is no man that wants him so much proven guilty as I do." Later Babcock was indicted "for conspiracy to defraud the revenue." He was a West Pointer, had a good Civil War record, had been Grant's aide, confidant and friend, and had been brevetted brigadier general. The President could not believe that Babcock was guilty and voluntarily testified by deposition to his good character. The Presidential secretary was acquitted but after that continued his duties at the White House only a short time. He was drowned in 1884 while on vacation off Mosquito Inlet, Florida.

The President was doubly embarrassed by the scandal because he himself had accepted a $6,000 gift—a span of trotting horses and a carriage with harness, whip and other trappings—from John McDonald, the illiterate superintendent of internal revenue at St. Louis. After McDonald had served sixteen months in prison, he published *Secrets of the Great Whisky Ring,* in which he asserted but did not prove that Grant as well as Babcock was implicated in the frauds. Grant resented Secretary Bristow's activities and forced him to resign on July 17, 1878, before he could complete the Whisky Ring prosecutions. Bristow, who was reputed to be an able lawyer and sincere reformer, received 126 votes for President in the Republican National Convention of 1876.

What were the Star Route Frauds?

In sparsely populated parts of the United States there are many post offices to which mail cannot be sent by railroads, steamboats, airplanes and other ordinary means of public transportation. Such mail is carried by independent contractors over postal lines known as "star routes," of which there are now some 12,000.

Up until 1845 the Post Office Department required coach transportation over numerous mail routes that did not justify that grade of service. Under date of October 18, 1827, President John Quincy Adams gives us a glimpse of the mail contractors of those days.

Mr. Clay came, and introduced the committee of the mail contractors, who had passed a written resolution that they would in a body visit the President and Secretary of State. . . . They then came in procession, upwards of a hundred in number. I received them in the winter parlor, shook hands with them all, and, at the suggestion of Mr. Clay . . . showed them the rooms on the lower floor and those above, with the exception of the bedchambers. There was cake and wine served to them, and I drank success to them all, through highways and by ways. . . . These are persons from all parts of the Union, who at this time of the year come to offer proposals of contracts for carrying the mails. Each contract is for three or four years, but a certain proportion of them expire every year, and this is the time for the renewal of them. As the post-roads and the number of mail conveyances increase, this body of men increases every year with them. This, I believe, is the first time that they have assembled and acted as a body.

In 1845 the Post Office Department was directed by law to provide for the transportation of mail "with certainty, celerity and security" without regard to the method of transportation. These routes were called star routes because in official documents of the Department they were distinguished from other routes by means of asterisks, "little stars."

The present system of star routes dates from 1870, when they numbered 7,295. At that time a star route was any line over which mail was carried by power other than steam. The star route carrier obtains a contract by competitive bidding to carry mail from railroad and steamboat stops to certain post offices regularly, safely and expeditiously by whatever mode of transportation he sees fit, whether by horseback, wagon, canoe, rowboat, motorboat, automobile or even on foot. On some star routes the functions of rural free delivery are performed; that is, the star route carrier places mail in individual boxes along the way. The longest star route in the continental United States in recent times has been that between Reno and Las Vegas in Nevada—nearly 450 miles. One of the most famous star route carriers has been John A. Thompson, who, during the twenty years from 1856 to 1876, carried the mail between Placerville, California, to Carson City, Nevada, a distance of ninety miles. His endurance, courage and daring in making perilous journeys over snow-covered mountains won him the nickname "Snowshoe Thompson." In 1943 it was reported that D. M. Brodehl, who had a contract to deliver mail from Tahoe City, California, to Crystal Bay only twelve miles away, fulfilled his contract, after heavy snows had made the roads impassable, by going to Crystal Bay by way of Reno and Carson City, Nevada—a round trip of 270 miles.

During the administration of Rutherford B. Hayes charges were made that the letting of star route contracts was becoming a corrupt political racket. Both houses of the Democratic Congress investigated but absolved from wrongdoing General Thomas J. Brady, head of the bureau in charge of star routes. Congressmen from the old States wanted to restrict the expensive star routes, while those from the new States wanted to extend them. President Hayes directed that no mail contract involving considerable expense or liability should be made or altered unless it was submitted to the Postmaster General and by him brought before the President and Cabinet.

In April, 1881, Postmaster General Thomas L. James investigated and concluded that a group of officials and former officials had conspired to defraud the Government of half a million dollars in connection with star route contracts. After the Cabinet discussion on the subject, President James A. Garfield removed Brady as second assistant postmaster general. Attorney General Isaac Wayne MacVeagh appointed Benjamin H. Brewster and George Bliss as special prosecutors to assist him in handling the cases against the offenders. Shortly after Garfield had died and Chester A. Arthur had succeeded him as President, MacVeagh retired from the Cabinet and Brewster became Attorney General. During the next three years the Star Route Frauds case virtually pre-occupied the Department of Justice and constituted the chief political scandal of the Arthur administration.

Among those indicted by a District of Columbia grand jury were Brady; Stephen W. Dorsey, a former carpetbag Senator from Arkansas, and the latter's private secretary, M. C. Reredell. The political implications were enhanced by the fact that Dorsey was a friend of President Arthur and, as a member and the secretary of the Republican National Committee during the Presidential campaign of 1880, had been informally accused of carrying Indiana with a slush fund of undetermined origin. At the trial the defendants were represented by Robert G. Ingersoll, then at the height of his fame as lawyer and orator. The defendants were charged with conspiring with the contractors in control of 134 star routes to defraud the Government by granting extravagant contracts and by uselessly increasing the postal service. In the first trial in 1882 the jury stood ten to two for convicting Brady and nine to three for convicting Dorsey; in the second trial in 1883 Reredell pleaded guilty, Dorsey was acquitted, and the charges against Brady were dismissed on the ground of insufficient evidence. There was much popular clamor that the real culprits had escaped justice. Both the prosecution and the defense brought charges of jury-bribing, which resulted in further indictments but no convictions.

How did *boodle* originate?

Boodle in the sense of political graft is believed to be from Dutch *boedel*, which means goods, stock or belongings, and which was introduced into America by the Dutch of New Netherland. As early as 1833 *boodle*, also spelled *caboodle*, was used in New England in the sense of pack, lot or crowd; as, "the whole kit and boodle of them." Possibly *boodle* in that sense is from old English *buddle*, which means the same. During the 1850's *boodle* was applied to counterfeit or illicit money, and a generation later to money obtained by bribery, collusive contracts, kickbacks, shakedowns and other forms of political graft. In the latter sense the term was popularized in 1880 during an investigation of a franchise for a Broadway railway granted by the New York City board of aldermen. Sometimes *boodle* was applied to political campaign funds. On October 29, 1884, Jay Gould, Cyrus Field, Andrew Carnegie and

[228]

other "captains of industry" and "money kings" sponsored an elaborate and expensive dinner at Delmonico's in New York City to honor James G. Blaine, the Republican candidate for President, and to raise funds for the campaign. It was estimated that $500,000 was raised as the result of this dinner, which the Democrats ridiculed as "Belshazzar's Feast" and "Blaine's Boodle Banquet."

What is meant by greenbacks and greenbackism?

Greenback is now sometimes applied loosely to any United States paper currency, but once it had a more specific meaning. What is known as the greenback movement had an important effect on American political history.

Edward Kellogg (1790-1858), author of books and pamphlets on financial reform, is known as "the father of greenbackism," although *greenback* and *greenbackism* were not coined until after his death. He advocated a complete scheme of monetary reform and financial control. Most of his theories were too radical to receive much political support, but one of his ideas was adopted by most of the radical political parties that sprang up after the Civil War. Kellogg believed that legal tender notes should be the only United States currency and that the Government should borrow and lend all money through such notes interconvertible at any time with Government bonds bearing interest at a rate corresponding to the rate of the accumulation of wealth in the country. The cost of the entire operation, he estimated, could be carried by a one per cent charge on loans. In the 1860's Kellogg's daughter, Mary Kellogg Putnam, published some of his writings under the title *A New Monetary System,* which attained wide circulation and gained many adherents.

On February 25, 1862, President Lincoln approved an act of Congress authorizing the issue of $150,000,000 in non-interest-bearing, legal tender Treasury notes to circulate as money. This was the first time that the United States under the Federal Constitution had issued paper money under its own name. Before that all paper money circulated in the United States consisted of national, State or local bank notes. Acts of July 11, 1862, and March 3, 1863, each authorized further issues of $150,000,000 in legal tender notes. By January 3, 1864, a total of $449,338,902 in these notes had been issued, and most of them were outstanding when the war ended.

The Treasury legal tender notes authorized in 1862 and 1863 were in effect fiat money. *Fiat* is a Latin word literally meaning "let it be done."

Fiat money is paper currency issued by a government and made legal tender for all debts by fiat or law alone. Such money has no intrinsic value, is not based in any way on specie or metal of any kind, carries with it no promise of redemption in specie, and is supported only by the credit of the government. A person who advocates fiat money used to be called a *fiatist*. *Inflationist* is sometimes used in the same sense, although that term generally has a wider application.

The legal tender notes issued in 1862 and 1863 were called greenbacks because the device on their backs was printed in green ink. For a similar reason Confederate notes were called *bluebacks*. *Greenback* itself was not a new word. It had been used as early as 1778, but only in the sense of a frog. On June 14, 1862, the New York *Tribune* said: "The greenbacks are popular; the people have had a fresh taste of a paper currency which will pay debts, and buy goods alike in New York and Nebraska."

The original greenbacks were issued solely as a means of financing the Civil War. Even their sponsors doubted the Constitutionality of the authorizing acts and referred to them as "a question of hard necessity." The generally accepted notion was that the Federal Government did not have the Constitutional power to issue legal tender notes or fiat money. The Constitution says, "The Congress shall have power . . . to borrow money on the credit of the United States . . . to coin money, to regulate the value thereof, and of foreign coin," and "No State shall . . . coin money; emit bills of credit; make any thing but gold and silver coin a tender in payment of debts," but it does not say specifically that the Federal Government may issue bills of credit to circulate as money.

During the war virtually everybody accepted the new fiat money at face value without question. But after the war creditors began to protest against accepting fiat money that was legal tender for all debts on a par with notes issued against specie. At one time the greenbacks depreciated to about thirty-five cents on the dollar. Creditors argued that the acts authorizing the greenbacks were unconstitutional because the legal tender notes were inflationary and enabled a person to pay in cheaper money debts contracted before the acts were passed. Many cases involving the payment of debts in greenbacks were taken to the courts and they resulted in a series of decisions known as the Legal Tender Cases.

Most of the early Legal Tender Cases were against the legality of the greenbacks so far as they involved the payment of debts contracted before the authorizing acts were passed. In *Hepburn* vs. *Griswold* (February 7, 1870) Chief Justice Salmon P. Chase, who was Secretary of the Treasury when the greenbacks were issued as a temporary war measure, wrote the majority opinion of the Supreme Court holding that the authorizing acts that made non-interest-bearing Treasury notes legal tender in payment of "all debts, public and private" were not within the express or implied powers of Congress granted by the Constitution and therefore invalid as far as they applied to debts contracted before passage of the acts. In effect Chase as Chief Justice had overruled Chase as Secretary of the Treasury. The decision held that contracts made before the greenbacks were authorized must be paid in gold, and the compulsory fulfillment of such obligations in greenbacks was an impairment of contracts and equivalent to the taking of property without due process of law as forbidden by the Fifth Amendment of the Constitution.

By act of April 10, 1869, the membership of the Supreme Court had been increased from seven to nine. One of President Grant's appointees to the new places on the court had been rejected by the Senate and another had died, with the result that the decision in *Hepburn* vs. *Griswold* was made by seven members. The President then appointed Joseph P. Bradley of New Jersey and William Strong of Pennsylvania to the two vacancies. In *Knox* vs. *Lee* (May, 1871), scarcely more than a year after the first legal tender decision, the court completely reversed itself and the Chief Justice. It then held that under the implied power theory and the elastic clause Congress could carry on war by any proper means. In 1884 the Supreme Court held that these acts were valid when applied to contracts made before as well as after their enactment, and that the power granted to Congress to borrow money on the credit of the United States and to regulate the currency included the power to issue legal tender notes.

Meanwhile what should be done about the greenbacks in circulation had become a political issue. This species of "cheap money" appealed especially to many farmers, laborers and small businessmen because it was reputed to reduce interest rates and make the payment of debts easier. The "hard money" men in control of the Government after the war took the position that the greenbacks should be retired as rapidly as possible and that all Government bonds should be paid in gold as they matured. They looked askance at all "soft money" and felt that to pay off Government bonds in anything but gold would be a partial repudiation of the debt contracted by the Government with the people to save the Union. Accordingly the Funding Act of 1866 authorized the Secretary of the Treasury to retire $10,000,000 of the greenbacks within six months and the remainder at the rate of $4,000,000 a month thereafter. Economic conditions at the time were such, however, that there was a popular demand to suspend the retirement of greenbacks to prevent further deflation of the currency.

In 1867 George H. Pendleton, who had been the Democratic candidate for Vice President in 1864 and who had his eye on the Democratic nomination for President in 1868, sponsored, if he did not conceive, what was known as the Ohio Idea, which was a proposal to withdraw all bank notes, substitute greenbacks, make greenbacks the only Federal currency, and pay off in greenbacks the principal of all Government bonds not specifically requiring payment in specie. The Ohio Idea caught the fancy of millions of people and became a burning issue in many States. "The same money for the bond-holder and the plough-holder" was the battle cry of the Greenbackers. In the Democratic National Convention of 1868 Pendleton was hailed as "Young Greenback," but the convention, after adopting Pendleton's greenback plan in substance, nominated Horatio Seymour of New York its permanent chairman, because it did not wish to enter the campaign with too much emphasis on a single issue. The Republicans stood firm for hard money and General John R. Hawley, chairman of the Republican National Convention, declared that "every bond is as sacred as a soldier's grave." Former Secretary of the Treasury William Pitt Fessenden's "Repudiate the Repudiators" became a Republican slogan during the campaign of 1868. But agitation over the Ohio Idea in 1868 forced passage of an act suspending further retirement of greenbacks, with the result that $356,000,000 in legal tender notes became a permanent part of the nation's currency.

Greenbackism was only scotched, not killed. Many farmers and workingmen still demanded that the amount of greenbacks in circulation be increased and reformers began to make attempts to unite these two groups on this issue. Both labor and agriculture in the United States had been slow to organize for political action. Feeble attempts to form workingmen's parties in the Northern States were made in the 1820's. During John Quincy Adams's administration a Workingmen's Party was formed in Philadelphia. It demanded judicial reform, revision of the militia system, free public education, and mechanics' lien laws, and opposed banks, religious legislation and debtor laws. In 1829 a Workingmen's Party was formed in New York City. Its chief purpose was to maintain the ten-hour day. About the same time "The New England Association of Farmers, Mechanics and other Working Men" was formed. These organizations had considerable success in State and local politics. On November 15, 1833, John Quincy Adams, referring to the election of Governor in Massachusetts, wrote in his diary, "The small detachment of the working-men's party has effected this." George Frisbie Hoar became a member of the Massachusetts house of representatives in 1852. In *Autobiography of Seventy Years* (1903) he wrote: "I made, in

1852, a speech in favor of reducing the time of labor in factories to ten hours a day which, so far as I know, was the first speech in any legislative body in this country on that subject. My speech was received with great derision." The early workingmen's parties were short-lived. Most of the "Workies," as members of these parties were called, joined the Jacksonian Democrats, and no serious attempt to organize a labor party was made until after the Civil War.

In 1866 the National Labor Union was formed. It incorporated several conflicting reform organizations and soon had a membership of 650,000. This movement, which had an auspicious beginning, was killed, it is said, by the "fatal malady, politics." In 1872 the Labor Reform Party was formed by a group of the National Labor Union. The nucleus of the Labor Reform Party was formed in Massachusetts by a trade union of shoemakers that called itself the Knights of St. Crispin. A Labor Reform Party convention, composed of delegates from seventeen States, met on February 21, 1872, and adopted a platform favoring the issue of greenbacks, exemption of Government bonds from taxation, civil service reform, an eight-hour working day, abolition of contract labor, exclusion of Chinese, Government control of railroad and telegraph rates, and free trade. For President the convention nominated David Davis of Illinois and for Vice President, Joel Parker of New Jersey. In June both Davis and Parker declined to run on the ticket, whereupon the Labor Reform Party recalled the convention and indorsed Charles O'Conor of New York, who had been nominated for President by the Straight Democrats but who finally refused to be a candidate. What few popular votes the Labor Reform Party polled in 1872, when Grant and Greeley were the major party candidates for President, are indistinguishable among the 29,489 accredited to the candidateless Straight Democratic Party. But the Labor Reform Party of 1872 prepared the way for the Greenback Party three years later.

In the meantime another national labor organization had been formed. It was called the Knights of Labor and was organized on Thanksgiving Day in 1869 as a sort of secret society with an elaborate ritual. Intended at first for garment workers only, it soon accepted members from other trades and developed into an over-all national labor organization to promote the interests of workingmen in general. The Knights of Labor grew slowly in the beginning, but in time they gained strength, discarded their secret ritual and took part in politics. In 1878 the Knights of Labor had a membership of 80,000. By 1886 its membership was 600,000. Many of the new members were in need of relief and were a liability to the organization. The Knights of Labor were somewhat discredited by a series of unsuccessful strikes and political activities. In 1886 the American Federation of Labor succeeded the Knights of Labor as the over-all trades union organization in the United States.

The first attempt to organize the farmers on a large scale was not made until after the Civil War. In 1865 Oliver Hudson Kelley, a clerk in the Bureau of Agriculture, conceived the idea of a national farm organization while he was on a trip through the country to make a survey of agricultural conditions for his Bureau. Two years later he resigned from the Bureau of Agriculture. He and several associates met in Washington on December 4, 1867, and formed The National Grange of the Patrons of Husbandry. Local units were called "granges" and members "grangers." Kelley traveled about the country to organize granges. The National Grange of the Patrons of Husbandry was ostensibly only a secret fraternal order for social and educational purposes and at first it grew very slowly. But discontent among the farmers, particularly during the Panic of 1873, caused the organization to expand rapidly. By 1874 the Grange, as it was called for short, had 20,000 granges and a total membership of 750,000. Though only a secret association for promoting agricultural interests and not actually a political party, the Grange entered politics and in a sense became a political party. It was an instrument of political power and was the first effort of farmers to take an active and effective part in politics. The Grangers and their allies gained control of the legislatures of several Middle Western States and passed what are known as the Granger Laws. In Illinois, Iowa, Wisconsin and Minnesota the Granger-controlled legislatures helped set maximum railroad rates and establish railroad commissions. The Granger Laws were challenged in the courts and led to a series of decisions known as the Granger Cases. In 1876 the Supreme Court of the United States upheld the Constitutionality of the principle of State regulation of public utilities. The original Granger movement reached its peak of power in 1876 and after that year began to decline, but it had taught farmers to take part in politics as they had never done before and it attracted many of them to greenbackism.

President Grant in 1874 vetoed a bill that would have raised the amount of greenbacks in circulation from $356,000,000 to $400,000,000. The Resumption Act of 1875, set January 1, 1879, as the date on which all greenbacks would be redeemed in specie, and the Treasury set aside $100,000,000 in gold for this purpose. On February 25, 1874, a group of men interested in "a sound money system" met at Indianapolis and formed an organization tentatively known as the Greenback Party. The Greenback Party went on record against resumption of specie payments and in favor of withdrawing all national and State bank notes, of substituting for them greenbacks exchangeable for interconvertible bonds bearing interest at sufficiently high rates to keep them at par with gold, and of using specie only in paying interest on the national debt. The basic idea was to increase the volume of greenbacks and to forbid any other kind of money. On May 17, 1876, the Greenback Party held a national convention at Indianapolis and adopted the name Independent Party. The original purpose of the Greenbackers was to gain control of the Democratic Party, which still showed leanings toward greenbackism, but that hope was destroyed by the nomination of Samuel J. Tilden of New York for President by the Democrats. Alexander Campbell of Illinois, who was elected to Congress as an Independent in 1874, is known as "the Father of the Greenback Party." The Indianapolis convention nominated for President Peter Cooper of New York, inventor, manufacturer and philanthropist, who had built the first American steam locomotive and who had founded Cooper Union in New York City "for the advancement of science and art." For Vice President the convention nominated Samuel F. Carey of Ohio, who had succeeded Rutherford B. Hayes in Congress in 1867. What was left of the Labor Reform Party of 1872 indorsed the Independent Party candidates. During the campaign hard-money men ridiculed greenbacks as "rag currency," and Thomas Nast, in a cartoon, fastened "Rag Baby" on the greenback idea. In the close election of 1876 between Tilden and Hayes the Independent Party ticket headed by Cooper and Carey received only 81,737 popular votes, most of them in the Western farm States. But greenbackism had many more advocates than those who voted for the Independent Party.

At a convention in Toledo on February 22, 1878, the Independent Party united with various labor groups, including the Labor Reform Party, and formed the National Greenback Labor Party. The convention adopted the original Greenback platform and added planks demanding an eight-hour day, exclusion of Chinese, women's suffrage and denouncing special grants to railroads and other corporations. It is estimated that in the Congressional and State elections of 1878 the National Greenback Labor Party polled a million votes. By fusions with various other parties it elected fourteen or fifteen members of Congress, among them Adlai Ewing Stevenson of Illinois, later Vice President of the United States, who had served in Congress as a Democrat from 1875 to 1877 but who had been defeated in 1876.

Meanwhile confidence in the greenbacks in circulation had been so strengthened by the Resumption Act of 1875 that few of them were presented on January 1, 1879, after which the greenbacks ceased to be fiat money. But a widespread demand for greenbacks persisted. In March, 1880, 250 delegates of the National Greenback Labor Party from twenty States met in convention in St. Louis and nominated Stephen B. Dellaye of New York for President despite the fact that he wired the convention he would not accept. B. J. Chambers of Texas was nominated for Vice President. The convention reassembled at Chicago in June and substituted the name of General John Baird Weaver of Iowa for President in place of that of Dellaye. Weaver was originally a Democrat, but became a Republican after being converted to Free-Soilism by reading Horace Greeley's New York *Tribune* and Harriet Beecher Stowe's *Uncle Tom's Cabin*. In 1868 he had been elected to Congress as a Greenbacker. The National Greenback Labor Party was unable to induce most of the Greenbackers in the country to leave the major parties in a Presidential year and in the election of 1880 Weaver and Chambers received only 308,578 popular votes. A few members of the original Greenback Party refused to give up their identity and join the National Greenback Labor Party. As late as 1948 a small group—the mere phantom of a party calling itself the Greenback Party—met in Indianapolis and nominated John G. Scott of New York for President and Grenville B. Leake of Indiana for Vice President.

In 1884 Benjamin F. Butler of Massachusetts was an avowed candidate for President and hoped to be the nominee of one of the major parties. A former Union general, Butler had been a Democrat and a Republican and had a considerable following among farmers and workingmen. Both the Republicans and the Democrats were worried for a time about his candidacy. On January 9, 1884, former President Hayes wrote in his diary: "The workingmen's party is on the threshold, under Butler and other demagogues, of organizing independently as a new third party." A group calling itself the Anti-Monopoly Organization of the United States held a convention in Chicago on May 14, 1884, and adopted a platform demanding economy in government, enactment and enforcement of equitable laws, an interstate commerce law, establishment of a labor bureau providing industrial arbitration, direct election of U.S. Senators, a graduated income tax, payment of the national debt as it matured, and "fostering care of agriculture." Tariffs and land grants to corporations were denounced. Butler was nominated for President and General Alanson M. West of Mississippi for Vice President. On May 28, Butler's and West's candidacies were indorsed by the National Greenback Labor Party and the joint ticket was known as the People's Party.

[236]

In the election of 1884, when Cleveland and Blaine were the Democratic and Republican nominees respectively, Butler received only 175,370 votes.

In 1887 the Union Labor Party was formed in the hope that it would be the successor of the defunct People's Party. It advocated greenbacks, the issue and control of currency only by the Federal Government, and the reform of laws relating to elections and trusts. Another group had organized and called itself the United Labor Party. A number of delegates to the State United Labor Party convention at Syracuse, New York, seceded and formed the Progressive Labor Party, which in 1887 held a convention, adopted a platform and nominated a candidate for Governor of the State, but its candidate received only 7,000 votes, most of them in New York City. On May 15, 1888, two labor party conventions met in Cincinnati. One called itself the Union Labor Party and the other the United Labor Party. The Union Labor Party nominated Alson J. Streeter of Illinois for President and Samuel Evans of Texas for Vice President, while the United Labor Party nominated Robert R. Cowdrey of Illinois for President and W. H. T. Wakefield of Kansas for Vice President. In the election of 1888, when Harrison and Cleveland were the major party candidates, Streeter and Evans received 146,836 popular votes, many of them cast by former members of the defunct People's Party, while Cowdrey and Wakefield received only a handful of popular votes.

In 1891 another People's Party was organized. It is known in history as the Populist Party because members of it were called Populists. The nucleus around which this People's Party was formed was the Farmers' Alliance, which originated in 1885 as the Texas State Farmers' Alliance. The movement spread rapidly and in 1890 the Southern and Northern Farmers' Alliances were responsible for the election of several members of Congress and the majority of the members in several State legislatures. This movement brought the farmers back into politics as they had not been since the heyday of the Grangers. Mrs. Mary Elizabeth Lease, writer and lecturer known as the "Kansas Pythoness," stumped her State advising the farmers "to raise less corn and more hell." The Farmers' Alliances disintegrated for want of financial support and an adequate and effective national organization, but their members were the chief backers of the new People's Party.

Large quantities of silver were being produced in the West and the emphasis shifted from greenbacks to silver. The People's Party advocated a safe, sound and flexible currency, an increase in the amount of currency, the free and unlimited coinage of silver and gold at the ratio of sixteen to one, public ownership and operation of railroads, telegraphs and telephones, the return to the Government of all lands granted to railroads and other corporations in excess of their actual needs, limitation on the ownership of land by aliens, postal savings banks, a graduated income tax, pensions, popular election of U.S. Senators, and an eight-hour working day. The People's Party National Convention at Omaha in 1892 nominated John B. Weaver, who had been the National Greenback Labor Party candidate in 1880, for President, and James G. Field of Virginia for Vice President. The Populists demanded the same privileges under the Government for the man who had three acres and a cow as for the man who had a large fortune, and "Three Acres and a Cow" became a Populist slogan. Long before election day the Republicans and Democrats, who had renominated Harrison and Cleveland, realized that the Populists were a genuine threat to them. In the election of 1892 Weaver and Field received 1,041,028 popular votes and the electoral votes of Colorado, Idaho, Kansas and Nevada and one electoral vote in both North Dakota and Oregon.

In 1896 the Democratic Party stole most of the thunder of the Populists. It nominated William Jennings Bryan for President and Arthur Sewall, Maine shipbuilder, for Vice President. The People's Party met in convention in St. Louis on July 22, 1896, and nominated Thomas E. Watson of Georgia for Vice President and then indorsed Bryan for President. The Republican Party nominated William McKinley for President and Garret Augustus Hobart of New Jersey for Vice President. It adopted a plank favoring the gold standard and opposing the coinage of standard silver dollars. Persons who favored the plank were called Gold Bugs. Hobart, the Republican candidate for Vice President, said in his acceptance speech that "an honest dollar, worth one hundred cents, cannot be carved out of fifty-three cents worth of silver plus a Government fiat," and this saying became a sort of slogan in the campaign. Many Republicans objected to the gold plank in the platform of their party. Senator Henry M. Teller of Colorado and thirty-three delegates withdrew from the Republican National Convention and issued a call for an Independent Convention. This group and other Republican seceders held a convention on July 22 in St. Louis—where the Populists were holding their convention on the same day—and adopted the name National Silver Party. After declaring in favor of free silver at the ratio of sixteen to one the National Silver Party Convention indorsed Bryan and Sewall for President and Vice President. This made Bryan the

Presidential candidate of the Democratic, the People's and the National Silver parties. He had two running mates—Sewall of the Democratic and the National Silver parties, and Watson of the People's Party.

The Gold Democrats were unwilling to support either Bryan or McKinley. Delegates from forty-one States and three Territories met in convention at Indianapolis on September 2, 1896, and adopted the name National Democratic Party. After denouncing the money planks in the Democratic and the National Silver platforms as "extreme" and "revolutionary," the convention nominated John M. Palmer of Illinois for President and General Simon Bolivar Buckner of Kentucky for Vice President. The Social Labor Party held its convention in New York City on July 4 and nominated Charles H. Mitchell of New York for President and Matthew Maguire of New Jersey for Vice President. In the election of 1896 the popular vote was: McKinley, 7,104,779; Bryan, 6,502,925; Palmer, 133,148, and Mitchell, 36,274. McKinley received 271 electoral votes and Bryan, 176. The total vote of Bryan, Palmer and all other candidates was not enough to make McKinley a minority President.

The indorsement of Bryan in 1896 virtually destroyed the Populist movement as a separate organization. In 1900 the Democratic Party, which had adopted several of the best vote-getting planks in the Populist platform, renominated Bryan for President and nominated Adlai E. Stevenson of Illinois for Vice President. The People's Party convention met at Sioux Falls, North Dakota, indorsed Bryan for President and nominated Charles A. Towne of Minnesota, a Silver Republican, for Vice President, although Towne declined to accept. A fragment of anti-Bryanites in the People's Party held a convention at Cincinnati and nominated Wharton Barker of Pennsylvania for President and Ignatius Donnelly of Minnesota, "the Father of the People's Party," for Vice President. Known as Middle-of-the-Road Populists, they believed the reforms they stood for could be obtained only by independent action. In the election of 1900, when McKinley and Bryan were again the major party candidates, Barker and Donnelly received only 50,373 popular votes. In 1904 the People's Party at a convention in Springfield, Illinois, nominated its own ticket again—Watson for President and Thomas H. Tibbles of Nebraska for Vice President, but the Populist ticket received only 117,183 popular votes in the election that year. Four years later the People's Party met in convention at St. Louis and nominated Watson for President again. Samuel W. Williams of Indiana was nominated for Vice President. In the election of 1908, when William Howard Taft and James S. Sherman were the Republican nominees, and Bryan and

Senator John W. Kern of Indiana were the Democratic nominees, the Populist candidates received only 29,100 popular votes.

Which Republican President served the longest?

Ulysses S. Grant has been the only President elected by the modern Republican Party who served two full four-year terms. Since the Republican Party nominated its first candidate in 1856, thirteen men have become President under its auspices, and twelve of them served for shorter periods than eight years. Abraham Lincoln and William McKinley were re-elected, but their second terms were cut short by assassins. Andrew Johnson, Rutherford B. Hayes, James A. Garfield, Chester A. Arthur, Benjamin Harrison, William Howard Taft, Warren G. Harding and Herbert Hoover served four years or less. Theodore Roosevelt and Calvin Coolidge both served a full term in addition to an unexpired term. Roosevelt was President seven years, five months and twenty days— the second longest Republican service.

Grant, the only Republican President to serve two full terms, was born in Ohio in 1822 and graduated at West Point in 1843 as number thirty-one in a class of thirty-nine. He remained in the Army until 1854 and took little interest in politics. Although he was Constitutionally eligible to vote for President in 1844, he was moving from place to place and did not vote that year. In 1848 Grant favored General Zachary Taylor, the Whig candidate for President, but did not vote in the election. He did not vote in 1852 because he was with troops in the Far West. In 1856 the Republicans nominated John C. Frémont and the Democrats nominated James Buchanan. Although Grant's father had been a Whig and joined the new Republican Party, Grant had married into a Southern Democratic family and regarded himself as a Democrat after the breakup of the Whig Party. In 1856, after a brief membership in the American or Know-Nothing Party, he supported and voted for Buchanan. According to an apocryphal story, when asked several years later why he had voted for the Democrat, he replied, "Because I knew Frémont." At any rate he did say, "I thought it would be a misfortune for the country if he should be elected." In 1860 Grant preferred Douglas, the Northern Democrat, to Lincoln, the Republican, and preferred Lincoln to Breckinridge, the Southern Democrat, but since he was doubtful whether he was eligible to vote in Illinois he did not vote in that election. After Lincoln's election Grant began to regard himself as a "moderate Republican." But the vote for Buchanan in 1856 was the only vote for a Presidential candidate Grant had cast when he became the Republican candidate in 1868. Some authorities say he did not vote in the elections of 1868 and 1872. If that is true, he did not vote for a Republican until 1876, after he had been a Republican President for nearly eight years.

Several other Presidents changed political parties. John Quincy Adams left the Federalists in 1808 to join the Democratic-Republicans, and wound up as an independent Whig. Martin Van Buren started out as a Democrat, switched to the Free-Soilers, and returned to the Democratic fold. John Tyler began as a Democrat, joined the Whigs, and rejoined the Democrats. Millard Fillmore was first a Whig, then a Know-Nothing, then a Republican, and finally a Democrat. Abraham Lincoln was successively a National Republican, a Whig and a Republican. Rutherford B. Hayes was another Whig who became a Republican. In 1896 President Grover Cleveland voted for Buckner, the Gold Democratic candidate for President, instead of for William Jennings Bryan, the regular Democratic nominee. In 1904 Franklin D. Roosevelt voted for Theodore Roosevelt, the Republican candidate. Theodore Roosevelt bolted his party in 1912 and ran as the candidate of the Progressive Party, and he was supported by Herbert Hoover, who became the Republican candidate in 1928.

What Presidents were born posthumously?

Two of the men who have been President were born posthumously. Andrew Jackson was born March 15, 1767, a few days after his father's death. Rutherford B. Hayes was born October 4, 1822, seventy-six days after the death of his father, and, to use Hayes's own words, his uncle Sardis Birchard "adopted me as his child."

A person born after the death of his father is said to have been posthumously born. *Posthumous,* however, does not literally mean "after death," as many seem to suppose. It is derived from Latin *posthumous,* a superlative of *posterus,* "the hindmost" or "the last." Originally a posthumous child was simply the last child of a parent. Referring to the widow of the Roman dictator Sulla, Plutarch wrote: "Valeria was afterwards delivered of a daughter, named Posthuma; for so the Romans call those who are born after the father's death." Under English common law a posthumous child is one born either after the father's death or after his will was made. In Shakespeare's *Cymbeline* Imogen's husband is named Posthumus Leonatus. Ben Jonson was born a month after his father's death and was a posthumous child. A literary composition first printed after the author's death is called a posthumous work. POSS-*choo-muss* is the preferred pronunciation of the word.

Post-mortem is the Latin phrase for "after death." A post-mortem child is one born alive after the death of its mother. Such births occur rarely.

When did *whitewash* acquire its political meaning?

Whitewash in the sense of glossing over blemishes and covering up faults was used as early as 1762. In that year the term was specifically applied to going through bankruptcy proceedings or clearing an insolvent of liability for debts by judicial process. A writer in the issue of the Boston *Evening Post* of August 2, 1762, said: "Another, lately white-washed—taken the benefit of the Bankrupt Act—proposed to me my setting him up again in business."

The earliest recorded use of *whitewash* in a political sense is dated 1800. In the issue of the Philadelphia *Aurora* for July 21 of that year an editorial said: "If you do not whitewash President Adams speedily, the Democrats, like swarms of flies, will bespatter him all over, and make you both as speckled as a dirty wall, and as black as the devil." Soon thereafter *whitewashing* acquired the meaning of a prearranged exoneration of a public official, accused of wrongdoing, after a perfunctory investigation by a committee composed of a majority friendly to him.

In 1824 former Senator Ninian Edwards of Illinois, while on his way to assume his duties as Minister to Mexico, sent the House of Representatives a "defensive address" in which he charged Secretary of the Treasury William H. Crawford with official misconduct, and the House appointed a committee to investigate the charges. On April 22, 1824, Secretary of State John Quincy Adams wrote in his diary: "A prodigious stir is made about catching him [Edwards] and bringing him here and preventing his escape; all which is to excite odium against him as an accuser, and to prepare for a whitewashing of Crawford." On March 20 and 27, 1828, President Adams referred to General Jackson's "Nashville whitewashing committee's report." On April 16, 1840, Representative Adams wrote: "In the House, Joseph Jones, Chairman of the Committee of Accounts, finished his whitewashing speech for the Clerk," and on February 16, 1841, he referred to "A man named Edmund Burke, the very thickest skull of all New Hampshire, Chairman of a committee of the last session to whitewash the Clerk." Elsewhere in his diary Adams, who knew the famous Edmund Burke in England, referred to this Edmund Burke as "a libel on his own name." In *Twenty Years of*

Congress (1884) James G. Blaine wrote that in 1865 Senator Charles Sumner likened President Johnson's message "to the 'whitewashing' message of President Pierce with regard to enormities in Kansas."

What was the Readjuster Party?

The Readjuster Party was formed in Virginia in 1877 when the State was unable to pay interest on its large debt and the people, regardless of former party labels, divided into "debt payers" and "readjusters." Harrison H. Riddleberger introduced a bill declaring that the State should not pay any interest on that part of the debt incurred during the Civil War and the Reconstruction period, that the debt should be cut from about $31,000,000 to about $20,000,000 and that no part of the revenues of the State should be applied to the debt unless no other use for it could be found. This bill passed the Legislature but was vetoed by the Governor. In 1881 the Readjusters got complete control of the State and passed three bills on the debt question, one of them being substantially the Riddleberger bill. During this period the Readjusters elected William Mahone to the U.S. Senate and John Paul and Abram Fulkerson to the U.S. House of Representatives. Shortly thereafter Riddleberger himself was elected to the U.S. Senate. In nine decisions—known as the Virginia Coupon Cases—the U.S. Supreme Court declared some of the Readjuster acts an impairment of the obligation of contracts by a State and therefore unconstitutional. Finally the State and its bondholders reached a compromise, and the Readjusters, deprived of their main issue, were defeated by the Conservative Democrats and petered out after 1887.

What was the Liberal Republican Party?

The Liberal Republican Party was a short-lived political party organized in 1872 to oppose the re-election of President Grant. Conspicuous leaders of the movement were Horace Greeley, Carl Schurz, David Davis, Lyman Trumbull, Charles Francis Adams, Charles Sumner and B. Gratz Brown, who were dissatisfied with the Grant administration because of its corruption, its abuse of patronage for political purposes and its reconstruction policy in the South.

In January, 1872, when it was apparent that Grant's renomination by the Republican convention could not be blocked, the Liberal Republican convention of Missouri called a national convention to meet in Cincinnati on May 1 of the same year. This convention, little more than a mass meeting of self-appointed delegates, adopted a platform endorsing civil service reform, universal amnesty for former Confederates, reconciliation with the South, resumption of specie payments, and states' rights. After considerable controversy the convention nominated Greeley for President. B. Gratz Brown, newly elected Liberal Republican Governor of Missouri, was nominated for Vice President. At first the Liberal Republican movement, supported by many Governors, Senators, Representatives and other Republican leaders, gained so much momentum that even prominent regulars in the Republican Party feared Grant would be defeated in the general election. On July 16, 1872, Rutherford B. Hayes wrote in his diary: "Altogether it is plain to my mind that Greeley will win, if the Democrats support him with their whole force. I think they can't do it, but I fear it. I fear that the thing is in great doubt . . . I must say that I have just a feeling that Greeley will be elected!"

But there was so much opposition to the Greeley-Brown ticket among the Liberal Republicans themselves that a group of them held a convention in New York under the name of Independent Liberal Republicans and nominated William S. Groesbeck of Ohio for President and Frederick L. Olmsted of New York for Vice President. The Democratic National Convention at Philadelphia that year endorsed the candidates and platform of the Liberal Republicans. It was the first and has been the last time the Democratic Party did not nominate candidates of its own. But so many Democrats objected to the Greeley-Brown ticket that a convention of Straight Democrats met at Louisville, Kentucky, on September 3 and nominated Charles O'Conor of New York for President and John Quincy Adams, grandson and great-grandson of a President, for Vice President. Although the Liberal Republican Party started out as a "third party," it immediately became one of the two major parties when it was endorsed by the Democratic convention.

The campaign between the Republicans and the Liberal Republican-Democratic coalition was one of the most bitter in American history. The Republicans, well organized and supplied with funds, waved the bloody shirt and accused Greeley with being everything from a traitor to a fool. Grant made no campaign speeches, but Greeley, wearing a linen duster, took the stump and made an intensive speaking tour. Although Greeley was honest and able and his speeches compare favorably with those of other Presidential candidates, he was eccentric and cut a somewhat grotesque figure. His record was so inconsistent that he was easily misrepresented by the Republicans. Because of his eccentricities in dress he was nicknamed "Old White Hat." He was so ridiculed and abused in articles and cartoons that he said he hardly knew whether he was a candidate for the Presidency or the penitentiary.

"Grantism" was the chief issue and "Turn the Rascals Out" was the slogan of the Liberal Republicans. "Turn the rascals out" is supposed to have been coined in 1871 by Charles A. Dana, editor and part owner of the New York *Sun,* in reference to William Marcy ("Boss") Tweed and the Tammany ring that controlled New York City politics at the time. The saying has not been found in the *Sun* in 1871 and possibly it antedates that period. It has since been used as a slogan several times by the "outs" against the "ins," when it meant little more than "Turn their rascals out and put our rascals in." During the campaign of 1872 the Greeleyites sang the following song to the tune of "Yes, My Darling Daughter":

> Mother, may I go out to swim?
> Yes, my dear, go freely.
> Put on your white hat, your old white coat,
> And vote for Horace Greeley.

The Greeleyites also sang the following song, to the tune of "I Want to Be an Angel":

> I want to be a Liberal,
>   And with the Liberals stand,
> A white hat on my forehead
>   And a ticket in my hand.
>
> There right before the ballot box,
>   A-battling for the right,
> I'll vote for Horace Greeley
>   And help him in the fight.

Greeley had to leave off speaking to hurry to the bedside of his sick wife, who died October 30. The election returns stunned him. He received only 2,834,079 popular votes against Grant's 3,597,070, and only the sixty-six electoral votes of six Border and Southern States against Grant's 286 of all the other States. Although O'Conor and Adams had declined to be the candidates of the Straight Democrats, they received 29,489 popular votes. Groesbeck and Olmstead, the Independent Liberal Republican candidates, received only a handful of popular votes, but, oddly enough, Groesbeck received one electoral vote for the Vice Presidency. Greeley, grief-stricken by the death of his wife, exhausted by the arduous campaign, shocked by being the "worst defeated man who ever ran for the Presidency" and humiliated because his

[245]

former colleagues refused to let him return to the New York *Tribune* in his capacity as editor-in-chief, suffered a complete physical and mental breakdown and died on November 29. The Liberal Republican Party, of which he was one of the chief founders, soon dissolved.

Who was Lemonade Lucy?

President and Mrs. Rutherford B. Hayes were subjected to much "fashionable ridicule" for rigorously excluding intoxicating beverages from the White House. The press called Mrs. Hayes "Lemonade Lucy" because she served lemonade and fruit juices at state functions. Some foreign diplomats arched their eyebrows when they learned of the new policy and Secretary of State William M. Evarts vainly tried to get the President to change it in the interests of international relations. Asked, as he came out of the White House, how the first "dry dinner" came off, Evarts was quoted as saying, "Water flowed like champagne." On February 28, 1878, President Hayes wrote in his diary in reference to the White House dinner for the diplomatic corps:

The exclusion of wine from the list of refreshments has turned out exceedingly well. There is a great deal of dissipation here. At the receptions of the British Minister, and that of the Mexican Minister, disgraceful things were done by young men, made reckless by too much wine. Hence the necessity of our course is obvious, and is commended in unexpected quarters. Many of the foreign gentlemen speak of it with approval. We shall stick to it.

A story went the rounds that the White House help slipped some of the guests rum-spiked punches concealed in frozen orange skins. When Hayes read this in Ben. Perley Poore's *Reminiscences,* he wrote in his diary on January 10, 1887: "The joke of the Roman punch oranges was not on us but on the drinking public. My orders were to flavor them rather strongly with the flavor that is found in Jamaica rum. . . . This took! There was not a drop of spirits in them! This was certainly the case after the facts alluded to reached our ears. It was refreshing to hear 'the drinkers' say with a smack of the lips, 'would they were hot!' " Hayes was accused of being a hypocrite who drank secretly and served liquor to others in disguise. A disappointed office seeker spread the story that he had been turned down merely because he drank. "The exclusion of wine at the White House," wrote Hayes on June 11, 1885, "is at the bottom of three-fourths of all the lies that are now told about me."

As a young lawyer and officer in the Union army, Hayes played poker, smoked cigars, took an occasional drink and did a little cussing, all of which he later quit. He joined the Sons of Temperance and made temperance speeches. On November 21, 1850, he wrote in his diary: "I am a sincere but not extreme or violent friend of the temperance cause .... The learning to speak as well as the notoriety (not to speak of the good I *may* do) are objects worthy of the pains." He liked to kid his mother about his drinking. On February 6, 1855, he wrote to his sister Fanny: "Mr. Rogers has quit 'the intoxicating bowl,' tell Mother, and is in improving health. By the way, that 'bowl' is a fiction of temperance lecturers; never saw a 'bowl' in a saloon in my life." Hayes thought "the only practicable and safe prohibition is self-prohibition," and on April 7, 1882, wrote in his diary: "Temperance is like religion. It gains nothing by force—by coercion. Neither the force of law nor of arms can promote it. It is advanced by religion, by argument, by education, by persuasion, and above all by example." On February 15, 1881, President Hayes wrote:

It seemed to me that the example of excluding liquors from the White House would be wise and useful, and would be approved by the good people generally. I knew it would be particularly gratifying to Mrs. Hayes to have it done. We had never been in the habit of using liquors in our own house, and we determined to continue our home custom in this respect in our official residence in Washington. Mrs. Hayes has been from childhood a total abstainer. I was not a total abstainer when I became President. But the discussions which arose over the change at the President's house soon satisfied me that in this matter, if our example was to be useful, there was no half-way house for me. During the greater part of my term and at least for the last three years, I have been in practice and in theory a consistent total-abstinence man, and I shall continue to be so. All statements inconsistent with the foregoing are without foundation.

On Washington's Birthday in 1881, ten days before his retirement from the Presidency, Hayes issued the following executive order:

In view of the well known facts that the sale and use in the Army of the United States of intoxicating liquors is the cause of such demoralization among both men and officers, and that such sale and use give rise to a very large proportion of the cases before general and garrison courts martial, involving great expense and serious injury to the service, it is therefore directed that the Secretary of War take suitable steps, as far as practicable consistent with vested rights, to prevent the sale of intoxicating liquors (as a beverage) at the camps, forts, and other posts of the army.

James A. Garfield, Hayes's immediate successor, was also a teetotaler, but on January 10, 1881, Hayes wrote in his diary:

It is said General Garfield will restore wine and liquor to the White House. I hope this is a mistake. . . . If General Garfield rejects the practice I have inaugurated, he will offend thousands and drive them into the hands of the temperance demagogues. He will lose the confidence of thousands of good citizens and get no strength in any quarter. His course will be taken as evidence that he lacks the grit to face fashionable ridicule.

A week later the President wrote the President-elect a long memorandum on the subject, but Garfield did not adopt a rigid rule against serving wine at the White House.

Mrs. Hayes was the first college graduate to become First Lady. Lucy Webb's two brothers enrolled in the Ohio Wesleyan University at Delaware when that institution opened in 1844, and by a special ruling of the trustees Lucy was permitted to be the only girl student. After her brothers graduated in 1848 Lucy entered the Wesleyan Female College in Cincinnati and graduated in 1850 at the age of nineteen. The next year she was married to Hayes, by whom she had six children.

In her younger days Lucy Webb Hayes was noted for her beauty and vivacity. On December 30, 1872, Hayes wrote in his diary: "Our wedding day, twenty years ago! A happy day. Darling is handsomer than she was then, with a glorious flow of friendly feeling and cheerfulness, a genuine womanly character, a most affectionate mother, a good, *good* wife. How I do love her! What a lucky man I was and am!" She was five feet four and a half inches tall, and weighed 170 pounds when she became First Lady. Simple in tastes, she disliked state affairs and felt unequal to formal society, but she presided over the teapot with charm and grace, and Associate Justice Lucius Q. C. Lamar of the Supreme Court thought her "the perfect mistress of the White House." Her objection to drinking and playing cards did not prevent her from liking dancing, fishing, horse-racing and all sorts of sports. Her husband described her as "a handsome matronly looking woman," and to her many friends and admirers she was known affectionately as "Aunt Lu." When Lucy was on a visit to Ohio in 1878, the Boston *Post* said: "Mr. Hayes, during the absence of Mrs. Hayes, will be acting President." On August 28, 1880, the President wrote in his diary: "Lucy is forty-nine today. I never loved her so much as now." Ten years later almost to a day he wrote: "The charm of life left me when Lucy died." His last words, uttered shortly before his death in 1893, were: "I know that I am going where Lucy is."

How did "waving the bloody shirt" originate?

Stirring up sectional animosity for political purposes after the Civil War was known as waving the bloody shirt. Radical Republicans felt that their party had saved the Union and was entitled to govern it. During the Presidential campaigns of 1868, 1872 and 1876 in particular

Republican demagogues in the North lauded the Republican Party for saving the Union, denounced the Democrats for starting the war, urged Union veterans to "vote as you shot," and appealed in other ways to the prejudices against the South to get votes. In 1869 Senator Charles Sumner of Massachusetts announced that he was seeking re-election on the sole issue, "Shall those who saved the Republic continue to rule it, or shall it be handed over to rebels and their allies?" There was a belief that no candidate could be elected to public office in New England without waving the bloody shirt. It was an accepted principle of practical politics that "the old soldier vote" was too large to be ignored. The most intense phase of the Bloody Shirt Era ended with the Grant administration and the inauguration of that of Hayes, but in a different form waving the bloody shirt continues unto this day.

It is often said that these tactics were first described as "waving the bloody shirt" by Oliver Hazard Perry Morton, a Radical Republican Senator from Indiana from 1867 to 1877. Morton's legs were crippled and he had a stationary bracket beside his desk on which to lean while speaking in the Senate. Of him George Thomas Lanigan (1845-1886) wrote in "The Bloody Shirt":

> With a crutch by way of a pole,
> With artistic flutter and flirt,
> A Senator in the Senate sat,
> Waving a bloody shirt.

But there is no evidence that Morton was the first to use the phrase to describe the political tactics in which he was proficient. The earliest recorded use of the phrase occurs in J. S. Reynolds's *Reconstruction in South Carolina* (1875): "A diligent attempt is now being made to hide with the 'bloody shirt' the appalling wrongs committed by the Republican party." In the *North American Review* for July, 1877, A. S. Black wrote: "To parade acts of violence and murder perpetrated within the jurisdiction of carpetbag government, was called, in the flash language of politicians, waving the bloody shirt, and considered a most effective means of electioneering." On July 21, 1880, after James A. Garfield had been nominated by the Republicans to succeed him, President Rutherford B. Hayes wrote in his diary: "The failure of the South to faithfully observe the Fifteenth Amendment is the cause of the failure of all efforts towards complete pacification. It is on this hook that the bloody shirt now hangs." When the Republicans nominated James G. Blaine in 1884 it was reported that they expected to "wring one more President out of the Bloody Shirt."

On September 11, 1885, Major William McKinley visited Rutherford B. Hayes at Fremont, Ohio. Under that date the former President wrote in his diary:

He is on a stumping tour . . . I criticised the bloody-shirt course of the canvass. It seems to me it is bad 'politics,' and of no use. This, even supposing it was sound in itself. The people are very weary of it. It is a stale issue. An increasing number of people are interested in good relations with the South. This tends to keep alive animosities. Two ways are open to succeed in the South: 1. A division of the white voters. 2. Education of the ignorant. Bloody-shirt utterances prevent division, etc.

The Republicans elected five Civil War veterans to the Presidency, while the Democrats never elected one. After the Reconstruction Period the Democrats of the South did some waving of the bloody shirt on their own account.

A bloody shirt is the symbol of any means used to influence people to zeal, anger or retaliation. In *Arcadia* (1586) Sir Philip Sidney wrote: "People . . . hauing no banners, but bloodie shirtes hanged vpon long staues." "The sacred duty of pursuing the assassins of Othman was the engine and pretence of his ambition," wrote Edward Gibbon in *The Decline and Fall of the Roman Empire* (1788). "The bloody shirt of the martyr was exposed in the mosch at Damascus." Mark Antony waved the bloody shirt when he raised the bloodstained mantle on Caesar's corpse and exposed the wounds to the mob. It was an ancient practice to exhibit the bloodstained garments of a slain person to incite his kin to vengeance. Criminal defense lawyers still sometimes wave the bloody shirt. On one occasion Patrick Henry placed the bloody clothes of a murdered man in the courtroom where they could be seen by the jurymen. Leon Foucher in France reviewed Jared Sparks's *Life of Washington,* and Lewis Cass, in *France, Its King, Court and Government* (1840), wrote that Foucher observed: "It is by spreading out the miseries of the workmen, the bloody shirt of some victim . . . that excites the people to take arms."

In a speech at New York City on September 17, 1880, Senator Roscoe Conkling said of *waving the bloody shirt:* "It is a relief to remember that this phrase is no invention of our politics. It dates back to Scotland three centuries ago. After a massacre in Glenfrein, not so savage as has stained our annals, two hundred and twenty widows rode on white palfreys to Stirling Tower, bearing each on a spear her husband's bloody shirt." John S. Farmer, in *Americanisms, Old and New* (London, 1889) accounted for *waving the bloody shirt* as follows:

[250]

The origin of the expression is to be sought in a Corsican custom now nearly, if not quite, obsolete. In the days of the fierce vendette—the feuds which divided the Corsicans family from family—bloodshed was a common occurrence. Before the burial of a murdered man the *gridata* was celebrated. This word, which literally means a crying aloud, may be translated "a wake." The body of the victim was laid upon a plank; his useless firearms were placed near his head, and his blood-stained shirt was hung above his head. Around the rude bier sat a circle of women, wrapped in their black mantels, who rocked to and fro with strange wailings. The men, relatives and friends of the murdered man, fully armed, stood around the room, and with thirst for revenge. Then one of the women—the wife or mother or sister of the dead man—with a sharp scream would snatch the bloody shirt, and waving it aloft, begin the vocero—the lamentation.

Who was the first ex-Confederate to serve in the Cabinet?

David McKendree Key (1824-1900) of Tennessee, Postmaster General in President Hayes's Cabinet from 1877 until he resigned in 1880, was the first former Confederate to serve in the Federal Cabinet.

On February 17, 1877, when it appeared that the Electoral Commission would decide in his favor, Hayes wrote in his diary:

The inaugural and Cabinet-making are now in order. I would like to get support from good men of the South, late Rebels. How to do it is the question. I have the best disposition towards the Southern people, Rebels and all. I could appoint a Southern Democrat in the Cabinet. But who would take it among the capable and influential good men of those States? General Joseph E. Johnston occurs to me. I must think of this.

Johnston, one of the chief generals of the Confederacy, had used his influence after the war to heal the nation's wounds, and William T. Sherman, General of the Army, told Hayes that he would be willing to take orders through his old antagonist on the field but questioned the wisdom of the proposed step.

The proposal was abhorrent to several Republican leaders, and Hayes passed over Johnston and appointed Senator Key, who had served as a lieutenant colonel in the Confederate army. The President often had to defend this decision. On April 11, 1880, he wrote:

My task was to wipe out the color line, to abolish sectionalism, to end the war and bring peace. To do this, I was ready to resort to unusual measures, and to risk my own standing and reputation with my party and the country. For the first time in our history a gentleman who had opposed the election of the President was by that President invited into his Cabinet. Judge Key, a Confederate soldier and a Democrat who supported Tilden against me, was made Postmaster General and one of my constitutional advisers.

As late as January 27, 1881, shortly before the expiration of his term the President wrote to William Henry Smith: "The fact is I first thought of General Johnston for a *place*—probably the Interior. I soon saw that of course the War (Department) would not do. But a place for some Southerner was in my mind. Johnston was not preferred and Key was. That is all there is of it."

When Grover Cleveland became President in 1885 he appointed two former Confederates to Cabinet posts—Lucius Quintus Cincinnatus Lamar of Mississippi, Secretary of the Interior, and Augustus H. Garland of Arkansas, Attorney General. When Cleveland became President the second time in 1893 he appointed as Secretary of the Navy Hilary A. Herbert of Alabama, who as a Confederate colonel had been wounded in the Battle of the Wilderness, and he was the first ex-Confederate to become head of one of the military departments of the Government.

Who was Parson Brownlow?

William Gannaway Brownlow (1805-1877), a stormy petrel of Tennessee politics, was known as "Parson Brownlow" and "the Fighting Parson" because he was a Methodist minister for ten years before he became an editor and politician. He was born in southwestern Virginia and moved to Tennessee in his youth with his parents. Parson Brownlow was an effective speaker and writer and gained a large political following. In 1842 Andrew Johnson defeated him for the nomination to Congress. Although not originally against slavery, he opposed secession and was the recognized Unionist leader in the State. In 1861 the Confederates arrested him and put him in jail, but later he was sent within the Federal lines. The Fighting Parson of the Tennessee mountains was received in the North as a national hero. In *Anecdotes of Public Men* (1881) John W. Forney wrote that *Parson Brownlow's Book,* published in 1862, "had an immense sale, and settled the reverend-editor a handsome little fortune." As Reconstruction Governor of Tennessee for two terms (1865-1869) he disfranchised all former Confederates and used the militia to check the Ku Klux Klan. He served a term (1869-1875) as a Union Senator from Tennessee but was physically unable to take an active part in the Senate. James G. Blaine described Parson Brownlow as "a quaint and eccentric man."

When did political parties first have national committees?

The early political parties in the United States were loosely organized and did not have permanent national committees. In 1804 the supporters of President Jefferson designated a leader in each State to manage his campaign for re-election, and four years later the Congressional Caucus that nominated Madison for President and Clinton for Vice President named, a "committee of correspondence." On January 23, 1808, John Quincy Adams, who attended the Republican Caucus, wrote in his diary: "A committee of correspondence was then chosen, consisting of a member from each State, but Connecticut and Delaware, not being present, had no members chosen." The Federalists also had a "general committee" in the same year, but these groups were informal and largely self-appointed, and they dissolved after each election. Lack of adequate party organizations on a national scale was an obvious weakness of both the National Republican and the Whig parties in their opposition to the Democratic-Republican Party from 1828 to 1852.

The Democratic National Convention of 1844, which nominated James K. Polk for President and George M. Dallas for Vice President, appointed a "central committee" to "promote the election of Polk and Dallas." Before that the Democratic Party had no national organization of any kind and its national conventions were called by the Democratic members of the New Hampshire legislature. The Democratic National Convention of 1848, which nominated Lewis Cass for President and William O. Butler for Vice President, organized the first Democratic National Committee to act as the permanent agency of the party during the intervals between conventions. B. P. Hallett, of Massachusetts, was the first chairman.

The first Republican National Convention, which met in Philadelphia in June, 1856, adopted a similar scheme of party organization, which had been agreed upon by a preliminary meeting of Republican leaders at Pittsburgh in the preceding February. This first Republican National Convention nominated John C. Frémont for President and William L. Dayton for Vice President and confirmed Edwin D. Morgan, of New York, as permanent chairman of the Republican National Committee, a position he held until 1864.

Members of the national committees are elected by the national conventions and candidates are nominated by State primaries, conventions, committees or delegations to the national conventions. At present the national committees are composed of one man and one woman from each State and each Federal Territory, District and insular possession that has votes in the national conventions. The national committees have no powers except those that the national conventions give them.

Both major parties have campaign committees in both houses of Congress. In 1866, when Congress and President Andrew Johnson were at odds, the Radical Republicans in the House of Representatives formed the Republican Congressional Campaign Committee to look after their own political interests independently of the National Republican Committee, which was controlled by the faction of the party friendly to President Johnson. The Republican Congressional Campaign Committee was made permanent in 1912 and the next year its name was changed to the National Republican Congressional Committee. In 1915 the House Democrats formed a permanent organization known as the Democratic Congressional Campaign Committee. The Republican Senatorial Campaign Committee was made permanent in 1916 and the Democratic Senatorial Campaign Committee about the same time. These Congressional and Senatorial campaign committees of each party co-operate with each other and with their party's national committee but they are separate political organizations concerned chiefly in promoting the election of members of their respective parties to their respective houses of Congress. In 1942 former Senator John G. Townsend of Delaware was appointed chairman of the Republican Senatorial Campaign Committee and that has been the only instance of a nonmember of Congress being chairman of one of the four Congressional campaign committees.

Who were the Red Shirts?

The volunteers who followed General Giuseppe Garibaldi in the Italian wars from 1859 to 1867 were called Red Shirts because their partisan uniform was distinguished by a red shirt. From this *red shirt* became synonymous with revolutionist.

During Reconstruction the term was applied to an armed political group in South Carolina organized to restore white supremacy and home rule. In 1868, under laws passed over President Johnson's veto by the Radical Republicans, South Carolina was "readmitted" into the Union under a regime that disfranchised and barred from office nearly all native whites and gave control to carpetbaggers, scalawags and former slaves. Eight years of disorder and corruption followed.

Native whites began to form "rifle" and "salute" clubs, which were organized throughout the State as the "Red Shirts" by General Martin Witherspoon Gary, descendant of John Witherspoon, Harvard law graduate and former Confederate cavalry officer. In 1876 the Straight Democrats, backed by the Red Shirts, nominated General Wade Hampton for Governor. Bands of mounted men in red shirts patrolled political gatherings and polling places and secured Hampton's election by persuasion, intimidation and fraud. Unlike the Ku Klux Klan, the Red Shirts worked openly and without disguises. Five thousand of them rode into Columbia to see that Hampton was installed as Governor. At first Governor Daniel H. Chamberlain, Massachusetts carpetbagger, refused to turn the State administration over to Hampton, but the Republican regime collapsed when President Rutherford B. Hayes withdrew the Federal troops in April, 1877.

The Red Shirts continued to control the elections for several years. On March 23, 1879, President Hayes asked rhetorically in his diary: "If the red-shirts can be present at the polls in South Carolina, why cannot the bluecoats be called in also?"

Who were the Knights of the White Camellia?

The Knights of the White Camellia was a secret order formed at Franklin, Louisiana, in 1867 to resist Reconstruction and carpetbag government and to restore native white supremacy. Its headquarters was at New Orleans and for several years its membership in the lower South was greater than that of the Ku Klux Klan. It was similar to the Klan in organization and purposes but more conservative and less spectacular in means and methods.

Camellia is the name of a genus of evergreen shrubs which includes the tea plant and which is native to the Orient. These shrubs have thick, dark and shining leaves and handsome white, pink or rose-colored flowers. A Moravian Jesuit missionary named George Joseph Kamel wrote an account of the plants in Luzon in the Philippines and it was published in 1704. Most of the cultivated varieties of camellia were developed from Camellia japonica, a native of Japan and China, which was introduced into Europe in 1837 by Lord Petre. Although Kamel had never seen any plants of this species, the Swedish botanist Linnaeus honored him in 1753 by calling the whole genus Camellia, a Latinized form of the name. In 1848 Alexander Dumas the Younger published La Dame aux Camélias, "The Woman of the Camellias," in which the camellia is the heroine's favorite flower. The name of the Knights of the

White Camellia was probably suggested by the popularity of Dumas's novel among the Louisiana French and the fact that camellias thrive out of doors in the South.

Another secret military organization in Louisiana during the Reconstruction Period was known as The White League or the Crescent White League. It was more violent in its campaign of terror against Negroes, carpetbaggers and scalawags than were the Knights of the White Camellia and the Ku Klux Klan. In 1874, after a battle with the police, the White League seized the government of New Orleans by force and controlled it until dispersed by Federal forces.

How did "ten acres and a mule" originate?

The authorship of this saying is unknown. It originated in America in 1862 and expressed the amount that the slaves expected to get from the Federal Government when they were emancipated after the Union victory. The Federal Government never made any such promise to the slaves. Later *forty* was substituted for *ten* in the expression and it became "forty acres and a mule."

This alteration may have been due to the fact that in a special field order issued at Savannah on January 16, 1865, General William T. Sherman said: "Every family shall have a plot of not more than forty acres of tillable ground." The Freedman's Act, approved by President Lincoln March 3, 1865, authorized the Commissioner to lease for three years to all male refugees and freedmen not more than forty acres of land in the South that had been abandoned by the owners or confiscated by the Federal Government, with an option to buy after three years and to acquire such title as the United States could convey. Freedmen obtained little advantage from this provision, because the owners reclaimed the abandoned land and confiscations could be, under the attainder clause in the Constitution, for only the life of the owners. Thaddeus Stevens, who subscribed to the "conquered province theory," advocated the confiscation of all the property of ex-Confederates and making a gift of forty acres to each former slave. After the Negroes in the South learned they were not to get the "forty acres and a mule" that they fondly yearned for and supposed had been promised, many of them went to work as tenant farmers.

The British counterpart of the saying is "three acres and a cow," generally ascribed to Jesse Collings, who, as a henchman of Joseph Chamberlain in the House of Commons, sponsored the "small holdings amendment" that defeated the ministry of Lord Salisbury in 1888.

During the 90's "three acres and a cow" was widely used by the Populists in the United States to designate the meager wealth of the common man.

How did *fixing fences* as a political term originate?

A politician in office, particularly a member of Congress or a State legislature, who visits his home district to look after his political interests, to compose differences among his followers and to prepare for his re-election, is said to be out mending or fixing his fences.

The phrase arose from a casual remark made in a speech delivered at Mansfield, Ohio, in 1879 by John Sherman, then Secretary of the Treasury in the Cabinet of President Rutherford B. Hayes. In his *Recollections of Forty Years in the House, Senate and Cabinet* (1895), the Ohio statesman—a brother of William Tecumseh Sherman—related the history of the expression as follows:

I went to Mansfield, and as my family was absent and the homestead occupied by comparative strangers, I stopped at the St. James hotel where, as was natural, I met a great many of my old neighbors and friends, both Democrats and Republicans, who welcomed me home.

Among my visitors were several reporters from different parts of the country who wanted to interview me and especially to learn if I was a candidate for governor, and why I came home. In the afternoon I visited my farm near by and my homestead of about twenty acres adjoining the city. I found them in the usual neglected condition of the property of a non-resident proprietor, with many fences down. In the evening I was serenaded at the hotel and made a brief speech to a large audience, commencing as follows:

"I am very happy to be again in your midst, to see your faces and to greet you as friends. The shaking of your hands is more grateful to me than the music of bands or any parade. I never felt like making an explanation in coming before you until now. I found when I arrived in my old home that the papers said I came west seeking the nomination for governor. I came purely on private business—*to repair my fences and look after neglected property.*"

The reporters seized upon the reference to my fences, and construed it as having a political significance. The phrase *mending fences* became a byword, and every politician engaged in strenthening his position is still said to be *mending his fences.*

Notwithstanding this naïve statement written long afterward, the suspicions of the reporters were probably justified. Sherman was an aspirant for the Republican Presidential nomination in 1880, 1884 and 1888. He returned to the Senate in 1881 and remained there until he resigned to become Secretary of State in William McKinley's Cabinet.

The Sherman Anti-Trust Act and the Sherman Silver Purchase Act bear his name.

Why is a political prize called a plum?

Plum in the sense of a public office or reward bestowed because of party service or political pull rather than personal qualifications is believed to have been popularized if not coined by Matthew Stanley Quay (1833-1904), who was for many years Republican boss of Pennsylvania.

Quay was the son of a Presbyterian minister, graduated from Jefferson College at Cannonsburg, and was awarded the Congressional Medal of Honor for distinguished service in the Union army. He mastered several languages, read the Greek and Latin classics in the original languages, and was fond of discussing literature. But he was such a consummate and successful politician that his name is almost synonymous with political plunder. While he was State treasurer (1885-1887) he placed large sums of State money in the People's Bank of Philadelphia and used it to buy stocks on margin. On one occasion Quay and his associates piled up orders for the stock of the Metropolitan Railroad of New York until only about $10,000 was left in the bank. John S. Hopkins, the cashier, became frightened and protested to the political boss. Quay sent the cashier the message: "Buy and carry a thousand Met for me and I will shake the plum tree." The stock rose from almost nothing to 160 and then began to fall, whereupon Hopkins committed suicide. On January 13, 1887, the year Quay became U.S. Senator and Chairman of the Republican National committee, the Louisville *Courier Journal* said: "Senator Beck gets the credit for most of the federal appointments in Mason County. The boys enjoying the plums will support anybody who is for him or them." The plum is a luscious and delicious fruit and previously the term had been applied both in England and America to a stroke of luck, a good thing, the pick of the lot or anything likened to a plum in desirability.

Why are standpatters called "the Old Guard"?

The Old Guard was first applied to Republican standpatters in 1880. In the Republican National Convention at Chicago in that year Senator Roscoe Conkling, in placing General U. S. Grant's name in nomination, said among other things: "Pull no skulkers from under the ammunition wagon; take the tried and true old hero—with the Old Guard behind him who have never kept step to any music but the music of the Union." The more than three hundred delegates who supported Grant for a third term and stood pat to the last adopted as their slogan, "The Old Guard dies, but never surrenders." From this circumstance the Old Guard came to be used in American politics to designate the conservative or standpat element in the Republican Party.

In the course of time the phrase was broadened to include any body or group opposed to change and known for its reactionary tendencies. Any conservative political philosophy was known as Old Guardism.

The Old Guard (*Vieille Garde*), Napoleon Bonaparte's original imperial guard organized in 1801, received its popular name in 1810 after "The Young Guard" was created as a recruiting unit for it. The Old Guard took part in many of Napoleon's campaigns and made the final French charge at the Battle of Waterloo.

The slogan used at the Chicago Republican convention in 1880 was a rough translation of French *La Garde meurt et ne se rend pas* ("The Guard dies and never surrenders"), which is the reply attributed to General Pierre Cambronne, a commander of the Old Guard, when Colonel Hugh Halkett demanded his surrender at Waterloo. In a speech at his home town of Nantes in 1835 Cambronne denied that he had uttered the heroic words. On another occasion he explained that such a statement would not have been called for, since he surrendered and did not die at the time. An eyewitness testified that Cambronne, as his horse was shot under him, said, *Je me rends,* "I surrender." There is a legend that General Cambronne, when Colonel Halkett demanded his surrender, uttered a five-letter French word that is unprintable, and this word is still known among the French as *le mot de Cambronne.*

In 1817 Nicholas Charlet used the words, *La Garde meurt et ne se rend pas,* as a motto on his famous lithograph entitled *"Grenedier de Waterloo."* Eduard Fournier (1819-1880), French historian, said in his *L'Esprit dans l'Histoire* that the saying was invented by a French journalist named Rougement, who was noted for his ability to coin *mots* and who used it two days after the Battle of Waterloo in an article in the Paris *Independent.*

But it is not certain that Rougement coined the saying. It appears to have been quoted as already familiar in a letter written on the evening of the battle by Captain Digby Mackworth to General Howland Hill. Perhaps the saying was already old. Victor Hugo, in *William Shakespeare* (1864), wrote: "Certain sayings which are in history, have no right to be historical; and it is well understood, for example, that the gendarme who fired a pistol at Robespierre at the Hotel de Ville rejoiced in the name 'The-guard-dies-and-never-surrenders.' " In any event, the words were engraved on a monument in memory of Cambronne at Nantes and they are popularly associated with his name.

After President John Tyler was repudiated by most of the Whigs in 1841 and became "a man without a party," the handful of Whig members of Congress who continued to support him were known as "the guard," "the Tyler guard" and "the corporal's guard." On December 29, 1842, John Quincy Adams wrote in his diary: "Upon the reading of the report the House began to heave convulsively with the agonies of the Tylerizing corporal's guard, and their sympathizing Democracy—manifested chiefly by Profitt, and by Gwin, of Mississippi."

How did *peanut politics* originate?

Until the early part of the nineteenth century peanuts were regarded as unfit food for the upper classes and were eaten only by poor whites and slaves in the South. Hence *peanut* came to be applied to anything small, trifling or of little or no value, and to any person who was low, mean, paltry or contemptible. "They were your peanut fellows I suppose," occurs in a temperance novel entitled *Thirty Years Ago; or, the Memoirs of a Water Drinker,* and written in 1836 by William Dunlap, American playwright and theatrical manager. In England a constable or petty police officer is called a peanut. Who first used *peanut politics* is not known. The earliest example of the phrase cited by *The Dictionary of American English* is dated 1887. Alliteration and usefulness have kept the term alive. Peanut politics is petty politics and a peanut politician is one who plays petty politics for his personal or party advantage to the detriment of the public interest.

What is a keynoter?

A keynoter is a person who makes the introductory declaration of party principles and policies in a political convention. Political parties in the United States had keynoters in their conventions long before that particular term was used. Apparently *keynote* entered the American political vocabulary at a comparatively late date. The term, of course, was borrowed from the vocabulary of music, where the keynote is the note or tune on which a key or system of tones is based. The unabridged Standard dictionary printed in 1913 does not include the term in its political sense. In addition to the technical meaning, that work defines *keynote* simply as "a ruling principle, motive, thought or sentiment, as, the keynote of a discourse or argument."

On June 18, 1880, President Rutherford B. Hayes wrote to William Henry Smith: "John Thomason's advice should be our keynote in advising." In *My Quarter Century of American Politics* (1920) Champ Clark, referring to a speech he made in Tammany Hall on July 4, 1893, wrote: "Later, *The St. Louis Republic* hailed it as 'A Key-note Speech,' and it was headlined throughout the land." In reference to the Democratic National Convention of 1904, Clark, in the same book, says: "The chief business of the temporary chairman is to make a key-note speech outlining the issues of the campaign. This stunt was accomplished by Hon. John Sharp Williams with great éclat."

The keynoter at a national political convention delivers the keynote speech and strikes or sounds the keynote of the essential issues before the assembly. The keynote address is one of the first made at a convention and is customarily delivered before the platform is adopted and the candidates nominated. Traditionally the temporary chairman is the keynoter. He generally reviews the record of the party, foreshadows future policies and "views with alarm" the policies of the opposition. He also tries to use a catch phrase or pithy sentence that can be used by his party as a campaign slogan. In recent years it has become customary for national conventions to have a woman as well as a man keynoter.

What is meant by practical politics?

The earliest known use of *practical politics* in print occurs in a novel published anonymously by Benjamin Disraeli in 1826 and entitled *Vivien Grey,* which contains the sentence: " 'Hargrave,' said his Lordship, 'if you want any information upon points of practical politics . . . there is only one man in the kingdom whom you should consult.' "

At first *practical politics* denoted political transactions in actual practice as distinguished from their theoretical discussion. Now the term signifies little more than *politics* unmodified and survives chiefly because of the alliteration in the two words. The practical politician ranks between the demagogue and the statesman, having neither the meanness of the former nor the principles of the latter. He likes to do the right thing when it is convenient and practicable to do so, but he is no reformer and not overly concerned with ethics. Being a realist rather than an idealist, the practical politician accepts conditions and people as they are and not as he or others think they ought to be and takes half a loaf when he knows he cannot get a whole loaf. He plays the game of politics for its and his own sake and operates on the principle that a politician must get elected in order to have the opportunity to serve the people.

"Practical politics," wrote former President Rutherford B. Hayes in his diary on November 26, 1882, "means selfish ends promoted by base means. Sunday-school politics means serve your party by serving your country."

What was the famous apple tree of Appomattox?

On June 5, 1880, in the Republican National Convention at Chicago, Roscoe Conkling named former President Ulysses S. Grant for a third term as President. The New York Stalwart was a powerful speaker and had a reputation as a wit, and when he mounted the table of a newspaper correspondent to speak, the convention hall was charged with expectancy. After waiting fifteen minutes while the convention applauded uproariously, Conkling began his dramatic speech with:

> And if asked what state he hails from,
> This our sole reply shall be,
> From near Appomattox Court-House,
> With its famous apple-tree.

The quotation is from the eighth stanza of "A Bumper to Grant" by Charles Graham Halpine (1829-1868), Irish-born newspaperman, poet, humorist and Union soldier, who during the Civil War wrote under the pen name Private Miles O'Reilly. The four preceding lines of Halpine's poem, written before Grant was elected President the first time in 1868, are:

> So boys! a final bumper
> While we all in chorus chant,
> "For next President we nominate
> Our own Ulysses S. Grant."

Conkling said afterward that until the night before he made his speech he had never heard of Halpine's poem. In spite of Conkling's speech and leadership in the 1880 convention Grant lost the nomination to James A. Garfield. In his *Memoirs* (1886) Grant explained the report about his meeting General Robert E. Lee on April 9, 1865, under an apple tree at Appomattox:

But I had no doubt about the good faith of Lee, and pretty soon was conducted to where he was. I found him at the house of a Mr. McClean, at Appomattox Court House with Colonel Marshall, one of his staff officers, awaiting my arrival. The head of his column was occupying a hill on a portion of which was an apple orchard, beyond a little valley which separated it from that on the crest of which Sheridan's forces were drawn up in line of battle to the south.

Before stating what took place between General Lee and myself, I will give all there is of the story of the famous apple tree.

Wars produce many stories of fiction, some of which are told until they are believed to be true. The war of the rebellion was no exception to this rule, and the story of the apple tree is one of those fictions based on a slight foundation of fact. As I have said, there was an apple orchard on the side of the hill occupied by the Confederate forces. Running diagonally up the hill was a wagon road, which, at one point, ran very near one of the trees, so that the wheels of vehicles had on that side, cut off the roots of this tree, leaving a little embankment. General Babcock, of my staff, reported to me that when he first met General Lee he was sitting upon the embankment, with his feet in the road below and his back resting against the tree. The story had no other foundation than that. Like many other stories, it would be very good if it were only true.

Did General Sherman turn down the Presidency?

When the Democratic National Convention met at Chicago on August 29, 1864, to nominate a candidate to oppose President Lincoln the name of General William T. Sherman was mentioned as a possibility. General Sherman, whose army was engaged in the famous Georgia campaign, heard about it and wrote to General Henry W. Halleck, chief of staff in Washington: "Some fool seems to have used my name. If forced to choose between the penitentiary and the White House for four years, I would say the penitentiary, thank you."

In 1884 Sherman, who had retired in 1883 as the General of the Army and who was living in St. Louis, was boomed for the Republican nomination for the Presidency. The leading candidates were James G. Blaine, President Chester A. Arthur and the General's brother, John Sherman. On May 25, 1884, General Sherman wrote to Blaine: "I will not in any event entertain or accept the nomination as candidate for President by the Chicago convention or any other convention . . . I would account myself a fool, a madman, an ass, to embark now, at sixty-five years of age, in a career that may at any moment become tempestuous by the perfidy, the defalcation, the dishonesty or neglect of a hundred thousand subordinates utterly unknown to the President of the United States, not to say the eternal worriment of a vast host of impecunious friends and old military subordinates." Apparently when he wrote this letter he had in mind the unhappy experience of President Grant, who was a victim of his "friends."

But the movement for General Sherman as a compromise candidate persisted until after the meeting of the convention. John Brooks Henderson of Missouri, chairman of the convention, was strong for his St. Louis

[263]

neighbor and friend. On June 5 Henderson wired General Sherman: "Your name is the only one we can agree upon. You will have to put aside your prejudices and accept the Presidency." General Sherman immediately wired Henderson an emphatic refusal. The original message has been lost and its exact wording is not known. One of Sherman's sons, who was at the convention and who saw the telegram, said afterward that the exact words, as he recollected them, were: "I will not accept if nominated, and will not serve if elected." The message, however, is generally quoted: "If nominated, I will not accept; if elected, I will not serve."

The fact that General Sherman's wife was a Catholic probably influenced his decision. In *Autobiography of Seventy Years* (1903) George Frisbie Hoar wrote: "When I came back to Washington, I called at John Sherman's house and talked over the convention with him. . . . He said he was not surprised, and that he believed the unwillingness to have the religious faith of his wife made matter of public discussion had a good deal to do with his brother's refusal to permit himself to be a candidate."

In 1829, when William Tecumseh Sherman was nine years old, he went to live with Thomas Ewing, who became the boy's guardian but who, contrary to a common impression, did not formally adopt him. Ewing's wife, nee Maria Wills Boyle, was a Catholic, and Ewing himself later became a convert to that faith. Sherman was engaged to Eleanor Boyle ("Ellen") Ewing, daughter of his guardian, in 1843 and was married to her seven years later. Thus his foster mother became his mother-in-law. Sherman's son Thomas became a Jesuit. On May 8, 1890, Rutherford B. Hayes wrote in his diary: "General Sherman told me of the excellent spirit of his boy, the Catholic priest; of his cheerfulness, etc., but complained that after he had spent thousands of dollars for his education they now took it all,—made him a teacher with almost no salary and so practically confiscated him." On February 19, 1891, Hayes noted that "Father Tom Sherman" was at the General's funeral in St. Louis. Although General Sherman was not a member, at the end, while unconscious, he received the last rites of the Catholic Church.

There is no means of knowing whether General Sherman would have been elected if he had been nominated. This is one of the "ifs" of American history. It is even doubtful whether he could have been nominated had he consented. Blaine, whose mother was a Catholic, was nominated on the fourth ballot and was defeated by Grover Cleveland by a narrow margin. General Sherman might have suffered the same fate. When Senator Hoar tried to line up the Massachusetts and New York delegates for General Sherman at the convention, many of them told him, "Our people do not want a Father Confessor in the White House," and Hoar wrote, "So we agreed we should have to give it up."

Despite General Sherman's emphatic refusal to be a candidate, Henderson persisted in his efforts to have him nominated and he received a few votes in the convention. So did John Sherman. That has probably been the only instance of brothers receiving votes for President in the same national convention.

In 1944 Franklin D. Roosevelt used General Sherman's language in reverse. On July 11 of that year the President, making known his availability for a fourth term, said: "If the convention should nominate me for the Presidency, I shall accept. If the people elect me, I will serve."

William T. Sherman was superintendent of a military college in Louisiana when the State seceded and he was offered a high commission in the Confederate army. While commanding in Kentucky in 1861 General Sherman incurred the enmity of the newspapers by keeping reporters out of his lines. Rumors were spread that his mind was giving away. These rumors were readily believed because at the time the General was nervous and frail in health. So seriously were these rumors taken in official circles that when General Sherman reported for duty under General Halleck at St. Louis the latter received him coldly and suspiciously. Sherman was so depressed that he contemplated suicide. At Shiloh Sherman had four horses shot under him and was promoted from brigadier to major general for his conduct in that second large battle of the Civil War. About that time rumors were circulated that General Grant was frequently incapacitated by strong drink. It is said that many years later, when General Sherman was pressed to reverse one of President Grant's policies, he refused, saying: "Grant stood by me when I was crazy, and I stood by him when he was drunk, and now we stand by each other." John Sherman was noted for his lack of a sense of humor, but General Sherman was "full of fun."

Who are the lily whites?

Republicans in the Southern States who desire to exclude Negroes from the party and from political affairs are known as "lily whites."

The name originated in Reconstruction days and was applied by the Negroes themselves to those who were in favor of building up a white Republican party. It may have been suggested in 1888 by a statement made by N. Wright Cuney, Negro national committeeman and Republican "boss" of Texas. The Negro leader said that the bolting Republicans regarded themselves as too good to associate with Negroes or to clasp their lily-white hands with those of men of darker hue.

Newspapers about that time took up the term *lily white* and it was already widely used at the Republican National Convention held that year. In most Southern States the Republicans are divided into two factions, the lily whites and the regulars or black and tans. The former desire to make their party a white man's organization capable of effective opposition to the Democratic Party among the whites themselves; the latter favor giving Negroes a voice in party councils corresponding to their numerical strength.

Since time immemorial the whiteness of the lily has been the symbol of purity, chastity and virginity, and in Christian art the white lily is the emblem of the Virgin Mary. According to a legend in the Holy Land, white lilies sprang up spontaneously on every spot touched by the feet of Jesus after he rose from the dead, and in the early church white lilies became the symbols of the Resurrection and were used to decorate churches at Easter. In *Love's Labor's Lost* Shakespeare has the French princess refer to herself as being "as pure as the unsullied lily," and in *Henry VIII* Archbishop Cranmer of Canterbury, in his prophecy about the infant Elizabeth, says she must die "a virgin, a most unspotted lily." Oddly enough, Negroes and chimneysweeps were known as lily whites in England during the eighteenth century, the term being suggested by the contrast.

Who was the first Negro chairman of a national convention?

The Republican National Convention at Philadelphia in 1872 that renominated Grant for President was the first national nominating convention of a major party in which Negroes took part as delegates. Three Negroes—William E. Gray of Arkansas, B. B. Elliott of South Carolina and John Roy Lynch of Mississippi—made speeches from the rostrum.

During the Republican National Convention of 1880 Permanent Chairman George F. Hoar turned the gavel temporarily over to Blanche Kelso Bruce, a Negro Senator from Mississippi.

John Roy Lynch was temporary chairman and keynoter of the Republican convention at Chicago in 1884 that nominated James G. Blaine for President. The contest was largely between President Chester A. Arthur and Blaine. A fight developed between Blaine's followers and "the reformers" headed by Henry Cabot Lodge and Theodore Roosevelt, then only twenty-five years old. Powell Clayton of Alabama was the choice of the Blaine men for temporary chairman. In opposition Lodge nominated and Roosevelt seconded Lynch, who was chosen by a vote of 424 to 384. At the time Lynch was thirty-seven years old and was the youngest temporary chairman of a national convention of a major party until thirty-two-year-old Harold E. Stassen was chosen Republican key-noter in 1940.

Lynch was born in slavery near Vidalia, Louisiana, in 1847, of a Negro mother and a white father. He and his mother were sold after his father's death and taken to Natchez, Mississippi, where, after emancipation, he went to school and studied photography and law. He was admitted to the bar and in 1869 became a justice of the peace. At the age of twenty-four he was elected to Congress, and when he took his seat in the House at twenty-six was the youngest member. He was a member of the House from 1873 to 1877 and from 1881 to 1883. Under President Benjamin Harrison (1889-1893) he was fourth auditor of the Treasury. In 1898 he entered the army as paymaster and retired in 1911 with the rank of major. He died in Chicago in 1939 at the age of ninety-two.

Who was Calico Charlie?

"Calico Charlie" was the nickname of Charles Foster (1828-1904), an Ohio Republican politician, who was a Representative in Congress (1871-1879), Governor of Ohio (1880-1884), and Secretary of the Treas-ury under President Benjamin Harrison (1891-1893). He lived most of his life and was buried at Fostoria, a town named after his father. In his youth he was his father's partner in a dry-goods store and became wealthy as a merchant and banker. During the Civil War he did not join the army but continued in business. When he ran for Governor in 1879 his political enemies tried to discredit him as "a man who knew no higher occupation during the war than measuring calico" and ridiculed him as "Calico Charlie." His supporters made political capital of the nickname and women wore gowns of calico and men neckties of the same material.

What President was a preacher?

No ordained minister of the gospel has become President, but James A. Garfield, the twentieth President, was a lay preacher in the denomina-tion known as the Disciples of Christ or Campbellites. He was succes-sively a student, teacher and principal of the Western Reserve Eclectic Institute (later called Hiram College because it is at Hiram, Ohio), which was the chief Campbellite institution of higher learning.

When John Adams, the second President, graduated from Harvard in 1755 he had some thought of becoming a clergyman, but he decided to study law instead of theology. James Madison, the fourth President, also had some thought in his youth of becoming a minister of the gospel, and, like all students there at the time, he studied divinity and theology at Princeton, but he early abandoned all thoughts of entering the ministerial profession.

Three Presidents were the sons of clergymen. When Chester A. Arthur, the son of a Baptist minister, retired from the Presidency on March 4, 1885, he was succeeded by Grover Cleveland, the son of a Presbyterian minister. Woodrow Wilson has been the only other President who was the son of an ordained minister of the gospel. His father was a Presbyterian minister. Herbert Hoover's mother, Hulda Minthorn Hoover, was a recorded lay preacher in the Society of Friends.

Four Presidents married daughters of clergymen—John Adams, Millard Fillmore, Franklin Pierce and Woodrow Wilson. James Buchanan's mother was the daughter of a Presbyterian preacher.

What President saw himself nominated for that office?

James A. Garfield has been the only President actually to see himself nominated for that office. Other delegates to national nominating conventions have been nominated for the Presidency, but Garfield has been the only successful Presidential candidate to be present in the convention hall when the ballots that nominated him were cast.

Garfield was opposed to a third term for Grant and went to the Republican convention at Chicago in 1880 as head of the Ohio delegation and floor manager for John Sherman, whose name he placed in nomination. On the thirty-fourth ballot Garfield himself received seventeen votes. He was recognized on a point of order and shouted: "I challenge the correctness of the announcement. The announcement contains votes for me. No man has a right, without the consent of the person voted for, to announce that person's name, and vote for him, in this convention. Such consent I have not given—." George F. Hoar, president of the convention, cut him off at that point with the firm statement: "The gentleman from Ohio is not stating a question of order. He will resume his seat. No person having received a majority of the votes cast, another ballot will be taken. The Clerk will call the roll." The Sherman delegates, realizing that further support of their man was futile, continued to vote for Garfield and he was nominated on the thirty-eighth ballot. Horatio Seymour was present in the convention hall and protesting when the Democratic convention nominated him for President in 1868, but he was defeated by Grant in the election.

In *Autobiography of Seventy Years* (1903) Hoar said of the Garfield incident: "I interrupted him in the middle of his sentence. I was terribly afraid that he would say something that would make his nomination impossible, or his acceptance impossible, if it were made. I do not believe it ever happened before that anybody who attempted to decline the Presidency of the United States was to be prevented by a point of order, or that such a thing will ever happen again." On June 15, 1880, William Henry Smith wrote to President Rutherford B. Hayes: "To the accidental presence of Garfield in the convention is to be attributed his nomination. Otherwise the opposition to Grant would have united as readily on another."

On December 1, 1865, when Hayes and Garfield were both members of Congress, Hayes noted in his diary, "General Garfield, a smooth, ready, pleasant man, not very strong." On June 15, 1880, Garfield spent several hours with Hayes at the White House and the President wrote in his diary:

He told me two omens. As he entered the convention the day of his nomination, a man distributing leaves of the New Testament handed him a leaf which he (Garfield) put in his pocket. Long after the nomination, emptying his pockets, the leaf was found. The verse that was apparent as it was folded read: 'The stone which the builders rejected, etc. etc.' At one o'clock P. M., the hour of the nomination, an eagle lit on Garfield's house in Washington and sat there several minutes and was seen by many persons.

Garfield was nicknamed "The Canal Boy" because in his youth he spent several months as boatman, deck hand and driver of a canal boat in Ohio. He once observed, "I never did care for the upholstery of office."

In the Republican National Convention of 1888 John Sherman was again an aspirant for the nomination and William McKinley was his floor leader this time. Several votes were cast for McKinley on a number of ballots and the delegates showed signs of stampeding for him. McKinley got recognition and in a brief speech said: "I do not request, I demand, that no delegate who would not cast reflection upon me shall cast a ballot for me." Benjamin Harrison of Indiana instead of John Sherman of Ohio got the nomination, but McKinley's loyalty to Sherman helped him to get the nomination himself in 1896.

What man was Representative, Senator-elect and President-elect at the same time?

James A. Garfield was a member of the U.S. House of Representatives, U.S. Senator-elect and President-elect of the United States all at the same time for a period of four days.

In 1862, while a Major General in the Union army, he was elected to the Thirty-Eighth Congress and was elected to the eight succeeding Congresses, including that ending March 3, 1881. On January 13, 1880, the Ohio legislature elected him to the U.S. Senate for the term beginning March 4, 1881, the date his service in the House would normally have ended. But on June 8, 1880, he was nominated for the Presidency by the Republican National Convention in Chicago. On November 8, 1880, he resigned his seat in the House, and on December 23 of the same year he declined to accept the Senatorship, having been chosen President November 4.

How did *junket* originate?

A trip made by members of Congress or other officials at public expense for private pleasure under the cloak of Government business is called a junket. The earliest use of the term in this sense recorded by the *Dictionary of American English* is dated 1886.

The root of *junket* is believed to be the Latin *juncus,* "rush" or "reed." In Old Northern French this word became *junc,* and its diminutive, *junquet* or *junket,* was applied to a basket made of rushes. A dish of flavored curds and sweatmeat topped with a layer of cream was called a junket because it was prepared or served in a junket or rush basket. Hence any sweatmeat, cake, confection or dainty food served as a dessert came to be known as a junket. In Shakespeare's *The Taming of the Shrew* old Baptista tells the wedding party, "You know there wants no junkets at the feast." Next the term came to signify a feast or banquet, particularly a picnic or eating and drinking party away from home.

Modern French *jonquille* means "little rush" and a species of narcissus is called jonquil from its long, narrow, rushlike leaves.

Who coined *rum, Romanism and rebellion?*

On October 29, 1884, James G. Blaine, the Republican candidate for President, received a delegation of about six hundred clergymen of many different Protestant denominations at the Fifth Avenue Hotel in New York City. The reception was held in the forenoon because Blaine was scheduled to view a businessmen's parade in the afternoon and to attend the dinner that became known as Belshazzer's Feast in the evening. The Reverend Dr. Robert Stuart McArthur, pastor of the Baptist Calvary Church in New York City, had been designated spokesman of the clergymen, but he was not present, and at the last minute the Reverend Samuel

Dickinson Burchard (1810-1891), pastor of the Murray Hill Presbyterian Church in New York City, was substituted. Many Republicans, known as Mugwumps, were supporting Grover Cleveland, the Democratic nominee, and the delegation of clergymen wanted to let Blaine know they were loyal Republicans. In his address to the Republican nominee Dr. Burchard, who spoke extemporaneously, said:

We expect to vote for you next Tuesday. We have higher expectations, which are that you will be the President of the United States and that you will do honor to your name and to the high office you will occupy. We are Republicans and don't propose to leave our party and identify ourselves with the party whose antecedents are rum, Romanism, and rebellion. We are loyal to our flag. We are loyal to you.

Blaine, who it is said was busy formulating his reply, did not realize the statement was loaded with political dynamite. According to one story, he supposed Dr. Burchard had referred to *Mormonism* instead of *Romanism*. It is more probable that he did not note the exact substance or words of the statement. At any rate, the Republican candidate let the statement pass unnoticed in his reply. This was seized upon by the Democrats as an indication that Blaine was anti-Catholic and their campaign managers made effective use of it in the remaining days of the campaign. The impression was even created that the obnoxious words had even been uttered by Blaine himself, and it was too late to make a convincing explanation.

On his father's side Blaine was of Scotch-Irish ancestry and he was a Protestant, but his mother was a Roman Catholic and his sister was the Mother Superior of a convent in Indiana. But *Romanism* was not the only politically dangerous word in Dr. Burchard's statement. Liquor was becoming a serious political issue, and, with the Civil War less than twenty years back, *rebellion* was a ticklish word in American politics. Before Dr. Burchard made his statement the betting was two to one in favor of Blaine and it was generally believed that he had the edge on Cleveland. The common impression is that this incident cost Blaine the Presidency. Such may have been the case, for he would have been elected had he carried New York, which he lost by only 1,049 votes. A switch of only 525 votes would have made him President. Cleveland's plurality in the nation was only 23,000.

Dr. Burchard, though embarrassed by the notoriety and criticism that his act brought, never apologized. He only said: "If I have been an instrument in the hands of Providence against my will, I am content to abide by the consequences." The New York *Sun* termed him "a Silurian or early Paleozoic bigot." Blaine himself is reputed to have observed, "I have been beaten by an ass in the shape of a preacher." Dr. Burchard had been a highly respected clergyman and had been pastor of the Houston Street Presbyterian Church for forty years. During a cholera epidemic in Kentucky in 1832 he was the only student not to leave Centre College and became known as "the student nurse of Danville" for his indefatigable care of the sick. The famous saying that made political history may have been merely an alliterative echo of what others had been saying. When it appeared that Tilden was elected and Hayes defeated in 1876 James A. Garfield in a letter attributed the result to "The combined power of rebellion, Catholicism and whiskey."

Who were the Mugwumps?

The original Mugwumps in the purely political sense of the term were the Independent Republicans who in 1884 "bolted" their party with Carl Schurz, George W. Curtis, Charles W. Eliot, Charles Francis Adams and other men of consequence.

They objected to James G. Blaine, the Republican nominee for President, partly because of his foreign policy while Secretary of State in Garfield's cabinet and partly because of his private character. At the same time they approved of Grover Cleveland, the Democratic nominee, partly because of his conduct while Governor of New York and partly because of his professed devotion to civil service reform.

In parts of the United States *mugwump* had been used as early as 1832 to designate a person who makes great pretensions but whose character and ability are not equal to them. The term at first expressed the idea of a pharisee, a conceited and self-important person, one who sets himself up above his fellows. It is said the term was employed in the sense of a political pharisee in the Indianapolis *Sentinel* as early as 1872, when the Liberal Republicans deserted Grant to support Horace Greeley for President.

On February 16, 1877, Isaac H. Bromley published an editorial in the New York *Tribune* entitled "IMPEACH LOGAN." Among other things he wrote: "Listen! John A. Logan is the head Centre, the Hub, the King Pin, the Main Spring, Mogul, and Mugwump of the final plot by which partisanship was installed in the Commission." Logan, known as "Black Jack," was a Union general during the Civil War and later a Senator from Illinois. Bromley referred to Logan's influence with the Electoral Commission appointed by Congress to pass upon the electoral votes of Florida, South Carolina, Louisiana and Oregon in the Hayes-Tilden contest.

MUGWUMP D. O. BRADLEY was a headline in the New York *Sun* March 25, 1884. The earliest known application of *mugwump* to the Republican Independents during the Blaine-Cleveland campaign was published by Charles A. Dana in New York *Sun* on June 15, 1884. Five days later the New York *Evening Post* declared that all the Regular Republican papers were referring to the Independents as "Pharisees, hypocrits, dudes, mugwumps, transcendentalists, or something of that sort." The "bolters" committed the unpardonable political sin of leaving their party "on principle" and were looked upon by the Regular Republicans with the utmost contempt. The Regulars asserted that the Independents regarded themselves superior to their party in virtue and intelligence and so they dubbed them "mugwumps." Thomas B. Reed called them "long-tailed birds of Paradise." The *Nation* defined *mugwump* as "a man who for some reason or other is unable to vote his regular party ticket." In an interview at Cleveland during the campaign Horace Porter supplied the bon mot: "A mugwump is a person educated beyond his intellect."

At the Republican National Convention of 1880 a West Virginian named A. W. Campbell said, "I am a Republican who carries his sovereignty under his own hat." Curtis quoted this saying at the convention in 1884 as justification for not supporting Blaine, and it was used as a slogan by the Mugwumps during the campaign.

The Republican insurgents of 1884 themselves adopted the appellation given to them in derision and the term soon lost most of its sting. In time *mugwump* came to signify any independent voter, one who votes according to his convictions regardless of party. President Harold Willis Dodds of Princeton is credited with saying that a mugwump is "a fellow with his mug on one side of the fence and his wump on the other." Since independence in politics has become quite general the term has lost most of its original significance and is now little used.

There are two theories regarding the origin of *mugwump*. According to one, it is a corruption of a similar word used by the early Virginians for a bullfrog in its intermediate stage between a tadpole and a frog, when it is neither a frog nor a tadpole. According to the other, which is generally accepted and is the more plausible, the term is a corruption of *mukquomp*, an Indian word meaning "great man" or "leader" in the Massachuset dialect of the Algonquian tongue. The components of the word are *moqki*, "great," and *omp* "man." When John Eliot, "the Apostle to the Indians," translated the Bible into the Algonquian language he employed *mukquomp* to render such English terms as *duke, lord, chief, captain, leader* and *great man*. For instance, Genesis 36:40-43 refers to certain descendants of Esau as "dukes." The Hebrew word

translated "duke" here literally signifies "leaders" and Eliot rendered it
mukquomps to make it intelligible to the Northeastern Indians.

Who were the Stalwarts and Half-Breeds?

Stalwarts and *Half-Breeds* were nicknames of Republican factions
during the administrations of Hayes, Garfield and Arthur (1877-1885).
In 1866 James G. Blaine of Maine and Roscoe Conkling of New York
became involved in a bitter feud that started in a debate in the House of
Representatives during which Blaine, while presenting a military affairs
committee report, charged Conkling with revising his remarks in the
Congressional Globe in such a way as to distort the meaning of Blaine's
replies. The New Yorker replied with some "cruel sarcasm" at the
expense of the Man from Maine, who then uttered the following ill-
tempered sentence: "The contempt of that large-minded gentleman is so
wilting, his haughty disdain, his grandiloquent swell, his majestic,
supereminent, overpowering, turkey-gobbler strut, has been so crushing
to myself and all the members of this House, that I know it was an act of
the greatest temerity for me to venture upon a controversy with him."

Cartoonists ever after depicted Conkling as a turkey-gobbler and he
never forgave Blaine this blow to his vanity. The breach between the two
Republican leaders could never be healed and eventually it split the
party into factions known as Stalwarts and Half-Breeds. Conkling's
antagonism as much as any other one thing prevented Blaine from
getting the Republican nomination for President in 1876 and 1880 and
prevented his election when he was finally nominated in 1884.

Stalwart is a sixteenth century Scottish form of *stalworth,* which
apparently is derived from two Anglo-Saxon words meaning "place" and
"worth." The underlying thought of *stalworth* is "foundation-worthy"
or "having a firm footing." Literally it means stable, sturdy, strongly and
stoutly built, robust and serviceable, and figuratively brave, courageous
and valiant. *Stalwart* with about the same meaning was popularized in
English by Sir Walter Scott.

In its political sense *Stalwart* was first used in 1877 by Blaine to
designate those Republicans who wanted to keep Federal troops in the
South and to continue to treat the former Confederate States like
conquered provinces. During the administration of Rutherford B. Hayes
(1877-1881) the Stalwarts opposed civil service reform and the President's
conciliatory policy toward the South. On December 4, 1878, after
sending his civil service reform message to Congress, President Hayes
wrote in his diary: "Such Stalwarts and irreconcilables as the New York

Times are severe in their strictures upon it." The Stalwarts contemptuously referred to the liberal and independent Republicans who supported Hayes as Half-Breeds, a term suggested by the fact that a half-breed or half-blood is the offspring of parents of different races and presumed to be inferior because mongrel.

In the Republican National Convention of 1880 the Stalwarts supported Grant for a third term, while the Half-Breeds supported Blaine. Conkling and more than three hundred Stalwarts stood by Grant through thirty-six ballots. Throughout the thirty-six ballots Grant led all other candidates with from 304 to 313 votes. The "306" Stalwarts became famous in politics for their stubborn stand. On the thirty-seventh ballot, however, James A. Garfield, a Half-Breed, was nominated for President, and Chester A. Arthur a Stalwart, was nominated for Vice President. President Garfield made Blaine, the original Half-Breed, his Secretary of State. After the election the New York *Daily News* referred to, "A Cabinet of Half-Breeds, as the party of Civil Service Reform are called." The fight between the Stalwarts and the Half-Breeds was extremely bitter during Garfield's short administration. It was more acute in New York than in any other State because Conkling and his colleague in the Senate, Thomas C. Platt, continued to lead the Stalwarts in their opposition to civil service reform. Both Senators resigned because President Garfield persisted in making independent appointments. Conkling and Platt expected the New York legislature to re-elect them as a rebuke to the President, but in this they were disappointed and Garfield won the first round in his contest with the Stalwarts.

After he shot President Garfield on July 2, 1881, Charles Guiteau, a disappointed office seeker, was reported to have cried, "I am a Stalwart of the Stalwarts." On July 7, 1881, when he had reason to think the President would recover, former President Hayes, a Half-Breed, wrote to Senator John Sherman: "Stalwartism, which is synonymous with extreme, not to say, bitter and savage partisanship, will lose power and thus the great calamity may turn out well for the President and for the country." But President Garfield died and Arthur became President. On February 24, 1882, Hayes wrote in his diary: "Speaking of Stalwarts. There are, says the *Tribune,* 'Stalwarts and Stalwarts.' I suppose they may be designated as Guiteau Stalwarts and Arthur Stalwarts. Brass-medal Stalwarts and Guiteau Stalwarts are identical." But President Arthur, a Stalwart, supported a civil service reform bill and made appointments so judiciously that the split in the party was superficially mended. On March 14, 1884, nearly a year before Arthur's term expired, Hayes wrote: "Sherman, Edmunds, Lincoln, either perhaps, can unite

Stalwarts, Half-Breeds, and Independent Republicans." Little was heard of Stalwarts and Half-Breeds as two factions in the Republican Party after Grover Cleveland defeated Blaine for the Presidency in the election of 1884. *Half-Breed* as a political term fell into disuse, but *stalwart* in the sense of a loyal and dependable party wheel horse, particularly an uncompromising and staunch conservative, survived as part of the political vocabulary. Even Blaine, the original Half-Breed, lived to hear himself called a Republican stalwart.

Who was the first Catholic nominated for President?

Charles O'Conor (1804-1884), a noted New York lawyer, was the first Catholic nominated for the Presidency. On September 3, 1872, the Straight-Out Democrats, who refused to support Horace Greeley, held a convention at Louisville and nominated O'Conor for President, and John Quincy Adams, grandson of the President of the same name, for Vice President. Both nominees declined, but no substitute nominations were made by the Independent Democrats. The Reform Labor Party, whose first nominees had refused to accept, called another convention late in 1872 and endorsed O'Conor for President. In the election the total popular vote of the Straight-Out Democrats and the Labor Reformers combined was only 29,408 in twenty-three States. O'Conor helped expose the Tweed Ring scandals, was counsel for Jefferson Davis in his treason trial, and represented Samuel J. Tilden before the Electoral Commission.

Governor Alfred E. Smith of New York, who was nominated by the Democratic National Convention at Houston in 1928, was the first member of the Catholic Church nominated for the Presidency by a major political party.

What is the unit rule?

Some delegations in Democratic national conventions operate under what is known as the "unit rule." Under this rule the entire vote of a State delegation is cast for a candidate determined by a majority regardless of the preference of the minority. If a State delegation with twenty-one votes is divided eleven to ten between two candidates, under the unit rule the full twenty-one votes are cast for the candidate favored by the eleven.

The unit rule is an old device in American politics. When the South Carolina legislature appointed John Rutledge, Christopher Gadsden and Thomas Lynch to attend the Stamp Act Congress at New York in 1765 it was agreed that they should act as a unit and be bound by a majority. One of the first acts of the First Continental Congress in 1774 was to decide that the delegation from each Colony should have only one vote. It was noted in the Journal that this was a temporary decision and not to be taken as a precedent. This method was retained and even the Declaration of Independence was adopted under the unit rule. When the Articles of Confederation were under consideration in Congress in 1777 there was much discussion whether the delegates from each State should vote as a unit or individually. In the end they wrote into the Articles of Confederation the provision that, "In determining questions in the United States in Congress assembled, each state shall have one vote," and that method continued in force until the Constitution went into effect in 1789. In the Constitution the unit rule was prescribed only in cases when the House of Representatives chooses a President.

The unit rule was adopted by national conventions soon after they were introduced as the method of nominating candidates and in the days when all delegates were appointed by State conventions or committees. In the Whig convention in 1839 at Harrisburg, when William Henry Harrison and John Tyler were nominated, all State delegations cast their votes under the unit rule. The Democratic Party adopted the same system, as also did the Republican Party, which practically supplanted the Whig Party after 1856.

Whether the unit rule should be permissible was an issue in the National Republican Convention of 1876 at Cincinnati, which nominated Rutherford B. Hayes and William A. Wheeler. James G. Blaine, who started out as the leading aspirant for President, advocated abolition of the unit rule and the right of each delegate to vote as he pleased. When Don Cameron, political boss of Pennsylvania, cast the entire vote of the delegation for Governor John F. Hartranft, four Pennsylvania delegates challenged Cameron's authority to cast their votes and asked to be recorded for Blaine. The presiding officer, a Pennsylvania delegate who had voted for Hartranft, ruled that each delegate could vote as he pleased and his ruling was sustained by the convention by a vote of 395 to 353.

In 1880 the State Republican conventions of New York, Pennsylvania and Illinois instructed their delegates to vote as a unit in the Republican National Convention for the candidate that should be agreed upon by the majority of the delegation. The Grant men in the National Convention at Chicago favored the unit rule, while the supporters of John Sherman and others opposed it. The rules committee, after a bitter struggle, brought in a recommendation to change the rules in conformity to the ruling of 1876 respecting unit voting and the recommendation was adopted 479 to 276. During the proceedings the chairman of the Alabama delegation reported the vote on a resolution as twenty for it, but a Negro delegate asked that his vote be recorded in the negative. No further serious effort was made to use the unit rule. James A. Garfield was nominated for President and the unit rule disappeared from Republican conventions. President Hayes, who favored "district representation" and called the unit rule "the corner-stone of the boss system," wrote in his diary on June 5, 1880, that, "The final overthrow of the unit rule is a solid achievement."

But the Democrats kept the unit rule. When a State delegation was not instructed to vote for a particular candidate, or when its instructions had expired, the delegation was permitted to caucus and to decide by a majority vote how the whole delegation was to vote. This was supposed to be in keeping with the States' rights tenets of the Democratic Party. The interpretation and application of the unit rule are governed by the terms of the resolution of the State party authority that imposes it, and the Democratic National Committee does not recognize or enforce this rule unless it is specifically imposed by the State party. Under the unit rule a majority of the delegates from a State cast the entire vote of the State regardless of the number of delegates present or refusing to vote. Since 1912 Democratic conventions have held that the unit rule is not applicable to delegates chosen by primaries under State laws. Delegates so chosen are regarded as being responsible solely to their constituents and are required to vote individually. The convention may abrogate the unit rule under a suspension of the rules, which requires a two-thirds majority.

Did General Sheridan ever run for President?

Philip Henry Sheridan (1831-1888), the outstanding Federal cavalry general during the Civil War, never held or sought any civil office. He was born in Albany, New York, graduated from West Point in 1853 and spent his life as a professional soldier.

General Sheridan was a Republican and was often mentioned as a presidential candidate but never encouraged suggestions that he seek the nomination. Perhaps the fact that he was a Catholic caused him to avoid becoming involved in party politics. He favored General Grant for a third term in 1880 and went to the Republican National Convention that year as a spectator. During the thirtieth ballot a delegate from

Wyoming Territory voted for him. The General, who was sitting on the platform, immediately stepped forward and said to the convention: "I am very much obliged to the delegate from Wyoming for mentioning my name in this convention, but there is no way in which I could accept a nomination from this convention, if it were possible, unless I should be permitted to turn it over to my best friend."

Senator George F. Hoar, president of the convention, then said: "The Chair presumed the unanimous consent of the convention to permit the illustrious soldier who has spoken to interrupt its order for that purpose. But it will be a privilege accorded to no other person whatever." Later Hoar wrote: "The General's prompt suppression of this attempt to make him a candidate was done in a direct and blunt soldierly fashion."

Why is the Republican Party called the G.O.P.?

G.O.P. as the nickname of the Republican Party is the abbreviation of *Grand Old Party*. Just how or when the phrase originated is not known for certain. Oddly enough, the earliest known use of *grand old party* was in reference to the Democratic Party. In 1879 Senator Benjamin H. Hill, of Georgia said in the U.S. Senate: "We are for national parties now. We come back to the grand old party of the north that never went off after secession, that never went after the Baals of consolidation. If there are any men on this earth for whom I have a higher regard than others, they are the democrats of the north." As late as 1888 Representative Edward Lane, an Illinois Democrat, said in the House of Representatives: "The Republican Party is responsible for all of this misrule, but a brighter day is about to dawn. I am glad that I am a member of that grand old party that assures a better trade to our people ... " In both of these cases, however, the phrase was used without capitals and probably was not intended to be specific.

Meanwhile the phrase had been applied specifically to the Republican Party. On May 4, 1887, the Louisville *Courier-Journal* ran the following headline: THE G.O.P., ON A STILL HUNT FOR A NATIONAL LEADER FOR THE BATTLE, and on May 1, 1888, an unidentified speaker in Congress said: "[A proposed protection tax] is the doings of the G.O.P.—the grand old party—the Republican party." The Democrats at first took up the nickname in derision. *Grand Old Party* as a specific nickname for the Republican Party may have been suggested by "the Grand Old Man," a phrase first applied to William E. Gladstone in April, 1882, by Lord Rosebery. At any rate, G.O.P. came into general use in the United States about two decades after the Civil War, when the Grand Old Man of

England was at the acme of his fame. Nowadays the Republican Party is referred to as the G.O.P. by persons of all political affiliations without any regard to the literal significance of the letters. In 1931 T. B. Dowden wrote that he, as a printer on the Cincinnati *Gazette,* abbreviated *Grand Old Party* as G.O.P. during the Cleveland-Blaine campaign in 1884, and it is very probable that the term was applied to the Republican Party as early as that.

How did *right* and *left* acquire their political senses?

Right and *left* as designations for political factions originated in Europe. In the National Assembly of France (1789) the monarchists and conservatives sat to the presiding officer's right, the republicans and radicals to his left, and the moderates in the center between the other two groups. From this seating arrangement, which is still observed in some Continental legislatures, *right, left* and *center* came to mean "conservative," "liberal" and "moderate" respectively. Often these terms are applied to factions within major political parties rather than to the major parties themselves. *Left* in the sense of a radical faction was introduced into English by Carlyle in *The French Revolution* (1837). *Rightist, leftist, rightism* and *leftism* came into use later. *Left wing* was suggested by military usage, the left wing of an army being that to the left of one facing the enemy. In Shakespeare's tragedy *Coriolanus* he refers to "us of the right hand file." In both the U.S. House of Representatives and Senate the Democrats sit to the presiding officer's right and the Republicans to his left.

How did General Rosecrans pronounce his name?

William Starke Rosecrans (1819-1898), a native of Ohio, pronounced his surname ROE-*suh-kranz*. The name is often pronounced as if it were spelled *Rosencrans,* which more closely approximates the early form of the name, which literally means "rosary." General Rosecrans was descended from Harmon Rosenkrans, who came to America from Norway about 1657. On his mother's side he was descended from Stephen Hopkins, a Rhode Island signer of the Declaration of Independence.

General Rosecrans was identified conspicuously with the battles of Rich Mountain, Corinth, Stone River and Chickamauga. At West Point Rosecrans was converted to the Roman Catholic faith and later converted a brother, Sylvester Horton Rosecrans (1827-1878), who became a

Catholic prelate and built a cathedral and forty churches. After the Battle of Stone River (called Murfreesboro by the Confederates), in which the total casualties were nearly 20,000 General Rosecrans had high mass celebrated in his tent. His official report of the battle to the Department of War ended with the words from the mass, *Non nobis, Domine, non nobis; sed nomine tuo da gloriam,* "Not unto us, O Lord, not unto us; but unto thy name give the glory." In 1863 General Henry W. Halleck, General in Chief of the Army, was accused of putting military commands on the "auction block" by offering a major-general-ship to either Rosecrans or Grant depending on which one of them first won an important victory.

Rosecrans has been called "the greatest strategist of the Civil War," although he met with misfortune at Chickamauga. To his soldiers he was known affectionately as "Old Rosy." After the war he settled in California and served as Minister to Mexico, a Democratic member of Congress, and Register of the Treasury.

Why are the elephant and the donkey the Republican and Democratic emblems?

The elephant and the donkey as the symbols of the Republican and Democratic parties respectively were popularized, if not invented, by Thomas Nast (1840-1902), the famous cartoonist, who was born at Landau in Germany, and who died as U.S. Consul at Guayaquil, Ecuador. Nast was the son of a German army musician and was brought to America by his mother when he was six years old. President Lincoln is reputed to have said toward the close of the war: "Thomas Nast has been our best recruiting sergeant."

Nast first used the donkey to represent the Democrats in a cartoon published in the January 15, 1870, issue of *Harper's Weekly.* This cartoon portrayed Edwin M. Stanton, who had recently died, as a dead lion being kicked over by a donkey labeled COPPERHEAD PAPERS. Under the picture were the words: "A live Jackass kicking a dead lion. And such a lion! and such a Jackass!" Later Nast, a Republican reformer and crusader, used the donkey to typify the Democratic party specifically.

The elephant as a party symbol was born nearly five years later. On November 7, 1874, *Harper's Weekly* printed a Nast cartoon in which the assembled animals and birds of the forest—representing various newspapers, States and issues—are shown as being frightened by a donkey in a lion's skin crying *Caesarism,* which alluded to the Democratic charge that President Grant was scheming for a third term. The elephant, labeled REPUBLICAN VOTE, is frightened also, and is running toward a pitfall loosely covered with deceptive planks labeled INFLATION, REPUDIATION, REFORM, etc. It was the cartoonist's way· of making good-natured fun of his own huge but timorous party. In this particular cartoon the donkey does not represent the Democratic Party, which is symbolized by a fox with a face suggesting that of Samuel J. Tilden. Nast continued to use the two symbols, which seemed to please the public fancy, and they have been used as popular symbols of the two major political parties ever since.

It is said that the idea of the cartoon printed on November 7, 1874, was suggested to Nast by an article in the New York *Herald* describing the escape of some animals from a local menagerie. But it is possible that both the elephant and the donkey had been used as party symbols in a general way before Nast's time. There is evidence that an elephant was used on one of the Lincoln banners carried at the Republican National Convention at Chicago in 1860. It is claimed that the figure of an elephant was used on a Salmon P. Chase badge about the same time. Lithographed and etched cartoons during the early 1830's portrayed President Jackson riding a "Jack (son) -ass." Others pictured Jackson's head on the body of an ass. The *Field Piece,* a Whig campaign paper published at Chicago, printed a woodcut on July 19, 1848, portraying the figure of a donkey on what was labeled the "Democratic platform." During the Civil War the Peace Democrats were represented as a donkey decorated with a Confederate flag, and in 1864, General George B. McClellan, the Democratic nominee for President, was portrayed mounted backward on a donkey urged on by August Belmont and other Democratic leaders. Perhaps Nast's use of the elephant and donkey were echoes of earlier usage.

The elephant and the donkey are used as cartoon and comic rather than as official party symbols. Various devices were originally used on party ballots to help illiterate voters to identify the party candidates. Many Democratic organizations adopted the rooster or gamecock as the party emblem after 1840, and many Republican organizations adopted the eagle as the party emblem soon after the party was organized in the the early 1850's. With these emblems printed at the top of party tickets it was easy for the local politicians to tell the Democrats to vote for the "big chick" and the Republicans to vote for "the bird on the dollar."

"The Democratic party is like a mule—without pride of ancestry or hope of posterity," is a saying of unknown authorship. It is sometimes attributed to Ignatius Donnelly (1831-1901), who was Lieutenant Governor and Congressman from Minnesota and who used the bon mot in a speech in the Minnesota legislature. The saying alludes to the fact that the mule is a sterile hybrid produced by breeding a female horse to a male ass. But Democrats insist that their popular party symbol is the donkey or ass, not the mule.

On November 7, 1929, Senator George H. Moses of New Hampshire made an address in Washington before the New England Manufacturers' Association in which he said: "Mournfully I prophesy that the program of these *sons of the wild jackass* who now control the Senate will probably go forward to complete consummation." He referred to a group of independent Republican senators who had joined the Democrats in blocking legislation providing higher tariff protection desired by the New England Republicans. The phrase used by Moses was resented by several of the insurgents and the subject was widely discussed in the newspapers. Various interpretations were placed on what the New Hampshire Senator had said. The utterance of the sharp-tongued Moses was the subject of a stormy debate in the Senate the following day. A feeble and futile effort was made to unseat him as chairman of the Republican Senatorial Campaign Committee and as president pro tempore. It is often supposed that *sons of the wild jackass* was borrowed from the Bible, but no such phrase occurs in the Scriptures, although it was undoubtedly suggested by a vague recollection and fusion of several Biblical passages. Senator Moses afterward explained that the phrase was inspired by Jeremiah 14:6, which says: "And the wild asses did stand in the high places, they snuffed up the wind like dragons; their eyes did fail, because there was no grass." *Jackass* does not occur in the King James Version and probably was not coined for more than a century after that version was made. Job 11:12 says: "For vain man would be wise, though man be born like a wild ass's colt."

Actually Senator Moses's phrase was a variation of an older political phrase. John A. Pickler served as a Republican member of Congress from South Dakota from 1889 to 1897. Speaker Thomas B. Reed observed: "I have read and heard much of the wild ass's colt of the desert, but I never had any clear conception of what manner of animal it really was till I saw Pickler in action." But as early as February 20, 1877, John Hay had written to William D. Howells: "We are in a bad way. That herd of wild asses' colts in Washington, braying and kicking up their heels, is an unsatisfactory result of a hundred years of Democracy." A group of anti-Cleveland Democrats in the House were called "The Wild Horses" because they kicked over the traces and would not stay hitched to the party program.

Who was the Old Roman?

Allen Granbery Thurman (1813-1895), who served as Representative and Senator in Congress and as chief justice of the State supreme court of Ohio, was known in his later years as "The Old Roman" because he was picturesque in appearance, sturdy in character, learned in the law and shrewd in politics. He was a native of Virginia, a nephew of William ("Ohio Gong") Allen, and a Democrat of the Jeffersonian school. The Old Roman carried a large red bandanna with which he frequently mopped his expansive brow. In 1888 he ran for Vice President on the unsuccessful Cleveland ticket. Senator Harrison H. Riddleberger of Virginia, when asked what he thought of the Democratic candidate for Vice President, replied: "I think you've simply nominated a pocket-handkerchief."

What President hanged two men?

Grover Cleveland hanged two men. In the election of November, 1870, Cleveland was elected sheriff of Erie County, New York, for a two-year term beginning the next year. During his term of office two murderers were sentenced to death within his jurisdiction. On February 14, 1872, Jack Gaffney, a notorious gambler, was hanged for shooting and killing Patrick Fahey in a card game in a Buffalo dive. Five months later, on September 6 of the same year, Patrick Morrissey was hanged for murdering his mother. In both instances Sheriff Cleveland, unwilling to shirk the unpleasant duty by delegating it to a subordinate, sprang the trap with his own hands. During the Presidential campaign of 1884 Cleveland was called "The Hangman" by his political enemies.

Why are fractional votes cast in political conventions?

There are several reasons for fractional votes in national political conventions. Political parties allot their adherents in each State a number of votes based on the State's representation in Congress. Originally the basic membership of a national convention consisted of two accredited delegates from each Congressional district and four accredited delegates at large from each State. In other words, each State had twice as many votes in a national convention as it had electoral votes. This is still the basis for membership in national conventions, but in recent years the major parties have adjusted the number of convention votes of States to their past voting records.

But the parties did not generally fix the number of delegates that a State might send to a national convention to cast its votes; they fixed only the number of votes. Local political leaders like to attend conventions and some States permitted an unlimited number of them to attend the national convention as delegates, in which case the convention vote was divided among the delegates on a fractional basis. Delegates from some States had as small as one-thirty-second of a vote each. It was a common practice to give district delegates a full vote but to designate two delegates at large for each vote and to give each half a vote. The delegates are chosen by State primaries, conventions or committees and the allotment of votes to delegates depended largely on the party organization in each State. There is a growing tendency to restrict the number of delegates and to eliminate fractional votes, although many delegates are still assigned half votes. Occasionally delegates from rival factions of the same party in a State are admitted into a national convention, the total vote allotted to the State is divided equally between the two delegations and each delegate is given half a vote. In the Democratic National Convention at Baltimore in 1912 Champ Clark received 440½ votes on the first ballot and Woodrow Wilson 224. The Democratic Party of Connecticut sent 20 delegates to the New York convention in 1924, but they could cast only 14 votes. Accordingly each delegate had only 0.7 of a vote and the result was that on many ballots William G. McAdoo received 4.9 votes and Alfred E. Smith received 9.1 votes from the Connecticut delegation. In the Missouri State Democratic Convention of 1872 Francis Marion Cockrell lost the nomination for Governor by one-sixth of a vote. When a delegation operates under the unit rule the fractional votes alter the result only in votes taken by the delegation to determine which candidate shall receive the total vote of the State.

Since 1896 the two major parties have allotted votes to delegates from the Federal territories, districts and insular possessions. Both parties admit delegations from Alaska, Hawaii, the District of Columbia and Puerto Rico. The Democratic Party also admits delegates from the Virgin Islands and the Canal Zone. Even the Philippines were represented in the national conventions until they became independent. These "courtesy delegates" from the Federal territories, districts and insular possessions are full-fledged members of the convention and they vote for candidates, although the territories they represent have no electoral votes and cannot take part in Presidential elections. The number of these delegates varies and is fixed by the national committees of each party under authority given to them by the conventions. The total number of votes in the national conventions varies considerably. In 1948 the total number of votes in the Republican National Convention was 1,094 and in the Democratic National Convention 1,234.

The State political organizations also send to the national conventions substitute delegates called "alternates." The number of alternates is the same as the number of delegates. They are seated on the convention floor behind the regular delegates. In the absence of a delegate his alternate has all the privileges of voting and debating that his principal has. The alternates also join in the demonstrations and help increase the din and confusion in the convention hall.

How does a majority differ from a plurality?

Plurality and *majority* are often confused. According to American usage, if a candidate for office in a race in which more than two are running receives more votes than any other candidate, he receives a "plurality"; if he receives more votes than all the other contestants combined—more than half of all the votes cast—he receives a "majority."

But according to British usage, in an election where more than two candidates are running the leading candidate is said to receive so many votes more than the second contestant. What is called a plurality in the United States is called an "absolute" or "clear" majority in Britain.

Thus in the language of American politics *majority* signifies a number that is more than half of the whole, while *plurality* signifies excess over some other number, generally the next largest. When there are only two candidates in the contest the plurality and the majority are the same. In Congress and State legislatures a "working majority" is one with enough dependables to pass party bills.

Who was the Plumed Knight?

"The Plumed Knight" was one of the popular nicknames of James Gillespie Blaine (1830-1893) after the Republican National Convention at Cincinnati in 1876. His name was presented by Robert G. Ingersoll in one of the most brilliant nomination speeches in the history of political conventions. Among other things the orator said: "Like an armed warrior, like a plumed knight, James G. Blaine marched down the halls of the American Congress and threw his shining lance full and fair against the brazen forehead of every traitor to his country and every maligner of his fair reputation."

It is hard now to appreciate the profound impression made by Blaine during the days he was one of the foremost political leaders in America. He was born and educated in Pennsylvania, and taught school and studied law there. In 1854, at the age of twenty-four, he moved to Maine, where he rapidly came to the fore as an editor, member of the legislature and pioneer Republican leader. At Washington College he was known as "Nosey Blaine" because of his large nose. He became a member of Congress in 1863 and served in the House until he resigned in 1876 to become a Senator. From 1869 to 1875 he was Speaker of the House. In Congress he became successively "Magnetic Blaine," "Blaine of Maine" and "The Man from Maine."

Blaine retired from the Speakership in 1875 with a spotless reputation and great prestige, and a majority of Republicans regarded him as the logical candidate for President in 1876. Then a scandal was attached to his name that closed the White House doors in his face and embarrassed him politically for the rest of his life. Rumors were circulated that he had corruptly acted as a private and secret broker of the bonds of a railroad while he was Speaker. On April 24, 1876, the former Speaker said in the House: "For some months past a charge against me has been circulating in private and was recently made public—designing to show that I had in some indirect manner received the large sum of $64,000 from the Union Pacific railroad company in 1871—for what services and for what purpose has never been stated." He emphatically denied the charge. But the charge was published again in a newspaper, and on May 2 the Democratic House ordered an investigation by its Judiciary Committee, which appointed a subcommittee of two Democrats and one Republican to hear testimony.

An important witness was James Mulligan, former bookkeeper to a railway official named Warren G. Fisher, Jr. Mulligan casually told the subcommittee that he had certain letters written by Blaine to Fisher. Blaine, who was present and who thought these letters had been returned to him, was panic-stricken by the information, got the Republican member to move an immediate adjournment. In a conference with Mulligan in a hotel room, Blaine obtained possession of the "Mulligan Letters" under false pretenses and refused to return them to Mulligan or to turn them over to the subcommittee. On June 5, nine days before the meeting of the Republican National Convention at Cincinnati, the leading aspirant for the Presidential nomination rose in the House to a question of personal privilege and read parts of the Mulligan Letters, commenting upon them and making his own defense as he went along, and winding up dramatically by charging Chairman Proctor Knott of the Judiciary Committee with holding back an important telegram from London which confirmed testimony favorable to Blaine but which he himself had inspired. This dramatic speech convinced many, but not all, of his innocence, and temporarily his enemies were routed. It was to this incident that Ingersoll referred in his convention speech.

On Sunday, June 11, Blaine fainted from a sunstroke on the steps of his church in Washington. His ensuing illness caused the investigation to peter out. On June 12, Governor Rutherford B. Hayes, who expected Blaine to be nominated at the forthcoming convention, wrote him from Columbus: "I have just read with the deepest sorrow of your illness. My eyes are almost blinded with tears as I write. All good men among your countrymen will pray, as I do, for your immediate and complete recovery. This affects me as did the death of Lincoln. God bless you and restore you." As late as June 14, the day the convention opened, Hayes wrote: "The indications, as I now read them, point to the nomination of Blaine on the first or some early ballot." But a few days later it was Hayes himself, not the Plumed Knight, who was nominated for President.

The Democratic platform of 1876 charged Blaine with "marketing his rulings as presiding officer." The extent to which Blaine yielded to improper influence or perjured himself is still a moot question among historians. On April 10, 1869, an amendment was offered in the House to emasculate a bill renewing a land grant to Arkansas for the Little Rock and Ft. Smith Railroad. Speaker Blaine, when asked by the friends of the railroad to save the bill, said he would rule the amendment out of order as not being germane, and he did so. So far as known Blaine was not then interested financially in this railroad and his ruling was in accordance with parliamentary precedents. On June 29 of the same year, in reply to some sort of proposal, he wrote to Fisher: "I do not feel that I shall prove a deadhead in the enterprise if I once embark in it. I see various channels in which I know I can be useful." On October 4 of the same year he asked Fisher to tell one of the promoters of the Little Rock and Ft. Smith Railroad that he had unconsciously done the company "a great favor" in making his ruling as Speaker on April 10. It appears that Blaine received a considerable sum in commissions on bonds of the railroad, later taken over by the Union Pacific, and that many of these bonds were sold to various persons in Maine upon Blaine's recommendation that they were a good investment. Blaine appears also to have received railroad bonds for himself at much less than the current price. When the bonds became virtually worthless Blaine lost heavily and reimbursed his friends who held the bonds. Senator George F. Hoar, in *Autobiography of Seventy years* (1903) wrote:

All Blaine did was to say when he applied for the purchase of the stock to the men who were then trying to dispose of it that "he should not be a dead-head." He meant by that only that he was able to be of advantage to any undertaking in which he should be interested, an assurance which his known ability and energy and large acquaintance with businessmen thoroughly warranted him in making.

On June 21, 1884, former President Hayes wrote in his diary:

Birch read Blaine's speech in June 1876 on the Mulligan letters. Blaine showed great apprehension of disgrace and ruin when he begged the letters of Mulligan. He spoke of suicide, the ruin of his family, etc. etc. Nothing in the letters seems to warrant this. There was evidently more in his transactions with Fisher, or his other railroad transactions, than has been made public. Otherwise his extreme agitation is unaccountable.

Soon after the convention of 1876 Blaine resigned from the House to accept appointment to the Senate. In 1880 he was again a leading aspirant for the Republican nomination, but lost to James A. Garfield. He became Secretary of State in Garfield's Cabinet but resigned a few months after the President's death. In 1884 the Republican convention nominated him for President on the first ballot. His followers still regarded him as the Plumed Knight. In a nomination speech in the convention a blind orator from Ohio named West declared that "wherever blows fell the thickest and fastest, there in the forefront of the battle was seen to wave the white plume of James G. Blaine, our Henry of Navarre." But the old scandals were immediately revived by the Democrats and many Republicans refused to support him. His political enemies followed Beaumarchais's precept: "Calumniate, Calumniate! Something will always stick."

As early as April 17, 1884, two months before the convention, *Puck,* the illustrated magazine, printed a cartoon by English-born Berhard Gillam portraying Blaine as the Greek hetaera Phryne before the Athenian judges with his robe thrown back and exposing his body tattooed with the names of the scandals with which he was associated. Gillam's cartoon was labeled THE TATTOOED MAN, which was suggested by George Constantine, a curiously and completely tattooed man exhibited by P. T. Barnum during the 1870's. Friends had difficulty in dissuading Blaine from prosecuting German-born Joseph Keppler, *Puck* publisher, on obscenity charges. This cartoon and others of the same type were widely circulated, and gave Blaine a new nickname, "The Tattooed Man."

One of Blaine's letters to Fisher in 1869 closed with "Kind regards to Mrs. Fisher," and had written on the back "Burn this letter." "Kind Regards to Mrs. Fisher" and "Burn This Letter" became Democratic campaign slogans in 1884, and Democrats chanted:

> Blaine, Blaine, James G. Blaine,
> The Continental liar from the State of Maine.
> Burn this letter!

A story was circulated that when Roscoe Conkling, Blaine's bitter political enemy, was asked to take the stump for the Plumed Knight, he replied: "No, thank you, I don't engage in criminal practice."

But the Republicans also had a card up their sleeve. The Democratic nominee was Governor Grover Cleveland of New York, a forty-seven-year-old bachelor. In its issue of July 21, 1884, the Buffalo *Evening Telegraph,* a newspaper published in Cleveland's home town, printed a story under the caption, A TERRIBLE TALE. It said that in the 1870's Cleveland had illicit relations with a widow named Maria Halpin, who had borne a son whom she named Oscar Folsom Cleveland, after the Democratic Presidential candidate and his law partner. Mrs. Halpin, according to the story, said she was willing to swear that Cleveland had promised to marry her and that he was the father of her son. The story further said that Cleveland had acknowledged paternity of the child and had contributed financially to the support of both mother and child; that the child had been taken forcibly from her and put in an orphanage, and that Mrs. Halpin was then in failing health.

When the frantic Democratic nominee was asked by his campaign managers what to say in reply to the newspaper story, he is reputed to have replied: "Whatever you say, tell the truth."

The truth, according to Cleveland, was that he had had illicit relations with Mrs. Halpin, that she did have a child who she claimed was his and had named it after him and his law partner, that he had contributed to the support of the mother and child, that nobody really knew who was the father of the child because other men were involved, that he doubted he was the father of the child, that he had not promised to marry the mother, that after she became addicted to drink he put the child in a reputable orphanage, that he had continued to help Mrs. Halpin financially from time to time, and that her present whereabouts was unknown to him.

The Republicans modified a popular song and sang:

Ha! Ha! Where's my pa?
Gone to the White House,
Ha! Ha! Ha!

The Democrats tried to laugh off the scandal by singing the jingle:

Hurrah for Maria,
Hurrah for the kid,
I voted for Grover,
And am damned glad I did.

Blaine was charged with being officially corrupt while his Democratic opponent was charged with being privately immoral. George William Curtis, Moorfield Storey, Carl Schurz, Charles B. Codman, Theodore Lyman and other Cleveland advocates met at a club in New York to discuss the prospects of success. The Mugwumps in particular were embarrassed and shocked by the publication of the Cleveland scandal, because they had made honesty and cleanness the chief issue of their campaign. According to Storey, an unnamed man from Chicago said to the group:

Do you want to know how this matter strikes me? Well, from what I hear I gather that Mr. Cleveland has shown high character and great capacity in public office but that in private life his conduct has been open to question, while on the other hand, Mr. Blaine in public life has been weak and dishonest while he seems to have been an admirable husband and father. The conclusion that I draw from these facts is that we should elect Mr. Cleveland to the public office which he is so admirably qualified to fill and remand Mr. Blaine to private life which he is so eminently fitted to adorn.

The Cleveland scandal helped Blaine by counteracting the Democratic and Mugwump attacks upon his integrity, but Dr. Burchard's unfortunate "Rum, Romanism and Rebellion" statement a few days before the election hurt Blaine considerably and he was defeated by a narrow margin.

In 1884 Blaine had published the first volume of *Twenty Years of Congress,* and after the election of 1884 he completed the second volume of that work. But he still had his eye on the Presidency and received substantial support for the Republican nomination in 1888. He became Secretary of State again in President Harrison's Cabinet and distinguished himself in that office. By 1892 he was regarded as an elder statesman and received some votes for President in the Republican convention. Thus he received votes for President in five successive Republican conventions—1876, 1880, 1884, 1888 and 1892. In 1890 his daughter Margaret was married to Walter Damrosch, the internationally known musical conductor.

Why is political corruption called graft?

Graft in the sense of political corruption originated as American slang during the latter part of the nineteenth century and its true origin may be lost beyond recovery. The Oxford dictionary indicates that this use of the term occurred as early as 1889. *Graft* in the sense of a cut shoot used in grafting trees is derived ultimately from Greek *graphion,* "stylus" or "writing pen." The grafting slip was so called because it was fancied to resemble a stylus. It is suggested that corruption may have been called graft because illegitimate profit was regarded as a graft or abnormal growth on legitimate business. Another theory is that the term was suggested by *graft* in the English sense of "work," "job" or "trade." In that connection *graft* comes from a root meaning "to dig," whence also comes "grave."

It is more probable that *graft* in the sense of ill-gotten gains originated in the underworld. In *Tramping with Tramps* (1899) Josiah Flynt (Willard) used it as a slang word among criminals. Two years later Flynt published a book entitled *The World of Graft. Graft* with all its present-day significance was popularized in connection with the campaign conducted by Joseph Wingate Folk (1869-1923) against a corrupt administration in St. Louis. Folk was elected "circuit attorney" in 1900 and during the next two years he started investigations that resulted in the indictment of twenty-four men for bribery and thirteen for perjury. Among those indicted were twenty-one city assemblymen, including the city boss. Twelve of them wound up in the penitentiary. In 1904 Folk was elected Governor of Missouri largely on the strength of his vigorous exposure and punishment of grafters among St. Louis officials and businessmen. The earliest use of *graft* recorded by *The Dictionary of American English* is dated 1903.

How did *tariff* originate?

Popular etymology regards *tariff* as a survival of the pirate's craft and derives it from *Tarifa,* the name of a Spanish seaport about twenty miles from the Pillars of Hercules, which, in the olden days, was the stronghold of the Moorish pirates who hovered in the vicinity of the Strait of Gibraltar waiting to plunder merchant vessels entering the Mediterranean Sea. Tarifa received its name from Tarif, whom Tariq sent to

Spain early in the eighth century as commander of the advance guard of the Moorish invaders. In time, according to the myth, the pirates became more businesslike and ceased to plunder vessels, but instead exacted a certain percentage of the cargo for the privilege of passing without further harm. Finally, the story says, the tribute was levied in accordance with a systematic scale. Thus when European nations began to impose duties on exports and imports they called the system *tariff* after the Tarifa pirates.

This picturesque derivation is plausible and it has been used frequently by popular orators and writers to indicate the questionable origin of all tariff systems. But, regardless of the origin of tariff systems, this derivation of the term is discredited by philologists. Reputable etymologists derive *tariff* from Arabic *tarif,* "knowledge," "information" or "an inventory." Originally a tariff was a schedule of duties.

A duty levied on imported goods to protect domestic industries from foreign competition is a protective tariff, while one levied on such goods only to raise revenue to maintain the government is a nonprotective tariff. The first is to help home industries, the second is merely to raise money to pay government expenses. Whether the new Federal Government should levy protective tariffs or merely nonprotective tariffs became a spirited issue soon after the Federal Constitution went into effect in 1789. On February 14, 1789, Samuel Breck of Boston wrote to Tobias Lear, secretary to George Washington, a letter about native broadcloth in which he said: "I do hope it will be worn by one whose example will be worth more than any other as encouragement that can be given to our *infant* Manufactures." When Washington was inaugurated President on April 30 of that year he wore a suit of homespun broadcloth made in New England. The second bill passed by Congress was approved by President Washington on July 4, 1789, and was "an act for laying a duty on goods, wares and merchandise imported into the United States."

The first protective tariff bill, sponsored by Henry Clay, was passed by Congress and approved by President John Quincy Adams in 1828. It was supported largely by the Northeastern States and opposed by the Southern States. Of this measure Philip Hone wrote in his diary on May 28, 1828: "It increases the duties on all those descriptions of manufactured goods imported from foreign countries which are supposed to come into competition with our manufactures. The success of this measure will be considered a triumph of the manufacturing over the mercantile interests." John Randolph of Roanoke said: "It is a pirate under a black Flag—its only manufacture being the manufacture of a

President." This measure came to be known as "The Tariff of Abominations" and opposition to it resulted in the Nullification crisis in Jackson's time, when it was modified.

The protective tariff continued to be a major political issue for generations. The Whigs and the Republicans favored protection, while the Democrats favored a tariff for revenue only and leaned toward free trade. In 1880, when Garfield and Arthur were the Republican candidates, the Democrats nominated General Winfield Scott Hancock for President and Thomas Dunn English for Vice President. Hancock has been the only West Pointer besides Grant nominated for President by a major party. He was a native of Pennsylvania and was named for General Winfield Scott, had a notable military record, and was the general who chose the battleground at Gettysburg. After the Battle of Williamsburg on May 5, 1862, General McClellan reported that "Hancock was superb," and after that he was known as "The Superb." General Grant rated him as "the most conspicuous figure of all the officers who did not exercise separate command."

General Hancock had spent his life as a soldier and knew little about politics. In an interview published in the Paterson (New Jersey) *Daily Guardian* on October 8, 1880, Hancock was quoted as saying "The tariff question is a local question." Since the Democratic candidate was running on a tariff-for-revenue-only platform, this statement was ridiculed by the Republicans as evidence that Hancock didn't understand the chief issue in the campaign. In view of the logrolling methods used in Congress to pass protective tariffs, some regarded Hancock's statement as a profound truth. In an editorial in the New York *Sun* on October 19, 1880, William O. Bartlett said "Winfield Scott Hancock is a good man weighing two-hundred and fifty pounds," but also described him as "pure, patriotic and good, a fit man to be President." Garfield beat Hancock 214 to 155 in electoral votes but received only 12,467 more popular votes than he.

While testifying before an industrial commission in 1899 Henry O. Havemeyer, a railroad official, observed: "The mother of all trusts is the customs tariff law." The Hawley-Smoot act, approved by President Hoover in 1930, was the last partisan protective tariff law passed by Congress. The Democratic platform of 1932, on which Franklin D. Roosevelt was elected President, declared: "We advocate a competitive tariff for revenue, with a fact-finding tariff commission free from executive interference, reciprocal tariff agreements with other nations. . . . " A "most-favored nation" provision was added to this law by amendment. It provided that all nations were entitled to tariff reductions granted to any one nation, unless specifically excluded from the privilege by Presidential proclamation for discrimination against American commerce. The Reciprocal Trade·Agreements Act of June 12, 1934, authorized the President to make trade treaties with other nations without requiring confirmation by the Senate. This act permitted tariff reductions up to fifty per cent and contained a most-favored-nation clause. In his *Memoirs* (1948) former Secretary of State Cordell Hull, chief sponsor of the trade agreements policy, wrote of the unconditional most-favored-nation clause: "The phrase is not the happiest. It gives the impression of getting or giving favor or special treatment. It merely means: 'I won't treat you any worse than the person I treat the best of all, provided you don't treat me any worse than the person you treat the best of all.' "

Who was Frederick Douglass?

Frederick Douglass (1817-1895) was a noted American Negro orator and journalist. His original name was Frederick Augustus Washington Bailey. He was born in slavery at Tuckahoe near Easton, Maryland, and was the son of an unknown white father and Harriet Bailey, a slave of mixed Negro and Indian blood. While a slave in the home of Hugh Auld in Baltimore he was taught to read by the wife of his master. With money secretly earned blacking shoes he bought his first book, *The Columbian Orator,* which was the foundation of his career as one of the most eloquent and effective orators ever produced by the Negro race in America.

At an early age he dropped *Augustus Washington* and called himself simply Frederick Bailey. In 1838, while apprenticed as a ship calker in Baltimore, he escaped from slavery disguised as a sailor and went to New York City. For greater safety he soon removed to New Bedford, Massachusetts, using the name Johnson to conceal himself from slavehunters. At New Bedford he was befriended by a white man named Nathan Johnson, who had just been reading Sir Walter Scott's *The Lady of the Lake* and who so admired the chief character in the narrative poem that he induced the runaway slave to abandon the name Johnson and to assume the name Douglas in order the better to conceal his identity and to avoid capture. Thus it came about that Frederick Augustus Washington Bailey, a Maryland slave boy, took his place in history as Frederick Douglass. In Scott's poem *Douglas* is spelled with one *s*, but Frederick Douglass always spelled his name with the double *s*. Two variant spellings of this Scotch name had prevailed for centuries. The ancestors of Stephen A. Douglas wrote the name *Douglass*.

An extemporaneous speech at a meeting of the Massachusetts Anti-Slavery Society attracted such favorable attention that Douglass was employed as a lecturer. Up to that time he had worked as a common day laborer. In 1845, when he was twenty-eight, he published *Narrative of the Life of Frederick Douglass*. Fearing that the facts about himself in the book would lead to his arrest as a fugitive slave, he spent several years in England and Ireland. Douglass was entertained at the White House by three Presidents—in 1864 by Lincoln, in 1878 by Hayes, and in 1885 by Cleveland. A convention that met in 1872 at Vineland, New Jersey, and styled itself the Equal Rights Party, nominated Mrs. Victoria Claflin Woodhull for President and Frederick Douglass for Vice President. During the Civil War Douglass actively aided in recruiting colored troops in the North. Douglass, who was married twice, said, "My first wife was the color of my mother; my second, the color of my father." From 1889 to 1891, during Benjamin Harrison's administration, Douglass was American Minister to Haiti, and it is often said that he was the first American Negro to be appointed to a Federal office and to occupy a diplomatic post; but that distinction belongs to Ebenezer Don Carlos Bassett, who was appointed U.S. Minister Resident and Consul General to Haiti by President Grant in 1869 and who served in that capacity until 1877. Bassett was born in Litchfield, Connecticut, in 1833 and attended Birmingham Academy, the State Normal School and Yale University. He settled in Philadelphia, where he became principal of a colored high school and professor of classics and mathematics. Like Douglass, Bassett had a strain of Indian blood. James Milton Turner, a Missouri schoolteacher, who was educated at Oberlin College, served as U.S. Minister Resident and Consul General to Liberia from 1871 to 1878 and was the second American Negro to hold a high Federal office.

When were women first allowed to vote?

Early settlers in America brought with them from Europe the belief that this is a "man's world" and that "woman's place is in the home." Women might rule nations as queens but were not supposed to hold office, vote or take part directly in public affairs.

Margaret Brent (1600-1671?), who migrated with her brothers and sisters from England to Maryland in 1638, was the first American woman landowner, taxpayer, lawyer, feminist and suffragist. "Mistress" Brent, who never married, became sole executrix of the will of Governor Leonard Calvert, who married her sister Ann, and attorney for Lord

Baltimore. In 1648 this Portia of Maryland, who was a Catholic and who lived at "Sisters Freehold" in St. Mary's County, demanded but was refused two votes in the upper house of the Maryland assembly, one as "Lady of the Manor" and one as attorney for Lord Baltimore.

Anna Maulin Zenger, wife of Peter Zenger, got out the New York *Journal* in 1734-1735 while her husband was in jail for libel and was the first woman editor and publisher in America. Ann Franklin, sister-in-law of Benjamin Franklin, became editor of the Newport (Rhode Island) *Mercury* in 1762 after her husband's death. Mrs. John Franklin, another sister-in-law of Benjamin Franklin, became postmaster at Boston in 1854 after her husband died. The first woman to be postmaster in the United States in her own right was Miss Mary Katharine Goddard, who was postmaster of Baltimore from 1775 to 1789 and who was the first woman to work for the United States Government.

After the Declaration of Independence was adopted in 1776, Abigail Adams, wife of John Adams, suggested in a letter to her husband that women should be given equality with men in the new republic. The first State constitution of New Jersey (1776) conferred suffrage on all inhabitants of full age who owned property worth fifty pounds. This provision was interpreted as applying to both sexes and a law passed under it in 1793 allowed women with the required property qualifications to vote, but the law was repealed in 1807, when suffrage was restricted to free white males. New York also for a time allowed women "to vote their estates."

In 1787 Mrs. Mercy Otis Warren, sister of James Otis, urged that equal rights for women be recognized in the new Federal Constitution. Although women were not qualified to vote in any of the original thirteen States in 1787, it is presumed that they were eligible to the Presidency under the Federal Constitution as originally adopted. Apparently, however, the founding fathers did not take this possibility very seriously. In the Constitution the masculine pronouns—*he, him, his*—are invariably used in reference to the chief executive. So far no serious effort has been made to have the Constitution amended in this respect in anticipation of a woman President. The masculine pronouns are presumed to apply to both sexes, since the English language contains no satisfactory pronouns for both. It is not probable that any delegate in the Constitutional Convention suggested "he or she," "him or her" and "his or her" in these connections.

President Jefferson wrote to Secretary of the Treasury Albert Gallatin in January, 1807: "The appointment of a woman to office is an innovation for which the public is not prepared, nor am I." On July 18,

1836, Abraham Lincoln, in announcing for the Illinois legislature, said: "I go for all sharing the privileges of government who assist in bearing the burdens. Consequently I go for admitting all whites to the right of suffrage who pay taxes or bear arms, by no means excluding females." In the same year Representative John Quincy Adams presented an antislavery petition signed by fifty-eight Massachusetts women and explained that he "had not yet brought myself to doubt whether females were citizens." Some members of Congress questioned the propriety of receiving petitions from women, and even Adams felt that women, though interested in moral issues, had no disposition to take part in public affairs as such.

Equal rights for women were advocated by Frances Wright, English-born reformer, who lectured in America during the 1820's, 1830's and 1840's. Philip Hone referred to her in his diary as "This Female Tom Paine" and shuddered at the prospect of "petticoat government," admitted that "wives and daughters are famous auxiliaries in a righteous cause." *Petticoat* literally means "little coat" and was first applied to a small coat worn by men. Later the term was applied to a woman's underskirt and became symbolical of women. In 1702 John Dunton wrote: "By *Petti-Coat Government,* I mean when Women Ascend the Throne, and Rule according to Law, as is the Case of the Present Queen Anne. Again, by *Petti-Coat Government,* I mean the discreet and housewifely Ruling of a Home and Family."

At first the antislavery, temperance and equal-rights movements went hand in hand. Woman's suffrage was only incidental to equal rights for women. The first equal rights convention met on July 19, 1848, at Seneca Falls, New York, under the auspices of Lucretia Mott, Mrs. Elizabeth Cady Stanton and other feminist leaders. It issued a Declaration of Sentiments, which was modeled on the Declaration of Independence and which severely indicted man for his injustice to woman through the ages. In 1849 Elizabeth Blackwell graduated from the Geneva Medical School in Western New York and became the first American woman physician with a regular medical degree and license. A national equal rights convention was held at Worcester, Massachusetts, in 1850. Antoinette Louisa (Brown) Blackwell, sister-in-law of Dr. Elizabeth Blackwell, completed the theology course at Oberlin College in 1850 but was refused a license to preach because of her sex. After preaching independently for two years she became the regular pastor of the Congregational Church at South Butler, New York. About this time a few women got clerical jobs with the Federal Government. In 1854 Clara

Barton, founder of the American Red Cross, became a copyist in the U.S. Patent Office at a salary of $900 a year.

In 1855 Lucy Stone (1818-1893), an early advocate of equal rights, was married to Henry Brown Blackwell, a brother of Dr. Elizabeth Blackwell and a brother-in-law of Antoinette Louisa Blackwell. Blackwell pledged his life to the cause of woman's rights, and he and Lucy issued a widely publicized protest against the legal discriminations against women. Lucy Stone kept her maiden name, but substituted *Mrs.* for *Miss,* and called herself Mrs. Lucy Stone. Her name became a byword and militant feminists, especially those who retain their maiden names after marriage, are known as "Lucy Stoners."

Kansas in 1861 granted women the right to vote in school elections, and gradually other States did the same. In the spring of 1862 Francis E. Spinner, Treasurer of the United States, persuaded Secretary of the Treasury Salmon P. Chase to let him hire a woman to cut and trim paper currency. Spinner hired Jeannie Douglas and afterward wrote that "her first day's work settled the matter in her and woman's favor." Before the end of that year the Federal Government employed five other women. While the Fourteenth Amendment to the Constitution was being considered in 1866 Lucy Stone and her husband tried to have "male" struck from Section 2. Shortly afterward the American Equal Rights Association and the National Equal Rights Association were formed. The first emphasized equal rights in the States and the second worked for a Constitutional Amendment. Later *Woman's Suffrage* was substituted for *Equal Rights* in the names of both organizations. In 1879, under the leadership of Alice Blackwell Stone, the only child of Lucy Stone, these two organizations were united under the name of The National American Woman's Suffrage Association.

Congress received the first petition for a woman's suffrage Amendment to the Constitution in 1866, and two years later Representative James Brooks, New York Democrat, introduced the first resolution for that purpose. The Territorial legislature of Wyoming granted women the right to vote in all elections in 1869, a right that was incorporated in the constitution when the Territory became a State in 1890. In 1870 the Massachusetts Republican State Convention admitted Lucy Stone and another woman as delegates.

It is often said that Belva Lockwood, who headed the ticket of the Equal Rights Party in 1884 and again in 1888, was the first woman nominated for the Presidency. That distinction, however, belongs to Mrs. Victoria Claflin Woodhull (1838-1927), who in 1872 was nominated for the Presidency at Vineland, New Jersey, by a convention styling itself the Equal Rights Party. Frederick Douglass, the Negro reformer, was the candidate for Vice President. Mrs. Woodhull, like Mrs. Lockwood later, received only a few thousand popular votes. Her supporters adopted the following campaign song, sung to the tune of "Comin' Thru' the Rye:"

> Yes! Victoria we've selected
> For our chosen head:
> With Fred Douglass on the ticket
> We will raise the dead.
>
> Then around them let us rally
> Without fear or dread,
> And next March, we'll put the Grundys
> In their little bed.

After a fashion Mrs. Woodhull, known as "The Terrible Siren," was a candidate for President again in 1880 and 1892. But in 1883 she married an Englishman named John Biddulph Martin and thereafter lived in England. She was abroad when she "ran for President" the third time.

In 1872 the National Prohibition Party also declared in favor of woman's suffrage, and in the same year the National Republican platform declared that the demand of women "for additional rights should be treated with respectful consideration." Woman suffragists insisted that denial of their right to vote abridged their privileges and immunities as citizens within the terms of the Fourteenth Amendment. A Missouri woman sued a registrar for refusing to put her name on the voting list in 1872 and thereby depriving her of the right to vote for Presidential electors, but two years later the Supreme Court upheld Missouri's Constitutional right to restrict voting to males. In 1872 Miss Susan B. Anthony and fifteen other women also tested the legality of woman's suffrage under the Fourteenth Amendment by registering and voting at Rochester, New York. Miss Anthony was arrested for violating the election laws. Her trial was postponed and she voted again in a city election in 1873. The jury, under the instructions of the judge, had no opportunity to pass on Miss Anthony's guilt, and she was convicted and fined $100, which she refused and persisted to the end in refusing to pay. She and her fifteen companions are believed to have been the first women to vote in the United States in a regular election.

In 1876 a motion was made to admit Miss R. Lavinia Goodell to practice before the State supreme court of Wisconsin. Chief Justice Edward G. Ryan denied the motion and among other things said in his opinion:

The law of nature destines and qualifies the female sex for the bearing and nurture of the children of our race and for the custody of the homes of the world and their maintenance in love and honor. And all lifelong callings of women inconsistent with these radical and sacred duties of their sex, as is the profession of the law, are departures from the order of nature; and, when voluntary, treason against it.

The peculiar qualities of womanhood—its gentle graces, its quick sensibility, its tender susceptibility, its purity, its delicacy, its emotional impulses, its subordination of hard reason to sympathetic feeling—are surely not qualification for forensic strife.

Our profession has to do with all that is selfish and malicious, knavish and criminal, coarse and brutal, repulsive and obscene, in human life. It would be revolting to all female sense of the innocence and sanctity of their sex—shocking to man's reverence for womanhood and faith in woman—that woman should be permitted to mix professionally in all the nastiness of the world which finds its way into the courts of justice. Discussions are habitually necessary in courts of justice which are unfit for female ears.

But when that was written there were already licensed women lawyers. Arabelle A. Mansfield of Mount Pleasant, Iowa, had been formally admitted to the bar and licensed to practice as early as June, 1869.

Upon the request of Miss Anthony, Senator Aaron A. Sargeant, Republican of California, introduced another joint resolution in 1878 proposing a woman's suffrage Amendment to the Constitution. In 1884 the Greenback Party endorsed such an Amendment. On April 24, 1884, the House Judiciary Committee reported unfavorably on a Constitutional Amendment. Thomas Brackett Reed of Maine, in a minority report that was later widely publicized by woman suffragists, wrote:

It is not surprising to find that the reasons on which the continuance of the inferiority of women are urged are drawn almost entirely from a tender consideration of their own good. The anxiety felt lest they should thereby deteriorate would be an honor to human nature were it not a historical fact that the same sweet solicitude has been put up as a barrier against every progress women have made since civilization began.

No women were employed in the White House except as cooks and maids until Benjamin Harrison's administration. On January 1, 1890, Miss Alice B. Sanger, who had worked for Harrison in Indianapolis, became a White House stenographer, with the title of clerk and a salary of $1,400 a year.

Other States joined Wyoming in granting woman's suffrage—Colorado in 1893, Utah and Idaho in 1896, and Washington in 1910. After 1913, when twelve States and Territories had adopted woman's suffrage, the various equal rights and woman's suffrage organizations began to concentrate upon adoption of a Constitutional Amendment. "The Army of the Hudson" commanded by "General Roselie Jones" marched on Washington. President Wilson was presented a petition containing half a million names. Suffragists held mass meetings, rallies and parades and picketed the White House and the Capitol. The joint resolution proposing the Woman's Suffrage Amendment to the Constitution was passed by Congress on June 4, 1919. It reads:

"The right of citizens of the United States to vote shall not be denied or abridged by the United States or by any State on account of sex. Congress shall have power to enforce this article by appropriate legislation."

This Amendment was ratified by the required three-fourths of the States and on August 26, 1920, became effective as the Nineteenth Amendment to the Constitution. At that time fifteen States had adopted woman's suffrage, and one woman had served in Congress and about sixty in State legislatures. On June 30, 1920, a woman presided over a major party national convention when Mrs. George Bass of Chicago, national committeewoman for Illinois, presided briefly over the Democratic National Convention in San Francisco. Millions of women voted throughout the country in the election of 1920.

The Nineteenth Amendment does not specifically confer the right to vote on women, but merely forbids discrimination against them in laws prescribing qualifications of voters, and it applies to men as well as to women. Under it the Federal Government and the States may not permit women to vote and deny that right to men. A law allowing persons of one sex to vote at eighteen and the other at twenty-one would be a violation of the Amendment.

Although often called the "Equal Rights Amendment," the Nineteenth Amendment deals only with voting. It does not forbid inequalities between men and women in respect to jury service, the administration of wills and estates, marriage relations and other legal matters. In 1923, the same year that equal pay for equal work was granted under the Classified Civil Service, Senator Charles Curtis, Republican of Kansas, afterward Vice President, introduced a joint resolution proposing an Equal Rights Amendment to the Constitution. It read: "Equality of rights under the law shall not be denied or abridged by the United States or any State on account of sex. Congress and the several States shall have power within their respective jurisdictions to enforce this article by appropriate legislation."

This Equal Rights Amendment was sponsored by the National Woman's Party, which was formed by a merger of other organizations in 1917 with Alice Paul as chairman of the national executive committee, but some women objected to the proposed Amendment on the ground that it would hurt rather than help women by nullifying laws and procedures giving women particular protection. Both the Democratic and the Republican platforms of 1944 and 1948 endorsed the Equal Rights Amendment. In 1948 the joint resolution was defeated in the Senate by a 38-35 vote, but on January 25, 1950, the Senate approved the resolution by a 63-19 vote, with an amendment providing that the general language of the Amendment to the Constitution should not prohibit present or future laws giving women special rights, benefits or exemptions. This version, contradictory in terms, was not approved by the House.

On June 4, 1920, Julia C. Stimson, superintendent of the Army Nurse Corps, became a major in the regular United States Army, and she was the first woman U.S. Army officer, although her rank was not equal in every respect to the same rank held by men. Florence A. Blanchfield, superintendent of the Army Nurse Corps, was the first woman to be commissioned a regular U.S. Army officer without restrictions on her rank. On July 18, 1947, she was commissioned a colonel with equality in every respect with men holding the same rank.

In 1867, when a Reform Bill was being considered in the British Parliament, John Stuart Mill moved that the suffrage privileges be extended to women, but the motion was lost by a vote of 106 to 73. New Zealand adopted complete woman's suffrage in 1893; Finland in 1906, and Great Britain in 1919. By 1950 woman's suffrage had been adopted by all but about a dozen of the nations of the world.

More women than men are eligible to vote in the United States. In the world as a whole about 106 males are born to every 100 females, but the longevity of females is generally greater than that of males, and the number of males and females has a tendency to become about the same. According to all the censuses from 1790 to 1940 inclusive, the number of males in the United States was greater than the number of females, but the percentage of females increased with each census. The 1950 census was the first to show more females than males in the country as a whole.

In 1940 it was estimated that forty-one per cent of all the individual wealth in the United States was owned by women.

Who was The Man of Destiny?

Napoleon Bonaparte was called "The Man of Destiny" because he rose from corporal to emperor within a few years and because he looked upon himself as an instrument in the hands of destiny. *Man of destiny* or its equivalent in other languages was an old phrase. Grover Cleveland was called "The Man of Destiny" because of his rapid rise in political office. He became mayor of Buffalo in 1881 and President of the United States four years later. A book about him entitled *A Man of Destiny* was published in 1885. Another nickname for Cleveland was "Stuffed Prophet," which was suggested during the campaign of 1892 by an editorial in the New York *Sun,* which charged the ex-President and Democratic Presidential candidate with "stuffing" the people with idle prophecies about tariff reform and sound money.

Who said: "We love him for the enemies he has made"?

"We love him for the enemies he has made" is a popular paraphrase of what General Edward Stuyvesant Bragg of Wisconsin said of Grover Cleveland in a seconding speech at the Democratic National Convention in Chicago in July, 1884.

Cleveland's name was placed before the convention by Daniel N. Lockwood of New York in a brief and formal address that has been forgotten. General Bragg, in seconding the nomination, made a fiery speech in which he used a happy phrase that did much to gain for Cleveland the Democratic nomination for the Presidency and that is still frequently referred to.

Grim and gray, personally fighting the battles of Democracy [declared Bragg], I stand today to voice the sentiments of the young men of my State when I speak for Governor Cleveland. His name is on their lips; his name is in their hearts. . . . They love him, gentlemen, and they respect him, not only for himself, for his character, for his integrity and judgment and iron will, but *they love him most for the enemies that he has made.*

The speaker referred to the "valuable enemies" that the New York Governor had made as a result of his rugged honesty in public office. The speech was especially effective because Bragg turned and faced the Tammany delegates when he came to the dramatic part of his oration. Cleveland has been the only man nominated for President by a major party convention without having the support of the majority of delegates from his own State.

Bragg, who was born in New York State in 1827, rose to the rank of brigadier general in the Union army in the Civil War, served four terms in Congress and was later appointed to several diplomatic posts in the American foreign service. He died at Fond du Lac, Wisconsin, in 1912. His name is often confused with that of General Braxton Bragg (1817-1876), the noted Confederate officer.

Rutherford B. Hayes had expressed a somewhat similar thought earlier. On February 28, 1882, he wrote to William Henry Smith: "I cannot but feel grateful that it was my good fortune to have all such men my enemies. I can well think, if I don't publicly say it, 'a man is known by his enemies.' Perhaps I ought to claim this as a *mot* of my own invention." Again on March 30 of the same year Hayes wrote to Smith: "I must repeat what I have often said to you. Such abuse is an encomium. The highest praise comes from that quarter in this form. A man is known quite as much by his enemies as by his friends." On January 16, 1881, President Hayes had written in his diary: "If there are any two men in the country whose opposition and hatred are a certificate of good character and sound statesmanship, they are Conkling and Butler. I enjoy the satisfaction of being fully endorsed by the hatred and opposition of both these men."

Cleveland himself knew how hard it is for a President to have friends. He wrote to his law partner, Wilson S. Bissell: "I am sick at heart and perplexed in brain. I almost think that the professions of my friends are but the means they employ to accomplish personal selfish ends. Henceforth I must have no friends."

What President had an artificial jaw?

In 1893, the first year of President Grover Cleveland's second term, the life of the President was endangered by a type of cancer on the roof of his mouth. On July 1 of that year he was operated upon. The entire left half of the upper jaw was removed. Other parts of the malignant growth were cut out on July 17. An artificial section of the jaw made of vulcanized rubber was then fitted into the opening by a dentist. These operations were performed on board Commodore E. C. Benedict's yacht *Oneida* in Long Island Sound and were kept a close secret. It was not until many years later that it became generally known that President Cleveland had been operated on for cancer of the mouth.

Who said we are confronted by a condition?

In his annual message to Congress in December, 1887, President Grover Cleveland said: "Our progress toward a wise conclusion will not be improved by dwelling upon the theories of Protection and Free Trade. This savours too much of bandying epithets. It is a condition which confronts us, not a theory."

There was then a surplus of $140,000,000 in the Treasury, due largely to customs revenue, and the Democratic President recommended a reduction in the tariff. In a speech on import duties delivered on April 25, 1843, Benjamin Disraeli declared: "Free trade is not a principle, it is an expedient." Cleveland considered the condition so pressing in 1887 that he devoted his entire annual message to Congress to the tariff. In response to this message the Mills bill, which put wool, lumber, hemp and flax on the free list and reduced the duties on pig iron and woolen goods, passed the House but failed in the Senate. James G. Blaine asserted that Cleveland's message of 1887 was a "free trade manifesto" and the Republicans defeated Cleveland in 1888 by making the protective tariff the issue.

Who was the Tall Sycamore of the Wabash?

Daniel Wolsey Voorhees (1828-1897), Hoosier criminal lawyer, orator and Democratic politician, was known as "The Tall Sycamore of the Wabash" because he was large and tall and lived at Terre Haute on the Wabash River in a region where grew many tall and massive trees of the species known in the United States as the sycamore or buttonwood and in Europe as the plane tree. He was born in Ohio but was taken by his parents to Indiana when a baby. Between 1861 and 1897 he served about thirty years in Congress as a Representative and Senator.

James G. Blaine considered Voorhees "by nature a fierce partisan, yet always filled with generous impulses." His courage is shown by the fact that one of his early cases involved going to Virginia to defend James E. Cook for taking part in John Brown's raid at Harper's Ferry. Voorhees was reputed one of the best stump speakers and forensic orators in the Middle West. In 1897, the year the Tall Sycamore of the Wabash died, Paul Dresser, assisted by his brother Theodore Dreiser, composed "On the Banks of the Wabash," which contains the lines:

> Thro' the sycamores the candle lights are gleaming,
> On the banks of the Wabash far away.

Voorhees's son, Charles Stewart Voorhees, sat in the U.S. House of Representatives as a Delegate from Washington Territory from 1885 to 1889 while the father was a U.S. Senator from Indiana.

How did *henchman* originate?

Henchman in the sense of a ward heeler is the ignoble descendant of a noble ancestor and represents a curious degeneration in the meaning of a word. It is believed to be derived from Anglo-Saxon *hengst,* "stallion" or "horse," and "man." Originally a henchman was a man who looked after the horses. Next it was applied to a groom, squire, or attendant of a knight. Shakespeare uses the term only once—in the sense of a page of honor. In *A Midsummer Night's Dream* Oberon says to Titania: "I do but beg a changeling boy, To be my henchman." During the seventeenth century the term became virtually obsolete in England but survived in Scotland in the sense of the gillie or attendant of a Highland chief. Through this usage it acquired the sense of a faithful and obedient follower. *Henchman* was used in the United States as early as 1839 in the sense of a servile political underling who does the bidding of his boss without asking embarrassing questions.

What State first adopted prohibition?

Soon after Georgia was chartered in 1732 the Trustees, with the approval of Parliament, prohibited the manufacture and importation of rum and brandy. In 1736 Colonel William Byrd of Westover wrote to the Earl of Egmont, president of the Trustees:

Your Lordship's opinion concerning Rum and Negroes is certainly very just, and your excluding both of them from your Colony of Georgia will be very happy; tho' with Respect to Rum the Saints of New England I fear will find out some trick to evade your Act of Parliament. They have a great dexterity at palliating a perjury so well as to leave no taste of it in the mouth, nor can any people like them slip through a penal statute. They will give some other Name to their Rum, which they may safely do, because it goes by that of Kill-Devil in this country from its baneful qualities. A watchful Eye must be kept on these foul Traders or all of the precautions of the Trustees will be in vain.

The prohibition of spirituous liquors was unpopular with the first settlers in Georgia, who were chiefly debtors and other distressed persons, and in 1741 the Trustees legalized the importation of rum after they saw they could not enforce the regulation.

The modern prohibition movement grew out of the earlier temperance movement. In 1774 Anthony Benezet published at Philadelphia a book entitled *The Mighty Destroyer Displayed, In Some Account of the Dreadful Havock Made by the Mistaken Use as well as the Abuse of Distilled Spiritious Liquors*. The Methodist General Conference in 1786 condemned both the manufacture and consumption of alcoholic beverages. A small temperance group was formed in 1808 at Saratoga, New York. On December 12, 1818, Thomas Jefferson, who drank wine but not "ardent spirits," wrote to M. deNeuville: "I rejoice, as a moralist, at the prospect of a reduction of the duties on wine. It is an error to view a tax on that liquor as merely a tax on the rich. Prohibition of its use to the middling class is condemnation of them to poison whiskey." In a report on the reduction of the army, dated December 14, 1818, Secretary of War John C. Calhoun recommended that the "spirit ration" to soldiers should be replaced by molasses and that hard liquor should be reserved for use before battle "when great efforts are necessary." The first temperance societies in the United States were organized after General Winfield Scott published *Scheme for Reducing the Use of Ardent Spirits in the United States* in a series of articles in the Philadelpia *National Gazette* in December, 1821. Scott favored the use of light wine and beer to the exclusion of hard liquor.

The American Society for the Promotion of Temperance was founded at Boston in 1826. During the 1830's the temperance movement gained considerable momentum. It was during that decade that *prohibition* began to acquire the specific sense of a restriction on the manufacture and sale of alcoholic drinks for common consumption. On December 18, 1840, Abraham Lincoln said in the Illinois house of representatives: "Prohibition will work great injury to the cause of temperance. It is a species of intemperance within itself, for it goes beyond the bounds of reason in that it attempts to control a man's appetite by legislation, and makes a crime out of things that are not crimes. A Prohibition law strikes a blow at the very principles upon which our government was founded."

In 1838 the Tennessee legislature repealed its laws taxing and licensing retailers of spirituous liquors, but this attempt at prohibition in the Volunteer State lasted only a few years. In Texas General Sam Houston made temperance speeches but cautioned his hearers to "do as I say and not as I do." On May 10, 1842, Philip Hone of New York wrote in his diary:

Hon. Thomas F. Marshall. The lion of the day is the gentleman whose name is at the head of this article, a member of the House of Representatives from Kentucky, a man of talents undoubtedly, a fierce, impassioned declaimer, and as he is proud of declaring to the world, a "reformed drunkard." He is now in this city, come on for the purpose of attending the temperance meetings, and going about from place to place, to tabernacles and taverns, churches and fire engine houses, all of which overflow when it is announced he is to speak, inveighing against the use of all liquors from wine down to whiskey, and extolling water as the only panacea for soul and body. His strongest argument is his own case.

Thomas F. Marshall was a nephew of Chief Justice John Marshall.

New York adopted a law forbidding the manufacture and sale of alcoholic beverages in 1846 but repealed it two years later. In 1849 Father Mathew, the Irish "Apostle of Temperance," visited the United States and gave a stimulus to the temperance movement. In 1838 Neal Dow of Portland began a crusade for outright prohibition in Maine, and in 1846 he induced the legislature to pass a law drastically restricting the sale of liquor. This law, however, did not satisfy the prohibitionists, and a stricter law was passed in 1851. New Hampshire, Vermont, Massachusetts, Connecticut, Rhode Island, Michigan, Pennsylvania, Delaware, Indiana, Illinois and Iowa experimented with mild prohibition and "local option" laws before 1855, but most of these early State laws were declared unconstitutional or were repealed. Although "The Maine Law of 1851" became a sort of model for other States, it was repealed in 1855 after rioting in Portland, of which Dow was mayor, but was re-enacted in 1858.

Interest in the temperance and prohibition movements subsided during the Civil War but revived soon after. James Black of Pennsylvania, an early advocate of temperance, founded the National Prohibition Party and in 1872 was nominated its first candidate for President by a convention at Columbus, Ohio. The National Prohibition Party has nominated a Presidential candidate in every Presidential election since 1872 and is the longest-lived of all minor political parties in the United States; although it has never received a single electoral vote. Black received only 5,608 popular votes. To appeal to women the National Prohibition Party included a woman's suffrage plank in its platform of 1872 and was the first political party to do so.

The women of Hillsboro and Washington Court House, Ohio, began a temperance crusade in 1873, and the next year the Woman's Christian Temperance Union (W.C.T.U.) was formed at Cleveland. In 1876 the National Prohibition Party nominated for President Green Clay Smith of Kentucky, Congressman, son of a Congressman, Mexican and Civil War veteran, lawyer and Baptist minister, who received 9,522 votes. In 1880 Kansas became the first State to incorporate prohibition into its constitution, and Maine followed suit four years later. But in spite of this progress in the prohibition movement, the National Prohibition Party polled only 10,305 popular votes in 1880.

John Pierce St. John, Union veteran and former Governor of Kansas, was nominated for President by the National Prohibition Party in 1884. In that election the party concentrated its campaigning in New York, where the supporters of Cleveland and Blaine seemed to be almost equally divided. William E. Evarts begged the Prohibitionists not "to throw away their votes" by "voting in the air" for St. John. Abraham S. Hewitt ran for mayor of New York City in the same year. Tony Pastor wrote a song with the refrain, "What's the matter with Hewitt?" When it was sung the audiences instinctively responded with "Oh, he's all right!" The Prohibition candidate had been a Republican and the Republican leaders, with the song in mind, asked ironically, "What's the matter with St. John?" Prohibitionists replied, "He's all right" and used it as their campaign slogan. St. John received 50,369 popular votes, about half of them in New York. Since New York's electoral vote was decisive, since Cleveland carried the State over Blaine by only 1,049 votes, and since most of the Prohibitionists were former Republicans, it is probable that St. John indirectly elected Cleveland, and he was the only third-party candidate between 1860 and 1912 who can be credited with having decided a Presidential election.

In 1888, when Cleveland and Harrison were the major party candidates, Clinton B. Fisk, the Prohibition candidate for President, received 246,876 votes. Four years later the National Prohibition candidate for President, John Bidwell of California, received 964,138 votes, the largest number ever received by any of its candidates. The Republicans and Democrats had both tried to keep prohibition from becoming a party issue, but the large vote of the Prohibition Party in 1892 forced them to take notice of it or let the minor party challenge their position. After that the National Prohibition Party became a permanent minor party in the usual sense of the term. In 1896 a fragment of the National Prohibition Party seceded and formed the National Party because they wanted to include in the platform, besides prohibition and woman's suffrage, other planks, such as the free coinage of silver, proportional representation, the initiative and referendum, and election of the President and Senators by direct popular vote. Meanwhile prohibition received another ally, the Anti-Saloon League, organized in 1894 to fight the liquor traffic in a practical way through the major parties. The National Prohibition Party used the fountain and the camel as its emblems.

States were lax in enforcing prohibition laws around the turn of the century, when a militant and sensational agitator named Carry Nation began to focus attention on the subject. She was born in Kentucky in 1846 and christened Carrie Amelia Moore, but her first name was always spelled *Carry* because her unlettered father wrote it that way in the family Bible when she was born. The family moved first to Missouri and then to Texas. In 1867 Carry Moore married Dr. Charles Gloyd, by whom she had her only child, a daughter named Charlien. She abandoned her first husband, who had become an alcoholic, and in 1877 she married David Nation, a country minister, lawyer and editor, who was nineteen years her senior.

Carry Nation swore eternal warfare against liquor in 1899 at Medicine

Lodge, Kansas, where she organized a local unit of the Women's Christian Temperance Union. She believed that she had received a divine commission to put saloons out of business, and since saloons were illegal in Kansas, she worked on the theory that they had "no rights anybody was bound to respect." She was nearly six feet tall, weighed a hundred and seventy-five pounds, and had a commanding presence, boundless energy and remarkable physical strength. Armed with a hatchet, she entered a saloon at Kiowa on June 9, 1899, and all but wrecked the place. Later she assailed other saloons and smashed doors, windows and mirrors, riddled pictures on the walls, pulled down fixtures, hacked bars and paneling, destroyed liquor supplies, drove out barkeepers and even threatened saloonkeepers with violence. Saloons hung up the sign, ALL NATIONS WELCOME EXCEPT CARRY. Early in 1901 Carry Nation was arrested and jailed in Topeka for smashing up a saloon and gambling joint. When brought into court she addressed the judge as "Your Dishonor" and refused to agree to a bond that would have released her on good behavior because she thought "it would be better to defer the decision as long as possible." In the same year her second husband divorced her for desertion. During the next ten years she was arrested and jailed thirty-three times, usually on charges of "disturbing the peace" and "disorderly conduct."

But despite her sensational methods of attracting attention, Carry Nation spoke well and lectured effectively to large audiences not only in the United States but also in Mexico, Canada and Great Britian. Enemies called her "Smashing Carry Nation," while admirers called her "The Loving Home Defender." She referred to her physical attacks upon saloons as "hatchetings" and "hatchetations." Although she was ridiculed unmercifully in the press and was regarded as half-crazy by millions, she whipped up public sentiment against liquor and did much to promote prohibition. She died in 1911 and was buried at Belton, Missouri, where friends and admirers erected a monument to her bearing the inscription, SHE HATH DONE WHAT SHE COULD. Her hatchet was placed in the Kansas State Historical Archives at Topeka.

The Anti-Saloon League's official organ said in 1908: "Prohibition, as the word is now used in the United States, means prohibition of the saloon, not of the personal use of alcoholic drinks. Liquor people mislead by saying temperance people favor enforcement of total abstinence by law." Soon, however, the Anti-Saloon League, the Woman's Christian Temperance Union and other antiliquor organizations were demanding Federal as well as State prohibition. In November, 1917, an act of Congress was approved prohibiting the manufacture of hard liquor as a war measure. This act did not affect wine and beer, but soon President Wilson ordered a reduction in the alcoholic content of beer. On December 18, 1917, Congress submitted to the States a Constitutional Amendment that reads:

Section 1. After one year from the ratification of this article the manufacture, sale, or transportation of intoxicating liquors within, the importation thereof into, or the exportation thereof from the United States and all territory subject to the jurisdiction thereof for beverage purposes is hereby prohibited. Section 2. The Congress and the several States shall have concurrent power to enforce this article by appropriate legislation.

A third section provided merely that the Amendment should be inoperative unless duly ratified within seven years after its submission.

On January 29, 1919, the Department of State certified that the Amendment had been ratified by the required three-fourths of the forty-eight States, and accordingly it became the Eighteenth Amendment to the Constitution, although by its terms it did not become effective till one year after ratification, which was January 16, 1920. Eventually every State except Rhode Island ratified the Eighteenth Amendment. When the Amendment went into effect thirty-three States were already "dry" as the result of State laws or constitutional provisions, and many counties and subdivisions in other States were so under local-option laws.

The Eighteenth Amendment did not define "alcoholic liquors." On October 28, 1919, Congress overrode President Wilson's veto of the National Prohibition Act, which was the Federal Act to enforce the Eighteenth Amendment and which prohibited the making, selling and carrying of all liquor containing more than one-half of one per cent of alcohol by volume, except for industrial, medicinal and sacramental purposes. This act was known as the Volstead Act because it originated in the House Judiciary Committee of which Representative Andrew John Volstead (1860-1947), Minnesota Republican, was chairman. Although Volstead, who was in Congress from 1903 to 1923, was a stanch Prohibitionist, the committee rather than the chairman drafted the act that bore his name.

The validity of the Eighteenth Amendment was challenged in the courts on the grounds that the resolution proposing it was not voted for by two-thirds of the total membership of both houses and that it was inconsistent with the so-called Bill of Rights. On June 7, 1920, the Supreme Court, in disposing of several cases in one decision, held, as it had held before, that the two-thirds vote in each house required by Article V in proposing Amendments is a vote of two-thirds of the members present—assuming a quorum—and not two-thirds of the total membership, present and absent. The prohibition of intoxicating liquors embodied in the Eighteenth Amendment, declared the Court, "is within the power to amend reserved by Article V of the Constitution. That Amendment, by lawful proposal and ratification, has become a part of the Constitution, and must be respected and given effect the same as other provisions of that instrument." The Supreme Court held that the first section of the Eighteenth Amendment "is operative thoughout the entire territorial limits of the United States, binds all legislative bodies, courts, public officers and individuals within those limits, and of its own force invalidates every legislative act—whether by Congress, by a State legislature, or by a territorial assembly—which authorizes or sanctions what the section prohibits." The Supreme Court also sustained the Constitutionality of the Volstead Act as "appropriate legislation" within the meaning of the Eighteenth Amendment.

Opponents of the Volstead Act insisted that its definition of intoxicating liquors was unreasonable and that it would not be sufficiently supported by public opinion to be enforceable. The 1920's are symbolized by beer, moonshine, bathroom gin, wood alcohol, blind pigs, hip flasks, speak-easies, bootleggers, rum-runners, hijackers, gangsters and general lawlessness. The Republican platform of 1924 declared in favor of law and order, and the Democratic platform of the same year asserted: "The Republican administration has failed to enforce the prohibition laws, is guilty of trafficking in liquor permits, and has become the protector of the violators of this law. The Democratic Party pledges itself to respect and enforce all laws."

In 1928 the Republican platform pledged the party and its nominees to a "vigorous enforcement" of the Eighteenth Amendment. Herbert Hoover never referred to prohibition as "a noble experiment" in those exact words. The common belief that he did arose from a letter that he wrote to Senator William E. Borah of Idaho on February 23, 1928. Borah had sent a questionnaire on the subject of prohibition to several of the leading men then seeking the Presidency. "Our country," replied Hoover in part, "has deliberately undertaken a great social and economic *experiment, noble in motive* and far-reaching in purpose." This statement was the original source of the popular expression frequently attributed to Hoover. Later Hoover quoted part of his letter to Borah in his address of acceptance at Stanford University, California, on August 11, 1928. In that address he said: "I do not favor the repeal of the Eighteenth Amendment. I stand for the efficient enforcement of the laws enacted thereunder. . . . Our country has deliberately undertaken a great social and economic experiment, noble in motive, far-reaching in purpose."

New York in 1926 voted overwhelmingly to ask Congress to modify the Volstead Act. Governor Alfred E. Smith was a modificationist and was therefore classed as a "wet" by the "drys." The Democratic National Convention at Houston in 1928 adopted, with the approval of Bishop James Cannon, Jr., as spokesman for thirty-one dry organizations, a plank in its platform pledging the party and its nominees to "an honest effort to enforce the Eighteenth Amendment" and all laws enacted to enforce it. Governor Smith, who was nominated on the first ballot, said in a telegram of acceptance that he would stand on the platform but thought the Volstead Act should be modified to give the States more power.

In 1932 the Republican Party declared in favor of prompt submission of a Constitutional Amendment repealing the Eighteenth Amendment but giving the Federal Government power to protect States where prohibition exists, while the Democratic Party advocated repeal of the Eighteenth Amendment and immediate modification of the Volstead Act. Congress submitted an Amendment repealing the Eighteenth on February 10, 1933, which became effective on December 5 of the same year. The Twenty-First Amendment, however, did more than repeal the Eighteenth. Section 2 provides that, "the transportation or importation into any State, Territory, or possession of the United States for delivery or use therein of intoxicating liquors, in violation of the laws, thereof, is hereby prohibited." Titles I and II of the Volstead Act lost their Constitutional support and were specifically repealed by an act approved August 27, 1935. Federal prohibition lasted thirteen years, ten months and nineteen days. By a popular referendum in 1948 Kansas repealed its sixty-eight-year-old constitutional prohibition, and after that only Mississippi and Oklahoma remained legally dry, although vast areas in other States were dry under local option laws.

Sweden tried national prohibition for a brief period in 1909. In 1919 Norway adopted prohibition against all beverages with an alcoholic content of more than fifteen per cent, but this limited prohibition was completely abandoned in 1927. Soviet Russia, Finland and eight of the ten provinces of Canada also adopted and abandoned prohibition.

Why is an unofficial poll called a straw vote?

Straw vote in the sense of an unofficial poll taken before an election to get an indication of the drift of public opinion is believed to have been suggested by the old proverb, "Straws show which way the wind blows."

In *The Merchant of Venice* Shakespeare has Solanio say, "I should be still Plucking the grass to know where sits the wind." John Selden (1584-1654) wrote in *Table Talk*: "Take a straw and throw it up into the air,—you may see by that which way the wind is." In 1774 Joseph Galloway, member of the First Continental Congress, wrote that the Massachusetts delegates were "warm in their Behaviour and Conversation very modest, yet not so much as not to throw out Hints which, like Straws and Feathers, tell us from which Point of the Compass the Wind comes."

Apparently *straw vote* originated in America. The earliest example listed in *The Dictionary of American English* is dated 1891, but the term is probably older than that. At first straw votes were taken merely at casual gatherings or in a single town or district. Later more extensive straw votes were taken by newspapers and magazines. Charles ("Calico Charlie") Foster, who was elected Governor of Ohio in 1879, is reputed to have been the first politician to use this method to forecast the result of an election. In the 1930's straw votes conducted commercially on a Statewide and nationwide scale came to be called public opinion polls.

Straw vote is applied also to a common method of election by drawing straws. One person holds in his hands a number of short and long straws, with the lower ends concealed, equal to the number of persons voting. Those who draw long straws get the offices. Some minor offices are still determined in this manner. But straw voting is a form of drawing lots, like casting dice or cutting cards, and is election by chance.

What is the difference between socialism and communism?

Socialism and *communism* originally had about the same meaning. As *socialisme* and *communisme* both terms were coined in France during the first half of the nineteenth century. *Socialism* is derived from Latin *socius,* "sharing in." The earliest use of French *socialisme* appears to have been in 1832, when it was used in contrast to *personnalité,* but within two or three years several French writers used the term in its modern sense. The earliest use of *socialism* in English recorded by the Oxford dictionary is dated 1839, but the writer of a letter in the *Poor Man's Guardian* as early as 1833 had signed himself "A socialist."

Communism stems from Latin *communus,* "common." Apparently French writers began to use *communisme* in the 1830's. *Commune* was the name of the smallest administrative district in France and the radical revolutionists who seized power in Paris in 1792 and brought about the Reign of Terror called their regime "The Commune" because it was composed of the representatives from the communes. This usage may have tended to give *communisme* a more radical and revolutionary meaning than *socialisme.* In 1843 the *New Age* referred to "Works on Communism, Religious, Political, and Domestic." Goodwin Barmby, who founded The London Communist Propaganda Society in 1843, wrote in the first number of the *Apostle* in 1848: "I also conversed (in 1840) with some of the most advanced minds of the French metropolis, and there, in the company of some disciples of Babeoeut, then called Equalitarians, I first pronounced the name of Communism, which has since . . . acquired that world-wide reputation."

Already in the early 1840's *socialism* and *communism* were applied interchangeably to any proposed social system in which all property would be owned and all instruments of production controlled by the whole community for the benefit of all its members.

The general concept of communal life was known to the ancients. Plato, who lived about 400 B.C., in his *Republic* portrayed perfect men living in a perfect state under a perfect social system. Many primitive peoples live under communal systems and some authorities suppose that such was the earliest form of human society. Acts 2:44-45, referring to the first Christian community in Jerusalem, says "all that believed were together, and had all things common, and sold their possessions and goods, and parted them to all men, as every man had need." On the strength of this and other New Testament passages many Christian communal organizations have been formed. Other groups, without the religious motive, have established co-operative communities as escapes from the world or as experiments in various types of communalism. In *Utopia* (1516) Sir Thomas More pictured an ideal commonwealth on an imaginary island.

In 1813 Robert Owen of Lanark published *New View of Society,* in which he advanced his ideas of an enlightened treatment of industrial workers. Later he undertook to put his theories into practice in several communities in Scotland and at New Harmony, Indiana. Owen was a successful manufacturer and his theories made a profound impression on Western Europe. Some authorities believe that *socialism* was first used during the 1830's in discussions of Owen's social and economic theories and practices. François M. C. Fourier (1772-1837) advocated a system under which people would live in federated "harmony communities." Horace Greeley advocated Fourierism, and communities were established in Texas and New Jersey. Brook Farm in Massachusetts was for a time Fourierist in organization.

Dozens of different theories of socialism and communism were being advocated when Karl Marx appeared as the leader of a new movement. In 1847 he and Friedrich Engels wrote a pamphlet entitled *Manifest der*

Kommunisten, "Manifesto of the Communists," in which they expounded their system. The Manifesto frankly and militantly called for a world-wide social and political revolution by the working classes. It declared: "The proletarians have nothing to lose but their chains. They have a world to win. Workers of the world, unite!" Marx and Engels wrote: "The theory of Communism may be summed up in one sentence: Abolish all private property." Although Marx and Engels used *Kommunist* in their Manifesto, they continued to use *socialism* and *communism* synonymously. In fact Marx himself applied *socialism* to his theories more often than he did *communism*.

In 1851, only three years after the Manifesto was published, Joseph Weydemeyer, a German disciple of Marx, migrated to the United States and started a newspaper to advocate Marxism. He made few converts and for many years about the only Marxists in the United States were among recent German immigrants. In 1861 Weydemeyer enlisted in the Union army as a captain and rose to the rank of brigadier general on President Lincoln's staff. As late as 1864 Marx was still corresponding with his disciple in America. Weydemeyer is called by some the first Marxist in the United States and in 1950 the Attorney General cited the Joseph Weydemeyer School of Social Science at St. Louis as an agency of the American Communist Party.

Marx wrote from London a series of letters on international affairs for Greeley's New York *Tribune* and received a guinea apiece for them. He held that his system would not work unless applied universally, and in 1864 he helped form the International Workingmen's Association (First International) to overthrow the capitalist system by the united workingmen of the world. The First International adopted as its emblem the red flag, which in ancient Rome had symbolized war and in Revolutionary France insurrection and terrorism. *Red* in the sense of an anarchist, revolutionist or violent communist was first used in 1864. A letter written by Marx was sent to President Lincoln by the First International. Charles Francis Adams, Lincoln's Minister in London, replied that the President accepted the letter "so far as the sentiments expressed by it are personal," but made it clear that the American Government did not approve of revolutionary propaganda and doctrines of force.

In 1869 the National Labor Union, which had been formed the year before, sent delegates to the First International. But Marxism gained few adherents in America and the Marxist philosophy had little influence on the political thinking of Americans for many years. The headquarters of the First International were moved from London to New York in 1872 in the hope of stimulating interest in Marxist socialism in the United States, but the attempt failed and in 1876 the organization was dissolved at a conference in Philadelphia. In 1876 a group formed the Social Democratic Workingmen's Party, which in 1877 changed its name to the Socialist Labor Party. This was the first use of *social* and *socialist* in American party names.

Meanwhile *socialist* and *communist* had entered the American vocabulary as synonyms of labor agitator, social revolutionist, nihilist and anarchist. During the late sixties and the seventies laws passed by some of the Western States to restrict and regulate the activities of large corporations were called socialistic and communistic by conservatives. On March 17, 1880, nearly a year before he became President, James A. Garfield said in a speech: "The people of the Pacific Coast, after two years of wrestling with the spirit of communism in the City of San Francisco, have finally grappled with this lawless spirit, and the leader of it was yesterday sentenced to penal servitude as a violator of the law." On January 13, 1888, ex-President Rutherford B. Hayes, then preparing a speech for delivery before the National Prison Congress at Boston, wrote in his diary: "I gave (the finishing touches) to my Boston talk—a little 'communistic' in its tendency, the 'privileged class' will say."

In his annual message to Congress on December 3, 1888, President Grover Cleveland said: "Communism is a hateful thing and a menace to peace and organized government; but the communism of combined wealth and capital, the outgrowth of overweening cupidity and selfishness, which insidiously undermine the justice and integrity of free institutions, is not less dangerous than the communism of oppressed poverty and toil, which, exasperated by injustice and discontent, attacks with wild disorder the citadel of rule." Hayes, after reading William D. Howells's *Killburn,* wrote in his diary on January 13, 1889: "It opens the democratic side of coming questions. I do not find a ready word for the doctrine of true equality of rights. Its foes call it nihilism, communism, socialism, and the like. Howells would perhaps call it justice. It is the doctrine of the Declaration of Independence and of the Sermon on the Mount. But what is a proper and *favorable* word or phrase to designate it?" The ex-President observed on December 12, 1890, "E. B. Bemis on socialism writes well. State action, state regulation, state control, are his words. No state socialism, nor communism, nor nihilism which is anarchy."

Socialism and *communism* were in the meantime gradually acquiring different shades of meaning. During his latter years Engels used *socialism* in a general sense and *communism* in the more specific sense of the teachings of Marx. On January 3, 1894, the year before he died, Engels said in a letter that in all his writings he was using *communist* in preference to *social democrat* because the latter was the term applied to themselves by the disciples of both Proudhon and Lassalle in Germany and France.

Henry George's *Progress and Poverty* (1879), which advocated the single-tax theory, and Edward Bellamy's *Looking Backward* (1888), a Utopian romance picturing Boston in A.D. 2000 under a socialistic form of society, did much to stimulate interest in social reform and socialism in America. "Bellamy's book," wrote a contemporary, "brought socialism up from the workshops and the beer-gardens into the libraries and the drawing-rooms."

Daniel De Leon (1852-1914), who was born on the island of Curaçao and was educated in Germany and Holland, joined the old Socialist Labor Party in 1890 and became its moving spirit. In 1895 Eugene Victor Debs (1855-1926) became a convert to socialism while serving a six-months sentence in the McHenry County jail at Woodstock, Illinois, after conviction for contempt of court in violating an injunction in connection with the Pullman Company strike. He supported Bryan for President in 1896, but in 1897 formed the Social Democratic Party of America, which was composed chiefly of seceders from De Leon's Socialist Labor Party and the remnant of Debs's old American Railway Union. Debs ran for President in 1900 on the Social Democratic Party ticket and received 96,116 popular votes. In the same year Joseph Malloney, the Socialist Labor Party candidate for President, received 39,759 votes. The latter Party continued in the field but attracted little following.

In 1901 the Social Democratic Party was renamed the Socialist Party of America, and in 1904 Debs received 402,321 popular votes as its candidate for President. Four years later Debs, as the Socialist candidate for President, toured the country on a train known as "The Red Special," and in the election he received 420,973 popular votes. He received 901,062 votes in 1912 and in that year more than six hundred State and municipal officers were elected on the Socialist ticket. By this time the Socialist Party of America had begun to drop *bourgeoisie, proletariat* and many other Marxian terms and to advocate many social and political reforms in addition to socialism. Many of the planks in the Socialist platform were later enacted into law under the sponsorship of the major political parties.

Allen Benson of New York took Debs's place as the Socialist Party's candidate for President in 1916 and received 585,113 popular votes. In April, 1917, a Socialist Party convention at St. Louis issued a manifesto denouncing the war and advising its members to resist it with all the means in their power. At the Socialist State Convention at Canton, Ohio, on June 16, 1918, Debs bitterly attacked the Government for prosecuting persons charged with sedition. He himself was indicted by a Federal grand jury, and, after a four-day trial, was convicted on September 14, 1918, of violating the Espionage Act and sentenced to ten years in prison. This conviction was upheld by the Supreme Court on March 10, 1919, and on April 13 of the same year he was put in the West Virginia State penitentiary at Moundsville. On June 13 he was moved to the Federal penitentiary at Atlanta. In *Labor and Freedom* Debs wrote: "While there is a lower class I am in it. While there is a criminal class I am of it. While there is a soul in prison I am not free." At his trial in Cleveland he said: "When great changes occur in history, when great principles are involved, as a rule the majority are wrong." In 1920, while a prisoner at Atlanta, Debs was nominated for President by the Socialist Party and received 919,799 popular votes. He had received nearly six per cent of the total vote in 1912. By 1920 the number of voters had about doubled by reason of the Woman's Suffrage Amendment and increase in population and in that year Debs received only about three per cent of the total. On December 24, 1921, Debs was released from Atlanta by order of President Harding without restoration of civil rights.

In 1905 Debs, De Leon, William D. Haywood and other Socialists met at Chicago and formed the Industrial Workers of the World, which was patterned after French syndicalism. Its purpose was to gain control of all means of production and distribution, and ultimately society itself, by federating all unions. Its methods were sympathetic strikes, sabotage, terrorism and other illegal means; and its members were miners, harvest workers, lumberjacks, longshoremen, sailors and railroad workers, many of whom were recent immigrants more interested in higher wages and better working and living conditions than in the philosophy of socialism and communism. Debs and De Leon soon withdrew from the I.W.W., but under Haywood's leadership it had a twenty-five-year career of labor agitation and turbulence. Haywood finally joined the Communists in Russia, where he died in 1928. The name of the organization lingers only as the label of a labor union, which still has units in two Cleveland plants. Several States passed "criminal syndicalism" laws to restrain the I.W.W., and more than 5,000 members, including Haywood, were convicted and imprisoned. Members were called Wobblies, which is of unknown origin. An article in the September 5, 1923, issue of *The Nation* quoted an old-time Wobbly as saying: "In Vancouver, in 1911, we had a number of Chinese members, and one restaurant keeper would trust any member for meals. He could not pronounce the letter *w* but called it *wobble*, and would ask: 'You I *Wobble, Wobble?*' and when the card was shown credit was unlimited. Therefore the laughing term among us was *I. Wobbly Wobbly.*" This has been accepted by some as the origin of the term. The earliest use of it given by the *Dictionary of Americanisms* is dated October 1, 1914. It was said facetiously that I.W.W. stood for "I won't work."

The Second International was formed in 1889 to celebrate the hundredth anniversary of the French Revolution and continued until it and the Vienna International (1921) were merged to form the Labor and Socialist International in 1923. In March, 1919, representatives from twelve countries met in Moscow and, under the sponsorship of Russian communists, formed the Third International as a protest against the inactivity and bourgeois character of the Second International and as an aid to the Russian revolutionists.

The new International Association of Workers [declared the organizers] is established for the purpose of organizing common action between the workers of various countries who are striving toward a single aim: the overthrow of capitalism, the establishment of the dictatorship of the proletariat and of the international Soviet Republic, the complete abolition of classes and the realization of socialism—as the first step in communist society.

This organization was also called variously the Moscow International, the Red International, and the Communist International (Comintern). Lenin himself had long before regarded socialism as a stepping stone to communism. "But," he had written, "striving for Socialism, we are convinced that it will develop into Communism." In 1918, following the October Revolution of 1917, the Lenin group formed the Communist Party, but used *Socialist* instead of *Communist* in the official name of the government they established—"The Union of Soviet Socialist Republics." It may be said in a general way that the Marxists first called themselves Communists, then Socialists or Social Democrats, and finally Communists again.

In the Brussels-London Congress of 1903 the Russian socialists and communists, who then called themselves Social Democrats, split into two factions. Lenin and his followers won on an important organizational question and got control of the party. Russian *bolshinstvo* means "majority" and *menshinstvo* means "minority." After that, from this accidental circumstance, the dominant and most radical faction in the Russian Social Democratic Party was called Bolsheviki and the smaller and more moderate faction Mensheviki. After the Communists seized control of the government it became a mark of distinction for a person to have been one of the original Bolsheviki, and the ruling party in Russia still calls itself "Communist Party of the Soviet Union (Bolsheviki)." In America *Bolshevism* became synonymous with Russian communism and radicalism of the deepest dye. In the July, 1918, issue of the *Metropolitan Magazine* ex-President Theodore Roosevelt used "Parlor Bolshevism."

Many left-wingers who wanted to affiliate with the Comintern seceded from the Socialist Party of America in 1919 and joined with others in forming the Communist Party and the Communist Labor parties. Another faction called itself the Communist Party of America. For a while the Communists in America were split up into a dozen or more factions or splinter parties. In 1920 the Communist Party and the Communist Labor Party merged and became the United Communist Party. Later in the same year the United Communist Party and the Communist Party of America merged and, after using the name Worker's Party for a while, the American Communists finally adopted the name "The Communist Party of the U.S.A."

William Z. Foster was the Communist candidate for President in 1924, 1928 and 1932 and received 36,386, 48,770 and 102,785 popular votes respectively. Earl Browder as the Communist candidate for President received 80,159 popular votes in 1936 and 46,251 in 1940. In 1943 the Comintern, which was dedicated to world-wide political and social revolution, was dissolved as a gesture toward the United States and her allies who were co-operating with the Soviet Union in the Second World War. On May 10, 1944, the Communist Party of the U.S.A. announced that it had been dissolved and replaced by a nonparty organization known as "The Communist Political Association." This association endorsed Roosevelt for a fourth term. On October 5, 1944, the President, in a White House radio speech, said: "I have never sought and I do not welcome the support of any person or group committed to communism, or fascism, or any other foreign ideology which would undermine the American system of government, or the American system of free competitive enterprise and private property." In 1947 representatives of Communist parties in nine countries met in Poland and formed a Fourth International, known as the "Cominform," and in 1948 the Communist Party of the U.S.A., which had been revived, endorsed Henry A. Wallace, the Progressive Party candidate for President. In the same year the Socialist Worker's Party, representing the Trotsky wing of the American Communists nominated Farrell Dobbs for President and he received 13,007 popular votes.

After the secession of the left-wingers in 1919 and the years following the Socialist Party of America became anti-Communist. It continued to advocate moderate socialism but became more and more a party of social reform to be introduced by Constitutional processes. In 1924 for the first time it made no nomination of its own for President but endorsed Robert M. La Follette, the Progressive Party candidate. For technical reasons La Follette ran on the Socialist ticket in some States. Norman Thomas was the Socialist Party candidate for President in 1928 and the five succeeding elections. He received 267,420 popular votes in 1928, 884,781 in 1932, 187,720 in 1936, 99,557 in 1940, 60,518 in 1944 and 132,138 in 1948. In the eleven elections from 1904 to 1948 inclusive the Socialist Party of America nominated only three different men for President—Debs, Benson and Thomas—and none ever received an electoral vote.

No Socialist Party candidate has ever been elected to the Senate and only three to the House of Representatives. The first Socialist Party candidate elected to the House was Victor L. Berger of Wisconsin, who served from 1911 to 1913. Later he was denied a seat in the House on three different occasions but served in that body again from 1923 to 1929. Mayer London was a Socialist Party member of the House from New York City from 1915 to 1919 and again from 1921 to 1923. Fiorello H. La Guardia of New York was elected to the House in 1924 solely on the Socialist Party ticket, but he had previously been elected as a Republican and was subsequently elected as a Republican and regarded himself as a progressive Republican rather than as a Socialist.

In view of the application of *socialism* and *communism* during the last century it is difficult if not impossible to distinguish between the two terms sharply and briefly. As the terms are now generally used all communists are socialists but all socialists are not communists. In *Economic Consequences of Socialism* (1926) G. W. Gough wrote: "The Communist is a Socialist in a violent hurry." A later version of this is: "Socialism is Communism with a longer time-fuse." Socialists generally advocate public ownership of important national resources, general utilities and the means of production, while Communists, in theory at least, advocate public ownership of all property; Socialists generally advocate adoption of their system by legal means, while Communists advocate adoption of their system by revolutionary methods. Socialists generally have been antagonistic to religion and Marxist and Leninist communists particularly so. Marx was the son of a German Jewish lawyer, who had his entire family baptized as Protestants when Karl was six years old. In the introduction of *A Critique of the Hegelian Philosophy of Right* (1844) Marx wrote: "Religion is the sign of the oppressed creature, the feelings of a heartless world, just as it is the spirit of unspiritual conditions. It is the opium of the people." And in the Communist Manifesto of 1847 Marx and Engels said: "Christian Socialism is but the holy water with which the priest consecrates the heartburnings of the aristocrat."

Indiana in 1933 was the first State in the Union to pass a law barring Communists from running for public office, and Kansas in 1939 passed a law providing "it shall be a felony for any person or persons, organizations or body of persons to fly, to carry, to exhibit or to display, or to assist in carrying, exhibiting or displaying any Red flag, standard or banner distinctive of Bolshevism, syndicalism or radical socialism." During the early 1930's Congress enacted as a rider on an appropriation bill a provision requiring public school teachers in the District of Columbia to take an oath that they were not Communists. A provision in the Labor-Management Relations (Taft-Hartley) Act of 1947 requires officers of local, national and international labor unions to file affidavits with the National Labor Relations Board that they are not members of, or affiliated with, the Communist Party and do not support any organization advocating the overthrow of the United States Government by force or any other illegal or unconstitutional methods. The Supreme Court, in upholding the Constitutionality of this provision, declared that the Communist Party differs from recognized political parties in that its aim is for a minority to seize power and to impose a system upon the majority.

What man was both son and father of a President?

John Scott Harrison, who was born in 1804 at Vincennes, Indiana, was the son of William Henry Harrison, ninth President, and father of Benjamin Harrison, twenty-third President. As a young man he studied medicine, but he abandoned the medical profession and became a farmer. From 1853 to 1857 he was a Whig member of Congress from Ohio. His death occurred in 1878 on Point Farm, near North Bend, Ohio, where President Benjamin Harrison was born. He was the only one of the five sons of William Henry Harrison to survive their father. John Scott Harrison was buried near the tomb of his father. The day after the funeral his body was found at the Ohio Medical College in Cincinnati. It was reburied in the same cemetery. He might have said, as did Nicholas Longworth of Cincinnati: "It is my fate to go down to posterity as the son of a distinguished father and the father of a distinguished son."

Who defined a statesman as a dead politician?

In 1880 Thomas Brackett Reed of Maine, later Speaker of the House of Representatives, received a letter asking him to define *statesman*. Reed, who was noted for his epigrams, replied: "A statesman is a successful politician who is dead." In *The Democracy of the Constitution* Henry Cabot Lodge wrote:

> The epigram was published, flew over the country, and has become a familiar quotation. But the sequel is less well known. The correspondent who asked the question telegraphed as soon as he received the answer, "Why don't you die and become a statesman?" Mr. Reed handed me the telegram and said: "Here is my answer: No, Fame is the last infirmity of mortal mind."

Simon Cameron, political boss of Pennsylvania and Lincoln's first Secretary of War, is reputed to have said about 1860: "An honest politician is one who, when he is bought, will stay bought."

Who was Pitchfork Ben?

"Pitchfork Ben" was the nickname of Benjamin Ryan Tillman (1847-1918), Governor of South Carolina from 1890 to 1894 and U.S. Senator from 1895 till his death.

Tillman had lost his left eye in his youth and was unattractive in personal appearance, irascible in disposition, careless in manners and had a rasping voice. From his marriage in 1868 till he began to take an interest in politics in 1885 he devoted himself exclusively to farming, at which he seems not to have been very successful. As a dissatisfied farmer with a large family he became bitter toward the planter aristocrats who ruled South Carolina under the leadership of General Wade Hampton, a one-legged Confederate hero. Although Tillman's oldest brother George was prominent in State politics and had been elected to Congress, nobody in the farm country suspected that their uncouth neighbor was destined to defeat Wade Hampton, dominate the politics of the State for nearly thirty years and to attain national notoriety as the rabble-rousing spokesman of Southern agrarianism, white supremacy and popular reform.

In his speeches in the Senatorial campaign of 1894 Governor Tillman denounced President Grover Cleveland and shouted to the crowds that came to hear him: "Send me to Washington and I'll stick my pitchfork into his old ribs!" Speaking in his official capacity as Governor of South Carolina at the Atlanta Exposition in the same year, he said: "There are some so infatuated that they think that all the financial wisdom of the country is monopolized by the East; and they say, 'Me, too,' every time Cleveland grunts. I should not have said anything about the President, as I expect to get a better chance at him with my pitchfork in Washington . . ." From that time Tillman became universally known as "Pitchfork Ben."

His original followers were popularly called "Wool-Hat Boys," because they were recruited chiefly from "poor whites," cracker farmers and "one-gallus men" who the year around wore cheap, sweat-soaked, broad-brimmed black hats made of wool or felt. "Wool hat" dates back to Colonial days, and the term is often synonymous with "rustic" or "yokel." Thomas Edward Watson (1856-1922), Tillman's counterpart in Georgia, applied "Wool-Hat Boys" to his rural supporters.

Who was Silver Dick Bland?

Richard Parks Bland (1835-1899), who served twelve terms in Congress, was known as "Silver Dick" because of his persistent advocacy of the free and unlimited coinage of silver. He was born in Kentucky and spent ten years as schoolteacher, miner and lawyer in the Far West before settling in Missouri. His free-silver bill, which gave him a national reputation, passed the House of Representatives in 1877 but was blocked by the Senate. The next year Congress passed over President Hayes's veto the Bland-Allison Bill, a compromise providing that the silver dollar should contain $412\frac{1}{2}$ grains troy of standard silver and that the Treasury should buy between two and four million dollars worth of silver bullion a month.

On August 11, 1893, Silver Dick made a speech known as "Parting of the Ways," in which he served notice that the Western Democrats would put free silver above party loyalty. Until the national convention met at Chicago, Bland was the leading candidate for the Democratic Presidential nomination. In placing Bland's name in nomination Senator George G. Vest of "Dog Speech" fame quoted the following lines from the Boat Song in Scott's *The Lady of the Lake:*

> Ours is no sapling, chance-sown by the fountain,
> Blooming at Beltane, in winter to fade.

Bland led on the first three ballots but withdrew his name when Bryan's nomination appeared inevitable. "The Bald Eagle of the Ozarks," as he was also called, though able and thorough, was not an eloquent speaker, lacked personal appeal, and was regarded by the public as a "one-idea man." The coins struck off under the Bland-Allison Act were popularly known as "Bland's Cart-Wheel Dollars."

What was Bryan's "cross of gold" speech?

In 1896 William Jennings Bryan, who had served in Congress from Nebraska from 1891 to 1895, was a delegate to the Democratic National Convention at Chicago. On June 8 he made a speech before the convention that is generally regarded as largely responsible for his nomination for the Presidency. At the time he was only thirty-six and widely known as "The Boy Orator of the Platte." In his famous speech he hurled defiance at the Cleveland "Sound-Money Democrats" and advocated the free and unlimited coinage of silver at the ratio of sixteen to one, which had been authorized in 1837 and discontinued by "the crime of 1873." It is known as the "cross of gold" speech because it closed with that phrase. Among other things, "The Peerless One," as some of his admirers liked to call him, declared:

The humblest citizen in all the land, when clad in the armor of a righteous cause, is stronger than all the hosts of error. I come to speak to you in defense of a cause as holy as the cause of liberty—the cause of humanity. . . .There are those who believe that, if you will only legislate to make the well-to-do prosperous, their prosperity will leak through to those below. The Democratic idea, however, has been that if you legislate to make the masses prosperous, their prosperity will find its way up through every class which rests upon them. . . . We do not come as aggressors. Our war is not a war of contempt; we are fighting in the defense of our homes, our families, and posterity. We have petitioned, and our petitions have been scorned. We have entreated and our entreaties have been disregarded. We have begged, and they have mocked when our calamity came. We beg no longer; we entreat no more; we petition no more. We defy them! . . . If they dare to come out in the open field and defend the gold standard as a good thing, we shall fight them to the uttermost. Having behind us the producing masses of this nation and the world, the laboring interests and the toilers everywhere, we will answer their demand for a gold standard by saying to them: "You shall not press down upon the brow of labor this crown of thorns; you shall not crucify mankind upon a cross of gold."

The nomination of Bryan in 1896 was not so accidental as many suppose. He had conducted a clever preconvention campaign, obtained the pledges of hundreds of delegates, and carefully timed his speech. His leading competitor, "Silver Dick" Bland of Missouri, lacked color and popular appeal. In *My Quarter Century of American Politics* (1920) Champ Clark wrote: "It is a pleasant fiction that his nomination was solely the spontaneous result of his glowing 'cross of gold and crown of thorns' speech. But the hogshead of Bryan buttons immediately turned loose did not grow out of this speech! Hardly." Substantially everything

[327]

in the speech had been used before by Bryan in and out of Congress. Even the "crown of thorns" and "cross of gold" phrases had been used in a free-silver speech delivered in Congress on December 12, 1894. Nonetheless, Bryan's convention speech on June 8, 1896, was the most effective he ever delivered.

Bryan ran for President three times and each time was beaten by a man with the same first name as his own—William. In 1896 and 1900 he was defeated by William McKinley, and in 1908 by William Howard Taft. During the campaign of 1896 the Republicans replied to Bryan's demand for the free and unlimited coinage of silver with the slogan "Open the mills and not the mints."

Who said: "I am a Democrat still—very still"?

This saying is attributed to David Bennett Hill (1843-1910), who as Lieutenant Governor became Governor of New York when Grover Cleveland resigned that office to become President. Hill was elected Governor in 1885 and 1888 and served until 1892, when he became a U.S. Senator. He was a "machine man," a party politician and the up-State Democratic boss, who was in the habit of saying, "I am a Democrat," in a tone intimating that President Cleveland was not a good Democrat. In 1888 many of the New York Democrats voted for Hill for Governor and Benjamin Harrison, the Republican nominee, for President. Four years later Hill was an unsuccessful aspirant against Cleveland for the Democratic nomination for President. Like most of the conservative Democrats at the time Hill was a "sound money man" and opposed the free-silver wing of his party. At the Chicago Democratic National Convention in 1896 he said: "I am a Democrat, but not a revolutionist." After William Jennings Bryan was nominated a friend asked him whether he was still a Democrat, and he is reputed to have replied: "I am a Democrat still—very still." Although Hill did not support Bryan actively, he entertained the Democratic Presidential candidate in his home during the campaign, and four years later seconded Bryan's nomination in the Kansas City convention.

Who was the Great Commoner?

William Pitt the Elder (1708-1778), who was one of the chief architects of the British Empire and who was largely responsible for making Canada part of that empire, was known as "The Great Commoner." Formerly all members of the House of Commons were called "Commoners" to distinguish them from the members of the House of Lords, who were called "Lords." As a member of the House of Commons Pitt came to be regarded as "The *Great* Commoner." Dr. Samuel Johnson said, "Walpole was a minister given by the King to the people, but Pitt was a minister given by the people to the King."

Pitt, after whom Pittsburgh was named, ceased to be The Great Commoner to the British in 1766 when he formed a new ministry and chose for himself the office of Lord Privy Seal, which necessitated his transfer to the House of Lords. Shortly thereafter he was created first Earl of Chatham and Viscount Pitt. His wife, Lady Hester Granville, a sister of Prime Minister George Granville, author of the Stamp Act of infamous memory in America, had been created Baroness of Chatham in her own right five years earlier. By accepting a peerage and a seat in the House of Lords, The Great Commoner lost as much in popularity as he gained in dignity and security. A great banquet and illumination of London had been prepared to celebrate his return to the premiership, but when it was learned that he had accepted a peerage the celebration was called off.

His son, William Pitt the Younger (1759-1806), became Prime Minister in 1783 at the age of twenty-four when he had been a member of Parliament only two years. It is probable that neither of the Pitts would ever have been Prime Minister of England had not an ancestor sold a diamond for a good price. Thomas Pitt (1653-1726), grandfather of William Pitt the Elder, was known as "Diamond Pitt" because, while governor of Madras in India, he somehow acquired an unusual diamond that he sold for £135,000, with which he raised his family to a position of wealth and political influence in England.

Lord Chatham was opposed on principle to the British war against the American Colonies, and many Americans have read "An English Plea for Peace with the American Colonies," reputed to have been delivered by Pitt in the House of Lords on November 18, 1777. It contains the famous sentence, "I venture to say, you CANNOT conquer America," and, "If I were an American, as I am an Englishman, while a foreign troop was landed in my country, I never would lay down my arms!—never! never! never!" There was no original record of this speech. Later Dr. Johnson reconstructed it from the recollections of others and printed it in the *Gentleman's Magazine.* Pitt habitually wrote and spoke in a formal and stilted style and it is suspected that both the thought and language of this famous piece of eloquence were Johnson's rather than Pitt's. Pitt was opposed to the military conquest of America because he thought conciliation by other means was possible, but he was opposed to all proposals to grant America her independence. In his last speech in the House of Lords he is reported to have said: "My lords, I rejoice that the grave has not closed on me, and that I am still alive to lift my voice against the dismemberment of this ancient and noble monarchy." Lord North, who is detested as much as Pitt is admired by Americans, was much more inclined toward granting America independence than Pitt was.

But Americans long cherished "The Great Commoner" as their champion and the phrase was applied to both Henry Clay and Thaddeus Stevens. William Jennings Bryan (1860-1925) was known to many of his admirers as "The Commoner" and "The Great Commoner" in allusion to his championship of the rights of the common people. There is a story to the effect that after Bryan made his "cross of gold" speech in the Democratic convention of 1896 and had won the nomination for President, a railroad president offered him a private car in which to campaign, but Willis John Abbott advised him to turn down the offer on the ground that "You are now the Great Commoner and can't afford to accept favors from railroad companies." During the Presidential campaign of 1896, when Bryan was only thirty-six, he was known as "The Boy Orator of the Platte" in allusion to the fact that he then lived in Nebraska through which the Platte River flows. He was also called "The Peerless One." But Bryan himself preferred "The Commoner" to all the other sobriquets applied to him in his long and notable political career. In 1901 he started a weekly newspaper called the *Commoner* to keep himself and his ideas before the people.

Why are ultraconservatives called standpatters?

Standpat entered politics from poker. *To stand* in the sense of being willing to play with one's hand as dealt is recorded as a card-playing word as early as 1824. In American poker this became *to stand pat*. A poker player stands pat when he plays his cards just as dealt and refuses to take a chance by discarding and drawing other cards. *Standpatter,* in the sense of a politician who sticks to an established policy, such as a high protective tariff, and who refuses to consider any change or reform, was used in American political slang as early as 1882 but did not become common until around the turn of the century. In 1900 when Senator Mark Hanna was asked by a reporter to state the chief issue of the Republican campaign to re-elect McKinley, the President-maker replied, "We'll stand pat."

Speaker Joseph "Uncle Joe" Cannon prided himself on being a standpatter. "America," he said, "is a hell of a success—why tinker with it?" President Theodore Roosevelt objected to the philosophy of stand-pattism. "The voters," he said, "don't understand the expression 'stand pat' and don't like it."

Bourbon is used in a similar sense. The term refers to the Bourbons, a royal family that ruled France most of the time from 1589 to 1848. In 1796 a French naval officer named Charles Louis Etienne said of the Bourbons that "They have learned nothing and forgotten nothing." M. Schele de Vere wrote in 1871: "We find the name of the royal Bourbons applied now politically to any old-fashioned party which acts unmindful of past experience." The term was defined in 1884 as "A Democrat behind the age and unteachable."

Who coined *benevolent assimilation?*

Benevolent assimilation was used by William McKinley (1843-1901) to describe the American policy in taking over the Philippines from Spain in 1898. On December 21 of that year President McKinley sent through Secretary of War Russell Alger a letter of instructions to General Harrison Gray Otis in which he said:

Finally, it should be the earnest and paramount aim of the military administration to win the confidence, respect, and affection of the inhabitants of the Philippines by assuring to them in every possible way that full measure of individual rights and liberties which is the heritage of free peoples, and by proving to them that the mission of the United States is one of *benevolent assimilation,* substituting the mild sway of justice and right for arbitrary rule.

Olcott, in his life of McKinley (1916) quotes the President as saying in 1898 to a delegation of Methodist ministers:

When I realized that the Philippines had dropped into our laps I confess that I did not know what to do with them. I sought counsel from all sides—Democrats as well as Republicans—but got little help. I thought first that we would take only Manila; then other islands, perhaps, also. I walked the floor of the White House night after night until midnight; and I am not ashamed to tell you, gentlemen, that I went down on my knees and prayed Almighty God for light and guidance more than one night. And one night late it came to me this way— I don't know how it was, but it came; (1) That we could not give them back to Spain—that would be cowardly and dishonorable; (2) that we could not turn them over to France or Germany—our commercial rivals in the Orient—that would be bad business and discreditable; (3) that we could not leave them to themselves—they were unfit for self-government—and they would soon have anarchy and misrule over there worse than Spain's was; and (4) that there was nothing else left for us to do but to take them all, and to educate the Filipinos, and uplift and civilize and Christianize them and by God's grace do the very best we could by them, as our fellow-men for whom Christ also died. And then I went to bed, and went to sleep, and slept soundly, and the next morning I sent for the chief engineer of the War Department (our map-maker), and I told him to put the Philippines on the map of the United States (pointing to a large map on the wall of his office), and there they are, and there they will stay while I am President.

In his instructions to the peace commissioners in 1898 President McKinley said: "Be magnanimous, the true glory and enduring interests of our country would best be served by an example of moderation, restraint and reason."

McKinley was noted for his pleasing personality, natural kindliness, and cordial handshake. His favorite flower was the red carnation. It is said that many a disgruntled politician who entered his office angry and frowning came out with a smile on his face and a red carnation in his coat lapel. The Ohio legislature chose the red carnation as the State floral emblem because it was the favorite flower of "a beloved and devoted citizen of Ohio." McKinley was born on January 29 and members of Congress from Ohio observe his birthday each year by wearing red carnations.

The name of McKinley is linked with that of Marcus Alonzo Hanna (1837-1904), Ohio capitalist and politician, who made a fortune as a wholesale grocer and coal operator, and who came to be known as the "Republican Warwick" and the "President-maker." Hanna was largely instrumental in making it possible for McKinley to be elected Governor twice and President of the United States twice. Except for a year, when his seat was successfully contested, McKinley served in Congress from 1877 until 1891, when he was gerrymandered out. Hanna was grooming him for the Presidential race as early as 1888. Four years later President Harrison stood in the way and Hanna had to hold back his candidate. McKinley endorsed notes for a friend and when the friend failed in 1893 McKinley, then Governor of Ohio, became liable for $130,000, which was more than the combined assets of him and his wife. Hanna, who could not afford to let his Presidential candidate go through bank-ruptcy proceedings, came to the rescue and chipped in with other friends of McKinley to extricate the Governor from this financial difficulty.

The President-maker himself paid from his own pocket most of the cost—nearly $100,000—of the preconvention campaign in 1896. "Elect McKinley, the Advance Agent of Prosperity" was the slogan used by Hanna in the campaign that followed. The sponsor of the McKinley Tariff Act of 1890 was known as "The Napoleon of Protection," and the

Republicans urged the people to vote for "McKinley, Protection and Prosperity." To finance the campaign Hanna levied upon individuals and corporations that had benefited by the tariff and other protective laws. His theory was that those who had fattened on the tariff should give up part of their gains to support the campaign of their benefactors. In 1888 John P. Forster, president of the League of Young Republican Clubs, wrote a letter in which he suggested "to fry the fat" out of the manufacturers to get campaign funds, and in 1896 Hanna was called "the fat-fryer," because of his "fat-frying methods" of raising money. Hanna's enemies pictured him as a coarse, ruthless businessman in politics. Homer Davenport portrayed the President-maker in a famous cartoon with his clothes dotted with dollar signs. Later Davenport came to think better of Hanna and apologized to him for the cartoon, which had wounded his sensibilities. While William Jennings Bryan toured the country making speeches and greeting vast crowds, McKinley remained at home in Canton and conducted a "front-porch campaign." Although Bryan made silver the issue, McKinley soft-pedaled the money question. In its issue of May 13, 1896, the New York *Sun* quoted Speaker Thomas B. Reed as saying: "McKinley isn't a gold-bug, McKinley isn't a silver-bug, McKinley's a straddle-bug."

McKinley wanted Hanna in his Cabinet, but Hanna insisted on going to the Senate, where there was no vacancy. McKinley, therefore, kicked Senator John Sherman upstairs by putting pressure on him to become Secretary of State to provide a place in the Senate for Hanna.

In his inaugural address on March 4, 1897, President McKinley said: "We want no war of conquest. . . . War should never be entered upon until every agency of peace has failed." But the country wanted war and got it.

Neither McKinley nor Hanna wanted Governor Theodore Roosevelt as the President's running mate in 1900. But Senator Thomas C. Platt, the "Easy Boss" of New York, wanted the Governor nominated for Vice President to get him out of State politics. Platt said that the Vice Presidency would be a good place to put the "young man" and that "he will do less damage there than any other place we could put him." Because he sensed that certain politicians were trying to shelve him politically, Roosevelt at first shied away from the Vice-Presidential nomination. McKinley is reputed to have said that Roosevelt was "a smart aleck, a rough and uncouth person." Senator Matthew S. Quay of Pennsylvania joined forces with Platt in forcing McKinley and Hanna to accept Roosevelt, who was a delegate to the convention at Philadelphia in 1900 and nominated for Vice President on the first ballot. He received every vote except his own. Had Roosevelt not voted against himself both McKinley and he would have been nominated unanimously on the first ballots. Four years later he was nominated unanimously for President.

On January 30, 1900, Governor-elect William Goebel of Kentucky was mortally wounded by an assassin's bullet and died February 3, after being sworn into office on his deathbed. In its issue of February 4, 1901, the New York *Journal* printed the followings lines by Ambrose Bierce:

> The bullet that pierced Goebel's breast
> Cannot be found in all the West;
> Good reason; it is speeding here
> To stretch McKinley on his bier.

President McKinley was shot at Buffalo on September 6, 1901, and died September 14. Both Bierce, the author of the quatrain, and William Randolph Hearst, publisher of the newspaper that printed it, were accused by many people of having instigated the assassination of President McKinley. On the train that carried McKinley's body from Buffalo to Canton, Senator Hanna, who had been reluctant to accept Roosevelt for Vice President in 1900, said to a friend, "Now look, that damned cowboy is President of the United States."

On election night in 1900 Hanna said: "The Republicans have received a clear mandate to govern the country in the interests of business expansion." After McKinley's death the President-maker was believed to have his eye on the Presidency for himself, but he never openly committed himself to entering the lists against Teddy for the nomination in 1904, and he died four months before the convention met.

When was the "full dinner pail" slogan used?

"The full dinner pail" figured prominently in two different Presidential campaigns. Formerly, when the midday meal was generally called dinner, workingmen, like schoolchildren, carried their lunch in small tin pails. As early as 1894 William Hope "Coin" Harvey, crusader for bimetalism, used "the full dinner pail" as a symbol of prosperity in his *Professor Coin's Financial School*. In 1896 William Jennings Bryan advocated free silver and William McKinley advocated the gold standard, but the Republican candidate soft-pedaled the money issue and insisted that restoration of the Republican protective tariff would mean "a full dinner pail" for every workingman. During the last six weeks of the campaign "a full dinner pail" was used as a Republican slogan.

Comparatively good times continued during the next four years, and in 1900 the Republicans adopted "Four More Years of the Full Dinner Pail" as their slogan. This second McKinley-Bryan campaign was a tame affair compared to the one four years earlier between the same two candidates. A picture of a large dinner pail bearing the legend "Four More Years of the Full Dinner Pail" was printed during the campaign in the comic magazine *Judge*. This picture was reprinted and widely circulated by the Republicans and is the basis for the common statement that the slogan was invented either by Victor Gillam, the cartoonist, or Grant Hamilton, the editor of the magazine. The cartoon bears Gillam's signature. Republicans paraded in industrial centers with large dinner pails to emphasize the prosperity of McKinley's first term and to appeal to the labor vote. In *Folkways* William Graham Sumner wrote: "Catchwords are actually adapted to stimulate desires. In the Presidential campaign of 1900 we see a catchword deliberately invented—*the full dinner pail*. Such an invention turns suggestion into an art."

Who was Sockless Jerry Simpson?

"Sockless Jerry" was the nickname of Jeremiah Simpson (1842-1905), a Populist member of the U.S. House of Representatives for three terms between 1891 and 1899. He was born on Prince Edward Island, Canada, and was taken to the United States by his parents when he was a boy. After serving as a seaman on the Great Lakes for many years and as a private in the Union army for three months, he settled in Kansas in 1879 as a farmer and stock raiser. Owing to a severe winter that killed his cattle and to "hard times" he went broke and became interested in politics. He was twice an unsuccessful candidate for the State legislature. Although Simpson had little formal education, he was well read, clever, witty and able. In his first race for Congress he ridiculed his opponent as a man of means who wore "silk socks." A newspaper reporter twisted this into a statement to the effect that Simpson himself wore no socks at all. The result was that the candidate was ever after known as "Sockless Jerry." Needless to say, he wore socks and dressed as other men in similar circumstances.

In Congress Sockless Jerry favored free silver, fiat money and other "agrarian measures" and opposed imperialism and military expansion. He introduced a few bills and seldom spoke on the floor, but was feared and respected by his colleagues for his pointed questions and salty comments. He was a single-taxer and on one occasion he and several colleagues had the full text of Henry George's *Progress and Poverty* read into the *Congressional Record*. Speaker Thomas B. Reed visited Kansas and told Sockless Jerry's Congressional district that for four years past "it had been represented by chaos." On the floor of the House Simpson referred to Reed as "a political cannibal autocrat." The Speaker is reported to have observed to a friend: "Tom and Jerry may mix in a bar-room, but not in the House of Representatives."

Did Hoover predict grass would grow in the streets?

There is a common notion that Herbert Hoover, while Republican candidate for re-election to the Presidency in 1932, predicted that the grass would grow in the streets of American cities if he was defeated and the national administration placed in the hands of the Democrats. That is a distortion of what President Hoover actually said. In an address at Madison Square Garden in New York City on October 31, 1932, on the eve of the election, he declared: "Whole towns, communities and forms of agriculture with their homes, schools and churches have been built up under this system of protection. The grass will grow in the streets of a hundred cities, a thousand towns; the weeds will overrun millions of farms if that protection is taken away."

The protective tariff laws to which Hoover referred were not repealed by the succeeding administration.

Hoover's figure of speech had been used more than a century earlier in reference to the "Tariff of Abominations," enacted in 1828. On October 1, 1831, Philip Hone rode out from Schenectady to see two ships launched on the Mohawk River, and that evening wrote in his diary: "The sight was beautiful—two ships at the same time and from the same yard, a strange accomplishment of the prediction of the anti-tariff men who prophesied that about these times the grass would be growing in our streets, and our vessels be rotting at the wharves." In the May 15, 1861, issue of the Richmond (Virginia) *Daily Examiner* Edward A. Pollard said that the North was so dependent upon the South economically that if the South should secede from the Union grass would grow on the streets of the chief Northern cities. In his "cross of gold" speech, delivered on July 8, 1896, in the Democratic National Convention at Chicago, William Jennings Bryan said:

You come to us and tell us that the great cities are in favor of the gold standard. We reply that the great cities rest upon our broad and fertile prairies. Burn down your cities and leave our farms, and your cities will spring up again as if by magic; but destroy our farms, and the grass will grow in the streets of every city in the country.

How many Vice Presidents have been re-elected?

Of the thirty-five men who were Vice President from 1789 to 1951, only six were re-elected to succeed themselves in that office and served more than four years. They were John Adams, George Clinton, Daniel D. Tompkins, John C. Calhoun, Thomas Marshall and John N. Garner. Both the Vice Presidents elected with James Madison—George Clinton and Elbridge Gerry—died in office. Only two Vice Presidents—Tompkins and Marshall—served two full terms of eight years, and no Vice President served more than two terms. The first term of Adams was curtailed nearly two months by the delay in organizing the Federal Government; Clinton died during his second term; Calhoun resigned during his second term, and Garner's first term was shortened about six weeks by operation of the so-called Lame-Duck Amendment. The six Vice Presidents who succeeded to the Presidency—John Tyler, Millard Fillmore, Andrew Johnson, Chester A. Arthur, Theodore Roosevelt, Calvin Coolidge and Harry S. Truman—were all first-termers in the Vice Presidency, and only three of them—Theodore Roosevelt, Coolidge and Truman—were elected to succeed themselves in the Presidency. When Marshall was re-elected in 1916 he was the first Vice President to be chosen to succeed himself in eighty-eight years. Between Calhoun, who was elected to succeed himself in 1828, and Marshall, not a single Vice President was elected for a second term, and after Marshall only Garner served a second term.

All the Vice Presidents who were re-elected served consecutive terms. None of them has returned to the Vice Presidency after retiring from the office. Adlai Ewing Stevenson of Illinois, who was Vice President under Cleveland from 1893 to 1897, ran again for Vice President on the Bryan ticket in 1900, and Charles Warren Fairbanks, who was Vice President under Theodore Roosevelt from 1905 to 1909, ran for Vice President again on the Hughes ticket in 1916, but they were both defeated. Fairbanks was a cold and reserved conservative and was known as "Icebanks."

What was the Australian ballot?

Australian ballot is applied to the modern system of secret voting in political elections because its essential features were first introduced in 1858 in South Australia. When the system was introduced into the United States it was often referred to as "Kangaroo voting."

Although voting by ballot had been introduced in Massachusetts,

Connecticut and Pennsylvania before 1770, voting by viva voce continued in most of the other Colonies and States until after the Revolution. In the early days there was no secrecy in voting, and ballots were provided by the candidates, the political parties or even by the voters themselves. George F. Hoar, in *Autobiography of Seventy Years* (1903), wrote:

David Henshaw in 1829 fought through to the State supreme court a suit which resulted in securing legal recognition for the printed ballot, the first step toward uniform ballots, and from 1849 Amasa Walker led a campaign for the adoption of the secret-ballot. The secret-ballot law eventually enacted by a liberal legislature was repealed by the Whigs in 1853 on the ground that it "insulted the manliness and independence of the laboring men."

The Australian ballot had a fourfold purpose: to insure absolute secrecy, to protect the voter from outside influence while voting, to facilitate counting the ballots, and to prevent dishonesty in tabulating them. These ends were accomplished to a large extent by giving each voter a separate ballot and compelling him to go alone into a booth where he indicated his choice by making a mark opposite the names of those candidates whom he preferred. The ballot was then folded and dropped into a locked box that was not opened until the ballots were counted by official committees on which members of all parties were represented. Under this system, for the first time the names of all candidates appeared on the same ballot, which was strictly official, being compiled, printed and distributed at the polls under the direction of public officials at public expense.

A system of voting modeled after that used in South Australia was adopted in England in 1872. Shortly thereafter Henry George, economist and founder of the single-tax movement, began to advocate adoption of the Australian ballot in the United States. Charles Allen Thorndike Rice, editor of the *North American Review,* began an active campaign for ballot reform in 1886. Kangaroo voting was first employed in local elections in Louisville, Kentucky, in 1888, and in the same year Massachusetts adopted it for all State elections beginning the next year. The Australian system of secret voting in one form or other was gradually adopted in every State in the Union, although it was not adopted by South Carolina until the election of 1950. Since voting, even for Federal officials, is largely a State matter, even under the Australian system the ballots are printed according to State laws and are not the same in the different States. Voting machines preserve the essential feature of the Australian ballot.

No State in the Union had adopted compulsory voting. In Australia, the home of Kangaroo voting, failure of any person over twenty-one to vote is punishable by a five-dollar fine.

Who was Fighting Joe Wheeler?

Joseph Wheeler (1836-1906), famous Confederate cavalry officer, was known as "Fighting Joe." He fought in six hundred battles and skirmishes, had sixteen horses shot under him, was severely wounded three times, and was a lieutenant general at twenty-seven. Fighting Joe, a native of Georgia and a West Pointer, weighed only about one hundred pounds and was proportionately small. After the Civil War he farmed and practiced law in Alabama, and was a Congressman from 1881 to 1900. Made a major general of volunteers during the Spanish-American War, he was chief cavalry commander in Cuba and commanded a cavalry brigade briefly in the Philippines. Owing to illness he went into the Battle of Santiago in an ambulance, but, when things were going wrong, he got out, mounted a horse and led a charge up San Juan Hill. According to an apocryphal story, when the Spaniards retreated, Fighting Joe, still a Confederate at heart, forgot in the excitement what war he was fighting in and shouted, "See those damned Yankees run." The Confederate cavalry commander, who had served in the United States Army both before and after the Civil War, died as a retired regular brigadier general and was buried in Arlington National Cemetery.

Who was Czar Reed?

Thomas Brackett Reed (1839-1902), known as "Czar Reed," is one of the few political leaders who made a lasting national reputation almost solely by virtue of membership in the U.S. House of Representatives. He was born in Portland, Maine, lived there all his life and was buried there. After graduating from Bowdoin College, he became a lawyer, and served successively as a member of the State house and senate, State attorney general, attorney general and city solicitor.

Reed was a member of Congress from 1877 to 1899 and was Speaker from 1889 to 1891 and from 1895 to 1899. He was six feet three inches tall, weighed three hundred pounds, wore number twelve shoes, had a disproportionately long face, and gave the impression of being bigger even than he was. In Congress he soon became noted for his parliamentary skill, dictatorial methods, confirmed conservatism and salty speech. During his first Congress his quick repartee and biting sarcasm won him the epithet of "the Terrible Turk." In 1889 Reed defeated William

McKinley for the Republican nomination for Speaker by two votes and was chosen by the House by a narrow margin.

Early Speakers, except perhaps Henry Clay, were mere moderators and had little political power. Not until after the Civil War did Speakers begin to use their office for party leadership. John G. Carlisle, Kentucky Democrat, who was Speaker from 1883 to 1889, made many partisan rulings, but he was generally considered a fair and impartial presiding officer. But business in the House had been virtually stymied for years by continual filibusters, in which Reed himself had taken part, and when he became Speaker he determined to put a stop to dilatory procedure and to make himself master of the House in the bargain.

Under the Constitution the House can compel attendance of members for quorum purposes. Minorities were in the habit of nullifying this power by "constructive absence," that is, by refusing to answer roll calls when present. Reed put a stop to this practice simply by including in the count members present but not voting. At that time the Russian Czar was the most conspicuous autocrat in the world and the term was often applied in America to any person who exercised arbitrary power. While Carlisle was still Speaker a newspaper, referring to the tying up of the business of the House by one member's insisting upon a strict enforcement of the rules, asserted that "a single member on the floor might play the role of Czar as successfully as the Speaker." When Reed first began to "count a quorum" on January 29, 1890, the Democrats howled their disapproval and called him czar, tyrant and despot. Senator John T. Morgan of Alabama soon after dubbed him "the White Czar" and the epithet stuck. Cartoonists began to picture him as the Czar of All the Russias with a scepter in his hand and a crown on his head. His vast bulk and brusque manner contributed to the popularity of the nickname.

Czar Reed wrote and got adopted a set of rules giving him more power than any other Speaker had ever possessed. Under "Reed's Rules," as they were called, the Speaker was chairman of the Rules Committee. He appointed all committees and referred bills to whatever committee he chose. A Speaker has the important power of recognition, known as "the Speaker's eye." Formerly Speakers had generally tried to recognize the first member who addressed the chair, unless directed by the rules to prefer certain chairmen or members of a committee in charge of bills, but Reed had a flexible and convenient Speaker's eye and recognized whomever he pleased. Nonetheless the Czar of the House got its business done promptly and efficiently. When the Democrats regained control of the House in 1891 they did not carry out their promise to abolish

"Reedism." Instead they adopted Reed's Rules in substance if not in form. Under the two terms of Speaker Charles F. Crisp they restored even the most objectionable parts of Reed's Rules that they at first omitted. When Reed became Speaker again in 1895 his rules were firmly established. Filibustering in the House had been all but eliminated and Reed said, "Thank God, the House is no longer the greatest deliberative body in the world." Representative Lafayette ("Lafe") Pence, Colorado Populist and Silver Democrat, referred to Reed as "the mentor of the Republicans and the tormentor of the Democrats." But even some Republicans groaned under his yoke. One of them said he sat up there in the Speaker's chair with his feet on the neck of the Republican Party.

After so many parliamentary battles Reed and Crisp became personal as well as political enemies. During his first term as Speaker, Reed had held that no member had the right to demand on what ground the Speaker had decided a point of order. Crisp as Speaker turned the tables on Reed as minority leader. When Reed demanded on what ground the Speaker had decided a point of order, Crisp emphatically declined to hear the gentleman from Maine, and when Reed persisted Crisp told him to take his seat and directed the sergeant-at-arms to see that he did so. As the former Speaker resumed his seat under compulsion, David B. Culberson of Texas observed, "See Jumbo go back to his stake!" Reed never forgave Crisp, and when the Democrat's service in the chair was coming to a close, Reed refused to offer the customary resolution of thanks to the outgoing Speaker and even refused to vote for it when it was offered by another Republican.

In 1896 the Presidential bee got under the Czar's crown and he took his candidacy seriously. "They might go further and do worse," was an old political saying. Reed's version of this was, "They might do worse, and probably will." But he was too cynical and sarcastic to be popular. Mark Hanna, without Reed's knowing what was going on, had a majority of the delegates in the bag for McKinley before the convention opened. "They were for me till the buying started," observed Reed bitterly. Embittered by failure to get the nomination and desirous of providing for his family, he resigned his seat in the House and the prospect of continuing as Speaker.

Reed's reputation for humor became so great that all sorts of smart things he never thought of were attributed to him. He spoke with a nasal drawl and sometimes it was not what he said but the way he said it that made it funny. Many of his saltiest sayings were uttered in or out of the House chamber in private conversation and were not intended for publication. Some of those uttered in the House were in a low voice and heard only by persons close to him. Few of the sayings of Reed are found in the official records of the House.

"The Democratic Party," Reed observed, "is like a man riding backward in a railroad car; it never sees anything until he has got past it." He said of Theodore Roosevelt's trust-busting policy that "An indefinable something is to be done, in a way that nobody knows how, at a time nobody knows when, that will accomplish nobody knows what." To Roosevelt himself he said: "Theodore, if there is one thing more than another for which I admire you, it is your original discovery of the Ten Commandments." On one occasion Speaker Reed wired all absent Republicans to return to Washington at once to vote on an important bill. A member delayed by a flood replied: "Washout on the line; can't get there." By mistake *washout* was printed in the telegram as two words. Reed wired back: "Buy another shirt and come on." He opposed American imperialism and the war against Spain. After the acquisition of the Philippines he observed: "We have bought two million Malays at two dollars a head unpicked, and nobody knows what it will cost to pick 'em." Another of his observations was, "One, with God, is always a majority, but many a martyr has been burned at the stake while the votes were being counted." He thought, "One of the greatest delusions in the world is the hope that the evils of the world can be cured by legislation. I am happy in the belief that the solution of the great difficulties of life and government are in better hands even than those of Congress."

The portrait of every Speaker is painted at Government expense and placed in the Speaker's Lobby adjoining the House chamber in the Capitol. That of Reed was painted in 1891 by John S. Sargent and was not considered one of the artist's best. When Reed first saw it he exclaimed: "My God, now all my enemies are revenged!"

When were primary elections first held?

Primary is from Latin *primus,* "first," and in the sense of a method of nominating candidates for public office by popular vote it is short for *primary election*. Originally all candidates were nominated by party caucuses, assemblies, congresses or conventions. Such gatherings were thought of as "preliminary elections," and outside of New England any meeting to nominate candidates, or delegates to a larger meeting, was called a *primary* meeting.

Senator Thomas H. Benton of Missouri was one of the first important political leaders to insist that the convention method of nominating candidates was undemocratic and dangerous. In *Thirty Years View*

[342]

(1854) he wrote, "I am for the people to select, as well as elect, their candidates." Crawford County, Pennsylvania, adopted a system of nominating candidates for local offices by popular vote in 1866, and this system was adopted by other counties in the same State. In 1868 New York and California passed laws giving their counties the option of adopting the "Crawford County System." Many other States, particularly in the South and West, followed suit. In 1898 Robert M. La Follette and his law partner, Robert E. Roe, induced the Wisconsin State Republican Convention to declare in favor of mandatory direct primaries. Wisconsin adopted the first mandatory primaries in 1903, and two years later extended the system to include the choice of delegates to national conventions for nominating Presidential candidates. In 1948 complete or partial primaries had been adopted in forty-five States, and only Connecticut, Rhode Island and Delaware chose all candidates by party conventions.

Primaries in the States have bewildering variations. In some States candidates "file" by petition; in others, by a simple declaration and payment of a fee. Although generally the high man wins, in some Southern primaries a clear majority is required and a second or "run-off" primary is held to decide between the two highest in the first primary. In a closed primary, voting is restricted to a single party; in an open primary all parties may take part. A nonpartisan primary is one in which no party designations or symbols occur on the ballots. A preferential primary gives the voters first and second choices. Under the California primary system candidates may "cross-file"; that is, they may have their names on the tickets of all parties, but they cannot be candidates of other parties unless they win the nominations of their own. In some States cross-filing is specifically forbidden by law. In so-called "one-party" States nomination is equivalent to election. In some States primaries are not required for minor parties; in others primary selections must be confirmed by conventions.

At first primaries were regarded as only local and State party affairs and not subject to interference, regulation or control by the Federal Government, even when Presidential and Congressional nominees were involved. In process of time, however, primaries came to be handled very much like regular elections and they became a recognized part of the election machinery. In 1921 the Supreme Court held that the Corrupt Practices Act of 1910 did not affect the selection of a candidate by a party. The theory was that no Constitutional provision authorized the Federal Government to interfere in the affairs of a political party. But in the Classic Case in 1941 the Supreme Court started a trend in the other direction by holding that "the authority of Congress includes the authority to regulate primary elections when they are a step in the exercise of the people of their choice of representatives in Congress."

Who said: "God hates a quitter"?

Joseph Homan Manley (1842-1905), Maine lawyer, journalist and politician, who was chairman of the Republican National Committee from 1896 to 1905, went to the St. Louis convention in 1896 as the leading backer of Speaker Thomas B. Reed for the Presidential nomination. Although many of Reed's supporters wanted to make a last-ditch fight, his candidacy collapsed after June 10, when Manley, sensing that Mark Hanna had the convention sewed up for McKinley, announced on his own responsibility that in his opinion McKinley would win on the first ballot. General Samuel Fessenden (1847-1908) of the Connecticut delegation after learning of Manley's statement met him in a hotel corridor and said to him: "Joe, God Almighty hates a quitter. I have been a soldier in actual war, and am a faithful soldier of Reed now, but my general has deserted." "God hates a quitter" is often attributed erroneously to Reed himself.

What was embalmed beef?

The most notorious scandal connected with the Spanish-American War involved canned meat sold by packinghouses to the Government. Much of the meat was found to be spoiled when the cans were opened in the field and some of it was so putrid that it made the soldiers sick. Colonel Theodore Roosevelt said one-tenth of the meat bought by the War Department was unfit to eat. General Nelson A. Miles, who probably picked up the phrase from the army, called it "embalmed beef" because it was supposed to have been treated with chemical preservatives. There was considerable public clamor against the so-called Beef Trust. Secretary of War Russell A. Alger became the whipping boy and was threatened with impeachment. Although an investigation whitewashed him, criticism of the embalmed beef and other scandals forced his retirement from the department on August 1, 1899. Commissary Charles P. Eagan, who called General Miles a liar, was court-martialed, convicted and sentenced to dismissal from the service, but President McKinley commuted the sentence to a suspension of six years.

In its report of May 7, 1899, the War Investigation Commission asserted that the charge that the packers had treated the meat with chemical preservatives was not established, that the spoilage was due to tropical weather and damage to containers in transportation, and that the quality of the meat sold to the Government was the same as that sold to the public. But excitement was so intense that the report was received as a whitewashing document. Widespread charges of graft by Government officials and private contractors, though generally believed at the time, were never proved before a competent tribunal.

Who compared McKinley's backbone to a chocolate eclair?

"It's a pity that President McKinley has no more backbone than a chocolate eclair" is popularly attributed to both Theodore Roosevelt and Thomas B. Reed, but there is no evidence that either ever said it. Louise Lamprey of New York, a former Washington newspaperwoman, said in 1949 that she first used this crack about President McKinley in an article published in 1897 in the *Capital Times,* a Washington weekly. Roosevelt, then Assistant Secretary of the Navy, favored, and Reed, then Speaker of the House, opposed the war with Spain, while President McKinley was at heart against it but permitted himself to be pushed into it by the jingoes. Roosevelt thought McKinley should have the backbone to fight while Reed thought the President should have the backbone not to fight.

Who said: "Speak softly and carry a big stick"?

This saying was popularized by Theodore Roosevelt, who quoted the adage as early as 1900, when he was Governor of New York. On January 26 of that year he wrote Henry L. Sprague: "I have always been fond of the West African proverb: 'Speak softly and carry a big stick, you will go far.'" Governor Roosevelt on that occasion expressed his attitude toward the Republican political machine in the Empire State.

Speak softly is an old English phrase. Shakespeare used *speak softly* twice and *tread softly* once. The "West African" proverb quoted by Roosevelt was probably originally an allusion to hunting and fighting in the jungle and was equivalent to "Tread softly and carry a big club." The saying embodies some of the idea expressed in the Biblical "A soft answer turneth away wrath" (Proverbs 15:1), the French "A cudgel carries peace," and the Hindu "A man without a stick will be bitten even by sheep." Roosevelt never believed in what he called "broomstick preparedness."

On September 2, 1901, four days before President McKinley was shot at Buffalo and twelve days before his death, Vice President Roosevelt said in an address at the Minnesota State Fair: "There is a homely old adage which runs, 'Speak softly and carry a big stick. You will go far.' If the American nation will speak softly and yet build and keep at a pitch of the highest training a thoroughly efficient navy, the Monroe Doctrine will go far."

Later *The Big Stick* became a sort of slogan to describe his strong foreign policy and his advocacy of military and naval preparedness. In an address at Chicago on April 2, 1903, President Roosevelt explained what he meant by the saying:

Boasting and blustering are as objectionable among nations as among individuals, and the public men of a great nation owe it to their sense of national self-respect to speak courteously of foreign powers, just as a brave and self-respecting man treats all around him courteously. But though to boast is bad, and causelessly to insult another, worse, yet worse than all is to be guilty of boasting, even without insult, and when called to the proof to be unable to make such boasting good. There is a homely old adage which runs: "Speak softly and carry a big stick, you will go far." If the American Nation will speak softly, and yet build, and keep at a pitch of the highest training, a thoroughly efficient navy, the Monroe Doctrine will go far.

William R. Thayer in *Theodore Roosevelt* gives the saying as "Speak softly, *but* carry a big stick," and says regarding it: "More than once in his later years he quoted this to me, adding that it was precisely because this or that power knew that he carried a big stick that he was enabled to speak softly with effect." In his life of Theodore Roosevelt, J. B. Bishop quoted Roosevelt as saying, "Don't hit at all if it is honorably possible to avoid hitting, but never hit soft."

What was the Ananias Club?

Ananias came to mean *liar* because, according to Acts 5, an early Christian named Ananias lied about the price he got for a piece of land. In 1906 Washington correspondents applied *Ananias Club* to all those critics of President Theodore Roosevelt whom he had branded as liars. Roosevelt was not the first to use the phrase, and it is not known who did. Membership in the mythical club included Senator Benjamin R. Tillman, Edward H. Harriman, many newspapermen and other prominent persons. A newspaper reporter at the time said the Ananias Club had a long "waiting list." Some of the reporters charged that the President was in the habit of making statements as "trial balloons" and then, if they proved unpopular, of calling those who reported them liars. In *My*

Quarter Century of American Politics (1920) Champ Clark wrote: "Roosevelt believed in calling a spade a spade. The word 'liar' was familiar to his tongue, and he founded the Ananias Club, chose its members and thrust them in."

What was the Brownsville Riot?

On the night of August 13-14, 1906, a dozen or so members of a colored battalion of the Twenty-Fifth Infantry Regiment, enraged because denied admission to saloons, took their rifles from their barracks at Fort Brown, Texas, went on a shooting rampage through Brownsville, killed a bartender, wounded a police officer, damaged some property and terrorized the town for several hours. President Theodore Roosevelt, unable to determine the culprits because the Negro soldiers refused to testify against one another, gave all members of the three colored companies dishonorable discharges.

The incident created a furor in the press and in Congress. Many insisted that the rioters had extenuating provocation for their violence and that the President was unjust in punishing 250 men for what fewer than fifteen had done. Senator Joseph B. Foraker of Ohio got the Senate to pass a resolution to investigate, which infuriated Roosevelt and led to a spirited impromptu debate between the Senator and the President at a Gridiron Club dinner in January, 1907. A court of inquiry was created by act of March 3, 1909, but only fourteen of the discharged Negro soldiers were ever reinstated. Foraker's part in the Brownsville affair is supposed to have destroyed what chances he may have had to get the Republican nomination for President in 1908.

Who were the muckrakers?

Muck is trash, manure, dung or dirt; a muckrake is a rake for scraping up muck.

Muckraker has long been used figuratively to denote a person with a morbid interest in foul or scandalous things. This use alludes to a character in John Bunyan's *The Pilgrim's Progress*. The man with the muck-rake was so intent upon raking up muck that he could not see a celestial crown just over his head. "The Interpreter," wrote Bunyan, "has them first into a room where was a man who could look no way but downwards, with a muck-rake in his hand. . . . The man did neither look up nor regard, but raked to himself the straws, the small sticks, and dust of the floor."

[347]

Theodore Roosevelt gave *muckrake* a new meaning by applying the term—perhaps unfairly—to a school of writers who soon after the turn of the century investigated and exposed graft and corruption in public office and private business. In an address at the laying of the cornerstone of the first House Office Building in Washington on April 14, 1906, President Roosevelt said:

In Bunyan's Pilgrim's Progress you may recall the description of the Man with the Muckrake, the man who could look no way but downward with the muckrake in his hand; who was offered a celestial crown for his muckrake but who could neither look up nor regard the crown he was offered but continued to rake to himself the filth of the floor. Muckraking leads to a slander that may attack an honest man or even assail a bad man with untruth. An epidemic of indiscriminate assault upon character does no good but very great harm. Muckraking is as bad as whitewashing. . . . The men with the muckrake are often indispensable to the well-being of society; but only if they know when to stop raking the muck, and to look upward to the celestial crown above them, to the crown of worthy endeavor. There are beautiful things above and round about them; and if they gradually grow to feel that the whole world is nothing but muck, their power of usefulness is gone.

Theodore Roosevelt did not mention by name any of the *muckrakers* he had in mind; but it was an open secret that he alluded to such writers as Ida M. Tarbell, Upton Sinclair, Lincoln Steffens, Ray Stannard Baker, Norman Hapgood, Mark Sullivan, Thomas W. Lawson, Samuel Hopkins Adams, Henry Demarest Lloyd, Leroy Scott, Fremont Older and David G. Phillip. Although these writers were known as "the muckrakers," they were actually public-spirited journalists and writers who investigated and exposed graft, corruption, dishonesty and abuses with a view of effecting civil, social and moral reforms. Most of them accepted the name the President gave them and gloried in it. There is a tendency now to apply *muckraker,* not to zealous and honest reformers, but to sensational journalists who habitually dig up "dirt" and publish it merely because "it makes a good and saleable story."

What President was nearly blind in one eye?

Theodore Roosevelt (1858-1919) virtually lost the sight of one eye because of a blow he received while boxing in the White House. This fact was not made known to the public until about a year before his death. In his *Autobiography* (1919) Roosevelt wrote:

While President I used to box with some of the aides, as well as play singlestick with General Wood. After a few years I had to abandon boxing as well as wrestling, for in one bout a young captain of artillery cross-countered me on the eye and the blow smashed the little bloodvessels. Fortunately it was the left eye, but the sight has been dim ever since, and if it had been the right eye I should have been entirely unable to shoot.

Who coined *malefactors of great wealth?*

On August 20, 1907, Theodore Roosevelt made a speech at the laying of the cornerstone of the Cape Cod Pilgrim Memorial Monument at Provincetown, Massachusetts. At the time the stock market was shaky and general financial conditions were bad. Many conservative businessmen charged that the "panic" was the result of the President's antitrust policies. In the Provincetown speech Teddy countered with the charge that certain businessmen had themselves encouraged the depression to force the administration to relax its campaign against corporations. One long, clumsy, dangling sentence was as follows:

Most of it I believe to be due to matters not particularly confined to the United States and to matters wholly unconnected with any Government action, but it may well be that the determination of the Government, in which, gentlemen, it will not waver, to punish certain *malefactors of great wealth,* has been responsible for something of the troubles, at least to the extent of having caused these men to combine to bring about as much financial stress as they possibly can, in order to discredit the policy of the Government and thereby secure a reversal of that policy so that they may enjoy the fruits of their own evildoing.

Malefactors of great wealth was picked up and given wide circulation by newspapers as being characteristic of T.R.'s antagonistic attitude toward "big business."

Who was a combination of St. Paul and St. Vitus?

John Morley, British statesman and author, is reputed to have said, after talking with Theodore Roosevelt about 1900, that "He seems to be an interesting combination of St. Paul and St. Vitus." He alluded to Teddy's extraordinary mental and physical activity.

What was the Tennis Cabinet?

The Tennis Cabinet was a group of President Theodore Roosevelt's friends and advisers who played tennis on the White House grounds or took other forms of physical exercise with him. The President was reputed to be influenced more by the Tennis Cabinet than by the regular

Cabinet. Roosevelt afterward referred to "The men with whom I then played, whom we laughingly grew to call the *Tennis Cabinet*," which "was an elastic term." Among the members of the Tennis Cabinet were Major Generals Leonard Wood and Thomas H. Barry; Surgeon General Presley Marion Rixey of the Navy; Secretary of the Interior James R. Garfield; Gifford Pinchot, Chief of the Forest Service, and Robert Bacon, who became Secretary of State during the last months of the administration. Three days before his term expired the available members of the Tennis Cabinet lunched with the President at the White House and presented him a bronze cougar as a parting gift. In his *Autobiography* (1919) Roosevelt wrote:

While in the White House I always tried to get a couple of hours' exercise in the afternoons—sometimes tennis, more often riding, or else a rough cross-country walk. . . . My companions at tennis or on these rides and walks we gradually grew to style the Tennis Cabinet; and then we extended the term to take in many of my old-time Western friends. . . . Often, especially in the winters or early spring, we would arrange for a point to point walk, not turning aside for anything—for instance, swimming Rock Creek, or even the Potomac if it came in our way. Of course under such circumstances we had to arrange that our return to Washington should be when it was dark, so that our appearance might scandalize no one. . . . If we swam the Potomac, we usually took off our clothes. I remember one such occasion when the French Ambassador, Jusserand, who was a member of the Tennis Cabinet, was along, and, just about as we were to get in to swim, somebody said, "Mr. Ambassador, Mr. Ambassador, you haven't taken off your gloves," to which he promptly responded, "I think I will leave them on, we might meet ladies."

President Herbert Hoover had a Medicine-Ball Cabinet. He and a group of officials and friends started every weekday at seven thirty with a medicine-ball game on the White House lawn. The Medicine-Ball Cabinet varied in number from six to eighteen and included Supreme Court justices, Cabinet officers, assistant heads of departments, newspapermen and other friends of the President. But the object was physical exercise and not the transaction of business. Hoover said in his memoirs that he suggested medicine-ball rather than tennis for this purpose because medicine-ball requires less skill than tennis and is faster and more vigorous and provides more exercise in a short time.

After the game [he wrote in 1951] we assembled for a few moments for a fruit juice and coffee. It was no Kitchen Cabinet. By common consent the conversation was kept off official matters and on the light side. The morning-star shells of humor from these trenches often illuminated the dreary no man's land of the depression and started the day with good cheer—even on the last morning of March 4, 1933.

Who was Uncle Joe?

Joseph G. Cannon (1836-1926), one of the few men to make a national and permanent reputation solely by service in the House of Representatives, was universally known as "Uncle Joe" in his latter days.

He was born in North Carolina of Quaker parents and was christened John Joseph Gurney Cannon after a great English Quaker. His wife was a Methodist and he joined her church when he was married. After attending the Cincinnati Law School six months, he finally established himself as a lawyer at Danville, Illinois. He was a State district attorney for seven years, and served in the U.S. House of Representatives forty-six of the fifty years from 1873 to 1923.

As a freshman Congressman, Cannon's countrified appearance and uncouth manners won him the epithet "the Hayseed Member from Illinois." He later became an understudy to Thomas B. Reed, who as Speaker in 1890 made the Hayseed his "lieutenant in parliamentary procedure." Chairman Cannon of the Appropriations Committee, Chairman William McKinley of the Ways and Means Committee, and Speaker Reed were the three Republican members of the Rules Committee and wrote "Reed's Rules," which were based largely on a report made by Cannon to the Rules Committee. In August, 1890, Cannon made a speech on the floor of the House so coarse and in such bad taste that it contributed to his defeat by a Democrat in the fall election. For a time he was ridiculed as "Foul-Mouthed Joe," but he was re-elected to the House two years later.

In 1903 Speaker John B. Henderson of Iowa, who had succeeded Reed in 1899, retired from Congress, and "Uncle Joe" Cannon, as he was beginning to be called, was chosen Speaker. He was then sixty-seven years, six months and three days of age and has been the oldest Speaker at the time he assumed that office except Frederick H. Gillett, who was a month older when he became Speaker in 1919.

Uncle Joe was the political heir of Czar Reed and as Speaker he followed in the footsteps of his old mentor. What had been called "Reedism" came to be called "Cannonism." His rulings from the chair, his committee appointments, his reference of bills to committees and his exercise of the power of recognition were frankly arbitrary and often brazenly partisan. Within a few years he made the Speakership almost as powerful as the Presidency, and Cannonism became a national political issue. No member of the House could get recognition on the floor and no bill had a chance to pass without the previous assent of the Speaker, who rewarded friends and punished foes at pleasure and whose smile and frown made and unmade reputations in Congress. Although his name is linked with no important measure, he steam-rollered bills through the House or smothered them in Committees with tyrannical efficiency. He seemed to enjoy power for its own sake and took delight in exercising it. On one occasion, after putting a question for a voice vote, he said: "The Ayes make the most noise but the Nayes have it." When a constituent asked Representative Nathan W. Hale for a copy of the House rules in 1907, the Tennessean sent him Uncle Joe's picture. "This House," observed Speaker Cannon in the same year, "could pass an elephant if the gentleman in charge of it could catch the Speaker's eye."

Uncle Joe was an aspirant for the Presidential nomination in 1908 but received only fifty-eight votes in the Republican National Convention that nominated William Howard Taft. As early as 1905 William Peters Hepburn, Iowa Republican, launched an attack against the Speaker's arbitrary control of the House, and in 1909 the Democrats under the leadership of Champ Clark made a vain fight to overthrow Cannonism. The wings of the Speaker were finally clipped in a parliamentary battle that began on St. Patrick's Day in 1910. Two days later a coalition of about thirty insurgent Republicans under Representative George W. Norris of Nebraska and the Democrats under Clark got through a resolution enlarging the Rules Committee, depriving the Speaker of the power to appoint its members and making him ineligible to serve on it, but a Democratic resolution declaring the Speakership vacant failed to pass. Speakers had been members of the Rules Committee since 1858 and adoption of the Norris resolution removed much of the Speaker's power.

After "The St. Patrick's Day Revolution" Uncle Joe was still Speaker with the power of recognition, reference of bills and appointing the members of all committees except the Rules Committee, but he saw the handwriting on the wall and played the tyrant no more. The Democrats won control of the House in 1911 and chose Clark Speaker. In 1912 Uncle Joe was defeated for Congress, but in 1914 he was re-elected and served as "the grand old man" of the House until his retirement in 1923 at the age of eighty-seven. He was a plain, blunt man, and a politician from first to last. The tall, cigar-smoking, picturesque Speaker acquired a prodigious reputation for salty sayings, cloakroom stories and homespun philosophy. He said many witty things and had many others attributed to him that he did not say. When he spoke he worked his hands like pumphandles. "If Uncle Joe had to speak standing still and without gestures," Champ Clark wrote, "he would be a complete failure." Despite his highhanded methods as Speaker, he was regarded as incorruptible and was personally liked by nearly all members of the

House. It was said that people loved "the old man" for his "orneryness and general cussedness." During the First World War Uncle Joe made the nation laugh by observing that a modern cavalry officer's only use for spurs was to hold his feet on a desk in Washington.

Was "Champ" Speaker Clark's real first name?

Champ Clark (1850-1921), Speaker of the House in the Sixty-First, Sixty-Second, Sixty-Third and Sixty-Fourth Congresses (1911-1919), was christened James Beauchamp Clark. In *My Quarter Century of American Politics* (1920) he says he performed the surgical operation on his name at the age of twenty-four because his mail was confused with that of another James B. Clark.

> I first lopped off the *James* [he wrote] but that left me with a name which nobody but a Frenchman could pronounce correctly, and Americans pronounced it in a half-dozen different ways, all wrong. I would have liked very much to retain it, as it was my mother's name. It means "fair field" and is a beautiful name, but it could not be pronounced in this country correctly. . . . I cut *Beauchamp* in two in the middle and retained the last half.

How did *throwing the hat in the ring* originate?

Throwing the hat in the ring, in the sense of entering a political campaign or announcing one's candidacy for office, was popularized in 1912 by Theodore Roosevelt. Early in that year the former President was asked to speak at the Ohio Constitutional Convention at Columbus. On February 21, while passing through Cleveland on his way to the State capital, newspaper reporters asked him whether he intended to run for President in the coming campaign.

"My hat's in the ring; the fight is on and I'm stripped to the buff," replied the former President. "You will have my answer Monday."

The phrase came directly from Western sporting slang, with which Roosevelt was familiar. When he was a young man it was customary in the West for a man to volunteer to enter a boxing or wrestling match by throwing his hat into the ring. "Ready to fight at the drop of a hat" alludes to the same practice.

Throwing a hat in the ring is a survival of the old gage of battle. *Webster's New International Dictionary* defines *gage* as "a pledge of a person's appearance to combat, or do battle, in support of his assertions or claims; especially, a glove, *cap,* or the like, cast on the ground to be taken up by the opponent." Contests in the ancient Roman arena were opened by dropping a napkin or handkerchief. In his lives of the Caesars, Suetonius wrote:

So after a trial exhibition in his gardens before his slaves and the dregs of the populace, he [Nero] gave all an opportunity of seeing him in the Circus Maximus, one of his freedmen dropping the napkin from the place usually occupied by the magistrates.

Spanish bullfighters used to toss their hats into the ring upon entering the arena. In *The Sincali; or, An Account of the Gipsies of Spain* (1841) George Borrow refers to a similar custom.

The intended combatants at length arrived; it was necessary to clear the ring, —always a troublesome and difficult task. Thurstall went up to the two Gipsies, with whom he seemed to be acquainted. . . . Then pushing the people aside, he strode to the ropes, over which he bounded into the ring, flinging his Spanish hat high into the air. Gipsy Will,—"The best man in England for twenty pounds!". . . No man would fight the Gipsy—Yes! a strong country fellow wished to win the stakes, and was about to fling in his hat in defiance, but he was prevented by his friends, with "Fool! he'll kill you!"

In *The Fancy* (1820) the English poet John Hamilton Reynolds ("Peter Corcoran") wrote:

> Throw in his hat, and with a spring
> Get gallantly within the ring.

Among the lumberjacks of the Northwest a fight used often to be started by the challenger throwing down his hat, coat or shirt, and "daring" anybody to take it up. A similar custom prevailed among the Cornwall miners, where wrestlers from different mines challenged one another by tossing their hats on the ground. In some parts of England and the United States wrestling matches are arranged by having the contestants throw down their hats, whereupon a blindfolded person shuffles them and hands them out in pairs, the owners thus being paired for a match. In *Tom Brown's School Days* (1856) Thomas Hughes describes the old sport of backsswording or singlestick, which is played with sticks handled like medieval heavy swords. The challengers enter the contest by throwing down their hats. Hughes says: "A tall fellow who is a down shepherd, *chucks his hat on the stage* and climbs up the steps."

When did three Presidents run at the same time?

In 1912 former President Theodore Roosevelt, Progressive; President William Howard Taft, Republican, and future President Woodrow Wilson, Democrat, were all candidates for the Presidency on major party tickets. That has been the only instance when more than two men on the list of Presidents ran in the same election. The three major candidates in 1912 occupied the Presidency from 1901 to 1921.

Why were the Progressives of 1912 called Bull Moosers?

The Progressive Party organized in 1912 by the followers of Theodore Roosevelt was nicknamed the Bull Moose Party from a remark made by the former President when he arrived in Chicago to attend the Republican National Convention. When asked how he felt, Roosevelt replied: "I feel as fit as a bull moose." The banner carried on the convention floor by the California delegation contained the following inscription of unknown authorship:

> I want to be a Bull Moose,
> And with the Bull Moose stand
> With Antlers on my forehead
> And a Big Stick in my hand.

The Republican convention renominated William Howard Taft for President and John S. Sherman for Vice President. "The Progressive Party" was hastily organized and nominated Roosevelt for President and Governor Hiram W. Johnson of California for Vice President. The bull moose was taken up by reporters and cartoonists and soon given a place as the popular emblem of the Progressive Party beside the Republican elephant and the Democratic donkey. *Bull Moose* was applied to the Progressive Party by the New York *Tribune* on June 26 and by the New York *Times* the next day.

On the evening of October 14, 1912, an attempt was made to assassinate Roosevelt in Milwaukee while riding in an automobile from a hotel to the auditorium where he was to speak. After he had received a bullet wound in the breast, the former President, it was reported, said: "It takes more than that to kill a Bull Moose." Roosevelt, an outdoor man, a hunter and an advocate of "the strenuous life," had compared his condition with that of a bull moose before the campaign of 1912. It was a favorite comparison with him. As early as 1894 he had written to Henry Cabot Lodge: "However, except for feeling a little blue, I passed a delightful fortnight, all the time in the open; and feel as rugged as a bull moose." On June 27, 1900, after he had been nominated for Vice President on the McKinley ticket, Roosevelt wrote to Senator Marcus A. Hanna, chairman of the Republican National Committee: "I wish in this campaign to do whatever you think wise—whatever is likely to produce the best results for the Republican ticket. I am strong as a bull moose and you can use me to the limit."

The basis of the Progressive Party that was hurriedly formed in 1912 by the pro-Roosevelt delegates who seceded from the Republican Party was the program of the Republican Progressive League founded in 1911. Its platform—"a covenant with the people"—advocated: election of Senators by the people, woman suffrage, conservation of natural resources, establishment of a department of labor, an eight-hour day, nomination of all officers by direct primaries, the initiative, referendum and recall of State officers, a change in the method of amending the Constitution, publicity on campaign contributions and expenditures, inheritance and income taxes, establishment of a scientific tariff commission, prohibition of child labor, recall of judicial decisions, abolition of injunctions in labor disputes, enactment of corrupt practices acts, appointment of Federal officers on the basis of fitness, the use of business methods in government, strengthening the Interstate Commerce Commission and the antitrust laws, and a dissolution of the "unholy alliance between corrupt business and corrupt politics." It was essentially the "Wisconsin Idea" and a modified and less progressive version of Robert M. La Follette's platform rather than that of Roosevelt, whose great prestige and dynamic personality enabled him to take the leadership of the movement from the Wisconsinite. In one of the most effective speeches in his career Teddy said at a preconvention rally in Chicago on June 17, 1912:

"We fight in honorable fashion for the good of mankind fearless of the future, unheeding of our individual fate, with unflinching hearts and undimmed eyes; we stand at Armageddon, and we battle for the Lord." In the Progressive Convention on August 5, 1912, he said: "To you men who have come together to spend and be spent in the endless crusade against wrong, to you who face the future resolute and confident, to you who strive in a spirit of brotherhood for the betterment of our nation I say now as I said here six weeks ago, we stand at Armageddon and we battle for the Lord."

The Progressive Party of 1912 started as a third party but ended up in the same year as the second party. The electoral and popular vote was Woodrow Wilson, 435—6,296,547; Roosevelt, 88—5,251,227, and Taft, 8—3,456,720. Roosevelt in 1912 received 27.4 per cent of the total vote and was the most formidable threat to the two major parties after the Civil War. The party was first named "The National Progressive Party" but soon became known simply as "The Progressive Party." La Follette himself, really the father of the Progressive Party, was so embittered because he lost the nomination of the new party to Roosevelt, that he supported Wilson. This Progressive Party rapidly petered out after 1912. It elected a few members of Congress in 1914 and Governor Johnson tried vainly to revive it as a national party in 1916. He himself ran and was elected Senator on the Progressive Party ticket. In 1916 the Progressive Party held its convention at Chicago on June 7 and nominated Roosevelt for President and John M. Parker of Louisiana for Vice President. Roosevelt declined the nomination, announced his support of Charles Evans Hughes, the Republican nominee, and advised his followers to do likewise. "The Progressive Party," observed William Allen White, an original Bull Mooser, "is all dressed up in its fighting clothes, with nowhere to go." The Progressive Party's national committee then "endorsed" Hughes, but Parker insisted on running for Vice President on the Progressive ticket, and Hughes and he, as Progressives, received 41,894 popular votes but no electoral votes in Maine, New York, Minnesota, Montana, Indiana, Georgia and Oklahoma, the only States where they were on the ballots.

The earliest use of *Progressive* in a political party name in the United States was in 1887, when a number of delegates who had seceded from the United Labor Party convention at Syracuse, New York, in 1886, formed the Progressive Labor Party, adopted a platform and nominated a candidate for Governor of New York, but most of the 7,000 votes received were cast in New York City. A small group of Midwestern Republicans under the leadership of La Follette and George W. Norris of Nebraska began to refer to themselves as progressive about 1908, when they began to oppose Joseph G. Cannon's re-election as Speaker of the House, although others at that time generally referred to them as "the Insurgents." Conference for Progressive Political Action, which had been organized in 1922, held a convention at Cleveland, Ohio, on July 4, 1924, formed "The Progressive Party" and nominated Robert M. La Follette for President and Senator Burton K. Wheeler of Montana for Vice President. The electoral and popular vote in 1924 was: Calvin Coolidge, 382–15,725,06; John W. Davis, 136–8,386,503, and La Follette, 13–4,822,856. The Progressive Party of 1924 received the electoral votes of only Wisconsin, but in eleven States west of the Mississippi ran second to the Republicans in the popular vote and received 16.6 per cent of the total popular vote in the country. On July 23, 1948, a convention at Philadelphia formed a new party officially styled "The Progressive Party" and nominated Henry A. Wallace for President and Senator Glen Taylor of Idaho for Vice President. The electoral and popular vote of 1948 was: Harry S. Truman, 303—24,105,812; Thomas E. Dewey, 189—21,970,065; James Strom Thurmond, 39—1,169,061, and Wallace, none—1,157,172. The Progressive Party ran fourth and the States' Rights Democratic Party third.

Seven former Vice Presidents have headed separate party movements, but all have failed. They were George Clinton in 1808; John Tyler in 1844; Martin Van Buren in 1848; Millard Fillmore in 1856; John C. Breckinridge in 1860; Theodore Roosevelt in 1912, and Wallace in 1948. Five of them were former Presidents as well as former Vice Presidents.

To what did "watchful waiting" refer?

Many people appear to be under the impression that Woodrow Wilson coined the phrase "watchful waiting" in reference to his policy of neutrality in connection with the war in Europe during his first administration. But "watchful waiting" referred to Mexico, not to Europe. In his annual message to Congress December 2, 1913, President Wilson said of American relations with Mexico: "We shall not, I believe, be obliged to alter our policy of watchful waiting."

What President said he had a single-track mind?

"I have a single-track mind," declared Woodrow Wilson in a speech at the National Press Club of Washington January 9, 1912, when he was Governor of New Jersey and a candidate for the Democratic nomination for President. On September 21, 1910, Wilson wrote George Harvey a letter beginning with the sentence: "Every day I am confirmed in my judgment that my mind is a one-track road, and can run only one train of thought at a time!"

Wilson's re-election in 1916 was the first re-election of a Democratic incumbent in the White House since Andrew Jackson's re-election in 1832—a period of eighty-four years.

Who coined *pitiless publicity*?

Under *Worship* in *Conduct of Life* (1860) Ralph Waldo Emerson wrote: "As gaslight is found to be the best nocturnal police, so the universe protects itself by pitiless publicity." The phrase was popularized by Woodrow Wilson when he was running for Governor of New Jersey in 1910. During the campaign a Republican Progressive leader named George L. Record in a series of questions asked Wilson how he proposed to abolish the boss and spoils system in politics. In reply the Democratic candidate said among other things: "I would propose to abolish it by the reforms suggested in the Democratic platform, by the election to office of men who will refuse to submit to it, and who will lend all their energies to break it up, and by pitiless publicity." The Emersonian phrase caught the public fancy and Wilson continued to use it. "Without publicity there can be no public spirit," said Benjamin Disraeli in a speech in Parliament in 1871, "and without public spirit every nation must decay." In an article in *The Saturday Evening Post* of January 2, 1915, Theodore F. McManus wrote: "In every field of human endeavor, he that is first must perpetually live in the white light of publicity."

Who was author of *deserving Democrats?*

On August 20, 1913, Secretary of State William Jennings Bryan wrote a letter to Walker W. Vick, receiver-general of the Dominican Republic, in which he said: "Can you let me know what positions you have at your disposal with which to reward *deserving Democrats?*"

Who was "the Grape Juice Secretary of State"?

William Jennings Bryan was a teetotaler and Prohibitionist and as Secretary of State served no intoxicating liquors at state banquets. Before accepting the appointment in 1913 he asked President Wilson "whether he would regard the exclusion of intoxicating liquors from our table as an insurmountable objection to my assuming the duties of the office," and was told that he might do as he wished in the matter. Newspapers made much of the fact that the foreign diplomats invited to Bryan's farewill dinner to Viscount James Bryce, retiring British Ambassador, were given the choice of drinking grape juice or water, and Bryan was ridiculed as "the Grape Juice Secretary of State." In his *Memoirs* Bryan explained, "Not that we thought of drawing a contrast between wine and grape juice, but because the glasses for plain and mineral water looked a little lonesome."

After Admiral Togo had drunk to Bryan's health in champagne, the Secretary of State said to the naval hero of the Russo-Japanese War: "You won your victories in water and I drink to your health in water. Whenever you win any victories in champagne I shall drink to your health in champagne." Once Bryan paid the following tribute to water:

Water, the daily need of every living thing. It ascends from the seas, obedient to the summons of the sun, and, descending, showers blessing upon the earth; it gives of its sparkling beauty to the fragrant flower; its alchemy transmutes base clay into golden grain; it is the canvas upon which the finger of the Infinite traces the radiant bow of promise. It is the drink that refreshes and adds no sorrow to it. Jehovah looked upon it at Creation's dawn and said—It is good.

Who originated the slogan: "He kept us out of war"?

The authorship of "He kept us out of war" has never been definitely determined. It was a Democratic slogan in the campaign of 1916 and undoubtedly was a decisive factor in the re-election of Woodrow Wilson.

The slogan may have been suggested by various statements made by President Wilson himself. In an address at Cleveland on January 29, 1916, he said: "You have laid upon me this double obligation: 'We are relying upon you, Mr. President, to keep us out of war, but we are relying upon you, Mr. President, to keep the honor of the nation unstained.' " In an address made two days later, at Cleveland on January 31, 1916, President Wilson said:

I know that you are depending upon me to keep this nation out of the war. So far I have done so and I pledge you my word that, God helping me, I will—if it is possible. But you have laid another duty upon me. You have bidden me see to it that nothing stains or impairs the honor of the United States, and that is a matter not within my control: that depends upon what others do, not upon what the Government of the United States does. Therefore there may at any moment come a time when I cannot preserve both the honor and the peace of the United States. Do not exact of me an impossible and contradictory thing.

The exact phraseology of the slogan apparently evolved during the Democratic National Convention at St. Louis in the following June. It appears to have been a crystallization of the convention sentiment on neutrality and the preservation of peace. It is variously attributed to William Jennings Bryan, Governor Martin H. Glynn of New York, and Senator Ollie M. James of Kentucky in their speeches before the convention. Governor Glynn was temporary chairman and keynoter; Senator James was permanent chairman, and Bryan was a principal speaker. But, notwithstanding frequent statements to the contrary, the words, "He kept us out of war," do not occur in the transcripts of the speeches of any of these men on that occasion, although the general idea was expressed by all three.

The nearest approach to it in James's speech was: "With critics all about him, with patience and strength and great foresight, he has kept a nation at peace with honor." In his speech Bryan said:

I have differed with our President on some of the methods employed, but I join with the American people in thanking God that we have a President who does not want this nation plunged into this war.... And I believe the American people, grateful for what this administration has done, grateful that we have peace here while war stalks throughout the world, will not be unmindful of the fact that it was a Democratic President, supported by a Democratic Senate and House, that thus saved the country the horrors of that war.

Governor Glynn touched upon the same theme but did not use the words "He kept us out of war." But the platform adopted by this convention contained the following sentence: "In particular, we commend to the American people the splendid diplomatic victories of our great President, who has preserved the vital interests of our Government and its citizens and *kept us out of war.*"

Robert W. Woolley, publicity director and a member of the Democratic National Campaign Committee in 1916, told the author in 1945 that the Democratic headquarters never used "He kept us out of war" officially. He said he suggested as a slogan "With honor he has kept us out of war," and that was the form of the slogan on all literature sent out officially. But the public and some of the Democratic field workers altered it to the simpler and more effective, "He kept us out of war," and as such it became the chief slogan of the campaign. One campaign pamphlet contained the lines:

> You are working, not fighting;
> You are living, not cannon fodder;
> Wilson kept you out of war.

"Wilson's wisdom wins without war" was another similar slogan used in the campaign. President Wilson never made an unqualified pledge that he would keep the country out of war if re-elected, and during the campaign he never used or alluded to the slogan, "He kept us out of war." As late as February 26, 1917, he told Congress: "I am the friend of peace and mean to preserve it for America so long as I am able.... War can come only by the wilful acts and aggressions of others." On April 2 of the same year he asked Congress to "declare the present course of Germany to be in fact nothing less than war against the government of the United States."

When did Wilson say: "We are too proud to fight"?

Woodrow Wilson never said, in so many words, as is generally supposed, that the United States was too proud to fight. The famous phrase originated in a speech made by President Wilson before a meeting of newly naturalized citizens at Philadelphia, May 10, 1915. On that occasion he said among other things:

The example of America must be a special example. The example of America must be the example not merely of peace because it will not fight, but of peace because it is the healing and elevating influence of the world and strife is not. There is such a thing as a man being too proud to fight. There is such a thing as a nation being so right that it does not need to convince others by force that it is right.

Too proud to fight was immediately given wide currency by the President's political enemies as a satirical description of his foreign policy in a world at war when the people of the United States were divided into pro-Ally and pro-German factions and three days after the *Lusitania* had been sunk. Wilson himself always maintained that what he said in that speech had been grossly misinterpreted. He used *proud* in the Southern sense of "self-respecting" rather than the Northern sense of conceited. In *Fighting Years* (1939) Oswald Garrison Villard wrote: "I had not been two days in Washington before I supplied the President through Tumulty with a phrase which brought down upon him a storm of abuse and denunciation. The words 'too proud to fight,' embodied in the President's speech of May 10, were mine."

Wilson had a good command of language and was fluent but often used words without calculating their political effect. His phrases, "peace without victory" and "with the cause and object of this war we have no concern," as well as several others, backfired on him politically.

Whom did Wilson call "a little group of willful men"?

In 1917, just before the United States entered the First World War, a bill proposing to "authorize and empower the President to arm merchant ships and otherwise provide for their protection" passed the House of Representatives by a vote of 403 to 13. A large majority of the members of the Senate favored the measure, but twelve Senators, seven Republicans and five Democrats, prevented it from being voted upon by conducting a filibuster that lasted until the adjournment of Congress on March 4.

The filibusterers were Robert M. La Follette of Wisconsin, George W. Norris of Nebraska, Albert B. Cummins and William S. Kenyon of Iowa, Moses E. Clapp of Minnesota, Asle J. Gronna of North Dakota, John D. Works of California (Republicans), James K. Vardaman of

Mississippi, William F. Kirby of Arkansas, James A. O'Gorman of New York, William J. Stone of Missouri and Harry Lane of Oregon (Democrats).

The armed neutrality bill was an administrative measure and President Wilson, in a formal statement to the country a few hours after the adjournment of Congress, said: "The Senate of the United States is the only legislative body in the world that cannot act when it is ready for action. A little group of willful men, representing no opinion but their own, have rendered the great government of the United States helpless and contemptible."

"A little group of willful men" became a famous phrase, and the persons it was intended to describe became the targets of a fusillade of popular denunciation throughout the country. It was at a time when the nation was in the grip of a war hysteria and anti-German sentiment was growing by leaps and bounds. Several State legislatures condemned the little group of willful men in strong terms, and the Kentucky senate went so far as to pronounce them "disloyal, unpatriotic, traitorous and cowardly" for resorting to a filibuster to carry out their "outrageous action."

Did Woodrow Wilson write the limerick "My Face"?

Once a quotation is widely ascribed to the wrong person, particularly if that person is famous, it is very hard to pin it to the name of the real author. Even ancient sayings are sometimes rejuvenated and given a new lease of life by being attached to prominent living persons.

The type of nonsense verse known as the limerick appealed to Woodrow Wilson's sense of humor. Because he quoted it so often and made it famous throughout the English-speaking world, the following limerick entitled "My Face" is frequently attributed to him:

> As a beauty I am not a star.
> There are others more handsome, by far,
> But my face—I don't mind it,
> For I am behind it.
> It's the people in front get the jar.

There are many famous limericks, but this is perhaps the most famous ever written. With variations in language it is widely cited to illustrate the typical verse of this class and is the only complete poem by a living author cited in *Webster's New International Dictionary*.

Of course, Woodrow Wilson was not the author of this limerick. It was composed by Anthony Henderson Euwer (1877—), writer, illustrator and lecturer, and published in 1898 in the Pittsburgh *Index,* where, as one of a series, it was accompanied with a drawing of a bulldog. The author says it was reprinted later in a small volume entitled *The Smile on the Face of the Tiger,* published by Henry Holt. The limerick, with a note explaining its history and authorship, was finally reprinted in 1916 in a little volume entitled *Rhymes of Our Valley* by Euwer himself. The version of "My Face" quoted above is that given in *Webster's New International Dictionary.* In a letter to the author dated April 10, 1946, Euwer says the version he prefers is as follows:

> As a beauty I'm not a great star,
> Others are handsomer far,
> But my face—I don't mind it,
> Because I'm behind it—
> 'Tis the folks in the front that I jar.

Who said: "Politics is adjourned"?

Woodrow Wilson was author of this saying. In a message delivered in person to a joint session of Congress on May 27, 1918, President Wilson said: "Politics is adjourned. The election will go to those who think least of it; to those who go to the constituencies without explanations or excuses, with a plain record of duty faithfully and disinterestedly performed." He meant merely that the country was united on war measures.

On October 24, 1918, just before the Congressional election, President Wilson issued an appeal to the country for the return of Democratic majorities in both houses of Congress. This, from the man who only five months before had declared politics adjourned, was widely greeted with ridicule. In the election the Republicans won control of both houses of Congress for the first time in eight years.

"Politics is adjourned" was an old thought in new dress. In a speech at Philadelphia on February 15, 1884, Thomas B. Reed said: "We should all be glad if we could step aside and say, 'Now let us have a day of rest. Politics are over and the millennium is begun.' But we live in a world of sin and sorrow."

Who coined "Food Will Win the War?"

This slogan was evolved and popularized during the First World War by the U.S. Food Administration, headed by Herbert C. Hoover. The exact wording of the slogan is believed to have been suggested in

1917 by Dr. Ray Lyman Wilbur (1875-1949), chief of the conservation division of the Food Administration. Dr. Wilbur was president of Stanford University for twenty-seven years and Secretary of the Interior in President Hoover's Cabinet. His brother, Curtis Dwight Wilbur, was Secretary of the Navy in President Coolidge's Cabinet. "Food Will Win the War" was used widely again by the U.S. Food Administration during the Second World War.

Who called the First World War "a war to end war"?

"A war to end war" is popularly credited to both Woodrow Wilson and David Lloyd George. There appears to be no evidence that Wilson coined the phrase or even so much as used it. The nearest approach to it in any of his published writings is in his message to Congress on January 8, 1918, in which he said: "This is the culminating and final war for human liberty." Prime Minister Lloyd George is reputed upon doubtful authority to have said about 1917: "This war, like the next war, is a war to end war." In the issue of *Liberty* dated December 29, 1934, H. G. Wells asserted that he himself was the first to call the First World War "a war to end war." Wells published a book in 1914 entitled *The War That Will End War*. Shortly before his death at Warm Springs, Georgia, on April 12, 1945, President Franklin D. Roosevelt prepared an address to be broadcast to the Jefferson Day dinners throughout the country on April 13. In that address he wrote: "More than an end to war, we want an end to the beginnings of all wars."

Who said: "The world must be made safe for democracy"?

This was the punch line in President Woodrow Wilson's address to a joint session of Congress on April 2, 1917, in which he asked for a declaration of war against Germany. "The world must be made safe for democracy" was vigorously applauded in Congress and immediately became the rallying cry of the whole nation. A joint resolution declaring a state of war with Germany was passed in the Senate by a vote of 82 to 6 on April 4 and in the House of Representatives by a vote of 373 to 50 on April 5.

What was the "smoke-filled room"?

Smoke-filled room in its political sense was popularized by Kirke L. Simpson of the Associated Press in connection with the nomination of Warren G. Harding by the Republican National Convention at Chicago in 1920. Before the convention opened Harry Micajah Daugherty, Harding's campaign manager, was reported to have predicted his candidate's nomination in the following words: "The convention will be deadlocked, and after the other candidates have gone their limit, some twelve or fifteen men, worn out and bleary-eyed for lack of sleep, will sit down, about two o'clock in the morning, around a table in a smoke-filled room in some hotel and decide the nomination. When that time comes, Harding will be selected." At five o'clock on the morning of June 12, 1920, Simpson filed a story beginning: "Harding of Ohio was chosen by a group of men in a smoke-filled room early today as Republican candidate for President." Later the same day the convention nominated Harding by an overwhelming majority and *smoke-filled room* took its place in the American political vocabulary. The next year Simpson was awarded a Pulitzer Prize for his report of the burial of the Unknown Soldier at Arlington Cemetery.

The nomination of Harding, however, was not quite so simple or accidental as legend makes it appear. Harding, who had been Lieutenant Governor of Ohio and had become a Senator in 1915, was a man of imposing presence and pleasing manners and was an effective public speaker. His friends began to groom him for the Presidency in 1916, when he was chosen as temporary chairman and keynoter of the convention that nominated Charles Evans Hughes for President. In the 1920 convention the Ohio Senator was known personally to more of the delegates than any of his rivals. The leading candidates for the nomination were Governor Frank O. Lowden, General Leonard Wood and Senator Hiram W. Johnson. Daugherty's preconvention strategy was to get enough first-choice delegates for Harding to keep his name before the convention and enough second-choice delegates to put him over after the leading candidates had eliminated one another. The deliberate plan was to play the leaders against one another in the convention and to force Harding up with votes from all the others.

The first ballot was scheduled for Friday, June 11. Thursday night was the deadline for filing for Federal offices in Ohio, and Daugherty and his colleagues were so confident of victory that they persuaded Harding not to file for renomination as Senator. Governor Frank B. Willis of Ohio placed Harding in nomination in a well-timed and effective speech. On the first ballot the vote was: Wood, 287; Lowden, 211; Johnson, 133; Governor Sproul of Pennsylvania, 84; Nicholas Murray Butler, 69, and Harding, 65. On the fourth and last ballot of that day the leading candidates had about the same number of votes and Harding had only 61.

That night Daugherty's forces worked intensively and incessantly to convince the delegates that the deadlock could not be broken by any of the three leading candidates and that Harding was the ideal compromise candidate. About two o'clock the next morning a group of leaders, many of them U.S. Senators, met in the reception room of Colonel George Harvey in the Blackstone Hotel to canvass the situation. Other groups of leaders met in other places during the night for the same purpose. The legend is that the group in Colonel Harvey's room agreed to break the deadlock by switching their delegations to Harding. Daugherty himself wrote that he did not hear of the meeting until afterward and doubted whether the men in Colonel Harvey's conference in Suite 804-5 in the Blackstone Hotel could have changed more than fifty votes. The evidence indicates that there was already an inclination on the part of the majority of the tired delegates to break the deadlock and wind up the convention by switching to Harding.

According to another story, probably a fable, Harding was invited to come at once to the smoke-filled room in the Blackstone, and, after he had arrived, was asked if there was anything in his life or background that would embarrass the party or the country if the convention nominated him. After excusing himself for meditation, he returned within a few minutes and replied that there was not.

On the first ballot taken on Saturday Lowden passed Wood and Harding received 78 votes. On the eighth ballot Harding received $133\frac{1}{2}$ votes and passed Johnson. At that point Chairman Henry Cabot Lodge declared a motion to recess adopted. During the recess there were many conferences, and Lowden released his delegates, Senator Boies Penrose in Pennsylvania gave Daugherty by telephone a message that would put his delegation behind Harding, and it was apparent that Harding would win. The coterie of Senators who thought they were in control of the convention did not dictate Harding's nomination. Their switch to him was more in the nature of a capitulation to the inevitable. On the ninth ballot, after the recess, Harding received 374 votes, and on the tenth, $692\frac{1}{5}$, which gave him the victory.

After the nomination reporters rushed to the candidate and asked him for a statement. Harding, a poker player, said: "We drew to a pair of deuces and filled." *To fill* in poker parlance means to get a "full house"—a pair and three of a kind.

The Democratic National Convention at San Francisco in 1920 nominated Governor James M. Cox of Ohio for President. It was the second time since 1860, when Lincoln and Douglas of Illinois were the Republican and Democratic nominees in the North, that both the major-party candidates were from the same State. It had occurred in

1904, when Theodore Roosevelt and Alton B. Parker of New York were the candidates, and it occurred again in 1944, when the nominees were Thomas E. Dewey and Franklin D. Roosevelt of New York.

During the campaign an organized effort was made to defeat Harding by flooding the country with anonymous circulars containing a pedigree so doctored as to make it appear that the Harding family had a trace of Negro blood. The Post Office Department refused to accept the circulars for mailing after President Wilson ordered the destruction of 250,000 copies in the San Francisco post office. The circulars, however, continued to be distributed by other means until the close of the campaign. The charge that the Harding family had Negro blood in it was not new in 1920. It appears to have originated in a feud among schoolchildren some sixty years earlier and had been raised against Harding in several of his earlier political campaigns in Ohio. Harding believed it to be false and malicious and never answered it in any public statement. The roorback was not effective and Harding won by a landslide.

Harding has been the only newspaperman to become President. At sixteen he became a printer's apprentice and cub reporter on the Marion (Ohio) *Star,* and at thirty-five was owner and publisher of that paper. While President he was a voting member of the National Press Club of Washington. Before his death in 1923 he sold his newspaper for $480,000. Only two other major-party candidates for President have been professional newspapermen—Horace Greeley in 1872, and James M. Cox, Harding's Democratic opponent in 1920. James G. Blaine and William Jennings Bryan both edited newspapers for several years.

The Ohio Gang was first applied contemptuously to Mark Hanna and the other politicians who were influential in the McKinley administration. "I *know* these Ohio men," Speaker Thomas B. Reed once told Representative James Franklin Aldridge. In 1921 *The Ohio Gang* was revived as an opprobrious designation of Attorney General Daugherty and the other Ohio politicians who were intimate with President Harding. "I frankly confess to a leadership in the so-called 'Ohio Gang' for about forty years," Daugherty wrote in 1932. "On the lips of rival politicians the 'Ohio Gang' is an epithet. I wear its badge as a mark of honor."

In 1927, four years after President Harding's death, Nan Britton published under her name a book entitled *The President's Daughter,* in which she claimed that Harding was the father of a daughter born to her in 1918. The book is written in such a way that it is hard to determine what part of it is truth and what part fiction. Positive and convincing evidence to prove or disprove Nan Britton's story has not been produced. Letters from her to Harding calling upon him to acknowledge the paternity of her child were found, but there is no evidence that he ever saw them. No letters from Harding to her have been produced. Miss Britton tried but failed in a Federal court at Toledo in 1931 to get a legal decision establishing the truth of her story. In *The Inside Story of the Harding Tragedy (1932),* Daugherty, who was an intimate friend of Harding for years and who drew up the President's last will, asserted that he had never heard of Nan Britton until the publication of her book, which he said was a fake.

Who became President because of a strike?

Calvin Coolidge became President largely because of a strike. In 1919 some members of the Boston police force, who had been permitted to have an organization of their own, formed a union to affiliate with the American Federation of Labor. The police department had an old rule against unionization and all members of the force agreed to it when they joined the service. The head of the department was appointed by the Governor of the Commonwealth, who ordinarily did not interfere with this city office. When the police persisted in their union activities, a committee appointed by Mayor Peters, a Democrat, urged Governor Coolidge, a Republican, to compel Commissioner Edwin U. Curtis to settle the dispute by arbitration. Although Curtis had been appointed by a predecessor, Coolidge backed him up because he could not see how it was possible to arbitrate the question of obedience to the department rules and the Commissioner's orders, which he thought had the force of law.

Curtis discharged twenty-nine policemen after regular hearings, and on September 9, 1919, three-fourths of the force, after urging the others to join them, left the service in a body. Boston was virtually without police protection and that night there was some rioting. On September 11, after Mayor Peters had called out the militia in the city for police duty, Governor Coolidge called out substantially the whole State Guard to protect the city. Under a special law the Mayor displaced Curtis, by putting a militia officer in command of the police, whereupon the Governor under a general law restored Curtis, directed policemen to obey his orders and called on the citizens for assistance. In his *Autobiography* (1929) Coolidge wrote: "This is the important contribution I made to the tactics of the situation, which has never been fully realized. To Mr. Curtis should go the credit for raising the issue and enforcing the principles that police should not affiliate with any outside body, whether of wage earners or of wage payers, but should remain unattached, impartial officers of the law, with sole allegiance to the public."

Samuel Gompers, AFL president, who had advocated arbitrating the dispute, wired the Governor asking Curtis's removal and the policemen's reinstatement. Part of Coolidge's reply to Gompers on September 14, 1919, read:

The right of the police of Boston to affiliate has always been questioned, never granted, is now prohibited. . . . Here the policemen's Union left their duty, an action which President Wilson characterized as a crime against civilization. Your assertion that the Commissioner was wrong cannot justify the wrong of leaving the city unguarded. That furnished the opportunity, the criminal element furnished the action. There is no right to strike against the public safety by anybody, anywhere, any time.

In a proclamation on September 24, Governor Coolidge said that the police who stayed on duty "are the real heroes of this crisis," that those who deserted their posts and let in the enemy "dispossess themselves of office" and "stand as though they had never been appointed," that "the authority of the Commonwealth cannot be intimidated or coerced," that "there is no middle ground," and that "every attempt to prevent the formation of a new police force is a blow at the government."

One sentence in the telegram to Gompers—"There is no right to strike against the public safety by anybody, anywhere, any time"—caught the public fancy throughout the country. Coolidge himself said he expected to be defeated in the fall election because of the Boston police strike. Instead he was re-elected Governor by an increased majority and was immediately talked of for President. The leading aspirants for the Presidential nomination in the Republican National Convention at Chicago were Governor Frank O. Lowden, General Leonard Wood and Senator Hiram W. Johnson, with Senator Warren G. Harding in the offing in the event of a deadlock. "We deny the right to strike against the government" was incorporated into the platform. Coolidge, placed in nomination by Frederick H. Gillett of Massachusetts, Speaker of the U.S. House of Representatives, with the support of the State delegation, received thirty-four votes on the first ballot and some on all ballots till the last one, when all but one of his supporters switched to other candidates.

After Harding was nominated for President, he indicated he would accept Johnson as his running mate, but the disappointed Californian declined. A coterie of U.S. Senators who thought they controlled the convention then got together on Senator Irvine L. Lenroot of Wisconsin. Coolidge indicated that he did not want the Vice Presidency and accordingly the Massachusetts delegation did not place his name before the convention for that office. After the convention had met to nominate a Vice President, Judge William McCamant of Oregon started a Coolidge boom by climbing upon a chair on the convention floor and shouting that Oregon had come to nominate Coolidge for President and now wanted him for Vice President. The North Dakota delegation seconded the nomination from the floor and the cry of "Coolidge!" spread from delegation to delegation. The result was a stampede to Coolidge and on the first ballot he received three-fourths of all the votes. The Democratic platform in 1920 asserted, "With respect to government service, we hold distinctly that the rights of the people are paramount to the right to strike."

A law approved August 24, 1912, recognized the right of Federal employees to belong only to organizations or unions whose constitutions forbid members to strike against the United States.

Who coined *normalcy?*

Normalcy was popularized by Warren G. Harding, although not coined by him, as commonly supposed. It means "normality" or "the state of being normal." In mathematics the term is used in a specific sense, as "the point of normalcy." The earliest use of the word recorded by the Oxford dictionary is from Davies and Peck's *Mathematical Dictionary,* published in 1857.

The term, in a popular sense, was brought to the attention of the American public when Harding used it in his speech accepting the Republican nomination for President. In that speech, delivered July 22, 1920, at Marion, Ohio, Senator Harding said: "We must stabilize and strive for *normalcy,* else the inevitable reaction will bring its train of sufferings, disappointments and reversals." This, however, was not the first time Harding had used the word. In an address before the Ohio Society of New York on January 20, 1920, he had said: "But there is a sane normalcy due under the new conditions, to be reached in deliberation and understanding." In a speech before the Market Club at Boston on May 14, 1920, he said: "America's present need is not heroics but healing, not nostrums but *normalcy,* not revolution but restoration, not agitation but adjustment, not surgery but serenity, not the dramatic but the dispassionate, not experiment but equipoise, not submergence in internationality but sustainment in triumphant nationality."

During the Presidential campaign of 1920 "Back to Normalcy" was used as a sort of slogan by the Republicans, and in his inaugural address on March 4, 1921, President Harding said: "Perhaps we never shall know the old levels of wage again, because war invariably readjusts compensations and the necessaries of life will show their inseparable relationship, but we must strive for *normalcy* to reach stability." The President used the term in the sense of sane stability, but his enemies distorted it to mean reaction, ultraconservatism and a return to the good old days.

What Vice President was known as Hell Maria?

Charles Gates Dawes (1866-1951), Vice President from 1925 to 1929 under Coolidge, was known as "Hell Maria" because he used that expletive at a Congressional investigating committee hearing on February 2, 1921. Representative Oscar E. Bland, Republican from Indiana, a member of the committee, which was investigating charges of waste, fraud and extravagance in the conduct of the First World War, asked General Dawes whether it was true that he, while purchasing agent of the A.E.F., had paid $400 for horses in France that he could have bought for half that amount in the United States.

This question, which intimated that the General had wasted Government money, made the witness "good and mad." Afterward Dawes explained: "I shouted, why, Hell Maria! I'd have paid horse prices for sheep if they could have drawn caissons and guns in the Argonne. Our boys were there getting hell from the Germans and they had to have artillery support. We needed horses to get them there and a horse was worth its weight in gold. I'd have paid anything for them." *Hell Maria* never fitted an occasion so appropriately. Newspapers gave the phrase wide circulation and after that the General was "Hell Maria Dawes." Some tried to soften it into "Hell and Maria" or "Helen Maria." But Dawes said "Hell Maria" was the phrase he used. He also told the investigating committee on the same occasion:

We were fighting a war. We did not have time for duplicate vouchers and double-entry bookkeeping. It is a hell-fired shame for everybody to be trying to pick flyspecks on the greatest army the world ever knew. We did more organization despite our unpreparedness than the French and the British. What do you suppose we went to war for? We went to France to win the war and we did it.

Dawes was born at Marietta, Ohio. After attending Marietta College and the Cincinnati Law School, he practiced law at Lincoln, Nebraska, before he settled permanently at Evanston, Illinois. He distinguished himself as a lawyer, businessman, soldier, statesman, diplomat and author. In 1896 he managed the Republican campaign in Illinois and became Comptroller of the Currency in McKinley's administration. He resigned that position in 1902 to seek the Republican nomination for Senator from Illinois. After he failed to get the nomination he observed: "I'm out of politics for good and all. I'm no politician." In the same year he organized the Central Trust Company of Illinois, which was later merged with the National Bank of the Republic and became the Central Republic Bank and Trust Company.

Dawes went to France in 1917 as a lieutenant colonel of engineers and came back twenty-six months later as a brigadier general. In 1921 President Harding appointed him the first Director of the Budget. After the Armistice in 1918 he had served on the Liquidation Commission of the A.E.F. and on the Liquidation Board of the War Department for disposing of army surplus stores and equipment. In 1923 Secretary of State Charles Evans Hughes suggested that the Allies form a commission of experts to study the reparations problem and Dawes was sent to Europe for that purpose. He became chairman of one of the committees of the international commission, and from the report of this committee, on which Owen D. Young and Henry M. Robinson also served, evolved what came to be called "The Dawes Plan," a revised schedule for the payment of reparations by Germany. This plan not only put German reparation payments on a sliding scale but also stabilized German currency. Dawes insisted that Young was the chief architect of the Dawes Plan, but Young insisted that it was based largely on the preliminary work done by Dawes. In 1925 Dawes was awarded jointly with Sir Austen Chamberlain the Nobel Peace Prize, his share of which was given to the endowment of the Walter Hines Page School of International Relations.

The General was a man of action rather than of words, but when he spoke his language was usually plain and to the purpose. After he had taken the oath as Vice President on March 4, 1925, he shocked "the greatest deliberative body on earth" by swearing in all the new Senators at one time instead of in groups of four as had been the time-honored custom. Then, in a spirited and blunt inaugural address, he severely criticized the Senate rules and procedure as outmoded and inefficient. In March, 1925, the Senate was tied forty-forty on a motion to confirm Charles B. Warren of Michigan as Attorney General. Had the Vice President been in the chair he could have broken the tie in favor of the administration, but he had been assured that no vote would be taken on the motion that day and was asleep in his room in the Willard Hotel. In response to frantic calls from the Republican leaders in the Senate he made a mad ride in a taxicab to Capitol Hill but was too late to save Warren. When the Vice President reached the chair a Democrat who had voted for Warren had switched his vote and there was no longer a tie to break. He was a descendant of that William Dawes who rode with Paul Revere on the historic night of April 18, 1775, and his ride up Pennsylvania Avenue was inevitably compared to the ride of his Revolutionary ancestor. The fact that the new Vice President was caught napping only a few weeks after he criticized the Senate for its dilatoriness gave his critics a field day.

From 1929 to 1932 Dawes was President Hoover's Ambassador to London, where he distinguished himself by refusing to wear knee breeches and other dress generally required at court functions. He was chairman of the finance committee of the World's Fair at Chicago in 1933-1934 and was largely responsible for the financial success of that enterprise. In February, 1932, when the Great Depression was nearing its most acute stage, President Hoover appointed Dawes the first president of the Reconstruction Finance Corporation, which had just been created with control of $2,000,000,000 to "aid the financing of agriculture, commerce, and industry, to encourage small business and to help maintain the economic stability of the country."

Dawes resigned from the RFC on June 6, 1932, to return to the Central Republic Bank and Trust Company in Chicago, which was having financial difficulties. Three weeks later the RFC approved an $90,000,000 loan to the Dawes bank. This loan was severely criticized by the Democrats as irregular and improper and during the 1932 campaign President Hoover defended it as a wise action to save not only one large bank but also the banking stability of the whole country. Later the Government sued some of the stockholders of the Dawes bank to recover double liability for the RFC loan. The Central Republic Bank and Trust Company went into receivership and ceased to function, its liabilities being assumed by the City Bank and Trust Company, a new Dawes bank. Dawes did not oppose the Government suits and promptly paid a $5,200 assessment on his own fifty-two shares of stock. The Dawes family paid a total of $1,027,000, of which $728,000 was paid by Dawes Brothers, Inc., the holding company of Dawes and his brothers. In the end the Government lost nothing in the deal.

General Dawes at one time habitually smoked and popularized a type of "underslung pipe," which appeared to be upside down. He was a good pianist and composed several pieces of music. His "Melody in A Minor" was played for some time by Fritz Kreisler before he or the public learned it was the work of Dawes.

[374]

Who was the first President born west of the Mississippi?

Although the Federal Constitution had been in effect 140 years when he was inaugurated in 1929, Herbert Clark Hoover was the first President born west of the Mississippi. He was born August 10, 1874, at West Branch, Cedar County, Iowa, where he lived until he was eleven years old, after which he went to live with an uncle in Oregon. West Branch was founded in 1854 by Hoover's maternal grandfather. His father, Jesse Hoover, was the local blacksmith, and his mother, whose maiden name was Hulda Minthorn, was a preacher in the Quaker congregation at the near-by village of Springdale. Hoover, who was a resident of California when elected, was the first President born west of the Mississippi to be nominated for President by a major party. John C. Frémont, who was born in Georgia but who was a resident of California in 1856, was the first resident of a State west of the Mississippi to receive a major-party nomination for the Presidency.

Harry S. Truman, who was born in 1884 at Lamar, Missouri, was the second President born west of the Mississippi. The first Vice President born west of the Mississippi was Charles Curtis of Kansas, who took office the same time Hoover did. The next three Vice Presidents were all born west of the Mississippi—John N. Garner of Texas, Henry A. Wallace of Iowa, and Harry S. Truman of Missouri.

Mrs. Hoover was the first First Lady to be born west of the Great River. Her maiden name was Lou Henry and she was born in Waterloo, Iowa, the daughter of Charles D. Henry, a banker. The family moved to Monterey, California, when she was a girl.

What President rode camels in his work?

As a mining engineer in Australia in 1897-1899, Herbert Hoover rode camels on inspection trips to the widely separated gold mines owned by the firm he worked for. In those days Afghan camels, driven and tended by Pathans from India, were the chief means of transportation on the deserts of central west Australia. Long afterward Hoover said that the sight of a camel made him seasick.

Why was President Hoover married by a Catholic priest?

Herbert Hoover, a Quaker, was married to Lou Henry, an Episcopalian, in her father's house in Monterey, California, on February 11, 1899, by the Right Reverend Monsignor Ramon M. Mestres, pastor of the San Carlos Church in that town, which was predominantly Spanish-speaking and Catholic. In his memoirs Hoover says that Miss Henry had "determined to join my Quaker faith" and wanted a Quaker wedding, but there being no Quaker meeting in that part of California and "at the moment no Protestant minister in town," they "compromised on one of her old family friends, a Catholic priest," who "secured a special dispensation from his bishop to marry Protestants." In January, 1928, Father Mestres wrote that when Miss Henry first asked him to perform the ceremony he replied that "I could not do it without a special permission from the Bishop, which I refused to apply for," but later at a reception to Bishop Montgomery "they themselves asked the Bishop to permit me to marry them and the Bishop gave a verbal permission."

In August, 1791, Andrew Jackson was married to Rachel Donelson Robards in the home of Thomas Marston Green, Jr., near Natchez, then under the Spanish flag. There is no record of this marriage and historians have been unable to determine who performed the ceremony. Mary Donelson Wilcox, a niece of Mrs. Jackson, said the ceremony was performed by a Catholic clergyman, while tradition in the Green family says it was performed by Green's father in his capacity as a civil magistrate of some sort.

Was Herbert Hoover ever a British subject?

During Herbert Hoover's campaigns his political enemies repeatedly charged that he was ineligible to the Presidency because he had forfeited his American citizenship and become a British subject by voting in English elections. For several years before the First World War Hoover lived in a rented house in London. As a rent payer Hoover's name appeared on London tax lists because taxes were assessed on rents. Preliminary voting lists were made up from these tax lists and Hoover's name appeared on such voting lists for several years. But aliens were not eligible to vote, even if their names were on the tax list and preliminary voting list, and no evidence exists that Hoover ever applied for British citizenship or tried to vote. During his twenty years abroad Hoover made frequent trips to the United States and always traveled with American passports, which are issued only to American citizens. After the income tax law was passed Hoover paid income taxes to the United States. Notwithstanding the facts, Hoover was repeatedly referred to as "Sir Herbert" with the implication that he had undergone "a corruption of his American spirit" by his long residence in England.

Was Herbert Hoover ever a Democrat?

Herbert Hoover was born and brought up a Republican. From 1897 to 1917 he was abroad much of the time and won an international reputation as a mining engineer, businessman and relief administrator. He took little interest in partisan politics in the United States and had never voted in a Presidential election when appointed Food Administrator by President Wilson in 1917. According to his own statement, he supported the Progressive rather than the Republican candidate for President in 1912. In his memoirs he says he joined the National Republican Club in 1909 and "in 1912 rooted for Theodore Roosevelt and supported him by financing others to root."

Hoover was accused of favoring a pro-Wilson Democratic Congress in 1918, but there is no evidence that he voted in the Congressional election of that year. He came through the war very popular and Democrats and Republicans alike boomed him for President. Since he served under a Democratic President, he took no public notice of the Presidential boom and was accused by political foes of not knowing whether he was a Democrat or a Republican and of "flirting with both parties."

After Hoover ceased to be Food Administrator on July 1, 1919, he announced he was and always had been a Republican, but this did not stop nonpartisan support of him for President. His name was entered early in 1920 in both the Democratic and Republican preferential primaries in Michigan and he led the Democratic ticket with 25,046 votes and ran fourth on the Republican ticket with 52,503 votes. Much applause came from the galleries but little from the delegates when he was nominated for President by Nathan L. Miller of New York in the Republican National Convention at Chicago in 1920. He got $5\frac{1}{2}$ votes on the first and $9\frac{1}{4}$ on the last ballot. In the election of that year he cast his first vote, which was for Harding, who appointed him Secretary of Commerce. Hoover was called "The Great Engineer," but his subordinates referred to him as "The Chief."

Did Hoover say: "Prosperity is just around the corner"?

"Prosperity is just around the corner" was a popular fusion of several statements made by President Herbert Hoover after the stock market crash of 1929. On October 29, four days after the first break in the stock market, the President said: "The fundamental business of the country is on a sound and prosperous basis." In the following January he declared that there were definite signs that the country had "turned the corner." The President predicted in March that the high point of unemployment would be passed in sixty days, and in May he assured the country: "We have now passed the worst and with continued unity of effort we shall rapidly recover." It was not until 1932, when the depression had become grim, that Hoover's political enemies began to charge him with having said that "Prosperity is just around the corner."

What President's surname is the root of a verb?

Herbert Hoover is the only President whose surname is the root of a verb. His name became a household word when he became Food Administrator in 1917 and began a campaign to persuade the people to help win the war by voluntarily eliminating waste in the use of wheats, fats, sugar and other essential foods. Meatless, wheatless and sweetless days once a week were part of his conservation program. *To hooverize* in the sense of to save or to economize, especially in the use of food, began to appear in newspapers a day or two after Hoover issued his first regulations. The new verb was included in the 1934 edition of *Webster's New International Dictionary,* although it is now little used. The names of other Presidents are the basis of adjectives and nouns, such as Washingtonian, Jeffersonian, Madisonian, Jacksonian, Jeffersonianism, Jacksonianism, Lincolnesque, Grantism, etc., but not of verbs. Political enemies blamed President Hoover for the depression during his administration and applied *Hooverville* to any group of huts and shacks that sheltered the unemployed.

What does *grass roots* mean?

In its political sense *grass roots* means close to or springing from the rank and file rather than from political leaders. *Grass roots* was used as early as 1880 in the sense of topsoil. "To get down to grass roots," meaning to get at the bottom of things, is supposed to date from around the turn of the century. In his keynote address at the Bull Moose Convention at Chicago on August 2, 1912, Senator Albert J. Beveridge of Indiana said: "This party comes from the grass roots. It has grown from the soil of the people's hard necessities." Calvin Coolidge is quoted as having said: "The real test of party strength is down close to the grass roots." After Franklin D. Roosevelt was nominated for President by the Democratic National Convention in Chicago on July 1, 1932, former Senator James A. Reed of Missouri made a plea for party harmony in which he said: "Prosperity will not be obtained from the Federal Government. It will come, when it comes, from the grass roots, from where it always must come." In 1934 John D. M. Hamilton, Kansas Republican national committeeman, used *grass roots* in a speech at a Republican celebration in Topeka. Hamilton gave the name "grass-roots convention" to a conference of Middle Western Republicans held at Springfield, Illinois, in June, 1935, to revitalize the party from the roots up and to try to make it an effective opposition to the New Deal.

Who coined *rugged individualism*?

Rugged individualism was popularized, if not coined, by Herbert Hoover. In a speech in New York City on October 22, 1928, the Republican candidate for President said:

During one hundred and fifty years we have builded up a form of self-government and a social system that is peculiarly our own. It differs essentially from all others in the world. It is the American system. When the war closed, the most vital of all issues both in our own country and throughout the world was whether governments should continue their wartime ownership and operation of many instrumentalities of production and distribution. We were challenged with a peace-time choice between the American system of rugged individualism and a European philosophy of diametrically opposed doctrines—doctrines of paternalism and state socialism. The acceptance of these ideas would have meant the undermining of the individual initiative and enterprise through which our people have grown to unparalleled greatness.

In *The Challenge to Liberty* (1934) former President Hoover wrote: "While I can make no claim for having introduced the term 'rugged individualism,' I should be proud to have invented it. It has been used by American leaders for over a half-century in eulogy of those God-fearing men and women of honesty whose stamina and character and fearless assertion of right led them to make their own way in life." Hoover may have been right in saying *rugged individualism* was an old phrase, but no recorded use of the term earlier than his has been found. *Individualism* in that sense is an old term and Hoover himself published *American Individualism* in 1922. *Rugged* acquired its meaning of "robust," "vigorous" and "sturdy" in America. In 1816 John Pickering wrote that "Englishmen notice our use of *rugged* in this sense as a peculiarity."

Who was the Happy Warrior?

On June 26, 1924, Franklin D. Roosevelt placed the name of Governor Alfred E. Smith of New York in nomination for President at the Democratic National Convention in Madison Square Garden in New

[379]

York City. He closed his address with these sentences: "He has the power to strike at error and wrongdoing that makes his adversaries quail before him. He has the personality that carries to every hearer not only the sincerity but the righteousness of what he says. He is the 'Happy Warrior' of the political battlefield." In *Franklin D. Roosevelt, a Career in Progressive Democracy* (1931) Ernest K. Lindley says "it was not Roosevelt but Smith's intimate adviser, Supreme Court Justice Joseph M. Proskauer, who chose the sobriquet, *The Happy Warrior*."

Four years later, on June 27, 1928, Roosevelt again placed the name of Smith in nomination for the Presidency at the Democratic National Convention in Houston. On that occasion he closed his address with these words: "We offer one who has the will to win—who not only deserves success but commands it. Victory is his habit—*the happy warrior, Alfred E. Smith*."

Many who are familiar with these references to Governor Smith as "The Happy Warrior" may not know the history of the phrase. Long before Roosevelt applied it to Smith it had been associated with two other leaders of the Democratic Party—Woodrow Wilson and Grover Cleveland. The source of the phrase is William Wordsworth's poem entitled "Character of the Happy Warrior," which was composed in December, 1805, or January, 1806, but not published until 1807. In a measure the poem was written in commemoration of the death of the poet's brother, John Wordsworth, who died in 1805. The poem opens with the question:

> Who is the happy warrior? Who is he
> That every man in arms should wish to be?

Then, after delineating an idealized happy warrior, the poet concludes with the answer:

> This is the happy warrior; this is he
> That every man in arms should wish to be.

That "The Happy Warrior" should have been applied to many different persons was only natural. The "Character of the Happy Warrior" was one of Woodrow Wilson's favorite poems. On one occasion, during their days at Princeton together, former President Cleveland heard future President Wilson read the poem and Cleveland was so impressed with Wilson's reading of it that he also adopted it as his favorite and requested to have it read at his funeral, which was done.

"The Happy Warrior" as a sobriquet for Governor Smith never really caught on. It was Roosevelt himself rather than Smith who became "The Happy Warrior" on American political battlefields. In 1928

Stanley Vestal published an impressionist biography entitled *Kit Carson, the Happy Warrior of the Old West.*

Did President Hoover promise a chicken in every pot?

The "chicken-in-every-pot" slogan used by the Republicans during the Presidential campaign of 1928 is often attributed to Herbert Hoover personally; but there is no evidence that he ever used it in his campaign speeches or elsewhere.

This slogan first came to the attention of the American public during that campaign when "A Chicken for Every Pot" appeared as the heading of a paid full-page advertisement that the Republican National Committee had inserted in a number of newspapers and that was signed by several prominent Republicans. One sentence in the advertisement read: "Republican prosperity has reduced hours and increased earning capacity, silenced discontent, put the proverbial 'chicken in every pot' and a car in every backyard to boot." The nearest approach to the slogan in the campaign speeches of the Republican candidate was the following: "The slogan of progress is changing from the full dinner pail to the full garage."

During the campaign of 1932, conducted in the midst of acute economic depression, President Hoover's political enemies attributed the "chicken-in-every-pot" slogan to him personally and used it as the basis of repeated ridicule.

As a matter of fact the slogan was a rough translation of an old French saying. When Henry IV became King of France in 1589 he sincerely desired to pacify and restore order to his war-torn countrymen. He expressed concern for the welfare of the common people, developed agriculture and industry, reduced the national debt, suppressed sinecures, reformed the finances and repressed many abuses in the government. "It is my wish," he was reported as saying, "that every peasant may have meat for dinner every day of the week, and a fowl in his pot every Sunday." He was seriously called Henry the Great and Henry the Good and facetiously *Le Roi de Poule au Pot,* "Chicken-in-the-Pot King." Sully, the French statesman, wrote in his *Memoirs* that "a fowl in the pot" was of great concern to Henry. In 1596, two years before his power over the French was complete, Henry IV wrote: "I have hardly a horse on which I could fight; my doublets have holes at the elbows, and my pot is often empty."

Alexander Smith (1830-1867), the Scottish poet, wrote: "Just consider what a world this would be if ruled by the best thought of men of letters! Ignorance would die at once, war would cease, taxation would be lightened, not only every Frenchman, but every man in the world, would have his hen in the pot."

Who addressed Roosevelt as "My Old Potato"?

Alfred E. Smith greeted Franklin D. Roosevelt with the words, "Hello, my Old Potato," at the New York Democratic convention in Albany, October 4, 1932. There had been an estrangement between the two men since the preceding July when Roosevelt defeated Smith for the Presidential nomination at the Democratic National Convention in Chicago, and the public was curious to see what would happen when the two former friends and political allies met at the Albany convention. Roosevelt was on the speakers' platform when Smith entered to place the name of Lieutenant Governor Herbert H. Lehman in nomination for Governor. Smith walked over to Roosevelt, shook hands with him and greeted him cordially with the words "Hello, my Old Potato." It has been said that the words were not Smith's but the invention of a reporter. In a letter to the author dated November 19, 1941, Governor Smith wrote: "Years ago *Old Potato* was an affectionate form of greeting. In Albany at the State Convention when I walked on the platform I shook hands with Franklin D. Roosevelt and did say, 'Hello, my Old Potato.'"

Alfred Emanuel Smith (1873-1944), known almost universally as "Al Smith," served four two-year terms as Governor of New York—1919-1920 and 1923-1928—and was a colorful figure in American politics. His brown derby hat, cigar, cane, salty speech and witty sayings have become proverbial. He was born on the New York East Side near the Fulton Street Fish Market. When "Silver-Tongued" W. Bourke Cockran placed Al Smith's name in nomination for the Presidency in the Democratic National Convention at San Francisco in 1920, a band played "The Sidewalks of New York," the first stanza of which is:

> East Side, West Side, all around the town,
> The tots sang, "Ring-a-rosie," "London
>   Bridge is falling down";
> Boys and girls together, me and Mamie Rorke,
> Tripped the light fantastic on the side-
>   walks of New York.

The words of this song, first published in 1894, were written by James W. Blake (1862-1935) and the music was composed by Charles B. Lawlor (1852-1925). "The Sidewalks of New York" became associated with Al Smith, and after he was nominated for President in 1928 it became the

[382]

Democratic campaign song. After newspapers published a report in 1933 that Blake was destitute, Smith saw to it that the author of the famous song was provided for.

When Franklin D. Roosevelt, who was crippled by polio, became a candidate for Governor in 1928 to succeed him, the Democratic Presidential candidate observed that "The Governor of New York State does not have to be an acrobat." In an interview on November 24, 1933, after President Roosevelt had devalued the gold dollar, Smith said, "I am for a gold dollar as against baloney dollars." "Slice it where you will," he said, "it's still baloney." The popular version of this became, "No matter how thin you slice it, it's still baloney." Referring to the use of relief funds for political purposes, Smith said, "Nobody shoots at Santa Claus." "Alphabet soup" was the term he applied to the various New Deal agencies known by their initials. According to an apocryphal story, when he was asked whether Roosevelt could be depended upon, Smith replied, "Did you ever try to nail a custard pie to a barn door?"

Why was Vice President Garner nicknamed Cactus Jack?

In 1901 the Texas legislature designated the bluebonnet the State flower. During the debate on the resolution in the State house of representatives John Nance Garner moved to substitute the cactus known as the prickly pear, which was more common than the bluebonnet in his part of the State. His colleagues after that called him "Cactus Jack" and the nickname stuck. In Washington the solidly built, medium-sized, bushy-eyebrowed and red-faced Texan was regarded as a sort of cross between the cactus and the sphinx.

Garner was born on November 22, 1868, in a log farmhouse in Red River County, Texas. In 1888 he entered Vanderbilt University at Nashville, Tennessee, but withdrew in about two weeks because of ill health. He studied law in Clarksville in his native county and was admitted to the bar in 1890. Believing he was threatened with tuberculosis, he sought a drier and more healthful climate at Uvalde in southwestern Texas where he became lawyer, newspaper publisher, banker, owner of many buildings and much ranch land, and public official.

When Garner ran for County Judge in 1892 a local girl named Ettie Rheiner campaigned against him because she understood that he drank whisky, played poker and was generally unfit for the office. Later she met the County Judge, changed her opinion and married him. She was his secretary throughout his long public career, and in Washington Garner and his wife were thought of as a team and generally referred to as "the Garners." In 1902 Garner was elected to Congress from a district he had carved out for himself while a member of the State legislature. He never made speeches or campaigned in his district during the thirty years he was in Congress. He made few speeches on the floor of the House, and when he did speak he usually did not permit his speeches to remain in the *Congressional Record*. Once Speaker Joseph G. Cannon said to him: "If anybody ever finds out where your district is, they'll beat you."

In 1913 Garner passed up a chance to become chairman of the Foreign Affairs Committee to take a bottom place on the more important Ways and Means Committee, which handles tax and tariff legislation. At the time Frank A. Munsey's Washington *Times* charged in an editorial that Garner owned more goats than any other man in the world and therefore would have a special interest in the next tariff bill. In all previous tariff bills wool and goat hair had been classed as one product and put on the free list. The Underwood bill of 1913, reported out by the committee of which Garner was a new member, left wool on the free list but imposed a duty on mohair, and the Republicans made much ado about this change. Representative Sereno E. Payne of New York, coauthor of the Payne-Aldrich Tariff Act of 1909, charged on the floor that the Democratic bill "taxes mohair while exposing shorn sheep to the arboreal blasts of free trade because Garner has got in his handiwork," while Representative J. Hampton Moore of Pennsylvania read to the House a doggerel poem of his own composition ridiculing the "Garner goat of Texas." The fact is that Garner never owned a goat in his life, but he felt that Moore's poetic attack on him required a reply in kind. So he went to the cloakroom, concentrated a few minutes and then wrote his first and last poem, which he then read to the House:

> Hampy Moore is a hell of a poet—
> He don't know a sheep from a goet.

Garner became Democratic Leader of the House in 1929. He and Speaker Nicholas Longworth, though leaders of opposing parties, were close personal friends. After the day's session they and a few colleagues often met in a room on the first floor of the House side of the Capitol to talk business, swap yarns and "strike a blow for liberty," which consisted of a drink of whisky with or without "branch water." Representative John McDuffie of Alabama dubbed this sanctum sanctorum of the leadership "The Board of Education."

The House provided the Speaker but not the Minority Leader with a car and chauffeur. Speaker Longworth often gave the Minority Leader a lift in the official car between the Capitol and the latter's hotel both in the morning and in the evening. The two, who could play together as solemnly as two small boys when not opposing the programs of each other's parties in Congress, fell into the habit of referring to the Speaker's automobile as "our car." The Congressional election of 1930 was so close that it was doubtful whether the Republicans or the Democrats would organize the House and choose the Speaker. It was assumed that Minority Leader Garner would be promoted to the Speakership if the Democrats controlled the next House and there was much kidding as to who would get "our car." After the election Longworth wired Garner from Cincinnati: "Whose car is it?" When the new Congress met on December 7, 1931, enough Republicans had died in office and been replaced by Democrats in special elections to give Garner the Speakership, but in the meantime Speaker Longworth had died and was not there to turn the gavel and "our car" over to his friend.

Garner was a consummate parliamentarian, an experienced legislator, had a thorough knowledge of the mechanics of government and the philosophy behind it, and was especially versed in Federal finance. He was simple in tastes and manners, picturesque in person, and salty and forthright in speech. As Speaker of the first Democratic House in twelve years and the highest-ranking Federal official, he attracted so much attention that, without any encouragement or promotion on his own part, millions of Democrats favored him for the Presidential nomination in 1932. He was elected Vice President on the Roosevelt ticket in 1932 and re-elected on the same ticket in 1936.

At first the Vice President and the President worked together as personal friends and leaders of the party. Although Garner never charged a purchase in his life, he went along with New Deal legislation that spent billions of dollars of borrowed money for relief. Gradually, however, Garner drifted away from the New Deal, which he had hoped would be only a temporary program, and he finally broke with Roosevelt because he opposed a third term for the President.

In *Garner of Texas* (1948) Bascom N. Timmons wrote: "To a radio sponsor who offered him a contract amounting to close to $100,000 a year, he replied: 'I am not worth it as John Garner, and any value I have attained as Vice President of the United States is not for sale.'"

Personal admirers and anti-New Dealers began to boom Garner for the Presidential nomination in 1940 to succeed Roosevelt, and Garner reluctantly consented to have his name used. On July 27, 1939, John L. Lewis, president of the United Mine Workers of America and of the Congress of Industrial Organizations, appeared before a special meeting of the House Committee on Labor called to consider proposed amendments to the National Labor Relations Act of 1935. Among other things the CIO leader said to the committee: "You know the genesis of this campaign against labor in the House of Representatives is not hard to find. It is within the Democratic Party. It runs across to the Senate of the United States and emanates there from a labor-baiting, poker-playing, whisky-drinking evil old man whose name is Garner."

When reporters showed Garner Lewis's statement, he chuckled and said: "I have no comment to make. I never make criticisms or comments on anything." Eight days later he was overheard to say to a friend at Dallas: "I'm going to get eviler every day. I'm going to be my natural self and a free man as long as I live." Although Garner acquired a prodigious reputation as a poker player in his younger days, actually he quit playing poker for stakes in 1920. The Garner boom subsided and the Democratic National Convention in 1940 nominated Roosevelt for a third term with Henry A. Wallace as his running mate. Garner returned to Uvalde to hunt, fish, feed his chickens, nurse his trees and shrubs, and "get full of chiggers and feel natural once again." He played on the Possum Trot team as a youngster in North Texas and always remained an ardent baseball fan. Visiting the zoo was one of his favorite relaxations while in Washington. November was his lucky month. He was born, married and elected to office twenty times in November.

Who coined *the forgotten man?*

The forgotten man is an old English phrase which was used by Lord Byron and even earlier writers but which was popularized by William Graham Sumner (1840-1910), professor of political and moral science at Yale University. Early in 1883 Sumner delivered a lecture at New Haven entitled The Forgotten Man, and the phrase is a chapter heading in his *What Social Classes Owe to Each Other,* first published later the same year. Sumner said:

Wealth comes only from production, and all that the wrangling grabbers, loafers and jobbers get to deal with comes from somebody's toil and sacrifice. Who, then, is he who provides it all? The Forgotten Man . . . delving away in patient industry, supporting his family, paying his taxes, casting his vote, supporting the church and the school . . . but he is the only one for whom there is no provision in the great scramble and the big divide. Such is the Forgotten Man. He works, he votes—generally he prays—but his chief business in life is to pay and he always pays. All the burdens fall on him, or on her, for the Forgotten Man is not seldom a woman.

And again, the Forgotten Man "is the clean, quiet, virtuous, domestic citizen, who pays his debts and his taxes and is never heard of out of his little circle."

In 1897 Walter Hines Page (1855-1918) delivered an address entitled The Forgotten Man at the North Carolina Teachers' College at Raleigh.

This address attracted considerable attention and popularized the phrase in the South. Sumner had used the phrase in the sense of the solid citizen and taxpayer, while Page used it more in the sense of the "average man." During the pre-Convention campaign in 1932 Governor Franklin D. Roosevelt of New York revived the phrase in the sense of the "under-privileged man" or the "underdog." In a radio speech from Albany on April 7, 1932, Governor Roosevelt said: "These unhappy times call for the building of plans that rest upon the forgotten, the unorganized but indispensable units of economic power, for plans like those of 1917 that build from the bottom up, and not from the top down, that put their faith once more in the forgotten man." In March, 1933, after President Roosevelt had announced his Cabinet, which included nine men and Miss Frances Perkins, Will Rogers observed: "They have found the forgotten man. There's nine of him and one woman."

How did *The New Deal* originate?

The New Deal as a political phrase and slogan was a blending of Theodore Roosevelt's *Square Deal* and Woodrow Wilson's *The New Freedom*. It was borrowed from card-playing. *New deal* is synonymous with *re-deal* and means a reshuffling of the cards and a new distribution to the players when there has been a mistake or *misdeal*.

New deal was used figuratively as early as Andrew Jackson's second administration. In a letter to Nicholas Biddle, dated January 18, 1834, John Rathbone used the expression "a new bank and a new deal." John Sherman wrote in 1863: "The war is prolonged, and but little chance of its ending until we have a new deal." Mark Twain used the phrase in *A Yankee at the Court of King Arthur* (1889). The Yankee, after observ-ing that he was in a country where only about six persons out of every 1,000 had any voice in the government, said "what the 994 dupes need is a new deal." In 1914 Ezra Pound, self-exiled and expatriated American poet, editor and translator, wrote:

> Come, let us on with the new deal,
> Let us be done with pandars and jobbery.

Albert Bushnell Hart, the historian, in 1923 defined a radical as one whose slogan is, "Let us have a new deal." In *Abraham Lincoln Traveled This Way* (1930) Fred L. Holmes wrote in reference to the Republican victory in 1860: "A new party had come into power; a new deal was being made." It is said that "Let's have a new deal" was used by the Democrats in Erie County, New York, during Governor Franklin D. Roosevelt's campaign for re-election in 1930, and that it was suggested by Daniel J. Sweeney, Buffalo newspaper editor and political leader. But *a new deal* did not become nationally associated with F.D.R. and his policies until July 2, 1932, after he closed his acceptance speech before the Democratic National Convention in Chicago with the words: "I pledge you—I pledge myself—to a new deal for the American people. Let us all here assembled constitute ourselves prophets of a new order of competence and of courage. This is more than a political campaign; it is a call to arms. Give me your help not to win votes alone, but to win in this crusade to restore America to its own people." On October 20, 1932, in a speech at Indianapolis, the Democratic candidate said: "This campaign marks the beginning of a new deal in American politics, and in the conduct of the American government."

A new deal is variously said to have been suggested to Governor Roosevelt by Samuel I. Rosenman, Herbert Bayard Swope, Raymond Moley and other early New Dealers and Brain-Trusters. In the June 24, 1939, issue of *The Saturday Evening Post* Moley wrote: "The phrase, 'a New Deal,' & which was publicly introduced in the speech of acceptance, I first used in the general philosophical statement prefacing this series of memoranda." Willard M. Kiplinger, in *Washington Is Like That* (1942), wrote of President Roosevelt: "His political thinking grew out of the ferment of the early 1900's, was shaped chiefly by the 'progressive' or 'liberal' ideas of T.R. and Wilson. His own 1932 slogan, 'a New Deal,' was a conscious union of the New Freedom and the Square Deal."

After Roosevelt became President in 1933 *The New Deal* was substituted for *A New Deal* as the designation for the program of economic recovery and social security sponsored by his administration. The measures generally associated with the New Deal were: National Industry Recovery Act (NIRA), Agricultural Adjustment Act (Triple-A), Public Works Act (PWA), Tennessee Valley Authority Act (TVA), Wagner Labor Relations Act, Securities and Exchange Act, Reciprocal Trade Act, Public Utilities Holding Act, Wage and Hour Act, Social Security Act and many others. In fact *The New Deal* was applied to the whole body of reform legislation passed during the first two terms of President Roosevelt, especially during his first term. One important New Deal measure, the Supreme Court enlargement bill of 1937, failed to pass. New Dealers, as supporters of the program were called, used the phrase as a badge of honor, but their opponents used it contemptuously. At one time people spoke of "The New Deal Party" as distinguished from the Democratic Party proper. The New Deal, as the term is now used, contained some measures that President Roosevelt himself at first opposed, such as the act guaranteeing Federal bank deposits.

Just before Christmas in 1943 President Roosevelt told a newspaper correspondent that *New Deal* was outmoded as a designation of the policies of the administration and suggested that *Win the War* be substituted. In 1949 President Harry S. Truman adopted *The Fair Deal* as the designation of his program. On January 5, 1949, he said in his State of the Union address to Congress: "I hope for cooperation from farmers, from labor, and from business. Every segment of our population and every individual has a right to expect from our Government a fair deal." In his Inaugural Address on January 20, 1949, President Truman said: "The old imperialism—exploitation for foreign profit—has no place in our plans. What we envisage is a program of development based on the concepts of democratic fair-dealing." It is believed that President Truman was personally responsible for the choice of *fair deal*. At any rate, *The Fair Deal* immediately took its place beside *Square Deal*, *New Freedom* and *New Deal*.

The New Freedom was coined by Woodrow Wilson and was used as a slogan during the Presidential campaign of 1912. It was also used as the title of a volume of his speeches, but the phrase never wa. applied specifically to Wilson's program to the same extent that *New Deal* was applied to Franklin D. Roosevelt's.

In a speech at Springfield, Illinois on July 4, 1903, President Theodore Roosevelt said: "A man who is good enough to shed his blood for his country is good enough to be given a square deal afterward. More than that no man is entitled to and less than that no man shall have." On November 4, 1904, just before the national election, President Roosevelt said: "If elected, I shall see to it that every man has a square deal, no less and no more." When suit was brought to dissolve the steel trust during the same year, President Roosevelt wrote in a letter: "We demand that big business give people a square deal." In a speech at Dallas, Texas on April 5, 1905, President Roosevelt explained what he meant by a square deal:

When I say I believe in a square deal I do not mean, and nobody who speaks the truth can mean, that he believes it possible to give every man the best hand. If the cards do not come to any man, or if they do come, and he has not got the power to play them, that is his affair. All I mean is that there shall not be any crookedness in the dealing.

How did *brain trust* originate?

Brain trust seems to have originated around the turn of the century when it was customary to refer to large corporations and monopolies as trusts. There was a steel trust, a sugar trust and a beef trust, and President Theodore Roosevelt was called "The Trust-Buster." In a syndicated article dated July 12, 1935, Hugh S. Johnson wrote that when Secretary of War Elihu Root established the first general staff in 1901 Commissary General Weston referred to it contemptuously as "a damned brain trust." "The Brain Trust" was the title of an article by William Allen White in the *Saturday Evening Post* of March 21, 1903.

After Franklin D. Roosevelt was nominated for President in 1932 he got three college professors—Raymond Moley, Rexford G. Tugwell and Adolph A. Berle, Jr.—to assist him and his secretary, Louis McHenry Howe, to prepare campaign material and to write speeches. Roosevelt referred to these men as his Privy Council. One day in August, 1932, John M. Kieran, New York *Times* reporter at Hyde Park, dubbed the group "the brains trust" and began to use the phrase in his dispatches. Roosevelt liked the phrase and adopted it himself, and soon the whole country was hearing about "the brains trust." *Brain trust* seemed more natural and it was not long before *brains* in the phrase had lost its *s*.

Later *Brain Trust* was applied not only to the original group but to a continually changing White House inner circle who helped President Roosevelt write speeches, draft bills, plan policies and distribute patronage. Some of the Brain-Trusters were Federal officeholders but many of them were not. Some of them were expert advisers on specific subjects, while others were general utility men of the administration. They helped Roosevelt formulate most of the measures that became known as the New Deal. Among those who were classed as members of the Brain Trust at one time or another were: Samuel I. Rosenman, Charles W. Taussig, Hugh S. Johnson, Basil D. O'Connor, Felix Frankfurter, Harry L. Hopkins, George E. Warren, Frank A. Pearson, Isador Lubin, Thurman W. Arnold, William I. Myers, M. L. Wilson, William C. Bullitt, John Dickinson, James P. Warburg, Mordecai Ezekiel, James H. Rogers, Arthur E. Morgan, Hermann Oliphant, Leo Wolman, Thomas G. Corcoran, Benjamin V. Cohen, O. M. W. Sprague, Gardiner C. Means, William O. Douglas, James M. Landis and Leon Henderson. *Brain trust* is now often applied to any staff of intimate, behind-the-scenes experts or advisers.

Who was the first President to fly?

Franklin D. Roosevelt was the first man to fly while President. In 1932 Roosevelt made a spectacular airplane flight from Albany to Chicago to accept his first nomination, but after he became President the Secret Service put thumbs down on flying for the President on the ground that it was dangerous. In 1943, however, President Roosevelt overruled the Secret Service and flew in a plane to the conference at Casablanca in Africa. Until that time no President had been up in a plane or any other kind of aircraft. Roosevelt made two other flights—to Teheran in 1943 and to Yalta in 1945. The first flight made within the United States by a President was made in June, 1945, when President Harry S. Truman flew from Washington to the Pacific Coast and back. Quentin Roosevelt, a son of Theodore Roosevelt, crashed and was killed while flying a French Nieuport plane in France during the First World War.

What was the Cuff Links Club?

At the close of the Presidential campaign of 1920, Franklin D. Roosevelt, the unsuccessful Democratic candidate for Vice President, gave a pair of cuff links to each newspaperman who had traveled with him during the campaign. This group called themselves the Cuff Links Club, and after Roosevelt became President in 1933 they often met with him at the White House for an evening of good fellowship around a poker table. In the group were Stephen T. Early, Marvin H. McIntyre and Kirke L. Simpson. There were also "honorary members." The Cuff Links Club was an informal social group and had no political significance.

How did boondoggling originate?

In the spring of 1935 the New York City Board of Estimate investigated the use of relief money. Robert C. Marshall, a "training specialist," testified that the artists' project was making "leather crafts, three-ply carving, and boondoggles." *Boondoggle* was picked up by reporters and shortly *boondoggling* was the accepted though derogatory name for any "made work" of little or no value provided and paid for by the Government. Critics of the New Deal pictured white collar workers on relief as frittering away their time and energy and the taxpayers' money on useless and wasteful projects. In an address on September 18, 1936, to New Jersey relief leaders at the Robert Treat Hotel in Newark, President Franklin D. Roosevelt said:

"There is a grand word going around—*boondoggling*. It is a pretty good word. If we can boondoggle ourselves out of the depression, that word is going to be enshrined in the hearts of the American people for years to come."

Apparently *boondoggle* was an American pioneer slang term for simple articles made by handicraft. Some authorities think they have traced *boondoggle* to an obscure British slang word. In 1935 a movie actor named Guy Kibee thought the people in the Ozarks called gadgets made of discarded materials *boondoggles* because Daniel Boone whiled away idle hours whittling out toys for his dog to play with. Robert H. Link, a former Boy Scout of Rochester, New York, said in the same year that he nicknamed his son "Boondoggle" when he was born in 1926. Link thought his use of the word was responsible for its adoption by the Boy Scouts during the Jamboree in England in 1929. An unidentified writer in the March, 1930, issue of *Scouting* said: "Boon-doggles are like old-type lanyards. They are made of plaited leather. Scouts have been making them for years for uniform ornaments all over the world." In its political sense American *boondoggling* became British *boonwiggling*.

When were "the three long years"?

In the keynote address at the Republican National Convention at Cleveland in 1936 Senator Frederick Steiwer of Oregon repeatedly used the phrase "three long years" in reference to the period the Democrats under Franklin D. Roosevelt had been in power. Governor Alfred M. Landon of Kansas was nominated for President and "three long years" became a sort of Republican slogan during the campaign. The Republican theme song was Stephen C. Foster's "O, Susanna," the chorus of which runs,

> O, Susanna! O, don't you cry for me,
> I've come from Alabama, wid my banjo on my knee.

Why was Huey Long called The Kingfish?

Huey Pierce Long (1893-1935) of Louisiana gave himself this title. Several species of fish, because of their size or other characteristics, are named kingfish. The term acquired the slang meaning of "king-pin," "king-bee," "big cheese" and "top dog." In his autobiography, *Every Man a King* (1933) Long wrote that he and his associates were in the habit of referring to various of their opponents as "The Kingfish." On one occasion Governor Long was sitting with the members of the Highway Commission when they were opening bids for the purchase of bonds. A prospective buyer made the point that under the law the sales had to be awarded by the Commission and not by the Governor. Long admitted the point was well taken, but said: "I am participating here anyway, gentlemen. For the present you can just call me The Kingfish."

Having dubbed so many of my political opponents by such a title [wrote Long], the newspapers instantly took advantage of the incident and heralded my name far and wide as the self-styled Kingfish. It has persisted ever since. It has served to substitute gaiety for some of the tragedy of politics. I have made no effort to discourage it. The sound of the name and the word "Long" over the telephone for some reason is a bit difficult to understand. It has saved time and effort on many occasions to say, "This is the Kingfish."

Long was admitted to the bar in 1915 and was a member of the Railroad Commission from 1918 to 1921 and of the Public Services Commission from 1921 to 1928. He became Governor on May 21, 1928, and in 1930 was elected to the U.S. Senate for the term beginning March 4, 1931. After the election he said he would not take the oath as Senator until the expiration of his four-year term as Governor. He said that "no term of office begins, whether it is constable, justice of the peace, Governor or Senator, until such officer is sworn in" and pointed out that Hiram W. Johnson of California, Robert M. La Follette of Wisconsin and David B. Hill of New York had postponed taking their seats in Congress until they had completed their terms as Governor. Finally, however, Long resigned as Governor and took his seat in the Senate on January 25, 1932, but received no Senatorial salary for the nearly two years that he was both Governor and Senator-elect. In 1930 he introduced into political campaigning the portable device known as the "sound truck."

Senator Huey Long advocated a "Share-the-Wealth" relief plan, which involved homestead exemptions, guaranteed minimum incomes for all families, shorter working hours, and limits on private fortunes, legacies and incomes. His phrase, *every man a king,* was suggested by William Jennings Bryan's, "Behold, a Republic! where every man is a king, but no one wears a crown." Chief Justice Taft was reported to have said that Long was one of the most brilliant lawyers who ever practiced before the U.S. Supreme Court. In 1949 Louisiana designated Long to represent the State in Statuary Hall in the U.S. Capitol by a life-size bronze statue.

As Governor, Long advocated cornpone and potlikker as wholesome and economical foods for the people. *Pone* is from an Algonquian Indian word meaning anything baked. Captain John Smith spelled it *ponap* in 1612. Cornpone is corn meal, mixed with salt and water, made into patties with round tops and flat bottoms and baked until hard. Pot liquor (usually spelled "potlikker") is the juice left in the kettle after boiling meat and green vegetables together. The Kingfish insisted that the most "delicious, invigorating, soul-and-body sustaining potlikker" is produced by boiling turnip greens and cut-up turnips with salt fat pork as seasoning.

It has always been the custom to eat cornpone with potlikker [wrote Long]. Most people crumble the cornpone into the potlikker. . . But, with the progress of education, the coming of "style," and the change of the times, I concluded that refinement necessitated that cornpone be "dunked" in the potlikker, rather than crumbled in the old-fashioned way. So I suggested that those sipping of potlikker should hold the cornpone in the left hand and the spoon in the right, sip of the soup one time, then dip the cornpone in the potlikker and bite the end of the bread. My experience showed this to be an improvement over the crumbling.

Long insisted that cornpone and potlikker be served in the Senate restaurant but the argument between the dunkers and crumblers was still going on when he was assassinated on September 8, 1935.

Mrs. Rose McConnell Long by appointment and election filled the unexpired term of her husband in the Senate and served until January 3, 1937. On November 2, 1948, Russell Billiu Long, a son of Senators Huey P. and Rose McConnell Long, became a Senator from Louisiana, and had the unique distinction of serving in the same branch of Congress in which both his parents had served.

Who coined "horse-and-buggy days"?

This is a popular version of a phrase used by President Franklin D. Roosevelt. On May 27, 1935, the U.S. Supreme Court, in *A.L.A.Schechter Corporation* vs. *United States,* held unanimously that the National Recovery Act was unconstitutional so far as the code-making powers were concerned. On May 31 President Roosevelt commented at length upon this court decision in the longest White House press conference he ever held. Among other things, he said: "The whole tendency over these years has been to view the interstate commerce clause in the light of present-day civilization. The country was in *the horse-and-buggy age* when that clause was written ..."

What Presidential candidate first made campaign speeches?

In the early days of the republic it was considered undignified to solicit support openly for the Presidency, and Presidential candidates did not make campaign speeches. Electors were chosen by State legislatures or by a restricted suffrage, candidates were designated by caucuses, and Presidential candidates did not appeal directly to the people. The practice of electioneering openly and frankly for the highest office evolved gradually.

The puritanical influence in the Northern States discouraged electioneering by candidates for public office, but the practice occurred early in Virginia. In 1777 James Madison was defeated for re-election to the legislature because he refused to provide the voters with free whisky. Distribution of free liquor to the voters appears to have been a custom brought from England by the early settlers. Some of Madison's constituents petitioned the legislature to set aside his opponent's election on the ground that he did "contrary to an ordinance of Convention, make use of bribery and corruption," but a privileges and election committee refused to construe giving liquor and other presents to voters as bribery and corruption.

Nearly all candidates for President after Washington played politics to maneuver themselves into positions where the lightning would have a good chance to strike them. It is probable that every one of Washington's successors has wanted the job and has made some effort to get it. No President since Washington has been "drafted" for the position. A few men have been nominated for President without any effort by them, but each one of these worked to be elected after receiving the nomination. Even those who succeeded to the Presidency from the Vice Presidency accepted the lesser office in the hope of getting the higher one.

But the early candidates for President did not openly electioneer, as campaigning was then called. Thomas Jefferson wrote numerous letters, conferred continually with his political supporters and inspired newspaper articles when he was seeking the Presidency. He was a master artist at getting others to fight his political battles while he remained in the background. On May 15, 1793, he wrote to Madison that "we have been trying to get another weekly or half weekly paper set up." In 1802 a Federalist wrote that soliciting votes was "a new Democratic device." In 1804 Charles Cotesworth Pinckney of South Carolina was the Federalist caucus candidate for President against Jefferson. It would not have been proper for Pinckney to have electioneered openly during the campaign, but a year earlier, preparatory to the contest of 1804, he toured New England. When he rode about Salem with Elias H. Derby, it reminded a Jeffersonian of Hezekiah showing Jerusalem to the Babylonians. Harvard, a Federalist stronghold, conferred an honorary degree on Pinckney, something it did not do for President Jefferson. Madison, James Monroe, John Quincy Adams, Andrew Jackson, Martin Van Buren and their opponents did not campaign openly for the Presidency, although Monroe had done some electioneering when he ran for the Senate in Virginia.

A typical campaign expedient occurred in connection with Jackson in 1823. Speaker Henry Clay, Secretary of the Treasury William H. Crawford, Secretary of State John Quincy Adams and Secretary of War John

C. Calhoun, as well as General Jackson, were all prospective candidates for the Presidency in 1824. Northern protectionists wanted to learn Jackson's position on the tariff, but he felt it would not be proper for him to make a formal statement on the subject. To get around this difficulty, William Patterson of Philadelphia sent the Hero of New Orleans "A Grass Bonnet or Hat, made by American hands, and of American materials" and expressed the hope that Mrs. Jackson would wear it as "an encouragement to domestic manufactures." Jackson replied in a personal letter that Mrs. Jackson would wear the Grass Hat made by two girls under twelve years of age and that "its workmanship . . . will be regarded as an evidence of the perfection which our domestic manufacturers may hereafter acquire, if properly fostered and protected." From this letter the Philadelphia protectionists knew, or thought they knew, how Jackson stood on the tariff. As early as 1820 Secretary of War Calhoun made a tour of the country to inspect coastal fortifications and to review troops. Everywhere he stopped he was wined and dined and it was an open secret that he was feeling out the possibilities for his candidacy for President in 1824.

After the legislature of his State had nominated him for the Presidency in December, 1821, William Lowndes (1782-1822) of South Carolina said: "The Presidency is not an office to be either solicited or declined." This saying, with variations in language, has often been quoted since. The author of the quotation was a son of Rawlins Lowndes, who was President of South Carolina in 1778. William Lowndes served in the U.S. House of Representatives from 1811 to 1822. His older brother Thomas had served in that body. Lowndes, who was six feet six inches tall, apparently was one of the most popular men who ever served in Congress. Fair, dispassionate and forthright but formidable in debate, he won the respect of political friends and foes alike. John Quincy Adams called him, "a man of irreproachable character, amiable disposition, and popular manners," and Henry Clay said he was "the wisest man I ever knew." For health reasons Lowndes declined appointments to the Cabinet and diplomatic missions. At forty he died on his way to England and was buried at sea. While in Congress he was chairman of the committee on "ways and means," a phrase supposedly coined by an English William Lowndes (1652-1724), who was secretary of the treasury during the reigns of King William, Queen Anne and King George I.

Some interesting sidelights on electioneering in those days occur in Adams's diary. On June 29, 1827, President Adams wrote:

Dr. Watkins showed me a letter from R. Peters, Jr. of Philadelphia, urgently recommending that I would attend the meeting for the celebration of the opening of the Pennsylvania Canal, so as to show myself among the German farmers and speak to them in their own language. I told Watkins I was highly obliged to my friends for their good purposes, but that this mode of electioneering suited neither my taste nor my principles. I thought it equally unsuitable to my personal character and to the station in which I am placed.

On October 29 of the same year the President wrote:

He (Clay) said also that the friends of the Administration in Kentucky were taking measures for acting in concert at the elections of the next year, and that he had received an application from a committee asking whether I should be willing to receive from them and answer certain direct enquiries in relation to my public accounts, and also relative to my conduct as a member of the Senate upon the acquisition of Louisiana. He observed that the misrepresentation with regard to my accounts, which had been circulated from speeches in Congress and in the newspapers, had been of the most pernicious influence upon the late election in Kentucky. I told him that I was aware of the uses which had been made, and were making, of these misrepresentations, but that I did not think there would be a propriety in my corresponding with an electioneering committee on these subjects. I was aware that it is the usage in Kentucky for candidates to offices conferred by the suffrages of the people to offer themselves and solicit votes—a natural consequence of which is, that they are called to account before the people, and to answering charges against them, or enquiries made of them, respecting their conduct or principles. But this has not been customary with reference to the office of President of the United States, and I should not be willing to set the precedent. As to my accounts, I had partly prepared a statement of them to be laid before Congress at the next or succeeding session. This appeared to me the most proper manner of exhibiting the facts to the public, and the Congressional documents will show my conduct in relation to the purchase of Louisiana.

Representative John Bailey of Massachusetts, upon the suggestion of Daniel Webster, asked President Adams whether he had five or ten thousand dollars to use secretly to influence the Kentucky elections in his favor. On March 8, 1828, President Adams wrote: "I answered that there was a sentiment expressed first by the late Mr. Lowndes, much repeated since by General Jackson and his friends, though not practiced upon by them, but hitherto invariably observed by me, that the Presidency of the United States was an office neither to be sought nor declined." On May 20, 1828, the President wrote: "General Metcalf, member of the House from Kentucky . . . is the Administration candidate for Governor of the State, and, according to the usage of that part of the country, must before the election travel round the State and offer himself to the people and solicit their votes . . . his competitor has already made his canvassing tour." And on August 27, 1831, the former President, when asked to run for President on the Anti-Mason ticket, replied that, "I never had asked, and never should ask, the vote of any person for any office."

Electioneering in the modern sense appears to have flowered first in Virginia and Kentucky. Clay, a native of Virginia but a resident of Kentucky where active campaigning was the custom, did not make campaign speeches in the modern sense when he was the National Republican candidate for President against Jackson in 1832. William Henry Harrison, a native of Virginia but a resident of Ohio, appears to have been the first Presidential candidate to make anything approaching present-day campaign speeches as a candidate for President. In 1836, when Harrison ran for President against Van Buren without a national Whig nomination and "pretty much on my own hook," he departed from the time-honored custom that a Presidential candidate should not electioneer. He made a grand tour of most of the Northern and Border States and showed himself to crowds everywhere he stopped. New York, New Jersey, Pennsylvania, Delaware, Maryland, Virginia and Kentucky were among the States he visited. He visited the Tippecanoe battlefield and went as far west as Illinois. He attended dinners, receptions and outdoor gatherings. Most of the speeches he made on these occasions were replies to the many honors he received, but some of them were political and frankly and openly in the interest of his candidacy for President.

In 1839 Clay, with his eye on the Whig nomination in 1840, made a tour of some of the Northern States, ostensibly to see Niagara Falls. He was wined, dined and partied at many places and he made long speeches with a decided political tinge. But Harrison, not Clay, received the Whig nomination in 1840 and the famous log-cabin, hard cider and coonskin campaign followed. In that campaign Harrison confined his active campaigning to his own State. He made a grand tour of Ohio, making speeches, receiving honors and shaking hands with the people. After that he remained at his North Bend home and received delegations and other visitors. President Harrison's death thirty days after taking office is believed to have been partly due to physical exhaustion resulting from his active and strenuous political campaign. During the summer of 1839 President Van Buren, who had become nervous about the activity of the Whigs and the increasing prospect that he might be defeated for re-election, visited his old home at Kinderhook. He was given an enthusiastic popular reception through Pennsylvania, New Jersey and lower New York, and the Whigs, perhaps with some justification, referred to this as an electioneering trip. On October 1, 1840, Adams wrote in his diary:

One of the most remarkable peculiarities of the present time is that the principal leaders of the political parties are travelling about the country from State to State, and holding forth, like Methodist preachers, hour after hour, to assembled multitudes, under the broad canopy of heaven. Webster and Clay, W.C. Rives, Silas Wright, and James Buchanan are among the first and foremost in this canvassing oratory, while Andrew Jackson and Martin Van Buren, with his heads of Departments, are harping upon another string of the political accordion by writing controversial electioneering letters. Besides the prime leaders of the parties, numerous subaltern officers of the Administration are summoned to the same service, and, instead of attending to the duties of their offices, rave, recite, and madden round the land.

On October 17, 1840, a committee notified Adams of his nomination for re-election to Congress. In his diary under that date he wrote:

I told them . . . that I had felt myself under a peculiar obligation to abstain from attendance at all the public meetings which had been held in the course of the present year having reference to the approaching Presidential election; that a sense of propriety had heretofore prescribed it as a rule to all ex-Presidents of the United States to abstain with interference in the election of their successors, and although the last President, Jackson, had departed from that rule, as the present President, Van Buren, had departed from another rule, forbidding any candidate for the Presidency to canvass for himself—disapproving of these practices, I am unwilling to give countenance to them by following the example.

Clay was a perpetual candidate for President and seldom made a speech in or out of Congress without having his weather eye on the White House, but in his early days he was careful to observe the custom that a Presidential candidate should not appeal openly for support—that the office should seek the man and not the man the office. After he was nominated by the Whigs in 1844 he opened his active campaign at a monster mass meeting in Nashville. His Democratic opponent, James K. Polk, made no campaign speeches. In 1848 neither Zachary Taylor nor Lewis Cass made political speeches during the campaign. Franklin Pierce observed the unwritten rule that forbade open electioneering by a Presidential candidate and did not take the stump in the campaign of 1852, but Winfield Scott, the Whig candidate, tried to get around the tradition by making a nonpolitical tour of the Northern and Border states. Congress had authorized a soldiers' asylum, and Scott, in his capacity as General of the Army, toured the country under the guise of inspecting possible sites for the institution. The Whig candidate made only nonpolitical speeches and carefully preserved the fiction that the trip was official and not political, but the public easily saw through the transparent device and it did Scott little good. A Democratic newspaper jeered: "General Scott says he is traveling to select a site for a military asylum; from present indications he ought to be the first candidate for admission."

New England especially was slow to accept electioneering by candidates for public offices of any kind. In 1857 Nathaniel Banks shocked the sensibilities of Massachusetts conservatives by stumping the State for the governorship.

John C. Frémont did not make campaign speeches in 1856, and James Buchanan remained at Wheatland, his residence near Lancaster, and conducted a "front porch" campaign, making political speeches and statements only to visiting delegations. In 1860 Abraham Lincoln remained at his home in Springfield and did not make campaign speeches; but Stephen A. Douglas, John C. Breckinridge and John Bell campaigned actively and made some speeches away from home. Even at that late date Douglas's active personal campaign was sharply criticised as "a regrettable innovation" below the dignity of a candidate for the Presidency. Neither President Lincoln nor George B. McClellan made campaign speeches in 1864.

In the fall of 1868 President Andrew Johnson made his famous swing around the circle to gain popular support in his fight with Congress. He traveled as far north as Detroit and as far west as St. Louis and made many political speeches. No President had ever done anything like this before and even many of his supporters thought it was beneath the dignity of a man holding the high office of President.

Ulysses S. Grant remained quiet in 1868, but Horatio Seymour took the stump in October and made an aggressive speaking campaign. In 1872 President Grant again remained quiet, but Horace Greeley took the stump and addressed large crowds and continued to do so until called home by his wife's illness. Neither Rutherford B. Hayes nor Samuel J. Tilden made campaign speeches in 1876, but both were active in directing their campaigns from behind the scenes. Tilden made public several vigorous statements on the issues. Hayes visited the Centennial Exposition at Philadelphia and attracted considerable public attention. On October 19, 1876, he wrote Carl Schurz: "I shall go to the Ohio Day next week, 26th, at the Centennial, but will avoid political demonstrations and the hospitalities which may be offered. This, according to a promise I made our managers if Ohio was right at the (October) elections. Following Tilden's example." But apparently the Republican candidate weakened when he got to the Quaker City. On October 29 he noted in his diary: "Returned last night from Ohio Day at the Centennial. It was an enthusiastic and prodigious crowd which greeted me. I managed to shake some four thousand people by the hand and to make half a dozen speeches from steps, windows and roof of the

Ohio Building, without saying anything that I regret—without 'slopping over.' " In 1880 Winfield Scott Hancock did not campaign actively, but James A. Garfield took the stump and made some seventy campaign speeches. Garfield's was the most active personal campaign made by a Presidential candidate up to that time and he was the first Presidential candidate who made campaign speeches to be elected after William Henry Harrison. Four years later James G. Blaine toured the country and made an active personal campaign, but Grover Cleveland made only a few short speeches and only a few public appearances, one of them being to review a parade in New York City.

Neither Cleveland nor Benjamin Harrison toured the country making campaign speeches in 1888 and 1892, but in 1888 Harrison did conduct an active "front porch" campaign. He remained at home during the campaign but made a large number of short speeches to visiting delegations. While he was President, however, Harrison, no doubt with renomination and re-election in 1892 in the back of his head, made an "official" and nonpolitical tour to the Pacific coast and back. He was a good orator and on that trip made one hundred and forty speeches without repeating himself.

In 1896 Mark Hanna, William McKinley's campaign manager, announced: "He will not take the stump." McKinley remained at his home in Canton, greeted visitors and read a few carefully prepared statements but made few formal addresses. Apparently *front porch campaign* was first applied to this type of campaign in reference to McKinley. In *My Quarter Century of American Politics* (1920) Champ Clark wrote, "That method of campaigning has lost its vogue because there are no more free railroad passes!" William Jennings Bryan, however, made the most energetic and aggressive speaking campaign in 1896 ever made up to that time by a Presidential candidate. He traveled 18,000 miles, spoke to 5,000,000 people, shook hands with tens of thousands, and frequently made from ten to twenty speeches a day. The Presidential campaign of 1896 was the last conducted with torchlight parades and the noise and hurrah started in the log cabin and hard cider campaign in 1840. After the Spanish-American War President McKinley toured the Central States in the interests of the Republican candidates for Congress. But in 1900 he remained quiet again. It still was not regarded as proper for a President to campaign openly for re-election and no President had done so. It was, however, all right for a mere candidate for President to do so and Bryan again stumped the country.

During the spring of 1903 President Theodore Roosevelt made a long tour of the West and made many speeches. Senator Marcus Hanna was then being groomed to oppose Roosevelt for the Republican nomination.

in 1904 and the President's tour was regarded at the time as political in purpose. On April 5, 1903, Secretary of State John Hay wrote to the President: "Your speeches have been admirable—strong, lucid and eloquent; they will make a splendid platform for next year." In 1904 Alton B. Parker, the Democratic nominee, made a short speaking tour. President Roosevelt did not make campaign speeches but issued some vigorous political statements in reply to his opponent. In a sense Theodore Roosevelt was the first President while in office not only to campaign for the nomination but also the first President while in office to issue political statements and take an active part in a Presidential campaign.

During the campaign of 1908 William Howard Taft and Bryan both made campaign speeches. In 1912 President Taft was urged to campaign actively for renomination. At first the President refused because he did not want to break the precedent that a President did not openly seek renomination. But former President Theodore Roosevelt was gaining strength every day and Taft finally yielded, saying, "Even a rat will fight when driven in a corner." During the Presidential campaign of that year past President Roosevelt, President Taft and future President Woodrow Wilson all campaigned openly. In 1916 President Wilson confined his campaigning to a few key speeches, while Charles Evans Hughes toured the country and made an active campaign. Four years later James M. Cox traveled and made campaign speeches, while Warren G. Harding remained at his Marion home and read a series of carefully prepared speeches and statements to visiting delegations, although finally he left his "front porch" and made a speaking tour through some of the pivotal States.

John W. Davis and Robert M. La Follette made active speaking campaigns in 1924, but President Calvin Coolidge made only one political speech and only a few public statements during the campaign. In his *Autobiography* (1929) Coolidge wrote of the 1924 campaign: "With the exception of the occasion of my notification, I did not attend any partisan meetings or make any purely political speeches during the campaign. I spoke several times at the dedication of a monument, the observance of the anniversary of an historic event, at a meeting of some commercial body, or before some religious gathering." Herbert Hoover and Alfred M. Smith both campaigned actively in 1928. Since then it has been customary for Presidential candidates, whether President or not, to take an active part in their political campaigns. Both President Hoover and Franklin D. Roosevelt made campaign speeches in 1932. In 1936, 1940 and 1944 President Roosevelt took to "the open road" and made many campaign speeches.

In 1948 Harry S. Truman made the most extensive speaking campaign ever made up to that time by a President seeking election. He himself said he would speak at every "whistle stop" on the railroads over which he traveled. Trains make two types of unscheduled stops. When a whistle stop is made the engineer on the train notifies the station with the locomotive whistle, while when a flag stop is made the station master flags the train. Truman as a youth had worked as a timekeeper on the Santa Fe Railway and was familiar with railroad lingo. *Whistle stop* became synonymous with *jerk-water town, tank-town* or any small town.

It is generally conceded that Clay, Blaine and Bryan have been the greatest campaign orators. All three were the Presidential nominees of their parties—Clay twice, Blaine once, and Bryan three times—yet none of them were elected. They were all members of Congress and all three served as Secretary of State. On June 27, 1888, after Benjamin Harrison had been nominated by the Republicans, former President Hayes wrote to William McKinley: "My old friend Judge Johnson used to say, 'The Presidency is unlike the Kingdom of Heaven,—those who seek shall never find.' " But eight years later McKinley, with the help of Mark Hanna, sought it and found it.

A person who has an excessive desire to become President is said to have the Presidential bee in his bonnet. His behavior is supposed to resemble that of a person who has a bee buzzing inside his hat. In *Autobiography of Seventy Years* (1903) George Frisbie Hoar wrote: "In Plato's day the bee lighted on the lips of the orator, and the sweet honey of Hymettus mingled with the discourse as it came forth. Today, the bee lights in his ear and fills his fancy with delightful dreams of a hive by the Potomac, thatched with flowers and redolent with the incense of flattery." Thomas Jefferson wrote in 1799: "Whenever a man has cast a longing eye on offices, a rottenness begins in his conduct."

During the early days of the republic men with the Presidential bee in their bonnets started to work early just as they do today. Early in 1821, even before President Monroe had started to serve his second term, several members of his official family already had their eye on the next Presidential election. The bee was buzzing particularly in the bonnets of Secretary of State Adams, Speaker Clay, Secretary of the Treasury Crawford and Secretary of War Calhoun. Four years later Adams got the prize, but in 1821 he pretended he would do nothing underhanded to get the Presidency. The state of his mind is indicated by an entry in his diary on February 25, 1821:

Hopkinson dined with us. . . . I told Mr. Hopkinson that I was perfectly aware of the exertions making by Mr. Crawford himself and his friends to secure the Presidency at the next election. If that office was to be the prize of cabal and intrigue, of purchasing newspapers, bribing by appointments, or bargaining for foreign missions, I had no ticket in that lottery. Whether I had the qualifications for a President . . . was, to say the least, very doubtful to myself. But that I had no talent for obtaining the office by such means was perfectly clear. I had neither talent nor inclination for intrigue. I can do nothing either to canvass for myself or to counteract the canvassing of others. I will have no stipendary editor of newspapers to extol my talents and to criticize or calumniate my rivals. I will devote none of my time to devising laws to increase my own patronage and multiply canvassers in my favor.

Judging from his diary and letters Adams thought of little during the next four years except his chances of being President. Behind the scenes he continually promoted his candidacy and encouraged others to do likewise. When he finally did become President he didn't forget Joseph Hopkinson, the early supporter to whom he told the things just quoted. He appointed him a Federal judge! All of which shows there is more than one way to skin a cat.

For many years after he had become a national hero, Andrew Jackson did not take himself seriously as a Presidential candidate. As late as 1821, when friends urged him to be a candidate, General Jackson replied: "I know what I am fit for. I can command a body of men in a rough way; but I am not fit to be President." On another occasion he said more emphatically: "Do they think that I am . . . damned fool enough to think myself fit for President? No, Sir." It was not until after the election of 1824, when he received more popular and electoral votes than any other candidate but still was not chosen, that he resolved to become President in spite of hell and high water.

On July 11, 1858, Hayes wrote to his friend and schoolmate Guy M. Bryan:

If you do get into the Senate, don't get the Presidential mania. It makes mad every man who is at all prominent at Washington either in the House or Senate. Scores of men, usually sound and sensible, fancy they can be President, who has no more right to think so than the autocrat of Russia. I have no knowledge of any tolerably conspicuous politician at Washington whose career is not colored and marred by his ambition to be President. I say this in all seriousness. It makes fools of all sorts from Webster down to Lewis Campbell.

In time the bug crept into Hayes's bonnet and stung him. On April 14, 1875, he wrote in his diary: "I am still importuned in all quarters to consent to run as Republican candidate for governor. Several suggest that if elected governor now, I will stand well for the Presidency next year. How wild! What a queer lot we are becoming! Nobody is out of the reach of that mania." He was elected Governor for a third term and the next year was elected President.

Clay, Webster, Calhoun, Blaine, Thomas B. Reed, Bryan, Champ Clark and perhaps others were embittered by their failure to win the Presidency or their party's nomination for it. One of these, Clark, wrote of another:

For a score of years there was a successful, scintillating, aurora-borealis statesman, known as "the Man from Maine," who strove with marvelous dexterity for the glittering prize of the Presidency, who kept the country in a turmoil for nearly a generation with his ambitions, and who finally went to his grave cut off before his time, bitterly disappointed, if not broken-hearted.

Who said: "Spend and spend, elect and elect"?

"We will spend and spend, tax and tax, elect and elect" is popularly attributed to Harry Lloyd Hopkins (1890-1946), who was successively Emergency Relief Administrator, Works Progress Administrator, Secretary of Commerce, Lend-Lease Administrator, and Special Assistant to President Franklin D. Roosevelt. Max Gordon, theatrical producer, said Hopkins made the statement to him at the Empire race track at Yonkers, New York, in August, 1938. Hopkins denied that he had ever said any such thing, but it was widely circulated as representative of the alleged cynical attitude of the New Dealers in spending billions of dollars for "pump priming," "made work," "boondoggling" and relief in general in order to win elections.

Who said: "I hate war"?

In a speech at Chautauqua, New York, on August 14, 1936, President Franklin D. Roosevelt said, "I hate war," and the saying is generally identified with him. But neither the phraseology nor the thought was original. While taking his regiment from Vera Cruz to Pueblo in August, 1847, Colonel Franklin Pierce, later President, wrote his family, "I hate war in all its aspects." John Hay in a letter to Theodore Stanton on May 8, 1808, wrote, "I detest war." Speaker John B. Henderson, who lost a leg from wounds in the Union army, began a speech to the Grand Army of the Republic at Indianapolis with: "My theme tonight is war; I hate it." In *Woodrow Wilson as I Know Him* Joseph P. Tumulty (1921) wrote: "All politicians pretend to hate and to dread war, but Woodrow Wilson really hates and dreads it in all the fibres of his human soul . . ."

What is a dogcatcher?

"He couldn't be elected dogcatcher" is an old American saying of unknown authorship. *Dogcatcher* is a popular name for a poundmaster, an officer whose duty is to round up stray livestock and pets and keep them in a pound until they are returned to their owners or otherwise disposed of. Formerly this officer was regarded as the lowest in dignity in the community and *dogcatcher* became a slang term for a contemptible person. An office seeker who couldn't be elected dogcatcher couldn't be elected to any office. "He couldn't be elected constable" is a similar and probably earlier expression of the same idea. In 1949 Neal D. Bishop, a State senator in Colorado, suggested to President Harry S. Truman that he appoint John L. Lewis, president of the United Mine Workers, as Ambassador to Russia, and on May 5 of the same year the President replied in a letter to Bishop that "for your information I wouldn't appoint John L. Lewis dogcatcher . . ." Poundmasters are now appointed, but formerly they were chosen by popular vote in some New England towns. In *The American Language* H. L. Mencken says "a dog-catcher is a *canine control officer* in Peoria, Illinois, and a *humane officer* in Tulsa, Oklahoma." The mayor of Auburn, Maine, appoints honorary dogcatchers, a distinction that carries with it a special gold certificate.

Who called one of his statements "campaign oratory"?

During a hearing conducted by the Senate Committee on Foreign Relations on February 11, 1941, Senator Gerald P. Nye of North Dakota asked Wendell L. Willkie (1892-1944) about several statements he had made the year before as Republican nominee for President. Nye finally said: "One more assertion of yours, that of October 30th. 'On the basis of his'—that is, Roosevelt's—'past performance with pledges to the people, you may expect we will be at war by April, 1941, if he is elected.' . . . Do you still agree that might be the case?" Willkie replied: "It might be. It was a bit of *campaign oratory*." Political opponents made much of the phrase and he never lived down the charge that in his offhand answer he had confessed insincerity and double-talk in his campaign speeches.

Willkie, a native of Indiana, was christened Lewis Wendell Willkie but reversed his first and middle names when he entered the army in 1917. He was originally a Democrat and did not register as a Republican until a year before his nomination for President. The sudden and spectacular preconvention drive was launched after a young attorney named Oren Root had received a flood of replies in response to a notice in the want-ad section of a New York newspaper asking those favoring Willkie for President to respond.

How many Speakers have become Vice President?

Only two Speakers of the House of Representatives have become Vice President of the United States.

John Nance Garner of Texas has been the only person who went directly from the Speakership of the House to the Vice Presidency. On March 4, 1933, he lighted a cigar as Speaker of the House and finished it as Vice President and presiding officer of the Senate. After adjourning the House as Speaker he walked across the Capitol from the House chamber to the Senate chamber and was immediately sworn in as Vice President. That has been the only instance of a man presiding over both branches of Congress on the same day. Technically his term as a member of Congress and as Speaker ended at midnight of March 3 and his term as Vice President began at that moment. Although he did not take the oath as Vice President until shortly after noon on March 4, he was technically Vice President when he presided over the last sitting of the House of the Seventy-Second Congress. Garner was elected to the Seventy-Third Congress in the same election he was elected Vice President but resigned from the Seventy-Third Congress without ever becoming a member.

Schuyler Colfax of Indiana, Vice President during Grant's first term, has been the only other person to serve as both Speaker and Vice President. He resigned as Speaker March 3, 1869, the day before he took the oath as Vice President, and Theodore M. Pomeroy of New York was elected Speaker for one day. Colfax was a suave, genial little man whose nickname was "Smiler."

Charles W. Fairbanks of Indiana, who was Vice President under Theodore Roosevelt, 1905 to 1909, was the only other person elected Vice President while a member of the House of Representatives. Thomas Riley Marshall of Indiana, Vice President during Wilson's two terms, in his early days declined a nomination for a seat in Congress on the ground that he might be elected.

John C. Calhoun, John C. Breckinridge, Hannibal Hamlin and Andrew Johnson were the only four persons who after presiding over the Senate as Vice President returned to that body as members.

Do delegates to nominating conventions receive pay?

The delegates to the national conventions for nominating Presidential and Vice Presidential candidates receive no salary or compensation of any kind for their services and they pay their own expenses. Individual aspirants for nomination or their backers may pay the bills of delegates, but the parties themselves make no provision for paying the delegates for their services. At one time the Democratic and Republican parties in Oregon and Minnesota provided pay for their delegates, but the practice was abandoned.

The general expenses of a national nominating convention are paid out of the party treasuries, which obtain their funds largely as campaign contributions. The national committee of each party chooses the city in which its convention is held. Such a convention brings considerable business to a city and it has long been customary for the commercial interests and various civic organizations to donate large sums of money to a party to induce it to hold its national convention in their city. When the members of a national committee vote upon the various cities suggested they take into consideration this fact as well as the hotel, convention hall and other facilities available.

National nominating conventions are not created by law but are purely the product of party custom and convenience. Their membership, machinery and procedure are determined by party rules and regulations.

At one time, because of poor transportation and great distances, the Western States had difficulty in getting men to serve as delegates to national nominating conventions. In 1860 Oregon designated Horace Greeley, the New York editor, to serve as head of its delegation at the National Republican Convention that met in Chicago and nominated Lincoln for President. The first Democratic National Convention was held in Baltimore in 1832 and renominated Andrew Jackson for President and nominated Martin Van Buren for Vice President. The delegates were nearly all officeholders. Tennessee sent no delegates, but a man from the Volunteer State named Rucker happened to be in the city, and he was accepted as a delegate and permitted to cast the fifteen votes for his State. Silliman Evans, newspaper reporter and publisher, served as a delegate to three Democratic conventions from three different States. He was a delegate from Texas in 1932, from Maryland in 1936, and from Tennessee in 1940—and each convention nominated Franklin D. Roosevelt for President.

Who has been the oldest President?

Andrew Jackson has been the oldest President. He was born March 15, 1767, and lacked only eleven days of being seventy when he retired from the Presidency on March 4, 1837. He was eleven days short of sixty-two when inaugurated the first time on March 4, 1829. On March 4, 1833, Philip Hone wrote in his diary: "The President held a levee after the ceremony of inauguration, and crowds went to the palace, I among the rest. But shortly before I arrived he had been compelled to retire from exhaustion . . . He looks exceedingly feeble. If it were delicate and respectful to bet on such a subject, I would bet large odds that he does not outlive the present term of his office." Jackson was so exhausted by banquets, receptions and other festivities during his journey to New England in the same year that his physicians insisted that the journey be abandoned so the President might "return to Washington alive." But the old warrior remained very much alive and lived to be past seventy-eight.

James Buchanan was Jackson's nearest competitor in respect to age. He lacked fifty days of being seventy when he yielded the Presidency to Abraham Lincoln on March 4, 1861. William Henry Harrison, who was born February 9, 1773, was the oldest President when inaugurated. He was sixty-seven when elected and sixty-eight when inaugurated on March 4, 1841. But he did not become the oldest President because he died a month after taking office.

Theodore Roosevelt was the youngest man to be President. He was born on October 27, 1858, and lacked forty-three days of being forty-three when he became President as the result of McKinley's death September 14, 1901. He also has been the youngest man *elected* to the Presidency, being only a few days past forty-six when he was elected in 1904. Ulysses S. Grant, his nearest competitor in respect of youth, was also forty-six, but a few months older, at the time of his election the first time.

Six Presidents took the oath while still in their forties—Theodore Roosevelt, forty-two; Grant, forty-six; Cleveland, forty-seven; Pierce, forty-eight, and Polk and Garfield, forty-nine. Six Presidents were in their sixties when they took the oath—John Adams, Jackson and Harry S. Truman, sixty-one; Taylor, sixty-four; Buchanan, sixty-five, and William Henry Harrison, sixty-eight. All the other Presidents were in their fifties when they took the oath—Fillmore, Arthur and Taft, fifty; Tyler, Coolidge and Franklin D. Roosevelt, fifty-one; Lincoln fifty-two; Van Buren, McKinley and Hoover, fifty-four; Benjamin Harrison and Harding, fifty-five; Madison, Johnson and Wilson, fifty-six; Washington, Jefferson and John Quincy Adams, fifty-seven, and Monroe and Hayes, fifty-eight. No man in his thirties or seventies has become President. Truman, sixty-one, was the oldest of the seven Vice Presidents to succeed to the Presidency as the result of the death of Presidents.

John Adams (October 30, 1735—July 4, 1826) lived longer than any other President—ninety years and nearly eight months. His nearest rival in longevity was James Madison, who died at eighty-five. Thomas

Jefferson died at eighty-three. James A. Garfield (November 29, 1831–September 19, 1881), who died when he was forty-nine years, nine months and ten days old, was the youngest of all Presidents either in or out of office at the time of his death. The second youngest President at the time of his death was James K. Polk, who died out of office at fifty-three years and seven and a half months. He had been the youngest ex-President. At fifty-five Chester A. Arthur became the second youngest ex-President. He died at fifty-six. The average age of the first thirty-two Presidents at the time of taking the oath of office was 54.8 years. The average age of the first thirty Presidents when they died was 68.6 years. There has been a tendency for the life expectancy of Presidents to diminish slightly and it may be said in a general way that now the Presidency shortens the lives of the occupants.

In early days men considered themselves old at a much younger age than they do today. George Washington underwent many hardships in the field from youth and suffered several serious illnesses, and he regarded himself as an old man at fifty. He had one critical illness while President. On May 15, 1790, Senator William Maclay of Pennsylvania wrote in his diary: "Called to see the President. Every eye full of tears. His life despaired of. Doctor MacNight told me he would trifle neither with his own character or the public expectation—his danger was imminent; and every reason to expect that the event of his disorder would be unfortunate."

On May 13, 1827, John Quincy Adams, then fifty-nine and President, wrote in his diary: "My own career is closed. My hopes, such as are left me, are centered upon my children. The capacity to write fails me from day to day. My duties are to prepare for the end with a grateful heart and an unwavering mind." After that date he wrote several more volumes of his diary, served nearly seventeen years in the House of Representatives as an active crusader against slavery, and lived to be past eighty.

How is the vacancy filled when a nominee for President dies or withdraws?

The national committee of each major political party has power to fill vacancies on the ticket from any cause, or to call a national convention together for that purpose. That power is usually conferred on the national committee by the national conventions that make the nominations. For instance, the Republican National Convention that met in 1928 and nominated Herbert Hoover for President and Charles

Curtis for Vice President adopted the following resolution empowering the Republican National Committee to fill vacancies on the ticket:

Resolved, That the Republican National Committee be and is hereby authorized and empowered to fill any and all vacancies which may occur by reason of death, declination or otherwise in the ticket nominated by the convention and that, in voting in said committee, the committee members representing any State, Territory, Territorial Possession or the District of Columbia, shall be entitled to cast the same number of votes as said State, Territory, Territorial Possession or the District of Columbia was entitled to cast in the national convention; or, that the National Committee in its judgment may call the national convention for the purpose of filling such vacancy.

Therefore if a party nominee for President or Vice President should die or resign before the November election the national committee of that party would designate another person to fill the vacancy or would call the national convention into session again for that purpose. Only twice has the national committee of a major political party had occasion to act in such an emergency. In 1860 the Democratic National Convention at Baltimore that nominated Stephen A. Douglas for President nominated Benjamin Fitzpatrick of Alabama for Vice President, but two days later he declined the nomination, whereupon the Democratic National Committee filled the vacancy on the Democratic ticket by designating Herschel V. Johnson of Georgia as the Vice-Presidential candidate. On October 30, 1912, a few days before the national election, Vice President James S. Sherman, who was running for re-election on the Taft ticket, died. The Republican National Committee, acting under the power conferred on it by the National Convention, which had met at Chicago and made the nominations, designated Nicholas Murray Butler of New York to fill the vacancy caused by Sherman's death. Only eight electors pledged to Taft and Butler were elected—four each in Vermont and Utah.

Which ex-Presidents held offices?

Generally Presidents are reluctant to accept either appointive or elective offices after they have retired or been defeated, but there have been a few exceptions.

When war with France seemed imminent in 1798 President John Adams appointed George Washington, the first ex-President, "Commander-in-Chief of the Army" with the rank of lieutenant general, and he accepted and served.

John Adams served as a Presidential elector in 1820 and voted for

James Monroe. Four years later James Madison and Monroe both refused to serve as Presidential electors. Monroe, however, did accept an appointment as justice of the peace.

Two ex-Presidents served in Congress—John Quincy Adams and Andrew Johnson. Adams's friends solemnly discussed "the propriety of my taking a seat in the House of Representatives," he says in his diary. Representative Joseph Richardson, the sitting and retiring member from the Plymouth district, told Adams that "he thought that the service in the House of Representatives of an ex-President of the United States, instead of degrading the individual, would elevate the Representative character." Adams wrote: "I said I had in that respect no scruple whatever. No person could be degraded by serving the people as a Representative in Congress. Nor, in my opinion, would an ex-President of the United States be degraded by serving as a Selectman of the town, if elected thereto by the people."

On October 13, 1830, after being nominated, Adams wrote: "And so I am launched again upon the faithless wave of politics." On November 6 of the same year, after he had been elected by an overwhelming majority over two other candidates, he wrote that "My return to public life in a subordinate station is disagreeable to my family, and disapproved by some of my friends" but that he was deeply grateful for "the testimonial of the continued confidence" of the people of his district. On December 16, 1831, soon after taking his seat, the ex-President wrote, "Mr. Clay asked me how I felt upon turning boy again to go into the House of Representatives." Clay predicted that Adams would find the service too laborious. Adams served in the House from March 4, 1831, until his death on February 23, 1848, a period of nearly seventeen years. He had never previously served in the House, but he had been a Senator from March 4, 1803, to June 8, 1808, and has the distinction of having served in Congress both before and after he was President. In 1892 ex-President Rutherford B. Hayes wrote in his diary that John Quincy Adams was "by all odds the most important figure in our history [in] his career after retiring from" the Presidency. Adams was defeated for Governor of Massachusetts after he was President and while in Congress.

Andrew Johnson has been the only ex-President to sit as a member of the U.S. Senate. In 1872, three years after retiring from the Presidency, he ran as an independent for Representative-at-large but was defeated. He was elected to the Senate by the Tennessee legislature on January 26, 1875. Ordinarily he would not have begun his duties as a Senator until December of the same year, but President Grant called a special session of the Senate to act on a treaty with the King of the Sandwich Islands, and accordingly the ex-President took the oath as a Senator March 6, 1875. On March 22, the ex-President made a speech in the Senate opposing the resolution approving Grant's conduct in reference to Louisiana. In this speech he reviewed the shortcomings of the whole Grant administration and appealed for justice to the South. The special session of the Senate ended two days later, and Johnson died on July 31 of the same year. He had previously served as a Senator from October 8, 1857, to March 4, 1862, and has the unique distinction of having served as a U.S. Senator both before and after he was President.

John Tyler was a delegate to the Confederate Provisional Congress in 1861, and a member-elect of the Confederate house of representatives when he died early in 1862. On January 18, 1886, former President Rutherford B. Hayes wrote in his diary: "I have avoided receiving any honors or office since I left Washington. My feeling is that as ex-President I have the highest place a citizen can hold and that it would be unseemly to take anything else." Ex-President Benjamin Harrison was attorney for Venezuela in a boundary dispute with Great Britain and served as a delegate to a conference at The Hague. Theodore Roosevelt acted as special ambassador at the funeral of King Edward VII in 1910. Ex-President Herbert Hoover carried out several official missions by Presidential appointment, and in 1949 he declined an appointment as U.S. Senator from New York offered to him by Governor Thomas E. Dewey.

Ex-Vice Presidents who did not reach the Presidency have not been so particular as ex-Presidents about holding public offices. John C. Calhoun was a Senator and Secretary of State. Richard M. Johnson served in the lower house of the Kentucky legislature. George M. Dallas was Minister to England. John C. Breckinridge served in the U.S. Senate and as Confederate secretary of war. Hannibal Hamlin was Senator and Minister to Spain. Levi P. Morton was Governor of New York. Charles G. Dawes was Ambassador to Great Britain and member of the Reconstruction Finance Corporation. Henry A. Wallace was Secretary of Commerce.

When were mechanical voting machines first used?

The first patent obtained by Thomas A. Edison in 1868 was for an electrical vote recorder. A mechanical voting machine in a simple form was tried out in England as early as 1870. The problem was to construct a practical and accurate machine that would retain the essential features of the Australian ballot. An elaborate mechanical voting machine such as those used now was first employed in an election at

Lockport, New York, in 1892, and six years later a similar machine was used in an election at Rochester in the same State. By 1948 about 45,000 such voting machines were in operation in some 25,000 cities, towns and villages in twenty-five states. Mechanical voting machines are largely an American development and are not yet (1952) used on a large scale in any other country.

Which Presidents were related?

There has been only one instance of a father and son serving as President. John Quincy Adams was the son of John Adams. Both were born in what is now Quincy, Massachusetts, and both are buried there in the same temple. The Adamses are the only two Presidents who celebrated their fiftieth wedding anniversaries. John Quincy Adams became President twenty-eight years after his father did. On February 9, 1825, Senator Rufus King of New York sat down at his desk in the Senate chamber in Washington and wrote the following note, which he sent by special messenger to Secretary of State John Quincy Adams:

My Dear Sir:—We have this moment heard the issue of the election, and I send you and your venerable father my affectionate congratulations upon your choice as President of the United States on the first ballot of the House of Representatives. I include your father, as I consider your election as the best amends for the injustice of which he was made the victim. To me and mine, the choice has been such as we have cordially hoped and expected.

The President-elect at once sent King's note by post to his father at Quincy:

My dear and Honored Father:—The enclosed note from Mr. King will inform you of the event of this day, upon which I can only offer you my congratulations and ask your blessings and prayers.

On February 18, 1825, John Adams at Quincy wrote as follows to his fifty-seven-year-old son:

I have received your letter of the 9th. Never did I feel so much solemnity as upon this occasion. The multitude of my thoughts and the intensity of my feelings are too much for a mind like mine, in its ninetieth year. May the blessing of God Almighty continue to protect you to the end of your life, as it has heretofore protected you in so remarkable manner from your cradle! I offer the same prayer for your lady and your family—and am Your affectionate father . . .

James Madison and Zachary Taylor were both great-grandsons of James Taylor and his wife, Martha Thompson and were second cousins. Taylor became President forty years after Madison did. When Taylor was a young junior officer in the Army he dined with President Madison at Montpelier and took advantage of this social occasion to solicit his distinguished second cousin for a Federal appointment. The President replied sharply that public offices were not granted for private or family reasons and the young officer left in a huff without taking leave of his host.

Benjamin Harrison was a grandson of William Henry Harrison. The second President Harrison was born in the home of the first President Harrison at North Bend, Ohio. Benjamin Harrison was seven years old when William Henry Harrison died and became President forty-eight years after his grandfather did.

The blood relationship between Franklin D. Roosevelt and Theodore Roosevelt was not so close as is generally supposed. They were only fourth cousins once removed, a degree of relationship seldom considered by families except for genealogical purposes. The first member of the Roosevelt family to come to America was Claes Martenszen Van Rozenfeldt who is supposed to have emigrated from Holland to New Amsterdam about 1650, the exact year not being established beyond doubt. *Claes*, the Christian name of the first immigrant, like *Claus* in *Santa Claus*, is a familiar derivative from the last part of *Nicholas*. *Martenszen* is equivalent to "son of Marten." It was not until two or three generations later than *Rozenfeldt*, which literally means "field of roses" or "red field," assumed the present spelling. *Roosevelt* with varying spellings is still a common family name in the Netherlands.

Claes Martenszen Van Rozenfeldt died in 1660 and left five minor children. Among them was Nicholas, the second and last common ancestor of the two Presidents in America. Nicholas had two sons—Johannes, born in 1689, and Jacobus, born in 1692. Theodore Roosevelt was descended from Johannes, and Franklin D. Roosevelt from Jacobus. *Jacobus* and *Jakobus* were the Latin and early forms of *James*, the form later adopted by the Roosevelts. The two lines of descent, with the dates of birth, are as follows:

Claes Martenszen Van Rozenfeldt
Nicholas, 1658

Johannes, 1689	Jacobus, 1692
	Isaac, 1726
	Jakobus, 1760
	Isaac, 1790
	James, 1828
Theodore, 1858	Franklin Delano, 1882

From this it will be seen that President Theodore Roosevelt and Franklin D. Roosevelt's father were fourth cousins. As a matter of fact, President Franklin D. Roosevelt, through his mother, was more closely

[415]

related to President U.S. Grant than he was to Theodore Roosevelt, and it is said that he was related in one way or another to eight or nine other Presidents.

The two Roosevelts were more closely related by marriage than by blood. In 1905 Franklin D. Roosevelt was married to Anna Eleanor Roosevelt, daughter of President Theodore Roosevelt's brother Elliot and therefore his own fifth cousin. The then President attended the wedding of his niece, and his daughter Alice, afterward the wife of Speaker Nicholas Longworth, acted as her first cousin's bridesmaid. Thus the children of President Theodore Roosevelt were fifth cousins to President Franklin D. Roosevelt and first cousins of his wife. The relationship of the children of the two Presidents is more complicated. Through their father the children of President Franklin D. Roosevelt are fifth cousins once removed to the children of President Theodore Roosevelt; through their mother they are second cousins once removed. The second President Roosevelt had no full brothers; he had one half brother, James, who was born in 1854.

No two of the first thirty-five Vice Presidents have been closely related. Adlai E. Stevenson, Vice President under Cleveland from 1893 to 1897, and one of the grandmothers of Vice President Alben W. Barkley were first cousins, and the relationship between these two Kentucky-born Vice Presidents is that of first cousins twice removed.

How did *steam roller* originate?

A steam roller is a leveling machine used to crush and flatten stones in a roadbed. The term is applied politically to high-handed methods of overcoming opposition, particularly opposition to a ticket prepared by party bosses and leaders.

In 1908 the Republican National Committee met at Chicago a week before the national convention to pass on contested delegates and to make up the temporary roll. At the time President Theodore Roosevelt was trying to dictate the nomination of William Howard Taft as his successor. The opposition consisted of Hughes, Knox, Cameron, Fairbanks and Foraker, each of whom had the support of the delegates from his own State, and the outcome of the fight between the Roosevelt-Taft delegates on the one hand and the Allies on the other depended on how the contests were decided by the Republican National Committee. With machinelike precision the Roosevelt-Taft members of the national committee decided the contests in favor of their faction and gave the Roosevelt-Taft delegates control of the convention to meet the next week.

Oswald F. Schuette was covering the meeting as the political writer for the Chicago *Inter-Ocean*. As he came out of the Coliseum after one of the sessions a steam road roller standing on a vacant lot caught his eye. The steam roller had on it a sign reading: THE STEAM ROLLER VAUDEVILLE AT THE AUDITORIUM THEATRE. It was merely an advertising stunt, but it suggested to Schuette the idea of comparing the methods of the Roosevelt-Taft committeemen with a steam road roller. In his report in the *Inter-Ocean* the next day he said that the Roosevelt-Taft men flattened out the opposition like a steam roller. Steam roller as applied to this highhanded method caught the popular fancy and was given wide currency by the newspapers. The term in its political sense is often erroneously said to have originated in the Republican National Convention of 1912, which renominated Taft in the teeth of Roosevelt's opposition.

Who was the tallest President?

Abraham Lincoln was about six feet four inches in height and has been the tallest President. He reached his full height at seventeen. In a brief autobiography that he wrote in 1859 upon the suggestion of Jesse W. Fell, Lincoln said: "If any personal description is thought desirable, I am in height six feet four inches, nearly; lean in flesh, weighing on an average, one hundred and eighty pounds." The records of the Black Hawk War, in which Lincoln served as a captain, gave his height as six feet four and a half inches. Henry C. Whitney, who traveled with Lincoln on the circuit in Illinois and often slept with him, wrote: "He was six feet and four inches in height, his legs and arms were disproportionately long, his feet and hands were abnormally large, he was awkward in his gait and actions." His great height was due largely to the unusual length of his legs from the knees down. Legend says that when a friend bantered him upon the length of his legs, Lincoln observed that he was so tall that his legs had to be long to reach the ground. Lincoln, even after he became President, was fond of having other tall men measure heights with him. When traveling Lincoln had considerable difficulty in finding a bed long enough to sleep in with comfort. In December, 1864, Mrs. Lincoln bought for him and had set up in the White House an eight-foot bed with canopy and curtains.

Just who was the second tallest President is hard to determine. Evidence indicates that George Washington was six feet tall at sixteen and six feet two inches in his prime. In 1760 George Mercer, his friend and companion in arms, wrote: "He may be described as being as straight as an Indian, measuring six feet two inches in his stockings, and weighing

175 pounds, when he took his seat in the House of Burgesses in 1759." David Anderson of Alexandria, Virginia, recorded that in 1778 Washington "seemed six feet and a half" but his "exact height was six feet two inches in his boots." George Washington Parke Custis, who was reared by Washington, agreed that he was six feet two inches in height. In 1761, in an order for clothes to his London agent, he wrote: "I enclose a measure, and, for further insight, I don't think it amiss to add, that my stature is six feet; otherwise rather slender than corpulent." In a clothing order dated April 26, 1763, he describes himself variously as "six feet high" and "about six feet high." In another clothing order, however, he described himself as "6 ft. 3 in. tall." John Hunter, a London merchant who visited Washington at Mount Vernon in 1783, noted in his diary: "The General is about six feet high, perfectly straight and well made; rather inclined to be lusty." Despite this evidence Tobias Lear, who was present when Dr. Elisha C. Dick measured Washington after death, reported that Washington's dead body measured "6 feet 3½ inches." On August 19, 1783, General Washington and ten of his officers weighed themselves at West Point and the Commander-in-Chief tipped the scales at 209 pounds in uniform.

The exact height of Jefferson is not known. It is often given as six feet three inches. James Sullivan, who knew him personally, said Jefferson "was a tall man, over six feet in stature." After visiting Monticello in 1824, Daniel Webster wrote that, "Mr. Jefferson is now between eighty-one and eighty-two, above six feet high." But his oldest grandson, Thomas Jefferson Randolph, who was brought up at Monticello, wrote that his grandfather was "six feet two-and-a-half inches in height." Jefferson, like Lincoln, had disproportionately long legs, was loose-jointed and gangling, and, when sitting, gave the casual observer the impression that he was much shorter than he was. Apparently he was more than six feet two inches in height.

Chester A. Arthur and Franklin D. Roosevelt were six feet two inches in height. Roosevelt weighed about 187 pounds. His family was the tallest who have occupied the White House. Mrs. Roosevelt is five feet eleven inches tall and their four sons range in height from six feet to six feet four. Andrew Jackson was six feet one inch in height. James Monroe, James Buchanan, John Tyler ("Long John"), James A. Garfield, William Howard Taft and Warren G. Harding were six-footers, and Woodrow Wilson was nearly so. The heights of Millard Fillmore, Grover Cleveland and Herbert Hoover are given as about five feet eleven inches; and those of Franklin Pierce, Andrew Johnson, Theodore Roosevelt, Harry S. Truman and Calvin Coolidge as five feet ten inches. Rutherford B. Hayes was five feet eight and a half inches and

Zachary Taylor five feet eight inches in height. James K. Polk whose exact height is not a matter of record, was probably about five feet eight inches tall. He was slender and had his clothes tailored to make him look larger.

Winfield Scott, unsuccessful Whig candidate in 1852, was six feet five inches in height and has been the tallest person ever to run for President.

William Howard Taft was the heaviest President. He weighed 332 pounds when he entered the White House and 354 when he left it. Senator Jonathan P. Dolliver of Iowa was reputed as having referred to President Taft as "a large good-natured body entirely surrounded by people who know exactly what they want." Taft's obesity was the source of many jokes. It was reported that he got stuck in the White House bathtub several times and had to call for help. The problem was solved by installing an extra large tub for his special use. Occasionally the President fell asleep and slept during conferences. In *As I Knew Them* (1936) Senator James E. Watson of Indiana wrote: "I was at the White House a good many times for lunch and dinner and observed his habits. He had a voracious appetite which he always satisfied to the limit. Often when I was talking to him after a meal his head would fall over his breast and he would go sound asleep for ten or fifteen minutes. He would waken and resume the conversation, only to repeat the performance in the course of half an hour or so." When Taft was Governor-General of the Philippines he once cabled Secretary of War Elihu Root "Rode 30 miles today to Baguio; feeling fine," to which Root replied "How's the horse?" Jokesters said that once on a streetcar Taft arose, bowed politely and gave his seat to two ladies, and that a man was told that he could not take a swim at a bathing beach because President Taft was using the Atlantic.

Cleveland weighed 250 pounds when he was inaugurated and was the second heaviest President.

James Madison is generally regarded as having been the shortest and smallest President. The exact height of "Little Jemmy" and "The Great Little Madison," as he was called, is not known for certain. Estimates range from five feet four inches to five feet six inches. He weighed only about one hundred pounds. Under date of February 22, 1790, Senator William Maclay of Pennsylvania referred in his diary to Madison, then a Representative in Congress, as "his Littleness." The next shortest President probably was Martin Van Buren, "Little Van" and "The Little Magician," who was barely five feet six inches tall. Benjamin Harrison, "Little Ben," was only a little over five feet six inches tall. His grandfather, William Henry Harrison, was small in stature and was probably about five feet eight inches in height. During the Presidential campaign of 1840 his partisans sang:

Come now, huzza for Harrison,
Just as we used to do
When first we heard of Proctor's fall—
When this old hat was new.

And during the campaign of 1888 the Democrats said "Grandpa's Pants Won't Fit Benny" and called him "The Man in His Grandfather's Hat." The Republicans countered with the jingle:

Yes, grandfather's hat fits Ben—Fits Ben;
He wears it with dignified grace, Oh yes!
So rally again and we'll put Uncle Ben
Right back in his grandfather's place.

Benjamin Harrison had unusually short legs and it was observed that when he and Cleveland sat beside each other during the inauguration they appeared to be about the same height.

John Quincy Adams was only about an inch taller than Van Buren and Benjamin Harrison. "My own height is five feet seven inches, English," he tells us in his diary on March 20, 1812. His father, John Adams, was probably about the same height. The height of William McKinley was five feet seven and one-fourth inches, and that of Ulysses S. Grant about five feet seven and three-fourths inches.

The tallest Vice President was about the same height as the tallest President. He was Charles Warren Fairbanks, who was six feet four inches tall. Aaron Burr, known as "Bantam Burr" in the Continental army, was probably the shortest Vice President. He was five feet six inches in height, a fraction of an inch shorter than Van Buren.

What is a demagogue?

Demagogue is used so loosely and recklessly that it is not susceptible of exact definition. The term is derived from Greek *demos,* "people," and *agogos,* "leading," and literally means leader of the people. In ancient Greece a demagogue was at first an orator or leader who took the part of the people against other interests in the state. But the demagogues so often led the people astray that the term gradually came to signify a misleader rather than a true leader of the people. "Demagogues," said the cynic Diogenes, "are the mob's lackeys."

The earliest use of *demagogue* in English given by the Oxford dictionary is dated 1650. As now used the term is applied to an unprincipled politician who tells the voters what they like rather than what they ought to hear in order to gain popularity and to get or stay in an elective office. The typical demagogue is a noisy opportunist who professes humility, pretends to love the people and often feels compelled to rise above principle. He votes as well as talks for the record. Demagogues thrive in times of depression and discontent and, to borrow a phrase from Herbert Hoover, play "politics at the expense of human misery." In Shakespeare's *Coriolanus* the Second Officer says "there have been many great men that flattered the people, who ne'er loved them." But many people apply *demagogue* to any politician with whom they disagree.

In Great Britain the methods and practices of demagogues is called *demagogism* or *demagogy*, while in the United States the more common form of the word is *demagoguery*, which is an Americanism. On June 14, 1855, the Georgetown (Kentucky) *Herald* said of a politician: "He is too familiar with the tricks of demagoguery and too loose in his political principles."

Who was the oldest Vice President?

Alben William Barkley of Kentucky was the oldest man elected to the Vice Presidency between 1789 and 1949. He was born November 24, 1877, and was seventy-one years and forty days old when he became Vice President January 20, 1949. His nearest rival in point of age was Charles Curtis of Kansas, who was born January 25, 1880, and who was past sixty-nine when he qualified March 4, 1929. Curtis was seventy-three when he retired. Elbridge Gerry of Massachusetts was sixty-eight, seven months and eighteen days old when he qualified March 4, 1813. George Clinton of New York, William Rufus De Vane King of Alabama and Thomas A. Hendricks of Indiana, all of whom died in office, were sixty-six when they qualified. Clinton lacked several months of being seventy-three when he died. Levi P. Morton of New York, Vice President under Benjamin Harrison, was the longest-lived of the Vice Presidents. He was born at Shoreham, Vermont, May 16, 1824, and was ninety-six when he died on his birthday in 1920.

In many cases the Vice Presidents have been older than the Presidents with whom they were elected. That is because there is a tendency for conventions to nominate for Vice President an old party wheelhorse "to balance the ticket." In 1904 the Democratic Party, after two successive defeats, was short of funds. The convention nominated eighty-one-year-old Henry Gassaway Davis of West Virginia as Vice-Presidential candidate on the Parker ticket because he was wealthy and expected to contribute largely to the campaign expenses. But the octogenarian was a dead loss on the ticket. He did not contribute to the hopeless cause and refused to make campaign speeches on the ground he was too old. Harry S. Truman and Barkley were the oldest successful team ever nominated for President and Vice President by a major party. Truman was sixty-four and Barkley seventy when they were nominated in 1948. Truman was the oldest of the seven Vice Presidents to succeed to the Presidency because of the death of a President. He was past sixty-one when he became President April 12, 1945.

Why is a political orator called a spellbinder?

An effective and eloquent campaign orator is called a spellbinder because he is said to hold his hearers as if bound in a spell. A typical spellbinder usually charms his audience by flowery words rather than by logic. The term is believed to have been coined by William Cassius Goodloe (1841-1889), a Republican politician of Kentucky. During the Harrison-Cleveland campaign of 1888 the Republican stump-speakers were so often referred to in the press as holding their listeners spellbound that Goodloe said on one occasion: "Here comes another of the spellbinders." The earliest known use of the term in print occurs in the New York *Tribune* dated November 15, 1888. Goodloe, the supposed originator of *spellbinder,* was killed in the Lexington post office in a sensational personal encounter in which his antagonist, Armistead M. Swope, was also killed. Spellbinding oratory is less common than formerly but is far from extinct in some sections of the country.

Which Presidents were left-handed?

Two Presidents—James A. Garfield and Harry S. Truman—were born left-handed. Garfield was naturally left-handed in childhood, but his parents and teachers insisted upon his learning to write and draw with his right hand, with the result that he became ambidextrous and was able to use both hands with almost equal ease. In the Union army he used his sword with his right hand. Essentially, however, he remained left-handed. One of his sons said he had been told that his father could write his name with both hands at the same time, but that the signature written with his left-hand was backward. Another story is that Garfield once demonstrated his ambidexterity by writing at the same time in Latin with one hand and in Greek with the other. The J. Q. Adams Ward statue of Garfield near the Capitol in Washington represents him with the right arm in repose and the left in action.

Truman was born left-handed, but as a child was taught to write with his right hand and continued to do so, but in eating, throwing a ball, etc., he gave preference to his left hand. Like Garfield, he really became ambidextrous. In opening baseball games after he became President he threw out the first ball with his left hand, but on April 18, 1947, he threw out the ball at the opening game in Washington with his right hand—just to kid the public and the photographers.

What is a landslide?

Literally a landslide is the slipping of a large mass of earth or rock from a mountain or shore. The term originated in America as a substitute for the earlier British *landslip*. An overwhelming victory at the polls is called a landslide because the candidate who wins by a large majority is thought of as bearing everything before him like a mass of earth sliding from a mountain side. The earliest use of the term in its political sense given by *The Dictionary of American English* is dated 1895, although it may be older than that.

Just what percentage of the total popular vote a winning candidate must get to justify calling his victory a landslide is hard to say. Andrew Jackson in 1828 and 1832, Ulysses S. Grant in 1872, Theodore Roosevelt in 1904, Warren G. Harding in 1920, Herbert Hoover in 1928 and Franklin D. Roosevelt in 1932 and 1936 won the Presidency by majorities sufficiently large to be called landslides. Theodore Roosevelt received 56.4 per cent of the popular vote in 1904; Harding, 60.3 in 1920; Hoover, 58 per cent in 1928, and Franklin D. Roosevelt, 54.7 and 60.7 per cent in 1932 and 1936 respectively. William McKinley's victory over William Jennings Bryan in 1896 was hailed as a landslide by the Republicans, although McKinley received only 51 per cent of the popular vote.

What Presidents had living parents?

Ulysses S. Grant is the only person to become President while both his parents were living. Jesse Root Grant died in 1873 at the age of seventy-nine, and his wife, Hannah Simpson Grant, died in 1883 at the age of eighty-five. President Grant survived his mother only two years.

Twelve other men have become President while one of their parents was living. George Washington, John Adams, James Madison, James K. Polk, James A. Garfield, William McKinley, Franklin D. Roosevelt and Harry S. Truman became President while their mothers were living, while John Quincy Adams, Millard Fillmore, Warren G. Harding and Calvin Coolidge assumed that office while their fathers were alive.

Mrs. Mary Ball Washington died in August, 1789, of a cancer of the

[423]

breast at the age of eighty-two only a few months after her son had become the first President of the United States. General von Steuben, who had been Washington's drillmaster at Valley Forge and who stood beside him when he was inaugurated the first time, was in conference with President Washington when he received the message that his mother was dead. Mrs. James Madison, Sr. ("Old Mrs. Madison") died in 1829 at the age of ninety-nine. President Madison, who died in 1836 at eighty-five, survived his mother only seven years. Mrs. Jane Knox Polk survived her son. On November 2, 1848, President Polk wrote in his diary:

This is my birthday . . . fifty-three years old. It will be twenty-one years on tomorrow since my father died. My mother is still living. Upon each recurrence of my birthday I am solemnly impressed with the vanity and emptiness of worldly honours and worldly enjoyments, and of the wisdom of preparing for a future estate. In four months I shall retire from public life forever. I have lived three-fourths of the period ordinarily allotted to man on earth. I have been highly honored by my fellow-men and have filled the highest station on earth, but I will soon go the way of all earth. I pray God to prepare me to meet the great event.

On the following June 15 the former President died at Nashville, Tennessee.

President James A. Garfield was also survived by his mother, Mrs. Eliza Ballou Garfield, whom the President called "Aunt Eliza." The aged, ailing, snow-white-haired Mrs. Garfield was the first woman to be present when a son was sworn in as President and to hear him deliver his inaugural address. Less than seven months later President Garfield died from an assassin's bullet. After he was shot he immediately sent his mother a note in which he made light of the wound. Mrs. Sara Delano Roosevelt, who died in 1941 at the age of eighty-six, lived to see her son Franklin sworn in as President three times. Mrs. Martha E. Truman, mother of President Harry S. Truman, who succeeded to the Presidency April 12, 1945, died July 26, 1947, at the age of ninety-four. Nathaniel Fillmore, when eighty years old, visited his distinguished son at the White House. When friends tried to persuade him to stay longer, he said: "No, no, I will go; I don't like it here; it isn't a good place to live; it isn't a good place for Millard either; I wish he was at home in Buffalo."

Why was twenty-one chosen as the voting age?

Under Roman law, the basis of civil law in Europe, a person came of age or reached his majority and acquired full legal and civil rights at twenty-five; but under the English common law both men and women came of age at twenty-one, which was regarded as the average age at which a person reached full maturity and discretion. English common law divided the twenty-one years from birth to manhood into three seven-year periods—infancy, childhood and abolescence. Actually a normal person may cease to grow at sixteen or may continue to grow until twenty-five. England adopted the legal age of twenty-one as the minimum voting age, and the Colonies and States of the Union adopted the same conventional standard. When women were granted the right to vote the same minimum age was required. In 1943, during the Second World War, Georgia amended its constitution by popular vote so as to lower the voting age from twenty-one to eighteen for both men and women on the theory that persons old enough to fight are old enough to vote. A similar proposal passed the Florida house in 1947 but was rejected by the senate. So far no State has forbidden elderly citizens from voting on the corollary theory that persons too old to fight are too old to vote.

Were any of the Presidents born during a war?

So far no person born during a major war in which the United States was engaged has become President. The nearest approach to a "war-baby President" was Martin Van Buren, who was born December 5, 1782, which was after the provisional treaty of peace ending the Revolution was concluded at Paris November 30, 1782, but before the final peace treaty was signed in 1783.

Presidents have been born in every month of the year except June. November is the lucky birth month for Presidents in respect to numbers. Five Presidents—Polk, Taylor, Pierce, Garfield and Harding—were born in November. March, April and October have been the birth months of four Presidents each. The names of the Presidents in the order of their birth are as follows:

Washington, February 22, 1732; John Adams, October 30, 1735; Jefferson, April 13, 1743; Madison, March 16, 1751; Monroe, April 28, 1758; Jackson, March 15, 1767; John Quincy Adams, July 11, 1767; William H. Harrison, February 9, 1773; Van Buren, December 5, 1782; Taylor, November 24, 1784; Tyler, March 29, 1790; Buchanan, April 23, 1791; Polk, November 2, 1795; Fillmore, January 7, 1800; Pierce, November 23, 1804; Johnson, December 29, 1808; Lincoln, February 12, 1809; Grant, April 27, 1822; Hayes, October 4, 1822; Arthur, October 5, 1830; Garfield, November 19, 1831; Benjamin Harrison, August 20, 1833; Cleveland, March 18, 1837; McKinley, January 29, 1843; Wilson, December 28, 1856; Taft, September 15, 1857; Theodore Roosevelt, October 27, 1858; Harding, November 2, 1865; Coolidge, July 4, 1872;

Hoover, August 10, 1874; Franklin D. Roosevelt, January 30, 1882 and Truman, May 8, 1884.

Fillmore was the last President born in the eighteenth century, and Pierce was the first born in the nineteenth century, assuming that the nineteenth century began with January 1, 1801. If the nineteenth century began with January 1, 1800, as some contend, then Fillmore was the first President born in the nineteenth century. Only twice has the same year produced two Presidents. John Quincy Adams and his immediate successor, Andrew Jackson, were born in 1767, and Ulysses S. Grant and his immediate successor, Rutherford B. Hayes, were born in 1822. Hayes lived until 1893 and he was alive during part of the lives of all the Presidents except Washington. Grant lived during the lives of all of them except Truman. Harding was elected President on November 2, 1920, which was his fifty-second birthday.

How many Presidents had previous Cabinet experience?

Only eight of the thirty-two Presidents from Washington to Truman had Cabinet experience before their election. They were Jefferson, Madison, Monroe, John Quincy Adams, Van Buren, Buchanan, Taft and Hoover. The Cabinet has been even a less fertile field for Vice Presidents. Only four of the thirty-five Vice Presidents from Adams to Barkley had previous Cabinet experience. They were Jefferson, Calhoun, Van Buren and Wallace. Calhoun and Wallace served in the Cabinet both before and after being Vice President.

Who received electoral votes in the most elections?

Franklin D. Roosevelt and George Clinton, both of New York, share the distinction of having received electoral votes in more elections than any other persons. Roosevelt received electoral votes in 1920 for Vice President and in 1932, 1936, 1940 and 1944 for President. Clinton received electoral votes for President in 1788, 1792, 1796 and 1808 and for Vice President in 1804. He was elected Vice President in 1804, and was renominated for Vice President by the Republican caucus in 1808, but he insisted that he was a candidate for President and not for Vice President. The result was that he received 113 electoral votes for Vice President and six for President. Electors did not vote separately for President and Vice President until the election of 1804, after the Twelfth Amendment to the Constitution became effective, and before that year the electoral votes for President were often scattered among many candidates. Franklin D. Roosevelt, Clinton, John Adams and Thomas

Jefferson all received electoral votes for President four times. Adams received electoral votes in 1788, 1792, 1796 and 1800, and Jefferson in 1792, 1796, 1800 and 1804. George Washington, Charles C. Pinckney, John Jay, Rufus King, John Quincy Adams, Andrew Jackson, Martin Van Buren, Henry Clay, Grover Cleveland, William Jennings Bryan and Theodore Roosevelt received electoral votes in three different elections.

How many men have been nominated for President three times?

Since Presidential candidates have been nominated by national conventions three men have received the Presidential nomination of a major party more than twice—Franklin D. Roosevelt, Grover Cleveland and William Jennings Bryan, all of whom were Democrats. Roosevelt was nominated for President by Democratic national conventions four times—1932, 1936, 1940 and 1944—and each time received a majority of both the popular and the electoral votes. Cleveland was nominated for President by Democratic national conventions in 1884, 1888 and 1892 and received a plurality of the popular votes all three times but failed to receive a majority of the electoral votes in 1888. Bryan was nominated for President by Democratic national conventions in 1896, 1900 and 1908 but failed to get a majority or plurality of either the popular or electoral votes at any time.

Thomas Jefferson was the Democratic-Republican caucus candidate for President three times—1796, 1800 and 1804. Jackson was a candidate for President in 1824, 1828 and 1832, but ran in 1824 and 1828 without a national caucus or convention nomination. Henry Clay was a candidate for President in 1824, 1832 and 1844. In 1824 he ran without either a national caucus or convention nomination, but he was nominated by the National Republican National Convention in 1832 and by the Whig National Convention in 1844. Martin Van Buren was nominated for President by Democratic national conventions in 1836 and 1840 and by the Free Soil National Convention in 1848, but the latter was a minor party and Van Buren received no electoral votes in 1848. The Socialist Party (the Democratic Socialist Party at first) nominated Eugene Debs for President five times—1900, 1904, 1908, 1912 and 1920, and Norman Thomas six times—1928, 1932, 1936, 1940, 1944 and 1948.

How many Presidents served in Congress?

Twenty-two of the first thirty-two Presidents served in the national legislature. Three of them—George Washington, John Adams and Thomas Jefferson—served only in the Continental Congress before the

Federal Constitution was adopted. James Madison and James Monroe served in the Continental Congress and in the Congress under the Constitution.

All of the first eleven Presidents served in the Continental Congress or the Congress under the Constitution, and Zachary Taylor, the twelfth President, was the first without service in the national legislature. The other nine who never served in Congress were: Ulysses S. Grant, Chester A. Arthur, Grover Cleveland, Theodore Roosevelt, William Howard Taft, Woodrow Wilson, Calvin Coolidge, Herbert Hoover and Franklin D. Roosevelt. Of these only Theodore Roosevelt, Calvin Coolidge and Franklin D. Roosevelt had served in State legislatures.

After the adoption of the Constitution, five Presidents served only in the Senate—Monroe, Martin Van Buren, Benjamin Harrison, Warren G. Harding and Harry S. Truman. Seven served only in the House of Representatives—Madison, James K. Polk, Abraham Lincoln, Rutherford B. Hayes, James A. Garfield and William McKinley. Seven served in both the House of Representatives and the Senate—John Quincy Adams, Andrew Jackson, William Henry Harrison, John Tyler, Franklin Pierce, James Buchanan and Andrew Johnson. John Quincy Adams's service in the House was after he was President. He served longer in Congress than any other President—five years and three months in the Senate and nearly seventeen years in the House—a total of more than twenty-two years. Buchanan served in Congress longer than any other President before election to the Presidency—ten years in the House and ten years and nearly three months in the Senate—a total of more than twenty years. Buchanan's service in the Senate was longer than the service of any other President in that body. Garfield served longer in the House than any other President—nearly eighteen years. He was Senator-elect when elected President but never served in the Senate. Harding was the only man elected President while a Senator. No man was elected President while a member of the House of Representatives, and no President after McKinley saw service in that branch of Congress. Three Presidents were chairman of the Ways and Means Committee of the House—Polk, Fillmore and McKinley.

Legislative experience is generally supposed to be useful to a President in dealing with Congress, but one of the Presidents with Congressional experience did not think that long Congressional service was helpful to a President. On April 25, 1881, former President Hayes wrote:

I see more clearly than ever, and I thought I saw before, that congressional life is not the best introduction for the President's house. Great and fully equipped as the general [Garfield] is, there are embarrassments growing out of his long and brilliant career in Congress, which Jackson and Lincoln, and Grant, and myself, escaped. The traditions and courtesies of the Senators and Representatives stand in the way of the Executive, however, as defined by the Constitution, and no man who is trained in the congressional school fails to suffer by them in a way that men of merely executive experience know nothing of.

But Calvin Coolidge, who held no Federal office until he became Vice President, thought otherwise. In his *Autobiography* (1929) he wrote: "The Presidents who have gone to Washington without first having held some national office have been at great disadvantage. It takes them a long time to become acquainted with the Federal office-holders and the Federal Government."

Twenty-seven of the thirty-five Vice Presidents from John Adams to Alben W. Barkley inclusive served in the Continental Congress or in one or both branches of the Congress under the Constitution. The eight who had no Congressional service when they became Vice President were Daniel D. Tompkins, Chester A. Arthur, Garret A. Hobart, Theodore Roosevelt, Thomas R. Marshall, Calvin Coolidge, Charles G. Dawes and Henry A. Wallace.

Why is the Vice President called the Veep?

Veep for *Vice President* seems to have made its first appearance in print in 1949. It quickly gained currency because newspapermen found it a convenient variant for *V.P.* and *Vice President* in headlines. Leonard Kirsten, vice president of the George Washington University Student Council, asked Vice President Alben W. Barkley whether he objected to the application of the term to Vice Presidents in general. In a letter dated September 2, 1949, the Vice President wrote to Kirsten: "Of course, the name 'Veep' is not copyrighted in the legal sense of the word, but it is a name that my children gave to me in connection with the Vice Presidency. They just took the two letters, v and p, and put a couple of small e's between, and it spelled Veep, and it has become rather familiar over the country as a new title for the Vice President." The wife of a Vice President is not customarily called the Veepess.

Alben William Barkley was born on November 24, 1877, near Lowes in Graves County, Kentucky. After graduating from Marvin College at Clinton in his native State and attending Emory College in Georgia and the University of Virginia Law School, he was admitted to the bar in 1901 and hung up his shingle in Paducah. His long and uninterrupted career as officeholder began in 1905, when he became county prosecuting attorney. He served in Congress as Representative and Senator from

March 4, 1913, till January 19, 1949, when he resigned to become Vice President the next day.

When Senator Joseph T. Robinson of Arkansas died on July 14, 1937, Assistant Leader Barkley and Senator Pat Harrison of Mississippi became candidates to succeed him as Majority Leader. The "court-packing plan" was pending before the Senate, feelings were running high and the contest for the Leadership was close. On the day after Robinson's death President Franklin D. Roosevelt wrote a letter on the importance of pressing for immediate "judicial reform," and addressed it to Barkley "because you are the acting majority leader in the Senate." The President's salutation was "My dear Alben." This letter, which indicated the President's preference for Barkley, undoubtedly tipped the delicately balanced scales in favor of the Kentuckian, who won over Harrison in the Democratic caucus by one vote. For some time after that the new Majority Leader was often referred to as "Dear Alben." On August 12, 1949, Congress voted a gold medal in recognition of Vice President Barkley's distinguished public service and outstanding contributions to general welfare. In reporting out the bill, the House Banking and Currency committee said: "In more than a third of a century of service to his country few men have ever so endeared themselves in the hearts of their fellow man as has the present Vice President of the United States." Barkley was seventy-one and a widower when he became Vice President. His marriage on November 18, 1949, to Mrs. Carleton S. Hadley, a thirty-eight-year-old widow of St. Louis, was widely publicized.

What is a pivotal State?

Pivot in the mechanical sense of a pin on which something turns is an old English noun, but *pivotal* as an adjective meaning "of critical importance" is an Americanism dating back at least to 1844. A large State in which the major political parties are almost evenly divided is called a pivotal State because the national election may turn, hinge or depend upon its electoral vote in a Presidential election. In 1844 Polk, to be elected, had to carry New York against Clay and he did so by a narrow margin. Before the Civil War Pennsylvania was the chief pivotal State, but since then New York has more often decided Presidential elections. In 1884 Cleveland carried New York over Blaine by only 1,049 votes. On September 28, 1900, John Hay wrote Samuel Mather: "I think the field is pretty well taken care of—Indiana, of the important, so-called *pivotal* States, seems doubtful." Party national committees generally neglect "sure" and "small" States and concentrate their funds and energies in pivotal States. Candidates for President and Vice President are often chosen from pivotal States on the theory that they can carry their own States.

What is the kiss of death?

In its political sense *the kiss of death* means the endorsement of a candidate by a person or organization whose support is a liability and fatal to the candidate's success. The phrase was popularized in 1926 when Governor Alfred E. Smith of New York applied it to William Randolph Hearst's support of Ogden L. Mills, the Republican candidate for Governor. Originally the kiss of death was a kiss given to one just before dying and symbolized a farewell or final leave-taking. "Kiss me before I die" occurs in Chaucer's *Canterbury Tales*. "The kiss of death is like taking hair out of milk" is used in Babylonian Talmud to denote an easy process. The hypocritical, treacherous or Judas kiss—kissing before killing—may have influenced the phrase as used by Governor Smith.

What State is known as the Mother of Presidents?

Virginia is the state known as the Mother of Presidents. Eight—one-fourth—of the first thirty-two Presidents were born in the Old Dominion. They were George Washington, Thomas Jefferson, James Madison, James Monroe, William Henry Harrison, John Tyler, Zachary Taylor and Woodrow Wilson. But the State acquired the nickname early in the nineteenth century because four of the first five Presidents were Virginians.

Three—one-fourth—of the twelve presidents of the Continental Congress, including the first and the last—were Virginians—Peyton Randolph, Richard Henry Lee and Cyrus Griffin. William E. Gladstone once said that "Virginia produced more contemporary great men than any other piece of real estate on earth, Greece and Rome not excepted."

"The Virginia Dynasty" was the popular name given to three Virginia Presidents—Jefferson, Madison and Monroe—who occupied the White House for twenty-four years, from 1801 to 1825, and who represented substantially the same political party and philosophy. In 1816, when Madison was still President and Monroe was President-elect, Correa de Serra, the Portuguese Minister at Washington, referred to them as "the past, the present and the future," and the next year he called them "the Presidential Trinity." On January 1, 1840, John Quincy Adams wrote in his diary that "this policy and drill, first organized by Thomas Jefferson, first accomplished his election, and established the Virginia Dynasty of twenty-four years, a perpetual practical contradiction of its own principles." Washington, the first President, was not included in the so-called Virginia Dynasty. The three members of the Virginia Dynasty sometimes met at Monticello, and one chronicler related that he once saw the three men who occupied the White House for twenty-four successive years walking arm in arm on the campus of the University of Virginia at Charlottesville, the building of which Jefferson was supervising. Madison, according to tradition at Monticello, was sitting one day with his back toward one of the large French windows on the first floor. In a moment of abstraction or merriment he rocked his chair too far back and fell out of the window. The hundred-pound President was not seriously injured, but the master of Monticello was greatly worried. The incident would probably have been forgotten except for the iron bars that Jefferson had put across the outside of the window the next day. Both Madison and Monroe looked upon Jefferson as their mentor.

Two counties in Virginia had the honor of giving birth to four of the eight Presidents born in the State. Washington and Monroe were born in Westmoreland County, and Harrison and Tyler in Charles City County. Harrison and Tyler were elected President and Vice President respectively on the same ticket in 1840, and when Harrison died a month after taking office he was succeeded by a man born in the same county. Five of the Virginia-born Presidents were residents of the State when they became President. Harrison was a resident of Ohio, Taylor of Louisiana, and Wilson of New Jersey when they were elected. "Virginia," Speaker Thomas B. Reed observed, "may be the Mother of Presidents, but it will be a long time before she is in a family way again." Since then only one man born in Virginia—Wilson—has become President. The five Presidents elected from Virginia served a total of thirty-five years and nine months, and the eight Virginia-born Presidents served a total of forty-five years and two months. Only two Vice Presidents were born in Virginia—Jefferson and Tyler—and both became President.

Ohio ranks second to Virginia as the nursery of Presidents. Seven Presidents were born in the Buckeye State—Ulysses S. Grant, Rutherford B. Hayes, James A. Garfield, Benjamin Harrison, William McKinley, William Howard Taft and Warren G. Harding. All of these except Grant and Benjamin Harrison were residents of Ohio when elected. William Henry Harrison was a resident of Ohio when he became President. The six Presidents who were elected from Ohio served a total of fifteen years and seven months, and the seven Ohio-born Presidents served a total of twenty-seven years and seven months. No resident of Ohio has been elected Vice President. Thomas A. Hendricks, Charles W. Fairbanks and Charles G. Dawes were born in Ohio but were elected from other States.

Six Presidents—Martin Van Buren, Millard Fillmore, Grover Cleveland, Chester A. Arthur, Theodore Roosevelt and Franklin D. Roosevelt—were residents of New York, but only four of them—Van Buren, Fillmore, and the two Roosevelts—were natives of that State. The six Presidents elected from New York served a total of thirty-seven years, seven months and twenty-three days, and the four New York-born Presidents served a total of twenty-six years, four months and eight days. Franklin D. Roosevelt served twelve years, two months and twenty-three days and his service was longer than the combined services of William H. Harrison, Taylor, Fillmore, Garfield, Arthur and Harding. New York leads all the States as a nursery of Vice Presidents. Eight of the first thirty-five Vice Presidents were born in New York, and ten of the first thirty-five were residents of that State when elected. Four Vice Presidents were elected from Indiana, but only one of them—Thomas R. Marshall—was born in the Hoosier State.

Which Presidents were Governors?

Thirteen of the thirty-two men who have been President served as Governors of their States. They were: Thomas Jefferson, James Monroe, Martin Van Buren, John Tyler, James K. Polk, Andrew Johnson, Rutherford B. Hayes, Grover Cleveland, William McKinley, Theodore Roosevelt, Woodrow Wilson, Calvin Coolidge and Franklin D. Roosevelt. In addition three Presidents served as Governors by appointment. Andrew Jackson was Governor of Florida Territory, William Henry Harrison was Governor of Indiana Territory and William Howard Taft was Governor-General of the Philippines. Five—Hayes, Cleveland, McKinley, Wilson and Franklin D. Roosevelt—were Governors when elected President. Two—Theodore Roosevelt and Coolidge—were Governors when elected Vice President, from which they succeeded to the Presidency. In addition Johnson was Military Governor of Tennessee when elected Vice President. Four Presidents were unsuccessful candidates for Governor—John Quincy Adams (after he was President), Millard Fillmore, Benjamin Harrison and Warren G. Harding. Harding and Coolidge were the only Presidents who were Lieutenant Governors of their States. Twelve Presidents were never State or Territorial Governors nor candidates for Governor—George Washington, John Adams, James Madison, Zachary Taylor, Franklin Pierce, James Buchanan, Abraham Lincoln, Ulysses S. Grant, James A. Garfield, Chester A. Arthur, Herbert Hoover and Harry S. Truman. In every Presidential election from 1884 to 1944 inclusive, with one exception, a State Governor or former Governor has won or lost the Presidency. Neither Taft nor William Jennings Bryan, the nominees in 1908, was the Governor or former Governor of a State. In many cases both major party nominees were Governors or former Governors. William Henry Harrison and John Tyler were the only two Presidents whose fathers were Governors.

Who coined *America first?*

America first was popularized, if not coined, by Woodrow Wilson. The earliest known recorded use of the phrase occurs in a speech delivered at the annual meeting of the Associated Press by President Wilson in New York City on April 20, 1915. On that occasion he said: "Our whole duty, for the present, at any rate, is summed up in the motto: America first." This so-called motto may have been suggested by the slogan "See America first," which is believed to have been coined in 1910 as an advertising slogan by President Louis W. Hill of the Great Northern Railway while promoting Glacier National Park with the view of increasing railway passenger traffic. When the First World War cut off American travel to Europe in 1914, other railroads and the National Park Service, took up the slogan.

America first became the motto of certain "isolationists" and "one hundred per cent Americans" after the First World War and the controversy over the League of Nations. Senator Warren G. Harding used the phrase in an address before the Ohio Society of New York on January 20, 1920. During the Presidential campaign later that year the Republican nominee made "America first" one of the chief issues and repeated in various forms what he had said before: "Stabilize America first, prosper America first, think of America first, exalt America first." It was not until the years immediately before the Second World War that a certain degree of popular odium became attached to *America first*.

How is a minority President elected?

Minority President is a term applied to a President who has been elected by a minority, or less than half, of the total number of popular votes cast. This is possible because the President and Vice President are not elected directly by popular vote, but by electors who are chosen by popular vote and who can, without violating their instructions, elect candidates who did not receive a majority popular vote in the election. Candidates for President and Vice President receive all or none of the electoral votes cast by a State, except in the rare cases when the electoral vote is split. There are many instances where candidates for President and Vice President with the largest popular vote have been defeated in the electoral colleges. The same thing can happen when the choice devolves upon the House of Representatives or the Senate.

In the early days of the Federal Government the legislatures of many States elected the Presidential electors and in those States the preference of the people was indicated only indirectly by their votes for members of the State legislatures. There is for that reason no trustworthy record of the popular vote for Presidents previously to 1824. In the election of that year, when seventeen of the twenty-three States in the Union chose their electors by popular vote, none of the four candidates for President received a majority of either the electoral or the popular votes. The electoral and popular votes were as follows: Andrew Jackson, 99–155,872; John Quincy Adams, 84–105,321; William H. Crawford, 41–44,282, and Henry Clay, 37–46,587. Since none of the candidates had a majority of the electoral vote the choice fell upon the House of Representatives, which chose Adams, who had received fewer electoral and popular votes than Jackson. Adams was chagrined by the fact that he was a minority President. At the end of 1825, after he had been President ten months, Adams wrote in his diary:

The year has been the most momentous of those that have passed over my head, inasmuch as it has witnessed my election at the age of 58 to the Chief Magistracy of my country; to the summit of laudable, or at least blameless, worldly ambition; not, however, in a manner satisfactory to pride or to just desire; not by the unequivocal suffrages of a majority of the people; with perhaps two-thirds of the whole people adverse to the actual result. Nearly one year of this service has already passed with little change of the public opinions or feelings; without disaster to the country; with an unusual degree of prosperity, public and private.

In 1828 there were only two candidates and Jackson received a decided majority of both the electoral and popular votes over Adams and was clearly a majority President. Four years later, when all the States except South Carolina chose their electors by popular vote, Jackson received a majority of both the electoral and popular votes over Clay, John Floyd and William Wirt. In 1836 Martin Van Buren received a small majority of the popular votes over William Henry Harrison, Hugh L. White, Daniel Webster and Willie P. Mangum.

Since 1840 James K. Polk (1844), Zachary Taylor (1848), James

Buchanan (1856), Abraham Lincoln (1860), Rutherford B. Hayes (1876), James A. Garfield (1880), Grover Cleveland (1884 and 1892), Benjamin Harrison (1888), Woodrow Wilson (1912 and 1916) and Harry S. Truman (1948) have been elected President without receiving a majority of the total popular vote and have been minority Presidents. In most of these cases minority Presidents were elected because several candidates were running. But in 1876 Samuel J. Tilden actually received more popular votes than Hayes did and still Hayes became President; and in 1888 the Cleveland electors received 5,540,050 popular votes and the Harrison electors received only 5,444,337, but of the 401 electoral votes Harrison received 233 as compared with 168 received by Cleveland, and Harrison became President.

Since the election of 1876 was somewhat irregular the election of 1888 is the best illustration of how a candidate may receive more popular votes and fewer electoral votes than an opponent. Suppose, for illustration, there were only two States in the Union at the time—Georgia and New York. The Harrison electors received 40,496 votes in Georgia and the Cleveland electors received 100,449. In New York the Harrison electors received 648,759 and the Cleveland electors received 635,757. Thus from these two States Cleveland received a total of 736,256 popular votes as compared with only 689,255 by Harrison. But a majority, even of only one, usually carries with it the entire electoral vote of a State. Accordingly Cleveland received only the twelve electoral votes of Georgia while Harrison received the thirty-six electoral votes of New York. When this principle is applied to all the States it is easy to understand how a candidate may receive a majority or plurality of the popular votes without receiving a majority or even a plurality of the electoral votes.

In 1832 Clay carried Maryland over Jackson by the slim margin of only four popular votes. The famous victory of William H. Harrison over President Martin Van Buren in 1840 was not the "popular landslide" that it is generally supposed to have been. Harrison received 1,275,017 popular votes, while Van Buren received 1,128,702, a difference of only 146,315. But Harrison received 234 electoral votes and Van Buren only 60.

The electoral and popular votes in 1860 were as follows: Lincoln, 180–1,865,913; Stephen A. Douglas, 12–1,374,664; John C. Breckinridge, 72–848,404, and John Bell, 39–591,900. Lincoln received 59.4 per cent of the electoral vote but only 39.2 per cent of the popular vote. He had a plurality, that is more than any other candidate, but not a majority of the total. It is a common error to say that Lincoln was elected in 1860 by a division of the opposition. If the Democrats had not split and had nominated only one candidate and that candidate had received the combined popular votes received by Douglas, Breckinridge and Bell, Lincoln still would have won, because the combined popular vote of the three would have changed the electoral vote in only California and Oregon and Lincoln would have received 173 electoral votes as against 130 for his opponent. All four candidates in 1860 were regional candidates to a large extent. Not one of them had an electoral ticket in every State in the Union. No Lincoln electors were on the ballots in ten Southern States, but he was strong in the large Northern States, which cast the majority of the electoral votes.

Four years later the electoral and popular votes were as follows: Lincoln, 212–3,216,007, and George B. McClellan, 21–1,808,725. Lincoln received a clear majority of the popular votes and was a majority President the second time, but the popular vote was so close in many key States that a shift of only about 5,000 votes would have given McClellan the majority of the electoral votes. Even if the Confederate States had been participating and all had voted for McClellan, Lincoln still would have been re-elected, although he might have been again a minority President. As a matter of fact, in many elections the redistribution of a small number of popular votes in key States would have reversed the result in the electoral vote.

In the election of 1884 the electoral and popular votes were: Cleveland, 219–4,874,986; James G. Blaine, 182–4,851,981; Benjamin F. Butler, 175,370, and John P. St. John, 150,000. Cleveland had a popular plurality of only about 25,000 in the country as a whole. He received the New York electoral votes by a plurality of only 1,049. St. John, the Prohibition candidate for President, received 25,000 popular votes in that State alone. If 1,049 of these votes, or only 525 of Cleveland's votes, had gone to Blaine electors, Blaine would have received New York's electoral votes and been President. The fact is that Cleveland, who ran for President three times and was elected twice, never received a majority of the popular vote at any time. There seems to be a widespread impression that William Jennings Bryan once received a majority of the popular vote for President without receiving a majority of the electoral vote, but he received neither a majority nor a plurality of the popular vote in any of his three races for President. Because of this false impression it is often said erroneously that William McKinley received only a plurality of the popular votes in 1896, but he received a clear majority of the popular votes over all other candidates in that election. He was the first candidate to receive a popular majority after 1872. In the election of 1912 the electoral and popular votes were: Wilson, 425–6,293,029; William Howard Taft, 8–3,484,956; Theodore Roosevelt,

88—4,119,507; Eugene V. Debs, 901,873; Eugene W. Chapin, 207,928, and Arthur E. Reimer, 29,259. The combined popular votes of Roosevelt and Taft alone were over 1,300,000 more than those of Wilson; yet Wilson received all the electoral votes except 98. In 1916 Wilson received 9,127,695 popular votes and Charles Evans Hughes, 8,553,507, but other candidates received a total of 806,661, which made Wilson a minority President by 212,475 popular votes, although he received 277 electoral votes as against 254 for Hughes.

In 1948 a total of 48,836,579 popular votes were cast. President Truman received 24,105,812; Thomas E. Dewey, 21,970,065; James Strom Thurmond, 1,169,021; Henry A. Wallace, 1,157,172; Claude A. Watson, 103,343, and others, 191,645. Truman came 433,310 votes short of a majority over all other candidates and therefore became a minority President. His electoral vote was 303 as against 189 for Dewey and 39 for Thurmond.

Under the Constitution a candidate cannot be elected President or Vice President by a minority of the electoral votes except when the choice devolves upon the House of Representatives or the Senate respectively.

Which Presidents were Masons?

Thirteen of the first thirty-two Presidents of the United States are known to have been Masons. They were: George Washington, James Monroe, Andrew Jackson, James K. Polk, James Buchanan, Andrew Johnson, James A. Garfield, William McKinley, Theodore Roosevelt, William H. Taft, Warren G. Harding, Franklin D. Roosevelt and Harry S. Truman.

John Adams, Thomas Jefferson, James Madison, John Quincy Adams, John Tyler, Zachary Taylor, Millard Fillmore, Abraham Lincoln, Ulysses S. Grant and Benjamin Harrison have been listed by one writer or another among the Presidents who were Masons but their Masonic affiliations have not been substantiated. There is a legend that Jefferson became a Mason before the American Revolution and that he attended a Masonic lodge meeting in Paris with Thomas Paine. A story has it that John Quincy Adams became a Mason in Boston in 1826 when he was President, but in his diary after that date he makes it clear that neither he nor his father, John Adams, was a Mason. In 1831 John Quincy Adams was elected to Congress with the support of the Anti-Masonic Party. No evidence has been produced to substantiate the oft-repeated story that Fillmore was once a Mason and that he recanted after the anti-Masonic excitement following the disappearance of William Morgan in 1826. It appears quite certain that Madison, Tyler, Taylor, Lincoln, Grant and Benjamin Harrison were never Masons.

On May 3, 1865, at the close of the Civil War, Major William McKinley became a Mason at Hiram Lodge No. 21 in Winchester, Virginia. Every Masonic official who took part in the initiation had been an officer in the Confederate army. William H. Taft became a Mason when he was President-elect. He received all three blue lodge degrees on February 18, 1909, in Kilwinning Lodge No. 385, at Cincinnati. Harry S. Truman became a thirty-third degree Mason in 1945 after he had succeeded to the Presidency. The only other President to be elected a thirty-third degree Mason was Warren G. Harding, but he died before the degree could be conferred.

Fourteen of the first thirty-five Vice Presidents, from John Adams to Alben W. Barkley inclusive, are known to have been affiliated with the Masonic order. Their names are: Aaron Burr, Daniel D. Tompkins, Richard Mentor Johnson, George M. Dallas, William R. D. King, Andrew Johnson, John C. Breckinridge, Schuyler Colfax, Adlai E. Stevenson, Garret A. Hobart, Theodore Roosevelt, Charles W. Fairbanks, Thomas R. Marshall and Harry S. Truman. Three of them—Johnson, Theodore Roosevelt and Truman—became President. In the administrations of Monroe, Polk, Buchanan and McKinley, and the part of the fourth term of Franklin D. Roosevelt, both the President and the Vice President were Masons.

Four Masons signed the Constitution—Washington, Benjamin Franklin, Alexander Hamilton and David Brearly.

How did *fellow traveler* originate?

Fellow traveler is an old English phrase in the literal sense of a traveling companion or one going the same way. In 1744 Dr. Alexander Hamilton of Maryland wrote in his diary that he was "sorry to hear that my fellow traveler Mr. Rhea was taken with an ague." On October 9, 1810, John Quincy Adams wrote in his diary that he told Count Romanzoff at St. Petersburg that "Mr. Jones had been a fellow-traveller with Mr. Poinsett, who had given him such a favorable idea of Russia that he had come, as a traveller, to visit the country." *Fellow traveler* acquired the meaning of one who sympathizes with the Communist party without being a member under Russian influence. It was first used by Communists as the English equivalent of Russian *poputchik*, which is from *po*, "with," *put* "road," and *chik*, Russian suffix indicating agent or doer and corresponding to English *or* and *er*. A *poputchik,* both literally and figuratively, is one who goes along the road with another fellow—a fellow traveler.

Which Presidents were bachelors?

Only three bachelors—Buchanan, Tilden and Cleveland—have been nominated for President by major parties. Two of them—Buchanan and Cleveland—were elected. All three were Democrats.

Samuel Jones Tilden, "The Sage of Greystone," received a majority of the popular votes in 1876 but lost to Rutherford B. Hayes in the official count of the electoral votes. He was the only bachelor nominated by a major party not to become President.

Grover Cleveland was a bachelor when he took office March 4, 1885. His sister, Miss Rose Cleveland, acted as mistress of the White House during his first fifteen months there, but the President hardly made a pretense of keeping house in the White House without a wife. On June 2, 1888, at the age of forty-nine, Cleveland was married in the White House to twenty-one-year-old Frances Folsom, daughter of his Buffalo law partner. The President wrote his own wedding invitations on White House stationery. The only child of a President born in the White House was his daughter Esther, born September 9, 1893, during his second administration.

James Buchanan (1791-1868), the only Pennsylvanian by birth or residence to become President, never married and is known as the Bachelor President. He was born at Cove Gap near Mercersburg, graduated from Dickinson College in 1809, admitted to the bar in 1812, began to practice law at Lancaster, then the State capital, served in the legislature two terms (1814-1815), Representative in Congress five terms (1821-1831), Minister to Russia (1832-1834), Secretary of State under President James K. Polk (1841-1845), Minister to Great Britain (1853-1856) and President one term (1857-1861). He was the only President of the United States to be president of a railroad. At forty he retired from law and business with a fortune large enough to enable him to devote himself exclusively to politics and public office. He started out as a Federalist but supported Andrew Jackson for President in 1824 and became a Democrat. He had considerable support for the Democratic nomination for President in 1844, 1848 and 1852, and got it in 1856.

When he was twenty-eight and already a successful lawyer, Buchanan fell in love with twenty-two-year-old Anne Coleman of Lancaster and they became engaged. On the strength of gossip that the young lawyer was keeping company with other girls, her father induced her to break the engagement and to refuse to see him again. Buchanan was refused an opportunity to explain or deny the truth of the gossip. Before a reconciliation could take place, Anne, telling her parents she was going to an opera in Philadelphia, locked herself in a hotel room and committed suicide. Buchanan wrote for permission to see her after death but even that was refused. Family tradition says he remained single because he secretly cherished his love for Anne, whose letters he treasured till death. He was often kidded about being a bachelor. In 1844 he wrote to Mrs. James I. Roosevelt:

I am now "solitary and alone," having no companion in the house with me. I have gone a wooing to several gentlemen but have not succeeded with any of them. I feel that it is not good for man to be alone; and should not be astonished to find myself married to some old maid who can nurse me when I am sick, provide good dinners for me when I am well, and not expect from me any very ardent or romantic affection.

In 1849 Buchanan bought "Wheatland," a twenty-two-acre estate near Lancaster, and there lived in a great mansion in baronial style. He kept on hand a plentiful supply of good whisky and once observed that he couldn't see how anybody could drink enough of it to become intoxicated. He was tall and handsome, and courtly but formal and aloof in manner. Some looked upon him as a "stuffy old bachelor," and in 1841 John Quincy Adams described him as "the speaking scrivener." On February 27, 1849, President Polk wrote in his diary of his Secretary of State: "Mr. Buchanan is an able man, but is in small matters without judgment and sometimes acts like an old maid."

During an acrimonious debate in the Senate in 1840 John Davis, a Massachusetts Whig, accused Buchanan of favoring "ten cents a day" as the proper pay for an American laborer, and thereafter the Whigs called him "Ten-Cent Jimmy." He was often called "Buck" for short, and, since half of the oxen in America were named "Buck" or "Bright," during the 1856 campaign Buchanan and his running mate, John C. Breckinridge, were fancied to resemble a yoke of powerful oxen and were called "Buck and Breck." But Buchanan gave himself his best known nickname when he referred to himself as "Old Public Functionary" ("O.P.F.") in allusion to the fact that he was an old, industrious wheelhorse who had served the public and his party faithfully for over thirty years. His political enemies responded with "Old Iniquity." After retiring he became "The Sage of Wheatland."

Buchanan brought up his sister Jane's orphaned daughter Harriet Lane, who is reputed to have been one of the most charming mistresses the White House has ever had. When Buchanan was Minister to England he and Alfred Lord Tennyson received honorary degrees from Oxford, but the American Minister's beautiful and attractive niece stole the show during the ceremonies. On January 11, 1866, Harriet Lane at the age of thirty-three was married at Wheatland to Henry Elliot Johnston, a wealthy Baltimore banker, with whom she had been in love seventeen years and by whom she had two sons who died in their early teens.

Old Public Functionary opposed slavery as an institution but favored protecting it under the Constitution. He was nominated in 1856 as a Northern man with Southern principles. Rufus Choate switched from the Whigs to the Democrats because he thought Old Buck carried "the flag and kept step with the music of the Union." As President he tried to please both the North and the South and disappointed both. During the dark days of 1860-1861 he was constantly in fear of assassination. After turning the reins of the Government over to Abraham Lincoln, he retired to Wheatland and announced his support of the new administration. When the funeral train of his assassinated successor passed through Lancaster in 1865 the seventy-four-year-old ex-President was observed sitting in his carriage in the throng. He died on June 1, 1868, and was buried in near-by Woodward Hill Cemetery. His fellow-townsman and political and personal foe, Thaddeus Stevens, one year younger and also a bachelor, died later the same year.

Many bachelors have served in both houses of Congress and other Federal positions, but comparatively few have risen high in American politics. Among those that did, besides Buchanan and Stevens, were John Randolph of Roanoke; Stephen F. Austin, Father of Texas; Richard Mentor Johnson of Kentucky, Vice President of the United States; Alexander H. Stephens, vice president of the Confederacy; Kenneth McKellar, President Pro Tempore of the Senate; Joseph W. Martin, Speaker of the House, and Hatton W. Sumners, Chairman of the House Judiciary Committee; John Paul Jones, naval hero; Jubal A. Early, Confederate general; Boies Penrose, U.S. Senator and Republican boss of Pennsylvania; John G. Whittier and Fitz-Greene Halleck, poets, and John Singer Sargent, artist, were bachelors.

In Colonial days the town of Providence in Rhode Island excluded bachelors from voting. Under the Articles of Confederation in 1782 Alexander Hamilton proposed flat taxes on land, houses, tobacco, salt, carriages, taverns, household servants, lawyers and bachelors. In 1943 Robert B. Yerkes, Republican leader of the Delaware State senate, introduced a bill to levy a five-dollar tax on bachelors, with exemptions for clergymen and servicemen. Alvin Peterson Hovey of Indiana was brevetted Major General in July, 1864, and directed to raise 10,000 recruits for the Federal army. He accepted only single men and his command was known as "Hovey's Babies."

What is a hair shirt?

A hair shirt is a rough garment made of coarse haircloth and worn as a shirt or girdle next to the skin by eccentrics and penitents by way of humiliation and mortification. The practice dates from the early Christian period and was probably suggested by the Biblical sackcloth. In the *Canterbury Tales* Chaucer refers to a woman who "had next to her body placed a shirt of hair" and says "bodily pain lies . . . in wearing shirts of hair or coarse wool, or habergeons next the naked flesh, for Christ's sake, and such other kinds of penance." During the Middle Ages hair shirts were worn by penitents on Ash Wednesday, and such garments of humiliation are still worn by members of certain religious orders.

On December 14, 1929, President Herbert C. Hoover said in a speech at the Gridiron Club in Washington:

In the Middle Ages it was the fashion to wear hair shirts to remind one's self of trouble and sin. Many years ago I concluded that a few hair shirts were part of the mental wardrobe of every man. The President differs only from other men in that he has a more extensive wardrobe. We have had tonight an indication of the great variety of persons and organizations who cheerfully and voluntarily insist on acting as hair shirts to the President.

Since then *hair shirt* has been used in the sense of criticism and needling. "What President Truman needs is a 'hair shirt', charges a prominent United States Senator," reported *Look* magazine on April 12, 1949.

Which Presidents never went to college?

Eight of the first thirty-two Presidents never attended any institution of learning rating the grade of college or university. They were George Washington, Andrew Jackson, Martin Van Buren, Zachary Taylor, Millard Fillmore, Abraham Lincoln, Andrew Johnson and Grover Cleveland.

Nineteen were college graduates. They were John Adams, John Quincy Adams, Theodore Roosevelt and Franklin D. Roosevelt, Harvard University; Thomas Jefferson and John Tyler, William and Mary College; James Madison and Woodrow Wilson, Princeton; James K. Polk, University of North Carolina; Franklin Pierce, Bowdoin College; James Buchanan, Dickinson College; Ulysses S. Grant, West Point;

[443]

Rutherford B. Hayes, Kenyon College; James A. Garfield, Williams College; Chester A. Arthur, Union College; Benjamin Harrison, Miami University; William Howard Taft, Yale University; Calvin Coolidge, Amherst College; and Herbert Hoover, Leland Stanford University.

Several of the twenty Presidents who went to college attended more than one college. Franklin D. Roosevelt attended the Columbia University Law School. Wilson graduated from the University of Virginia Law School, and received a Ph. D. degree from Johns Hopkins University. Taft attended the Cincinnati Law School, and Hayes the Harvard Law School. Coolidge graduated from Amherst in 1895, the same year his immediate successor, Hoover, graduated from Leland Standford University.

Also several Presidents attended college without graduating. James Monroe attended William and Mary College for two years, but left to serve in the Continental army and never returned to college. William Henry Harrison attended Hampton-Sidney College for a year. William McKinley entered Allegheny College at Meadville, Pennsylvania, when he was seventeen but quit the first year because of ill health. Warren G. Harding studied for three years at Ohio Central College, an institution of academy grade at Iberia, Ohio, but left at sixteen without graduating. Both McKinley and Harding are sometimes included among the Presidents without college education. John Quincy Adams studied in Paris and at the University of Leyden and has been the only President to attend foreign schools. President Harry S. Truman took the three-year course in the Independence High School, but did not attend college in his youth. However, in 1923, when he was thirty-nine, he enrolled in Kansas City Law School and studied in the law department of that institution until 1925, when he was forty-one years of age.

Nine Presidents taught school—John Adams, Jackson, Fillmore, Garfield, Arthur, Cleveland, McKinley, Wilson and Harding. Garfield and Arthur, who were elected President and Vice President on the same ticket, both taught at different times in the same school near Pownal in the southwestern corner of Vermont. The building, still standing, is known as the Presidents' School. Wilson was the only President who made teaching his profession. Garfield was principal of Hiram College, where he had been a student, and Wilson was president of Princeton. Jefferson founded the University of Virginia, and Hayes was "Father of Ohio State University" at Columbus. Washington and Tyler were both chancellors of William and Mary, and Fillmore was the first chancellor of the University of Buffalo. John Quincy Adams was the first professor

[444]

of rhetoric and oratory at Harvard. Taft was a professor of law at Yale and Cleveland lectured at Princeton after they had been President.

Washington, Jackson, Taylor, Lincoln and Johnson had the least formal education, while Wilson had the most. Washington's schooling corresponded to about the fifth grade in a modern public school. He was good in mathematics, which he largely taught himself, and though a reader, he did not read assiduously like Lincoln. Jackson went to school but his academic training was rather limited. It is said that the only book he ever read completely through was Oliver Goldsmith's *The Vicar of Wakefield*. Taylor never went to school and his only formal education was by private tutors. Although poorly educated in the formal sense, he was far from illiterate, as he is sometimes represented. Fillmore barely went to school at all and received most of his early education from his pioneer parents. Lincoln's total schooling was less than a year. Jackson, Fillmore and Lincoln all "read law" and became successful lawyers.

That Andrew Johnson was taught to read and write by his wife after their marriage is a cherished but somewhat exaggerated legend. Johnson was born in a shack in a back street in Raleigh, North Carolina, on December 29, 1808, and he was about seven weeks older than Lincoln, whom he succeeded as President. Johnson's parents were both illiterate. His father, who made a meager living as a porter, was drowned while trying to save a friend's life when Andrew was five. At ten the boy was apprenticed to a tailor for a term of eight years. After six years he ran away from his apprenticeship and later set up as a tailor on his own in Greenville, Tennessee. A Raleigh newspaper published an advertisement offering a $10 reward for his capture. So far as known Johnson never went to school a day in his life. But before he left North Carolina he had learned to read and probably write a little. He had a craving for knowledge and education and he is known to have studied *The American Speaker,* which contained specimens of the orations of Pitt, Fox and other famous statesmen. He was married to Eliza McCardle of Greenville on May 27, 1827, when he was eighteen and she was sixteen. His wife, daughter of a Scotch shoemaker, had gone to a local academy and had a fair education for a girl of her age and part of the country. Mrs. Johnson helped her tailor husband improve his writing and reading and encouraged him to prepare himself to take part in public affairs. She has been the youngest bride to become a First Lady, and Johnson was younger when married than any other President.

Washington and Jackson were both poor spellers, but both wrote and spoke with clarity and force. Washington's spelling and capitalization were highly irregular, as a few examples will illustrate: Avocado pear,

"Avagado pair"; raccoon, "Rakoon"; smallpox, "small Pox"; oil, "oyl"; blue, "blew"; lie, "lye," and pleurisy, "ploo Reese." He had a tendency to misspell familiar words and to spell unusual words correctly. He also had a tendency to spell phonetically but he had no regular system and sometimes spelled the same word more than one way in the same letter. Often he misspelled the names of friends and associates. But he was a good penman and wrote in a strong, orderly and legible hand. Washington was a voluminous writer of letters, diaries, ledgers and account books. The number of letters he wrote is estimated by experts all the way from 26,000 to 75,000. No one person has ever read all of the extant writings of Washington. Gaillard Hunt, who was long in charge of them, said the Washington manuscripts in the Library of Congress is the largest collection of papers of one person in the world. Washington had a large library and read many books but was not a studious man. Besides writers on farming and military affairs, his favorite authors appear to have been Addison, Goldsmith, Shakespeare, Swift, Smollett, Sterne, Fielding and Cervantes.

Jackson was a poorer speller than even Washington, and his grammar was much worse. In 1898 Walter Preston Brownlow of Tennessee said in the House of Representatives: "Andrew Jackson spelled *God* with a small *g* and *Europe, Urop,* but he was a great general and incorruptible judge, and a capable President. He always believed the earth was flat instead of round, and insisted that the proper pronunciation of *development* was *devil-ope-ment,* but he had great ruling qualities nevertheless." When Theodore Roosevelt, a poor speller and an advocate of simplified spelling, was reminded in 1906 that Jackson had written "I will hold New Orleans in spite of Urop and all hell," he asked: "If that doesn't spell *Europe,* what does it spell?" In 1828, when Jackson was running against John Quincy Adams for President, the House of Representatives directed that a report to the War Department be printed. President Adams wrote in his diary that the purpose of this "was to expose to public view the ferocious letter of General Jackson to G. W. Campbell, with all its sins of orthography and of syntax upon its head." Secretary of War Barbour, according to Adams, "observed that besides the numerous unequivocal misspellings; such as goverment, solem, secratary, gurantee, reguard, &c, there were others probably, though not certainly, misspelled, and about which he was doubtful how to direct that the copy should be made." But the printers corrected all of Jackson's misspellings, much to the chagrin of his enemies, who wanted to create the impression that he was ignorant because a poor speller. It is sometimes said that English spelling was not yet fixed and uniform in the time of Washington and Jackson and that they spelled as well as others according to the standards of those days; but the fact is that most other Presidents and statesmen of that time, even those that had little formal education, were good spellers.

The practice of conferring honorary degrees on Presidents started with Washington. Harvard University conferred the degree of Doctor of Laws on General Washington soon after the British evacuated Boston in 1776. In 1781, just before Yorktown, the same honor was conferred on him by Yale University, and the University of Pennsylvania did likewise in 1783. An academy at Chestertown, Maryland, was raised to college rank and named Washington College with the General's consent. He headed the subscribers to the new college, which, in 1789, conferred on him the degree of Doctor of Laws, which President Washington acknowledged with a formal letter. Brown University made him a Doctor of Laws in 1790. Washington was a trustee of the academy at Alexandria and in 1788, the year he was chosen President, he was elected chancellor of William and Mary College. He financed a number of young men through college.

In 1784 the Virginia legislature chartered the James River Company for building canals and the next year awarded $50,000 of its securities to Washington in recognition of his services to the project. Washington refused to accept the gift for his personal benefit but agreed to hold it in trust for a worthy purpose and asked the legislature to designate a recipient. The legislature suggested an institution of learning in the "upper country." Accordingly in 1790, when the securities had begun to pay dividends, Washington gave the securities to Liberty Hall Academy at Lexington, now Washington and Lee University. The James River Company evolved into the Chesapeake and Ohio Railroad Company and the securities presented by Washington eventually brought the school considerable income.

When Andrew Jackson visited New England in 1833 his escort in Massachusetts was Josiah Quincy, Jr., son of the President of Harvard University. Young Quincy was so impressed by Jackson that he persuaded his father that Harvard should confer an honorary degree on him. Josiah Quincy, Sr., called a rump meeting of the Harvard overseers and obtained their consent to honor Jackson. Ex-President John Quincy Adams, who had been defeated by Jackson in 1828 and who was related to Quincy, didn't like the idea. On June 18, 1833, Adams was called from his nursery and garden at Quincy by the President of Harvard. That night Adams wrote in his diary:

He told me also that as President Jackson is about visiting Boston, the Corporation of the university had thought it necessary to invite him to visit the colleges; that he (Mr. Quincy) should address him in a Latin discourse, and confer upon him the degree of Doctor of Laws; and he intimated that I should receive an invitation to be present at the ceremonies. I said that the personal relations in which President Jackson had chosen to place himself with me were such that I could hold no intercourse of a friendly character with him. I could therefore not accept an invitation to attend upon this occasion. And, independent of that, as myself an affectionate child of our Alma Mater, I would not be present to witness her disgrace in conferring her highest literary honors upon a barbarian who could not write a sentence of grammar and hardly could spell his own name. Mr. Quincy said he was sensible how utterly unworthy of literary honors Jackson was, but the Corporation thought it was necessary to follow the precedent, and treat him precisely as Mr. Monroe, his predecessor, had been treated. As the people of the United States had seen fit to make him their President, the Corporation thought the honors which they conferred upon him were compliments due to the station, by whomsoever it was occupied. Mr. Quincy said it was thought also that the omission to show the same respect to President Jackson which had been shown to Mr. Monroe would be imputed to party spirit—which they were anxious to avoid.

Adams was not satisfied with these reasons and adhered to his determination to stay at home. Four days later he sat in his house and wrote: "There was much cannonading this afternoon at the President's reviewing of the military companies. The distant report of them gave me a double relish for the solitary tranquillity of my own occupations."

Honorary degrees were declined by at least two of the Presidents who did not go to college. In 1855 Oxford University offered the degree of Doctor of Civil Law to Ex-President Millard Fillmore, who declined it on the ground that he had no literary or scientific attainments to justify the honor. At the time of its 250th anniversary in 1886, Harvard University offered President Cleveland a degree, which he turned down because he thought he was not scholar enough for the distinction. Herbert Hoover leads all the Presidents in the number of such honors. He received more than fifty honorary degrees from institutions of higher learning throughout the world.

Wilson has been the only President who had an earned doctor's degree before he was President. He received the Ph. D. degree at Johns Hopkins University in 1885. His thesis was *Congressional Government*, a book he had published the preceding year.

Who promised "Milk for the Hottentots"?

In an address delivered on May 8, 1942, Vice President Henry Agard Wallace said: "The object of this war is to make sure that everybody in the world has the privilege of drinking a quart of milk a day." Political enemies distorted this into "Milk for the Hottentots," a phrase that the

Vice President denied using. By conservatives Wallace was regarded as "a starry-eyed liberal and mystic." In a speech in Congress on February 9, 1943, Representative Clare Booth Luce of Connecticut said that "much of what Mr. Wallace calls his global thinking is, no matter how you slice it, still *globaloney*."

Henry A. Wallace, his father, Henry Cantrell Wallace, and his grandfather, Henry Wallace, all were agricultural editors and all wrote books on agriculture. As Secretary of Agriculture in President Franklin D. Roosevelt's Cabinet from 1933 to 1940, Henry A. Wallace advocated a program that he called "the ever-normal granary." The public was under the impression that this program was suggested by the Biblical story of Joseph and the seven lean and the seven fat years in Egypt, but in a speech on February 8, 1943, Vice President Wallace explained that he got the idea from a book on the economics of Confucius that he came across in the Des Moines public library.

Who was Pig-Iron Kelley?

William Darrah Kelley (1814-1890), who represented a Philadelphia district in Congress from 1861 to 1890, was known as "Pig-Iron Kelley" because he staunchly supported a high tariff to protect American manufacturers and frequently referred to the Pennsylvania iron and steel industry. He was the son of a jeweler and served an apprenticeship to a jeweler before he became a lawyer. Originally a Democrat and free-trader, he helped form the Republican Party because of his views on slavery. Pig-Iron Kelley was a good speaker and writer and in Congress supported the impeachment of President Johnson, bayonet-rule over the South and inflation of the currency to help workingmen and farmers. From 1881 to 1883 he was chairman of the House Ways and Means Committee.

How many Presidents were lawyers?

Twenty-three of the first thirty-two Presidents were admitted to the bar and practiced law. Three others—Theodore Roosevelt, Warren G. Harding and Harry S. Truman—studied law briefly but were never admitted to the bar. The six who never studied law were: George Washington, farmer and soldier; William Henry Harrison, soldier and farmer; Zachary Taylor, soldier and farmer; Andrew Johnson, tailor; Ulysses S. Grant, soldier, and Herbert Hoover, mining engineer. Theodore Roosevelt was a writer, Harding, a newspaperman and Truman, a farmer and haberdasher.

Some of the lawyer Presidents did not practice law long. Thomas Jefferson was a successful lawyer for several years but was primarily a farmer. James Madison, Andrew Jackson and John Tyler were planters who practiced law incidentally. Woodrow Wilson graduated from the University of Virginia law school, was admitted to the bar and practiced one year in Atlanta, but became a teacher by profession. After retiring from the Presidency on March 4, 1921, Wilson formed a law partnership with Bainbridge Colby, his last Secretary of State, but illness prevented his taking an active part in the work of the firm. Franklin D. Roosevelt attended Columbia University law school for three years without graduating, but he was admitted to the bar and became a lawyer by profession.

Johnson never had any trade or profession other than that of tailor. To the end of his life he took a tailor's interest in good clothes and was always neat in dress and personal appearance. He visited the barber often and was one of the few public men of his day who took a bath every day without waiting for Saturday night. Millard Fillmore was apprenticed to a fuller and clothier at fifteen and learned to card wool and dress cloth, but later became a lawyer. Grant worked in his family's tannery for a time but never became a tanner. Although Truman is referred to as having been a harberdasher, actually he ran a men's furnishing store only a short time. Washington and Lincoln had experience as surveyors. Jefferson's father was a surveyor and Jefferson himself could run a line as straight as Washington or Lincoln.

All but six of the thirty-five Vice Presidents from John Adams in 1789 to Alben W. Barkley in 1949 were lawyers by profession or had studied law. Elbridge Gerry, Henry Wilson and Levi P. Morton were businessmen; Andrew Johnson was a tailor, and Schuyler Colfax and Henry A. Wallace were editors. Theodore Roosevelt and Truman studied but never practiced law.

How many Presidents had naval experience?

There has never been a sailor President or Vice President. None of the Presidents and Vice Presidents or the major-party candidates for President and Vice President has been an Annapolis graduate or had any experience as a private seaman or as a member of the naval forces. In 1900 Admiral George Dewey, the hero of Manila Bay, made a futile bid for the Republican nomination for President. Both Presidents Theodore and Franklin D. Roosevelt served as Assistant Secretary of the Navy, which was a civilian office. There are two reasons why sea service has not been a good steppingstone to political preferment. Isolation of the service has prevented the necessary political contacts and the number of water veterans has been comparatively too small to comprise an effective bloc of voters. In his youth George Washington wanted to go to sea, and historians have speculated as to what the effect upon American history might have been had his mother not thwarted his ambition to become a sailor.

How many Presidents had military experience?

Twenty of the thirty-two Presidents from George Washington to Harry S. Truman inclusive had some military training or experience, although several of the twenty saw little or no active service. Only twelve of the thirty-two never had any military training or experience of any kind. Eleven Presidents, more than a third of the thirty-two, were generals—Washington, Andrew Jackson, William Henry Harrison, Zachary Taylor, Franklin Pierce, Andrew Johnson, Ulysses S. Grant, Rutherford B. Hayes, James A. Garfield, Chester A. Arthur and Benjamin Harrison. Both Johnson and Arthur held the rank of brigadier general during the Civil War but neither served with troops in the field. Washington is the only one to be commissioned a general after he was President.

John Adams and John Quincy Adams had no military service. In 1770 Thomas Jefferson was commissioned lieutenant and chief commander of the Albemarle County militia by Lord Botetourt, lieutenant governor of Virginia. As ranking military officer of the county, Jefferson was entitled to be called general. He was again commissioned lieutenant and chief commander of the Albemarle County militia by the Committee of Safety in 1775. Some authorities believe that Jefferson technically held that office when he wrote the Declaration of Independence. Although Jefferson never saw active military service, as Governor during the Revolution he gave some directions to the militia when the State was invaded by the British. Washington and Jefferson were the only two Presidents who had held militia commissions under the British Crown.

James Madison enlisted in the Orange County Independent Company in 1775 and trained with it for several months, practicing rifle marksmanship, but he was physically frail and his "experience during the exercises and movements" of the militia company warned him "against a continuance." James Monroe served in the Revolution and became a lieutenant colonel. He and Washington were the only Presidents who fought in the Revolution in uniform. Jackson did some fighting in the Revolution but not as a regular member of the army or militia. In 1780, when only thirteen, he acted as courier and orderly to William Richardson Davie's partisan band and witnessed the action at Hanging Rock.

The next year the fourteen-year-old boy and his next older brother Robert were taken prisoners when a party of irregulars tried to capture a body of British at Waxhaw Church. When a Tory officer named Johnson ordered Andrew to black the officer's boots the boy refused on the ground that he was a prisoner of war, whereupon the Tory officer struck him with a saber. Andrew's left hand, raised to ward off the blow, was cut to the bone, and the saber then made a deep gash on his scalp that left a mark for life. Both of the Jackson boys contracted smallpox while in jail. Their mother finally obtained their exchange and release, but Robert died soon after of neglected wounds or disease. Meanwhile Andrew's oldest brother Hugh had died of the exposure and fatigue suffered in the irregular military service. The mother of the three boys died in 1781 of "prison fever" while nursing the sick. Andrew Jackson's loss of his mother and two brothers in the Revolution caused him to hate the British and this hatred no doubt contributed to his efficiency at the Battle of New Orleans. Jackson was the only President to be a prisoner of war.

Martin Van Buren was never a soldier. Jackson, William Henry Harrison, John Tyler, Taylor and James Buchanan served in the War of 1812. William Henry Harrison had entered the regular army in 1791 as an ensign and retired from the service in 1797 as a captain. Tyler was in uniform only a month as captain of a company of volunteers called out to defend Richmond against a threatened attack that did not materialize. Despite his brief military experience, he was ever after known as "Captain Tyler." Buchanan enlisted as a private in a company of dragoons captained by Judge Henry Shippen and marched from Pennsylvania to the defense of Baltimore, where he served under Major Charles Sterret Ridgely, but was discharged a couple of weeks later without seeing much service. He was the only President with military experience who never held rank higher than that of private. Neither James K. Polk nor Millard Fillmore had any military experience. Taylor was the only President who fought in both the War of 1812 and the Mexican War and he was the only President who spent most of his adult life as a professional soldier. Abraham Lincoln's only military service was as a captain of an Illinois militia company in the Blackhawk Indian War. Even before the Civil War was over, Lincoln was opposed in the election of 1864 by one of his generals, George B. McClellan.

Andrew Johnson was given the rank of brigadier general of volunteers when he was appointed Federal military governor of Tennessee in 1862. His commission was signed by President Lincoln on March 4, 1862. Grant, Hayes, Garfield, Benjamin Harrison and William McKinley all took an active part as soldiers in the Civil War. From April 15, 1865, to March 4, 1885, nearly twenty years, the White House was occupied by men who had been generals in the Union army—Johnson, Grant, Hayes, Garfield and Arthur; but no man who has been a general has occupied the White House since. They all were chosen as President or Vice President on the Republican ticket. No Democrat who served in the Union army has been elected President, and no former Confederate has ever become President. Harry S. Truman has been the only son of Confederate parents to attain that office. Grant has been the only West Pointer to become President. The only other West Pointer ever nominated for President by a major party was General Winfield Scott Hancock, the Democratic nominee in 1880. Jackson, William Henry Harrison, Taylor and Grant were the only Presidents who served in the regular army. When Garfield ran for President in 1880, he defeated three other former generals—James E. Weaver, Hancock, and Neal Dow. Two other former generals have been nominated by major parties but were defeated—Lewis Cass in 1848 and Winfield Scott in 1852. Scott was the highest ranking officer in the army when he was a candidate for President. John C. Frémont, the Republican candidate in 1856, and John C. Breckinridge, the Southern Democratic candidate in 1860, became generals afterward. Grover Cleveland avoided military service during the Civil War by availing himself of the privilege of hiring a substitute under the draft law. In 1884 his Republican opponent, James G. Blaine, was without a military record. In 1888 Cleveland was defeated by General Benjamin Harrison, but four years later Cleveland defeated General Harrison.

William McKinley enlisted at seventeen as a private, rose to the rank of captain and was brevetted major for meritorious service. Hayes and McKinley served for a time in the same outfit and future President Hayes often mentions future President McKinley in his diary and letters. On December 13, 1862, Hayes wrote in his diary: "Our new second lieutenant, McKinley, returned today—an exceedingly bright, intelligent, and gentlemanly young officer. He promises to be one of our best." Hayes wrote his wife on August 30, 1863: "McKinley (the former sergeant), tearfully and emotionally drunk, has been boring me for the last half hour with his blarney. He uttered a great many prayers for 'madame and those little boys, God bless them.' So, of course, I was civil to him." In the spring of 1864 McKinley became a quartermaster on Hayes's staff and Hayes wrote his wife that McKinley had been "very gallant" in the fighting around Winchester. On November 4, 1864, Hayes wrote his son Birchard: "Captain McKinley is on General Crook's staff. He has not been wounded, but every one admires him as one of the bravest and finest young officers in the army. He had two or three horses shot under him." Hayes noted in his diary on December 13, 1864: "Sleigh-ride with Captain McKinley to Winchester Depot. Run against hay team." And on November 8, 1885, the ex-President wrote of the future President: "McKinley is a friend worth having."

Theodore Roosevelt fought in the Spanish-American War as Colonel of the Rough Riders. He resigned the office of Assistant Secretary of the Navy to enter the Army. His only previous military experience was three years' service in the New York National Guard, in which he was a captain. Grover Cleveland excepted, every President from Pierce to Theodore Roosevelt inclusive had some military experience. Theodore Roosevelt was followed in the White House by six Presidents without any military experience—William Howard Taft, Woodrow Wilson, Warren G. Harding, Calvin Coolidge, Herbert C. Hoover and Franklin D. Roosevelt. Truman fought in France during the First World War and held the rank of major when discharged. After graduating from the Independence (Missouri) high school, Truman took an examination in the hope of receiving an appointment to West Point, but failed to pass the examination because of defective vision and never received the appointment. No President except Grant ever received an appointment to West Point.

Monroe and Hayes are known definitely to have been seriously wounded in battle by action of the enemy, although several others were touched by enemy missiles. In his *Autobiography* (1913) Roosevelt, referring to the fighting on the eve of the Battle of Santiago in Cuba, wrote: "Early in the morning our artillery began firing from the hill-crest immediately in front of where our men were encamped. Several of the regiment were killed and wounded by the shrapnel of the return fire of the Spaniards. One of the shrapnel bullets fell on my wrist and raised a bump as big as a hickory-nut, but did not even break the skin." At Buena Vista a bullet passed through General Taylor's left coat sleeve and grazed the skin of his arm, and another bullet tore the lining of his coat.

Washington was never wounded in battle, but at Braddock's Defeat he had two horses shot under him and had one bullet through his hat and three through his clothing. William Henry Harrison had a musket ball through the brim of his hat at Tippecanoe, but the evidence seems to be that he was never actually wounded in battle. The question whether he was ever wounded in battle was asked by the Baltimore *Republican* during the 1840 Presidential campaign. The Louisville *Journal* replied: "No. Was General Jackson or General Washington? As a matter of fact General Harrison received two wounds at Tippecanoe—one grazed his neck, one broke the skin of his hip—mere trifles that left no mark—but what a difference a few inches would have made."

During the fighting around Mexico City, Pierce, a "political briga- dier," was injured twice. At Contreras an exploding Mexican shell caused his horse to rear violently, to throw him against the saddle pommel and to give him a painful blow in the groin. The horse fell and badly wrenched the General's knee. At Churubusco Pierce hurt his injured knee and again fell in a faint. During his campaign for the Presidency on 1852 the Whigs sneeringly referred to him as the "Faint- ing General."

Grant, who saw more actual fighting than any other soldier President, never received even a minor wound in battle. In February, 1866, General Grant accidentally shot himself in the hand while inspecting a new breech-loading rifle. The incident took place in Grant's hotel apartment in the presence of his family and several officers and the bullet lodged in the wall of the room. "I am not hurt," exclaimed the General. Although the wound was dressed by a surgeon and was painful, it did not keep Grant from going to a party that evening. GENERAL GRANT'S FIRST WOUND was the headline on the story in the Philadelphia *Inquirer* on February 26, 1866.

Monroe was an eighteen-year-old lieutenant when, at the Battle of Trenton, he was struck in the left shoulder by a British musket ball, which he carried for the rest of his life. Jackson was wounded in a duel and in a brawl, and once slightly in battle. In the Creek War a bullet nicked his left shoulder above the wound that had been inflicted a short time before by one of the Bentons, but this wound gave him little trouble and quickly healed up.

Hayes was the most wounded of all the soldier Presidents. He enlisted as a private, served four years in the Union army, and was a major general by brevet when discharged. He was wounded five times, twice badly, and had four horses killed or disabled under him. At South Mountain a musket ball passed through the center of his left arm, and at Cedar Creek he was hit in the head by a spent Minié ball and dashed violently to the ground when his horse was killed. On January 6, 1871, Hayes wrote, "My legs have the marks of Rebel missiles," and on January 19, 1884, he said in the postscript of a letter, "During the present winter I have been forced to use a crutch a short time from the effects of the injury received at Cedar Creek—a combination of rheumatism and the old wound." In 1864 Hayes was nominated for Congress without his consent and friends in Ohio asked him to get a furlough from the army and come home to stump his district. On August 24, 1864, he wrote William Henry Smith: "An officer fit for duty who at this crisis would abandon his post to electioneer for a seat in Congress ought to be scalped.

You may feel perfectly sure I shall do no such thing." He was elected without taking any part in the political campaign.

Not a single one of the soldier Presidents ever claimed or admitted that he personally killed or wounded a man in battle.

Two Presidents served as Secretary of War—Monroe and Taft. In 1867 President Johnson appointed Grant Secretary of War in Edwin M. Stanton's place, on the theory that the General would hold the office until the Constitutionality of the Tenure of Office Act could be tested in the courts, but Grant returned the commission to the President when the Senate refused to consent to Stanton's dismissal.

Many of the Vice Presidents had some military experience, and some of them distinguished themselves in war—such as Aaron Burr, George Clinton, Richard Mentor Johnson, John C. Breckinridge and Charles G. Dawes—but no professional military officer has ever been elected Vice President.

How many Presidents were born in log cabins?

Millard Fillmore, James Buchanan, Abraham Lincoln and James A. Garfield were born in log cabins, one-room structures made of unhewn logs notched at the corners and the interstices filled with clay. Garfield lived in such a log cabin until he was fifteen. Chester A. Arthur was born in a log house rather than a typical log cabin. Andrew Jackson is supposed to have been born in a log farmhouse. Shadwell, Jefferson's birthplace, was on the frontier and was probably a log structure. The house at Raleigh in which Andrew Johnson was born was a small cottage in the yard of Casso's Inn, where his father, Jacob Johnson, was a porter. George Washington, James Madison, William Henry Harrison, John Tyler, Benjamin Harrison, William Howard Taft and the two Roosevelts were born in mansions. All the other Presidents were born in ordinary frame houses. No President has been born in a hospital. Only two Presidents have been city born—Theodore Roosevelt, New York City, and Taft, Cincinnati.

Who was Private John Allen?

"Private John" was the familiar name of John Mills Allen (1846-1917) of Tupelo, Mississippi, who served throughout the Civil War as a private in the Confederate army, and who later became a successful lawyer. In 1884 Allen and a former Confederate general named Tucker both sought the Democratic nomination for the seat in Congress that had been occupied since 1877 by Colonel Henry Lowndes Muldrow. On one occasion, when the candidates spoke from the same platform, General Tucker wound up his appeal to the voters in words substantially as follows:

"Twenty years ago last night, my fellow citizens, after a hard-fought battle on yonder hill, I bivouacked under yonder clump of trees. Those of you who remember, as I do, the time that tried men's souls will not, I trust, forget your humble servant on election day."

In reply Allen said: "What General Tucker says to you about having bivouacked in yonder clump of trees on that night is true. It is also true that I was vidette picket and stood guard over him while he slept. Now then, fellow citizens, all of you who were generals and had privates to stand guard over you while you slept, vote for General Tucker, and all of you who were privates and stood guard over the generals while they slept, vote for Private John Allen."

The voters chose "Private John Allen" and continued to do so until he retired from Congress sixteen years later. Although the sayings of Private John Allen have not found their way into standard quotation books, he acquired a national reputation for wit and humor and is still quoted on Capitol Hill. Speaker Champ Clark referred to Private John as "a humorist of the first order" and "one of the greatest humorists who ever lived."

Private John began his "maiden speech" with the words: "Mr. Chairman, I desire to say to those present that their perfect attention will not embarrass me in the least." When the Chairman of the Committee of the Whole reminded him that his time on the River and Harbor Bill had expired, he said: "This is a pity; for I had many other things of great interest to say, but as my time has expired, and not wishing to further interrupt the proceedings, I would at least like to have permission to print some remarks in *The Record* and insert 'laughter and applause' in appropriate places. Now I will retire to the cloak-room to receive congratulations." The House took him at his word and after that Private John's speeches were followed by congratulations in the cloakroom.

His most famous speech was on a Federal fish hatchery at Tupelo. On February 20, 1901, two weeks before his retirement from Congress, he asked and obtained unanimous consent to insert in a bill, and to speak for twenty minutes on an amendment providing "for the establishment of a fish hatchery and fish-culture station at the town of Tupelo, State of Mississippi, $20,000." After relating an extravagant and humorous history of his home town, he said: "This, Mr. Chairman, is a proposition to establish there a fish hatchery. We have the ideal place for a fish hatchery. Why, sir, fish will travel over land for miles to get into the water we have at Tupelo. Thousands and millions of unborn fish are clamoring to this Congress this day for an opportunity to be hatched at the Tupelo hatchery." The amendment passed unanimously and the Private John Allen Fish Hatchery at Tupelo is still a going concern. He was in the habit of signing himself "Private John Allen, Tupelo, U.S.A."

How many Presidents' sons have served in Congress?

From 1789 to 1951 six sons of Presidents served in Congress. Charles Francis Adams, John Scott Harrison, David Gardiner Tyler and Franklin D. Roosevelt, Jr. served only in the House of Representatives. John Quincy Adams served in the Senate before he was President and in the House after he was President. Robert A. Taft served only in the Senate. He and John Quincy Adams are the only two Presidents' sons to become Senators.

Thomas Jefferson's two sons-in-law, John Wayles Eppes and Thomas Mann Randolph, served in the House together while he was President.

Only three grandsons of Presidents have served in Congress—Charles Francis Adams, grandson of John Adams; Benjamin Harrison, grandson of William Henry Harrison, and William Henry Harrison, grandson of Benjamin Harrison. Of these, only Benjamin Harrison, who was himself President, served in the Senate.

Only two brothers of Presidents have served in Congress. Charles Phelps Taft, older brother of President William Howard Taft, served in the House as a Republican from Ohio from 1895 to 1897, and James Isaac Van Alen, half brother of President Martin Van Buren, served in the House as a Federalist from New York from 1807 to 1809. Bushrod Washington, a nephew of President George Washington, and James Monroe, a nephew of President James Monroe, served in the House.

Three sons of Presidents have served in the Cabinet—John Quincy Adams, Secretary of State under Monroe; Robert T. Lincoln, Secretary of War under Garfield and Arthur, and James R. Garfield, Secretary of the Interior under Theodore Roosevelt.

What Presidents had foreign-born parents?

Andrew Jackson has been the only President whose parents were both born abroad. Andrew Jackson, Sr. and his wife Elizabeth Hutchison Jackson, the parents of the President, were born in Northern Ireland. They migrated to America in 1765 with their two young sons, Hugh and Robert. Their third son, Andrew, was born two years later. Andrew Jackson's parents and his two brothers all died before the close of the Revolution.

President James Buchanan's father, James Buchanan, was born in 1761 in County Donegal in Northern Ireland, and migrated to America in 1783, eight years before his distinguished son was born. James Buchanan, Sr. married Elizabeth Speers, who was born in Pennsylvania in 1767 but whose father had come from Northern Ireland in 1756.

William Arthur (1797-1875), the father of President Chester A. Arthur, was born at "The Draen" near Ballymena in County Antrim in Northern Ireland. He emigrated to the United States in 1817 and, after teaching and studying law, became a Baptist minister, writer and antiquarian. In 1821 he married Malvina Stone, who was American born.

Thomas Jefferson's mother, whose maiden name was Jane Randolph, was born in London in 1720 while her Virginia parents were making an extended stay in England. Her husband, Peter Jefferson, named his home "Shadwell" after the London parish in which she was born. Jane Randolph Jefferson died on March 31, 1776, about three months before her distinguished son wrote the Declaration of Independence.

Woodrow Wilson's mother, whose maiden name was Janet Woodrow, was born at Carlisle, England, in 1826, and migrated to the United States with her parents when she was nine.

The mother of Herbert Hoover, whose maiden name was Hulda Minthorn, was born in 1848 in North Norwich Township, Oxford County, Ontario Province, Canada. She was one of the seven children of Theodore and Mary (Wesley) Minthorn, who both were born in Canada and who migrated to the United States when Hulda was eleven years old. Both the Minthorn and Wesley families had migrated from the United States to Canada in the early 1800's.

What candidate told a voter he was too dumb to understand?

During the Presidential campaign of 1932 Vice President Charles Curtis, seeking re-election as the running mate of President Hoover, told a heckler at the Clay County Fair at Spencer, Iowa, that he was "too damn dumb to understand."

When critics of the New Deal ridiculed the Works Progress Administration projects for white collar workers in New York in 1935, WPA Administrator Harry L. Hopkins was reported as saying that they were "too damned dumb" to appreciate the finer things of life.

Who was *That Man?*

During the 1930's some anti-New Dealers disliked President Franklin D. Roosevelt so intensely that they referred to him as "That Man in the White House" or simply as "That Man" instead of by his name.

Referring to an unmentionable or detested person as "That Man" or "That Woman" is old in English usage. Neither the thought nor the language was original with Anti-New Dealers. William Richardson Davie (1756-1806) of North Carolina, who was a delegate to the Constitutional Convention in 1787 and who became a strong Federalist, refused to accept appointments from Thomas Jefferson and referred to the President as "that man."

What two Presidents were married in England?

Two men who became President of the United States were married in London, England. They were John Quincy Adams and Theodore Roosevelt.

On July 26, 1797, John Quincy Adams then U.S. Minister to the Netherlands, wrote in his diary:

At nine this morning I went, accompanied by my brother, to Mr. Johnson's, and thence to the Church of the parish of All Hallows Barking, where I was married to Louisa Catherine Johnson, the second daughter of Joshua and Catherine Johnson, by Mr. Hewlett. Mr. Johnson's family, Mr. Brooks, my brother, and Mr. J. Hall were present. We were married before eleven in the morning, and immediately after went out to see Tilney House, one of the splendid country seats for which this country is distinguished.

Joshua Johnson was a Marylander who had been employed more or less in Europe from the outbreak of the Revolution and his daughter Louisa Catherine was born in England.

When Adams was seeking re-election to the Presidency the fact that his wife was born in England became a political issue. On May 10, 1828, the President wrote in his diary:

Mr. Marks, a Senator from Pennsylvania, showed me a letter that he had received from an editor of a newspaper in the western part of Pennsylvania, mentioning reports circulated industriously there, that my wife was an Englishwoman, and others of a similar character, but the more readily believed for their absurdity. Mr. Marks asked me to mention so much of the facts as would enable him to deny these ridiculous tales. I told him that I was married in London; that my wife was the daughter of Joshua Johnson, a native of Maryland, then Consul of the United States at London, and brother of Thomas Johnson, a member of the Congress of 1774, first Governor of Maryland after the Revolution, and appointed by General Washington a Judge of the Supreme Court of the United States, with all which information Mr. Marks was much gratified.

Joshua Johnson, Mrs. John Quincy Adams's father, and Thomas Johnson, her uncle, were members of a family of twelve children. For some unaccountable reason many writers say that Thomas Johnson

(1732-1819) was one of the Maryland signers of the Declaration of Independence. The only signers from Maryland were Samuel Chase, William Paca, Thomas Stone and Charles Carroll of Carrollton. Thomas Johnson was an active patriot before the Revolution and was chosen a delegate to both the First and the Second Continental Congresses. On June 15, 1775, upon the suggestion of John Adams, he nominated George Washington to be supreme commander of the Continental army. He was not in Philadelphia when the Declaration of Independence was adopted and he never signed that document. He had returned to Maryland to help frame a State constitution and on July 6, 1776, he voted at Annapolis for the Declaration of the Delegates of Maryland, which declared the separation of Maryland from the mother country. Later in the same year he raised 1,800 Maryland militia and as brigadier general led them to the relief of Washington in New Jersey. While in camp he was chosen the first Governor of Maryland and served three terms. Thomas Johnson was one of Washington's intimate and confidential friends. As head of the board of commissioners he was largely responsible for naming the new Federal City "Washington." In his old age he said he firmly expected meeting Washington in heaven.

Theodore Roosevelt was married the first time in 1880 to Alice Hathaway Lee, daughter of George Cabot Lee. The first Mrs. Roosevelt died in 1884, leaving one child, Alice, who married Nicholas Longworth in 1906. On December 2, 1886, twenty-one months after the death of his first wife, Roosevelt was married in St. George's Church, Hanover Square, London, to Edith Kermit Carow, daughter of Charles Carow of New York. By this union five children were born—Theodore, Kermit, Archibald, Quentin and Ethel.

Only one other President was married on foreign soil. Andrew Jackson was married to Rachel Donelson Robards in 1791 in the "Natchez District," which was then still under nominal Spanish jurisdiction.

Who was James Proctor Knott?

James Proctor Knott (1830-1911) was a U.S. Representative, Governor of Kentucky and law professor who is remembered chiefly for a humorous speech in Congress about Duluth. As attorney general of Missouri in 1861 he opposed secession but was imprisoned a short time because he refused to take the oath of allegiance to the Federal Government. He returned to Kentucky, his native State, and acquired a reputation as a public speaker.

On January 27, 1871, Congressman Knott was largely responsible for killing a joint resolution authorizing an extension of time for a land grant to build a railroad from the St. Croix River to Duluth on Lake Superior. The first permanent settlement at Duluth was made in 1853 and in 1871 it was still little more than a wilderness village. The Kentucky Congressman ridiculed the "future metropolis" in a witty speech that put the House in a roar and made him nationally famous. In this speech he said:

Duluth! The word fell upon my ear with a peculiar and indescribable charm, like the gentle murmur of a low fountain stealing forth in the midst of roses, or the soft sweet accent of an angel's whisper in the bright, joyous dream of sleeping innocence. It was the name for which my soul had panted for years, as the hart panteth for the water-brooks.

One phrase in Knott's speech, "The zenith city of the unsalted seas," was adopted by Duluth as a sort of slogan. Many years later, after Duluth had realized the orator's satiric forecast, he was given an enthusiastic reception by the Duluthians. Knott County, Kentucky, was formed while he was Governor of the State.

Did George Washington use tobacco?

Although George Washington raised tobacco for sale as a "cash crop," he did not habitually use tobacco in any form. Some authorities think he may have smoked a pipe and used snuff for a period before the Revolution. Later, however, he seems to have been definitely allergic to tobacco smoke. George Washington Parke Custis wrote that Washington could not endure tobacco smoke and had the "utmost abhorrence" of it. According to Custis, who was reared by Washington, the Father of His Country, even when compelled by courtesy and custom to take a whiff from the calumet while conferring with Indians, "drank" as little of the smoke as possible, made a wry face and passed the pipe of peace quickly along to the next person. But on July 11, 1794, John Quincy Adams attended a reception given to a delegation of Chickasaw Indians by President Washington and wrote in his diary:

"As soon as the whole were seated, the ceremony of smoking began. A large East Indian pipe was placed in the middle of the Hall. The tube, which appeared to be of leather, was 12 or 15 feet in length. The President began, and after two or three whiffs, passed the tube to Piomingo; he to the next Chief, and to all round."

Under date of April 2, 1767, Washington noted in his *Ledger A:* "By 1 Paper Snuff Box 7/6." This appears to be the only entry of its kind in his accounts and does not prove that he was a snuff user. In those days snuffboxes were a common present and Washington received and gave away many of them.

A majority of the Presidents have used tobacco in one form or other. John Adams, the second President and the first occupant of the White House, pinched snuff, smoked a pipe and "chewed a little." Thomas Jefferson, James Madison and James Monroe, though they raised tobacco, never used it in any form except when they smoked the pipe of peace with Indians. Irving Brant, author of a monumental life of Madison, wrote the author in 1948: "Madison did not use tobacco in any form, at any time in his life, though it was the principal cash crop from which he drew his livelihood." In 1822 Dr. Waterhouse sent ex-President Madison a series of lectures denouncing the use of tobacco and ardent spirits. Madison said in reply: "In every view, your remedial efforts are highly meritorious, since they may check, if they cannot cure, the evil, and since a partial success may excite co-operating efforts which will gradually make it compleat; and I join heartily in every wish that such may be the result."

In describing his day's routine John Quincy Adams noted in his diary under date of June 30, 1796: "Then take a very slight supper and my segar, and retire to bed at eleven." Under date of July 2, 1814—twenty years later—the diplomat wrote: "Prince Henry left the city about noon. I dined at the table-d'hote, at one. The other gentlemen dined together at four. They sit after dinner and drink bad wine and smoke cigars, which neither suits my habits or my health, and absorbs time which I cannot spare." On September 24, 1829, after he had retired from the Presidency, Adams wrote: "I smoked tobacco and read Milton at the same time, and from the same motive—to find out what was the recondite charm in them which gave my father so much pleasure. After making myself four or five times sick with smoking, I mastered that accomplishment, and acquired a habit which, thirty years afterwards, I had much more difficulty in breaking off."

During the eighteenth century many men of all classes in the North chewed tobacco, but in the South the habit was restricted to the lower classes. Southern gentlemen seldom smoked and when they did smoke they did so in private. The notion that no Southern gentleman smoked in public persisted far into the nineteenth century. Very few of the early statesmen of Virginia and South Carolina smoked or chewed, although some of them used snuff. It was said that when John C. Calhoun took a pinch of snuff all South Carolina sneezed.

But Andrew Jackson, a border man, chewed tobacco and smoked a pipe with equal energy and didn't care who saw him do it. Admirers in

[463]

all parts of the world sent pipes to the Hero of New Orleans. He once told a visitor that the fancy specimens would do to look at but he would stick to his corncob because it was the sweetest and best pipe. At one time he was fond of a long-stemmed Powhatan bowl pipe that he rested on his lap. Another favorite was the old-fashioned clay pipe. Jackson was in the habit of smoking and chewing at the same time. After he became President he paid $12.50 a piece for twenty elaborate spitoons for the White House. While visiting Philadelphia in 1833 he got sick and was treated by Dr. Philip Syng Physick. "Now, Doctor," Old Hickory told the most famous physician in America. "I will do anything you ask me to except give up tobacco and coffee."

Martin Van Buren was a snuff-user. On March 7, 1834, Daniel Webster presented to the Senate a petition from the master builders of Philadelphia asking Congress to do something to remedy financial conditions. Henry Clay seconded the motion to refer and print the memorial and then, in mock seriousness, appealed directly to Vice President Van Buren to take a message to Jackson and to use his great influence with the President to persuade him to take action to relieve the distressed people. In *Thirty Years View* Thomas H. Benton wrote:

> During the delivery of this apostrophe, the Vice-President maintained the utmost decorum of countenance, looking respectfully, and even innocently at the speaker all the while, as if treasuring up every word he said to be faithfully reported to the President. After it was over, and the Vice-President had called some senator to the chair, he went up to Mr. Clay, and asked him for a pinch of his fine maccoboy snuff (as he often did); and, having received it, walked away.

William Henry Harrison, though the son of a Virginia tobacco planter, used tobacco in no form and was annoyed when his sons took to smoking. John Tyler, himself a Virginia tobacco planter, never used tobacco. Neither did James K. Polk. Zachary Taylor, Virginia born and Kentucky reared, did not smoke but was a habitual chewer, as his vest often bore evidence. Neither Millard Fillmore nor Franklin Pierce were tobacco users. James Buchanan smoked cigars and in later years often had an unlighted cigar in his mouth. Abraham Lincoln never used tobacco in any form. Andrew Johnson was a cigar smoker.

At West Point Ulysses S. Grant tried smoking but gave it up because it made him sick. In Mexico he took up smoking light cigars and cigarettes. Later he became a habitual pipe smoker and smoked cigars only occasionally. After he sent his "Unconditional Surrender" message to Buckner and won the sensational victory at Fort Donelson, the Union general was reported to have had a cigar in his mouth at the time of the capitulation. Newspapers described and pictured the victorious general smoking a cigar. The result was that admirers thoughout the North sent him more than a thousand boxes of cigars. Grant himself said he became an inveterate cigar smoker while trying to smoke up these gifts. Thereafter he was seldom seen without a cigar in his mouth.

Rutherford B. Hayes smoked cigars in his younger days but gave them up because of weak lungs and a chronic throat ailment. James A. Garfield smoked cigars. Chester A. Arthur was the first occupant of the White House to smoke cigarettes. Of all the Presidents who used tobacco, he appears to have been the only connoiseur of fine tobacco. He smoked cigarettes of Turkish, Egyptian and other imported brands with the relish of an Oriental. Grover Cleveland and Benjamin Harrison were both perpetual cigar and pipe smokers. William McKinley was reported to have smoked cigarettes during his Presidency, but he seems to have preferred strong black cigars. When he was being photographed with William Allen White he held his cigar behind him to keep the public from seeing him pictured smoking in the presence of a young newspaperman. Theodore Roosevelt and William Howard Taft are known to have smoked an occasional cigarette or cigar to make others feel at home, but neither was a habitual smoker. Woodrow Wilson did not use tobacco. He once said that he tried to smoke only once and that the cigar made him so sick that he never tried it again. Warren G. Harding smoked a pipe and cigarettes, preferring the latter. He also chewed tobacco but his wife made him give up the habit after he became President. Calvin Coolidge was an inveterate smoker of cigars and started the custom of passing around cigars at Cabinet meetings. Herbert Hoover started smoking in college and continued to enjoy both a pipe and cigars. Franklin D. Roosevelt smoked a pipe in his younger days but later became an inveterate cigarette smoker. Harry S. Truman never used tobacco in any form.

Who was Kicking Buck Kilgore?

That was the nickname of Constantine Buckley Kilgore (1835-1897), Texas Congressman from 1887 to 1895. Before 1890 he was known as Buck Kilgore. In that year, on one occasion when Czar Reed had ordered the doors closed and had begun to "count a quorum," Kilgore, determined not to remain in the hall and be counted, kicked open a door leading into the lobby and damaged the nose of Representative Nelson Dingley of Michigan, who was standing outside. Newspapers played up the incident and ever after Kilgore was known as "Kicking Buck." Kilgore entered the Confederate army as a private and rose to the rank of colonel. He was wounded at Chickamauga, captured, and confined in Fort Delaware for a year as a prisoner of war. Champ Clark said Kicking Buck was six feet tall, straight as a ramrod, lithe as a panther, unusually handsome, with snow-white hair and imperial mustache, and was an inveterate joker. After his defeat for renomination he was appointed a Federal judge in Indian Territory. Kilgore in Gregg County, Texas, was named after him.

Who was the first President to be photographed?

John Tyler was the first President to be photographed while in office, and John Quincy Adams was the first man who was President to be photographed. George Washington, John Adams, Thomas Jefferson, James Madison and James Monroe all died before the invention of photography.

Louis Daguerre, French scene painter and physicist, announced the discovery of his process of photography early in 1839. On December 4, 1839, Philip Hone, who lived in New York City, wrote in his diary:

"I went this morning by invitation of M. Francois Gourand to see a collection of the views made by the wonderful process lately discovered in France by M. Daguerre, which is called by his name. M. Gourand is the pupil and friend of the inventor, and comes to this country to make known the process."

In either 1839 or 1840 Professor J. W. Draper of New York University Medical College made the first photograph of a living person in America. His sister, Miss Dorothy Catherine Draper, had to sit rigid for ten minutes to get a good "daguerreotype likeness." In 1842 or 1843 Mathew B. Brady, then only twenty years old, established a portrait studio at the corner of Broadway and Fulton Street in New York City and went into the photographic business. When daguerreotypes were first made in the United States they were popularly known as "chemical pictures."

Under date of November 13, 1843, Ex-President John Quincy Adams, then in Cincinnati, wrote in his diary: "Before returning to the Henry House, we stopped at a daguerreotype office, where three attempts were made to take my likeness. I believe neither of them (successful)." On April 12, 1844, Adams noted at Washington: "At the request of J. M. Edwards and Anthony, I sat also in their room while they took three larger daguerreotype likenesses of me than those they had taken before. While I was there President Tyler and his son John came in; but I did not notice them." Three daguerreotypes of Andrew Jackson were made after he was President. The best of these was made April 15, 1845, by

Brady, who took his cumbersome equipment to Tennessee and "shot" Old Hickory in the Hermitage two months before he died. In 1846 Congress voted Zachary Taylor a gold medal for his exploits in Mexico, and on October 5 of that year Secretary of War William L. Marcy asked Old Rough and Ready to send a portrait, miniature or daguerreotype for the use of the artist. General Taylor replied that he had no such likeness of himself and that there were no photographers in his army, but that he would have his picture taken as soon as possible. Under date of February 14, 1849, shortly before his retirement from the White House, President James K. Polk wrote in his diary: "I yielded to the request of an artist named Brady, of New York, by sitting for my daguerreotype today. I sat in the large dining-room." Every President after Polk was photographed.

Brady became America's most famous photographer. The *Illustrated London News* published daguerreotype pictures of Crimean War battle scenes made in 1854 by Roger Fenton, "the first war photographer," and when the Civil War began Brady, already a popular and successful photographer with studios in New York and Washington, decided to make a pictorial record of the conflict. From President Lincoln and Allan Pinkerton of the secret service he got permission for himself and assistants to accompany the Federal armies to make photographs of actual battle scenes. Brady was a small, genial, polite man of Irish descent who wore a mustache and pointed beard and who was generally seen in a linen duster and broad-brimmed flat straw hat.

In July, 1861, Brady loaded his cumbersome camera, plateholder, black cloth, chemicals for developing pictures and other paraphernalia on a wagon and set out from Washington for the Bull Run battlefield in Virginia. This first attempt to photograph a battle did not turn out well. The photographer lost his darkroom on wheels, his camera and all his equipment in the battle and was found lost in the woods by a Federal officer after the rout of the Union army. But Brady persisted in his enterprise and during the next four years made about 3,500 photographs of battles, places devastated by gunfire, troops on the march and in camp, groups of officers and other scenes. In 1874 Congress appropriated $2,840 for 7,200 negatives, and the next year it appropriated $25,000 for another 2,000 of these priceless glass negatives. Several thousand others are preserved. But despite his industry, enterprise, artistry and personal popularity, Brady failed financially on his Civil War venture. He died in New York in 1896 at the age of seventy-three as the result of an injury received when a carriage ran over him. He always insisted on spelling his first name *Mathew,* with only one *t,* and he was himself uncertain what his middle initial stood for. Brady was noted for his tinted daguerreotypes on ivory and had received a dozen or more medals for the excellency of his work before he undertook to record the history of a war in pictures.

Next to Brady, the most famous early photographer was William Henry Jackson (1843-1942), who began to work in his father's portrait gallery at Troy, New York in 1857, served in the army during the Civil War and who became the photographer of the West. His work is a pictorial record of covered wagon days and consists of thousands of photographs of Indians, pioneers, mountains, geysers and other Western scenes.

Why is public office called the toga?

Toga (from Latin *tegere,* "to cover") was the name of the mantle, cloak or loose outer garment worn in public by ancient Roman citizens. It consisted of a single almost semicircular piece of undyed woolen cloth without sleeves or armholes and was worn in a flowing fashion over the shoulders and body. The *toga virilis,* "manly toga," was assumed by Roman youths at the age of fourteen. Roman officers wore togas with special borders as distinctive badges of rank. Later *toga* became synonymous with "classical," "stately" or "majestic." The word is spelled *toge* in Shakespeare. Coriolanus, soliciting votes for consul, asks, "Why in this woolvish toge should I stand here. . . ?" Iago in *Othello* refers to "the toged consuls." In time *toga* came to denote a professional gown or official robe. Now a candidate for office is said to seek the toga; if successful, he is said to don the toga. *Mantle* is used in a similar sense. When a person succeeds another in office he is said to assume the other's mantle. This alludes to Elisha's taking up of Elijah's mantle, as related in II Kings 13.

When did Presidents start mass handshaking?

The early Presidents did comparatively little handshaking. President Washington did not shake hands with guests at official receptions because his advisers thought the practice was out of keeping with the dignity of such occasions. Handshaking increased with the extension of suffrage. Wholesale handshaking did not become common until the Jackson era, when the ability to shake hands became an essential qualification of a politician.

On February 11, 1841, Philip Hone wrote in his diary in reference to

President-elect William Henry Harrison, who had just arrived in Washington: "They say his arm is so lame at overexercise in shaking hands that he can no longer use it in that way." On March 4 of the same year, the day Harrison was inaugurated, Hone wrote: "He does not shake hands, having experienced some injury by the frequent and too forcible use the 'dear people' have made of that avenue to his heart."

President James K. Polk wrote in his diary after a New Year's reception at the White House on January 1, 1847: "I stood on my feet shaking hands with the immense crowd from half past eleven o'clock A.M., till three o'clock P.M. . . . I was very much exhausted by the fatigue of the day." On January 1, 1849, after a similar reception, President Polk wrote:

I received the crowd in the circular parlour and for three hours shook hands with a dense column of human beings of all ages and sexes . . . I must have shook hands with several thousands persons. Towards the close of the day some gentlemen asked me if my arm was not sore, and if I would not suffer from the day's labour. I answered them that judging from my experience on similar occasions I thought not. I told them that I had found that there was a great art in shaking hands, and that I could shake hands during the whole day without suffering any bad effects from it. They were curious to know what this art was. I told them that if a man surrendered his arm to be shaken by some horizontally, by others perpendicularly, and by others again with a strong grip, he could not fail to suffer severely from it, but that if he would shake and not be shaken, grip and not be gripped, taking care always to squeeze the hand of his adversary as hard as he squeezed him, that he suffered no inconvenience from it. I told them also that I could generally anticipate when I was to have a strong grip, and that when I observed a strong man approaching I generally took advantage of him by being a little quicker than he was and seizing him by the tip of the fingers, giving him a hearty shake, and thus preventing him from getting a full grip upon me. They were much amused at my account of the operation, which I gave them playfully, but admitted that there was much philosophy in it. But though I gave my account of the operation playfully, it is all true.

Abraham Lincoln was a prodigious handshaker. On the night of his first inauguration on March 4, 1861, Lincoln shook hands at the White House from 8:15 until 10:30 at the rate of twenty-five hands a minute. Herman Melville, who attended the reception, wrote his wife that Lincoln "shook hands like a good fellow—working hard at it like a man sawing wood at so much per cord." After delivering his second inaugural address on March 4, 1865, Lincoln at a White House reception shook hands with 6,000 persons in three hours. In 1864 the New York *World* reported that Lincoln's style of shaking hands was neither the pump handle, the twist, nor the reach, but a sudden thrust and a corkscrew burrow. But these handshaking ordeals often left Lincoln's right hand so badly swollen that he could not use it for hours.

In *My Quarter Century of American Politics* (1920) Champ Clark wrote of Grover Cleveland during his second administration: "He had a sort of patent way of shaking hands which he probably invented for self-protection. He grabbed the visitor's hand, gave it a slight squeeze, and dropped it like a hot potato. He never under any circumstances whatsoever permitted a visitor to grip his large, fat hand."

William McKinley shook hands at the rate of 2,500 persons an hour. Theodore Roosevelt shook hands at the White House on New Year's Day with 8,100 persons in 1902, with 8,000 in 1906 and with 8,513 in 1907. William Howard Taft shook hands with 6,000 persons at the New Year's reception in 1910 but his right hand was so swollen on the next day that it had to be bandaged. Describing his daily routine in the White House, Calvin Coolidge, in his *Autobiography* (1929), wrote: "At twelve-thirty the doors were opened, and a long line passed by who wished merely to shake hands with the President. On one occasion I shook hands with nineteen hundred in thirty-four minutes, which is probably my record. Instead of a burden, it was a pleasure and a relief to meet people in that way and listen to their greetings, which was often a benediction." Herbert Hoover found it a burden, especially after a hard day's work, to shake hands with thousands of visitors and to offer a friendly attitude and greeting to each one of them. "Often," he wrote in his memoirs, "my hand would be so swollen that I could not write with it for days. On one occasion a husky Westerner with a turned-in diamond ring gave me such a warm clasp as to cut my hand badly. We had to terminate the session in a trickle of blood." Franklin D. Roosevelt, who avoided the full impact of hard-squeezing, bone-crushing handshakes by grasping their fingers, could shake hands with about 1,000 persons in succession without excessive fatigue, but beyond that he began to show strain and had to desist. Harry S. Truman worked out his own technique for shaking hands with the least damage to himself. It was suggested to him by his experience on a farm and consists of grasping the visitor's hand as if it were a cow's teat.

Many politicians set great store by handshaking and count each handshake as a vote. On September 11, 1950, Senator William Benton of Connecticut and some political associates, while calling at the White House, asked Truman how to get elected, and the President was reported as telling them "to shake hands with 25,000 people between now and November 7."

What is a straw man?

The original "man of straw" or "straw man" was probably an effigy, a suit of clothes stuffed with straw, like an old-fashioned scarecrow. Later the term came to mean a person of no substance, a counterfeit, a sham or a dummy put forward as a substitute, whipping boy or surety for another. In *Second Frutus* (1591) John Florio wrote that "A man of straw is worth more than a woman of gold." As early as 1624 the term was used in the sense of an imaginary adversary or a fictitious argument set up to be easily knocked down or refuted. In that year a Puritan divine and critic named Thomas Gataker wrote, "To skirmish with a man of straw of his own making." James Gallatin wrote in his diary at Paris in March, 1817: "I have just heard that a man called Cantillon has been arrested. They say he is but a man of straw and that his arrest was made to appease the English and that he will never be tried." On Februrary 12, 1841, Representative John Quincy Adams wrote in his diary: "This shuffling trick of misstating the question, and setting up a man of straw to make a pompous demonstration of knocking him down, is a measure of the capacity of Edward Black and of the majority of the House."

How many Presidents were slaveholders?

Ten of the men who have been President were owners of Negro slaves at one time or other. They were George Washington, Thomas Jefferson, James Madison, James Monroe, Andrew Jackson, John Tyler, James K. Polk, Zachary Taylor, Andrew Johnson and Ulysses S. Grant. The first eight of these were slaveowners in the full sense of the term and all of them owned slaves while President.

Washington owned forty-seven slaves when he was married in 1759. The estate of Daniel Parke Custis, first husband of Martha Dandridge, included about three hundred slaves, many of whom Mrs. Washington inherited. A list of his slaves made by Washington in 1783 indicates that he then had two hundred and sixteen slaves, including the "dower Negroes" in which his wife had a life interest. Jefferson inherited thirty slaves from his father and acquired about one hundred and thirty-five through his wife. During the Revolution the British carried away more than thirty of his slaves from his James River plantation. In 1809 he had one hundred slaves at Monticello and about eighty-five at Poplar Forest—a total of one hundred and eighty-five. It is believed that at the height of his prosperity he had two hundred slaves. Madison inherited many slaves from his father and at one time owned one hundred and sixteen. Monroe, though a Virginia planter on a small scale, was never wealthy and owned few slaves compared with Washington, Jefferson and Madison.

Jackson bought a Negro girl for $200 when he first went to Nashville in 1785 and after that he bought and sold slaves. In 1810 he had twenty slaves. When he was President he had about one hundred slaves at the Hermitage plantation and sixty at the Melton Bluff plantation in Alabama—a total of one hundred and sixty, and probably the largest number he ever owned at one time. So far as known, Jackson never uttered a word against slavery. Tyler was a Virginia planter and owned a large number of slaves. Polk, though reared in a nonslaveholding family, owned plantations in Tennessee and Mississippi and at one time owned about eighteen slaves. Taylor, Virginia-born and Kentucky-reared, who owned a large plantation in Louisiana, had about three hundred slaves when he became President and was the largest slave-holder of all the Presidents.

During his younger years Johnson bought several slaves whom he kept as household servants and field hands, and he continued to own these slaves until the Civil War broke out, but he never sold a slave. William Andrew Johnson, who died at Knoxville, Tennessee, in 1943 at the age of eighty-seven, is believed to have been the last surviving person who had been a slave of a President. His mother was purchased by Johnson when she was fourteen and her son was born in slavery in 1856 on Johnson's estate near Greenville while he was Governor of Tennessee. The slave boy was named after his master and was nineteen when the former President died in 1875. In 1937 William Andrew Johnson, the former slave of a man who had been President, visited Franklin D. Roosevelt at the White House and was presented with a silver-headed cane by the President.

Grant was born in Ohio and was brought up in an antislavery family. He never trafficked in slaves and was a slaveowner only in a limited sense. After he graduated from West Point he was sent to St. Louis, Missouri, for garrison duty. Near that city lived one of his classmates, Frederick T. Dent, whose father owned a large plantation known as "White Haven" and eighteen slaves. In 1848, upon his return from the Mexican War, Grant was married at White Haven to Julia Dent, sister of his classmate. Julia Dent had already been presented with a slave girl by her father, and when she was married he gave her a slave boy. Later Mrs. Grant acquired a third slave in her own name. After Grant had left the army and started farming in Missouri, he expressed a desire to give his wife's three slaves their freedom as soon as he was able. About this same time Grant in his own name purchased from his father-in-law a slave named William Jones. On March 29, 1859, Grant appeared in a St. Louis court and filed emancipation papers giving William Jones his freedom. Jesse R. Grant, son of the President, writing to the author from Santa Cruz, California, under date of February 6, 1925, said: "My mother's family had slaves from the beginning of that institution in America until the close of the War. My nurse was a slave born on the Gravois Farm. These slaves were probably well pleased at the farm, because when one ran away to Illinois he would soon come back and be glad to get *back home*." Grant himself did not pretend to be opposed to slavery in his earlier days. On one occasion he said he "was never an abolitionist, nor even what could be termed a protagonist of anti-slavery." In 1856, only four years before the outbreak of the Civil War, he voted for Buchanan, a Northern man with Southern principles, instead of for Frémont, a Southern man with Northern principles.

Martin Van Buren was the only Northern-born President who was brought up in a slaveholding family. His Dutch parents in New York State inherited six Negro slaves, but the evidence indicates that he himself never owned a slave.

Whether William Henry Harrison, the son of a Virginia slaveholder, ever owned slaves himself is hard to determine. In 1791, when eighteen, he went to Philadelphia to study medicine. When he arrived there he learned that his father had died. He never returned to Virginia to live, but, after serving seven years in the regular army, settled in the Northwest Territory. His father left him three thousand acres of land in Virginia but apparently all the slaves went to his mother and to his two older brothers. Ohio, which Harrison made his home most of his adult life, became a State in 1803, and he became Governor of Indiana Territory, which included the present States of Indiana, Illinois, Michigan, Wisconsin and part of Minnesota. Slavery was prohibited in the Territory by the Ordinance of 1787, but southern Indiana and Illinois were settled largely by Southerners and there was a strong demand for the legalization of slavery. On December 20, 1802, Governor Harrison presided over a convention at Vincennes that memorialized Congress to suspend the prohibition against slavery in the Territory for ten years. The argument was that many desirable emigrants from the South were going to Missouri rather than to Indiana Territory. Congress seriously considered but rejected the request. In 1802 Governor Harrison and the judges adopted a Virginia law permitting masters to make agreements with their slaves for "lifelong slavery." Under "voluntary" agreements slavery existed in Indiana and Illinois for a generation. Apparently Harrison favored this modified form of slavery. When Harrison inherited eleven Negroes from his mother he had them brought from Virginia and they worked for him as "voluntary slaves." According to a family tradition, these slaves were emancipated. Whether they became "free" by formal emancipation in Virginia or by removing to free territory is not clear. His failure to be re-elected to the State senate in 1820 was attributed to the fact that his views on the slavery question were not sufficiently positive, and, when a candidate for President in 1836 and 1840, his Northern political opponents accused him of having once been a slaveholder.

Who owned the largest number of Negro slaves in the United States at one time is hard to say. Nathaniel Heyward (1766-1851), South Carolina planter, owned between 3,000 and 4,000 and is reputed to have had more slaves than any other person who ever lived in the United States. He still owned 2,000 slaves when he died at the age of ninety-five. A few years earlier he had given 100 slaves to his son and 200 each to his three daughters for their plantations in South Carolina and Georgia. Wade Hampton (1752-1835) of South Carolina owned 3,000 slaves when he died and was probably the second largest slaveholder in the nineteenth century. His grandson, Wade Hampton (1818-1903), owned about as many slaves before the Civil War. James Bruce of Virginia, who died in 1837, is believed to have owned nearly 3,000 slaves at the time of his death. Howell Cobb (1815-1868), Speaker of the U.S. House of Representatives, Secretary of the Treasury, Governor of Georgia and Confederate general, owned 1,000 slaves. William Aiken of South Carolina, who was defeated for Speaker by Nathaniel P. Banks in 1856, owned 1,000. Robert F. W. Allston, Governor of South Carolina just before the Civil War, owned 590 slaves when he died in 1864. Richard Bennett of Maryland owned 1,300 slaves in the seventeenth century, and Henry Middleton (1717-1784) of South Carolina, father of a signer of the Declaration of Independence, owned 800 slaves. The largest contemporary slaveholder in Virginia was Robert "King" Carter, who had between 900 and 1,000.

Who rode off in all directions?

President Wilson is credited with having said of the indecisiveness of his first Secretary of State: "Mr. Bryan came out hurriedly, mounted his horse, and immediately rode off in five different directions." In *Nonsense Novels: Gertrude the Governess* (1911) Stephen Butler Leacock, the

Canadian economist and humorist, wrote: "Lord Ronald said nothing; he flung himself from the room, flung himself upon his horse, and rode madly off in all directions."

May the President and Vice President be from the same State?

It is not true, as often supposed, that the President and the Vice President cannot Constitutionally be residents of the same State. In its original form the Constitution provided that the electors in casting their ballots for two persons for President, "one at least shall not be an inhabitant of the same State with themselves." This restriction was carried over into the Twelfth Amendment in substantially the same language. That Amendment, which provides that the electors should vote for President and Vice President separately, says in part: "The electors shall meet in their respective States, and vote by ballot for President and Vice President, one of whom, at least shall not be an inhabitant of the same State with themselves."

No party has ever nominated candidates for President and Vice President from the same State, and obviously it would be unwise politically to do so, because the electors from that State could vote for only one of them if the party carried the State, and in the event of a close election it might by that reason fail to elect either the Presidential or Vice-Presidential candidate on its national ticket. But the electors from all the other States could vote for both candidates.

In 1840 William Henry Harrison and John Tyler, both born in Charles City County, Virginia, were elected President and Vice President respectively, but Harrison was at that time a resident of Ohio. Some authorities suppose that Andrew Jackson was born in South Carolina. If that is true, Jackson and John C. Calhoun, elected President and Vice President respectively in 1828, were born in the same State, but Jackson was then a resident of Tennessee. Only twice have both the President and the Vice President been residents of States south of the Mason and Dixon line—Jackson and Calhoun, and Harry S. Truman of Missouri and Alben W. Barkley of Kentucky.

From the beginning of the Federal Government it was customary to choose a President from the South and a Vice President from the North or vice versa. That was true in the case of Washington and Adams, Jefferson and Burr and Clinton, Madison and Clinton and Gerry, and Monroe and Tompkins. After the Missouri Compromise of 1820, when slavery became an acute issue, this tendency was even more pronounced. John Quincy Adams felt that he was hurt politically in 1828 when his followers nominated Richard Rush of Pennsylvania, another Northern man, to run as the candidate for Vice President on his ticket. Calhoun would probably not have been chosen to run with Jackson had not he already been Vice President under Adams. After the Civil War it was more usual to choose the President from the East and the Vice President from the West or vice versa.

Only three times from 1789 to 1949 were the men chosen President and Vice President residents of adjoining States—Harrison of Ohio and Tyler of Virginia in 1840, Ulysses S. Grant of Illinois and Schuyler Colfax of Indiana in 1868, and Truman of Missouri and Barkley of Kentucky in 1948. West Virginia had not been separated from Virginia in 1840 and at that time Virginia and Ohio were adjoining States. In only four cases have both the President and Vice President been residents of States not among the original thirteen—Abraham Lincoln of Illinois and Hannibal Hamlin of Maine in 1860, Grant of Illinois and Colfax of Indiana in 1868, Herbert Hoover of California and Charles Curtis of Kansas in 1928, and Truman of Missouri and Barkley of Kentucky in 1948. On every other occasion either the President or the Vice President has been a resident of one of the original thirteen States.

What is the lunatic fringe?

Apparently *lunatic fringe* was original with Theodore Roosevelt. On February 27, 1913, four months after he had been defeated as the Presidential candidate of the Progressive Party, Roosevelt wrote to Senator Henry Cabot Lodge: "The various admirable movements in which I have been engaged have always developed among their members a large lunatic fringe." In his *Autobiography* (1919) he wrote: "As I have already said, there is a lunatic fringe to every reform movement." Roosevelt, of course, referred to cranks, nuts and people with obsessions rather than actual lunatics.

Have many Presidents been musicians?

Most of the Presidents liked music but few of them have been notable for their musical talents. George Washington had a decided appreciation of music and is supposed to have tried his hand at playing the flute but without much success. Thomas Jefferson loved music and was an accomplished amateur violinist. He also played the cello passably well. In his younger days he practiced on the violin for several years under the direction of an Italian instructor. Tradition says he wooed and won the lady whom he married by singing to her and by playing his violin, an instrument that he referred to as a "never ending source of delight." The house at Shadwell, his birthplace and boyhood home, burned down during his absence, and when he returned he anxiously asked a Negro servant whether his library had been saved. "No, sir, master," replied the servant, "but we saved your fiddle." While he was Governor of Virginia, Jefferson wrote to a friend in Europe: "If there is a gratification which I envy any people it is, to your country, its music. This is the favorite passion of my soul, and fortune has cast my lot in a country where it is in a state of deplorable barbarism." While American minister at Paris Jefferson strained his wrist, which prevented him from playing his violin, so as a substitute he hummed tunes as he rode on horseback.

John Quincy Adams agreed with Jefferson regarding the musical talent of Americans. He told the French representative at The Hague in 1795 that there was little taste for music in America and that "we had neither cultivated nor were attached much to music; that it had always appeared to me a singular phenomenon in the national character, and I could not account for it otherwise than by supposing it owing to some particular construction of our fibres, that we were created without a strong devotion to music." The American minister continued:

> I pretend not to trace the cause of the fact, but music is not an object of enthusiasm in America; and that Marseillaise hymn, that your band are now playing, reminds me of a forcible proof of the fact I have stated. The Americans fought seven years and more for their liberty. If ever a people had occasion to combine the sensations of harmony with the spirit of patriotism, they had it during that time. Yet there never was during the whole period a single song written, nor a single tune composed, which electrised every soul, and was resounded by every voice, like your patriotic songs.

Adams, according to his own account, told the Frenchman:

> ... that if I could be permitted to cite myself as an instance, I am extremely fond of music, and by dint of great pains have learnt to blow very badly the flute—but could never learn to perform upon the violin, because I never could acquire the art of putting the instrument in tune—that I consoled myself with the idea of being an American, and therefore not susceptible of great musical powers; though I must do my countrymen the justice to say that few of them are so very dull as this; that I knew many who had a musical ear, and could tune an instrument with little or no instruction at all.

Next to Jefferson, perhaps John Tyler was the most musical of the Presidents. He, like Jefferson, found relaxation in playing the violin while a student at William and Mary College. His boyhood ambition was to be a musician. His fondness for music probably saved his life on one occasion. When it was announced on the *Princeton* that the big gun would be fired he lingered below deck to listen to a song. Had it not been for this delay he probably would have been on deck and near the gun when it exploded and killed two Cabinet officers and several other persons. It is said that the President won his second wife, Julia Gardiner, whose father was killed on the *Princeton,* by composing a serenade to her. He composed both the words and music of the song, which was entitled "Sweet Lady, Awake."

Abraham Lincoln, when asked whether he could play the violin, replied that he didn't know, since he had never tried. But he probably had a fairly good ear for and appreciation of music. In 1860 he wrote to a musical society: "I will tell you confidentially that my greatest pleasure when taking a rest after splitting rails, was to play a solo on the jew's harp."

Ulysses S. Grant had no ear for music and could hardly tell one tune from another. At West Point he had difficulty keeping in step on the drill field and he disliked to hear bands play. A clergyman reported him as saying that "all music seemed to affect him as discord would a sensitive ear" and "in church he always experienced a feeling of relief as each stanza of the hymn was sung and so disposed of." Later he said he could whistle only two tunes; one was "Yankee Doodle" and the other wasn't. Grant's daughter Nellie was married to an English singer named Algernon Sartoris. William McKinley had a good singing voice. William Howard Taft was so tone deaf that he couldn't recognize the national anthem and had his secretary nudge him so he could know when to rise when it was played at public functions. Woodrow Wilson was a good singer, sang in college glee clubs, often sang solos in later years, and could hold the high note at the close of "The Star-Spangled Banner." Warren G. Harding played several different wind instruments in bands in his youth and once organized a concert band. He used the first fifty dollars he ever earned to buy a trombone and later won a $200 prize in a band competition. As President he expressed the desire of making Washington the musical center of America. Calvin Coolidge played the mouth organ but cared little for music. Harry S. Truman, an amateur pianist, studied music as a youth and seriously considered making it a career.

Why is an enthusiastic supporter called a rooter?

Rooter is an old English word in the sense of one who digs up roots but a comparatively modern Americanism in the sense of a fan or enthusiastic and vociferous supporter. When and by whom it was first used is not known. It occurs in the American slang sense in the New York *Press* of July 8, 1890, but is probably much older than that. One who encourages his favorite political candidate or athletic team by applauding and shouting may have been compared to one who helps another dig up roots, or perhaps the excited fan was compared to a razorback hog in the act of rooting vigorously.

Who was the first President to play golf?

William Howard Taft was the first President to play golf and he was regarded as a good player. In August, 1909, the first year of his Presidency, a man bet another $1,000 that President Taft couldn't play the difficult Myopia Golf Course in Boston within the required hundred strokes. Taft turned in his clubs at ninety-eight.

Woodrow Wilson and Warren G. Harding were regular golfers, and Calvin Coolidge played occasionally. Wilson used to play in the snow with balls painted red. When he became President in 1913 he refused to accept honorary membership in the fashionable Chevy Chase Golf Club near Washington. Ulysses S. Grant is reputed to have said when he saw a man playing golf in England: "That looks like good exercise, but what's the little white ball for?"

Exactly when golf was first played in America is not easy to say. Alexander H. Findlay, who learned the game in Scotland, laid out a six-hole golf course on Edward C. Miller's Murchiston Ranch in Nance County, Nebraska, in 1887. John G. Reid, a native Scot, and several friends began to play golf at Yonkers, New York, in 1888, with clubs and balls brought from Scotland by Reid's friend Robert Lockhart. Later in the same year they formed the St. Andrew's Golf Club at Yonkers. The Shinnecock Hills Golf Club on Long Island was formed in 1891. Findlay did much to popularize golf in America by inducing Harry Verdon to make a golf-playing tour of the country in 1896.

How did *off the record* originate?

Off the record and *on the record* entered the political vocabulary from the courtroom. When court proceedings were suspended for an informal conference between judge and lawyers, the judge told the recorders that "This is off the record," and when the conference was over and official proceedings were resumed, the judge told the recorders that "This is on the record." In judicial review only what was "in the record" could be considered. The earliest use of *on the record* listed by *The Dictionary of*

American English is dated 1900, and *off the record* is not listed at all, but both terms are probably older than that.

Since 1873 the official proceedings of Congress have been published daily in the *Congressional Record,* and members fell into the habit of referring to informal statements as "off the record" and formal ones as "on the record." When an official speaks confidentially to reporters singly or at press conferences, he speaks off the record, his statements being merely for "background" or information and not to be quoted, printed or attributed to him. Although the term did not become common until after the First World War, the practice of speaking off the record was old. In an informal talk to the members of the Democratic National Committee at the White House on February 28, 1919, President Woodrow Wilson said: "Now what I wanted to suggest is this: personally, and *just within the limits of this room,* I can say very frankly that I think we ought to." Some politicians believe they are justified in denying off-the-record statements if they are published without their consent. One prominent official in Washington was in the habit of prefacing all confidential statements with the condition: "Outside of this room what I am going to tell you is a damned lie." A member of Congress who speaks on the floor for "home consumption" rather than to influence the proceedings, is said to "talk for the record."

Off the record, because of confusion with another saying, is often attributed to Governor Alfred E. Smith, the Democratic nominee for President in 1928. He believed in the Biblical principle "by their fruits ye shall know them," and used the expression "Let us take a look at the record," so often that it is identified with his name. But substantially the same phraseology had been used earlier. According to the official record of the Democratic National Convention at Baltimore in 1912, a New York delegate named John B. Stanchfield said in a speech on the floor: "Let us look at *The Record* for a passing moment."

What President was bald-headed?

Several Presidents had a tendency toward baldness in their old age, but John Quincy Adams has been the only one to be bald-headed while President. In his younger days he wore a wig on formal occasions to conceal his baldness. While he was at St. Petersburg as U.S. Minister to Russia the French Ambassador gave a ball in honor of Napoleon's marriage. Czar Alexander I attended this ball and chatted a few minutes with the American Minister. Under date of May 23, 1810, Adams noted in his diary that the Emperor "said that the difference in my looks in the street, without a wig, from that in which he had usually seen me, had been the cause that the first time he had met me he did not recognize me." Adams construed this remark by the Czar as excusing him from wearing a wig at court functions and he never again wore one. On December 24, 1811, Adams attended court on the occasion of the Emperor's birthday and wrote in his diary: "The Emperor noticed that I had at last left off my wig. I said I had considered his Majesty's example as a permission, and accordingly followed it. He said it was not so showy, but more convenient, to go without it."

Although Adams was conspicuously bald on top, he was not completely bald when President. A portrait of him painted at Ghent by Peter von Huffel in 1815, soon after he left Russia, shows him with a considerable fringe of hair, but perhaps the Dutch artist was over-generous in giving the American diplomat more hair than he had. A portrait of Adams made in 1826, during his second year in the White House, shows him with a decreasing but still considerable fringe of hair. His baldness was mentioned in the press when he was a member of the House of Representatives. In October, 1837, the Washington *Democratic Review* wrote: "Our attention is now attracted to a ray of light that glistens on the apex of a bald and noble head; it proceeds from the wonderful man who in his person combines agitator, poet, philosopher, statesman, critic, and orator—John Quincy Adams." His father, President John Adams, was partly bald when he died at the age of ninety. Martin Van Buren's hair was getting sparse on the front top when he was President and he was pretty bald on top later in life. On October 4, 1873, more than three years before he became President, Rutherford B. Hayes wrote in his diary: "I am fifty-one years old today. Gray hairs are getting into my brow; hair grows perceptibly thinner, but no baldness yet."

How did *ovation* originate?

The ancient Roman senate conferred two grades of ceremonial honors upon victorious commanders. The highest was the triumph *(triumphus),* which was granted only to generals who won important or decisive victories over foreign foes. For his triumph a general wore a laurel crown and a toga embroidered with gold stars and carried a scepter in one hand and a laurel branch in the other. He rode into Rome in a circular chariot drawn by four horses, preceded by the senators, magistrates and musicians and followed by his captives in fetters, the spoils of victory and his entire army in marching formation. The solemn and stately procession marched through the city to Capitoline Hill, where sacrifices were offered and the hero was entertained at a public feast. If a commander won a minor victory, such as one over slaves or insurgents, he was not entitled to a full triumph but was granted only a secondary triumph known as *ovationem,* from *ovare,* "to rejoice" or "to exult." A general receiving an ovation entered the city on foot or horseback and was crowned with myrtle instead of laurel. *Triumph* is an important word in English, but *ovation* is restricted to the sense of popular applause or a mass tribute to or reception of a public person.

Which President knew the most foreign languages?

Thomas Jefferson was the best linguist among the Presidents. He could read and write Greek, Latin, Gaelic, Anglo-Saxon, French, Italian, Spanish and German, and studied and compiled the vocabularies of several American Indian tongues. He lived in France several years and spoke French fluently. John Quincy Adams could read and write Greek, Latin, French and German and tried his hand at several other languages, including Hebrew and Russian, without success.

Most of the Presidents who went to college studied ancient and modern languages, but few of them could speak any foreign language fluently. James A. Garfield could read Greek, Latin and Hebrew, and knew German well enough to make campaign speeches in that language. Theodore Roosevelt was somewhat of a linguist. He studied Latin, Greek, French, German, Dutch and Gaelic. On October 17, 1903, Secretary of State John Hay, after hearing Roosevelt talk to a Frenchman at the White House, wrote in his diary: "The President talked with great energy and perfect ease the most curious French I ever listened to. It was absolutely lawless as to grammar and occasionally bankrupt in substantives; but he had not the least difficulty in making himself understood, and one subject did not worry him more than another." Woodrow Wilson studied several foreign languages but could speak only French and that hesitatingly. At Amherst College Calvin Coolidge studied Latin, Greek, French, German and Italian, but says in his *Autobiography* (1929) that he "never became very proficient in the languages." Franklin D. Roosevelt could speak German and Spanish to a limited extent and spoke French well enough to converse and speak in public in it. Ulysses S. Grant picked up a smattering of Spanish during the Mexican War.

George Washington, Andrew Jackson, Abraham Lincoln, Andrew Johnson, Grover Cleveland, William McKinley, Warren G. Harding and Harry S. Truman never learned any foreign language. Although he associated with the French for years as enemies and allies, Washington never learned the French language. At Fort Necessity he carelessly signed articles of capitulation in the French text in which he admitted that he was the *assassin* of a French officer named M. de Jumonville. The interpreter translated *l'assassinat* as "causing the death of."

Who said an appointment makes nine enemies and an ingrate?

In *Siècle de Louis XIV* Voltaire quotes the Grand Monarch of France as having said: "Every time I fill a vacant office I make a hundred malcontents and one ingrate."

Various versions of this saying have cropped up in American politics. In *Figures of the Past* Josiah Quincy quotes former President John Adams as observing in 1825 when he learned that his son, John Quincy Adams, had been chosen President: "No man who ever held the office of President would congratulate a friend on obtaining it. He will make one man ungrateful, and a hundred men his enemies, for every office he can bestow." On December 9, 1837, John Quincy Adams himself wrote in his diary: "He (President Van Buren) says he considers it as a misfortune when any office to be filled by him becomes vacant, and thinks patronage rather a burden than a benefit."

On January 7, 1847, President James K. Polk wrote in his diary: "In every appointment which the President makes he disappoints half a dozen applicants and their friends, who, actuated by selfish and sordid motives, will prefer any other candidate in the next election, while the person appointed attributes the appointment to his own superior merit and does not even feel obliged by it."

President Rutherford B. Hayes wrote in his diary on August 9, 1878: "Nothing brings out the lower traits of human nature like office seeking. Men of good character and impulse are betrayed by it into all sorts of meanness. Disappointment makes them unjust to the last degree." On December 27, 1892, former President Hayes wrote to Governor William McKinley of Ohio: "*All* appointments *hurt*. Five friends are made cold or hostile for every appointment: no new friends are made. All *patronage* is perilous to men of real ability and merit. It aids only those who lack other claims to public support."

Speaker Thomas B. Reed's version of the famous saying was: "Every time a Congressman recommends a postmaster he makes one ingrate and eight enemies." Governor Bibbs Graves of Alabama gave it another twist: "Every time I make one appointee I make nine disappointees."

Abraham Lincoln summed up the situation after his first inauguration when he said in reference to the throng of office seekers at the White House: "The trouble is there are too many pigs for the teats."

Which Presidents used shorthand?

Four Presidents used shorthand of one kind or other. Thomas Jefferson wrote that he had studied a book published in 1793 and entitled *The System of Shorthand Practiced by Mr. Thomas Lloyd in Taking the Debates in Congress.* Apparently, however, Jefferson used shorthand very little. James Madison reported the proceedings of the Constitutional Convention (1787) in a system of shorthand of his own invention. His system consisted chiefly in abbreviations rather than symbols.

On October 10, 1810, John Quincy Adams, then Minister to Russia, wrote in his diary regarding the laborious work of making complete records of his interviews: "It would be prodigiously facilitated if I were master of short-hand writing. I lament that I did not learn this effectually in my youth. It is now too late." But on May 4, 1814, Adams wrote: "Employed the day in writing and copying, for which purpose I resumed the practice of writing in short-hand. I have so long disused it that I find myself awkward at recommencing, and for the present save no time by it." On October 30, 1826, President Adams wrote a sonnet upon his father's birth and inserted it in his diary in shorthand because he thought it was not good enough to record in longhand. He wrote on September 5, 1841 that he had "learnt and practiced Byrom's shorthand writing, but no one could read it but myself." The system he referred to was invented by the English poet John Byrom, whose book, *The Universal English Shorthand,* was published after his death in 1763.

Woodrow Wilson was proficient in the system of shorthand invented by and named after Isaac Pitman (1813-1897), who was knighted by Queen Victoria. Wilson was a good typist and wrote his speeches on his own typewriter while he was President. Herbert Hoover did some writing on a typewriter in his youth.

How many Presidents died on the Fourth of July?

Three Presidents died, one became fatally ill, and one was born on the Fourth of July.

Thomas Jefferson, eighty-three, and John Adams, ninety, died on July 4, 1826, the fiftieth anniversary of the adoption of the Declaration of Independence, with which both had been intimately indentified.

They had been friends in their earlier years, enemies in their middle years, and friends again in their old age, although they never saw each other after Jefferson defeated Adams in 1801. Jefferson died at Monticello at 1:30 P.M., and Adams died at Quincy between five and six o'clock in the evening.

On July 21, 1826, President John Quincy Adams wrote in his diary of his father's last hours: "Mrs. Clark [his granddaughter] said to him that it was the 4th of July, the fiftieth anniversary of independence. He answered, 'It is a great day. It is a good day.' About one, afternoon, he said, 'Thomas Jefferson survives,' but the last word was indistinctly and imperfectly uttered. He spoke no more. He has sent as a toast to the celebration at Quincy, 'Independence forever.' " Jefferson was also thinking of the great event fifty years before. On July 3 he had feebly asked, "Is this the Fourth?" The next day he rallied a few minutes and, apparently thinking of the old committee of safety, held his hand as if writing and said: "Tell the committee to be on the alert." When Adams said "Thomas Jefferson still survives," Jefferson was already dead.

Two of the three sons of John Quincy Adams were born on July 4 and both were named after Presidents. George Washington Adams was born in 1801 and John Adams in 1803. The former, who was born in Germany on the twenty-fifth anniversary of the adoption of the Declaration of Independence, was at his illustrious grandfather's bedside when he died on his own twenty-fifth birthday.

On the same Fourth of July on which Jefferson and Adams died, Stephen Collins Foster, America's most famous songwriter, was born in Pittsburgh.

On June 16, 1826, Mayor R. S. Weightman of Washington, D.C. invited the three surviving signers of the Declaration of Independence—Jefferson, Adams and Charles Carroll—to attend a fiftieth anniversary celebration in the capital. None of them could attend but letters from all three were read at the ceremonies in Washington on July 4. Jefferson's letter, dated June 24, was the last important letter he wrote and was a final testament of his faith in the principles of the document he wrote fifty years before.

Five years later James Monroe, seventy-three, died at half-past three in the afternoon of July 4, 1831, at the home of his daughter, Mrs. Samuel L. Gouverneur, in New York City. "The venerable patriot," wrote Philip Hone in his diary at the time, "has been ill and his life has been despaired of for several months past, and he seems to have lingered to this time to add to the number of Revolutionary patriots whose deaths have occurred on the memorable anniversary." Five years later

James Madison, eighty-five, died on June 28, 1836. "It is a pity," observed Hone, "that he had not lingered six days longer, that his death might have occurred . . . on the anniversary of the political birthday . . ." In *Retrospect of Western Travel* (1838) Harriet Martineau wrote:

> I was told a story of an American physician which is characteristic (if it is true), showing how patriotic regards may enter into the practice of medicine. But I give it only as an *on dit*. It is well known that Adams and Jefferson died on the 4th of July of one year, and Monroe of another. Mr. Madison died on the 28th of June last year. It is said that the physician who attended Mr. Monroe expressed regret that he had not the charge of Mr. Madison, suspecting that he might have found means to keep him alive (as he died of old age) till the Fourth of July. The practice in Mr. Monroe's case is said to have been this: When he was sinking, someone observed what a remarkable thing it would be if he should die on the anniversary, like Adams and Jefferson. The physician determined he would give his patient the chance of ending so. He poured down brandy and other stimulants, and omitted no means to keep life in the failing body. On the 3rd of July, the patient was sinking so rapidly that there seemed little chance of his surviving the day. The physician's exertions were redoubled; and the consequence was, that, on the morning of the 4th, there seemed every probability of the patient's living to the 5th, which was not exactly desired. He died (much as he wished to oblige his friends to the last) late in the afternoon on the 4th. So the story runs.

On July 4, 1850, President Zachary Taylor, sixty-five, took part in the ceremonies in connection with the laying of the cornerstone of the Washington Monument. He suffered from the intense heat and drank large quantities of cold water. After returning to the White House the President ate some cherries and drank iced milk. That night he became ill with cholera morbus and fever and died four days later.

Calvin Coolidge was born at Plymouth, Vermont, on July 4, 1872. Hannibal Hamlin, who was Vice President during Lincoln's first term died on July 4, 1891, at the age of eighty-two. George Washington suffered a humiliating experience on a July 4 before that day became famous in American history. On that day in 1754 he surrendered his little Virginia army to the French at Fort Necessity on the Western frontier.

On July 4, 1863, General John C. Pemberton surrendered the confederate army at Vicksburg to General Ulysses S. Grant. This cut the Confederacy in two, and on August 26, of that year President Lincoln wrote to James C. Conkling: "The Father of Waters again goes unvexed to the sea." Grant's first terms were unconditional surrender and there was a reason why the Confederates permitted to let the strategic town fall on the Fourth of July. As a public holiday the Fourth of July never had the sentimental interest to Southerners that it had to Northerners. Possibly Pemberton could have delayed the fall of the city for another day. His personal inclination was to make a desperate attempt to cut his way out of the besieged town. But he was a Pennsylvanian and knew that nothing would please the Union army more than to capture Vicksburg on the Fourth of July. To his last council of war Pemberton said: "I am a Northerner and I know my people. I know their peculiar weakness and their national vanity. I know we can get better terms from them on the Fourth of July than any other day of the year. We must sacrifice our pride to these considerations." He capitulated on the Fourth and got more lenient terms.

When American Samoa changed from the Eastern to the Western hemisphere calendar in 1892, the Fourth of July was celebrated for two days.

Which Presidents were inventors?

Thomas Jefferson was the most versatile and inventive President. Besides being a planter, lawyer, statesman, politician, diplomat, parliamentarian, architect and philosopher, he was an amateur musician, landscape gardener, horticulturist, archaeologist, geologist, botanist, ethnologist, economist, astronomer, meteorologist, linguist, artist, surveyor and mechanical inventor. Few branches of art and science failed to receive his attention. He was a good horseman and traveled widely. He was surgeon enough to tie an artery or set a broken bone and mathematician enough to calculate an eclipse accurately. His extant writings, including some 18,000 letters, are a treasury of useful and interesting information on nearly every conceivable subject. He is quoted more often and on more different subjects than any other President.

Among the mechanical devices that Jefferson designed, invented or improved were a letter-copying press, sundial, wheelbarrow, swivel chair, two-way elevator or dumb-waiter, sheltered weathervane, adjustable bookcase, portable writing and reading desk, lock door for laying up vessels, leather buggy top, folding ladder, hexagonal lantern, folding chair, pedometer for measuring walks, hemp machine or brake, walking stick, and light sulky or phaeton for use on heavy Virginia roads. He never patented or profited by his inventions. For the most part he designed and invented devices, machines and gadgets for his own use and was willing for anybody else to have the benefit of them.

Jefferson is known as "The Father of the American Patent System" because as Secretary of State he was the chief of three Cabinet officers who administered the first Federal patent act, approved by President Washington in 1790. Secretary of State Jefferson, Secretary of War Henry Knox and Attorney General Edmund Randolph met inventors and examined their claims for patents and were the first patent examiners in the United States. At first the granting of a patent required the meeting of a majority of the Cabinet. During the first year the law was in effect only three patents were granted.

In the eighteenth century the plow most commonly used consisted of a wooden moldboard, which was sometimes sheathed with iron plates. After observing the plows used by French peasants, the American Minister to France in 1788 worked out a mathematical formula for the most efficient curve for moldboards. At the time he made rough models, some of which are still preserved in Paris. Jefferson continued his experiments with moldboards, and in 1798, when Vice President, he read a paper on the subject to the American Philosophical Society in Philadelphia. This paper, with drawings, was published under the title, *Description of a Mould-Board of the Least Resistance, and of the Easiest and Most Certain Construction*. In 1805, when he was President, Jefferson was elected an associate member of the French Academy of Agriculture and awarded its grand gold medal.

It is a common mistake to suppose that Jefferson invented an all-metal plow. What he devised was a formula by which any rural smith could make a better moldboard from a block of wood with ordinary tools. The first all-metal plow, with both share and moldboard made of cast iron, was patented by Charles Newbold of New Jersey in 1797, but it was not practical, and it was not till many years later that steel plows were generally used. That Jefferson did not claim to have invented an entire plow is shown by the following in a letter to Robert Fulton on April 16, 1810:

The Agricultural Society of the Seine sent me one of Guillaume's famous ploughs, famous for taking but half the moving power of their best ploughs before used. They, at the same time, requested me to send them one of our best, with my mould board to it. I promised I would, as soon as I retired home and could see to its construction myself. . . . I have made the plough and am greatly deceived if it is not found to give less resistance than theirs. In fact I think it is the finest plough which has ever been constructed in America.

Most of the virgin sod of the vast Louisiana Territory, purchased by Jefferson, was broken by plows with moldboards made more or less according to his formula.

On March 19, 1760, when Jefferson was still a student, George Washington wrote in his diary: "Peter (my Smith) and I after several efforts to make a plow after a new model—partly of my own contriving—was feign to give it out, at least for the present." Seven days later the First Farmer of Virginia wrote: "Spent the greater part of the day in making a new plow of my own invention." The next day he "Sat my Plow to work and found she answered very well . . ." On April 5 of the same year he reported, "Made another Plow the same as my former, excepting that it has two eyes and the other one." After the Revolution, Washington invented and used a grain drill, which consisted of a barrel with holes bored in it at intervals and which he called his "barrel drill" and "barrel plow."

Martin Van Buren, an admirer of Jefferson, tried his hand as a household inventor and designed a revolving bookcase and a coffee percolator. Abraham Lincoln has been the only President to obtain a patent. On May 22, 1849, when he was a member of Congress, the U.S. Patent Office issued him a patent on a "Method of Lifting Vessels Over Shoals" by means of "expansible buoyant chambers." Herbert Hoover, a mining engineer by profession, never took out a patent, but one of his sons, Herbert Hoover, Jr., also trained as a mining engineer, has been granted many patents.

Who was Tama Jim?

James Wilson (1835-1920), agriculturist, Congressman and Secretary of Agriculture under Presidents McKinley, Theodore Roosevelt and Taft (1897-1913) was known as Tama Jim because he lived at Tama, Iowa. He was born in Ayrshire, Scotland, and migrated to the United States when he was seventeen. James Falconer Wilson (1828-1895), a Democratic Representative and Senator from Iowa, was known as Jefferson Jim because he lived at Fairfield in Jefferson County.

Why was Kenesaw Mountain Landis so named?

Kenesaw Mountain Landis (1866-1944), Federal district judge in Illinois from 1905 to 1922 and high commissioner of professional baseball from 1920 until his death, was named after a mountain in Georgia.

Kenesaw Mountain is a 1,800 foot elevation in Cobb County about twenty miles northwest of Atlanta. On June 27, 1864, General Joseph E. Johnston's Confederate army was attacked at Kenesaw Mountain by part of General William T. Sherman's Federal army under Generals Thomas, McPherson and Schofield. The Federals were repulsed and their casualties were about 3,000, while those of the Confederates were only about 800. Among the Federal soldiers severely wounded was Abraham H. Landis. When a son was born to Landis at Millville, Ohio, on November 20, 1866, he commemorated the battle in the name of the son.

For two years Kenesaw Landis was private secretary to Walter Q. Gresham, who was Secretary of State in President Cleveland's second Cabinet and who had commanded the Union army corps at Kenesaw Mountain in which Abraham H. Landis was wounded. In 1907 Judge Landis tried the rebate cases in which the Standard Oil Company of Indiana was indicted on 1,400 counts. The judge won considerable fame by fining the company more than $29,000,000, but his decision was reversed upon appeal and the Government had to pay the court costs. Two of Judge Landis's brothers, Charles Beary Landis and Frederick Landis, were Representatives in Congress from Indiana.

The United States Geographic Board decided that the proper spelling of the name of the mountain and town in Georgia is *Kenesaw,* with one *n,* but later reversed itself in favor of *Kennesaw,* with two *n*'s. On some maps the name of the town is spelled *Kenesaw* and that of the mountain *Kennesaw. The U.S. Official Postal Guide* gives the Georgia town, as well as one in Nebraska, as *Kenesaw.*

Who coined *ghoulish glee?*

Grover Cleveland coined *ghoulish glee.* On November 8, 1886, the President, who disliked newspapers and alienated most of the press of the country, attended a banquet in Cambridge celebrating the 250th anniversary of the founding of Harvard, and in his speech he referred to "the silly, mean, and cowardly lies that every day are found in the columns of certain newspapers, which violate every instinct of American manliness, and in ghoulish glee desecrate every sacred relation of private life."

Which Presidents played football?

No President of the United States distinguished himself as a football player. Theodore Roosevelt was interested in football at Harvard and helped revise the rules of the game, but on October 1, 1903, he wrote from the White House to his son Ted: "I greatly admire football— though it was not a game I was ever able to play." Woodrow Wilson was a part-time football coach during his teaching years at Princeton. Calvin Coolidge did some football coaching at Amherst. Herbert

Hoover, though not on the team, was business manager of the Leland Stanford football team. Franklin D. Roosevelt played tackle and full-back at Harvard.

Soccer or association football was introduced in American colleges in the 1860's. The first intercollegiate soccer game in the United States was played at New Brunswick, New Jersey, on November 8, 1869, when Rutgers beat Princeton six to four. Rugby football was introduced into the United States from Canada a few years later. In the early 1870's the Harvard team visited Canada and played several games under Rugby rules.

Why was The Man Bilbo so called?

Theodore Gilmore Bilbo (1877-1947) of Mississippi served as State senator, Lieutenant Governor, Governor and U.S. Senator. During his first term as Governor (1916-1920) a Mississippi editor referred to him as "The Man" in connection with State-wide gossip about his prowess with women. "If these stories about the man Bilbo are true," Governor Bilbo told an audience of women in 1920, "you've got to admit, sisters, that he's a man." After that the Governor often referred to himself in speeches as "The Man Bilbo" and that became a common designation of him by others. Bilbo, after attending three universities, taught school six years before becoming a lawyer. He was licensed a Baptist minister but was never ordained.

How is the surname of Harold L. Ickes pronounced?

The surname of Harold Loy Ickes (1874—) of Illinois, who was Secretary of the Interior under Presidents Franklin D. Roosevelt and Truman from 1933 to 1946, is pronounced ICK-us by the family. Ickes was head of several New Deal agencies and was noted for his salty speech and writing style. In 1943 he published *Autobiography of a Curmudgeon. Webster's New International Dictionary* defines *curmudgeon,* an old English word of unknown origin, as "an avaricious, grasping fellow; a miser; niggard; churl."

Who was Puddler Jim?

This was the nickname of James John Davis (1873-1947), Secretary of Labor from 1921 to 1930 under Harding, Coolidge and Hoover, and U.S. Senator from Pennsylvania from 1930 to 1945. He was born in Wales, the son of an iron puddler, and was brought to the United States by his parents in 1881. At eleven Davis began work as a puddler's assistant in a western Pennsylvania ironworks and at sixteen became a puddler. In 1922 he published an autobiographical book entitled *The Iron Puddler.* Since the early part of the eighteenth century *puddling* has been used in iron manufacturing to denote the process of converting pig iron into wrought iron or steel by heating it in a small furnace and stirring it frequently to eliminate carbon and other impurities.

How did Sunset Cox get his nickname?

Samuel Sullivan Cox (1824-1889), politician and writer, was called "Sunset" because of a florid description of a sunset that he wrote for the *Ohio Statesman,* published at Columbus. He became editor of that paper in 1853 when only twenty-nine and on May 19 of the same year he published an article entitled "A Great Old Sunset." This article fastened upon its author a nickname that clung to him throughout his long and distinguished career as a member of Congress, first from Ohio and later from New York. The first paragraph of the article follows:

What a stormful sunset was that of last night! How glorious the storm and how splendid the setting of the sun! We do not remember ever to have seen the like on our round globe. The scene opened in the west, with a whole horizon full of golden impenetrating luster, which colored the foliage and brightened every object in its own rich dyes. The colors grew deeper and richer, until the the golden luster was transformed into a stormcloud, full of finest lightning, which leaped in dazzling zigzags all around and over the city.

Another Ohio statesman and journalist with the same surname but not related, James Middleton Cox, who was the Democratic candidate for President in 1920, was so given to the use of superlatives such as *astonishing* when he was a young reporter that he was nicknamed "Astonishing Cox."

Who was Cyclone Davis?

James Harvey Davis (1853-1940), of Sulphur Springs, Texas, was known as "Cyclone Davis" because of his conspicuous whiskers and breezy manner of speaking. He was born in South Carolina and taken to Texas as a child by his parents. After teaching school, serving as county judge, practicing law and speaking for the Farmers' Alliance, he helped form the Populist Party and was a leading spirit in that movement. As a Populist he was defeated for State attorney general in 1892 and for Congress in 1894. He served one term (1915-1917) as a Democratic Representative-at-large but was defeated for renomination, after which he farmed and lectured on the Chautauqua. Another sobriquet of James Harvey Davis was "Methodist Jim."

Who was author of "Addition, division, and silence"?

In March, 1867, William H. Kemble, State treasurer of Pennsylvania, wrote a letter to Titian J. Coffey in which he recommended a man named George O. Evans for political preferment. Among other things Kemble said: "He understands addition, division, and silence." The saying became famous after the letter was published in the New York *Sun* on June 20, 1872. It is sometimes attributed to Matthew Stanley Quay (1833-1904), who later said that "Addition, division and silence" are the qualifications of a political boss. Matt Quay was a U.S. Senator from 1893 to 1899 and from 1901 till his death. Like James Donald Cameron before him and Boies Penrose after him, he was in absolute control of the Republican Party in Pennsylvania.

Does the Government pay the funeral expenses of Presidents who die in office?

After the burial of President William Henry Harrison in 1841 the marshal of the District of Columbia presented a claim to Congress for the expenses of the funeral. Congress directed the claim to be referred to the proper accounting officer, who was instructed to allow what was "reasonably due." In 1850 Congress appropriated $8,000 to pay the funeral expenses of President Zachary Taylor, the second President to die in office. Another $4,000 was appropriated to pay for the transportation of his body from Washington to Kentucky. Since then it has been customary for the Government to pay the funeral expenses of Presidents who die in office. Congress appropriated $14,500 in 1945 to pay the funeral expenses of President Franklin D. Roosevelt. That amount was inserted in an omnibus appropriations bill as part of the funds available for the office of the President.

How can the electoral vote of a State be split?

The electoral vote of a State may be but rarely is split. Presidential electors are chosen in each State on general party tickets and usually if a Presidential candidate carries a State he receives all the electoral votes of that State, but sometimes there are exceptions, due to the fact that in some States the lists of the names of the candidates for electors are printed on the ballots and the candidates for electors in a party list do not always receive exactly the same number of popular votes. At one time several States made the experiment of choosing electors by Congressional districts, and under that system it was easy for the electoral votes of the State to be divided between two Presidential candidates, because one section of the State might be dominantly for one party and another section dominantly for another party; but the Congressional-district system of choosing Presidential electors was abandoned and now all States choose them on general tickets.

Where the names of electoral candidates do not appear on the popular ballots all the candidates on each list are accredited with exactly the same number of popular votes and the Presidential and Vice-Presidential candidates of a party receive all or none of the electoral votes of a State. But in some States where the individual names of the electoral candidates are printed on the popular ballots the voters may vote for each electoral candidate separately and the popular votes are counted individually. Occasionally when the popular vote of a State is close it happens that the electoral vote of a State is divided.

Originally the candidates for electors were voted upon individually by name, whether they were chosen by popular vote or by State legislatures. When lists of electoral candidates were first put up by political parties they were careful to select for electoral candidates only persons who were likely to poll the most votes. But as the electors gradually ceased to exercise their own judgments in voting and became mere figureheads who performed the perfunctory task of registering the will of the voters, less and less attention was given to the vote-getting qualities of the candidates for electors. Later some States began to omit the names of the electoral candidates from the ballots and a vote for the candidates for President and Vice President was a vote for the whole list of electoral candidates of that party. In States where the names of the electoral candidates are left off the ballots, there is usually a statute requiring each party to file the list of its electoral candidates with the State secretary of state. In some States where the list of the names of electoral candidates are printed on the ballot the voter must vote for an entire party list, while in other States he is permitted to vote for individual electoral candidates if he wishes to. Because of the excessive length of the printed ballots and the introduction of mechanical voting machines there has been a tendency for more and more States to leave the names of the electoral candidates off the ballots. In fact in some instances the original motive of States for excluding the names of electoral candidates from the ballots appears to have been primarily to prevent "scratching" the party "slate." The purpose was to prevent the local popularity or unpopularity of electoral candidates from affecting the result of the Presidential election.

Splits in the electoral vote of States have been rare since the Civil War. One of the six Democratic electoral candidates in California in 1880 was personally unpopular and failed to be elected, with the result that there was a split in the electoral vote of the State, and Winfield Scott Hancock received five electoral votes and James A. Garfield one. In 1892 the popular vote was so close in North Dakota that Benjamin Harrison, Grover Cleveland and James B. Weaver each received one of the three electoral votes of the State. The electoral vote was split in four other States in that election—Michigan, five for Cleveland and nine for Harrison; Ohio, one for Cleveland and twenty-two for Harrison; Oregon, three for Harrison and one for Weaver, and California, eight for Cleveland and one for Harrison. In 1896 William McKinley received twelve electoral votes in Kentucky and William Jennings Bryan received one, and in the same election McKinley received eight in California and Bryan one. Theodore Roosevelt received one electoral vote in Maryland in 1904 and Alton B. Parker received seven.

A notable case of this kind occurred in West Virginia in 1916. One of the Republican electoral candidates withdrew just before the national election and a man named Scott was chosen by the State Republican committee to take his place on the Republican ticket, but in the meantime the ballots had been printed in several counties and Scott's name, of course, was omitted. He lost his votes in those counties and the Democratic electoral candidate having the highest number of popular votes had more than he and accordingly was elected, with the result that Woodrow Wilson received one electoral vote in West Virginia and Charles E. Hughes received seven, although the total popular vote in the State was 143,124 for Hughes and 140,403 for Wilson. The same thing could happen if an electoral candidate on one party ticket were disqualified at the last minute. But under the present system such cases are not permitted to occur often. In 1948 one of the Tennessee Democratic electors exercised his legal right to vote for whom he pleased, with the result that Harry S. Truman received eleven of the State's twelve electoral votes and James Strom Thurmond, the States' Rights candidate, received one.

Can a Presidential elector vote for himself for President?

Nothing in the Federal Constitution prevents a Presidential elector from voting for himself for President or Vice President. When James Wilson of Pennsylvania, in the Constitutional Convention of 1787, first suggested an intermediary electoral system for choosing the President his motion provided that the electors should not vote for anybody "out of their own body." On July 20, 1787, according to Madison's notes, Elbridge Gerry of Massachusetts and Gouverneur Morris of Pennsylvania made a motion with a provision that the electors themselves should not "be eligible to the supreme magistracy." Although the motion was agreed to without objection, the provision relating to the eligibility of the electors themselves to the Presidency and Vice Presidency was omitted from the final draft of the Constitution. A candidate for the Presidency may serve as a Presidential elector if he is not barred by virtue of being a Federal officer.

Can one run for President and Congress at the same time?

A person can be a candidate for President or Vice President and for a seat in either branch of Congress at the same time. Candidacies for the Presidency or the Vice Presidency and for membership in the Senate or House of Representatives are not mutually exclusive because the President and Vice President, unlike members of Congress, are not "elected" in the national election in November but by the electors in December. In 1932 Speaker John N. Garner of Texas had already been nominated by a primary for re-election to the House of Representatives when he was nominated for the Vice Presidency. Consequently he was a candidate for both offices at the same time and was elected to both. He could not qualify for both and resigned his seat in Congress. Likewise a person may be a candidate for President or Vice President while a member of either branch of Congress, but he cannot be a candidate for both the House and the Senate at the same time.

Can the electoral colleges be recalled into session?

There is no Federal constitutional or statutory provision for a second meeting of the Presidential electors, and presumably after they meet on the prescribed date and cast their ballots for President and Vice President they cease to be electors and have no further legal status as such. If their ballots fail to choose a President and Vice President the task of making a choice devolves upon Congress.

The Presidential electors of each State meet, but the electors as a whole do not meet in their official capacity. In 1933, after Franklin D. Roosevelt was elected President the first time, a Philadelphia lawyer named Michael Francis Doyle suggested that the 531 persons who had just served as Presidential electors meet in a body and attend the inauguration on March 4. James A. Farley, chairman of the Democratic National Committee and an elector from New York that year, adopted the suggestion and appointed Doyle chairman of a committee to invite the electors of that year to meet in Washington. About 218 of them responded, met at the Capitol in Washington on March 3, took part in the inaugural parade, had their own section in the reviewing stand and attended a banquet on March 4. This was the first attempt to bring together the Presidential electors as a whole. The experiment was repeated and a larger number of the Presidential electors of 1936 attended the inauguration on January 20, 1937. In 1941 the electors formed a permanent organization known as the Electoral Colleges of the United States to perpetuate the custom of taking part in inaugurations as a body and to foster interest in the electoral system. Most of the former electors were Democrats who had voted for Roosevelt and such meetings are social and not official gatherings of the electors.

What is a two-thirds majority?

To say that a candidate received a two-thirds majority in an election is merely a popular way of saying that he received two-thirds of all the votes cast. Suppose, for instance, that 3,000 votes were cast, and one candidate received 1,000 and the other 2,000. The latter received a two-thirds majority in the general acceptation of the term; that is, two out of three of all votes cast. In this case the actual majority over the other candidate was only one-third of all the votes, and literally *two-thirds majority* would mean that the difference between the two figures was two-thirds of the total number of votes. To illustrate: If one candidate in the case supposed had received 500 and the other 2,500, the difference—2,000—would have equaled two-thirds of the total. But in the common parlance the term is employed to express the idea of two-thirds of all the votes, regardless of the number received by other candidates.

The two-thirds vote required by the Constitution in each House of Congress to propose Amendments to the Constitution, to pass bills over the President's veto, to remove disability resulting from participation in rebellion and to expel a member has always been interpreted as meaning a vote of two-thirds of the members present—assuming the presence of a quorum—and not a two-thirds vote of the entire membership, present and absent. The Constitution provides specifically that when the Senate sits as a court of impeachment "no person shall be convicted without the concurrence of two thirds of the members present," and that the President "shall have power, by and with the advice and consent of the Senate, to make treaties, provided two-thirds of the Senators present concur."

What is meant by power politics?

Power politics is international politics. It is played by nations instead of by parties and individuals. The term came into use in the United States around the turn of the century. It has a derogatory connotation and refers particularly to the diplomacy pursued by great powers to extend their territory or sphere of influence by the use or threatened use of military force.

What President was related to a famous author?

President Rutherford B. Hayes was a first cousin once removed of Elinor Gertrude Mead of Brattleboro, Vermont, who married William Dean Howells, editor, author and critic. Elinor was the daughter of Larkin Goldsmith Mead, sculptor, and sister of William Rutherford Mead, architect. Howells, a native of Ohio, met Elinor in Columbus during the winter of 1860-1861 while she was visiting her Hayes kin, and they were married in Paris in 1862. When Hayes ran for President in 1876 Howells wrote his campaign biography. On June 27 of that year the Republican nominee wrote to Howells that "you don't know how fond we are of managing to let folks know in a casual way that the editor of the *Atlantic,* the author of etc., etc., is our cousin." After his wife, Lucy Webb Hayes, died in 1889, the former President tried unsuccessfully to get "the dean of American letters" to write her biography.

Who was Colonel William Byrd of Westover?

Colonel William Byrd of Westover was the ancestor of the famous Byrd family of Virginia. In 1670 William Byrd, the eldest son of a London goldsmith of the same name, went to Virginia at the age of eighteen and later settled near the falls of the James River on a vast tract of land inherited from his uncle, Thomas Stegg. This William Byrd became a prominent planter, merchant and Indian trader and served the colony as member of the House of Burgesses, member and president of the council of state, and auditor general. In 1691 he moved down the river from near the present site of Richmond and established himself at "Westover" in Charles City County.

His eldest son, known as Colonel William Byrd of Westover, went to England for his education but returned to Virginia after his father's death and became a planter, lawyer, member and president of the House of Burgesses, receiver general of the colony, member of the council of state, and last but not least, one of the first wits and men of letters in America. Several times he acted as agent for Virginia in England, where he resided from 1697 to 1705 and from 1717 to 1726.

Colonel Byrd of Westover increased his land holdings from 26,251 acres, which he inherited from his father, to 179,000 acres. His slaves were numbered by the hundred and he lived in baronial style. He read the classics in Greek, Latin and Hebrew, had a large collection of paintings, and his library, one of the largest in Colonial America, contained 5,000 volumes. In 1728 he served on the joint commission that ran the boundary line between Virginia and North Carolina, and *The History of the Dividing Line* deals with that experience and is one of the first American classics. He acquired a large tract of land in Carolina just south of this line and called it "The Land of Eden." In *A Journey to the Land of Eden,* written in 1735, he relates how he *founded* Richmond on his own land:

When we got home, we laid the foundation of two large Citys, one at Shacco's, to be called Richmond, and the other at the Point of Appamattuck River, to be nam'd Petersburgh. These Major May offered to lay out into Lots without Fee or Reward. The Truth of it is, these two places being the uppermost Landing of James and Appamatux Rivers, are naturally intended for Marts, where the Traffick of the Outer Inhabitants must Center. Thus we did not build Castles only, but also Citys in the Air.

He also wrote *Progress to the Mines.* All of these were first printed in 1841 as the *Westover Manuscripts.* His secret diary written in his own peculiar shorthand has been deciphered and parts of it published. It is one of the most curious and interesting documents in existence bearing on Colonial life in Virginia. Colonel Byrd was twice married, first to Lucy Parke and second to Maria Taylor. By his first marriage he had two sons, both of whom died in infancy, and two daughters. By his second marriage he had three daughters and one son. His eldest daughter, Evelyn, was a famed Colonial beauty. When she went to England and was presented at court, King George I couldn't resist the pun, "Certainly our colonies produce *beautiful Byrds.*" She died unmarried in 1737 at the age of thirty. Her father named one of his ships after her. *Evelyn* is still cherished by members of the Byrd family and it occurs in the names of many of them. In that family it is always pronounced EEV-linn, whether used as a masculine or feminine name. Two of Evelyn's sisters, Maria and Anne, married brothers. They were the second wives respectively of Landon and Charles Carter, both of whom married three times.

The three famous Byrd brothers of our own time—Tom, Dick and Harry—are descended from the only son of Colonel William Byrd of Westover. The complete chain of descent, beginning with the first colonist, is as follows: William Byrd (1652-1704), William Byrd of Westover (1674-1744), William Byrd (1728-1777), Thomas Taylor Byrd (1752-1821), Richard Evelyn Byrd (1801-1872), William Byrd (1828-1898) and Richard Evelyn Byrd (1860-1925), who was the father of Harry Flood Byrd, Governor and U.S. Senator; Richard Evelyn Byrd, naval officer and explorer, and Thomas Bolling Byrd, farmer and orchardist. Admiral Byrd, recipient of all the medals of honor authorized by Congress, was the first man to fly over both the North and South poles.

What was Coxey's Army?

In 1894, during Cleveland's second administration, Jacob Sechler Coxey (1854-1951), of Massillon, Ohio, marched into Washington at the head of what he called "The Army of the Commonweal of Christ."

Coxey was born in Pennsylvania and started life as a stationary engineer in rolling mills. Later he became successful in the silica sandstone quarrying business. Early in the year following the Panic of 1893 he organized the "J. S. Coxey Good Roads Association of the United States" and called for a march of jobless men on Washington to petition Congress to authorize a roads and public works program to provide employment. The essence of the Coxey plan was to have the Government issue $500,000,000 in currency based on the non-interest-bearing bonds of States, counties and cities. The march of the jobless to present their grievances personally to Congress was known as "the petition in boots."

Small bands of men started from many parts of the country in response to Coxey's call. All groups were to meet in Washington for a demonstration on May Day. Owing to bad weather "General" Coxey and "Marshal" Carl Browne, his chief organizer and publicity man, set out from Massillon on March 25 with an "army" of fewer than 500. Although the army was met by large crowds along the way, "enlistments" were few. On April 28 it reached the outskirts of Washington, where it was reinforced by about a thousand men from other parts of the country who had answered the call.

At first the authorities made no attempt to interfere with Coxey's Army, but when it appeared on Capitol Hill on May 1 General Coxey and Marshal Browne were arrested by local police on charges of holding a meeting without a permit, carrying banners and walking on and injuring the shrubbery and grass. A few days later a police court found them guilty and sentenced them to $5 fines and twenty days in jail.

From this incident comes the saying, "Coxey was arrested for walking on the grass," which means punishing a person for a trifling technical trespass when he is doing something objectionable without violating an important law. "Ragged as Coxey's Army" also became a byword.

In 1914 General Coxey led another but smaller march upon Washington for a similar purpose, and in 1944, the 50th anniversary of the first march, when he was ninety years old, he spoke from the Capitol steps with the permission of the authorities. He was an unsuccessful candidate on various tickets for U.S. Representative, Governor of Ohio, U.S. Senator and President of the United States. In 1932-1933 he was Mayor of Massillon. He christened one of his sons "Legal Tender."

Who was Alfalfa Bill

William Henry Murray (1869–), Congressman and Governor of Oklahoma is almost universally known as "Alfalfa Bill." Murray was born at Collinsville, Texas, and edited newspapers and practiced law in the Lone Star State for several years before he moved to Indian Territory in 1898. He settled at Tishomingo and grew the first alfalfa ever planted south of the Canadian River, which divides Oklahoma into two nearly equal parts. About 1903, when cotton prices were low, Murray began to urge the farmers in that section to diversify their crops and to plant Irish potatoes. At a meeting in Tishomingo early in 1903 a group of farmers raised enough money to buy two carloads of seed potatoes for the experiment. When the seed-potato business was concluded, George W. Watkins suggested to the gathering that Murray make a speech on how to grow alfalfa. Murray responded, and later, at the request of Indian Territory farmers, made many speeches on the advantage of growing alfalfa.

A young man from Michigan named Arthur Sinclair had attended the meeting and saw humor in the transaction. Arthur Simpson, editor of the local newspaper, met Sinclair outside while the meeting was still in progress and asked him what the news was. "When I got up there they were planting taters," replied Sinclair, "but when I left they were contemplating planting Alfalfa Bills, and Alfalfa Bill himself was making a speech." Simpson put the witticism in his paper. A few weeks later a farm paper printed near Muskogee got Murray to write a series of articles entitled "Alfalfa and Hogs," in which he pointed out the most profitable way of combining the two. The editor put the first article on the front page and headed it ALFALFA BY ALFALFA BILL HIMSELF. Presumably he had seen Sinclair's article in the Tishomingo paper.

That is Alfalfa Bill's own story as to how he got one of the best-known nicknames in American politics. In a letter to the author dated August 6, 1942, Alfalfa Bill wrote:

From then on the nickname stuck and I adopted it because all my life I have had some nickname and I used this one because it was a good one for identification. Hence it has stayed with me ever since. In a political way it has both helped and injured me, as the great body of farmers and the multitudes in general took to the name, but it was a little too *rustic* for the effete of the population. It has also impressed the general public that I was too much of a rustic to be a scholar.

What is dollar diplomacy?

Dollar diplomacy is applied contemptuously to a foreign policy whose chief object is to obtain commercial and trade advantages, particularly when the negotiations are conducted with a weak or backward nation under the guise of friendship. The earliest known use of the phrase occurs in the April 23, 1910, issue of *Harper's Weekly,* where it is applied opprobriously to the policy of Philander C. Knox, President Taft's Secretary of State, who was charged with using diplomacy to promote and protect American investments abroad.

In 1909 Secretary Knox proposed that the powers adhering to the open-door policy supply China with capital to buy the Manchurian railroads from Russia and Japan. This venture in dollar diplomacy failed because Russia and Japan regarded it as an encroachment upon their special interests in that part of Asia. The next step in dollar diplomacy was made in 1910 when the U.S. Government aided American banks to make loans for use in China proper. In 1911 the United States made treaties with Nicaragua and Honduras under which private loans would be used to stabilize those governments by reorganizing their finances and removing customs from the reach of revolutionists, but these treaties were never ratified. The Republican administration regarded dollar diplomacy as a departure from the policy that the Democrats had branded as imperialism, which was intervention in foreign countries backed with military force. In 1912 Secretary Knox visited the Caribbean republics to allay any suspicions that the United States had imperial intentions.

The diplomacy of the present administration [said President Taft in the same year] has sought to respond to modern ideas of commercial intercourse.

This policy has been characterized as substituting dollars for bullets. . . . It is an effort frankly directed to the increase of American trade upon the economic principle that the government of the United States shall extend all proper support to every legitimate and beneficial American enterprise abroad.

But in the public mind *dollar diplomacy* in respect to Latin-America became associated with commercial concessions, exploitation of natural resources, protectorates and even the protection of American capital by armed force. Soon after assuming office in 1913 President Wilson, in a speech at Mobile, Alabama, specifically repudiated dollar diplomacy in the later sense of the term. At a White House press conference in 1933 President Franklin D. Roosevelt said that the cancellation of the Standard-Vacuum Oil Company leases in Ethiopia "is one more proof that since March 4, 1933, dollar diplomacy is no longer recognized by the American government."

When did the Government quit distributing free seeds?

Members of Congress and the Department of Agriculture still receive requests for free seeds, notwithstanding all free seed distribution was discontinued in 1926.

Thomas Jefferson, John Quincy Adams and other American diplomats abroad were continually trying to improve agriculture and horticulture in the United States by introducing into the country new and improved varieties of garden, orchard and field crops. On April 12, 1827, President Adams wrote in his diary:

I spoke again to Mr. Rush [Secretary of the Treasury Richard Rush] respecting the project of procuring seeds and plants from foreign countries which may be usefully naturalized in this country. There was a letter from Mr. Crawford [Rush's predecessor] to our Consuls abroad on this subject, but which has produced no result, because it authorized no expense. . . . I thought we might venture upon some small expense to collect certain specific seeds or plants and have them planted in the garden of the Columbian Institute.

On May 5 of the same year the President wrote:

Mr. Rush brought a draft of a letter to Dr. Mease upon the subject of enquiries relating to the natural history and cultivation of useful foreign plants which might be advantageously introduced into this country. This is a subject which will require long and persevering attention and a systematic pursuit, the issue of which, after all, must be doubtful. Mr. Rush had already made some enquiries at Canton in China, not concerning foreign plants, but of varieties of those which we have as garden vegetables and fruits, and particularly the cotton-plant. He read me an answer received from Canton, and one from Calcutta, neither of which is encouraging. They state that all the garden plants and fruits are far inferior to the same kind of vegetables in Europe. But Canton is on the tropic, and Calcutta nearly so, and could not be expected to produce fruits to thrive in our northern climate.

President Adams wrote five days later:

I spoke to Mr. Southard [Secretary of the Navy Samuel L. Southard] of my desire to obtain information of the natural history and cultivation of foreign plants, fruits, and forest-trees of special usefulness, with a view to introduce the cultivation of them into this country; and suggested the expediency of a circular letter of instructions to the captains of our public ships who visit distant parts of the world, to lend their assistance in cooperation with the Consuls to effect that object.

Little progress was made in the project until after June 15, 1835, when Henry Leavitt Ellsworth, lawyer, farmer and agriculturist, became head of the Patent Office, which had been set up in the Department of State on April 10, 1790. The United States was then an agrarian nation and the patents in the field of agriculture outnumbered all others. Commissioner of Patents Ellsworth was interested in promoting Government aid to agriculture and at his own expense and without Congressional authorization distributed seeds and plants from foreign countries given to him for the purpose. In his annual reports for 1837 and 1839, dated January 1, 1838 and 1840 respectively, Ellsworth asked Congress for funds for use in collecting and distributing seeds and plants and in compiling agricultural statistics. In 1839 Congress gave him permission to use $1,000 of the patent appropriation for such purposes. He set up the Agricultural Division in the Patent Office and his successors continued to distribute free seeds until 1862, when "the Department of Agriculture" was created. One of the special functions of the new Department was "to procure, propagate and distribute among the people new and valuable seeds and plants."

Since Senators, Representatives and Delegates in Congress represented every State and Territory in the Union, it was natural for Ellsworth to ask them to help distribute the free seeds. Members of Congress soon found that sending free seeds to their constituents was good campaign medicine. Representative Abraham Lincoln of Illinois sent some of the seeds to William H. Herndon in Springfield for distribution in the Congressional District. Herndon neglected to distribute them and threw them on a table piled high with books and newspapers. The roof leaked, the seeds sprouted, and when Lincoln returned in 1849 his law office looked like a vegetable garden. On February 2, 1866, Representative Rutherford B. Hayes wrote to an Ohio constituent: "Do you want any books, apple seeds, or oats? I am in that trade now." Appropriations for free seeds were increased and gradually Congressmen got a virtual monopoly on their distribution. In 1887 Congress passed a bill to enable the Commissioner of Agriculture to make a special distribution of seeds in the drought-stricken counties of Texas and appropriated $10,000 for that purpose. President Cleveland vetoed the bill and in his veto message said:

It is here suggested that the Commissioner of Agriculture is annually directed to expend a large sum of money for the purchase, propagation, and distribution of seeds and other things of this description, two-thirds of which are upon the request of Senators, Representatives, and Delegates in Congress, supplied to them for distribution among their constituents. The appropriation of the current year for this purpose is $100,000, and it will probably be no less in the appropriation for the ensuing year.

The "Veto President" suggested that Congressmen share some of their free seeds with the unfortunate Texas farmers.

Although some new and valuable plants were introduced by this method, most of the seeds were of the standard vegetable and flower varieties and the first attempt to give Federal aid to farmers gradually degenerated into a Congressional "racket." Beginning in 1896 Congress so worded the seed appropriations acts that the department had to allot five-sixths of all its seeds, bulbs, shrubs, vines, cuttings and plants to members of Congress for distribution to their constituents. The other sixth was distributed directly by the department. In time the "Seed Division" became a big business. It became impractical to fill all the orders with strictly new varieties of seeds and the tendency was to lose sight of the original intention of the service and to send out more and more seeds of common varieties. For years most of the Federal funds appropriated for agriculture were used to buy and distribute seeds, which were bought by the department through competitive bids in the spring from commercial seed growers and dealers. When the "Congressional seed distribution" system was at its peak each member of Congress was entitled to 20,000 packages of vegetable and 2,000 packages of flower seed. Each package consisted of five packets of seed of different varieties. At one time the Congressional seed amounted to nearly a million pounds a year—about 500 tons, or enough to fill twenty freight cars. The seeds were assembled and packeted by the Seed Division and a member of Congress could have them sent directly to him for distribution or mailed by the Department under his "frank" to designated persons. Seeds were sent out much as yearbooks and other free documents are now. Congressmen were permitted to "swap seeds" to adjust their quota to the demands of their constituents.

In *Recollections* (1925) Thomas R. Marshall wrote: "And it was his neighbor who ordered so many cow peas from the Department of Agriculture as to excite curiosity. On investigation the Department found that they were not being planted but eaten." Several Secretaries of Agriculture pronounced the free-seed business as little more than a national disgrace. After the system had been the butt of criticism for nearly a quarter of a century the appropriation for Congressional seed distribution was discontinued June 20, 1923, and that for new and rare seed distribution June 30, 1926, and since then the Department of Agriculture has had no seeds or plants of any kind available either for free distribution or for sale.

Who first called America a melting pot?

The fusion of many peoples into a new race in America was compared to the melting of metals in a crucible before the end of the Revolution. In 1782 J. Hector St. John de Crèvecœur, a Frenchman naturalized in America, wrote in *Letters from an American Farmer:* "Here individuals of all nations are *melted* into a new race of men, whose labors and posterity will one day cause great changes in the world." But *melting pot* is not found until the early part of the nineteenth century. *The Melting Pot,* a play written by the English-Jewish author Israel Zangwill, was first produced in New York in 1908. "America is God's Crucible, the great Melting Pot where all the races of Europe are melting and reforming," is a sentence in that play. "There is here a great melting pot in which we must compound a precious metal," declared President Wilson in an address at Washington on April 19, 1915. "That metal is the metal of nationality." On September 9, 1917, Theodore Roosevelt said in a speech: "We Americans are children of the crucible."

The conception of America as an asylum for the unfortunate of foreign lands goes back to Colonial days. In a speech in the Virginia House of Delegates in 1783 Patrick Henry foreshadowed the Statue of Liberty and its inscription by Emma Lazarus: "Make it the home of the skilful, the industrious, the fortunate, the happy, as well as the asylum of the distressed. . . . Let but this, our celebrated goddess, Liberty, stretch forth her fair hand toward the people of the old world—tell them to come, and bid them welcome." The Marquis de Chastellux reported General Washington as saying in the spring of 1788: "It is a flattering and consolatory reflection, that our rising republics have the good wishes of all the Philosophers, Patriots, and virtuous men in all nations; and that they look upon them as a kind of asylum for mankind. God grant that we may not disappoint that honest expectation, by our folly or perverseness." President Washington's proclamation declaring February 19, 1795, a day of thanksgiving contained, "Render this country more and more a safe and propitious asylum for the unfortunate of other countries." On December 2, 1823, Secretary of State John Quincy Adams wrote in his diary that Speaker Henry Clay "said he had thought of offering a resolution to declare this country an asylum for the fugitives from oppression." Former Mayor Philip Hone of New York City wrote in his diary on September 20, 1833: "The boast that our country is the asylum for the oppressed in other parts of the world is very philanthropic and sentimental, but I fear that we shall before long derive little comfort from being made the almshouse and place of refuge for the poor of other countries." America was called "Asylum of the oppressed of every nation" in the Democratic platform of 1856.

How is *Bayard* pronounced?

Bayard as a family name in America is generally pronounced *BY-urd*. That is the way it is pronounced by the Bayard family of Delaware, which is notable for the great number of its members who have held public office. Formerly Delaware was popularly known as "the pocket borough of the Bayard family."

This line of Bayards is descended from Samuel Bayard, a French Huguenot, who married a sister of Peter Stuyvesant, Director General of New Netherland.

John Bubenheim Bayard (1738-1807), merchant, judge and soldier of distinction, was a Pennsylvania delegate in the Continental Congress. He had a twin brother whose son, James Asheton Bayard (1767-1815), served in the U.S. House of Representatives and Senate. The latter married a daughter of Richard Bassett (1745-1815), one of the original Senators from Delaware in the U.S. Congress.

James Asheton and Ann Bassett Bayard had two sons, Richard Henry Bayard (1796-1866) and James Asheton Bayard, Jr., both of whom were Senators from Delaware. Thomas Francis Bayard (1828-1898), son of Thomas Asheton Bayard, Jr., served as a Senator from Delaware and as Secretary of State in Cleveland's first cabinet. In 1893 Cleveland appointed him Ambassador to the Court of St. James. His son, Thomas Francis Bayard, Jr. (1868-1942) was a Delaware Senator from 1922 to 1929.

Thus it will be seen that six members of the Bayard family have served in the American Congress. Five of them, representing four consecutive generations, have served as United States Senators from Delaware.

What is Senatorial Courtesy?

Senatorial courtesy and *the courtesy of the Senate* do not refer to the ordinary courtesies exchanged between Senators in the course of debate, although that was probably the earliest meaning of the phrases. They are now applied particularly to two different unwritten rules of the U.S. Senate.

One is that the Senate as a whole will defer to the wishes of the Senators from any given State in respect to the confirmation of nominations of persons from that State. Generally any Senator of the party in power can prevent the confirmation of any person whom the President nominates for Federal office within the Senator's State by simply letting the Senate know that the nominee is "personally objectionable and obnoxious" to him. The rule does not now apply to nominees for national offices such as members of the Cabinet and the Supreme Court, and generally Senators of a minority party do not invoke the traditional rule.

When the Federal Government was established in 1789 the Senators interpreted the Constitutional phrase, "by and with the advice and consent of the Senate" quite literally. President Washington, without consulting William Few and James Gunn, the first two Senators from Georgia, nominated Benjamin Fishbourn for naval officer in the customs house at Savannah. Senators Few and Gunn induced the Senate to reject the nomination of Fishbourn, a Revolutionary veteran held in high esteem by the President. On August 6, 1789, the President sent a message to the Senate in which he nominated Lachlan McIntosh for the place and in which he said:

Whatever may have been the reasons which induced your dissent, I am persuaded they were such as you deemed sufficient. Permit me to submit to your consideration whether on occasions where the propriety of nominations appear questionable to you it would not be expedient to communicate that circumstance to me, and thereby avail yourselves of the information which led me to make them, and which I would with pleasure lay before you. Probably my reasons for nominating Mr. Fishbourn may tend to show that such a mode of precedure in such cases might be useful.

Washington then detailed his reasons for making the appointment in the first place.

On February 18, 1791, Senator William Maclay of Pennsylvania, who was very critical of President Washington, wrote in his diary: "A number of communications were handed in, respecting the appointment of David Humphries, resident at the court of Portugal. The President sends first and asks for our advice and consent afterward."

On January 29, 1805, Senator John Quincy Adams wrote in his diary: "There was a nomination of a Consul this day, negatived—the first instance since I have been in the Senate; and it was done on General Smith's declaring that he knew the man, and that he was every way unfit for the office. He complained of our Consuls abroad in general, and appeared dissatisfied that the appointment had been made *without* consulting him." William Walton, who had been appointed commercial agent at San Domingo, was from Maryland, the State General Smith represented as a Senator.

During the struggle between President Andrew Johnson and Congress for power there was little important legislation passed except by a two-thirds majority in both houses and the members of Congress acquired the notion that they were entitled to control all appointments of civil officers in their own States and Districts. Some, but not all, of this arrogant insistence of control over appointments disappeared during the two terms of Ulysses S. Grant, who had his own notions as to who should control appointments from his State. For some reason not quite clear, Grant gave control of all Massachusetts patronage to General Benjamin F. Butler, then a Representative. Upon Butler's recommendation, Grant appointed William A. Simmons to be Collector of Boston. The Massachusetts delegation in Congress sent George Frisbie Hoar, the junior Senator, to protest to the President. Hoar found the President walking along the east side of Lafayette Park and in his *Autobiography of Seventy Years* tells what happened:

I told the President that I thought the Republicans of Massachusetts would be much dissatisfied with the nomination of Simmons, and hoped it might be withdrawn. The President replied that he thought it would be an injustice to the young man to do so, and that the opposition to him seemed to be chiefly because he was a friend of General Butler. I combatted the argument as well as I could. The whole conversation was exceedingly quiet and friendly on both sides until we turned by Mr. Sumner's house, when the President, with great emphasis, and shaking his closed fist toward Sumner's house, said: "I shall not withdraw the nomination. That man who lives up there has abused me in a way which I never suffered from any other man living."

Simmons was confirmed by the Senate. Once at a banquet President Grant was told that Sumner did not believe the Bible. "That's because he did not write it himself," observed the President.

In 1877 President Rutherford B. Hayes, who was committed to civil service reform and taking "Federal appointments out of politics," removed Chester A. Arthur as Collector and Alonzo B. Cornell as Surveyor of Customs of the Port of New York because they persisted in ignoring his order to keep their offices out of politics. The President's nominations were blocked in the Senate by Senator Roscoe Conkling, who had not been consulted in making the appointments. The man appointed to succeed Arthur was Theodore Roosevelt, father of President Theodore Roosevelt. It was during this contest that *senatorial courtesy* in this sense came into general use.

On December 8, 1877, President Hayes wrote in a letter: "In the end, the claim of a single Senator to control all nominations in his State will be found so preposterous that it will fall of its own weight." The next day he wrote in his diary: "I am now in a contest on the question of the right of Senators to dictate or control nominations. Mr. Conkling insists that no officer shall be appointed in New York without his consent, obtained previously to the nomination." Three days later he wrote: "In the language of the press, 'Senator Conkling has won a great victory over the Administration.' My New York nominations were rejected thirty-one to twenty-five. But the end is not yet. I am right, and shall not give up the contest."

Hayes was as good as his word and persisted. Without consulting Conkling he sent the names of Merritt and Graham to the Senate for the two offices. "The political event of last week is the opposition of Conkling to the New York appointments," he wrote in his diary on December 16, 1878. "This is a test case. The Senators generally prefer to confirm Merritt and Graham. But many, perhaps a majority, will not oppose Conkling on the question. Senatorial courtesy, the Senatorial prerogative, and the fear of Conkling's vengeance in future, control them." Arthur and Cornell, both powerful in New York politics, backed Conkling to the limit in his fight against Hayes, but on February 4, 1879, the President was able to report in his diary: "We are successful. The New York nominations, Merritt and Burt, were confirmed against Arthur and Cornell, after five or six hours' debate by a vote of thirty-three to twenty-four."

Hayes, however, suspected that the victory was not complete. On November 7, 1780, he noted in his diary that "there is an evident purpose to reestablish the doctrine that the Senators from a State are entitled to control the federal offices of that State." Meanwhile Cornell had been elected Governor of New York and Arthur had been elected Vice President of the United States, and the two men were in a stronger position than ever. When James A. Garfield became President in 1881, he shifted E. A. Merritt, Hayes's appointee, to a diplomatic post to make room in the New York customs house for Judge William H. Robertson, who had broken politically with Senator Conkling and headed the movement that resulted in Garfield's nomination for President by the 1880 convention. Again Conkling invoked Senatorial courtesy. Vice President Arthur went to Albany to help Governor Cornell whip up sentiment in New York in favor of Conkling in his fight with the President.

Ultimately Robertson was confirmed, whereupon Conkling resigned from the Senate. His colleague, Senator Thomas C. Platt, joined in a "sympathy resignation" and earned the nickname "Me Too Platt." On May 17, 1881, former President Hayes noted in his diary: "Conkling and Platt . . . have both resigned. They expect no doubt to be re-elected as Republicans opposed to Garfield's Administration. It is a wretched business." But neither Conkling nor Platt was re-elected by the Legislature to succeed himself, although Platt returned to the Senate fifteen years later.

In recent years the unwritten rule of Senatorial courtesy has been somewhat weakened and a number of Senators have advocated throwing it permanently in the discard, but it still operates in many cases.

The other unwritten rule referred to as senatorial courtesy is that a Senator or former Senator nominated for Federal office is confirmed promptly as a matter of course without investigation or reference to a committee. After President Roosevelt had incurred the displeasure of many Senators in 1937 by attempting to reform the Supreme Court by increasing the number of its members, he appointed Senator Hugo Black to fill a vacancy. The President, it was widely suspected at the time, named the Alabama Senator largely because under the traditional senatorial courtesy rule the Senate would be compelled to confirm him, while they might have been tempted to reject any nominee who was not a member of their "exclusive club."

What brothers were Governors at the same time?

John Bigler (1805-1871) was elected Governor of Pennsylvania on September 3, 1851, the same day his younger brother, William Bigler (1814-1880) was elected Governor of California. The former served two years and the latter four. They were the sons of a Pennsylvania German farmer and both were Democrats. The California Legislature named a large lake on the California-Nevada boundary Lake Bigler in honor of Governor William Bigler, but the people ignored the official name and continued to call it Lake Tahoe, an Indian name meaning "big water."

Although not elected at the same time, Enoch Lincoln (1788-1829) was Governor of Maine while his brother, Levi Lincoln (1782-1868), was Governor of Massachusetts. The former was Governor of Maine from

1827 till his death in 1829, and the latter was Governor of Massachusetts from 1828 to 1834. They were sons of Levi Lincoln, who was Attorney General under Jefferson, and were distant relatives of Abraham Lincoln.

Israel Washburn, Jr., was Governor of Maine from 1861 to 1862, and his brother, Cadwallader Washburn, was Governor of Minnesota from 1872 to 1874. Sam Houston was Governor of Tennessee from 1827 to 1829 and Governor of Texas from 1859 to 1861. He resigned from the first office and was deposed from the second. A period of about thirty years intervened between the time he ceased to be Governor of Tennessee and the time he became Governor of Texas. James Bennett McCreary was Governor of Kentucky from 1875 to 1879 and from 1911 to 1915. He took the oath the second time thirty-six years after he had taken it the first time. Preston H. Leslie was Governor of Kentucky from 1871 to 1875 and Governor of Montana Territory from 1887 to 1889. George Clinton was Governor of New York from 1777 to 1795 and from 1801 to 1804—a total of nearly twenty-two years; and his nephew, DeWitt Clinton, was Governor from 1817 to 1821 and from 1825 to 1828—a total of nearly eight years.

In 1886 Robert Love Taylor (1850-1912) Democrat, defeated his brother, Alfred Alexander Taylor (1848-1931), Republican, for the governorship of Tennessee in one of the most remarkable campaigns ever conducted in any State. The contest between the brothers was spirited but good-tempered. It was called "The War of the Roses" because the candidates traveled over the State together and Bob wore a red rose and Alf a white one so their followers could tell them apart. Their father presided over a meeting at Happy Valley on the eve of the election and gave them both his blessing. One writer says the weapons used in the campaign were "droll anecdotes, scintillating repartee and a matching of their skill as fiddlers." Robert was elected. He was Governor from 1887 to 1891 and again from 1897 to 1899. Finally—thirty-four years after his race with his brother Alfred Taylor was elected Governor of Tennessee in 1920 and served from 1921 to 1923.

The first general conference of the Governors of all the States was held in Washington in 1908 during Theodore Roosevelt's administration.

How many Presidents kept diaries?

George Washington, John Adams, John Quincy Adams, James K. Polk, Rutherford B. Hayes, James A. Garfield and William Howard Taft kept diaries. Washington, John Quincy Adams, Polk, Hayes and Garfield have been the only Presidents known to have kept diaries while

President. Polk kept a diary only while President. Although he did not keep an extensive diary as such, Thomas Jefferson made extensive current records and notes. Washington, John Quincy Adams, Hayes and Garfield all began to keep diaries at an early age and continued to do so intermittently throughout their lives. John Quincy Adams kept a daily record of his life more or less continuously for more than sixty years and his is the most extensive and complete of the Presidential diaries. On September 8, 1831, Adams wrote in his diary:

One of the best objects of practical perseverance with which a young man should begin life and pursue to the end is the keeping of a diary. This I began at twelve years of age; but I have failed of perseverance in keeping it at least twenty times, and often for long and important intervals. Few men, however, have in this point had perseverance equal to mine, and they were assuredly useful men. But I have filled my journals with trash, and with every whimsy that passed across my mind. This has been an idle waste of time, and a multiplication of books to no end and without end.

Fifteen years later—October 31, 1846—Adams wrote: "There has perhaps not been another individual of the human race, of whose daily existence from early childhood to fourscore years has been noted down with his own hand so minutely as mine. At little more than twelve years of age I began to journalise..."

Hayes began to keep a diary regularly in 1841 to improve his composition and for amusement. His last entry, written on January 15, 1893, two days before his death, ends with "Doing well." James Madison kept a detailed journal of the proceedings of the Constitutional Convention in 1787.

John Adams, Jefferson, Martin Van Buren, Ulysses S. Grant, Theodore Roosevelt, Calvin Coolidge and Herbert Hoover wrote autobiographies or memoirs. For the most part these Presidential autobiographies are only fragmentary and deal chiefly with the early lives of their authors. Few Presidents have published books other than autobiographies and compilations of addresses. Jefferson, a prolific writer, published only one book—*Notes on Virginia*. Both Adamses published books, but Theodore Roosevelt, Woodrow Wilson and Herbert Hoover have been the only real book authors among the Presidents. Hoover and his wife translated *Agricola de Re Metallica* from Latin.

Franklin D. Roosevelt made careful arrangements before his death for the preservation of his private papers, but Millard Powers Fillmore, the only son of President Fillmore, in his will directed his executors to destroy all his father's papers, and this mandate was carried out at Buffalo in 1891.

[513]

Who was Cotton Ed?

Ellison DuRant Smith (1866-1944) of South Carolina, who served in the U.S. Senate from March 4, 1909, until his death, was known as Cotton Ed (from his initials) because he was identified with and spokesman of the cotton interests. He was one of the chief organizers of the Southern Cotton Association in 1905 and was for several years field agent and general organizer of the cotton protective movement in the South.

Who was Ralph Izard?

Ralph Izard (1742-1804) was a South Carolina planter who bought property in London and settled there in 1771. After the outbreak of the Revolution he moved to Paris and in 1777 was appointed commissioner to Tuscany by the Continental Congress. He opened negotiations with the Tuscan court, but it refused to recognize or receive him, and he stayed in Paris, where he pledged his private fortune as security to buy warships for America. Because of his property in England, the Tory connections of his wife and the fact he sided with Arthur Lee in a bitter controversy with Benjamin Franklin, his loyalty to the United States was unjustly suspected and in 1779 he was recalled. He returned to South Carolina and became a member of the Continental Congress and one of the first U.S. Senators from his State. He was a friend of George Washington and an ardent supporter of the first President's administration.

George Izard (1776-1828) was one of Ralph Izard's fourteen children and was born in England. He was a Major General in the U.S. Army during the War of 1812 and was Territorial Governor of Arkansas at the time of his death. Izard County, Arkansas, is named after him. The name is pronounced izz-*erd*.

Who was the first President to have an automobile?

William McKinley was the first President to ride in an automobile. He took his first automobile ride in a Stanley Steamer in 1899. After he was shot on September 6, 1901, by Leon Czolgosz, President McKinley was taken to a Buffalo hospital in an "electric automobile ambulance."

Theodore Roosevelt occasionally rode in automobiles while he was President but did not own one. He was a great horse lover and preferred horses to automobiles. On October 14, 1903, President Roosevelt wrote from the White House to his son Kermit: "Yesterday afternoon Ethel on Wyoming, Mother on Yaganka and I on Renown had a long ride, the only incident being meeting a large red automobile, which much shook Renown's nerves, although he behaved far better than he has hitherto been doing about automobiles. In fact, he behaved so well that I leaned over and gave him a lump of sugar when he had passed the object of his terror—the old boy eagerly turning his head around to get it." During the latter years of Teddy's administration, the Secret Service kept an automobile at the White House, but the President did not care much for it and seldom rode in it. William Howard Taft was the first man to use an automobile regularly while President. A motor brougham was purchased for his use at the beginning of his administration in 1909. About the same time President Taft bought a motor landaulet for the use of his wife. Mrs. Taft was the first wife of a President to ride in a motor car with her husband from the Capitol to the White House on inauguration day. Warren G. Harding was the first man elected President who had driven a car himself, and he was the first President to ride to his inauguration in an automobile. President Franklin D. Roosevelt, despite the fact he was physically handicapped, sometimes drove his own car while at Hyde Park and Warm Springs.

Who said the Presidency is "a splendid misery?"

On March 9, 1789, soon after his election as the first President of the United States, George Washington wrote to Benjamin Harrison: "My movements to the chair of government will be accompanied by feelings not unlike those of a culprit who is going to the place of execution." Later, while he was subjected to unmerciful criticism and threatened with impeachment, he said, "I would rather be in my grave than in the Presidency." The first President did not enjoy the high office and was happy when he was relieved of its responsibilities and could return to Mount Vernon.

In *Figures of the Past* Josiah Quincy wrote that when John Adams first learned that his son had been elected President, the aged former President observed: "No man who ever held the office of President would congratulate a friend on obtaining it. He will make one man ungrateful, and a hundred men his enemies, for every office he can bestow." Shortly after his term expired in 1801 John Adams wrote: "If I were to go over my life again I would be a shoemaker rather than an American states-man."

In 1796, when Thomas Jefferson was a candidate for President but was chosen Vice President, he wrote to Edward Rutledge: "No man will bring out of the Presidency the reputation which carries him into it."

The next year Vice President Jefferson wrote to Elbridge Gerry: "The second office of the government is honorable and easy; the first is but a *splendid misery*." In 1807, after he had been President six years, he wrote to John Dickinson: "I am tired of an office where I can do no more good than many others who would be glad to be employed in it. To myself, personally, it brings nothing but unceasing drudgery and daily loss of friends." Two months before the expiration of his second term in 1809 Jefferson wrote to Dupont de Nemours: "Never did a prisoner, released from his chains, feel such relief as I shall on shaking off the shackles of power." When Jefferson turned over the Presidency to Madison he told Margaret Bayard Smith that he was much happier at the moment than his friend.

On May 18, 1825, George Sullivan called at the White House and asked President John Quincy Adams what he should say for him to Governor Lincoln when he returned to Massachusetts. "I said," wrote the President in his diary, "he should give my compliments to him, and congratulations upon his election, with my hope that he would find the Chair of Massachusetts a bed of roses, which I could assure him the Presidential Chair was not." Under date of November 28, 1880, President Rutherford B. Hayes wrote in his diary: "Mr. Alley also said that Mr. Charles Francis Adams said that his father, John Quincy Adams, habitually spoke of his Presidential term as the unhappiest four years of his life."

Ralph Waldo Emerson, in *Compensation* (1841), wrote: "The President has paid dear for his White House. It has commonly cost him all his peace and the best of his manly attributes. To preserve for a short time so conspicuous an appearance before the world, he is content to eat dust before the real masters who stand erect behind the throne."

On January 28, 1847, when he had been in the White House nearly two years, President James K. Polk wrote in his diary: "Since that time I have performed great labor and incurred vast responsibilities. In truth, though I occupy a very high position, I am the hardest working man in this country." He wrote on the following November 7: "With me it is emphatically true that the Presidency is 'no bed of roses.' " And on March 4, 1849, the day his term as President expired, Polk wrote: "I feel exceedingly relieved that I am now free from all public cares. I am sure I shall be a happier man in my retirement than I have been during the four years I have filled the highest office in the gift of my countrymen." Three months later he was dead.

As he left the White House on March 4, 1861, James Buchanan said to Abraham Lincoln: "If you are as happy, my dear sir, on entering this house, as I am in leaving it and returning home, you are the happiest man in this country." But Lincoln's stay in "this damned old house," as he once called the White House, brought him grief and sorrow and an untimely and tragic death. "If to be the head of hell is hard as what I have to undergo here," he observed, "I could find it in my heart to pity Satan himself." When a friend asked him how it felt to be President, he replied: "I feel like the man who was tarred and feathered and ridden out of town on a rail. To the man who asked him how he liked it, he said, If it wasn't for the honor of the thing, I'd rather walk."

Several years before he became President, James A. Garfield wrote in his diary: "The Presidency is the one office in the nation that for peace of mind no one should set his heart on." On December 31, 1880, when he was President-elect, Garfield wrote: "I close the year with the sad conviction that I am bidding goodbye to private life and a long series of happy years." Soon after he moved into the White House he said: "My God, what is there in this place that a man should ever want to get in it." Less than nine months later he died from the effects of an assassin's bullet.

When Grover Cleveland was about to begin his second term as President, he wrote: "I look upon the next four years to come as a self-inflicted penance for the good of the country. I see no pleasure in it." As his second term neared its end, Cleveland said: "I am tired of abuses. I am going to know how it feels to be really a sovereign, for that every American citizen is." After he had retired from the White House for good, he was asked how he felt with no Congress to fight and no official responsibilities. "I feel," he replied, "like a locomotive hitched to a boy's express wagon."

Theodore Roosevelt was one of the few Presidents who thoroughly enjoyed the job. On June 21, 1904, he wrote his son Kermit: "Incidentally, I don't think that any family ever enjoyed the White House more than we have." Later he said, "I had a corking time in the White House." On another occasion he said: "I enjoy being President and I like to do the work and have the hand on the lever. But it is worrying and puzzling." When he left the White House in 1909, Teddy observed: "No President ever enjoyed himself as much as I have. I shall miss having my hand on the lever of the great machine." Yet, in an interview with Henry L. Stoddard on life in the White House, he said: "You don't live there. You are only Exhibit A in the country."

The Presidency brought worry, strain and a physical breakdown to Woodrow Wilson. He didn't like being put in "the same category with the National Museum, the Smithsonian Institution, or the Washington

Monument." But, he once observed, "There are blessed intervals when I forget by one means or another that I am President of the United States."

Calvin Coolidge enjoyed his first year in the White House, but, he says in his *Autobiography* (1929), the power and the glory of the Presidency departed when his son Calvin died in 1924.

Franklin D. Roosevelt liked being President so well that he ran and was elected four times, but the strain of war broke his health and probably hastened his death.

On April 4, 1900, Admiral George Dewey, in announcing his availability for the Presidency, said: "If the American people want me for this high office, I shall be only too willing to serve them. . . . Since studying this subject I am convinced that the office of President is not such a very difficult one to fill, his duties being mainly to execute the laws of Congress." Charles Evans Hughes, who was nominated but defeated for the Presidency in 1916, said: "The Presidency is the greatest honor that could come to any man; it is also the greatest burden."

Why is the Vice Presidency low-rated?

The Vice President has no official duty except to preside over the Senate and even that duty is generally performed by a Senator. The sole purpose of the office is to have a person constitutionally qualified and elected to be ready to step into the President's shoes. Making the Vice President presiding officer of the Senate was suggested to the framers of the Constitution by the fact that such was the duty of the lieutenant governor in some of the States.

Vice as a prefix to such titles as *President, Admiral, Consul* and *Chancellor* has no connection with vice in the sense of moral depravity or evil-doing. It is the ablative of Latin *vicis*, "turn," "change" or "stead" and now means "in place of" or "substitute." *Vicar* and *vicarious* are from the same source. Dictionaries say that *vice,* when used as a preposition in its more literal sense, as "Frank Dennis was appointed postmaster *vice* Jack Levy," is pronounced in two syllables—VIE-*sa*.

The records of the Constitutional Convention of 1787 indicate that there was little discussion of the Vice Presidency when the Constitution was drafted, but there was objection to the office almost from the beginning. Somebody, Benjamin Franklin according to some, is reputed to have suggested that the Vice President be given the title of "His Superfluous Excellency." The Vice Presidency was among George Mason's objections to the Constitution, which he helped write but

[518]

refused to sign. He wrote in 1788: "Hence also springs the unnecessary officer, the Vice President, who for want of other employment is made president of the Senate, thereby dangerously blending the executive and legislative powers, besides always giving to some one of the States the unnecessary and unjust predominance over the others." Governor George Clinton of New York, who opposed the Constitution, argued that there was no valid reason for a Vice President. Sixteen years later he was elected to that office. In the Federalist Papers Hamilton took pains to reply to the critics of the Vice Presidency.

John Adams, the first Vice President, described the position as "the most insignificant office that ever invention of man contrived." On August 18, 1790, Adams wrote to Benjamin Rush: "I wish very heartily that a change of Vice-President could be made to-morrow. I have been too ill-used in the office to be fond of it;—if I had not been introduced into it in a manner that made it a disgrace. I will never again serve in it upon such terms." But Adams did serve another term as Vice President under Washington. The second Vice President, Thomas Jefferson, wrote to Elbridge Gerry in 1797: "The second office of the government is honorable and easy." Gerry later became Vice President himself. Abolition of the Vice Presidency has often been advocated on the ground that it is a useless office that is vacant too often to serve the purpose it was designed for. As early as 1803, when the Constitutional Amendment for choosing the President and Vice President separately was under consideration, Senator Jonathan Dayton, a signer of the Constitution moved that the Vice Presidency be abolished.

With few exceptions the Vice Presidents have been inferior to the Presidents and the Secretaries of State in stature as statesmen and national leaders. This is due in part to the common practice in later years of nominating "first rate second-class" men for Vice President "to balance the ticket." After a candidate for President is nominated, a convention seldom nominates the next best preconvention candidate for Vice President. Instead the Vice-Presidential nominee is generally chosen to compose party or sectional factions. With few exceptions the candidates for President and for Vice President come from widely separated parts of the country. The result has been that the Vice-Presidential candidates often are party wheelhorses whose chief qualification is that they have been good vote getters in a pivotal State.

Only three men—John Adams, Jefferson and Martin Van Buren—were elected President while they were Vice President, and Jefferson was the only one of these elected President twice. Seven Vice Presidents succeeded to the Presidency by reasons of the death of Presidents. The first four—John Tyler, Millard Fillmore, Andrew Johnson and Chester A. Arthur—failed to get the nomination to succeed themselves, although they all wanted it. The last three—Theodore Roosevelt, Calvin Coolidge and Harry S. Truman—were elected to the Presidency to succeed themselves. While the Vice President is always a potential President—it being said that there is but one heartbeat between the Vice Presidency and the Presidency—the second office is regarded as a poor position for further political advancement on merit. Thomas R. Marshall observed that the only duties of the Vice President are to preside over the Senate and to inquire each morning about the health of the President.

When the Federal Government was organized in 1789 the salaries of the President and Vice President were fixed at $25,000 and $5,000 respectively. Vice President Adams didn't think it was enough and complained that "it is difficult to maintain a menage in Philadelphia" on that amount. But that salary ratio of five to one was maintained until 1949, when the President's salary was fixed at $100,000 and the Vice President's at $30,000. The low salary for the Vice President is based on the theory that he is paid as the presiding officer of the Senate rather than as potential President and is regarded as being comparable in function and dignity to the Speaker of the House.

The Vice President has never been furnished with a residence at the seat of government at Federal expense. Many bills to provide such a residence for him have been introduced but none has passed. Once a wealthy Washington woman offered a pretentious mansion for the Vice President's use as a "Little White House," but the offer was not accepted by the Government. In his *Autobiography* (1929) Calvin Coolidge wrote:

But my experience has convinced me that an official residence with suitable maintenance should be provided for the Vice President. Under the present system he is not lacking in dignity but he has no fixed position. The great office should have a settled and permanent habitation and a place, irrespective of the financial ability of its temporary occupant. While I was glad to be relieved of the responsibility of a public establishment, nevertheless, it is a duty the second office of the nation should assume. It would be much more in harmony with our theory of equality if each Vice President held the same position in the Capital City.

A number of men failed to realize their Presidential ambitions because their pride would not permit them to seek the nomination for Vice President. Either Webster or Clay could easily have had the Whig nomination for Vice President in 1840 and in 1848. In both instances the Whig candidates were elected and in both instances the President died in office. The Conkling-Cameron group in the convention of 1880 suggested to Benjamin Harrison that he accept the nomination for Vice President with Ulysses S. Grant on the ground that Grant was in bad health and would die in office. "I am not ambitious to enter the White House following a hearse," replied Harrison, who received the Presidential nomination in 1888 and was elected. In 1920 Warren G. Harding wanted Senator Hiram Johnson to be his running mate. Had Johnson played ball with his successful rival for the Presidential nomination he instead of Calvin Coolidge would have succeeded Harding in the White House. According to an apocryphal story, President Coolidge suggested that Senator William E. Borah be his running mate in 1924, and when the Idaho Senator heard of it he asked, "Which end of the ticket?" A group of Republican leaders at the convention that year in Cleveland telephoned Borah in the middle of the night and told him they wanted him to be the Vice-Presidential candidate with Coolidge, but Borah replied he would not take it and went back to bed.

No man has turned down the nomination for the Presidency after it was made by a major party, but two have refused to accept the nomination for Vice President after it was made. In 1924 Frank O. Lowden of Illinois was actually nominated for Vice President on a winning ticket and declined the nomination. On May 24, 1844, Samuel F. B. Morse gave the first public demonstration of the telegraph line between Washington and Baltimore. The Democratic National Convention met in Baltimore four days later and the proceedings were reported by telegraph in Washington by manuscript bulletins hung up on the walls of the rotunda of the Capitol. On May 29 the convention nominated James K. Polk for President unanimously. Then, as a sop to former President Van Buren, who had been defeated for the Presidential nomination by the two-thirds rule, nominated his friend and political ally Senator Silas Wright of New York for Vice President with an almost unanimous vote. When Wright learned the news in the Capitol he had the telegrapher send the following: "Washingt. Important! Mr. Wright is here, and says, say to the New York delegates, that he can not accept the nomination." Fearing that this message might be construed as a threat to bolt the ticket, Wright asked the telegrapher to send another message: "Again. Mr. Wright is here, and will support Mr. Polk cheerfully, but can not accept the nomination for vice-president." The skeptical delegates in Baltimore were incredulous and jeered when the message was read to the convention and voted to adjourn. But the next day the delegates learned by a messenger on horseback that Professor Morse's magic wires had told the truth. George M. Dallas of Pennsylvania was then nominated for Vice President and was elected.

After he was nominated for Vice President in 1900 Theodore Roosevelt wrote to General Leonard Wood: "By the time you receive this you will have learned from the daily press that I have been forced to take the veil." Vice President Thomas R. Marshall continually poked fun at his job. In 1920 he observed: "The Vice President of the United States is like a man in a cataleptic state; he cannot speak; he cannot move; he suffers no pain; and yet he is perfectly conscious of everything that is going on about him." Marshall was fond of telling the following story: "There were once two brothers. One ran away to sea, the other was elected Vice President, and neither was ever heard of again." In *Recollections* (1925) Marshall wrote: "In the city of Denver, while I was vice-president, a big husky policeman kept following me around, until I asked him what he was doing. He said he was guarding my person. I said: 'Your labor is in vain. Nobody was ever crazy enough to shoot at a vice-president. If you will go away and find somebody to shoot at me, I'll go down in history as being the first vice-president who ever attracted enough attention even to have a crank shoot at him.'" As late as 1949 Vice President Alben W. Barkley declined the offer of Secret Service protection for similar reasons but in 1950 he accepted such protection, and was the first Vice President to do so. Three Presidents have been assassinated but no Vice Presidents. Vice President John N. Garner described the Vice Presidency as "the no man's land somewhere between the executive and the legislative branches" and the Vice President as "a figure of slight importance with a title of great impressiveness." In 1934 he referred to the Vice President as "a spare tire on the automobile of government." Bascom N. Timmons, in *Garner of Texas* (1948), quotes Garner as saying: "A Vice President may move into the Presidency and be a great President. A great man may be Vice President but he can't be a great Vice-President, because the office in itself is unimportant." On August 18, 1841, after Vice President John Tyler had succeeded to the Presidency, Philip Hone wrote in his diary: "Mr. Tyler was a sort of adjunct to the administration, a kind of fifth wheel to the political coach, which we now discover could have gone on much better without him."

How did *strike* originate?

To strike in the sense of to quit work to obtain or to resist a change in working conditions dates back at least to 1768. *Strike* as applied to an organized cessation of work by employees came into use about sixty years later.

The term smacks of the sea and is probably of nautical origin.

Striking is supposed to have received its name from the fact that merchant seamen who refused to go to sea because of some grievance would halt all movements on shipboard and tie up the vessel by "striking," which is a nautical term for lowering the yards on sailing vessels. When the sailors lowered the yards all activities on the ship were halted.

Efforts to form trade unions and to strike were made in ancient times. The sit-down method of striking was practiced by Egyptian workers three thousand years ago. More than three hundred years B.C. a Greek flute-player named Aristo called out his fellow musicians on strike because they were forbidden to eat in the temple of Jupiter. Some of the medieval guilds were essentially trade unions. The London tailors and woolcombers formed the earliest trade unions in England. In the time of Edward VII, son of Henry VIII, a person who tried to unionize workers was liable to have his ears cropped or to be branded with an F (Felon). A statute of 1546 imposed severe penalties upon "artificers, handicraftsmen and laborers" who swore "mutual oaths" regarding the kind of work they would do, the amount they would do in a day and what hours and times they would work.

All the laborers at Jamestown went on a sit-down strike in the early days of the first permanent English colony in America. A number of Poles at Jamestown refused to work until they were permitted to vote like the English for members of the House of Burgesses. In 1674 the corn and wine porters in New York City complained that the brewers and bakers were getting day laborers to carry corn and do other work that rightfully belonged to them. The Mayor's Court ruled that "The brewers have the wine porters to carry out their beer as formerly was accustomed and the bakers are not to hire or permit any corn to be carried up or down in their houses or garrets by any other persons than their own servants or the corn Porters." Ten years later the carmen (licensed by New York City to haul goods in hand-pulled carts) were not so successful in a strike for more pay. On March 29, 1684, the Common-Council dismissed all carmen on strike and permitted anyone except strikers and slaves to take their places. In 1741 the journeymen bakers of New York City all quit work in protest against a municipal ordinance regulating the price of bread.

Probably the first American strike in the modern sense of the term took place in Philadelphia in 1786 when about twenty-five journeymen printers struck against their employers and prevented a reduction in their wages from $6.00 to $5.83 a week. In 1792 one of the earliest known workers' associations or trade unions in the United States was formed by the Philadelphia shoe workers. It went on strike in 1796, 1798 and 1803. At that time trade unions were forbidden by law throughout the British Empire and there was no regulation of wages, hours or living conditions for workers either in England or the United States. The early working-men's associations were more or less secret unions in a single trade and city. Striking was illegal and continued to be for many years. Strikes directed by organized labor unions did not become common in America until after about 1825.

In 1833 several local trade unions in New York City formed a loose federation with a central committee. On May 11, 1833, Philip Hone reported in his diary that the New York journeymen carpenters were "parading the streets in great numbers to draw away from their work men who would rather work than starve." He added: "This unlawful proceeding is conducted, however, in a very orderly manner. They want $1.50 per day, and their employers refuse to pay more than $1.37." In 1836, a period of inflation, an epidemic of strikes and walkouts occurred in New York. On March 5 of that year Hone wrote of a strike of journeymen masons that "it appears they strike tolerably high," and on June 6 he recorded that some twenty of the "knights of the thimble" had been convicted by the courts of conspiring to raise their wages and to prevent others from working for less than the wages for which the trade union had "struck." *Strike* both as a noun and a verb was coming into general use. Harriet Martineau, in *Retrospect of Western Travel* (1838) wrote: "I heard one merry lady advise that the professors should *strike* for higher wages, and thus force the council and supporters of the university into a thorough and serious consideration of its conditions and prospects in relation to present and future times."

The right of workers to strike in Massachusetts was first recognized in a decision handed down by Chief Justice Lemuel Shaw in 1842. Referring to the Civil War Period, Carl Sandburg wrote in *Abraham Lincoln: the War Years*: "As if by instinct and with no traditions nor practice for guidance, the working class began using the weapon termed the strike. The very word *strike* was so novel that some newspapers put it in quotes as though it were slang or colloquial, not yet fully accepted in good language."

Speaking at New Haven in 1860, when thousands of workers in the New England shoe factories were on strike, Abraham Lincoln said: "Thank God that we have a system of labor where there can be a strike." But as late as 1926 Associate Justice Louis D. Brandeis, in the opinion in *Dorchy* vs. *Kansas,* declared: "Neither the common law nor the Four-teenth Amendment confers the absolute right to strike." Gradually, however, the right to strike had become a recognized weapon of labor in settling industrial disputes.

In 1902 John Mitchell, president of the United Mine Workers, obtained substantial concessions for the anthracite miners in eastern Pennsylvania by negotiating with the operators. At that time most of the hard-coal mines were owned and controlled by railroad companies and were what are known as "captive mines." The operators, however, repudiated the agreement, and on May 12 of that year 140,000 anthracite miners struck. The chief spokesman of the operators was George F. Baer, president of the Philadelphia and Reading Railroad, which controlled the Reading Coal and Iron Company. When Mitchell had appealed for arbitration of the dispute, Baer had replied that "anthracite mining is a business, not a religious, sentimental or academic proposition." Much publicity was given to a letter reputed to have been written by Baer on July 17 to W. Y. Clark of Wilkes-Barre, in which the capitalist was reported as saying: "I beg of you not to be discouraged. The rights and interests of the laboring man will be protected and cared for—not by labor agitators, but by the Christian men to whom God in his infinite wisdom has given the control of the property interests of the country." Baer denied writing the letter and its authenticity is still in doubt.

Hard coal rose in price from five to thirty dollars a ton and it looked as if the country would enter the winter without an adequate fuel supply. There was considerable demand that President Theodore Roosevelt intervene, if necessary by taking over the anthracite mines and operating them with soldiers unless the owners came to terms with the miners. The President disclaimed any right or duty to intervene, but finally called the representatives of the owners, miners and government to meet with him in conference at Washington. In his capacity as a private citizen, backed by public opinion, he finally induced the disputants to submit to arbitration and on October 23 the miners went back to work. This was the first time that the Federal Government had intervened to settle rather than to break a strike. Although the strike had cost the loss of $100,000,000, in the end the miners got shorter hours, higher wages and better living conditions.

On February 27, 1939, the Supreme Court of the United States outlawed the sit-down strike as a weapon of labor in industrial warfare. Three years later the Supreme Court declared that a sit-down strike aboard a ship in an American port is a mutiny. *Stay-in strike* is the British equivalent of American *sit-down strike*.

In 1896 the Cigarmakers Union of San Francisco adopted a trade mark to be placed on all articles made in a union shop and under union rules. That was the beginning of what is now known as the union label.

President Harry S. Truman on May 25, 1946, asked a joint session of Congress for "emergency power" to draft into the armed forces persons on strike against basic industries in cases where other methods of settling the strike had failed, but a bill embodying this recommendation failed to pass.

What is a lame duck?

Lame duck is applied to a politician, especially a member of a legislative body, who had been defeated for re-election and whose term of office has not expired. Ordinarily the term is not applied to a legislator who is serving after the election but who did not seek re-election. By extension the term is applied to Congress collectively after the general election in November and before its expiration.

The Constitution, as originally adopted, provided that "The Congress shall assemble at least once in every year, and such meeting shall be on the first Monday in December, unless they shall by law appoint a different day." Since the biennial election was held on the first Tuesday after the first Monday in November, the new members of a Congress did not take their seats for about thirteen months, unless a special session was called by the President. There was a long session and a short session of Congress. The short session lasted only from the first Monday in December until March 4, when the entire Congress automatically expired. This was called "the lame duck Congress" or "the lame duck session," because many of the members, who had been elected two years earlier, then had been defeated for re-election and the body supposedly no longer represented public opinion as expressed by the voters at the polls.

Although Congress itself had the authority to set a different date for its meetings, it never did so, and this unsatisfactory system continued until the adoption of the Twentieth Amendment to the Constitution, which became effective January 23, 1933. It is called the "Lame Duck Amendment" because it eliminated the short or "Lame Duck session" by providing in part that Congress should "assemble at least once in every year, and such meeting shall begin at noon on the 3rd day of January, unless they shall by law appoint a different day." *Lame Duck* was applied to this amendment long before it was adopted. As early as February 21, 1925, Senator George W. Norris, sponsor of the Amendment, wrote in the *Independent* that "The proposed Constitutional amendment . . . has usually been designated as the 'lame-duck' amendment." Even the Department of State's announcement on February 6,

1933, that the Amendment had been duly ratified referred to it in parentheses as the "Lame Duck" Amendment.

Despite the Twentieth Amendment, *lame duck* still survives in the sense of a member of Congress who has been defeated in a primary or in a general election and whose term has not yet expired. But the Lame-Duck Amendment reduced the length of the "lame duck period."

The Twentieth Amendment created an odd situation in respect to the Vice President after there has been a change in administration. A new Congress begins on January 3 after the general election and the term of the Vice President does not terminate until January 20 every fourth year, with the result that a "lame duck Vice President" may preside over a new Senate for seventeen days. Likwise an outgoing President remains in office seventeen days after the new Congress begins and may be called upon to make recommendations in the closing days of an administration that has been defeated.

Lame duck in its political sense was borrowed from stock market slang. In England a lame duck was originally a defaulter, bankrupt broker or stock jobber who would not or could not make good his losses and who was said to "waddle out of the alley like a lame duck." At first, it seems, a member of the London Stock Exchange who was absolutely bankrupt was called a dead duck, while one that was seriously crippled was called a lame duck. In 1761 Horace Walpole wrote in a letter, "Do you know what a bull and a bear and a lame duck are?" and twenty years later he wrote, "I may be lame, but I shall never be a duck, nor deal in the garbage of the alley." Macauley in *Mirabeau* (1841) referred to "Frauds of which a lame duck on the stock exchange would be ashamed." In Thackeray's *Vanity Fair* (1847) is this passage: "I don't like the looks of Mr. Sedley's affairs. . . . He's been dabbling on his own account, I fear . . . and unless I see Amelia's 10,000 down you don't marry her. I'll have no lame duck's daughter in my family."

In this sense *lame duck* was brought to America at an early date. In the second edition of his *Dictionary of Americanisms* (1859) John Russell Bartlett defined *lame duck* as "a stockjobber who has failed, or one unable to meet his engagements." M. Schele De Vere, in his *Americanisms; the English of the New World* (1872), wrote: "Bulls and bears strive here [in Wall Street] for the mastery . . . and pitying the *lame duck*, a stock-jobber who is unable to meet his engagements." One writer, without giving his authority, says it was so used in America already in the time of the Jefferson-Burr Presidential contest in 1800.

When or by whom *lame duck* was first used in its political sense is not known, but the transition was easy and natural. On May 7, 1844, former

President Andrew Jackson wrote to Francis P. Blair that "Clay [is] a dead political duck." On February 22, 1866, President Andrew Johnson spoke to a large group who went to the White House to applaud his veto of a civil rights bill. Somebody in the group shouted, "Give it to Forney." The President replied: "Some gentleman in the crowd says, 'Give it to Forney.' I have only to say that I do not waste my ammunition upon dead ducks." Thomas Nast caricatured President Johnson himself as a dead duck in a famous cartoon. Meanwhile, under date of January 14, 1863, the *Congressional Globe* referred to "A receptacle of 'lame ducks' or broken-down politicians," and that is the earliest known use of *lame duck* in its political sense.

Some authorities, without positive evidence, say that President Lincoln introduced *lame duck* into our political vocabulary. A Western Senator called at the White House in 1864 to introduce his successor to the President and to put in a request for himself as Commissioner of Indian Affairs. After the two men left Lincoln is quoted as having said: "I hate to have old friends like the Senator go away. And another thing I usually find out is that a Senator or Representative out of business is a sort of lame duck. He has to be provided for." Soon after Lincoln's second inauguration in 1865 Noah Brooks gave the President a list of "good party men" who had lost out in the fall election. Brooks quoted Lincoln as having referred to those on the list as "each like a lame duck, to be nursed into something else." In his *Memoirs and Letters of Charles Sumner* (1893) E. L. Pierce wrote that President Lincoln chose former Senator John Parker Hale of New Hampshire to be Minister to Spain "out of general kindness and good will to the lame ducks."

Who said the Government should not support the people?

In 1887 Congress passed a bill authorizing the Commissioner of Agriculture to spend $10,000 to make a special distribution of seeds in drought-stricken Counties of Texas. President Grover Cleveland vetoed the bill and in his veto message on February 16, 1887, said: "I can find no warrant in such an appropriation in the Constitution, and I do not believe that the power and duty of the General Government ought to be extended to the relief of individual suffering which is in no manner properly related to the public service or benefit. A prevalent tendency to disregard the limited mission of this power and duty should, I think, be steadfastly resisted, to the end that the lesson should be constantly enforced that though the people support the Government the Government should not support the people." Cleveland was sympathetic with the suffering Texas farmers and suggested they be aided by private means.

Did the Continental Congress try to control prices?

On December 31, 1776, nearly six months after the declaration of independence by the Continental Congress and when prices and wages had begun to rise rapidly, the Rhode Island legislature passed a law denouncing "the unbounded avarice of many persons," declaring that profiteering "disheartens and disaffects the soldiers who have nobly entered into service" and whose pay "is not sufficient to subsist them," and fixing ceilings on the wages of tradesmen and prices on certain commodities. The daily wages of carpenters were limited to seventy cents and those of tailors to forty-two cents. Barbers were not permitted to charge more than 3½ cents for a shave. The ceiling price on rum was 63 cents a gallon, on turkeys nine cents a pound, on milk nine cents a gallon, and on tobacco five cents a pound. Taverns were permitted to charge travelers not more than five cents for a night's lodging and not more than twenty-one cents for a dinner of "roast meat, with other articles equivalent, exclusive of wine."

INDEX

Backbone, McKinley's chocolate éclair, 345

Badge, campaign, 126-128

Baer, George F., coal strike, 525

Bahamas, American Tories, 19

Balancing tickets, 475

Bald Eagle of the Ozarks, Silver Dick Bland, 326

Bald-headed President, 480-481

Ballot, Australian, 337; origin, 173; ticket, 26-27

Baltimore, The Convention City, 48

Band-wagon vote, 187

Bank of the United States, removal of deposits, 93-94

Banners, campaign, 127

Banquet, Boodle, 228

Barkley, Alben W., Veep, 429-430; oldest Vice President, 421; and Adlai E. Stevenson related, 414-416

Barnburners and Hunkers, 149

Barre, Isaac, Sons of Liberty, 15-16

Barton, Clara, Federal clerk, 298

Baseball, Landis first high commissioner, 489

Bassett, Ebenezer Don Carlos, first Negro U.S. Minister to foreign country, 296

Battle, political, 25

Bayard family of Delaware, 507

Beast Butler, Benjamin F. Butler, 213

Bedfellows, politics makes strange, 107

Bee, Presidential, 403

Beef, embalmed, 344

Bellamy, Edward, *Looking Backward*, 319

Belmont, August, election bet, 159

Belshazzar's Feast, boodle, 228

Benevolent Assimilation, 331-334

Benson, Allan, socialist, 319

Benton, Thomas Hart, 71-73; Expunging Resolution, 94-96; Mint-Drops, 71; refused son-in-law support for Presidency, 180

Berger, Victor L., socialism, 323

Bets, election, 159

Beveridge, Albert, J., grass roots, 378

Bible, politics and politicians, vii-viii

Biddle, Nicholas, Jackson Day, 98; removal of deposits, 93-94

Bierce, Ambrose, McKinley assassination, 334

Big stick, speak softly and carry, 345

Bilbo, Theodore G., The Man, 491

Birney, James Gillespie, Liberty Party, 135-138

Birth dates, Presidents, 425-426

Birthplaces, Presidents, 456

Black, James, founder Prohibition Party, 309

Black and Tan, Lily Whites, 265

Black Dan, Daniel Webster, 118-121

Black Republicans, 192

Blackwell, Elizabeth, first woman physician, 298

Blaine, James G., Plumed Knight, 286-292; Boodle Banquet, 228; Rum, Romanism and Rebellion, 270; Stalwarts and Half Breeds, 274-275

Bland, Richard P., Silver Dick, 326; Cartwheel Dollars, 326

Bloody Bill, 215

Bloody shirt, Waving the, 248-251

Blue Jeans Williams, 221-222

Blue Whisky Van, Martin Van Buren, 115-117

Bluelight Federalists, 50-51

Board of Education, U.S. Capitol, 384

Bolsheviki, socialism and communism, 321-322

Bolt, origin, 175

Bonnet, bee in, 403

Boodle, 228

Books, written by Presidents, 512-513

Boondoggle, 391

Borah, William E., declined Vice Presidency, 521

Border States, solid South, 222

Boss, 223-225; qualifications, 493

Boston Police Strike, 369-371

Bourbons, standpatters, 330

Bovay, Alvan E., Republican Party, 189

Boy, whipping, 150

Boy Governor of Michigan, 73-74

Boy Orator of Platte, 327, 330

Brady, Mathew B., photographer, 467

Bragg, Edward S., We love him for his enemies, 304

Brain Trust, 389-390

Brant, Irving, James Madison and tobacco, 462-465

Breckinridge, John C., 184-185

Brent, Margaret, first feminist, 296

Bristow, Benjamin H., Whisky Ring, 225

British Army, American Tories in, 19

British Government, best in world, 26

British lion's tail, twisting, 201

British subject, first President not born, 114

Britton, Nan, 368

Brothers, Governors, 511-512

Browder, Earl, communism, 322

[540]

Man, of Destiny, 303
Man, Old, Eloquent, 64-66
Man, straw, 471
Man, That, Jefferson and Roosevelt, 459
Man, The Man Bilbo, 491
Manifest destiny, 171-173
Manifesto, communist, 317
Mantle of office, 468
Marcy, William L., spoils system, 99-100
Maria, Hell, 372-374
Marshall, John, related to Thomas Jefferson, 56; on Vice Presidency, 522
Marx, Karl, socialism and communism, 315-324
Maryland, solid South, 222
Mason, Stevens Thomson, Boy Governor of Michigan, 73-74
Masons, Anti-Mason Party, 75-81; Presidents, 438
Match, friction, loco-foco, 111
McClellan, George B., 209-211
McKinley, William, 331-334; chocolate éclair backbone, 345; front porch campaign, 401; full dinner pail, 334; manifest destiny, 172-173
Medicine Ball Cabinet, 349-350
Melting Pot, 506-507
Mending fences, 257
Mensheviki, socialism and communism, 321-322
Methodist Jim Davis, 492
Mexican War, Benton sought chief command, 72; Wilmot Proviso, 141-143
Michigan, Boy Governor of, 73-74; Toledo War, 123
Miles, Nelson A., embalmed beef, 344
Military experience of Presidents, 451-458
Milk for Hottentots, 448
Millboy of the Slashes, 67-69
Millions for defense, etc., 31-34
Milton, John, Old Man Eloquent, 64
Minor parties, socialist and prohibition, 53
Minority Presidents, how elected, 434-438
Mississippi River, first President and Vice President born west of, 375
Mississippi State, Yazoo land frauds, 27-28
Missouri, Bullion State, 71; solid South, 222
Mistress of White House, Harriet Lane, 441-442
Mitchell, John, miner's union leader, 525

Mixed ticket, 27
Mobocracy, 2
Moccasin, highland, and copperhead snakes, 217-218
Monarchy in America, 2
Money, Benton's Mint-Drops, 71; first U.S. paper money, 229
Monroe, James, Era of Good Feeling, 60-61; not re-elected unanimously, 61-63; tours through country, 221; wife daughter of Tory officer, 20
Monticello, dynasty, 432; Jefferson's tomb, 63-64
Moonlight, shines and stinks like rotten mackerel by, 52
Moore, J. Hampton, Garner's goat of Texas, 384
Moose, Bull, 355-358
Morey Letter, roorback, 173-174
Morgan, William, Anti-Mason Party, 75-81
Morley, John, T. R. a combination of St. Paul and St. Vitus, 349
Morris, Gouverneur, brother a Tory, 20
Morton, Oliver Hazard Perry, bloody shirt, 249
Mosby, John S., solid South, 223
Moscow International, 321
Moses, George H., sons of the wild jackass, 283
Mossback, 22
Most-favored nation clause, 295
Mother of Presidents, Virginia, 431
Mothers and fathers of Presidents, 458-459, 423-424
Mott, Lucretia, woman's suffrage, 196
Mr. Madison's War, 54
Muckrakers, 347-348
Mudsill, theory of society, 196
Mugwumps, 272-273
Mule, jackass, without pride of ancestry or hope of posterity, 282-283; ten acres and a, 256
Mulligan Letters, 287-288
Murchison Letter, roorback, 173-174
Murray, William H., Alfalfa Bill, 501
Music, campaign, 124-128
Musical Presidents, 476-478

Napoleon, Little, 209-211
Napoleon of protection, 332
Napoleon of the stump, 165
Nast, Thomas, Boss Tweed, 223-225; donkey and elephant emblems, 281-282
Nation, Carry, 310-311

without a party, 148; only Garfield saw self nominated, 268; only name root of verb, 378; only one nominated in a church, 147; only one Speaker became, 161; poet, 66; Presidential elector voting for self, 495; professions, 449-450; related to each other, 414-416; Republicans select five Civil War veterans President, Democrats none, 250; running for President and Congress at same time, 496; school teachers, 444; service in Congress, 427-429; seven Vice Presidents became, 519; shorthand, 484; slave holders, 471-474; son and father of President, 324; sons in Congress and Cabinet, 458; southernmost and northernmost born, 164; swear or affirm in oath, 179; tallest and shortest, largest and smallest, 417-420; the Fatal Twenties, 135; three entertain ex-slave Douglass, 296; three, in same year, twice, 129; three ran same time, 354; three sons of clergymen, 267; Truman and Barkley, oldest elected team nominated by major party, 420; two married in England, 460; two born posthumously, 241; Tyler's death unnoticed, 200; use of tobacco, 462-465; war baby, 425-426; Warren G. Harding, 365-369; what, said about Presidency, 515-518; when most Ex-Presidents living, 198-200; which candidate did not learn of nomination for month, 176; who changed parties, 240; wife smoked pipe, 84-86; William McKinley, 331-334; women candidates for, 299-300; wounded in battle, 454-455

Press conference, longest ever held, 394

Price control by Continental Congress, 529

Primary elections, 342-343

Prince Hal, Henry Clay, 67-69

Prince Henry of Prussia, offered American throne, 3

Prince John Van Buren, 115-117

Prince of Humbugs, Thomas H. Benton, 71

Private John Allen, 456

Professions of Presidents and Vice Presidents, 449-450

Progressive Labor Party, 237, 357

Progressive Party, 1912 and 1924, 355-358

Prohibition, Lemonade Lucy, 246-248; William J. Bryan, 359; Winfield Scott, 182

Prohibition Party, 307-314

Prosperity, advance agent of, 332; just around the corner, 377

Protective Tariff, 292-295

Proud, Too, to fight, 361

Proviso, Wilmot, 141-143

Public office, toga, 468

Public safety, right to strike against, 370

Publicity, pitiless, 358

Puddler Jim, 491

Pure democracy, 4

Purification of politics, iridescent dream, 106

Quay, Matthew Stanley, political plums, 258; addition, division and silence, 493

Quids, first third party, 51-53

Quitter, God hates a, 344

Quorum, counting, 339-342

Raccoon, Whig emblem, 126

Radical Democracy, 204-205

Rag currency, greenbacks, 235

Raise less corn and more hell, 237

Randolph, John of Roanoke, doughface, 35-36; Kitchen Cabinet, 89; Quids, 51-53; Yazoo land frauds, 27-28

Rascals, Turn the, out, 245

Rat, Even a, will fight when driven in a corner, 402

Reactionary, conservatives, 21-22

Readjuster Party, 243

Reciprocal Trade Agreements, 295

Reconstruction Finance Corporation, Dawes loan, 374

Record, Let us look at, 479-480; off the, 479-480

Red carnation, Ohio floral emblem, 332

Red flag, communism and socialism, 317

Red Fox of Kinderhook, Martin Van Buren, 115-117

Red International, 321

Red Shirts, 254

Reed, Thomas Brackett, 339-342; Reed's Rules, 339-342, 351-353; Sockless Jerry, 335; statesman a dead politician, 325; Virginia's motherhood, 432

Reedism, 351-353

Reform, civil service, "snivel service," 104

Regency, Albany, 118

Relief, boondoggling, 391; domestic and foreign, first Acts, 122

Religion, early woman preacher, 298; John C. Frémont, 180; opium of the

[551]